# A History of the Human Community

Volume II

*FIFTH EDITION*

# *A History*
# *of the*
# *Human Community*

## Volume II: 1500 to the Present

### William H. McNeill

*Professor of History Emeritus*
*University of Chicago*

PRENTICE HALL, Upper Saddle River, New Jersey 07458

*Library of Congress Cataloging-in-Publication Data*

MCNEILL, WILLIAM HARDY,
    A history of the human community : prehistory to the present /
William McNeill, — 5th ed.
        p.     cm.
    Includes bibliographical references and index.
    ISBN 0-13-266297-3
    1. World history.   I. Title.
D20.M485 1996
909—dc20                                                96-19658
                                                        CIP

Acquisitions editor: Sally Constable
Editorial/production supervision and
    interior design: Judith Winthrop
Manufacturing buyer: Lynn Pearlman
Copy editor: Kristen Cassereau
Photo editor: Lorinda Morris-Nantz
Cover design: Kiwi Design
Cover art: Lyonal Faininger's "Newspaper Readers 11,"
    1916, Acquavella Galleries, Inc.

© 1997, 1993, 1990, 1987, 1963 by William H. McNeill.
Simon & Schuster/A Viacom Company
Upper Saddle River, New Jersey 07458

Printed in the United States of America

10  9  8  7  6  5  4  3  2

ISBN 0-13-266297-3

Prentice-Hall International (UK) Limited, *London*
Prentice-Hall of Australia Pty. Limited, *Sydney*
Prentice-Hall Canada Inc., *Toronto*
Prentice-Hall Hispanoamericana, S.A., *Mexico*
Prentice-Hall of India Private Limited, *New Delhi*
Prentice-Hall of Japan, Inc., *Tokyo*
Simon & Schuster Asia Pte. Ltd., *Singapore*
Editora Prentice-Hall do Brasil, Ltda., *Rio de Janeiro*

# Contents

*Map List* *xi*

*Preface* *xiii*

—————————— Part III ——————————
THE FAR WEST CHALLENGES THE WORLD
1500 TO 1850

## 15 *The Great European Discoveries: 1480 to 1550* *361*

Problems of Seafaring 363
Portuguese Trade and Exploration 369
Growth of Spain's Overseas Empire 372
  *Montezuma* 376
Indirect Consequences of European Explorations 383
Conclusion 385
Bibliography 386

## 16 *Europe's Self-Transformation 1500 to 1650* *388*

Politics and Religion 389
  *Luther's Kidnapping* 395
Religious and Dynastic Wars 401
The Realm of Thought 406
The Pursuit of Beauty 410

Conclusion   412
Bibliography   413


# 17 The World Beyond Europe: 1500 to 1700                                    415

The World of Islam   416
Hindu Revival   425
The Celestial Empire of China   427
Japan's Sharp Shifts of Policy   430
The Rise of the Russian Autocracy   434
The New World   437
Africa and Oceania   440
Conclusion   443
Bibliography   444


# 18 Europe's Old Regime: 1650 to 1789                                        446

Social and Economic Changes   447
Politics and War   454
*Maria Theresa and the Hungarian Diet*   462
New Challenges to Royal Absolutism   462
European Culture   464
Conclusion   473
Bibliography   473


**ILLUSTRATED ESSAY: DEVELOPMENT OF HUMAN COMMUNICATION   475**


# 19 World Reactions to Europe's Expansion: 1700 to 1850                      478

Withdrawal from Contact with Europeans   479
The World of Islam   480
*Ali Pasha of Janina*   487
Hindu and Buddhist Asia   488
China's Reversal of Roles   491
The Land of the Rising Sun   496
Less-Developed Regions of the World   499
*Shaka, the Zulu Chief*   501
Conclusion   504
Bibliography   505

# 20 The Democratic and Industrial Revolutions: 1776 to 1850                        506

Emergence of Europe's New Regime   507
The American Revolution   508
The French Revolution   510
    *Declaration of the Rights of Man and of the Citizen*   512
    *Napoleon' Coronation*   519
The Industrial Revolution   526
Conclusion   534
Bibliography   535

## ILLUSTRATED ESSAY: BREAKTHROUGHS IN THE USE OF ENERGY AND FUEL    536

## Epilogue: Part III          540
## The State of the World: 1850

---
## Part IV
### BEGINNINGS OF WORLD COSMOPOLITANISM: FROM 1850
---

# 21 The Decisive Years 1850 to 1865                                                 543

The Breakdown of Traditional Social Order   544
Europe's Irresistible Impact   545
The Crimean War and Its Consequences   547
    *The Lady with the Lamp*   548
Reforms in India   554
Collapse of the Far Eastern Citadels   557
Civil War in the United States   563
The Rest of the World   564
Conclusion   566
Bibliography   566

# 22 Europe: 1850 to 1914                                                            568

Political Changes   569
    *Sentences Selected from the Communist Manifesto*   570
Economy and Society   577

Thought and Science  581
Art and Literature  586
Conclusion  588
Bibliography  590

## 23 World Reactions to Europe's Achievements: 1850 to 1914                591

Transportation and Communication  592
Population Growth  593
The Impact of European Skills  593
How the "Inner Ring" Got Along  594
The Asian "Outside Ring"  601
The Fate of Africans and Amerindians  610
Conclusion  615
Bibliography  616

**ILLUSTRATED ESSAY: TRANSPORTATION AND COMMUNICATION      617**

## 24 World Wars of the Twentieth Century: 1914 to 1945                623

Outbreak of World War I  624
    *The Sealed Train*  630
The Peace Settlement: 1918–1923  631
Stabilization and Renewed Crisis: 1923–1933  635
    *The Lone Eagle*  636
The Drift Toward War: 1933–1939  637
World War II: Initial Axis Victories, 1939–1941  640
Turning the Tide: American Mobilization and Allied Offensives, 1942–1945  645
    *The Second Best Is Not the Pacific*  646
Conclusion  649
Bibliography  650

**ILLUSTRATED ESSAY: WORLD VIEWS      652**

## 25 The World Since 1945: Public Affairs                658

Political and Economic Rivalries, 1945–1991  661
    *Charter of the United Nations*  664
    *The Conquest of Mount Everest*  667
Population and Society  678

Conclusion   685
Bibliography   686

## 26 Thought and Culture: 1914 to the Present     688

Rise of Popular Culture   689
The Sciences   694
     *The Double Helix*   698
Music, Art, and Literature   700
Religion and Philosophy   703
Conclusion   707
Bibliography   707

## Epilogue: Part IV The Study of History and Its Meaning     708

The Meaning of History   711

## Photo Credits     713

## Index     I-1

# Map List

Early 15th Century Chinese and Portuguese
   Voyages    365
Spanish and Portuguese Conquest and
   Discovery in the New World,
   1492–1550    377
Religious Diversity in Europe, ca. 1600    397
Rival States of Europe in 1648    403
The Realm of Islam, ca. 1700    417
Russian Expansion, 1500–1700    419
European Expansion in the Americas,
   ca. 1700    438
Europe in 1789    456
European Expansion Overland and Overseas,
   1650–1789    457
Europe in 1750    459
Retreat of Moslem Power, 1699–1856    482
Russian Territorial Expansion,
   1689–1855    484
China, Manchu Dynasty    492
Napoleonic Europe, 1810–1812    520–521
European States After 1815    524–525
Ottoman Empire, 1865    553
China in the Era of the Taiping Rebellion,
   1850–1864    559

Unification of Germany, 1866–1871    573
Unification of Italy, 1859–1870    574
United States Expansion, 1783–1959    597
Latin America (After the Wars for
   Independence)    599
World of Western Dominance, 1914    602
British Imperial Expansion in Asia and Africa,
   1800–1914    608
Africa, 1914    613
World War I, 1914–1918    627
States of Europe, 1923–1939 Interwar
   Boundaries and Alliance Structure    634
European and Mediterranean Theaters,
   in World War II, 1939–1945    641
World War II Asian and Pacific Theaters,
   1941–1945    644
Occupation Zones of Germany and Austria,
   1945    659
New States in Africa and Asia, 1947–1987    660
Cold War in Europe, 1947–1990    662
Arab-Israeli Wars and Boundaries
   1946–1989    668
Union of Soviet Socialist Republics,
   1947    675

# Preface

This book is built around a simple idea: People change their ways mainly because some kind of stranger has brought a new thing to their attention. The new thing may be frightening; it may be delightful; but whatever it is, it has the power to convince key persons in the community of the need to do things differently.

If this is true, then contacts between strangers with different cultures become the main drive wheel of history, because such contacts start or keep important changes going. The central theme of human history, after all, is change—how people did new things in new ways, meeting new situations as best they could.

It follows that world history can and should be written to show how in succeeding ages different human groups achieved unusual creativity and then impelled or compelled those around them (and, in time, across long distances) to alter their accustomed style of life to take account of the new things that had come to their attention by what anthropologists call "cultural diffusion" from the center of creativity. There remains a central mystery: How does important creativity occur? Accident, genius, and breakdown of old habit patterns all play a part in provoking inventions. Even more important (because it is commoner) is the need to readjust other elements in daily life after borrowing something from an outsider. So here, too, I am inclined to emphasize contacts between strangers as a basic force in increasing the variety and multiplying the openings for all kinds of creative inventions.

This angle of vision upon human affairs came to me from anthropology. In the 1930s anthropologists studied simple, isolated societies; only a few of them tried to think about relations between such "primitive" peoples and the more complicated civilized societies that occupied so much more of the face of the earth. One of the men who did wonder about the relationships between simple and complex societies was Robert Redfield. My most fundamental ideas took form while sitting in his classroom at the University of Chicago in the summer of 1936.

But even very simple general ideas have to be applied to the data of history with some care before we can really be sure whether they are much use. This took me about twenty-five years. Not till I had written *The Rise of the West: A History of the Human Community* (published in 1963) could I know how the history of humankind, insofar as modern scholars have been able to find out about it, would fit into this sort of anthropological framework.

Since then much new research has improved historical understanding. Most research corrects small details, and enough details can add up to give us, for example, a much enlarged and corrected view of the history of Africa, about which little was known a generation ago. But the greatest change in overall perspective on world history came when scholars pointed out the leading role of China in developing a trading network that bound all of the civilizations of Eurasia together after about A.D. 1000. This meant that before western Europe took over world leadership, there was a period of about 500 years when China played the same sort of role, though on a more restricted geographical scale, since, of course, the Americas remained unknown to them.

This and many other corrections of understanding are incorporated into this book. Intended for students, this book differs from *The Rise of the West* not just in being more up to date but also by spelling out more fully some of the basic information upon which the study of history is based. This risks overloading you, the student, with new names and unfamiliar technical terms. Keeping a balance between overall structure and local detail is *the* central challenge of world history, and I have tried to highlight the framework with just enough detail to give that framework meaning and substance. If you try to focus always on the question of how each part of the world fitted into the overall balance in each successive age, the burden of detail will prove bearable. For as details fit into place in your mind, this book can satisfy your natural curiosity about how we got to be the way we are. It is a curiosity everyone shares to some degree. I invite you to try and see.

William H. McNeill

# A History of the Human Community

## Volume II

# The Great European Discoveries

## 1480 to 1550

# 15

**High Technology in the Age of Discovery**    Between 1450 and 1550 new devices allowed European sailors to navigate the oceans of the entire earth and know at all times where they were and how to get back home. Compass, astrolabe, and hourglass (can you identify them?) made this possible when combined with maps and astronomical tables compiled by learned men like the one shown here.

In our modern age when computers, TV, radio, and telephone enable us to maintain instantaneous contact all round the world, it takes an act of imagination to think what it was like to live in a world bounded on every side by the gray shadow of regions utterly unknown, and at a time when news of great happenings in the more distant parts of the known world might take many months to reach even the best-informed persons. Yet this was the sort of world in which everyone lived 500 years ago.

Of course some people knew more than others about distant lands. The immense majority were peasants, who seldom knew or cared anything about regions more than twenty or perhaps fifty miles from where they labored in the fields. Merchants knew more. Some of them traveled thousands of miles to and fro along caravan routes or by sea during all of their active lives. Many such adventurers wandered off the beaten track once in a while; but unless they found something new they could use in trade, they would seldom go back a second time, and whatever they reported about their explorations soon faded from the memories of other merchants and travelers.

Merchants' lore about routes and markets, wars and famines spread by word of mouth and was seldom written down. Even such a remarkable adventure as that of Marco Polo, who traveled from Venice to China and back again in the thirteenth century, was recorded by merest chance. In later life, Marco Polo found himself imprisoned together with a writer of romances who chose to record the strange tale Marco Polo had to tell. For many centuries it was treated as fiction until modern scholars tested, and came to believe in, its essential accuracy. Except for these unusual circumstances, we would know absolutely nothing of Marco Polo's adventures at the court of Kublai Khan.

Side by side with the flow of gossip exchanged by long-distance travelers was another and usually quite separate tradition of knowledge about the geography of the earth based on books. From the time of the ancient Greeks, learned Europeans all knew that the earth was spherical. They even had a map of the world based on one made about 150 C.E. by the astronomer and geographer Ptolemy of Alexandria. Moslems shared this Greek inheritance and added to it a substantial body of travelers' reports about remote regions of the Eurasian world. The learned classes of other civilizations were less influenced by the mathematical calculations made by Ptolemy and his predecessors. The Chinese, for instance, took the view that their own land was the center of everything and measured all others by their distance from the "Middle Kingdom." Hindu tradition located a great mountain (the Himalayas?) at the center of the earth. Other people had still different traditional maps of the world's geography. But even the most learned, just like merchants and like simple peasants, always faced a limit beyond which the layout of the earth's surface was a blank.

In the half century between 1492, when Columbus bumped into America, and 1542 or 1543, when a Portuguese ship first visited Japan, European seafarers filled in many of the blanks that had existed for so long in western Europeans' knowledge of the geography of the earth. Discoveries were pushed inland by missionaries who set out to convert Asians and Amerindians to Christianity, and by military men who overwhelmed the Aztec and Inca empires in the Americas and probed other less-developed regions of the Americas, Africa, and the Spice Islands (the Moluccas) of Indonesia.

It took a while for other civilized people to hear of these great European discoveries; but within Europe itself the news spread rapidly, even among very humble people. Europeans broke down the old separations between learned tradition and the experience of travelers. News of important voyages got into print within a year or two. Books of exploration found ready sale as stay-at-homes were eager to read about the wonders of far places. Map makers, too, charted the new discoveries and arranged all the newly discovered lands in their proper places according to mathematical methods for projecting the earth's curved surface onto the flat surface of a map.

New knowledge of the world's geography was not the only lasting consequence of the European discoveries. For when the habitable seacoasts of all the earth had been linked together more closely than ever before by European shipping, trade began to follow new routes. Exchanges of goods attained greater volume than before in many parts of the globe. New crops and new diseases spread widely. Enlarged food supplies and heavier death rates from hitherto unknown diseases resulted.

Reactions in the different parts of the world differed sharply, Western Europe profited most directly. New products, new techniques, new ideas, and a new perspective on the world as a whole all swarmed in upon the nations that had initiated the new patterns of contact among the peoples of the earth. They were free to pick and choose among all the new things that competed for their attention, with no sense of being threatened or endangered by novelty, since they could come and go at will, and choose what to pay attention to and what to disregard, with perfect freedom. Others had to respond to European initiatives, and often reacted defensively by trying to stave off the intruders. As a consequence, Europeans felt free to experiment and inquire more recklessly than others. This openness to change put a special energy behind Europe's self-transformation throughout early modern times.

Eventually, Europe's willingness to try out new techniques and ideas put European or Western civilization ahead of all the other civilizations of the world in some very important ways. But for a long time, Europe's superiority was not very obvious. Both the Moslems and Far Easterners preferred their own habits and customs to anything the Europeans had to offer. The strength and skill these people had at their command, together with the distances that separated them from the European center, allowed them to follow their own paths for centuries.

Nevertheless, a new era of world history dawned when the Americas entered for the first time into the interacting circle of civilized humanity and when Europe's restless probing and self-revolution launched a force upon the world with which the rest of humanity, sooner or later, had to cope. The Eurasian Far West, previously at one extreme edge of the civilized world, therefore became central to the subsequent history of all humankind. When that happened, modern history began.

## Problems of Seafaring

The seas and oceans of the world are by no means uniform. Winds, tides, and currents all make an enormous difference, especially to ships that do not have powerful motors to drive them through the water. Only when seafarers learned how to make their ships sail upwind as well as downwind could they hope to travel safely in the stormy, tidal waters of the North Atlantic that wash Europe's western shores. On the other hand, abundant fish life provided a constant lure, for anyone who could sail those stormy seas in safety could make a living by catching fish.

Other seas are not as dangerous as the North Atlantic. In the Mediterranean Sea, for example, for about half the year the tradewinds blow steadily from the northeast, and storms do not occur. This was the season when Greek and Roman mariners sailed. A voyage late in the year was considered very risky, for then storms might blow the ship ashore on a rocky coast. Oars could help guide the ship into harbor or out again; but on the open sea sails were essential, even for war galleys with hundreds of rowers. The Romans never mastered the northern seas, where storms might occur at any season. Even crossing the channel from France to Britain was a risky enterprise. Longer voyages were rarely attempted.

In the Indian Ocean, however, the monsoons made seafaring comparatively simple. Half the year the winds blew from one direction at almost an even pace; half the year they reversed themselves, so that return voyages were particularly easy. The broad tradewind zones of the Pacific and Atlantic oceans were like the Mediterranean during the summer months. Throughout these zones a steady northeast wind in the Northern Hemisphere, or a southeast wind in the Southern Hemisphere, could propel sailing ships through bright, clear air every day in the year. To be sure, tropical storms can interrupt the regularity of the tradewinds. But they occur only during a well-defined season (August to October in the Northern Hemisphere) and affect the weather for only a few days of the year.

In the tropical zone between the two tradewind belts the air is often dead calm. Winds are local and usually die away after a few hours. In this region the air is thinned as the sun warms it and then gets pushed aloft by the inrushing denser and cooler air from more northerly and more southerly latitudes. It is this that creates the trade winds, which push toward the tropics to take the place of the thinned and heated air of that region.

Navigation of the tropic zone offered a problem to sailing ships, since light and variable winds might leave a vessel becalmed for weeks on end. Still, there was no great danger in lying becalmed, and ocean currents might allow a skilled captain to travel even without wind in the direction he desired. Conversely, if he had planned his course without due regard for winds and currents, he might find himself traveling backward, willy-nilly. Experiences of this sort quickly taught European navigators where favorable and unfavorable winds and currents could be expected; and as that knowledge spread, voyaging across the vast distances of the oceans became quite easy. Anywhere in the tradewind zones—and they occupied a large part of the entire ocean area of the earth—a sailing ship could move at least a hundred miles a day. These regions, therefore, became the throughways of the age of the sail.

As soon as European sailors learned how to navigate successfully in the stormy North Atlantic, the tradewind and tropic zones of the oceans offered no serious dangers. On the contrary, sailing in such gentle waters was easy by comparison with the problems sailors had to solve in the coastal waters of northern Europe.

## European Shipbuilding and Navigation

Throughout the Middle Ages, European shipbuilders and sailors made progress in mastering the dangers of the North Atlantic. But not until shortly before 1500 were all the technical and financial problems worked out successfully. The reason was that European mariners decided, from early in the Middle Ages, to try something radically new, building a ship big enough and strong enough to cut through the waves instead of riding upon them, as smaller and lighter vessels did.

Long before the developments of the Middle Ages, a different solution to the problems of navigating on the stormy seas of the North Atlantic had been tried, quite successfully, by early navigators. Small, saucer-shaped craft, made of wickerwork and covered with watertight animal skins, could only carry a few persons—usually no more than three or four. But such *coracles* (to give them their proper name) could sail before the wind across very rough seas, rising and falling with the waves like a cork. Vessels such as these carried Irish missionaries as far as Iceland in the early Middle Ages; and similar craft carried the ancient megalithic folk to and fro along the Atlantic shores of Europe and Africa, beginning about 2000 B.C.E. Coracles were light enough to be picked up and taken safely ashore by two or three persons, and they were small enough to be rowed or paddled for short distances against the wind. They were, in short, quite seaworthy so long as they stayed close to shore where refuge against headwinds could be found. Coracles actually remained in use for fishing off the shores of Ireland until about 1900.

By 900 the Vikings put an end to long-distance travel by coracles. The Viking ships were far bigger and carried crews of forty to a hundred men. Coracles were easy prey for such ships; and when travel in small, unprotected vessels ceased to be safe, sailors soon lost the skills needed for long-distance coracle navigation.

Viking ships were superior to coracles in having a keel, and a steering oar attached at the back of the ship. When the wind blew at an angle to the ship's desired course, the rudder and keel checked the ship's sidewise slip through the water. But, like coracles, Viking ships could not sail against the wind and had to wait on shore until the wind blew from a suitable direction. Since the seas in which the Vikings sailed were in the zone of prevailing westerlies, where cyclonic storms succeeded one another week after week throughout the year, they never had to wait long before the wind changed direction.

*The Development of Rigid Hulls and Multiple Masts*    Medieval shipbuilders made two major advances over the level attained by the Vikings. First, they made the hulls of their ships stronger and more rigid. This was done by enlarging everything about the Viking hull structure: heavier keel, stouter ribs, double planking attached inside and outside the ribs, and a deck to add strength and keep out water splashed over the gunwales. Medieval shipbuilders eventually learned how to make a hull strong enough to stand the strain of being picked up by two

great waves at the bow and stern, leaving little or no water to sustain the weight of the middle portion of the ship. These, then, were the large, stout ships that could safely cut through the waves instead of bouncing about on top of them as light, small vessels had to do.

European sailors also learned that a much safer and more maneuverable ship could be created by substituting rudders for steering oars. Rudders, being larger and attached directly to the rear end of the ship, could exert more force to steer the ship in any desired direction. A second major improvement was to make it easy to adjust sails according to the force and direction of the wind. This was done by placing several masts on the same vessel and dividing the sails

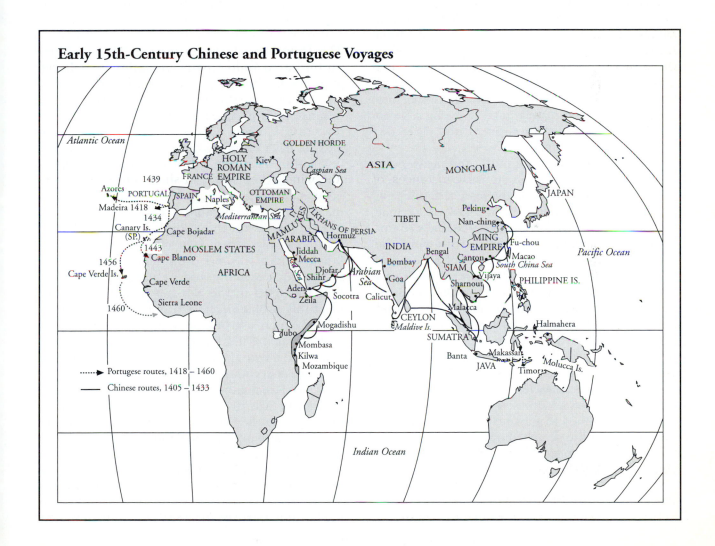

**Early 15th-Century Chinese and Portuguese Voyages**

on each mast into several different pieces of canvas. If the wind blew very hard, most of the sails could be taken down. By displaying only small storm sails of heavy canvas to the gale, a captain could keep his ship moving through the water fast enough to give the rudder steerage way and thus maintain his course even in stormy weather. With light winds, extra canvas could be spread to make the most of the slightest breath of air.

Sturdy and maneuverable ships built along these lines had another advantage that came by accident. For when European gunsmiths began to make large cannons, the ships European shipbuilders had learned how to design proved able to withstand the recoil of a heavy gun as easily as they could withstand the buffetings of wind and wave. Lighter and less rigidly constructed ships could and did sail safely in Mediterranean waters and in the Indian Ocean or South China Sea. But such vessels could not carry heavy artillery; the recoil would simply shake them apart. Hence, vessels built for the rough seas of the North Atlantic enjoyed an additional and critically important advantage in being able to carry heavier guns than ships of any other design could bear up under.

Multiple masts, rigid hulls, and heavy guns came together in the century between 1400 and 1500. The Portuguese took the lead in developing ships and sail designs. From 1418 on, Prince Henry the Navigator set out systematically to improve the sailing quality of ships with which he wished to explore the Atlantic coast of Africa. Until Prince Henry's death in 1460, Portuguese ships sailed southward almost every year. On his return each captain reported what lands he had found and how his ship had performed. These reports were studied and compared; and when it came time to rig out a new expedition, the practical lessons of preceding years were acted upon. In this way, reliable knowledge of winds, currents, reefs, and harbors accumulated rapidly. The same spirit when applied to ship design led to rapid improvements in the seaworthiness and maneuverability of Portuguese "caravels," as these new oceangoing ships were called.

### The Development of Cannon

Big guns had a different history. When the Mongols invaded central Europe in 1240—1241, they brought Chinese explosives with them, and European artisans probably learned more about Chinese gunpowder and guns during the century that followed. The first important use of guns in European wars took place at the Battle of Crécy in 1346, where the noise of the explosion scared the horses but did little real damage. The further development of guns was closely tied to the mining and metal industries in which Europeans already excelled as early as 1300. Comparatively abundant supplies of metal, in turn, allowed Europeans to outdistance others in the manufacture of artillery by about 1450. For example, the Turkish sultan Mehmed II, when he besieged Constantinople in 1453, employed European artisans to cast enormous guns outside the city's walls, and then batter them down on behalf of the Turks.

### The Progress of Navigation

The combination of stout hulls, maneuverability, and heavy guns made European ships clearly superior to all others. Yet before the exploration of the oceans could proceed, sailors had also to learn how to find their way across the trackless sea and get back home again. This called for skill in navigation. Here, too, Prince Henry of Portugal played a critical role. European sailors had long been accustomed to sighting the North Star and measuring its angle above the horizon in order to tell how far north or south they were. But as soon as a ship crossed the equator, this method failed. There was no prominent star near the southern pole that could be used as the North Star was used in the Northern Hemisphere. To meet this problem, therefore, Prince Henry employed expert astronomers and mathematicians to make tables that would show how high the sun stood above the horizon at noon of each day in the year at different latitudes. Then a sea captain could estimate how far north or south of the equator he was by sighting the sun at its highest point in the sky and measuring the angle between the sun and the horizon.

Prince Henry's captains, as soon as they discovered some new cape or estuary along the African coast, put ashore and took careful measurement of the sun's altitude, thus establishing the latitude fairly accurately. This in turn meant

**How to Navigate Accurately**   This woodcut from a French book illustrates how an explorer, by going ashore and setting up a sighting device on dry land, could measure the highest point in the sun's course with considerable accuracy. The exact angle of the sun's noontide elevation could then be compared with tables, prepared in advance by learned astronomers and mathematicians, that listed the latitude north or south of the equator corresponding to the angle for the particular day of the year on which the measurement was made. The text that accompanied this woodcut explains what must be done to find latitude, but the artist who made the woodcut obviously did not bother to understand what he was supposed to illustrate, for he shows the man sighting away from the sun.

that a ship could head for a particular place by sailing far out to sea, safe from the dangers of shoals and rocks, until it reached the right latitude, and then head east until the African coast appeared. Landfalls within thirty to forty miles of the intended goal could regularly be achieved by this method.

Measuring longitude was a different matter. No solution to this problem was discovered until 1761, when John Harrison designed a marine clock that could keep accurate time, even on a pitching ship and for long periods at a stretch. The clock kept Greenwich time; and by noting exactly when the sun reached its noontime height, it became possible to know how far the observer was east or west of the Greenwich meridian. Hours and minutes and seconds, east or west of the Greenwich meridian, could then easily be translated into actual distances (which varied with latitude) by use of tables.

At the time of the great European discoveries, however, ships' captains had no way of telling exactly how far east or west they might be and, as a result, sometimes blundered far off

course. Brazil, in fact, was discovered in this way in 1500, when a Portuguese expedition heading for India put farther out to sea than was necessary to clear the coast of West Africa and ran into South America.

But for most purposes, informed guesswork quite adequately took the place of accurate measurement of longitude. This required knowing the ship's speed through the water and then correcting for the speed and direction of ocean currents. The ship's speed through the water was measured by an interesting method. A slender rope with knots tied in it at regular intervals was attached to a "sea anchor" made of canvas and designed to offer so much resistance to being dragged through the water that it would remain almost still while the rope was paid out over the side of the ship. By counting the number of knots that went overboard in a given period of time, the captain would have a fairly accurate measure of how fast his ship was sailing through the water.

Detection of ocean currents was impossible by direct measurement. Instead, captains kept logs in which they entered the estimated distance traveled each day. Then when some large error showed up (for example, when the ship reached land either sooner or later than would be expected by adding up each day's mileage), the difference could be attributed to some current in the ocean. And by comparing records made by many different ships traveling along different courses, the direction and speed of the ocean currents could be defined with reasonable accuracy. The Portuguese became expert in this kind of rule-of-thumb calculation, before other Europeans knew much about oceanic navigation.

The idea that the earth was flat and that if a ship sailed too far it might fall off the edge of the world and never come back may have frightened some sailors. But European navigators and scholars knew better. Measurements of latitude along the coast of Africa had given the Portuguese an accurate idea of how big the earth was. Therefore, when Columbus came to the Portuguese court with his plan for sailing westward to China and the Indies, the experts in Lisbon knew that the Indies were much farther away than Columbus believed. They had their own plan for reaching the Indies by sailing around Africa and, quite correctly, decided that Columbus' route was far longer than the one they proposed to take. From the Portuguese point of view, there was absolutely no point in bringing in an ignorant stranger who wanted full rights for himself in anything he might discover. And so they turned Columbus down!

### The Value of Navigation Secrets

The Portuguese court treated information about the African coast and ocean navigation as secrets of state. The idea was to keep the trade along the coast for Portuguese ships exclusively. Exactly how much the Portuguese captains and navigators knew about the Atlantic Ocean before Columbus and the other great explorers opened up knowledge of the New World to all of Europe is still debated. Perhaps the Portuguese already knew of the existence of Brazil and the Americas. Or perhaps the store of myths and sailors' yarns about a beautiful land in the west, where the souls of the dead went—an idea as old as Egypt and the megalithic sailors—was all that lay behind the scattered hints about lands beyond the Atlantic that survive in medieval records for modern scholars to read and wonder about.

The Vikings had certainly reached North America from Greenland, where a colony existed until the 1340s. Reports of Leif Ericson's "Vinland" (first visited ca. 1000) were known in northern Europe; but Viking settlements in the New World did not take root and flourish, though the site of one of them was recently identified and excavated in northern Newfoundland.

A generation or more before Columbus' time, humble fishermen had also begun to sail far out into the Atlantic, and there is some reason to think that Basque and Breton fishermen from the Bay of Biscay may have sailed after cod all the way across the North Atlantic. But fishermen, like members of the Portuguese court, kept their secrets to themselves and certainly did not write books about where the best fishing grounds were to be found.

## Problems of Organizing Exploration

Whatever the exact facts were, it is clear that by 1480 European seafarers and shipbuilders had solved the problem of navigating the stormy ocean waters of the North Atlantic so well that no other seas were difficult for them to sail across. The remaining problem was one of money and organization. Who would pay for long voyages to unknown destinations, and how would newfound lands be treated? Spain and Portugal, the two nations that pioneered Europe's ocean contacts with the rest of the world, found two quite different answers to these questions. Under the leadership of Prince Henry the Navigator, Portugal started ocean voyaging and exploration in 1418. At first Prince Henry had to operate on a very modest scale. Funds came from the income of a crusading Order, of which Prince Henry was head. The Order was supposed to devote its resources to fighting the Moslems, and Prince Henry conceived his explorations as part of a grand plan for outflanking the entire Moslem world. Rumor had reached Europe of a great Christian ruler named Prester (that is, Presbyter or Priest) John, whose kingdom was located somewhere in Asia or, perhaps, in East Africa. Prince Henry hoped to be able to find a way to Prester John's kingdom by sailing around Africa. Then, he thought, a combined assault on the Moslem world might lead to final victory over Christendom's traditional enemy.

The existence of Christians in Ethiopia, of Christians in India (said to have been converted by St. Thomas), and of small communities of Nestorian Christians in central Asia provided the basis in fact for the stories of Prester John. But when a Portuguese diplomat named Pedro de Covilhão actually reached Ethiopia in 1487, what he found was disappointing. The Ethiopian Christians were not ready or indeed able to help against the Moslems who surrounded their kingdom.

Dependence on Prester John therefore proved a flimsy hope, and the resources of Prince Henry's Order soon became inadequate to pay for fitting out ships year after year. Borrowing was the next step. Bankers were quite accustomed to lending money to kings for wars and other royal undertakings. They were ready enough to finance the rulers of Portugal, if proper security for the loans could be found. At first this was difficult, for Portugal was not a rich country. But when Prince Henry's ships passed the barren Saharan coast and reached as far south as the Senegal River (1444), a lively trade with the local peoples began to develop. Slaves, gold, and ivory were the main products the Africans offered the Portuguese. Tools, weapons, and knickknacks, offered in exchange, made a trade that seemed advantageous to both sides. This sort of business the bankers of Italy and southern Germany understood. They were ready enough to finance such ventures, making loans and advances against a share in the profits to be expected from each voyage.

# Portuguese Trade and Exploration

Trade with the African coast sustained the costs of continued exploration, and new exploration added to the extent of trade. The process, in short, became self-sustaining, and the pace of Portuguese discovery picked up accordingly. New and better ships, together with a growing body of experienced crews and captains, could be supplied year by year, since the voyages paid off and new financing was therefore easy to find.

A few examples will show how rapidly progress was made once these operational problems were solved. When Prince Henry died in 1460, Portuguese ships had worked their way as far south as the Gambia River and the Cape Verde Islands. Twelve years later (1472) Fernando Po reached the island that still bears his name, located near the big bend where the African coast turns south again. Ten years later Diogo Cão discovered the mouth of the Congo River (1482). Five years thereafter Bartholomeu Dias rounded the Cape of Good Hope (1487).

The pace of exploration was interrupted briefly by quarrels with Spain arising from Columbus' discovery in 1492. But progress around Africa was resumed when Vasco da Gama (1497) sailed south through the mid-Atlantic to the latitude of the Cape of Good Hope, then turned eastward until the coast of Africa appeared, after ninety-seven days at sea without sight of land. After coasting along the east shore of Africa, da Gama arrived in Mombasa, where he picked up a pilot who guided him across the Indian Ocean to Calicut in southern India. There the Portuguese were able to load their ships with valuable cargo, and returned in triumph to Portugal (1499). Africa had been rounded at last. The way to the Indies had been discovered in sober fact.

*The Spice Trade*   The Portuguese set out energetically to develop the possibilities of trade in the Indian Ocean. "Spices" were especially in demand in Europe. Spices meant almost anything that came from the Indian Ocean coastlands and adjacent islands that could be used to flavor food or as a medicine or dye. But the familiar spices of the modern kitchen were always the most important: pepper, cinnamon, cloves. From medieval times, rich Europeans had become accustomed to consuming surprisingly large quantities of these spices. The reason for this was that without refrigeration the meat they ate was nearly always spoiled. Used in large enough quantities, pepper and other spices disguised the taste and smell of decaying meat and were valued accordingly. Spices were also believed to have medicinal effects; and because they were expensive, they also had show-off value.

Different spices came from different parts of the Indian Ocean area. Before da Gama appeared, spices had been gathered by Moslem merchants and shipped from southern India or southern Arabia through the Red Sea to Egypt. From Egypt the spices were forwarded to Venice and other Italian cities and then distributed over western Europe. This trade route involved many exchanges and a large price markup with each exchange. Taxes and tolls at each end of the Red Sea also added to the cost of the spices as delivered in Europe. Vasco da Gama interfered with this route by collecting spices in southern India and carrying them in a single, unbroken voyage to Lisbon. This made Lisbon, instead of Venice, the main port for delivery of spices to Europe.

The Portuguese quickly followed up da Gama's successful voyage by sending out a fleet in 1500 (the same fleet that, incidentally, discovered Brazil on its way to India). Other fleets followed. This new route around Africa obviously threatened the Moslem merchants who had been accustomed to making a living by sending spices via the Red Sea route; but the Moslems were not able to stop the Portuguese from doing anything they wanted to do on the high seas. Portuguese ships had guns that could sink enemy vessels at a distance of 100 yards or more. The lightly constructed ships used in the Indian Ocean could not arm themselves to match the Portuguese, since the recoil of heavy guns was almost as damaging to their ships as cannonballs. Hence, when the Moslems assembled a great fleet in 1509, the handful of Portuguese ships that sailed against them had no difficulty in winning a decisive battle off the port of Diu in northwestern India.

This battle marked a drastic revolution in naval tactics as far as the Moslem sea powers of the Indian Ocean were concerned. For at least 2000 years, ramming and boarding had been the methods of fighting at sea in both Mediterranean and Indian Ocean waters. But these close-in tactics became suicidal when cannon fire could sink an approaching vessel before it came close enough even to touch its enemy. In face of such catastrophic change in old patterns of naval warfare, the seafaring peoples of the Indian Ocean did not even try to borrow Portuguese techniques. They submitted instead to paying tolls or risking capture at Portuguese hands.

*Portuguese Land Bases Overseas*  Having demonstrated their command of the seas in such a convincing fashion in 1509, the next problem for the Portuguese was to seize strategic points on land for the control of trade. The port of Goa on the western coast of India (captured 1510) became their headquarters. Ports and naval stations at the mouth of the Persian Gulf (captured 1515) and at Malacca, in the straits between Sumatra and the mainland (captured 1511), made naval control of the whole Indian Ocean possible. Links with home were secured by means of a series of African coastal stations. Still farther east lay the Spice Islands themselves—that is, the Moluccas—and China. A Portuguese explorer reached the south coast of China as early as 1513, and by 1557 the Portuguese had founded a permanent colony at Macao, near Canton. Japan was visited first in 1542–1543.

All these naval operations cost large sums of money. At first, the Portuguese king had no trouble raising the sums needed to build and equip the fleets that sailed to the Indies. Individual voyages came home with cargoes that paid the total costs two or three times over when the spices had been sold in Europe. But windfalls of this sort soon disappeared. The Moslems reorganized themselves to compete once more with the Portuguese. After all, the route around Africa was at least three times as long as the route through the Red Sea, and the costs of building and maintaining the stout oceangoing ships used by the Portuguese were greater than those that had to be met by the flimsier ships of the Indian Ocean. Thus by lowering tolls and taxes and reducing the markup at each change of hands along the route, it was possible for the old pattern of the spice trade to adjust to Portuguese competition within about twenty years.

**Portuguese Ship in Japan**   This large folding screen records the visit of a European ship to Japan. It was made soon after 1542 when such contacts began. Clearly the artist was interested in details of the ship's structure: masts, crow's nests, sails, rigging, guns—all quite accurately portrayed. The white cloud in the foreground represents smoke from a ceremonial salute fired by guns in the bow of the vessel. Fittingly perhaps, it envelops a welcoming party of Japanese on shore, while the visiting Europeans in the foreground remain clearly visible, complete with a horse, perhaps newly landed from the ship. Acute interest in foreign technology—especially guns—evidenced here was characteristic of the earliest Japanese reaction to contact with Europeans. From a European point of view, Japan was the most distant new land they discovered where profitable trade could be conducted. Accordingly, Portuguese ships continued to find a welcome at Japanese ports for nearly a century.

This in turn meant that the financing of the Portuguese enterprises in the Indian Ocean became more difficult. Local garrisons had to find ways of paying for themselves. Supplies from home came more rarely and in smaller quantity. The first great burst of energy died away, and the Portuguese began to fit into the Indian Ocean scene simply as one group of traders operating in competition with others, with special advantages in the strength of their vessels but with handicaps, too—above all, the difficulty of supplying themselves adequately from a distant and by no means wealthy homeland.

In some places, nevertheless, the Portuguese continued to prosper. They carried on trade between Japan and China for nearly a century for example, and reaped the usual middleman's profits. Macao thrived on such a role, without any particular support from home. Local merchants could afford to buy the supplies they needed and to equip their ships from their profits. This was a special case, however, made possible by the fact that the Chinese government treated all Japanese merchants as pirates and prohibited direct dealings with them but allowed the Portuguese (who were not, to begin with, much less piratical) to act as go-betweens.

In the Spice Islands, too, the Portuguese were able to extract cloves and other trade goods by demanding them from local rulers as the price for being left in charge of a particular town or island. Since Portuguese ships and crews were equipped with weapons far superior to those that the local people had access to, it was relatively easy for the Portuguese to punish disobedience with sudden catastrophic violence. After a few terrorist acts, local chiefs and princes found it wise to do what was demanded of them and required their people to work for the Portuguese by gathering cloves or whatever other products the island could produce.

*Variations in Local Trade Patterns* Various local trade patterns arose elsewhere. The export of Asian goods to the African coast and exchanges between different regions of the Indian Ocean area offered some trade possibilities. But in general, local traders were in a better position than the Portuguese to develop these commercial relations, since they knew languages, market conditions, and local political relationships better than the European intruders. The Portuguese could demand protection money from the ships engaged in such trade, by virtue of their superior armament—and did so with considerable success.

The enduring handicap that the Portuguese faced in the Indian Ocean area and in the Far East was that there were almost no European products that anyone in Asia seemed to want. European manufactured goods were generally coarse and unattractive to Indian, Chinese, or Japanese consumers. Even in Africa, Asian goods were cheaper and better adapted to African use. Metal and guns interested the Japanese from the start. Elsewhere even these had little market. In any case, it was obviously unwise to sell too many guns to people who might use them to drive the Portuguese away.

A second problem, almost as difficult, was that the king in Portugal had no effective way of controlling his agents in Africa, India, and distant China. The king financed the major expeditions and claimed to rule the forts that had been set up along the trade routes. As early as 1505 a governor went out to India to represent the king. Governors continued to be sent to Goa until 1961, when Portugal finally lost control of that city. But the governors could not easily control the activities of agents scattered over thousands of miles. It was a standing temptation for official representatives of the king of Portugal to trade on their own account. Under these circumstances, profitable undertakings tended to pass into private hands, and dealings that lost money or returned little profit tended to stay on the king's accounts. The result, therefore, was that the king of Portugal seldom had anything to show for his imperial venture in the Indian Ocean. Soon he could not get loans to keep up his forts and ships abroad. Local enterprises, particularly in Macao, did not suffer; but after about 1520 support from home began to slacken, and new ventures into still more distant seas came to a halt. Individuals still might profit handsomely; but the king and the great bankers who had financed the king, in the beginning stages of Portuguese exploration, were not receiving a return on their investment. Accordingly, they stopped advancing money for further expansion.

## Growth of Spain's Overseas Empire

The Spaniards came into the business of overseas empire by the back door. Indeed, in 1492 there was no such thing as a kingdom of Spain, for even after the marriage of Ferdinand of Aragon to Isabella of Castile (1469), the two kingdoms retained separate governments. Since it was Isabella who financed Columbus' voyage, her kingdom of Castile fell heir to the Americas. But Castile was an inland kingdom, concerned, over the centuries, with crusading wars against the Moslems. Castile's crusade against Islam reached a climax in 1492, when the last remaining Moslem state in the Spanish peninsula, the kingdom of Granada, was finally conquered. Ferdinand and Isabella followed up this victory by expelling from their kingdom all Jews (1492) and Moslems (1502) who refused to become converts to Christianity. In this way the crusade was carried through to its logical conclusion at the very moment when a vast new field of missionary endeavor opened up in the Americas before the astonished eyes of the Spanish rulers.

## The Voyages of Columbus

The fact that Isabella took Columbus seriously was itself an indication of how little experience the Spaniards had in overseas operations. As we just saw, the Portuguese knew better and turned him down cold. But Isabella was impressed by his piety and energy; and when Granada fell, she decided that she could afford the cost of outfitting the three little ships Columbus used on his famous voyage to the "Indies." Moreover, Isabella agreed to make Columbus "Admiral of the Ocean Sea," with wide rights to any new lands that he might discover. The pattern she had in mind, presumably, was the familiar one of lord and vassal. Anything Columbus might find could be treated as another fief of the kingdom of Castile.

Columbus sailed from Spain in August 1492 and headed south to the Canary Islands,

**European Encounters with Cannibalism and Idolatry**   These two woodcuts show how shocking Europeans found the habits of some of the peoples whom they discovered in the century after 1500. Above is a scene from Brazil, showing both nudity and an all-too-human barbecue. The artist took some pains to suggest that the cannibals enjoyed their feast—making their behavior even more shocking. Below are crudely drawn images of three Indian gods, illustrating a popular book that attacked the idolatrous errors of the Hindu religion. Printing allowed information of this kind, as well as much else about newly discovered lands, to circulate widely in Europe in the sixteenth century. On first encountering scenes like these, Europeans reacted with mingled fascination and revulsion. Sharpened awareness of the variety of human habits and customs made older moral certainties harder (and, often, more important) to maintain.

which had belonged to Castile since 1344. Then he headed west and sighted one of the Bahama Islands after only thirty-six days out of sight of land. Since the Canaries lie in the tradewind zone, Columbus simply let the northeast trades blow his ships straight across the ocean. For the return, he headed north until he reached the zone of prevailing westerlies and then turned east toward Spain. Columbus was a skilled navigator and knew before he started how to take advantage of these favoring oceanic wind patterns. From a technical point of view, in fact, his famous voyage was not in the least difficult. Its significance lay in the fact that he opened regular contact between Europe and the Americas for the first time.

Ironically enough, Columbus refused until his dying day to admit that he had discovered a new continent. He believed instead that he had found islands lying somewhere off the coast of Asia. Before his death in 1506 he made three more voyages, discovering Hispaniola, Cuba, and other islands of the Caribbean Sea, and touching also upon the coast of South America in the region near the Orinoco River. He found small amounts of gold in Hispaniola. Rumors of untold riches, just over the horizon, ran swiftly through the Spanish court. Footloose nobles and penniless adventurers eagerly took ship to seek their fortunes. The queen continued to make grants of lands yet to be discovered, usually to captains who undertook to organize an expedition at their own expense.

### Establishment of Direct Royal Rule
The result in the Americas was wild disorder and bitter quarrels. Columbus soon proved unable to deal with the situation. A royal judge, dispatched from Castile to look into the situation, sent Columbus back to Spain as a prisoner in 1499. The grant of governmental powers to Columbus was canceled; and in principle, though not yet in fact, direct royal administration was extended to the newfound lands on the far side of the Atlantic.

The decision was simply an extension across the ocean of a struggle going on in Castile itself between the royal government and the great feudal nobles, who resisted any increase of royal authority over their lands. The royal gov-

ernment in Castile was making rapid advances, influenced, as it was, by Ferdinand's royal government of Aragon, which was much more centralized. As soon as troubles broke out in Columbus' possessions, therefore, officials took the opportunity to establish direct royal administration over the newly discovered lands.

Such a policy was all very well on paper. But at first the government lacked sufficient income from the New World to pay for the fleets, soldiers, judges, governors, and other officials needed to make royal administration a reality. Hence, the policy of making generous land grants to anyone who would equip an expedition continued to be followed. Such grants sometimes overlapped, since no one knew exactly what was being granted in the first place. Small-scale civil wars and threats of violence therefore continued to break out among the Spaniards in the New World. Royal court decisions and the law applied only spottily, if at all, since there was no way to enforce theoretical rights except by force of arms.

In other words, the turbulent struggle between king and nobles, which had been decisively won by the agents of the king in Castile just before Columbus sailed, shifted overseas.

### Adjustment of Claims Between Spain and Portugal
For a while, news of Columbus' discovery aroused great excitement all over Europe. In 1493 the pope divided the world equally between Spain and Portugal, along arbitrarily chosen meridians of longitude. During the following year, the two governments agreed to modify the pope's line of demarcation by moving it a hundred leagues to the west. The new line brought Brazil within the Portuguese half of the world, but because of the difficulties of measuring longitude, no one was really sure where the line fell in the Far East.

Other European kings did not like to admit the rights of Spain and Portugal, but only the English tried to do anything about it. Henry VII sent John Cabot across the Atlantic to explore more to the north (1497). Cabot discovered no passage to China or the Indies. On the contrary, he found only empty and forbidding forests that offered no obvious attraction to Europeans. After this single venture, therefore, for more than a century the English gave up western exploration as a bad business. No other country even tried.

## The Discoveries of Vespucci, Balboa, and Magellan

As for the Spaniards, it looked for a while as though the whole venture would soon fall through. Expedition after expedition went out to look for the fabled wealth of the Indies, and each discovered new stretches of the American coast. By 1507 most experts were ready to agree that what had been discovered was not Asia but a new continent. In that year a German scholar, Martin Waldseemüller, published a map on which he entered everything he could find out from the reports of the explorers. For his information about the more southerly parts of the coast of South America, he relied on the report of an Italian captain, Amerigo Vespucci, who had sailed almost as far south as the estuary of La Plata in 1502. In recognition of Amerigo Vespucci's discoveries, Waldseemüller proposed to call the new land America. The name stuck, although at first it applied only to South America, and it was not until after 1600 that Europeans agreed that the term should apply to both North and South America.

Any remaining doubt as to what Columbus had discovered was removed when Vasco Nuñez de Balboa, a Spaniard, crossed the Isthmus of Panama in 1513 and sighted the ocean we call the Pacific. Soon thereafter Ferdinand Magellan, a Portuguese sea captain sailing for Spain, discovered the straits that bear his name, at the tip of South America. He then sailed up the western coast of what is now Chile until he reached the tradewind zone. With the southeast tradewinds at his back, Magellan boldly set out across the vast Pacific. The voyage was long and perilous, for Magellan was heading for the Spice Islands, which he knew to be north of the equator. This required him to head northwest so that somewhere in the mid-Pacific he left the tradewind zone behind and entered the region of tropic calms, where his ships made slow and halting headway. But Magellan was a skilled navigator and eventually made his way to the Philippine Islands, where he was killed in a skirmish with the natives. His companions continued on their way around the world; and one of the five ships with which he had started finally made it back to Spain, arriving in 1522 after three years at sea.

Such feats of seamanship were exciting and impressive but left unanswered the question of how Spain's overseas ventures were ever going to pay for themselves. The gold Columbus gathered from the natives of Hispaniola did not amount to much. Other American products, however interesting, did not command an immediate market in Europe. The Amerindians whom the Spaniards first met were simple subsistence farmers and fishermen and did not even make good slaves because they died so rapidly from European diseases.

## The Conquests of Mexico, Peru, and Chile

Castile's overseas enterprise was saved by the reckless venture of Hernando Cortes against the Aztec Empire of Mexico. Cortes started off from Cuba in 1518 with 600 men and 17 horses under his command. After sailing for a while along the Mexican coast, he put ashore at Veracruz and set out to march inland toward the Aztec capital, Tenochtitlán. The Spaniards were helped by Indian tribes who resented the Aztec lordship. Montezuma, the Aztec ruler, was nonplused, believing the Spaniards to be supernatural beings. He allowed himself to be taken prisoner and died in captivity. When the Aztecs revolted against the Spaniards in 1520, Cortes was forced to retreat from Tenochtitlán; but the next year, with help from Indian allies, he once more besieged and captured the city. This time he destroyed it and founded Mexico City nearby, as the capital of the new Spanish domain.

What made Cortes' feat so important to the authorities back home was that he discovered enormous quantities of gold and silver in the Aztec capital. Here at last was something really valuable that could pay the cost of exploration and development. The news made credit easy to find and recruits eager to go adventuring overseas.

Cortes' brilliant and brutal success was quickly followed by Francisco Pizarro's conquest of Peru (1531–1536). Only 180 men and 27

# MONTEZUMA

In the year 1502 a handsome young Aztec chieftain succeeded his uncle as ruler of Mexico. The Aztecs were a warrior people, chosen, they believed, by the Sun god to feed him human hearts every day so that he would be strong enough to rise again each morning and dispel the darkness. In the year 1325 the Aztecs took possession of a swampy island in Lake Texcoco and made it their stronghold. By Montezuma's time, the island had become the site of a great city, Tenochtitlán. It was connected with the mainland by narrow causeways. Drawbridges allowed the Aztecs to halt an approaching enemy with ease. The city of Tenochtitlán was therefore a secure base. From it the Aztec warriors raided far and wide, seeking always to take prisoners alive so as to be able to sacrifice them to the Sun god. Peoples and tribes round about soon agreed to pay tribute rather than run the risk of being captured and sacrificed. So Aztec raiding parties traveled farther and farther to find captives for their god and, doing so, rapidly created a large empire. This was what Montezuma inherited. He was a capable and pious ruler. Each day priests sacrificed human beings to the Sun god by cutting their still-beating hearts from their bodies; each day the Sun rose victoriously in the east, refreshed by human sacrifice. But the Aztecs knew of another god. Quetzalcoatl, who had disappeared long ago after promising to return. Quetzalcoatl was white and bearded, a rival to the Aztec Sun god. What he would do when he returned, no one knew.

When Montezuma had ruled for fifteen years, disturbing news came from the eastern coast. Ships as big as houses had been seen; they carried white strangers, wearing beards. Was this a sign that Quetzalcoatl was coming back? Did this foretell the overthrow of the Sun god and of his blood-stained servants, the Aztecs?

Many inhabitants of Mexico thought so. Then, in 1519, a few hundred men and some horses actually came ashore and started to march inland. Hernando Cortes was on his way!

What should Montezuma do? Ought he to welcome Cortes as a god? Should he fight him? No one in Tenochtitlán knew. Montezuma tried at first to persuade the strangers to go back where they had come from. When they refused, he tried to cut off their food supply. But that failed, too, because peoples along the way decided that the Spaniards were gods—or at least so powerful that it was best to treat them as gods.

In the end Montezuma did the same. When Cortes came close to his capital, he went out to welcome him, escorted him into the center of his city, and gave the Spaniards everything they asked for. Montezuma soon found out that Cortes was not Quetzalcoatl, but that did not make him harmless. Quarrels began, and Cortes took Montezuma prisoner. When a riot broke out against the Spaniards, Montezuma tried to tell his people to stop. Instead, they stoned him; soon after, he died, a helpless prisoner. Within a year the empire he ruled and the Sun god he served vanished utterly because the Aztecs' former subjects all rebelled, led and organized by Cortes and his men.

## Spanish and Portuguese Conquest and Discovery in the New World, 1492 – 1550

horses started out with Pizarro in 1531. Yet the Inca Empire he conquered was larger and much better organized than the Aztec Empire had been. Gold and silver were even more abundant than in Tenochtitlán.

Such amazing adventures led other Spaniards to start off in every direction, looking for still more cities of gold. A grant from the Spanish government and a few promises to eager followers were enough to get the necessary credit for equipping an expedition. In such a fashion, Hernando de Soto explored what is now the southern United States and discovered the Mississippi River (1539–1542). Francisco Vásquez de Coronado explored what is now New Mexico, Texas, Oklahoma, and part of Kansas in 1540– 1543. Yucatan, the home of the Mayas, was explored a little earlier (1527–1535) without yielding returns comparable to the wealth of Mexico and Peru. Similar energies were spent in conquering Chile (complete by 1561), Colombia (1536– 1538), sailing down the Amazon from Peru (1541), and exploring lower California and other nearby regions.

### The Organization of Mining

By 1545 it had become clear that no more great empires remained to be conquered and no more Indian hoards of gold and silver awaited Spanish discovery. The great days of the conquistadors had lasted no more than twenty-five years. It was time for officials and administrators, missionaries and bureaucrats, to take over and make Spain's vast overseas empire of the Americas into a more orderly affair.

The first step was to organize mining to keep a flow of precious metals moving toward Spain. Precious metals would pay for everything and keep the authorities at home happy. Gold was found in small quantities at widely scattered locations, mostly as nuggets in stream beds. But the really important new mines produced silver in enormous quantities. The richest mine was located at Potosi, in the high Andes. This mine came into regular operation in 1545. Similar mines in central Mexico came into production soon afterward, but the viceroyalty of Peru remained the largest single source of precious metal. The Spaniards brought the best European techniques to the mines of the New World. The returns were spectacular. Vast quantities of precious metal kept coming year after year after year.

Safe delivery of the silver was a problem, since pirates from other European nations had no scruples about attacking a treasure-laden Spanish ship on its way home. A convoy system was therefore set up. Silver from Peru was brought by ship to Panama, carried across the isthmus on muleback, shipped again in armed convoy through the Caribbean islands, and then headed for home through the Straits of Florida following the path that Columbus had first sailed in 1492.

Administration according to standard bureaucratic methods became possible as soon as the flow of precious metals had been organized, since the mines paid, and more than paid, for all official salaries. The grants made to the conquistadors in the first days of exploration were canceled. Instead the Spanish lands of the New World were divided between a viceroyalty of Peru, with its capital at Lima, and a viceroyalty of New Spain, with its capital at Mexico City. The viceroy (that is, substitute king) was appointed from Spain and represented the royal authority in the New World. He was assisted by a council of high officials, but all important business had to be approved by a special Council for the Indies that sat in Spain. Various provinces were carved out of each viceroyalty. In these a subordinate council, like that which advised the viceroys, exercised official authority. Each town had a council, too, presided over by an appointed officer of the crown.

The wild excesses of the conquistadors' generation were thus effectively tamed. Lawsuits replaced naked force as the way to get and hold land and other forms of property. What had been the wildest and most unruly part of the Castilian kingdom became the most carefully and exactly governed portion. This surprising transformation was not only the work of mining engineers and lawyers; it was also the work of the Catholic Church.

## The Missionary Thrust

The Spanish kings were accustomed to working closely with the Church. At each stage of the long reconquest of Spain from the Moslems, newly won territory had been made part of the kingdom of Castile through the efforts of royal and Church officials. Indeed, royal officials and Church officials were nearly the same thing. In 1478 Ferdinand and Isabella organized a special Church court system known as the Spanish Inquisition. Its purpose was to search out heretics, particularly former Jews and Moslems who pretended to be Christians but secretly remained loyal to their old faiths. Four years later, in 1482, the pope agreed to give the monarchs of Castile and Aragon almost complete control over appointments to all high Church offices in their respective kingdoms.

These new powers became of the utmost importance to the royal administration. In particular, the Inquisition was almost the only institution that functioned freely and uniformly in both Castile and Aragon. Inquisitors had the power to arrest anyone on suspicion and could hold a prisoner secretly for months, or even for years, while they inquired into the "correctness" of his religious views. Such methods did indeed reveal a good many Jews and Moslems who pretended to be Christian. But the same methods could be and were used against any opponent of the royal administration. Even if no heresy could be found, the king's critics might simply disappear for an indefinite period. Efforts to inquire what had happened were likely to lead to the disappearance of the person who did the asking. Such arrests, therefore, quickly broke the back of opposition to Ferdinand and Isabella and prepared the way for greater and greater coordination between the two kingdoms.

*The Church in the New World*    One of the first things the Spanish monarchs did after the

**The Oldest American Cathedral**    This is the west doorway of the Cathedral of Santo Domingo in the Dominican Republic. Inside is a tomb of Christopher Columbus, though exactly where his bones are located is a matter of dispute. The building was dedicated in 1540, when this city was still the principal Spanish headquarters in the New World. Its architecture is wholly European, since Indian workmen who constructed it had no tradition of building with stone. The size and grandeur of this cathedral demonstrate the importance of the church in Spanish colonial administration. Its location on the central square, next to the vice-regal residence occupied initially by Christopher Columbus, aptly symbolizes the way churchmen were half-rivals, half-subordinates to secular administrators in managing the Spanish king's new subjects overseas.

news of Columbus' discoveries reached them was to make sure that the Church in the Indies would be under their full control. The pope agreed to this in 1493 and gave Spanish royal authorities the right to appoint bishops and other Church officials in all their overseas possessions. The Inquisition was not established in the New World until 1569, however, perhaps because it was not needed.

Individual priests and friars accompanied nearly every expedition undertaken by the conquistadors. Believing that millions of souls awaited salvation, the Spanish Church undertook an enormous effort, sending missionaries to every part of the territory that came under Spanish rule. Because the missionaries were interested in the religious welfare of the Indians, they became the special spokesmen for the interests of the native peoples. The most famous defender of Indian rights was Bartolemé de Las Casas (1474–1566), a priest, later bishop, who went to Hispaniola in 1502 and spent the rest of his life trying to plead and argue against enslavement of the Indians. He was successful. When law codes for the Americas were published (1542), Indians were classified as legal dependents, or wards, of the Spanish crown. Their enslavement and mistreatment were prohibited, although Spanish landholders were able to find other ways of controlling Indian labor when it suited them.

Las Casas also made one of the earliest experiments at systematic conversion. He wished to persuade the Indians to become Christians freely and without use of force. But the Indians preferred their own ways and if left really free would disappear into the forests. Later missions, therefore, combined an element of force with the element of persuasion. Friars and soldiers together rounded up groups of Indians and invited them to accept Christianity. Those caught in such a net seldom refused.

Sometimes a group of Indians tried to sneak away from the mission. Then the soldiers went after them and brought them back. But in general the Indians readily submitted to the friars and priests. The priests and medicine men of their old religions had demanded obedience. So did the Christian priests. It was not difficult for simple farmers to transfer loyalty and obedience from one to the other, particularly when the native religion and political leadership could offer no effective resistance to the Spaniards.

When the great conquistador expeditions ceased about 1540, missions became the means by which the Spaniards continued to extend their hold over the native peoples. The lack of hoarded gold was no obstacle to the expansion of missions. Each mission was expected to pay for itself. This meant putting the Indians to work. Accordingly the Spanish missionaries set out not only to convert the Indians to Catholic Christianity but also to teach them new skills.

Farming methods changed little, since the Indians knew a great deal already about how to raise American food crops. But new metal tools—hoes, axes, spades—often made an enormous difference. Cattle, sheep, and horses, unknown to the Indians before Columbus, also changed the pattern of land use in some parts of Mexico and South America. The missionaries built great churches with Indian labor and taught the Indians how to make all the things needed for church services and for the daily life of the whole community.

In this way, missions could become self-sufficient very quickly. Indeed, missionaries in Paraguay and in some other parts of the New World were later to make missions financially profitable. Indian labor could, after all, be used to produce goods for export. Such commodities when sold in Europe brought in funds that could then be used anywhere in the world; but this was a later development. Most missions were merely self-supporting. This was enough to permit rapid and continuous expansion of their scope within limits set by the number of available Spanish missionaries and companies of soldiers needed to back them up.

The mission system was important all along the fringes of the Spanish domains in the New World. In the central areas, however, and wherever there were silver mines of any importance, the mission pattern broke down. Indian labor was needed for the mines. It was also needed by the ordinary Spanish immigrant who had come to make his fortune and was not willing to work with his own hands. A common pattern was to lend goods or money to the Indians, who had no idea of what a loan meant and normally could not repay it. Then, as defaulting debtors, they could legally be required to work for their creditors. Low wages and easy credit at the store could then keep the Indians forever in debt and forever bound to work for their creditor. This relationship was called *peonage,* and it differed only in legal form from slavery.

In this way, Spaniards were able to compel Indians to work for them as cultivators, household servants, and as miners and artisans. Where this occurred, Indians and Spaniards both came under the spiritual control of parish priests and bishops, as was customary in Europe. In theory, the Church continued to make efforts to protect the Indians, and government officials backed the priests. In practice, though, loopholes in the law allowed the immigrant Spaniards to compel Indians to do all the menial tasks of the new colonial society. Since the Indians ranked at the bottom, half-breeds—with a Spanish father and an Indian mother—came in between. In regions where African slavery became important, other in-between groups arose from intermarriages between blacks and Indians, and blacks and Spaniards.

In time these in-between groups became increasingly numerous. This meant that the original simplicity of the Spanish-Indian relationship blurred. But the Church retained its importance always and so did the official bureaucracy. The two supported each other and together kept the society of the New World in order. Every effort was made to be sure that only Catholics in good standing came from Spain to the New World—and religious doubt or opposition to the Church

**Spanish Mission of the Alamo**   This woodcut from the eighteenth century illustrates the social structure of Spanish frontier missions. It shows the clergy, who were in charge, emerging in solemn procession from the church building. In the foreground, four uniformed soldiers bow reverently, while a group of Indians in the background show rather more mixed reaction—some piously on their knees while others stand and stare. In addition to these three groups, a seated figure by the corner of the building, who seems entirely inattentive of the ceremony, is wearing European clothes and may therefore represent a local landowner. Such persons often found themselves competing with clergymen for the control of Indian labor. The figure's apparent indifference to the religious ceremony in progress may therefore have been intended by the artist to give visual form to a pervasive social tension of Spanish colonial society.

was energetically suppressed in the Americas. The result was an ordered, stately society sustained by both the silver from the mines and the splendor of church services—all carefully controlled by officials appointed from Spain by the royal council.

## Portuguese Missions

Portuguese missionary enterprise had a different history. To outflank Islam had been Prince Henry the Navigator's great goal; and when at last Vasco da Gama rounded Africa, the missionary idea was not forgotten. Friars and priests accompanied the Portuguese explorers; and when regular shore stations were set up, missionary churches were established also. The trouble was that the local inhabitants were not willing to accept the teaching of the missionaries. In India and China, Christianity was already familiar, and Hindus and Confucians had no use for it. They regarded Christianity as the faith of an unimportant group of outsiders, who might indeed have good ships and guns but who certainly did not know the truth about the nature of God and the universe.

Wherever the Portuguese met Islam—and that was almost everywhere on the shores of the Indian Ocean—the followers of Mohammed were in direct competition with Christian missions. The Moslems usually proved more persuasive perhaps because they asked local peoples to give up fewer of their customs and habits than the Christians did. Sufi Islam, after all, had become a very elastic doctrine. Preachers of Islam recognized different ways to God. Christians required observance of all the sacraments. In particular, Christianity prohibited a man from marrying more than one wife, whereas in Africa and in parts of Southeast Asia, rich and important men took several wives and indeed measured their importance, in part, by the number of their wives. This situation made the Christian gospel unwelcome.

Even when Portuguese missionaries won initial success, long-term results were slight. In the kingdom of Kongo, for example, a usurping ruler became Christian in 1506 and took the name Afonso. King Afonso tried hard to spread Christianity throughout his kingdom, but he also wanted to increase his power by monopolizing the export of slaves. This alienated his subjects; and in fact his kingdom soon broke up, leaving little trace of King Afonso's conversion behind.

Africans mostly preferred to keep their old ways and religion. Nothing had happened to African society to discredit traditional rites and beliefs. The additional fact that Portuguese and other Europeans soon became deeply engaged in the slave trade with the Americas may also have helped to discredit Christianity.

In one land, however, Christian missions had a different reception, for when St. Francis Xavier reached Japan in 1549 he aroused a remarkable response. Many Japanese took a liking to European novelties and, for a while, even imitated European clothing and other outward aspects of their behavior. Christianity benefited from this interest in foreign things. A community of Japanese Christians soon came into existence and flourished for about a century.

Nowhere else did Portuguese efforts to spread Christianity meet with much success. The Portuguese Empire remained, therefore, a naval and trading empire almost entirely limited to the ports and the high seas. Nothing remotely resembling the vast inland territories that the Spaniards controlled in the New World resulted from Portuguese exploration. The mark they made on the world was correspondingly temporary, whereas the Spanish conquest of the Indians of the New World gave shape and definition to the society of most of South and Central America.

Brazil was an exception, for here the Portuguese met with Indians similar to those the Spaniards confronted elsewhere. The Portuguese government did not set up a centralized official administration like that which made the Spanish Empire so orderly. Instead, Brazil was divided into a large number of separate local governments. Without silver to pay for everything, officialdom could not keep local energies under control. Efforts to use Indian labor on plantations (especially sugar plantations) proved disastrous, since the Indians died from the unfamiliar diseases brought in by the Portuguese and by slaves from Africa. Soon African slaves began to bear the main burden of producing sugar.

Missionary enterprise in the backwoods never really got started. Portuguese settlers in Brazil wanted laborers, and they raided inland, far and wide, in search of manpower for their sugar fields. The Spanish pattern of protected missions could not arise under such circumstances. On the other hand, plantation owners usually wished to save their slaves' souls while exploiting their bodies. By enslavement, therefore, Brazilian Indians and blacks from Africa were at least superficially Christianized.

# Indirect Consequences of European Explorations

The great European discoveries altered prevailing concepts of the relationships among the major branches of humankind in far-reaching ways. But in addition to conscious changes, there were three worldwide and fundamentally important consequences that resulted from the new patterns of communication, of which contemporaries were largely or completely unaware. These were the so-called price revolution, the spread of diseases to new regions and among new populations, and the spread of American food crops to Europe, Africa, and Asia. Each of these deserves brief explanation.

## The Price Revolution

The supply of American silver was so large that the supply of goods that might be bought with coins of silver could not keep up. The result was a rapid rise in prices. More and more silver was needed to buy the same amount of useful goods. Naturally enough, the price revolution was felt first and most strongly in Spain. There prices rose by about 400 percent in a century. In other parts of Europe increases may have been a little less, and they came more slowly. But no part of the European world escaped the effect, since a sharp rise in prices in one market attracted goods from other markets, where prices promptly rose, until some sort of rough balance could be established once more. The effect was not limited to Europe, but spread to the Ottoman Empire and to both India and China.

But as the price revolution spread through the civilized world, it became less important. In Europe more of the people engaged in the purchase and sale of goods than was the case in most of Asia, where the peasant majority bought and sold very little because they supplied their social superiors with food in the form of rents and taxes in kind. Changes in the price system in China, therefore, did not do much to change relations between peasants and landlords. The same was true in India and in most parts of the Moslem world. In Europe, however, the price revolution disrupted traditional relationships between buyers and sellers, landlords and tenants, government and taxpayers, borrowers and lenders. Some classes benefited, others suffered. Everyone felt uncertain. Nearly everyone believed that greedy, wicked individuals must somehow be responsible for the rise of prices. But in an age when no one understood the relationship between silver supply and price levels measured in silver, it was difficult to find out who was responsible or to pin the blame on anyone in particular.

This did not make the general disturbance of traditional day-to-day relationships any less important or easier to accept. When many suffered and everyone faced new uncertainties in economic matters, the European public was eager to find a scapegoat. The religious quarreling provoked by the Lutheran movement in Germany owes much of its fierceness to the economic dislocation caused by price revolution. The resulting economic upheaval ran through Europe's history for the next hundred years and changed men's lives in detail in innumerable ways. Nothing could be quite the same when prices changed so sharply and, of course, unevenly.

## The Spread of Disease

A second, no less important, change was the result of the circulation of disease by ship. Where populations had previously had little contact with the outside world, new diseases brought by sailors from Europe had truly devastating consequences. In particular, the Indians of the Americas suffered enormous loss of life. They lacked any sort of established immunity to the standard childhood diseases of Europe; and thousands died in epidemics of measles, influenza, and whooping cough as well as from the disease more serious to Europeans, smallpox. On top of this exposure, the Amerindians soon had to face diseases brought from West Africa in slave ships—yellow fever, malaria, and the like.

Exposed to such a series of killing diseases, many Indian tribes died out completely. In Mexico and Peru, where millions of farming peasants lived when Cortes and Pizarro first appeared on the scene, the loss of life was even greater. It has been estimated, for example, that in the central part of Mexico the population was between 11 million and 20 million when Cortes arrived. By 1650, when smallpox, measles, malaria, and other diseases had done their work, only about 1.5 million people remained, including half-breeds and, of course, all the immigrants from Spain. In other words, more than 85 percent of the population had been wiped out in 130 years. Similar sharp decreases took place in Peru and other parts of South America. The same thing happened wherever a dense population that had not had earlier exposure to civilized diseases came into contact with Europeans.

Old World populations reacted differently. New plagues and epidemics reached European and Asian port cities by ships. But soon the number of ships and the frequency with which they came and went meant that every active port was infected with a more or less standard assortment of germs, varying only with the climate and living habits of the people.

When diseases became endemic in this manner, heavy loss of life from disease ceased to be an important control on population. Children either died in infancy or early childhood, or else survived by acquiring sufficient immunity to all the standard local diseases. It was not possible any longer for a disease that had not been around for fifty years of more to arrive in a town and kill half of the inhabitants because the townspeople had lost their acquired resistances to it.

In Europe during the later Middle Ages, after the opening of overland trade routes with China under the Mongols, this sort of occasional pestilence had been very common. The Black Death was among the earliest and most severe, but by no means the only example of sudden outbreaks of disease, killing off a large proportion of a town's population in a single summer. But after about 1750 communication had become so much more regular, and levels of infection had become so uniform throughout the civilized world, that such disasters almost ceased to afflict Europe; and they became much less important in India, China, and the Middle East as well.

The result was a remarkable increase in population. From about 1750 disease-experienced populations seem everywhere to have started to grow at a rate unknown before. The new immunity to epidemic diseases was one of the main reasons.

## The Spread of New Crops and Livestock

A third result of opening the world's oceans to shipping was the rapid spread of some important food plants and animals into new regions. The Americas gave tobacco, maize, potatoes, sweet potatoes, cassava, peanuts, and tomatoes to the rest of the world. In return came the domesticated animals of Europe: horses, cattle, sheep, and goats. The horse revolutionized Indian life on the Great Plains of North America, for mounted on horseback the Indians were able to hunt buffalo with much greater success than before. They developed a warlike hunting way of life, similar in some interesting ways to the life of the nomads of the Eurasian steppelands. (This, incidentally, is the kind of Indian who entered modern legends of the Wild West. But their way of life was still very new when the cowboys from the east arrived to dispute possession of the plains with them.)

Maize and potatoes came to have great importance in Europe and Africa. Sweet potatoes became a major food crop in southern China as well as in West Africa, where cassava and peanuts also flourished. Tobacco changed European and Turkish habits and made the fortune of the first English colony in North America. Tomatoes provided Indian and Mediterranean peoples with a valuable source of vitamins.

Taken together, the spread of the food plants from the Americas to the rest of the world greatly increased human food supplies. For example, until maize came from America, Africa had never before had a really high-yielding cereal plant that would do well in the climate of that continent. As maize spread, the food supply expanded and African populations started to grow. This, in turn, allowed black Africa to withstand the losses due to the slave trade. In southern China, likewise, peasants could plant sweet potatoes on hilly land, too steep for rice paddies, and thereby add considerably to the local food resources. Potatoes and maize had similar importance for Europe, although not until after 1650.

The increase in the food supply and the decrease in epidemic diseases, therefore, worked together to allow Old World populations to grow. The depopulation that new diseases brought to other parts of the world made the expansion of civilized disease-experienced populations easier than it might otherwise have been, since local populations often withered away when put into contact with settlers who brought dangerous new diseases with them. Taking the whole globe into account, the European discoveries radically tipped the balance between civilization and simpler, more isolated communities by favoring the more complex, better armed, more diseased, but also more resistant, populations we call civilized.

## Conclusion

After about 1550 the first drive and energy of the Portuguese and Spanish expansion slackened. The Portuguese came to depend on tolls and trade profits to support their string of coastal stations in Africa and Asia. The Spaniards had put their new empire on a self-sustaining basis, thanks to the new silver mines. But the period of

great, sudden windfalls, of surprising new discoveries, and of derring-do and adventure faded rapidly into the past.

Yet, in the short period of not more than two generations after Columbus returned with the news of his voyage, European discoveries had changed the relationships among the civilizations of the world in a fundamental fashion. The seacoasts of the world had become the most important zone where different civilizations met.

To be sure, the frontier between the steppe nomads and civilized peoples, which had played such a large role in political and military history since the time of the Scythians and Assyrians, did not disappear. As a matter of fact, India and China were conquered from the north by peoples coming directly or indirectly from the steppe in the centuries after the European discoveries had opened up the world's oceans for shipping.

But coastal ports where European ships put in began to rival the old steppe frontier as a critical zone of encounter. Here Europeans had a chance to learn about the strange ways of other peoples, and other peoples had a chance to study European skills and ideas, if they cared to do so. Goods and ideas, settlers, diseases, techniques, and art styles could travel more speedily by sea than overland, and did so.

At first the new pattern of movement by sea did not seem to make a great deal of difference in the Far East and India. Merchant ships had traversed the calm waters of the Indian Ocean and the South China Sea for many centuries before Portuguese ships rounded the Cape of Good Hope. The newcomers took over part of the trade and seized some strategic ports, but the goods from Europe which they had to offer were of little interest, and their ideas were quite unconvincing to most of the people who bothered to listen to them at all.

Even their techniques of seamanship and naval artillery, which were clearly superior to what had been known before in these southern seas, did not make the local peoples change their ways. The costs were too high, and too many changes in old skills would have been required. For ordinary trading, the traditional kind of ship construction, already familiar in those waters, was superior because it was so much cheaper. Simply by paying tolls to the Portuguese, local merchants and seafarers could avoid the costs of trying to construct floating castles like those the Portuguese brought to the Indian Ocean, and could thus escape all the uncertainty of radical innovation.

In the Americas, by contrast, the arrival of Europeans changed everything. The Amerindian civilizations were ruthlessly decapitated by the conquistadors. Old priests and chiefs were utterly discredited. The rank and file transferred obedience to the Spaniards. Native traditions sank to the village level and the lore of Aztec and Inca priests was almost completely forgotten.

Africa found itself more closely tied in with the rest of the world than before. Sea trade opened new possibilities, particularly in western Africa and in the whole southern half of the continent. Previously, connections with the civilized world had run northward across the Sahara or by caravan across the open savanna country. In both cases, the civilization with which African communities came in touch was Islam. With the Portuguese explorations, however, Christian contacts opened up, and Africans often found themselves in a position to choose between Moslem and Christian styles of civilization. Usually they preferred Islam, even though the Moslems were as active slave traders as were the Christians.

Islam continued to expand, not only in Africa but in Southeast Asia and in southeastern Europe. European discoveries did upset the Moslem's spice trade for a while, but, as we saw, it recovered after a few years. Trade overland between China and the Moslem lands was also affected somewhat by the opening of sea contact between Europe and China. But as long as the Ottoman Turks continued to win victories against Christian armies, it certainly did not seem as though the great explorations had made any vital difference for Islam.

Yet Islam had been outflanked, just as Prince Henry the Navigator had hoped. The whole of the Americas had been brought, at least potentially, within the circle of European civilizations. The southern seas had been penetrated by European shipping, and Moslem merchants faced new and dangerous rivals—even if the Portuguese failed to drive them from the seas.

With the benefit of hindsight, we can now see that the long-range effects of the great European discoveries had yet to show themselves in 1550. It was, in fact, the uses to which Europeans put their discovery of the New World that eventually allowed the Far Western style of civilization to outstrip its rivals in Asia.

The stimulus to Europe's own development was therefore the most important single consequence of opening the world's oceans to European shipping. New wealth, new ideas, new perspectives, new adventures all poured in upon Europe. The various internal deadlocks that had seemed about to freeze European civilization into a "medieval" mold were soon left behind. Europe plunged recklessly and relentlessly into a self-transformation that made the era 1500–1650 the divide between what historians have traditionally called medieval and modern times. We shall examine some of the aspects of that transformation in the next chapter.

# Bibliography

On the Medieval background for European transoceanic expansion, see Pierre Chaunu, *European Expansion in the Later Middle Ages* (1979), and Richard Unger, *The Ship in the Medieval Economy, 600–1600* (1980). Columbus's own words about his most famous voyage are accessible in Christopher Columbus, *The Diario of Christopher Columbus's First Voyage to America, 1492–1493, Abstracted by Bartolemé das Casas*, Oliver Dunn and James E. Kelley, Jr., eds. (1989). Hernan Cortes, *Letters from Mexico*, Anthony Pagden, ed. and trans. (1986), allows a similar access to the mind and person of the greatest of the Conquistadores. But by far the most vivid and readable text recording the early phases of European expansion is the work of a simple soldier of Cortes's little army, written in his old age and available in English translation as Bernal Diaz del Castillo, *Memoirs* (John Lockhart, trans., 1884 and often reprinted). The great explorations provoked a very lively European interest in geographical discovery. Reprints of reports of all the important early voyages have been painstakingly produced by the Hakluyt Society of England and are available in many libraries.

As for modern accounts, J. H. Parry, *Europe and a Wider World 1415–1715* (1949), and J. H. Parry, *The Age of Reconnaissance* (2nd ed., 1966), are among the best general introductions to the European discoveries as a whole. On Columbus, Samuel E. Morrison, *Admiral of the Ocean Sea: A Life of Christopher Columbus* (1942), is standard and laudatory; William D. Phillips, Jr., and Carla Rahn Phillips, *The Worlds of Christopher Columbus* (1992), is more balanced, recognizing costs as well as gains of Columbus' accomplishment.

For the Portuguese, Edgar Prestage, *The Portuguese Pioneers* (1933), and C. R. Boxer, *The Portuguese Sea Borne Empire, 1415–1925* (1969), are readable, perspicacious accounts. For the Spanish, John H. Elliott, *Imperial Spain 1469–1716* (1963), and John H. Elliott, *The Old World and The New, 1492–1650* (1992), are standard. Peggy K. Liss, *Mexico under Spain, 1521–1556* (1975), and James Lockhart, *Spanish Peru, 1532–1560: A Colonial Society* (1968), are authoritative within their respective domains.

On the biological exchanges inaugurated by the crossing of the oceans, Alfred Crosby, *The Columbian Exchange* (1972), and Alfred Crosby, *Ecological Imperialism* (1987), are fundamental. In addition, W. H. McNeill, *Plagues and Peoples* (1976), and P. M. Ashburn, *The Ranks of Death: A Medical History of the Conquest of America* (1947), discuss the impact of diseases on native American populations. The profound impact on both Old and New Worlds of the arrival of crops and domesticated animals from the other side of the ocean is dealt with in Herman Viola and Carolyn Margolis, eds., *Seeds of Change* (1991).

The view from the American Indians' side is explored in two interesting books that tap non-European sources: Miguel Leon-Portilla, ed., *The Broken Spears: The Aztec Account of the Conquest of Mexico* (rev. ed., 1992), and Nathan Wachtel, *The Vision of the Vanquished: The Spanish Conquest of Peru through Indian Eyes, 1530–1570* (1977).

On the history of cartography, G. R. Crone, *Maps and Their Makers: An Introduction to the History of Cartography* (5th ed., 1978), is a good place to start.

# Europe's Self-Transformation
## 1500 to 1650

# 16

**This-Worldliness**   This portrait of Venus, Roman
goddess of love, was made by Sandro Botticelli in
1485 to decorate the residence of a wealthy Florentine
citizen. Such harking back to the pagan past was a way
of challenging and altering Europe's medieval Christian
outlook, making more room for the new discoveries of
the era.

Between 1500 and 1650 Europeans began a new age. The Church and religion were transformed by the Reformation, beginning in 1517, and by the Catholic reform that gathered headway a generation afterward. Politics altered as peoples fought and struggled over religious doctrines, dynastic interests, and economic resources. Economic relations were transformed by the price revolution resulting from the influx of American silver, and by new forms of business organization that dominated large-scale enterprises and long-distance trade. Finally, European intellectual horizons enlarged dramatically as voyages of exploration and missionary reports brought in a flood of information about the vast and varied world that lay beyond the seas.

The shock of so many innovations coming so fast was severe. Many people were dismayed and alarmed, and popular movements of the age were all aimed at getting back to a purer, simpler past. But a handful of venturesome persons reacted differently and found new ways to act and think, taking advantage of fresh possibilities that opened before them year after year. Grumbling and protesting, the mass of the European population was dragged along and had to accept more and more novelties because specialists and experts organized, directed, and controlled human and material resources in such ways as to make new techniques and ideas work better than older, customary methods.

Asians did not respond to novelties nearly so actively between 1500 and 1650. This was, therefore, the time when western Europeans began to pull ahead of other civilizations in several important respects, preparing the way for the dominance Western civilization was later to acquire over the rest of the globe.

# Politics and Religion

Ever since the Roman emperor Constantine had allied himself with the Christian Church in 312, politics and religion had been closely intertwined in Europe's history. The medieval Church had been in the thick of politics. The popes headed an international government that shared authority with secular rulers differently in different places and at different times. Until about 1300 the power of the papacy tended to increase. Thereafter, royal governments in France, Spain, and England took a larger share in church affairs and left less and less real power to the popes. In Germany, however, no strong national government existed. The Holy Roman Empire of the German nation had been wrecked by the quarrel with the popes. When the empire was restored in 1273, the first man elected to the imperial dignity was Rudolph of Hapsburg, a relatively obscure, petty noble who could not possibly challenge the power of the great dukes and princes who ruled the larger states into which the empire had divided. Rudolph did have the rights of his office, however, including the right to reassign any fiefs that happened to fall vacant due to a lack of heirs. During his lifetime a large fief in Austria fell vacant. Rudolph took it for himself, thus planting the Hapsburg family on lands it continued to rule until 1918.

The emperor's powers were limited. In 1356 a constitutional document called the Golden Bull defined how the emperor should be chosen. Seven great princes were named electors, with the right to choose the emperor. In addition, there was a Diet (an assembly or council like the English Parliament) to which all the princes and free cities sent representatives. Both the electors and the Diet were interested in keeping the imperial government weak, so as to leave as many rights to themselves as they could. Hence the empire remained a confusing collection of states, almost but not quite independent of one another, presided over by an emperor who, most of the time, could not get his subjects to obey him, pay him taxes, or pursue common policies.

# The Hapsburg Empire of Charles V

This situation was changed when the house of Hapsburg acquired new and important territories through a series of fortunate marriages. First, Emperor Maximilian (reigned 1493–1519) married the heiress to the Burgundian lands. This marriage brought the Low Countries (present-day Belgium, Netherlands, and Luxembourg) and nearby territories under Hapsburg rule. He then married his son Philip to the heiress of Spain. Their son, Charles V, therefore, succeeded to the crown of Spain in 1516 when Ferdinand died. Charles succeeded, also, in securing election as Holy Roman Emperor when his grandfather Maximilian I died in 1519.

As emperor, Charles V used his authority to bring together a tremendous though scattered territory. Spain was the greatest power in Europe. Beginning in 1502, Spanish soldiers had conquered part of Italy, and the empire overseas began to pay off after Cortes (1521) and Pizarro (1535) started the flow of precious metals from the Americas to the Spanish royal treasury. In addition, the Low Countries were one of the richest parts of the continent. Austria and nearby lands constituted still a third power cluster, plus whatever Charles V could make out of his imperial title to all the German lands. No European ruler since Charlemagne had presided over such an empire. If the German princes could be brought to heel, as Ferdinand and Isabella had brought the Spanish nobles to heel, Emperor Charles V could hope to become supreme, or very nearly supreme, in all western Europe.

However, Charles V's enemies were as numerous as his subjects and his lands lacked any real cohesion. Spaniards, Dutch, Austrians, and Germans had little in common except the same ruler; and Charles was never able to govern them all from a single center or by the same set of laws. From 1522 he gave his brother, Ferdinand I, responsibility for German and Austrian affairs, taking Spain and the Low Countries as his own personal responsibility.

The big issue in Charles' eyes was who was going to control Italy. The French had invaded that country in 1494, upsetting the balance of power between the dozen or so little states into which Italy was divided. Spaniards came in by sea from the south and captured the kingdom of Naples by 1504. The pope and other Italian rulers twisted and turned, caught between the French in the north and Spanish in the south, but they were quite unable to escape foreign control. Time and again, Francis I of France (reigned 1515–1547) marched his armies into Italy. Each time he did so, Charles V went out to meet him, and

both sides gathered whatever allies they could find in Italy and elsewhere. Each time Charles won. Bit by bit, Spanish influence seeped northward through the peninsula, snuffing out Italian political independence (except in Venice) and choking off the more pagan aspects of Italian Renaissance culture with the fierce crusading spirit of Spanish Catholicism.

A second problem was almost as critical as the fate of Italy in Charles V's eyes: defense against the Turks. From its new capital of Istanbul (as Constantinople was renamed), the Ottoman Empire continued to be a formidable and aggressive military state. After 1499, however, wars waged against the shah of Iran turned Ottoman attention eastward. That did not stop expansion of Turkish power, however, for Sultan Selim the Grim was able to conquer Syria, Palestine, and Egypt between 1512 and 1520. In the next generation, Sultan Suleiman the Lawgiver (ruled 1520–1566) brought the Ottoman Empire to its peak. In 1526 he invaded Hungary, killed the king, and took control of most of that land. A claim to the Hungarian crown, however, passed to Ferdinand of Hapsburg, who had married the sister of the Hungarian king. The Hapsburgs therefore took over the part of Hungary that escaped Turkish control. This meant that later Turkish campaigns against Christendom pitted the sultan's forces against Hapsburg imperial armies. In 1529, for example, Suleiman besieged Vienna but failed to capture it. Border warfare became normal, and every once in a while the sultan set forth with his field army to settle accounts with the Christians. Suleiman died on such an expedition in 1566.

Defense against the Turks by land was the special concern of Ferdinand rather than of Charles V. This was also the case with the third of Charles's great problems: how to cope with the disturbance in Germany created by Lutheranism and the religious excitement stirred up by Luther's quarrel with the papacy. From Charles' point of view his wars with the Turks and against the French in Italy were defensive. They were necessary to prevent his enemies from driving his friends and supporters from their rightful positions. However, any systematic effort to suppress heresy in Germany required Charles to exercise powers that had not been in the Ger-

**Magnificence in Church and State**   Architects of the Renaissance era rejected the Gothic principles of construction that their predecessors in western Europe had used so successfully and sought inspiration instead in surviving structures from Roman antiquity. In practice this meant round arches and domes in place of pointed gothic arches and vaults. Above is the Cathedral of St. Peters, Rome, the seat of papacy, as constructed between 1506 and 1615. Below is the Palace of Chambord on the Loire river, erected as a royal hunting lodge and rural retreat for King Francis I of France after 1519. St. Peters is one of the largest churches in Christendom; Chambord, with no fewer than 444 separate rooms, was large enough to accommodate a swarm of courtiers as well as the king himself. Both buildings, deliberately echoing Roman imperial style, were designed to express the greatness and magnificence of the popes and kings whose wealth and will had called them into being.

man emperor's hands for centuries. Moreover, his Spanish and Netherlandish subjects were not eager to see their money or soldiers used to strengthen the emperor's position in Germany. It is therefore not really surprising that Charles could spend only a small part of his time and energy in trying to do something about the Lutheran movement. He had too many other matters to attend to.

Yet in European history, the Protestant Reformation that Luther started in 1517 turned out to be far more significant than the long wars over Italy, for the Reformation divided Europe into opposing religious camps and changed the lives of nearly everyone to some degree. To understand what the great dispute was about, we must know something of Luther's life and his personal pursuit of salvation, for it was these experiences that made him so certain and so persuasive, and gave him courage to defy the highest authorities of church and state when they commanded him to change his views.

# Luther's Reformation

Martin Luther was born in 1483, a miner's son. He started to study law but gave it up to become first a monk, then a priest, and in 1508 a professor of theology at the University of Wittenberg in Saxony. Such a career was unusual only because the young Luther advanced so rapidly. But he took religion far more seriously than most people did. He became a monk because he felt the need of assuring his soul's salvation. In the following years he worked hard to win that salvation. But his best efforts seemed fruitless. He remained—in his own judgment—a sinful man who deserved damnation. How could he, or anyone else, escape the just punishment for sin? How indeed?

The question was an agonizing one for Luther, until one day in 1515 he was reading St. Paul's Epistle to the Romans and came upon the verse that says: "The just shall live by faith." This simple phrase struck Luther with the force of revelation. Here was his answer: God asked only faith—total, unquestioning faith. God did the rest. Faith freed men and women of sin. All efforts to wipe out the penalties of sin by penance

and good works were futile, and indeed misleading, since sinners might think that their accounts with God were square when in fact they had failed in the great essential: to have faith and commit all else to God.

The radical consequences of his position became clear to Luther only by degrees. He did not set out to split the Christian Church in two. On the contrary, he always clung to the idea that somehow God would again unite all Christians. When he found his quarrel with the papacy could not be compromised, he appealed to a council of all the bishops, with the idea that this body might reform the Church—always, of course, according to the truth as Luther understood it.

*Luther's Attack on Indulgences*    What triggered the Lutheran Reformation was a campaign to raise money in Germany for the building of St. Peter's cathedral in Rome. One of the ways the popes collected money was by selling indulgences. These were pieces of paper that canceled the penalties of sin. The idea was that the pope could arrange the transfer of merits, accumulated by Christ and the saints, to an individual soul in need of help. By buying such indulgences, pious persons believed they could relieve themselves or others from having to suffer for their sins in purgatory. The sale of such indulgences had become an important source of income for the popes.

Luther was appalled by such an approach to sin, salvation, and finance. In 1517, therefore, when a seller of indulgences came to a nearby town, Luther publicly challenged the usefulness of indulgences. He did this in the customary way, by posting a series of theses on the church door in Wittenberg. These theses were short statements about controversial questions that Luther was prepared to defend in public debate with anyone who chose to argue against him.

Learned theologians were soon able to prove that Luther's views led to heresy. If Christians needed only faith for salvation, what happened to the power of priests to channel God's saving grace to sinners through the rites of the Church? Luther eventually admitted in public that on this and other points he agreed with John Hus, the Czech heretic, who had been burned at the stake for his opinions in 1415.

Even when he had been forced to recognize the radical implications of his position, Luther did not change his convictions. He felt, instead, that the pope must be wrong, because he knew that he was right about faith and salvation—the important thing—and had the words of the Bible to prove it. He put the whole issue before the German public in 1520 by writing three pamphlets in rapid succession: *Address to the Christian Nobility of the German Nation: The Babylo-*

---

**Luther and Pope Leo X**   These paintings suggest the contrasting character of the protagonists of the earliest phase of the Reformation. On the left, Martin Luther's craggy face and introverted gaze reveals the inward turmoil and firm conviction that impelled him to defy the busy man of affairs, portrayed on the right, who became Pope Leo X. As such, he governed the Church for eight turbulent years, 1513 to 1521, starting when he was just 37 years of age. As befitted a son of Lorenzo the Magnificent, who had ruled renaissance Florence after its peak, the new pope made Rome a center of the arts as never before. Building the Cathedral of St. Peters was only one of his many projects, and selling indulgences to pay for St. Peters was only one of the ways he set out to raise money for them. Italian politics was an even more urgent concern for Pope Leo X, for he had to steer between rival French and Spanish invaders, who both demanded that local Italian rulers, including the Pope, should support them. By comparison with these urgent and practical concerns, news from Germany of Luther's protest against sale of indulgences counted for little. In 1520 Pope Leo condemned Luther for heresy and left it at that. The next year Leo died. His successors on the papal throne continued to be so entangled in the Italian wars (1494–1559) that they had little time to bother with Lutheranism or the religious challenge coming from Germany until the 1540s.

*nian Captivity of the Church;* and *The Liberty of a Christian Man.*

In emphatic language Luther argued his cause, accused the popes of having twisted true doctrine, and invited the German nobility to reform the Church along the lines laid down in the Bible. Appeal to the Bible as the only reliable source of religious truth was, in fact, Luther's strongest and most convincing argument. It soon became obvious that many of the practices of the Church did not have any definite biblical basis. For example, confession, which had been defined as a sacrament only in 1215, in the time of Pope Innocent III, was not clearly authorized by any scriptural passage.

The public response in Germany to Luther's words was tremendous. His arguments seemed convincing to most Germans. Nearly everyone agreed that the Church needed reform—and furthermore, no one in Germany really liked to see good German money being shipped off to Rome to build the new cathedral of St. Peter's. Many Germans were eager to agree with Luther when he accused priests of having taken to themselves rights that were in fact enjoyed by every faithful Christian. The salvation of souls was, after all, a matter of highest importance; and if, in fact, Luther was right, and the popes had been misleading the Christian community for centuries, something had to be done about it, right away.

The newly elected emperor Charles V therefore made the Lutheran question one of the important items of business to be taken up at his first Imperial Diet, which met at the city of Worms in 1521. Luther came in person, on the strength of the emperor's promise that he would not be harmed. Luther reaffirmed views that expert theologians condemned as heretical. This was enough to satisfy the emperor, who persuaded the Diet to put Luther under the imperial ban. This meant that anyone who killed Luther would not be tried in an imperial court. Such an act, in effect, invited his assassination.

But the Elector of Saxony, Luther's immediate sovereign, continued to protect his controversial subject. For safety he hid Luther in the Wartburg castle, where he lived incognito for nearly a year. Luther used this time to translate the New Testament into German. A little later, with help from others who knew Hebrew, he also translated the Old Testament. Luther's Bible was widely read. Many ordinary Germans tried to puzzle out religious truth from its pages for themselves. The result was sharp disagreement, since different parts of the Bible lend themselves to very different interpretations.

A few radicals, known as Anabaptists, decided that infant baptism was an error because the baptisms recorded in the Bible involved only adults. Other doctrines often combined with this idea. Poor and unhappy people pored over the biblical passages announcing the end of the world and began to expect the opening of the skies at any minute. If the end of the world were really near, people ought to give up most ordinary pursuits, cease from sinning, and prayerfully await the end.

### Luther Denounces the Peasant Revolt

Religious views of this kind easily spilled over into social and economic protest. In 1524–1525, peasants in southwestern Germany tried to throw off their obligation to pay customary rents and services to their lords. Radical religious views were part of the movement, too. This frightened and angered Luther. He felt that the peasants were distorting the meaning of Christian liberty as he had explained it in his famous pamphlet. Faithful Christians, according to Luther, were free because they served their neighbors spontaneously and of their own free will, not because they had no duties or obligations to others. Luther also feared that the peasants and other radicals might discredit his reform in the eyes of the German nobles and princes. The result was another pamphlet in which Luther denounced the peasant rebels in extremely harsh language and exhorted their lords to kill them mercilessly.

The peasant revolt was indeed suppressed in blood. Thereafter, the Lutheran movement lost much of the white-hot enthusiasm that Luther's words had stimulated during the first eight years of the Reformation. Instead, Luther and his followers set out to order the Church as it should be ordered—that is, according to the Bible—wherever the secular ruler would agree to undertake the task of reform. Many, but not all, German princes went along with Luther in this task. They had much to gain, for the Lutherans decided that Church property was unneces-

# LUTHER'S KIDNAPPING

When Martin Luther accepted the emperor's summons to the Imperial Diet at Worms in April 1521, he and his friends recalled how John Hus had gone to the Council of Constance a little more than a century before and, in spite of the emperor's pledge for safe conduct, had been condemned as a heretic and then burned at the stake. Parallels with Christ's visit to Jerusalem and the arrest, trial, and crucifixion that followed also flickered in the minds of Luther's followers. But the young emperor Charles V allowed the troublesome professor to leave Worms unhindered, even though he was about to declare Luther an outlaw.

When Luther was nearing his home in Wittenberg, armed horsemen suddenly appeared along a lonely stretch of road, seized the famous reformer, and with oaths and threats carried him off before the eyes of his horrified companions, who thought he was about to be murdered. Indeed, shortly thereafter a body was discovered and identified as the mortal remains of Dr. Martin Luther. His followers were dismayed but not surprised. Such an event fulfilled the parallels they already had in mind.

Yet his close friends soon began to receive letters from the "dead" Luther; and in December he even visited Wittenberg secretly, disguised as a knight. But it was not until March 1522, eleven months after he had disappeared so dramatically, that Luther returned openly to Wittenberg and publicly took charge of the tumultuous reform movement he had so suddenly called forth.

The inside story then came out. Frederick the Wise, Elector of Saxony, was Luther's immediate sovereign. He did not want to see Luther killed as an outlaw. Yet he also felt that the famous Wittenberg professor of theology was a hothead and troublemaker. While still at Worms, the Elector decided to take Luther into custody secretly, thus making sure that no harm could come to him and that he could do no further harm himself. So that he might be able truthfully to deny that he knew where Luther was, the Elector ordered his servants to capture the reformer without letting the Elector himself know anything about the details.

When one of the Elector's officers explained the plan to him, Luther agreed, for he was in fear of his life and could not afford to defy the pope, the emperor, and his own prince all at once. The kidnapping was therefore arranged as a device for throwing Luther's enemies off the track. Accordingly, as soon as Luther's abductors were safely hidden in the woods, they paused to allow their "captive" to cast off his monk's cowl and put on a knight's clothing. Then the little party rode, by a roundabout way, to one of Frederick the Wise's more remote castles, the Wartburg. There Luther went into strict seclusion until his hair and beard had grown, disguising the monkish tonsure he had worn up to that time.

Luther used his spare time at the Wartburg to translate the Bible into German. He also carried on a busy correspondence with his friends and never lost touch with the Lutheran movement that continued to convulse Germany. As may be imagined, Luther's reported death and subsequent resurrection did nothing to weaken his hold on the popular imagination of Germany.

sary, that monasteries should be suppressed, and that Church appointments should be treated as another (though supremely important) branch of the governmental bureaucracy. Rulers who accepted Lutheran principles were therefore able to confiscate Church property and expand their power very substantially.

When Luther died in 1546, reform along these lines had been firmly established in most of northern Germany and in Scandinavia. Emperor Charles V had been far too busy in Italy and elsewhere to check Lutheranism effectively. When he did find time to turn to internal German affairs, it was too late. Confiscated lands and abandoned monasteries could not be restored; in such matters the German princes would not submit to the emperor's will without a fight. Charles V tried to use force, but that failed. In 1555 he therefore reluctantly agreed to the Peace of Augsburg, which gave every German ruler the right to impose either Lutheranism or Roman Catholicism upon his subjects.

# John Calvin and the Reformed Churches

Luther's challenge to the papacy did not pass unnoticed outside of Germany. Especially among townspeople in France, Switzerland, England, and the Low Countries, long-standing discontents with the papacy and with the Church burst into flame as news of what had happened in Germany spread through Europe.

In many places the reform party was unable to gain control of the government. Without such power they could only form a church, according to their taste, by withdrawing into some sort of separate body of their own. But in Switzerland, where local cantons (or districts) and cities ruled themselves, religious reformers had only to convince a majority of the city council in order to begin reform. In this fashion, a fiery preacher, Huldreich Zwingli (1484–1531), started reformation in Zurich in 1518. His ideas paralleled those of Luther on many points, although the two reformers differed on the meaning of the sacrament of the Eucharist. Church reform spread to other Swiss towns, but high in

the mountains more conservative communities clung to the old faith. Civil war broke out, and Zwingli was killed in battle. Soon afterward a peace was concluded that left each canton free to choose its own form of religion.

Zwingli's death, however, left the Swiss reformers without a leader. This gap was filled by John Calvin (1509–1564), a Frenchman, who first came to Geneva in 1536 but took up permanent residence there in 1541. Calvin was a far more cool-headed man than Luther. He thought out his opinions carefully and stuck to them with a will of iron. Through his learning and conviction he impressed his views upon all around him.

Like Luther, Calvin took the Bible as the only reliable source of religious truth. In the main, he drew the same lessons from the Bible that Luther had drawn. In his famous book, *Institutes of the Christian Religion*, Calvin gathered together the biblical passages that supported his views on all issues under debate. Calvin arranged his discussion of doctrine systematically so that anyone eager to find out what the Bible had to say about salvation, predestination, faith, and innumerable other questions could discover answers in his book. The *Institutes*, therefore, became a standard reference work for all of the reformed churches.

*Calvin's Divergence from Luther*      In some matters, however, Calvin disagreed with Luther. Like Zwingli, Calvin interpreted the Eucharist as merely commemorative of the last supper that Jesus Christ had taken with the Apostles. Calvin also emphasized predestination in a way that Luther did not. Luther accepted the idea of predestination, but he never felt it to be particularly important. What mattered was faith in God. Calvin, on the other hand, drew the logical conclusion: Some persons have faith and are saved, but some lack that faith and are therefore damned for all eternity. God makes the choice, not the individuals concerned. God does so for reasons of his own that mere human beings cannot understand.

Such a doctrine emphasized the role of God as judge and ruler. It did not, however, persuade Calvin and his followers to sit back and wait for God to do whatever He had decided to

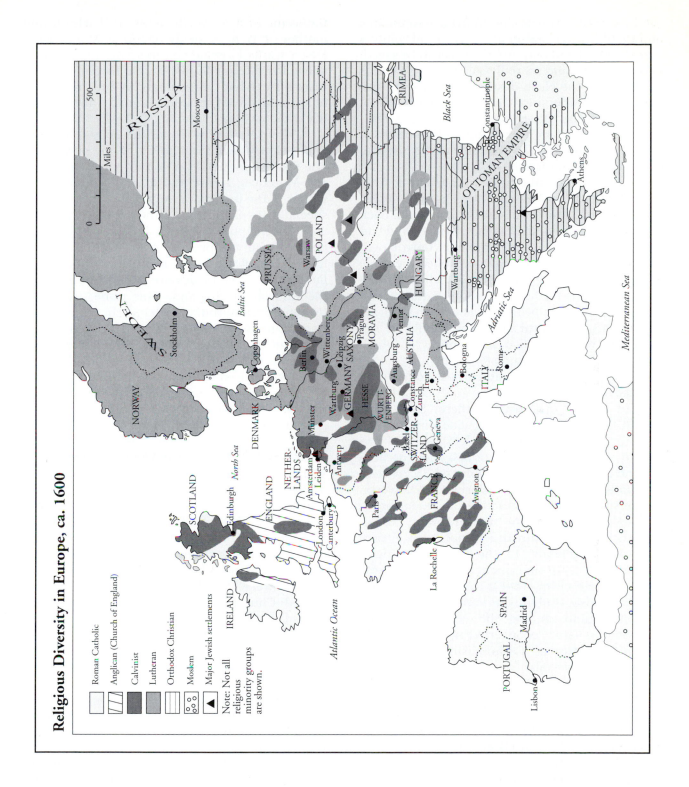

## Religious Diversity in Europe, ca. 1600

**Legend:**
- Roman Catholic
- Anglican (Church of England)
- Calvinist
- Lutheran
- Orthodox Christian
- Moslem
- ▲ Major Jewish settlements

Note: Not all religious minority groups are shown.

**Scale:** 500 / 0 Miles

**Labels on map:**

RUSSIA · Moscow · CRIMEA · Black Sea · Constantinople · OTTOMAN EMPIRE · Athens · Wartburg · Warsaw · POLAND · PRUSSIA · Baltic Sea · SWEDEN · Stockholm · Copenhagen · DENMARK · NORWAY · Berlin · Wittenberg · Leipzig · GERMANY · SAXONY · MORAVIA · Prague · Vienna · AUSTRIA · Augsburg · Constance · HUNGARY · Adriatic Sea · Bologna · ITALY · Rome · Mediterranean Sea · Wartburg · HESSE · WÜRT-ENBERG · Zürich · Trent · SWITZER-LAND · Geneva · Münster · Antwerp · Amsterdam · Leiden · NETHER-LANDS · North Sea · SCOTLAND · Edinburgh · ENGLAND · London · Canterbury · Paris · FRANCE · Avignon · La Rochelle · IRELAND · Atlantic Ocean · SPAIN · Madrid · PORTUGAL · Lisbon

397

do. Instead, Calvinists developed a tremendous moral drive. No one could ever be absolutely sure that God had chosen him or her to be saved. But a person could try to live as though he or she were among the elect, destined for Heaven. Under Calvin's leadership, Geneva became a school of righteousness. Dissent was suppressed. Morality was enforced by preaching and instruction, and when that failed, by the force at the disposal of the city government.

Calvin's ideas about the proper relation between Church and state were quite different from Luther's. After 1525 Luther had fallen back upon the support of the German princes and had agreed to their all but complete control over Church administration. Calvin combed the Bible for evidence of how the early Church was managed, and came to the conclusion that ministers and elders ought to be in charge of each separate congregation. General questions should be decided by representative assemblies in which both ministers and laymen took part.

Calvin attracted many earnest young men to Geneva to see and study the godly community he had helped to construct there. Such men spread Calvin's ideas far and wide through Europe. In Scotland, John Knox (1505–1572) was able to convert a whole kingdom by fiery preaching and a skillful appeal to nobles who were restless under royal authority. Elsewhere, however, Calvinism spread by attracting the assent of individuals most of whom lived in towns. Calvinists, therefore, remained a minority in France and the Rhinelands. In the Dutch provinces, Calvinists became dominant during a long war against Spain (1568–1648). In both Poland and Hungary, also, Calvinism had a considerable success, mainly among the nobility. Catholic missionaries later reconverted nearly all Polish Calvinists to Roman Catholicism; and in Hungary the majority also returned to Catholicism, although in the eastern parts of Hungary important Calvinist communities still survive.

## England's Reformation

The Reformation in England began when Henry VIII (ruled 1509–1547) came to the conclusion that the reason he did not have a male heir was that he had married his dead brother's widow,

Catherine of Aragon (the aunt of Charles V and mother of Henry's sickly daughter Mary). King Henry wanted a male heir to assure the continuance of the Tudor family on the English throne. Also, his eye had been caught by the pretty face of a young lady of the court named Anne Boleyn, whom he wished to marry.

The difficulty was that the pope refused to annul Henry's marriage to Catherine of Aragon. The Spanish influence in Rome opposed any such act. Moreover, Henry had married his brother's widow in the first place only on the strength of a special dispensation from the pope; it was awkward for the pope to contradict what before had been officially approved. After waiting in vain for a favorable decision. King Henry asked Parliament in 1534 to declare him to be head of the Church of England. This done, the archbishop of Canterbury declared the king's marriage annulled, freeing him to marry Anne Boleyn. But the king was again denied a male heir, for Anne gave birth to a girl, Elizabeth. King Henry soon tired of Anne and had her head cut off on the charge of unfaithfulness. He later married four other wives in succession, one of whom gave birth to a son, Edward VI (reigned 1547–1553).

Although he quarreled with the pope, Henry VIII had no intention of tampering with doctrine or even with rituals. But Lutheran and, presently, Calvinist ideas could not be prevented from seeping into England. Henry opened one important breach in the old order by seizing lands belonging to monasteries as a way of increasing his income. Under his son, distinctly Protestant phrases were introduced into the officially approved Church rituals. Queen Mary (reigned 1553–1558), daughter of Catherine of Aragon and wife of Philip II of Spain, tried to bring England back into the Roman Catholic fold. Her successor, Elizabeth I (reigned 1558–1603), returned to Protestantism, and in 1563 Parliament approved thirty-nine articles summing up Christian doctrine. They became the official theological position of the Church of England by Act of Parliament.

These articles had been drawn up with care so as to allow anti-papal Christians of many different shades of opinion to accept them. They have remained in force in England ever since. Because Protestantism and English patriotism

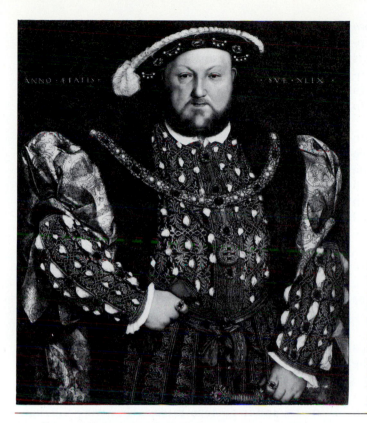

**His Majesty, King Henry VIII of England**
Henry VIII (ruled 1509–1546), portrayed here by
German artist Hans Holbein, was a man who liked
to have his own way. When his first wife failed
to provide him with a male heir, he decided to
divorce her. But the pope refused to approve
the plan, so Henry inaugurated a religious
reformation by declaring himself head of the
Church of England, and proceeded to divorce his
wife, suppress monasteries, and reluctantly allow
Protestant doctrines to filter into the land.

came to be firmly identified with each other under Queen Elizabeth, most of the English people
were well satisfied with the theological compromises of the Thirty-nine Articles. But some enthusiasts felt that the English Church needed
still further reformation. These "Puritans," as
they came to be called, were under Calvinist influence. Some felt it possible to work within the
established church. Others withdrew to form
their own congregations, to preach and practice
true and purified Christianity as they understood it.

## Roman Catholic Reform

For nearly twenty years the popes in Rome paid
little attention to the Protestant movement. They
were caught, like all the other rulers of Italy, in
the complicated struggle between France and
Spain for control of the Italian peninsula. When
Charles V's soldiers took Rome and sacked it
in 1527, how could the pope cooperate effectively with that same emperor to put down the
Lutherans in Germany? Moreover, the Renaissance popes were rulers, diplomats, and art patrons—far too much concerned with these affairs to take Luther seriously.

For a long time, too, there was a real ambiguity about the cry for reform. Luther and Calvin
never intended to set up separate churches, and
they always remained true to the ideal of one
universal Church to which all Christians ought
to belong. When asked what to do about the corruptions of the papacy, their answer was to appeal to a general council. This sounded like a return to medieval ideas for reforming the Church
by means of a council, and the popes could not
be expected to welcome revival of this issue.
They suspected anyone who urged the need for
reform of trying to undermine the authority of
the papal office.

*Pope Paul III and the Council of Trent*
Nevertheless, Protestant arguments and the advance of Protestant opinions in so much of Europe could not be overlooked forever. Pope Paul
III (reigned 1534–1549) began major reform by

appointing scholars and pious individuals to positions of power within the Church. He also approved the establishment of the Society of Jesus (1540), revived the Inquisition (1542), and eventually yielded to widespread demands for reform by calling the Council of Trent. It lasted from 1545 to 1563, with many recesses.

The Council of Trent took care of the main Protestant challenge by declaring that the Bible was not the only source of religious truth. The tradition of the Church, descending without a break from the Apostles, was of equal validity. In other matters of detail, the Council also explained doctrine in an anti-Protestant sense. The gap between the two camps was thus defined clearly, as had not at first been the case. The Council of Trent also reaffirmed the sovereign power of the papacy over the Church and entrusted to the pope the task of carrying out practical reform.

*The Jesuit Order*     The Society of Jesus played an active part in the deliberations of the Council of Trent. This was a new religious order, founded by St. Ignatius of Loyola (1491–1556). Loyola was a Spanish nobleman, who started out to be a soldier. While recovering from a battle wound, he decided to become a soldier for Christ. His first idea was to concentrate on converting the heathen, and for this he needed theological training. Loyola, therefore, took up study at the University of Paris, where he soon formed a small circle of similarly minded young men. They organized themselves into a religious order in Rome in 1534, and six years later were given papal blessing as the Society of Jesus.

The Society of Jesus differed from other religious orders in several respects. Its members offered themselves for any sort of service and, like soldiers, swore absolute obedience to their superiors. At the head of the order was a general—to begin with, Loyola himself—and the general took orders only from the pope. The Society of Jesus was thus like the royal standing armies that were coming into existence all over Europe: a body of trained and disciplined men at the disposal of the papacy. They quickly distinguished themselves as teachers, missionaries, and diplomats and became a power in Europe and the world comparable to that of an established state.

To train his shock troops, Loyola developed what he called Spiritual Exercises. Every member of the Jesuit order—as the Society of Jesus is often called—had to undergo special Spiritual Exercises once a year, and in case of need, more frequently. They lasted about a month, during which time the candidate was kept apart from others and commanded to reflect upon his sins, pray for forgiveness, and concentrate his entire attention upon key doctrines of the Church. The Exercises were so emotionally intense as to alter the personalities of those who experienced them. The aim was to strengthen individual character, producing men who would be fully conscious of their religious duty—resolute, self-disciplined, obedient at all times. St. Ignatius of Loyola was remarkably successful. Thanks largely to the Spiritual Exercises, thousands upon thousands of men who entered the Society of Jesus, from Loyola's day to the present, became new men to a degree seldom equaled by other religious orders or communities.

The Jesuits soon succeeded in checking the advance of the Protestant movement in Germany, and in eastern Europe they were the main agents in reconverting Poland and most of Hungary to Catholicism. Long efforts to bring England back to papal obedience eventually failed. Overseas, however, Jesuits were among the most active and successful Catholic missionaries, both in the Americas and in Asia.

Other important steps were taken to strengthen the Roman Catholic Church. Simple catechisms were introduced to teach the doctrines of the Church to everyone. The papal Inquisition sought out heretics in Italy and punished with death those who refused to recant. The Council of Trent created an Index of prohibited books. The popes kept the Index current by adding titles of new books that were judged damaging to the faith. In countries where the rulers cooperated, such books could not be printed or sold legally. School systems were much enlarged. The Jesuits distinguished themselves by making their schools the best in Europe, combining a thorough training in Latin and mathematics with religious instruction.

The upshot of the Protestant Reformation and the Roman Catholic response was to make Europeans far more conscious of religious duties and doctrines. Both the new Protestant churches of Germany and England and the revived Catholic churches in France, Italy, and Germany were more devout, learned, and serious organizations than had been true before Luther disturbed the religious balance of his time.

Yet religious division was the exact opposite of what everyone sought. There could be only one true Church and only one correct doctrine. All agreed on that. And the salvation of souls depended, everyone believed, on the correctness of beliefs and action in accordance with those beliefs. With these assumptions, no one could rest quietly when confronted by religious error. Their own immortal souls, and those of all persons around them, depended on suppressing mistaken and misguided opinions. It is not strange, therefore, that wars became religious, as Catholics and Protestants tried to impose their different versions of religious truth on each other.

# Religious and Dynastic Wars

Charles V abdicated in 1556 (effective 1558). He retired to a monastery and died soon after. The bulk of his possessions he left to his son Philip II of Spain. His brother Ferdinand I, however, inherited the Austrian lands and the title of Holy Roman Emperor. The two branches of the Hapsburg family continued to cooperate with each other in most matters, just as had been the case in Charles V's lifetime. Between them, Philip and Ferdinand inherited all the concerns that had distracted Charles V: the Turkish danger from the east, the rivalry with France, the Protestant movement in Germany and elsewhere. But Philip II tended to put a different priority upon the problems he faced. The suppression of Protestantism ranked higher for him than it had for Charles V, and the rivalry with France ranked correspondingly lower.

There was good reason for this, since France passed through a period of internal weakness from 1559 to 1598. In the first of these years, the French signed the Treaty of Cateau-Cambrésis with Philip II, withdrawing from Italy and also surrendering French claims to the Low Countries. For the next few years, weak French kings succeeded one another, and it became more and more obvious that the Valois royal family was about to die out. This raised the question of succession to the throne.

During the same years, Calvinist preaching was particularly active in France, and a party of Huguenots, as the French Calvinists were called, came into existence. They fought a series of low-grade civil wars against a rival Catholic faction, headed by the family of Guise. After the death of the last of the Valois kings in 1589, Henry of Navarre, a Protestant and first of the Bourbon line, laid claim to the throne. In 1594 he gave up his Protestantism for the Catholic faith, saying, "Paris is worth a Mass," and was crowned king. But Henry IV did not become really secure on the throne until he had come to terms with his former Huguenot allies. This he did through the Edict of Nantes (1598), which allowed great nobles and some towns to maintain Calvinist forms of worship and guaranteed them the same political rights as Catholics. Philip II of Spain died in the same year, and so he never had to face the strength of a reunited France.

As for the Turks, Philip II continued to wage war against them in the Mediterranean on and off until 1580, when he made a peace that recognized Turkish rights over the north coast of Africa as far west as Algiers. This agreement represented a considerable gain for the Turks, though in fact they were never able to control North Africa from Istanbul. Instead, Algerian pirates preyed upon any and all ships that came their way, with scant regard for their supposed obedience to the Ottoman sultan.

Philip concentrated on the struggle against heresy and met with much success. As we have seen, the energy and religious conviction of the Roman Catholic Church increased greatly, beginning with the pontificate of Pope Paul III (1534–1549). Spanish piety and Spanish ideals played a large part in this revival. Cooperation between the reformed papacy and the two branches of the Hapsburg house remained very close. All of central and eastern Europe felt the impact. Hapsburg officials, Jesuit confessors, and Catholic schools worked together to overwhelm Protestant heresy throughout a broad band of territory that reached from Italy northward across the Alps into Austrian, south German, Hungarian, and Polish lands. Only northern Germany and Scandinavia, together with the parts of Hungary under Turkish rule and areas of the Rhineland under Protestant German princes, escaped the force of this Catholic counteroffensive.

## The Limits of Hapsburg Power

In the western parts of Europe, however, Philip II of Spain met with serious setbacks. His wife, the English queen Mary, failed to bring her country back permanently into the Catholic fold. Worse still, the Netherlands revolted in 1567. Seasoned Spanish troops reconquered the southern part of the Netherlands (roughly, modern Belgium), but in the north the Dutch provinces could not be subdued because the Dutch held command of the sea and were able to move supplies and troops to any threatened place more easily than the Spaniards could move overland against them.

The rebels received some help from Queen Elizabeth of England. English pirates, such as John Hawkins and Francis Drake, had also begun to prey upon Spanish ships on the high seas and to plunder Spanish towns in the New World. This eventually persuaded King Philip to try to settle accounts with the English, instead of concentrating everything against the Dutch. He therefore sent a great fleet northward in 1588, intending that it should pick up Spanish troops from the southern Netherlands and then attack England.

But Philip's plan failed. When his fleet, the Spanish Armada, sailed through the English Channel, it suffered repeated attacks from Queen Elizabeth's ships, whose cannon fire damaged the Spanish galleons so badly that the plan of invading England had to be given up. Instead of trying to fight its way back through the Channel, the Armada's commander decided to return to Spain by sailing north around Scotland and Ireland. But his ships were caught in violent storms. Almost none of them got back safely to Spain.

King Philip's death in 1598 marked a turning point in Spanish fortunes. For nearly a century, Spain has been the greatest power in Europe, as well as mistress of the New World. After Philip's death, a reunited France, led by the new Bourbon dynasty, challenged Spain's political dominance in western Europe. Fifty years later, by 1650, the French monarchy had clearly become more powerful than the Hapsburgs of Spain. During the same years, the naval strength of England and of the Dutch Republic increased on all the oceans of the world at the expense of Spain and Portugal. Within Europe, it became more and more difficult for the Spanish government to keep up the armies required to defend the imperial position that the country had won between 1492 and 1598.

*The Thirty Years' War*    On the other hand, between 1618 and 1635, the Austrian branch of the Hapsburg house came close to winning control over all Germany. The progress of the Catholic Reformation in German lands strengthened the position of the Hapsburgs. In 1618, Protestant Bohemian nobles, fearing the consolidation of Catholic power, attempted to throw off Hapsburg control. This action started thirty years of bitter war that soon spread through most of Germany. On the one side stood Ferdinand II, Holy Roman Emperor and champion of Catholicism (reigned 1619–1637). On the other side gathered an unstable collection of Protestant princes. Early in the Thirty Years' War, Ferdinand overcame the Bohemian rebels (1620) and made that extensive kingdom thoroughly subject to his government for the first time. This resulted in a great expansion of his effective power, for Bohemia (modern Czech Republic) was richer as well as bigger than the Austrian lands.

Ferdinand also discovered that he could create a vast army by allowing soldiers to live off the land. Albert of Wallenstein was the imperial general who first showed how to create and support an overwhelming force by plundering what they conquered. Each time Wallenstein's army entered a new district, his soldiers ravaged it completely. As imperial armies occupied more and more territory, the resulting devastation was enormous.

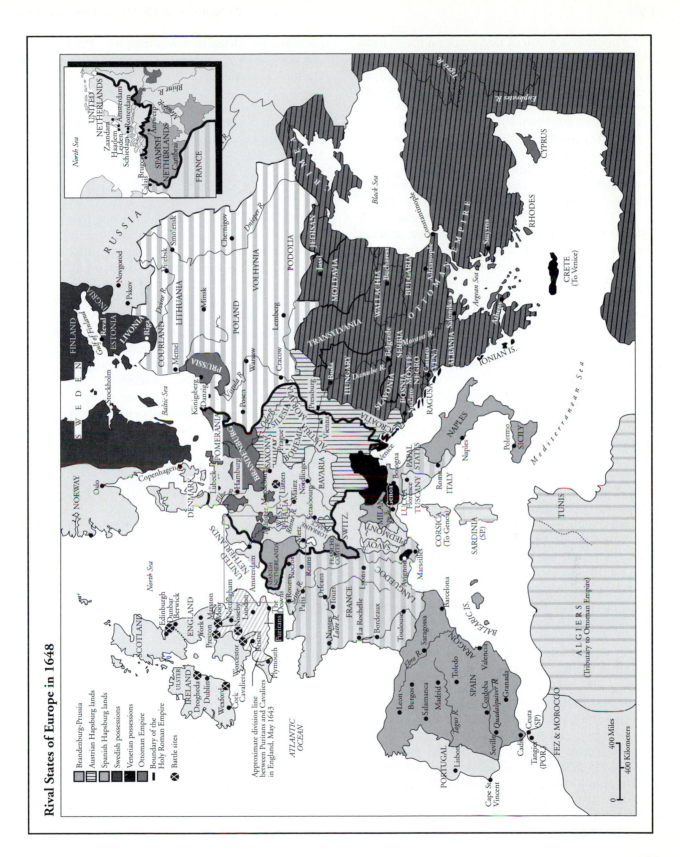

**Rival States of Europe in 1648**

Legend:
- Brandenburg-Prussia
- Austrian Hapsburg lands
- Spanish Hapsburg lands
- Swedish possessions
- Venetian possessions
- Ottoman Empire
- Boundary of the Holy Roman Empire
- ⊗ Battle sites

Approximate division line between Puritans and Cavaliers in England, May 1643

400 Miles
400 Kilometers
0

The intervention of Denmark on the Protestant side (1625) did not check the progress of the emperor's armies; but when Gustavus Adolphus, king of Sweden, entered the war against the emperor in 1630, his army temporarily reversed the balance. Sweden thus burst upon the European scene as a great power after centuries of poverty and weakness partly because the king succeeded in taming Swedish nobles by mobilizing the peasantry; and partly because Dutch ships developed a far more vigorous trade with all the Baltic lands. Tolls from traders gave Gustavus Adolphus money to equip a formidable army; and his Protestant convictions and desire for territorial expansion persuaded him to use it on German soil.

The Swedes won several famous victories but could not destroy their opponents. In 1632 Gustavus Adolphus died in battle. Two years later Wallenstein, Emperor Ferdinand's most successful general, was assassinated. He had quarreled with his imperial master and may have planned to make himself and his army supreme in Germany.

By now almost everybody was sick and tired of the war, which had become more destructive than any in memory. The aging Emperor Ferdinand died in 1637. He was succeeded by Ferdinand III (reigned 1637–1657), who wanted to make peace. The hope of uniting all Germany again no longer seemed worth the cost. The danger to the Hapsburgs of an over-mighty general, such as Wallenstein, and of an army of plunderers had become quite obvious. Nevertheless, the war went on until 1648. The main reason was that the French intervened in 1635, hoping to keep the Austrian Hapsburgs busy in Germany so that they could not come to the aid of their Spanish relatives, who began a war with France in 1622. The war between France and Spain lasted until 1659, when the reluctant Spaniards were compelled to cede a few towns in the Netherlands and territories along the Pyrenees frontier to France.

The Treaty of Westphalia finally ended the Thirty Years' War in 1648, leaving Germany devastated and divided into literally hundreds of separate little states. The Dutch Republic and Switzerland were both formally recognized as separate and independent countries, no longer part of the Holy Roman Empire. France and Sweden emerged as great powers, the one in western Europe, the other in the northeast. The weakened Hapsburgs were no longer a match for the combination of their French, Swedish, and Protestant German enemies. A new era of French predominance in European politics began.

## Internal Political Development

In 1500 nearly every ruler in Europe had to bargain with his subjects over paying taxes. Usually a meeting of "Estates" (Diet or Parliament) authorized the ruling king or prince to collect certain taxes for particular purposes and for a limited period of time. The Estates represented the nobles, clergy, and townspeople who paid taxes or helped to collect them from the peasants. Only in Italy did governments have standing professional armies and a large enough income to pay salaries to civilian officials.

By 1650 in Spain, France, Italy, and the Germanies, rulers generally had become absolute monarchs. This did not mean that they could do anything they wanted to do. It did mean that they did not have to consult representative bodies before collecting taxes or before spending tax income for whatever purposes the ruler and his personal advisers thought good. The religious wars in France, the Thirty Years' War in Germany, the Counter-Reformation in Italy, and the suppression of internal revolts in Spain had led to this result.

In fact, European rulers kept the interests of their subjects constantly in mind. They knew very well that their power depended on being able to supply their armies with guns and ammunition, food, clothes, and all the other things soldiers need. Equipping an army depended on industry and on trade. It meant trying to collect as much ready money inside the kingdom as possible, so as to be able to buy whatever might be needed. It meant, in short, close cooperation with bankers and businessmen.

One important European government did not follow this policy. The Spanish rulers actually persecuted townsfolk who were not good Catholics, and they banished Jews and Moriscos (converted Moslems) from the country. These latter two groups had been among the most active businessmen of Spain, and their departure helped to bring on the economic decay from which Spain began to suffer after 1600. In general, the Spanish government fostered the interests of the Church and of the clergy more than of any other group in the population. The policy was successful in uniting Spain under the king and gave the Spaniards a cause for which to fight. But it weakened Spain economically, and other kings were not eager to follow such a policy.

The countries that lay around the edges of Europe's center did not become absolute monarchies before 1650, although England came close to it under the Tudors (1485–1603). Parliament became almost a rubber stamp for Henry VIII and Elizabeth I. Under the Stuart kings, who succeeded Elizabeth, however, Parliament reasserted its claim to a controlling voice in royal policies, and civil war eventually led to the establishment of full-blown parliamentary government after 1688. The nobility of Portugal, Ireland, and Scotland, continued to be able to defy their respective kings with armed force when it suited them. In Poland and Hungary noble Diets kept sovereign political and military power in their own hands, for elected kings of these two countries had no administrative machinery to make their will effective.

Scattered through the heartland of Europe were the remnants of medieval city-states. In the Dutch Republic and in Switzerland, such cities managed to create powerful and important new confederations. The Dutch, in fact, became the leading sea power of the world and handled the big business interests of all of Europe. As for the Swiss, they were famous soldiers and mercenaries. The Swiss Confederation was dominated by self-governing cities, such as Geneva, Zurich, and Berne, just as the Dutch Republic was dominated by Amsterdam, Rotterdam and lesser cities. Venice, in Italy, and a score or so of imperial free cities in Germany carried on medieval traditions of republican self-government; but in these old-fashioned city-states, political power nearly always lodged in the hands of a privileged and wealthy upper class.

Only a few religious radicals supposed that the people had the right to govern themselves. It seemed self-evident that God had created separate social classes or, as they were usually called, Estates. Some people were peasants, some were artisans; others were kings or nobles. Society was like a body. It needed a head, but it also needed feet and hands. Each class, or Estate, had its appropriate part to play. If any class refused to fulfill its proper function, then the body politic was diseased. Nothing would go right until the disorder ended. The gap between rich and poor, educated and uneducated, peasant and master, was very great. Differences in clothing showed at a glance who was who. Manners and the way a person walked and talked showed his or her class as well as where he or she had come from. Each rank had its duties as well as its rights, and there was always the possibility for a gifted or lucky individual to rise through government service, since the king or prince could issue patents of nobility to anyone he chose. A rich businessman could buy such titles or an official might be rewarded for faithful service with a title to nobility.

On top of the whole system stood kings and princes, who recognized no superior but God. They held their positions by God's choice. Hence they ruled by divine right, just as their subjects served and obeyed by doing whatever they were born to do, according to God's will. Revolution, by such standards, was always wrong. Any injustices of this world would be corrected in the next. Only false religion, which might keep souls from Heaven, could justify rebellion. Hence, it is not really surprising that the wars and revolts, of which the century and a half between 1500 and 1650 was unusually full, were justified in religious terms by the combatants.

A glaring gap in this social theory was that no rules or limits applied to the relations of one ruler with another. Each ruler claimed absolute sovereignty within his own territory. Each claimed the right to make war or peace with any or all neighbors. Scholars tried to find a natural law that would instruct and guide rulers in their dealings with one another. A Dutchman, Hugo Grotius (1583–1645), wrote a famous book entitled *On the Law of War and Peace* with this purpose in mind. But kings and princes followed Grotius' rules only when it pleased them.

In effect, the problem that had troubled Europe since feudal times—how to maintain public peace—was simply shifted to a different level. Rulers who succeeded in suppressing the war-making power of the nobility brought a higher level of peace and order to their kingdoms than Europe had known since the days of the Roman Empire. But they used the same military force that kept peace at home to attack one another—with results that could be disastrous, as the Thirty Years' War showed.

## The Realm of Thought

The basic fact in Europe's intellectual history in these years was the breadth and depth of uncertainty that became apparent everywhere. The Reformation made the question of authority in matters of religion acute for everyone. Discoveries made by European explorers proved that the classical authors of antiquity had often been wrong about geography and knew nothing about the plants and animals of the New World. A series of important inventions, starting just before 1600, also allowed experts to see and measure things far more accurately than ever before. The microscope (invented ca. 1590), the pendulum clock (invented ca. 1656), the thermometer (invented ca. 1607), the telescope (invented ca. 1608), and the barometer (invented ca. 1643)—all sharpened human senses and extended the range of observation as dramatically as the explorations a century earlier had done. Discovery of microorganisms in drops of water was no less surprising than the moons of Jupiter. Things of which no one had ever dreamed suddenly became obvious. But such new knowledge discredited old authorities. Who and what should be believed? Was the Bible really infallible?

## The Search for Certainty

Europeans responded to the tremendous uncertainty of the years 1500–1650 in two contradictory ways. Some, probably the majority, tried desperately to mend the chinks in their world view by finding a total and complete answer to all important questions through an act of faith. Calvin and his fellow Protestants, for example, made one basic assumption: God had told human beings all they needed to know in the Bible. Careful study of the Scriptures would, therefore, answer all important questions. Anything omit-

**The Agony of Uncertainty**   This detail from an altarpiece showing the Crucifixion was painted in 1515, on the very eve of the Reformation, by Mathias Grunewald at Isenheim, Alsace. It portrays Mary Magdalene at the foot of the Cross, despairing at Christ's impending death. Her hands are especially eloquent of the agony of uncertainty—an agony felt by Christ's followers who had expected the Messiah to restore the Kingdom of David in Jerusalem. This torment was felt almost as acutely by those who followed Luther in denouncing the Pope for leading Christians away from the true path of salvation. This painting suggests the intensity of religious feeling and anxiety that the Lutheran movement tapped in Germany; in fact, the artist did associate with Lutherans in his later life.

ted from the Scriptures was by definition unimportant, and the only things that really mattered were the issues of salvation and righteousness with which the Scriptures dealt. The appeal of Calvinism rested largely on the logical simplicity of this assumption and on the skill with which Calvin was able to find answers from Scripture for the burning issues of the day. Roman Catholics, when stirred again to action by the Protestant challenge, also offered a complete system of belief. The more complicated origins of canon law and Catholic theology (based upon the Church Fathers, upon natural reason, upon Roman law, and upon decrees of the popes and councils, as well as upon the Holy Scriptures) were counterbalanced by the greater completeness of the intellectual system and the detailed rules for personal conduct that Catholic priests could offer the faithful in nearly every circumstance.

The effort to find an authoritative answer for every important question was shared also by the greatest philosopher of the age, René Descartes (1596–1650). Descartes was a Frenchman, Jesuit-trained. He had a powerful bent for mathematics and invented analytic geometry by combining the ideas and techniques of algebra and geometry. Descartes believed that mathematical reasoning could arrive at truths that everyone would have to accept. Each step followed logically and necessarily from the one before. A handful of simple self-evident assumptions were all that mathematicians needed to arrive at surprising and useful results. Why not, therefore, try the same thing with the age-old questions of theology and philosophy, about which everyone was quarreling so bitterly?

Descartes eagerly set out and found that he could logically doubt everything except the fact of his own existence. "I think, therefore I am" was his famous phrase. From this slender assumption he then set out to answer all important questions by logical deduction. The existence of God; the nature of the soul; how the world machine, sun, moon, and stars worked; and how animal bodies functioned could all be demonstrated, according to Descartes, by careful reasoning.

The trouble, of course, was that the biblical, the Catholic, and Descartes' mathematical answers did not agree with each other. No one of them, even if complete and persuasive by itself, could command the acceptance of all Europeans. This indeed was what all the argument was about and what gave rise to so much persecution and bloodshed.

A few thinkers responded to this distressing situation by concentrating attention on whatever happened to interest them, leaving the big questions unanswered. In this way separate sciences and branches of a study made great progress. Sometimes, indeed, scientific advances upset older ideas that had been made part of official Church doctrine. In such cases the difference in outlook came clear between specialists who cared for detail and accuracy and others who felt that overall certainty was the only thing that really mattered. Calvin, no less than the papal Inquisition that condemned Galileo's astronomical discoveries, could not let specialists pull down sacred doctrine. But the specialists had a way of winning in the end because they based their work on more and more exact observation, measurement, and experiment.

## The Development of Science

The scientists who took such pains to observe and measure and calculate had special reasons for doing so. Two great theories about the world were in conflict: One was based on Aristotle's logic and other writings while the other, mystical and mathematical, looked back to Plato. Aristotle's way of thinking had been skillfully worked into a Christian mold by the great medieval Scholastics, chief of whom was St. Thomas Acquinas. Aristotle's physics and astronomy, revised in the light of more recent information, had also been well worked out before 1500. There was nothing important left to discover along these lines, a fact that made it all the easier for the Roman Catholic Church to make Aristotelian science official.

During the Renaissance, however, men had rediscovered Plato and ancient "Pythagorean" writers. During his student days at the University of Padua in Italy, for example, Nicolaus Copernicus (1473–1543) accepted Pythagorean ideas about the mystical power and special qualities of numbers. He later argued that the earth revolved around the sun because a circular path for the planets were more "perfect" than the complicated movements required by the Ptolemaic-Aristotelian theory that made sun, moon, and planets revolve around the earth. Johannes Kepler (1571–1630) corrected Copernicus' theory by discovering that the path of the planets around the sun was not circular but elliptical. This required exact observation and measurement of the positions of the planets. It also required, or at least was inspired by Kepler's conviction, that mathematical ratios between the orbits of the different planets created the "music of the spheres" of which Plato and Pythagoras had written.

In medicine, too, an extraordinary character, who called himself Paracelsus (1493–1541), challenged the authority of Galen on mystical grounds. Only then did careful surgeons, such as Andreas Vesalius (1514–1564), discover errors that resulted from the fact that Galen had used pigs instead of human corpses for dissection. Once Galen's authority had been shaken by such discoveries, doctors began to experiment with new drugs and treatments for disease—often, perhaps, more to the injury than to the benefit of their patients. All the same, knowledge increased. William Harvey (1575–1657), for example, laid the foundation for modern physiology by figuring out that the heart was a pump and that it circulated blood throughout the body by means of the arteries and veins. He was led to this theory, however, by the same complex of Platonic-Pythagorean lore that treated the human body as a microcosm of the universe, and the heart as equivalent to the sun around which, by the new Copernican theory, everything else revolved.

The thought of Francis Bacon (1561–1626) and of Galileo Galilei (1564–1642), like that of their contemporary René Descartes, marked the coming of age of a new era in European science. Francis Bacon was a successful English lawyer, but in his spare time he set out to invent a new sort of logic that would improve on Aristotle's. He believed that if people would only stop arguing about abstract matters and instead use their senses to observe nature and keep careful count of what they saw, all sorts of new and useful in-

formation could be discovered. Bacon was no scientist himself, nor was he, like Descartes, a great mathematician. His ideas remained apart from the mainstream of scientific development; and, in fact, no one ever really followed his inductive method of scientific discovery in arriving at important new ideas and theories. Yet Bacon put a new challenge to old Aristotelian ideas in the field and helped to give English thought its own distinct character, more concrete and down to earth than the theories that had greater appeal on the continent of Europe.

Galileo, on the contrary, was a great practical inventor and discoverer, as well as a theorist. Unlike Descartes, he did not try to use mathematical reasoning to construct a complete system of knowledge. Galileo merely found ways to measure exactly how physical bodies moved, and put his results into mathematical form. He never tried to answer every question the way Descartes did. Instead he stuck to a limited range—to what we call physics and astronomy today. He was an ingenious experimenter and pioneered the use of the telescope, discovering not only Jupiter's moons and Saturn's rings, but sunspots as well—thus, incidentally, disproving one of Aristotle's principles about the perfection of heavenly bodies.

More than any other single person, Galileo can be considered the founder of modern science. He tested theories by observation and experiment, and he argued for his own discoveries and theories with unusual literary skill. Near the end of Galileo's life, the papal Inquisition compelled him to state publicly that some of his astronomical theories were wrong. Galileo submitted in order to keep out of trouble, but in private he made it quite clear that his opinions had not changed just because some officials of the Church made him say he had been in error.

Overall, the tensions and points of friction between those who tried to find complete answers to all questions in a total system of belief and those who kept searching for new information and knowledge in detail proved extraordinarily fruitful. Neither the one nor the other could long relax and assume that there was nothing more to find out, or no new point to defend.

**New Sciences** Galileo was born in Pisa, Italy, and started his career by lecturing on mathematics at the University of Pisa, within sight of the cathedral bell tower pictured above. The bell tower leans because of faulty foundations and was already famous in Galileo's day for its tilt. After Galileo discovered that falling bodies accelerate uniformly regardless of their weight—a proposition that refuted a doctrine of Aristotelian physics—someone invented the story that he proved his point by dropping different-sized cannon balls from this tower. But by the time Galileo worked out his new mathematical physics, he was far away at Padua and never returned to his native city for any such demonstration.

Below, Rembrandt's painting, "The Anatomy Lesson" illustrates another side of European science—exact observation and the use of drawings to record what had been discovered. Human anatomy became accurately known through such methods—an advance of intense interest to artists as well as to medical students, like those being instructed here.

Europeans pursued truth along many different lines. Sometimes, perhaps, the yawning uncertainties seemed dreadfully frightening. But the effort to do something about uncertainties meant rapid increases in knowledge and a restless testing of every idea and belief. The birth of modern science, with all the consequences that it had in later times, was the unexpected result. Human minds had never engaged in more fruitful or more fateful endeavor. The society and technology, the ideas and beliefs, and the power and the risks of our own age arise largely from the continued development and practical applications of science as pioneered in the age of Galileo, Bacon, and Descartes.

## The Pursuit of Beauty

The efforts Europeans made to discover truth were matched by almost equally fruitful efforts to give expression to their sense of beauty. In literature, the century and a half from 1500 to 1650 was the time when most of the existing literary languages of western Europe achieved their definition. Miguel de Cervantes (1547–1616) in *Don Quixote* mocked medieval romances and created literary Spanish. French owed its literary definition largely to John Calvin, who wrote a version of his *Institutes of the Christian Religion* in that language. Luther's Bible shaped modern German. The King James Bible (1611), together with William Shakespeare (1564–1616) and other Elizabethan poets, established modern English.

Latin remained the usual language for scholarship and science. It was also used for literary expression by men of letters such as Desiderius Erasmus (1466–1536) and Thomas More (1478–1535). In *Utopia,* More indirectly criticized injustices of the England of his day by describing a never-never land where people behaved rationally.

In the field of art, the force of Italian example was very strong. Especially in Catholic Europe, a more elaborate art style, called baroque, spread from Italy over southern Germany and eastward into the Austrian lands and Poland. The same style took root in the New World, where great baroque churches attested to the power of the clergy to organize the labor and loyalty of the Amerindians.

Distinct national schools of painting arose in Germany, Spain, and the Low Countries. Painters such as the German Albrecht Dürer (1471–1528), the Spaniard Diego Velásquez (1599–1660), the Fleming Pieter Brueghel (1525–1569), and the Dutchman Rembrandt van Rijn (1606–1669) were each able to express something of the distinct national character of their homeland.

In Italy, the great days of Renaissance art ended with the disastrous wars that began with the French invasion of 1494. Particularly after the sack of Rome by Charles V's soldiers in 1527, one of the main centers of patronage for art was gone. The Catholic Reformation was less friendly than before to artists and to secular pursuits in general. Nevertheless, in Venice a school of painters carried on, including many well-known artists among its followers—Titian (1490–1576), Tintoretto (1512–1594), and Paolo Veronese (1528–1588) being the most famous.

Differing local traditions of art were sometimes mingled in the work of a single artist. The career of Domenico Theotocópuli (1541–1614)—born in Crete, trained in Italy, and active during his mature years in Spain, where he was commonly called El Greco (the Greek)—clearly showed the influence of all three of the environments he inhabited, allowing him to create a style that was distinctly his own.

In northern Europe (particularly in the Dutch provinces), artists took on new roles in society. Paintings intended for private display in homes could be bought and sold like other luxuries. This contrasted with older ideas about art, displayed in churches and other public places and intended to edify and instruct as well as to please the public.

In accordance with their new social role, a distinct Dutch school of artists came into existence which, along with Venetian, Spanish and German schools, added greatly to the variety of European painting. But all these separate schools belonged together in some fundamental ways. They all accepted the techniques of per-

**Middle Class Comfort**   Despite all the religious and political conflict in Europe, town life flourished in the sixteenth and seventeenth centuries, and a growing number of private families began to enjoy new standards of domestic comfort. This painting by Jan Vermeer (1632–1675) shows some of the things a private family could expect to possess: glass windows to let in light and keep out the weather, for instance, together with table and chair, silverware for serving food and drink, a map hanging on the wall, and varied kinds of cloth covering the table, draped over the back of the chair and, of course, used also for clothing. Vermeer's wife suffered bankruptcy after his death, and he may have ranked as a poor man in his native town of Delft, but his pictures breathe an atmosphere of quiet comfort and tranquility that was enjoyed by the more prosperous citizens of his age.

spective that had first been worked out in Italy about 1440, and all agreed that a good painting should create an illusion of three-dimensional reality. These areas of agreement corresponded to the larger fact that Europe continued to have a loose but very real cultural unity throughout this age of sharp transition, despite all the fighting and quarreling in which Europeans continued to indulge.

Music, also, began to broaden. Systematic notation made possible more formal compositions. Court rituals and military parades gave new occasions for musical performances. Improved instruments opened new possibilities for harmony and rhythm. Singing and accompaniments became more closely linked to each other. In Italy the beginnings of opera date from before 1650. Congregational singing was a prominent part of Protestant services. Musical culture spread with Luther's hymns and Calvinist singing of psalms, as well as with the more stately and elaborate organ music that the Roman Catholic Church permitted after the composer Giovanni Palestrina (1525–1594) showed what could be done by combining choral voices with organ music.

Europe's artistic life was thus vigorous and varied, open to new ways of doing things. Patterns of thought and patterns of art and literature that had been created in the Middle Ages were not treated reverently, as though they were models that could not be tampered with. Even the ancients, who had been held up as models by the humanists of the Italian Renaissance, were found to be in error on important points. People were thrown back on their own resources—to pick and choose from the past and from what they could find in the world around them.

Such an open situation positively invited experiment and a more or less free personal invention in the fields of art, as well as in thought. In both these fields, Europeans responded to their opportunity much as they were doing in practical lines of activity, that is, with extraordinary energy, imagination, and creativity.

## Conclusion

The common denominator of all the confusing changes that came to Europe between 1500 and 1650 was this: Western Europeans learned how to expand and intensify activity in almost every sphere of human concern. Overall, this meant a great increase in the power of their civilization, both at home and in contacts with peoples of other cultural traditions.

New kinds of organization allowed larger numbers to cooperate in peaceable and in warlike undertakings. The joint stock company, for example, was perfected just after 1600. Under a legal charter, it allowed the shared ownership of a company through the purchase of stock. The joint owners were liable in case of bankruptcy for only the amount of money each of them had invested. And, of course, as long as the company prospered, a joint owner could sell his share, sometimes at a price higher than he paid for it. Modern corporations are built on the same principles. This kind of business organization allowed thousands to work together over long periods of time for goals defined by a small group of managers. Savings could be pooled, risks spread out, and special skills put to fuller use by this kind of organization than was possible with family businesses or partnerships.

In politics, nothing quite so novel as the joint stock company was invented. Bureaucracy and standing armies were very old. But they became much more efficient and took charge of more and more activities. Local self-help and the authority of separate town governments suffered; so did the rights of noble lords over their peasants. Simultaneously, it became easier for merchants to buy or sell anywhere within the kingdom without having to submit to local guild rules.

Royal and princely governments also learned how to mobilize a larger proportion of the resources of their subjects for public pur-

poses. Everything became more complicated as it assumed a larger scale. A handful of knights, supported by local peasants, no longer had any value on the battlefield. Instead, by the end of the period, dozens of cannons and thousands of muskets were what mattered, along with men carefully trained to use these weapons effectively. Skilled artisans, financiers, miners, smelters, wagon train drivers, riverboat captains and crews of seagoing vessels, tax collectors, army officers, drillmasters, and literally thousands of other specialists were needed to create and maintain such armies. But the cooperation of so many specialists produced more effective armies. Every new invention or improvement that worked spread rapidly, for no government could long afford to be without an armed force that could hold its own against neighboring states.

In thought and in culture, too, Europeans were able to find many new ways to mobilize greater energies. Sale of printed books, for example, allowed a man such as Erasmus to make a living as an author and scholar without having to take a post in a university or with the Church. The theater, too, by charging admission, created a livelihood for actors and playwrights such as William Shakespeare. Together, these changes gave secular literature a wider scope than before.

The printing press also had great importance in spreading new ideas more rapidly and more accurately than previously. Luther's pamphlets, for example, made it practicable for anyone who could read to learn the full details of his challenge to the papacy from Luther's own words—and to hear the arguments of his opponents, as well. In less controversial fields, too, the printing press made exchange of information far more efficient. Travelers' reports of new lands, woodcuts portraying newly discovered objects, maps drawn according to the latest information, anatomical and botanical drawings, mathematical proofs, philosophical or theological arguments—any sort of data, in fact—could be made public through printing.

This meant that those who cared about any particular line of inquiry could secure the latest and best information much more easily than before, even when they happened to live far away from the place where a new invention or new things had first been discovered. Once again, human energies over wider areas could be mobilized more efficiently: Each new idea or new bit of knowledge that entered European learning gave people more to think about. And just as the best-supplied and best-organized armies usually won battles, so also the best-informed and most experienced minds usually won arguments—and in doing so, enriched, enlarged, and expanded the intellectual inheritance of Europe as a whole.

Nowhere else in the world were these centuries nearly so full of fundamental novelties and departures from old ways. The appearance of well-armed European vessels along the shores of Asia did not make much difference to the old civilizations of that part of the world. Moslems, Hindus, Chinese, and Japanese were interested in retaining what they had and in keeping any necessary changes to a minimum. Only Europeans found it possible and necessary to question the assumptions of their ancestors so drastically—and so fruitfully. As a result, Europeans slowly but surely began to leave other peoples behind.

# Bibliography

Contemporary literary materials begin to multiply so enormously that it is difficult to choose which to mention here. Shakespeare's plays in English and Rabelais, *Gargantua and Pantagruel*, in French are among the most obvious literary monuments of the age. Luther, *Christian Liberty*, offers the most condensed and powerful statement of Luther's ideals; Loyola's *Spiritual Exercises* provides a window upon the Catholic counter thrust. Both of these are available in English in several editions. Galileo, *Dialogue Concerning the Two Chief World Systems—Ptolemaic and Copernican* (Stillman Drake, trans., 2nd ed., 1967), is both readable and an important landmark of the scientific revolution. Drake has also translated some of Galileo's other writings dealing with motion, comets, sunspots, and the like. Anyone wishing to understand more about Europe's self-transformation might profitably spend time with any and all of the above.

Brief but penetrating general overviews of the age are available in Eugene F. Rice, Jr., *The Foundations of Early Modern Europe, 1460–1559* (1970), and A. G. Dickens, *Reformation and Society in Sixteenth-Century Europe* (1966). Equally interesting, but much longer, are the two most influential works of twentieth-century scholarship pertaining to this age: Max Weber, *The Protestant Ethic and the Spirit of Capitalism* (1930), and Fernand Braudel, *The Mediterranean and the Mediterranean World in the Age of Philip II* (2 vols., rev. ed., 1977).

On the religious upheaval, Euan Cameron, *The European Reformation* (1991); A. G. Dickens, *The Counter Reformation* (1969); and Louis W. Spitz, *The Protestant Reformation, 1517–1559* (1985), are authoritative. For the underside of European religious controversy, see Brian P. Levack, *The Witch Hunt in Early Modern Europe* (1987). On the transformation of science, A. Rupert Hall, *The Scientific Revolution, 1500–1800* (2nd ed., 1962), and Herbert Butterfield, *The Origins of Modern Science 1300–1700* (rev. ed., 1957), are reliable standbys. For background and continuities, David C. Lindberg, *The Beginnings of Western Science: The European Scientific Tradition in Philosophical, Religions, and Institutional Context, 600 B.C. to A.D. 1450* (1992), is up to date and magisterial. Reappraisal of the contribution of mystical traditions to modern science are reflected in Frances Yates, *Giordano Bruno and the Hermetic Tradition* (1964). For the collision between Galileo and the papal Inquisition, see Giorgio de Santillana, *The Crime of Galileo* (1955).

On military matters four books are of special interest: Geoffrey Parker, *The Military Revolution 1500–1800* (1988); J. R. Hale, *War and Society in Renaissance Europe, 1450–1620* (1985); W. H. McNeill, *The Pursuit of Power: Technology, Armed Force and Society since A.D. 1000* (1982); and a clear and concise summary by Michael Howard, *War in European History* (1976). On printing, see Elizabeth L. Eisenstein, *The Printing Press as an Agent of Change: Communications and Cultural Transformations in Early Modern Europe* (2 vols., 1979).

Two other books deserve mention: Garrett Mattingly, *The Armada* (1959), because it is a literary work of extraordinary power; and Jan DeVries, *European Urbanization, 1500–1800* (1984), because it looks at the social and economic transformation of Europe in a new way by focusing on cities rather than on countries.

Art historians tend to specialize by countries and often write on individual artists. For introductory purposes, a standard textbook like H. W. Janson, *History of Art* (4th ed., 1991), is the easiest way to get a feel for the age by looking at and reading about some of Europe's principal works of art.

# Technology, Transport, and Communication; 1400 to present

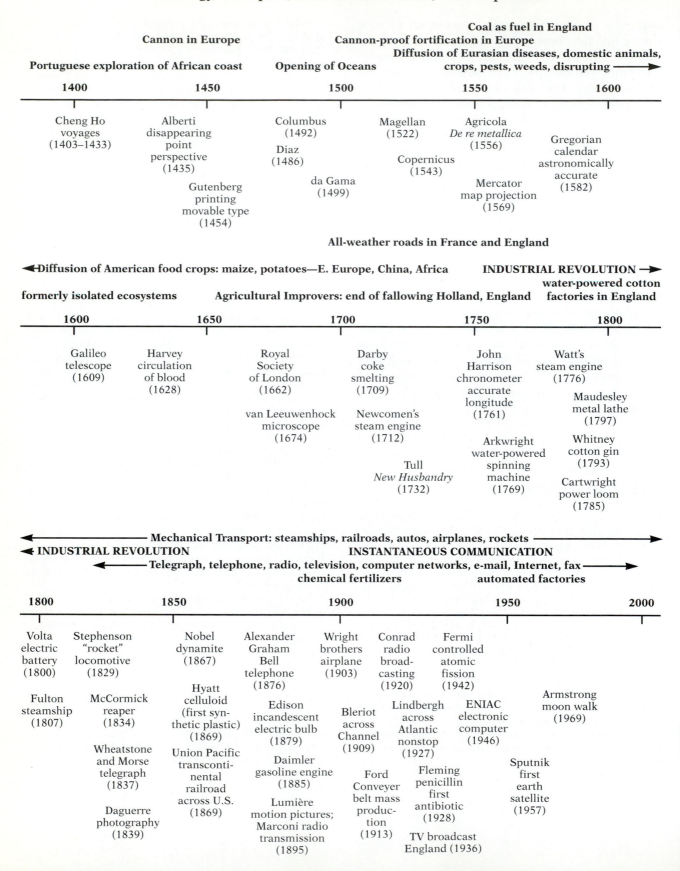

**Coal as fuel in England**

**Cannon in Europe**   **Cannon-proof fortification in Europe**

**Diffusion of Eurasian diseases, domestic animals,**

**Portuguese exploration of African coast**   **Opening of Oceans**   **crops, pests, weeds, disrupting** ——▶

| 1400 | 1450 | 1500 | 1550 | 1600 |

Cheng Ho voyages (1403–1433)

Alberti disappearing point perspective (1435)

Gutenberg printing movable type (1454)

Columbus (1492)

Diaz (1486)

da Gama (1499)

Magellan (1522)

Copernicus (1543)

Agricola *De re metallica* (1556)

Mercator map projection (1569)

Gregorian calendar astronomically accurate (1582)

**All-weather roads in France and England**

◀—**Diffusion of American food crops: maize, potatoes—E. Europe, China, Africa**   **INDUSTRIAL REVOLUTION** —▶

**formerly isolated ecosystems**   **Agricultural Improvers: end of fallowing Holland, England**   **water-powered cotton factories in England**

| 1600 | 1650 | 1700 | 1750 | 1800 |

Galileo telescope (1609)

Harvey circulation of blood (1628)

Royal Society of London (1662)

van Leeuwenhock microscope (1674)

Darby coke smelting (1709)

Newcomen's steam engine (1712)

Tull *New Husbandry* (1732)

John Harrison chronometer accurate longitude (1761)

Arkwright water-powered spinning machine (1769)

Watt's steam engine (1776)

Maudesley metal lathe (1797)

Whitney cotton gin (1793)

Cartwright power loom (1785)

◀————**Mechanical Transport: steamships, railroads, autos, airplanes, rockets** ————▶
◀ **INDUSTRIAL REVOLUTION**   **INSTANTANEOUS COMMUNICATION**
◀——— **Telegraph, telephone, radio, television, computer networks, e-mail, Internet, fax** ——▶
**chemical fertilizers**   **automated factories**

| 1800 | 1850 | 1900 | 1950 | 2000 |

Volta electric battery (1800)

Fulton steamship (1807)

Stephenson "rocket" locomotive (1829)

McCormick reaper (1834)

Wheatstone and Morse telegraph (1837)

Daguerre photography (1839)

Nobel dynamite (1867)

Hyatt celluloid (first synthetic plastic) (1869)

Union Pacific transcontinental railroad across U.S. (1869)

Alexander Graham Bell telephone (1876)

Edison incandescent electric bulb (1879)

Daimler gasoline engine (1885)

Lumière motion pictures; Marconi radio transmission (1895)

Wright brothers airplane (1903)

Bleriot across Channel (1909)

Ford Conveyer belt mass production (1913)

Conrad radio broadcasting (1920)

Lindbergh across Atlantic nonstop (1927)

Fleming penicillin first antibiotic (1928)

TV broadcast England (1936)

Fermi controlled atomic fission (1942)

ENIAC electronic computer (1946)

Armstrong moon walk (1969)

Sputnik first earth satellite (1957)

# *The World Beyond Europe*
## 1500 to 1700

# 17

**African Majesty**  Here you see the Obo of Benin,
ruler of a powerful state in West Africa, flanked by
two courtiers. The kingdom arose in the thirteenth
century and flourished until the nineteenth,
maintaining an art tradition of its own, as this bronze
casting shows. The big head and short legs were
conventional ways of expressing the Obo's dignity
and power.

The pattern of communication created by the conquest of the world's oceans by European seafarers just before and just after 1500 did not upset the age-old balance among the major civilizations of Eurasia all at once. Both the Moslem and Chinese worlds continued to expand their territory very successfully until after 1700. Even the Hindus, although subjected to Moslem rule, gained new self-consciousness and energy through religious revival.

Outside of western Europe itself, the really radical changes during the centuries 1500–1700 were limited to the Americas, where the arrival of Europeans had disastrous impact on Amerindian peoples. Africa remained apart, although the slave trade brought throngs of Africans to the New World. On the other hand, Australia and Oceania were scarcely affected by European seafaring before 1700.

The new age that began about 1500 favored civilized peoples. This was dramatically evident in Asia and in eastern Europe, where the development of guns gave civilized infantry a growing military superiority over nomad steppe cavalry. As a result, by 1700 Chinese and Russian armies had divided almost the entire Eurasian steppe between them. The eclipse of the nomads as a serious element in the military balance of Eurasia made land frontiers upon the steppe less and less critical, while the importance of seaboard regions, where European ships arrived and departed with growing frequency, became correspondingly greater for all the world's peoples.

Yet the challenges that European ideas and techniques offered to other civilized communities were not so pressing that they could not be disregarded, when it seemed easier to do so. Between 1500 and 1700, each of the Asian civilizations chose to take this path. It was especially tempting because the spread of heavy artillery to all parts of the civilized world allowed great imperial states to consolidate their hold over wide territories. Vast and mighty empires seemed in no danger from the occasional visits of European (or any other kind of) ships to their port cities.

Continuities are therefore more evident than revolutionary change in the history of the Asian civilizations during the first 200 years of European overseas expansion. Only in Japan, where an independent style of civilization was still comparatively new, and in Russia, where western Europe's pressure was felt more sharply because the distances were less, did far-reaching and drastic internal changes come to older patterns of life between 1500 and 1700.

# The World of Islam

In 1500 Moslems had no reason to doubt that the tide of world history was running with them, as it had done ever since the prophet Mohammed first proclaimed his revelation of God's truth in Mecca, centuries before. To be sure, the political unity of Islam lay in ruins, and civil war was constant. But this was nothing new. However reluctantly, Moslem thinkers had already come to terms with these political failures.

## Moslem Territorial Advances

They could find reason to console themselves by considering the frontier successes that continued to come to Moslem warriors and to Moslem missionaries. In Africa and Southeast Asia, Islam continued to expand throughout the two centuries that we are concerned with here. No single great event led to this result. Rather, Islam spread through a series of local conversions—sometimes of a city, of a tribal leader, or just of individuals—until they constituted a majority of the politically powerful persons in the region. Moreover, conversion to Islam was a gradual matter. Reverence for Sufi mystics led to acquaintance with the Koran and the Sacred Law. This in turn was prologue to familiarity with the entire cultural heritage of Islam. Mastery of the Koran required a knowledge of Arabic, and knowledge of that language opened wide the door to the treasures of Moslem learning.

On the battlefield, Moslem arms also did well. All of India came under Moslem domina-

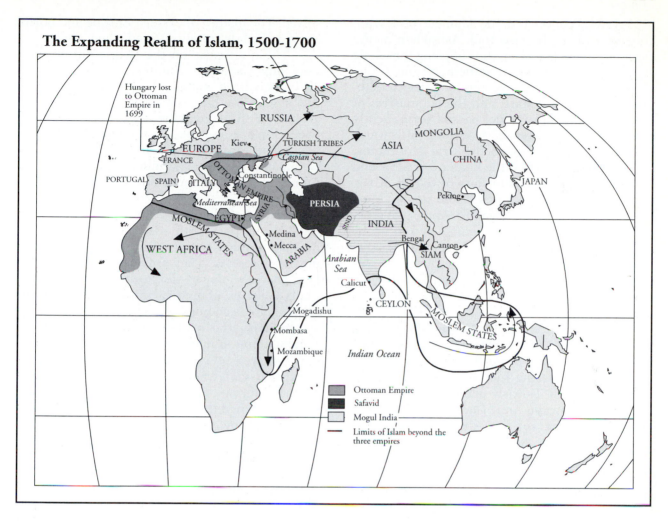

**The Expanding Realm of Islam, 1500-1700**

tion after 1565, when the Hindu Empire of Vijayanagar fell to a coalition of local Moslem rulers. Java became Moslem by 1526 in the same way. Against Christian Europe, Ottoman arms reached their high-water mark in 1683. The long naval duel in the Mediterranean between the Turks and the Spaniards ended by the Truce of 1580 was a Turkish success. They kept control of the eastern Mediterranean Sea and excluded the Spaniards from North Africa, except for small footholds at Ceuta, just opposite Gibraltar and Mellila on the Atlantic coast. By land, Ottoman armies extended their power all around the Black Sea and, year after year, kept up a generally successful local frontier war with the Hapsburgs. In 1683 the Turkish imperial army again besieged Vienna, as in the days of Suleiman the Lawgiver, and again failed to take the city. The long war that followed ended in 1699 with the first really serious defeat the Turks had ever suffered in Europe. By the Treaty of Karlowitz, which ended the war, the Turks had to cede most of Hungary to the Hapsburgs.

## Moslem Setbacks on the Steppe

This was not the first serious territorial loss that the Moslems had suffered at Christian hands. In 1552 the Russian czar, Ivan the Terrible (reigned

1533–1584), conquered the khanate of Kazan. Four years later he also took Astrakhan at the mouth of the Volga River, thus opening the whole of that river to Russian settlement and trade. These victories added tremendous new territories to the Russian state; and the old masters of Russia, the Golden Horde, passed permanently from political existence. Not long afterward, Russian pioneers crossed the Ural Mountains. By 1588 they destroyed the khanate of Sibir and took control of the headwaters of the Ob River. Here, in the central regions of the steppe, Moslem states and peoples began to topple like ninepins in the face of Russian guns, backed up by Russian settlers. The reversal of relations between steppe cavalry and civilized infantry was nowhere demonstrated more emphatically, or earlier, than along Russia's eastern and southern frontiers.

Farther east, also, the Moslems suffered a different sort of setback when Buddhists moved onto steppe lands of Central Asia that had been vacated by conquering Turkish tribes. This began in 1515 when a Turkish confederation, called Uzbeks, overran the Amu Darya and Syr Darya valleys. In doing so, they dislodged bands of Persianized Turks who ruled the region. The Turks fled southward into India, and eventually erected the Mogul Empire there.

This sort of domino action was age-old and completely traditional. What was different this time, however, was that the region that the Uzbeks vacated when they moved southward was taken over by a pagan tribe known as Kalmucks. Instead of becoming Moslem, as the Uzbeks and their predecessors in that part of the steppe had done, the Kalmucks preferred Lamaistic Buddhism. The same faith spread also among the Mongols and held its own among the Tibetans, who had created it in the first place.

Thus, a distinct nomad religious community came into existence in eastern and central Asia, holding itself consciously apart from Islam as well as from China. In the end it was the Chinese, not the Moslems, who conquered these communities, although China's victory was not complete until 1757 when the Kalmuck confederacy, ravaged by smallpox as well as by Chinese guns and cavalry, finally broke up. With this defeat, the last significant steppe cavalry force dissolved. The history of eastern Europe and northern Asia had definitely entered a new phase.

These setbacks on the steppe did not provoke any sustained countermove on the part of the civilized states of the Moslem world. The steppe was in itself poor and unpromising ground. With the opening of the ocean route between Europe and the Far East, trade caravans, which had formerly crossed the steppe between China and the west, lost much of their business. Animal packtrains could not compete with ship transport.

Moreover, the steppe route was soon outflanked on the north also. Russian pioneers quickly mastered the art of traveling through the northern forests. They traveled in summer by boat and in winter by sleigh along the rivers that made a series of natural highways. Relatively short and easy portages connected one river system with the next, and the native inhabitants—simple hunters and fishers for the most part—offered no effective resistance to Russian backwoodsmen who carried guns as part of their normal equipment. Hence, by 1638 Russian explorers reached the Pacific Ocean at present-day Okhotsk. They were attracted by furs, which they forced the local peoples to collect for them as a form of tribute. These furs were exported to both China and Europe, where they were in great demand. Tea and other Chinese goods were then carried back to Russia along the same river route.

As long-distance overland trade shifted northward in this fashion, the old caravan routes across the steppes declined in importance. As a result, the political retreat of Islam from the impoverished central portions of the steppe seemed no great matter to the men who controlled the great Moslem empires.

## The Rise of the Safavid State

Far more significant from the Moslem point of view was a great religious and political upheaval that came into the open in 1501, when Ismail Safavi openly proclaimed himself the descendant of the seventh Imam and therefore the true and only legitimate leader of the Moslem community. Ismail was a Shi'a. That is to say, he belonged to

# Russian Expansion, 1500–1700

Bering Str.

KAMCHATKA
Petropavlovsk

JAPAN

KOREA

Magadan
Okhotsk
1638

Vladivostok
Khabarovsk

Yakutsk
Albazin

Amur

CHINA

L. Baikal
Irkutsk

Lena

MONGOLIA

Krasnoyarsk

Yenisei R.

Arctic Ocean

Tomsk
Ob
Irtysh

Omsk

NOVAYA
ZEMLYA

Tobolsk

Karaganda

L. Balkhash

Tashkent

Murmansk

Svendlovsk

Aral
Sea
Khiva
Geok-Tepe
Merv

Archangel

Kazan

Volga R.

Moscow

Tsaritsyn

PERSIA

Caspian Sea

NORWAY

SWEDEN

St. Petersburg

Baltic Sea

Kiev
Dnieper R.

UKRAINE

HUNGARY

BULGARIA

Black Sea

OTTOMAN EMPIRE

500

Miles

0

Russia in 1533

Russia in 1598

Russia in 1689

Ceded to Poland, 1618

Ceded to Sweden, 1617

Area occupied by Sweden, 1612–13

Area occupied by Poland, early 1613

one of the sects of Islam that refused to recognize the legitimacy of the Omayyad caliphs and claimed instead that only descendants of Ali, Mohammed's son-in-law, could legitimately lead the Community of the Faithful. The Safavid sect had been in existence for many years and a secret propaganda had spread its ideas far and wide over Iran and eastern Anatolia. Ismail's Turkish soldiers were organized tribally, just as Mohammed's soldiers had been in the first days of Islam. The fanatical spirit of the Shi'a movement was also similar to the spirit that had kept the original Moslem community together.

As a result, Ismail won a series of rapid victories. In 1502 he took Tabriz in Iran and crowned himself shah. He captured Baghdad and Mesopotamia in 1508 and defeated the Uzbeks in 1510. In 1514 a widespread rising of Ismail's sympathizers took place in Anatolia against the Ottoman sultan. Selim the Grim had to mobilize the whole strength of his imperial army to suppress the Shi'a rebels. When he had drowned the uprising in blood, Selim drove ahead toward Tabriz to try to stamp out the source of the infection. He was able to defeat Ismail's troops in battle, thanks largely to the Ottoman artillery; but he could not capture Tabriz or destroy his rival.

Instead, Selim decided to eliminate any possible allies Shah Ismail might be able to find within the heartlands of Islam by conquering Syria, Palestine, Egypt, and the part of Arabia

**Persian Pomp and Splendor**   Court life at the three great Moslem empires of the sixteenth and seventeenth centuries achieved remarkable elaboration. Traces survive through works of art, like the carpet on the right and the painting above. Carpets like the one illustrated here served rulers and other powerful men as floor coverings both in private living quarters and also in rooms for public ceremonies, such as that portrayed above, where one sees Shah Tahmasp (ruled 1524–1576) of Iran receiving an embassy sent by one of the early Mogul rulers of India. Tahmasp was the son of Ismail Safavi and inherited his father's claim to be the only legitimate Moslem ruler. This made diplomatic relations with other Moslem rulers delicate. But political and religious quarrels could be softened by diplomatic ritual and courtly entertainments, like the professionalized music and dancing illustrated here.

where the holy cities of Mecca and Medina were located. This he did in two years' campaigning, 1515–1517. But Iran was too far away from Istanbul to allow the Ottoman armies to conquer it. The Turkish cavalrymen had to return to their estates after each campaigning season, and the sultan had to get back to his capital to assert his personal control over the central government. Hence the Ottoman armies operated within definite limits. Vienna lay at one extreme of the Turks' effective campaigning range, Tabriz at the other. Neither city could be captured, given the methods of transport and military organization available to the Ottoman Empire.

## The Religious Issue: Shi'a versus Sunni

Shah Ismail's claim to be the only legitimate political and religious leader of Islam was profoundly troublesome to all other Moslem rulers. It opened up again all the difficult problems of righteousness in social and political matters. What claim, indeed, did Turkish upstarts like the Ottoman sultans have to rule Moslems? Who was the rightful successor to the Prophet? What was the true and proper basis of religious and political authority?

These questions were strikingly similar to the issue of authority in matters of religion that was raised by the Protestant Reformation in Europe at almost exactly the same time. In Europe, Luther's challenge to papal authority provoked centuries of argument and a strenuous reexamination of biblical and early Christian texts. No universally accepted conclusion was reached, of course; but in the struggle for an answer, the depth and breadth of European knowledge and scholarship were greatly increased.

The Sunni Moslems of the Ottoman Empire responded to the Shi'a challenge differently. The pattern of their response was defined under Sultan Sulieman (ruled 1520–1566), whom Europeans called "the Magnificent" but who was called "the Lawgiver" by his own people. Suleiman put the full weight of his government behind Sunni orthodoxy. Schools for training experts in Sunni law were set up; and a carefully controlled hierarchy of religious officials, much resembling the hierarchy of the Orthodox Church, was established in every Ottoman town. Unorthodox dervish communities were not usu-ally persecuted. Rather, the Ottoman government allowed them to set up permanent residences, called *tekkes*. These were often out in the country, where the dervishes could pursue the mystic vision of God in their own way, without dangerously exciting the religious sentiments of the people as a whole.

Suleiman's efforts to reorganize and reinvigorate Sunni Islam proved effective. Revolt did not break out afresh. Shi'a believers went underground, pretended to accept the official form of Islam, and passed on their doctrine only to small, secret, initiated groups. This was as before. What was new was the official organization and control of the teachers and lawgivers of Sunni Islam—an intervention on the part of the state in the affairs of religion of which earlier Moslem empires never dreamed.

Ottoman success in controlling Shi'a heresy was made easier by the fact that the raw religious excitement of Shah Ismail's time faded rapidly. Ismail's heirs soon quarreled with Shi'a experts in the Sacred Law, who were called ayatollahs. The shahs claimed God-given, absolute power; the ayatollahs wanted to subordinate the shah's government to their own interpretation of God's will. Both did agree, however, that all traces of other forms of Islam should be destroyed.

Accordingly, the Safavid government launched a great effort to make all the shah's subjects into true believers according to the doctrines of the so-called "Twelver"* sect of Shi'a Islam. Special catechisms and schools taught the people what to believe. The former tolerance of religious variety and even of skepticism—a spirit very much in evidence in some medieval Persian poetry—abruptly disappeared. Persian culture took on a new, intolerant Shi'a coloring. The change that came to Iran under the Safavids was therefore similar to the change that came to Italy under the influence of the Counter-Reformation. In both countries, religious uniformity was achieved at the cost of cultural creativity.

---

*"Twelvers" were those who recognized twelve legitimate successors to Mohammed before the line of Ali's descendants came to an end. Other Shia sects recognized different lines of descent from Ali and fewer legitimate successors to the Prophet.

The Moslem rulers of India also had to come to terms with the Safavid claim to universal authority over all true believers. Both Babur (ruled 1526–1530), the founder of the Mogul Empire, and his successor, Humayun (ruled 1530–1556), publicly accepted the Shi'a faith at times when they badly needed help from the Safavids; but both renounced their Shi'ism when they were not in need of help. Akbar (ruled 1556–1605), who first put the Mogul Empire on a stable basis, tantalized everyone by experimenting with all sorts of religious views. Christian missionaries who came to his court were sure that he was about to become Christian; in fact he probably thought of himself as following Shah Ismail's example by becoming the head of his own religious community, experimenting with truth and seeking answers to all sorts of ultimate questions with a more or less open mind.

Akbar's successors adopted orthodox Sunni Islam, and the emperor Aurangzeb (ruled 1658–1707) tried to suppress both Hindu idolatry and Shi'a error. In doing so, he conquered previously independent Shi'a states in southern India and expanded the Mogul Empire to its greatest extent. But he also aroused Hindu hostility. Guerilla actions against the Moguls, which started in Aurangzeb's lifetime, quickly undermined the power of the central government in the years that followed his death.

## The Splendor of Moslem Art

Moslem art entered upon a particularly splendid period with the development of the Ottoman, Safavid, and Mogul empires. The Safavid Shah Abbas I the Great (reigned 1587–1629), for example, created a new capital for himself at Isfahan and made it one of the architectural wonders of the world. The Taj Mahal in India, built for the Mogul emperor Shah Jahan (reigned 1628–1657), was erected only a little later. Persian miniature painting also attained its highest excellence in these centuries, when expert craftsmen were gathered together at court and given every facility for their work. Traces of Chinese and European techniques are easy to find, but the gemlike coloring and minute detail of the Persian miniatures make them one of the world's great art traditions.

In India a similar and closely related style of painting developed around the Mogul court. Hindu painters used Persian technique to portray scenes from Hindu mythology, creating what is called the Rajput school of art. Other arts, like carpet weaving, furniture design, and jewelers' work, also attained a very high refinement in the imperial workshops, where only the very best could satisfy sophisticated courtiers' tastes.

## Moslem Thought and Literature

Intellectually, however, Islam showed far less creative energy. Formulas inherited from the first centuries of Islam were emphatically reasserted, memorized, and repeated. New thoughts were actively discouraged, perhaps because they threatened always to uncover once again the raw wound created by the Safavid challenge to political and religious legitimacy. Even such subjects as geography, in which Moslems had long taken a special interest, failed to respond to the stimulus of the European discoveries. Pious Moslems refused to read Christian authors, and so the new geographical knowledge that flowed into Europe was disregarded.

Literature escaped stagnation only by calling new literary languages into being at both the Ottoman and the Mogul courts—Turkish in Istanbul and Urdu in Delhi. Turkish and Urdu writers drew heavily upon Persian literary models, for the great Persian poets of the Middle Ages continued to command the admiration of all Sunni Islam. But they were banished from their homeland, for the Shi'a religious teachers could not abide the delicate ambiguities of religious doubt upon which classical Persian poetry depended for much of its effect.

## Weaknesses of Islamic Societies

Despite its brilliant success, Moslem civilization had an important weakness. In almost every part of the Moslem world, just a tiny minority of rulers and landowners really shared in Islamic high culture. Peasants were left out, and of course they were the great majority. Poor townspeople, too, had little in common with the lords and governors who employed some of them to build splendid mosques or tombs or to work in the luxury trades. Western Europe was, by comparison, much more coarse and vulgar. Even peasants entered the market. Refinement in western Europe may have been less, but what there was spread further down the social scale than in the Moslem lands.

In the Ottoman Empire, an important new circumstance arose from the fact that after 1638 the Turks stopped enslaving children from the Christian villages of the Balkans and training them to become soldiers and administrators of the empire. Instead, new members of the sultan's slave household came to be recruited from

**Two Mosques**  On the left is the dome of a mosque built outside Cairo by a mamluke ruler of Egypt, Qait Bey, between 1472 and 1474. It was intended to serve as his tomb. On the right is a mosque built on top of the highest hill of Istanbul by Suleiman the Lawgiver between 1550 and 1557. It also housed a school for students of the Sacred Law. Each of these buildings celebrated the power of the rulers who commissioned them, but Suleiman's mosque had a further significance. In size and elegance it surpassed the famous Byzantine church of Sancta Sofia that Emperor Justinian had constructed almost a millennium earlier in the same city, and thereby proclaimed the superiority of Islam to Christianity and of the Ottoman empire to its predecessors. Both of these buildings are elegantly precise in their proportions and decoration. Religious prohibition of images in human form had stimulated Islamic architects to perfect a distinctive and delightful style of geometric decoration, as Qait Bey's mosque shows. The two buildings thus expressed a self-confidence and vigor in Islamic civilization that was entirely unaffected by the achievements of a few European sailors and adventurers in the early modern era.

among the sons of those who already served the sultan. The result was to cut off what had been an important link between the Ottoman government and the Christian peasantry of the Balkans. As long as the high administrators of the Ottoman Empire had begun life as ordinary villagers, they could never lose a certain underlying sympathy with the communities from which they had come. When, however, officials came to be mainly sons of officials, all sympathy with the Christian peasantry disappeared. Discontented peasant boys, who in an earlier time might have become soldiers and administrators of the empire, became outlawed brigands instead.

This change weakened Ottoman society. It was also weakened by the unfortunate way palace officials sought to make succession to the throne peaceful and secure. Instead of allowing the dead sultan's sons to fight it out, as had often happened earlier in Ottoman history, potential heirs were instead confined to the harem until the moment when one of them was picked to succeed his father. This meant that after 1581 the reigning sultans were nonentities and rival cliques of palace officials actually ran the administration.

Economic decay, noticeable after about 1650, reinforced these changes in administrative personnel. Perhaps what happened was that the businessmen of the Ottoman Empire turned away from trade and used their funds instead to buy the right from government to collect taxes from a district, a town, or even from an entire province. This is known as tax-farming. It allowed the tax-farmers to make a handsome profit by collecting more from the public than they had paid for the right to fleece them. On the other hand, funds invested in this way were not economically productive; indeed, it probably became dangerous to invest in trade and manufacturing, for anyone who did make money from such activities was a natural target for the tax collectors. At any rate, the foreign trade of the Ottoman Empire passed almost entirely into the hands of Italian, French, Dutch, and English merchants, who took raw materials from Turkey and brought woolen cloth and other manufactured goods into the empire in exchange.

In the Indian Ocean also, the arrival of Dutch and English traders after 1600 began to cut into Moslem sea trade as the Portuguese had never done. The Dutch and English put great effort into developing trade between Asian ports, for their own manufactures were difficult to sell in India. The Dutch East India Company (organized 1602) took on the task of managing the agriculture of Java and adjacent islands, forcing local rulers to make their subjects plant whatever crops the Dutch judged would command the best sale in world markets. The English East India Company, organized in 1600, developed a flourishing trade in Indian cotton cloth. English agents made cash advances to Indian weavers and told them what kind of cloth to produce. In this way the English were able to take on the management of cloth production and sale throughout the whole Indian Ocean area.

The increasingly active and dominant role played by European traders in the economic affairs of the Moslem empires was a sign of things to come. But in 1700 no one could have foreseen that the English East India Company would become the successor to the Mogul emperors as rulers of India, or that the might of the Ottoman sultans would crumble before European interlopers. Moslem rulers cared next to nothing about who carried the trade from their ports or planned and controlled cotton manufacturing in their dominions. Such activities were the concern of humble folk who, as long as they paid their taxes and kept quiet, did not interest the rulers of the Moslem world in the slightest. The care most European governments (except Spain) took to foster trade and manufactures differed sharply from the attitudes of Moslem rulers and reflected the fiscal dependence of rulers on townspeople that prevailed in Europe. The Moslem rulers' view that it was not their responsibility to foster the welfare of taxpayers was as old as civilization itself in the Middle East. It was European governments that were unusual, largely because of their heritage from the Middle Ages, when kings and burghers had come together to repress unruly noblemen.

The economic history of the great Moslem empires thus reflected the general weakness of

Islamic society arising from the wide gap between rulers and everyone else. This gap was nothing new. Only the comparison with Europe made it potentially dangerous. Indeed, by every standard except the standard set by Europe's contemporary development, Islam was in a flourishing condition between 1500 and 1700. Moslems' dismay, when after 1700 they discovered they had been left behind, was correspondingly profound.

# Hindu Revival

The fact that after 1565 no independent Hindu state survived anywhere except in the remote island of Bali did not paralyze Hindu culture. On the contrary, Hinduism entered upon a new stage of development that gave it the ability to withstand Moslem and, later, Christian missionary efforts with ease. What happened was that two great poets and a famous holy man gave a new focus to Hinduism. The holy man was named Chaitanya (d. 1527). He was born a Brahman but in early manhood began to experience intense mystic experiences, during which his followers believed he actually became the great god Krishna.

A god incarnate was no ordinary thing, even in India. A religious sect soon developed around Chaitanya and flourished particularly in Bengal, where Chaitanya himself lived. His followers eliminated all caste distinctions. This undercut the main attraction of Islam for Indian minds. Until Chaitanya's time, members of the lower castes, especially in Bengal, had often become Moslem. After the new sect had come into existence, conversion to Islam almost ceased. The emotional conviction felt by Chaitanya's followers found expression in warm manifestations of common feeling expressed through public ceremonies. This proved far more attractive than Islam, even in Sufi form.

The two great Hindu poets Sur Das (d. 1563) and Tulsi Das (d. 1623) took stories from the two great Hindu epics, the *Mahabharata* and the *Ramayana*, and put them into the common language of northern India. The effect was comparable to what happened when Protestants translated the Bible into the everyday languages of western Europe. Ordinary people memorized long passages from the two poets. Schoolboys studied them. The lessons of piety and good manners their poems emphasized became standard. Hindu self-consciousness and religious uniformity increased.

Of the two, Sur Das was the less influential. He chose to celebrate the deeds of Krishna, and in later life he was admitted to Akbar's court. His poems have a Persian touch about them. Tulsi Das, on the other hand, concentrated his religious devotion upon Rama and escaped all taint of foreignness. Tulsi's poems entered very deeply into all later Hindu religious and cultural life. They emphasized Rama's role as both god and man and expressed intense personal devotion to him.

This was, indeed, the effect of all three men's work. Worshipers identified themselves with a holy figure, who was both god and man at the same time. Other deities and myths in the Hindu tradition were not rejected outright. But in practice each devotee focused his attention on a single god-man. The result was to create something rather like different sects in Hinduism—some preferring the worship of Krishna, others concentrating upon Rama. But both these deities were held to be incarnations of Vishnu, so there was no ultimate conflict between their worshipers.

Devotion to Shiva, the other great god of earlier Hinduism, tended to fade somewhat. So did the crude magic of Tantrism. On the other hand, the most ancient layer of Hinduism—the Sanskrit rituals based on the Vedas and administered by Brahman priests—continued to be necessary for all ordinary crises of human existence. The Brahmans, with their unintelligible Sanskrit chants, had to be called in for birth, coming of age, marriage, and death. Only the followers of Chaitanya refused to honor Brahmans because they upheld caste, and distinctions based upon caste.

In the practical sense, too, Hindus continued to play an important part in the Mogul Empire. Emperor Akbar relied very much upon

**European Intruders as Seen by Indian Eyes**   This ivory carving was made by local craftsmen in Sri Lanka about 1540. It shows an exotic scene: a European couple dining at a table, with servants on the alert behind each chair. All around them crowd Hindu symbols of wealth and good fortune unfamiliar to us, but the glimpse of European manners was what seemed odd and surprising to the artist who carved this little casket.

Hindu administrators and tax collectors, and his successors continued to do the same. Many Hindus continued to possess large estates and served in the Mogul army as warriors alongside the Persian-speaking Turks who constituted the core of Mogul power. The Hindu upper classes tended to take on much of the secular culture of their Moslem rulers. They, for example, were the patrons for whom Rajput painting was produced.

The overwhelming majority of the population of India remained Hindu. They treated the thin layer of foreigners who held the Mogul Empire together as a sort of caste—to be endured but not to be imitated or regarded as anything but what it was: an alien body in the midst of Indian society.

The missionary force of Islam was blunted by such attitudes. Hinduism had found a popular, emotional appeal through Chaitanya and the poets. There was no need to wrestle with Moslem accusations of idolatry any longer. Except in the extreme south, Hindu temples had been destroyed. The new forms of worship took place in public places out of doors and did not focus on idols but on hymns and prayers and congregational rejoicing. Hindus readily believed that the tremendous antiquity of their sacred texts made them superior to the Koran or, for that matter, to the Christian Bible. Hinduism, in other words, had nothing to fear from outside, being rooted securely in the feelings of the Indian people as a whole.

In Java, however, Hinduism crumbled before Islam, as we have already seen. But on the mainland of Southeast Asia and in Sri Lanka, Buddhism remained vigorous, partly, at least, because it allowed the Burmese, Siamese, Vietnamese, and Sinhalese peoples to preserve their national identities in the face of Islamic and other foreign pressures.

# The Celestial Empire of China

When the first Portuguese reached the coast of southern China in 1513, the Ming dynasty was already beginning to suffer from the signs of decay that had often before afflicted Chinese dynasties. Heavily taxed peasants were ready for revolt. Unruly generals intrigued for power. Tax income ceased to flow smoothly to the imperial court, and the nomads along the northern and western frontiers were restless.

In addition, the Ming government had to cope with piratical attacks from the sea that soon assumed a serious scale. Many of the pirates were Japanese. By 1555, they were strong and numerous enough to sail up the Yangtze River as far as Nanking to besiege that great city. Nothing in Chinese experience had prepared the Ming rulers for this kind of attack. Efforts to organize a Chinese navy that could police the seas and suppress piracy were sometimes successful, but the emperors always decided to economize and disband the naval force when it had done its work. The result was that discharged sailors often joined up with pirate crews—confirming the court's worst suspicions about sailors, and at the same time making it necessary to organize a fresh campaign to clear the seas of pirates once again.

The Portuguese fitted into this disorderly picture with no difficulty at all. The Chinese soon recognized the fighting qualities of Portuguese ships and made a sort of informal alliance with them. In return for allowing the Portuguese to trade from Macao, near Canton, the Chinese got a promise of Portuguese help against the Japanese pirates (1557). On the other hand, when it suited them, the Portuguese turned to piracy themselves.

In 1592, the Japanese warlord, Hideyoshi, attempted to cap his victorious career by attacking and conquering China. He sent a large Japanese army to Korea, where the Ming armies fought a long, hard campaign against the invaders. The struggle was undecided when Hideyoshi died in 1598. His successors simply withdrew. In an effort to stabilize political conditions at home, the new rulers of Japan, the Tokugawa shoguns, first restricted and then completely closed Japan to contact with foreigners. Strict laws prohibited Japanese ships from sailing to other countries from Japanese ports. Foreigners were also, of course, refused the right to sail into Japanese harbors. The result was to remove the main pirate threat. The Chinese were therefore spared having to do anything about improving sea defenses—a situation that cost them dearly two centuries later when European gunboats began to demand access to Chinese ports.

The drastic steps Chinese and then Japanese rulers took to suppress piracy and seafaring among their subjects had a remarkable side effect. Europeans moved swiftly into the vacuum official policy created since, from the 1550s, silver from America gave them something Asians wanted. Starting in 1567, a Spanish galleon carried Mexican silver directly across the Pacific to Manila each year; and American silver also reached Asia from Europe itself after crossing the Atlantic. In exchange came a flow of Asian manufactured goods and raw materials—porcelains, tea, spices, silk, muslins, and much else. A globe-girdling exchange network thus set in for the first time in history, uniting New World mines with Asian workshops in a single market, managed, for the most part, by Europeans. The modern global economy thus dawned,

**Palace and Castle in China and Japan**   On the left is the gateway to the enclosure where Chinese emperors lived between 1431 and 1911 and from whence they conducted the imperial government. The tourists flocking toward it would not have been admitted when this, the so-called Forbidden City, served its original purpose. Then, only persons who had business to transact with the government were allowed to enter; but what kept unwanted visitors out was the order and discipline of Chinese society, not fortification. The fact that the Chinese made no effort to guard the imperial palace from cannon fire is especially striking, for in the century that followed the original laying out of the Forbidden City, a revolution in warfare gave heavy guns the power to break down all older forms of local defense. In Japan, this military revolution had drastic consequences, as the White Heron Castle, shown on the right, suggests. Built by Hideyoshi, an upstart warlord, in 1581 to hold down the southern part of Honshu, it perches on top of heavy stone fortifications, carefully sloped to absorb cannon fire without crumbling. Yet Japan's long-standing connection with Chinese civilized traditions still rises above the heavy presence of new-fangled fortification, as indicated by the resemblance of roof lines in these photographs.

though at first only expensive luxuries were much affected.

## The Manchu Conquest

Neglect of China's sea frontier reflected the fact that the Ming were under increasingly dangerous attack from the north and could not stop rebellion from within. In 1615, Manchurian horsemen formed a powerful confederation and began nibbling away at Chinese territories. Then, in 1644 the commander of the Manchu confederation entered Peking, supposedly as a supporter of a Ming general who was trying to put down rebellion. Once inside Peking, however, the Manchus ceased pretending to serve the

Ming emperor and instead proclaimed a new dynasty. Manchu forces soon overran the rest of China; but the island of Taiwan held out until 1683, when it, too, submitted to the new rulers of China.

Like many steppe conquerors before them, the Manchus tried to keep their own people separate from the Chinese. Special garrisons of Manchu soldiers were set up at strategic places, mostly outside big cities, and high military command was rigorously reserved for Manchus. The civil administration, nevertheless, remained entirely Chinese. Indeed, the Manchus were already half won over to Chinese culture before they invaded the country and had none of the Lamaist foreign taint that made the Mongols so unpopular among the Chinese. However, many

Mongols were recruited into the ranks of the Manchu army, for there were not enough Manchus to overawe all of China. Some Chinese also served as soldiers, but they always remained in subordinate posts.

The new emperors busily set out to improve defenses against the steppe peoples to the west and met with such solid success that by 1755 the danger from the steppe was forever destroyed. Incidentally, the Chinese Empire as we know it today was created by the Manchu annexation of Tibet, Sinkiang, Mongolia, and, of course, Manchuria, too. The territory administered by the Chinese emperor almost doubled as a result. Traditional China acquired a fringe of half-empty borderlands in which to expand. As a result, a massive, centuries-long process of frontier settlement by migrants from the overcrowded Chinese heartlands set in and is still underway today.

The Manchus also cultivated Neo-Confucian learning and conformed gladly to Chinese imperial precedents in all matters affecting the internal administration of the country. Population grew rapidly, both because of an improved level of internal peace and because introduction of the sweet potato and other American food crops allowed the Chinese to supplement their older food resources by cultivating hill slopes that were too steep for rice paddies.

## Christian Missions to China

All foreigners were barbarians in Chinese eyes. They became worthy of courteous attention only when they had taken the pains to learn Chinese and become gentlemen. The first European to accomplish this feat was Matteo Ricci, a Jesuit missionary, who hoped to convert China to Christianity by winning over the emperor and his court. In 1601 Ricci gained permission to travel to Peking, where his mastery of Chinese learning made him acceptable to the officials and scholars who governed China.

Other Jesuits followed Ricci and soon proved that they had more accurate knowledge of astronomy and calendar making than the official court astronomer did. A Jesuit accordingly was appointed to this office, giving the mission an official status from which it could not easily be removed. Correct calculation of the calendar was thought to be of great importance, since lucky and unlucky days for undertaking new enterprises depended on having a calendar that accorded correctly with the motions of the heavenly bodies.

The Chinese also found European geographical knowledge interesting and delighted in mechanical toys and pendulum clocks that the Jesuits imported from Europe. But these were trifles. Educated Chinese felt sure that everything important was already well taken care of by traditional Confucian wisdom. Jesuit efforts to convince the Chinese of the truth of Christianity therefore fell on deaf ears, though poor children and others who were helped by the missionaries with food or medical service did sometimes become Christian.

The missionaries themselves faced an interesting dilemma. How could the technical terms of Christian theology be translated into Chinese? Or, put in another way, how did Chinese religious ideas and terminology fit into a Christian framework? Was ancestor worship idolatrous? Or was this only a family ceremony, honoring but not worshiping the dead? The Jesuits, after some hesitation, decided that ancestor worship was not worship at all, but simply a civil ceremony. They also decided that the Chinese word "Tien," usually translated "Heaven," was a suitable equivalent for the Christian word "God." These decisions meant that the Jesuits could point out to a Confucian scholar that he was already half-Christian and did not need to change family custom to become fully Christian by admitting the truth of divine revelation as recorded in the Bible and interpreted by Catholic tradition.

Such arguments did not convince many Chinese, and they profoundly shocked other Christian missionaries who had come to the Far East to convert the heathen and wished to have no truck with pagan ways. Serious controversy began in 1628 and dragged on until 1742. The Jesuits, of course, tried to defend their policies, and in doing so wrote extensive accounts of Chinese society and civilization. Learned Europeans in this way acquired a remarkably full, somewhat idealized stock of information about China.

As a result, appreciation for Chinese art and admiration for Chinese principles of government found a considerable lodgment in Europe. Even more important, quite a few Europeans tried to understand Chinese civilization as a whole and in itself, apart from their own inherited prejudices and opinions. This marked a new kind of relationship between different civilizations. Nothing could stand in sharper contrast to the sublime self-satisfaction of the Chinese educated class, who continued to believe that nothing of value could come from the Europeans, whom they called "south sea barbarians."

## China's Cultural Conservatism

Given such attitudes, little really new could arise in Chinese culture. Scholars became more and more rigorous and set out to scrape away Buddhist and Taoist ideas in order to get back to the authentic Confucian point of view. Paintings and poetry continued to be produced in quantity, for every cultivated man had to be able to paint and write good verse. But all this fell into well-worn, thoroughly traditional patterns. Experts agree that the works of the writers and artists of the Ming and Manchu periods were inferior to earlier paintings and poems. Prose tales, smelling of the street, did break into print for the first time, and a new, more popular dimension to Chinese culture thus entered the literary record. But that is about all that changed.

Chinese social structure remained what it had been ever since Sung times. Growth of manufacturing and trade was matched by the increase in agriculture that resulted from the intensified use of American food plants. Merchants and businessmen accepted the low social station to which Confucian doctrine assigned them. As soon as they could, they escaped by buying land and sending their sons to school to become gentlemen. As a result, upward social mobility fed energetic and capable men into government and strengthened the existing social order at the same time.

Thus the Manchus brought stability within a busy, prosperous, and extremely successful traditional order. Confucian ideals asked for nothing else. In 1700, reality came closer to matching the universally accepted principles of Chinese society than at most times before or any time since.

## Japan's Sharp Shifts of Policy

The Japanese welcomed the first Europeans to visit their shores more warmly and with a livelier interest in what the strangers had to offer than any other Asian people. St. Francis Xavier arrived in Japan in 1549, only six or seven years after the first Portuguese adventurers had come. His proud and imperious bearing impressed the Japanese. The Jesuit mission he inaugurated soon met solid success. Japan lacked any national religion of its own. Its religious loyalty was divided among Buddhist sects, Neo-Confucianism, and the still undeveloped imperial cult of Shinto. This undoubtedly helped the progress of Christianity.

Another contributing factor was the political division of the country. Local lords found it very much to their advantage to welcome Christian missionaries. Missionaries could attract European ships to the ports where they were well treated and could warn them away from places where Christian preaching was not permitted.

European ships were important in two ways. They had guns for sale, and a European cannon or two could knock down castle walls with ease. This often made all the difference in the local wars that had long been chronic in Japan. In addition, the Chinese government officially prohibited trade with Japan because Japanese pirates were raiding the Chinese coast all the time. But a Japanese gentleman needed silks and other elegancies from China. The Portuguese were able to import such commodities and carried silver from Japanese mines to China in exchange. Portuguese merchants profited handsomely from this trade and cooperated

# A Christian Daimyo Asks for Guns

The Jesuit missionary, St. Francis Xavier, arrived in Japan in 1649 and succeeded in converting several hundred Japanese to Christianity in the following three years. After returning to India in 1652, he reported his success to the Society of Jesus in Rome, expressing warm admiration for "a nation so ingenious, moderate, so desirous of instruction, so much guided by right reason and so well adorned with other eminent qualities." The letter below, written in 1568 to a Portuguee bishop in Macao, China, shows how a Japanese Daimyo sought to win advantage from his conversion to Christianity in the warring political world in which he lived.

Letter from the Lord of Bungo to Dom Belchior Carniero

I am saddened to hear . . . of your departure for China and of your illness. What makes me all the sadder is that these developments will make it difficult for you to come to Japan. I had looked forward to your visit to our province, as I had heard about your person and about the fact that through your suggestion the Governor General of Goa [in India] had sent me some guns. It is unfortunate that they were lost somewhere during the voyage from Malacca, but I owe you an expression of gratefulness just as if they had arrived. I have not had the fortune of attaining those guns, and I have not abandoned the hope to procure some guns. My faith in God and the protection I have extended to Christians and Portuguese in my province should sufficiently indicate that I am the servant and friend of the King of Portugal. . . . Therefore I hope that you will write a letter to the Governor General and inform him that I am entitled to be given guns as presents. I ask for them as we live on the coast, sharing borders with our enemy, and they are needed for self defense. If I succeed in defending my province and enabling it to prosper, the church, missionaries, Christians, as well as all the Portuguese who come will prosper. . . . There are many other things that I would like to tell you, but I do not want to make the letter longer.

Otomo Sorin, Lord of Bungo

Reproduced from William H. McNeill and Mitsuko Iriye, *Readings in World History*, Vol. 9, pp. 29–30, Mitsuko Iriye, translator.

closely with Christian missionaries to make sure that both silk and guns were channeled into friendly Japanese hands.

## Unification of Japan

Nevertheless, only a minority of the Japanese nation accepted Christianity, and the missionaries suffered, as well as profited, from their involvement in politics. This became obvious when, after a series of more and more violent wars, the whole of Japan came under the control of a successful warlord, Toyotomi Hideyoshi (1537–1598). Hideyoshi started out as a stable-boy, but his ruthlessness and ability carried him to supreme power by 1590. He viewed foreign missionaries as political rivals and in 1587 issued a decree banishing them from the country. Yet, strangely enough, he did not enforce his own decree. Perhaps he was afraid that if he acted too harshly against the missionaries, the

**Japan's Unifier**   Toyotomi Hideyoshi (1536–1598) was a self-made man who rose to supreme power in Japan by virtue of political daring and military success. Starting as a common soldier, he first became a general in the service of a nobleman named Nobunaga and then, after Nobunaga's death, set out on his own. By 1590 he emerged supreme over all of Japan and promptly sent an army to invade Korea, with the intent of conquering China as well. His death brought an end to this adventure, but the military upheaval that brought Hideyoshi to power resulted in a lasting unification of the country under the Tokugawa shoguns.

1600, one of Hideyoshi's lieutenants, Ieyasu Tokugawa, came out on top.

Ieyasu Tokugawa was a much more cautious man than Hideyoshi. After his victory, he sought only to keep what he had won by making his new position as secure as possible. He made Tokyo his capital and planted reliable family retainers as fief holders in most of Japan. In outlying regions, however, he permitted independent "outside lords" to retain their possessions. Ieyasu kept careful watch on all fief holders and required each ruling family to leave hostages in Tokyo to guarantee good behavior. In addition, the shoguns suppressed the use and manufacture of guns that had done so much to upset older Japanese society. By making skilled sword play the decisive factor in battle once again, the old samurai class of professional warriors could and did reclaim social primacy; and the shogun's power, backed by his faithful followers, was made safe from upstarts armed with new weapons like those the Europeans had first brought into the country.

The imperial family and court continued to exist at Kyoto, but the Tokugawa family made sure that the emperors had little to do with the realities of power. The new system of government is referred to as the Tokugawa shogunate because the head of the ruling Tokugawa family took the title *shogun* (commander of the imperial army). The regime lasted until 1867. Succession rested within the Tokugawa family, regulated by private rules. But the family possessions were so extensive that what amounted to a bureaucracy of officials had to be invented to administer the lands held by its members. Hence, while old feudal forms survived, something quite different grew up underneath.

## The Closing of Japan by the Tokugawa Shoguns

During the first decades of Tokugawa rule, the family was deathly afraid of renewed struggles for power among the warrior class. Hideyoshi's son, for example, was killed in 1615 to eliminate a possible rival. A code of conduct for warriors,

Portuguese would break off trade relations just when he was eager to build up his armaments for the invasion of China.

In 1592 Hideyoshi launched his great adventure on the Asian mainland by invading Korea. Early victories were followed by a long and difficult stalemate; and when Hideyoshi died in 1598, the Japanese forces were quickly withdrawn. The reason was that his followers soon quarreled. Each lord wanted all of his troops on hand at home. In a great battle fought in

THE WORLD BEYOND EUROPE

emphasizing loyalty to the feudal superior, was formally published in 1615. Active persecution of Christians began in 1617. When a body of Japanese Christians revolted in 1637, the shogun reacted by stamping out every trace of the foreign religion he could discover. Since the Japanese Christian community had numbered a quarter of a million or more, this involved large-scale violence and much bloodshed. All foreign missionaries were killed. Japanese Christians who refused to renounce their religion were also executed, with great cruelty.

At the same time, the shoguns established a new policy of total isolation from the rest of the world. In 1636 Japanese were forbidden to leave the home islands. Anyone who did so was refused the right to return. In 1638 Portuguese traders were driven from Japan. Three years later arrangements were made with the Dutch whereby a single ship was allowed to come to Nagasaki once a year. Even then, it could only dock at an island in the middle of the harbor. In this way the shogun felt that foreign intrigues could be prevented and imports from abroad could be thoroughly controlled.

Intervention in Japanese political-military affairs, which had allowed the first Christian missionaries to attain such important successes, thus backfired after less than a century, to the bitter cost of their converts. At the same time, Japan lost an opportunity to create a sea empire in the Far East similar to the Japanese Empire created during World War II, for the shogun's policy of isolation compelled Japanese mariners to stay home and stop raiding and trading across the seas surrounding Japan which they had begun to dominate.

# Divergent Forms of Japanese Culture

A time of such profound political shifts might be expected to create important new forms of cultural expression. That was, in fact, the case. Hideyoshi's age was a time for bigness and brashness. Hideyoshi himself was a great egoist, a religious skeptic, and flamboyant in everything he did. He built a bigger palace than had ever been seen before in Japan; and when he invaded Korea, he announced that his aim was the conquest of the whole world, beginning with China.

Japanese artisan skills developed rapidly in Hideyoshi's time. Chinese and Korean captives established or expanded new industries such as fine pottery manufacture and silk weaving. Eager efforts to imitate European gunsmiths were also successful, though shortages of iron always hampered Japan's armament industry. City life developed with the new wealth that came from overseas ventures, as well as from trading within Japan.

The Tokugawa regime was tamer and much more conservative. In 1608 Ieyasu made Neo-Confucianism official. His successors continued to patronize this Chinese school of learning, since its emphasis upon deference toward superiors could be made to justify the Tokugawa system of government. Yet the active, unruly life of the cities, which had taken such a spurt of growth in the age of the civil wars, did not disappear with the end of political disorder. On the contrary, peace provided still greater opportunities for trade within the Japanese islands.

The merchant class and other city dwellers, therefore, continued to support the popular, vigorous, and, at least occasionally, crude and sensuous culture that had come to the fore in Hideyoshi's time. In strong contrast to this tradition, the samurai class cultivated a heroic ideal, from which all forms of self-indulgence were banished. Loyalty and courage, even to the sacrifice of personal life and fortune, were the supreme virtues. Suicide by hara-kiri was an accepted and admired solution for any personal failure to live up to the warrior ideal. In the realm of art, this ideal found its own appropriate expression in the manufacture of magnificent swords and in such spare entertainments as the "tea ceremony" or the art of flower arrangement.

Japan therefore developed a curiously double face under the Tokugawa regime. Officially all was controlled, traditional, and strongly colored by Chinese models. But underneath, in the cities particularly, a sharply different cultural tone prevailed. Friction between these two worlds could not be avoided. Constant tension mirrored political strains, never entirely suppressed, between the Tokugawa family and the outside lords, and between the shogun and the emperor.

This situation kept Japanese minds open to new thoughts in a way that was not true of China. In China practice and theory matched one another so closely, after the Manchu conquest had again established a strong imperial authority, that no one could doubt the essential rightness of China's inherited wisdom and skills. The Japanese, on the contrary, had plenty of reason to wonder about a system that valued warrior skills above all others yet gave the samurai no chance to use their skills—and which officially put merchants at the bottom of the social scale but in practice allowed them to grow richer than true and faithful warriors ever did. Such disproportions between theory and practice meant that the Tokugawa government was like a corset for Japanese society, enclosing something quite at odds with, and very difficult to fit inside of, the official framework.

# The Rise of the Russian Autocracy

The effectiveness of firearms, together with the furious energy of war captains such as Hideyoshi, united Japan. Russia's dramatic expansion over all of northern Asia was likewise the direct result of the revolution in warfare that came with the spread of gunpowder weapons.

For more than 200 years, Moscow and other Russian towns, except for Novgorod far in the north, paid tribute to the so-called Golden Horde. The Horde was a nomad confederacy, ruled by heirs of Genghis Khan from headquarters at Kazan on the Volga River. When Ivan III, the grand duke of Moscow, repudiated his subjection to Kazan in 1480, he continued to collect tributes that had once been forwarded to the

Golden Horde. Ivan simply used them to support his own army and his own set of officials. This made Moscow by far the most powerful of Russian cities. But the Muscovites found themselves militarily inferior to their western neighbors, the Swedes and Poles, whose wealth and armament, commercial development, and level of culture were all superior to those existing in the Russian lands.

This presented Ivan IV (ruled 1547–1584) and his successors with a difficult problem. Constant effort was needed to keep their western neighbors from taking over Russian lands. Russia obviously required large and well-equipped armies, but the government could not afford to pay for everything that was needed. The solution that Ivan IV adopted was a violent revolution from the top which earned him the nickname "The Terrible." He seized the lands of most of the old, noble families of Russia and assigned them to his own personal followers. These men were then required to serve the czar (literally Caesar or emperor), as Ivan started to call himself. To make their lands worthwhile, peasants had to cultivate them and pay rents. To assure the necessary labor power, the Russian government passed laws that made it more and more difficult for peasants to run off into the woods or southward to the open steppe. In this way, a burdensome form of serfdom, approaching slavery, was fastened upon the Russian peasantry.

In theory, there was a rough sort of justice in the system. The peasants served their lords, who in turn served the czar; and the czar served God by protecting the Russian lands and the Orthodox faith from foreign encroachment. Moreover, the system worked, though not without difficulty. As long as Ivan IV lived, he kept his western enemies more or less in check, losing only minor border territories to them. Meanwhile, as we have seen, Russia profited enormously by expansion south and east at the expense of the steppe nomads. But Ivan left an incapable son to succeed him who died without a direct heir. A confused "Time of Troubles" followed. Poles invaded and occupied Moscow for a couple of years and claimed the crown for the king of Poland. The Swedes also overran important new territories inland from the Baltic coast.

## The Time of Troubles

Inside Russia, the greatest confusion reigned. Old noble families were interested in getting power back into their own hands. Far to the south, a rude, democratic Cossack community of warriors had arisen in the steppe. The Cossacks joined the fray, opposing the nobles and sympathizing with the peasants, but also robbing them as they marched to and fro across the countryside. The new "service nobility" that Ivan the Terrible had created lacked cohesion and leadership, once the legitimate line of czars died out. Several pretenders, each claiming to be the son of Ivan the Terrible, only added to the confusion.

In this situation, merchants and townspeople, together with the leaders of the Orthodox church, played a critical role. The Poles were Catholic, and their invasion of Russia was partly a crusade to bring that land under the pope. In 1595 the pope agreed to permit the eastern churches to continue to conduct services in Church Slavonic and to keep some other peculiarities of ritual—making the sign of the cross with three fingers instead of two, for example. These concessions persuaded the high clergy of the Ukraine to accept the papal claim to headship of the entire Christian church. Those who followed them were known as Uniates, and the branch of the Roman Catholic Church that thus came into existence was commonly referred to as the Uniate Church.

Russian national feeling, however, was deeply committed to the idea that the one true Orthodox Christian faith had found refuge in Russia after the fall of Constantinople in 1453. To admit that the pope's claims to rule the Church were actually valid seemed a dreadful heresy to most Russians. Hence it was not difficult for the head of the Russian church, the patriarch of Moscow, to rally widespread popular feeling against the Polish Catholic invaders. He was aided by the merchants and townspeople, who in turn rallied Ivan's new service nobility

**Cathedral of St. Basil, Moscow** This extraordinary church was built by Czar Ivan the Terrible to celebrate victories over the Tartars of Kazan and Astrakhan between 1552 and 1556. Byzantine, Persian, and Italian architectural traditions all contributed to this splendidly colorful and strangely effective array of domes and towers; but the dominant element in the design was authentically Russian, for medieval churchmen had learned to build elaborate churches of wood, complete with domes and arches like those Ivan's architects translated into stone when they constructed this church. This architectural monument gave an enduring expression to the remarkable political achievement by which Ivan and his predecessors pressed Tartar and European foreigners into the service of the Muscovite state, using their skills to exalt the autocratic power of the czar. The way foreign art traditions were here mingled with and subordinated to an inherited Russian style exactly matches the way foreign military and administrative skills were adopted and adapted by the rulers of Russia to serve Russian purposes and increase the power of the state.

and peasant sentiment behind a movement to throw the Poles out and to reestablish a Russian czar to defend the true Orthodox faith.

In 1613 a national assembly representing different classes of the Russian state chose Michael Romanov, the son of the patriarch of Moscow as czar. Reorganized Russian forces soon drove back the Polish invaders and reestablished the autocracy. The early Romanovs, like the Tokugawas, were cautious rulers who adopted a policy of keeping strangers at a distance, as far as possible. Japan could close itself off completely, being an island. Russia had more difficulty in isolating itself because of its long, open land frontiers. All the same, the first Romanovs reduced communication with the outside world. Foreign traders were required to live in special ghetto quarters in the towns, for example, and contact with them was reduced to a minimum.

## Church Reform

But pressure from the west was unrelenting. In particular, Jesuit missionaries, who had been extremely successful in eliminating Protestantism from Poland, kept up a telling assault upon Orthodox "errors." The trouble was that the Russian church books were full of mistakes that had crept in through scribal errors of translation or of copying. Jesuit scholars delighted to point these out, and some of them were so obvious that they could scarcely be denied. Yet Russian clerics could not admit that the Jesuits were right without seeming to endanger their whole claim to Orthodoxy.

In 1667 a new and masterful patriarch, Nikon, decided to take the bull by the horns. He set out to revise the Russian prayer books and service manuals by going back to the Greek originals and correcting whatever errors had accumulated over the centuries. Since the Greek Church was undeniably older than the Roman Church, the appeal to Greek church books seemed like an effective reply to Catholic propaganda.

On the other hand, any change in the familiar phrases of the church services shocked many Russians. An important party, known as "Old Believers," refused to accept Nikon's reforms and, indeed, accused him of being Antichrist.

The czar soon quarreled with Nikon, but even after deposing him, maintained Nikon's policy of church reform. What to do with those persons who refused to accept the revised forms of church ritual then became a serious problem. The czar resorted to persecution, but this simply drove religious dissent underground.

Communities of Old Believers spread over Russia and became particularly numerous in fringe areas, where the power of the state was weak. Some groups developed extreme doctrines, expecting the end of the world at any minute and seeing in the acts of the czar fulfillment of the prophecies in the book of Revelation.

## Costs and Gains of Russia's First Encounter with the West

Russian society thus came to be sharply divided. The upper class accepted the restored czardom and the revised forms of church worship. But they ruled over a "dark and deaf" peasantry, many of whom felt that their masters had betrayed true religion as well as elementary social justice. Peasant revolts expressed the anger of the lower class, but the uprisings always failed. Such experiences merely confirmed the Old Believers in thinking that the Antichrist was on the march and that the end of the world was truly at hand. Expecting God to set right the injustice from which they suffered, they remained, for the most part, sullen but passive when Czar Peter the Great (ruled 1689–1725) undertook still another revolution from the top to bring Russia more fully into touch with the western European world. But since Peter did not begin his reform until 1698, we shall wait until a later chapter to consider his career and its importance for Russia and the world.

One point, however, deserves emphasis here. The very real and profound troubles that Russia had in coping with the west and in keeping the Poles and Swedes in check had the effect of making the Russians extremely successful in their dealings with the peoples to the south and east. Thus, the time when Russia's problems with the west were especially acute was also the time when the vast Russian Empire took shape.

Siberia and the Russian Far East in the Amur Valley were occupied under the first Romanovs. Even more important, the Ukraine was annexed to Russia in 1667.

Russia in fact became, with China, the principal gainer from the gunpowder revolution that undermined the battle effectiveness of steppe cavalrymen. In 1689, after minor collisions in the Amur Valley, the two powers signed the Treaty of Nerchinsk, defining boundaries and regulating trade between them. By this treaty, a buffer zone, including Mongolia and the lands around the Ili River, was declared off limits for both China and Russia. But by thus delimiting the zone of nomad life, the two great agricultural empires of northern Asia were also signing the death warrant of independent nomad power.

However costly in themselves, Russia's troubles in adjusting inherited ways so as to repel western attacks therefore paid off handsomely across Russia's other frontiers.

## The New World

The Amerindians, like the Russians, had to change their ways drastically between 1500 and 1700 to adjust to the presence and activity of western Europeans. Moreover, the gap between Amerindian and European society was too great to allow the inhabitants of the New World to gather the same kind of compensation that came to the Russians. Instead, wherever they came into close contact with Europeans, Amerindian communities suffered cruel disruption and soon lost all effective independence.

## Spanish Empire in the Americas

In the most highly developed regions of the New World—Mexico and Peru—Spanish policy was to make Christians out of the native peoples whom they called Indians but otherwise leave the traditional institutions of their village communities in place. Nevertheless, as new diseases cut into the native population, the Spaniards and their de-

scendants needed to use a large proportion of the remaining Indian labor to keep their mines and other economic enterprises going. Ways were found of breaking into the Indian villages despite the legal protections that Spanish law gave them.

In particular, Indians who failed to repay their debts could legally be required to work off their indebtedness. This made it easy for Spanish ranchers to assure themselves of a steady supply of labor. The mines had more difficulty, for their labor needs were much greater. Labor shortage, however, promoted labor-saving improvements. As a result, the Mexican mines became among the most technically advanced in the world. After about 1650 the tremendous destruction of population by disease came to a halt. But by then the population of central Mexico had been reduced from between 11 million and 20 million to a mere 1.5 million. Recovery was slow at first, for death rates remained high. In the Caribbean islands and coastlands, African slaves largely replaced the indigenous population, which was particularly exposed to both European and African tropical diseases. This added a third element to the racial and cultural mixture of Spanish America.

Despite the drastic depletion of the native population, Spanish America, before 1700, became the seat of a flourishing provincial version of Spanish Catholic civilization. Mexico City and Lima were great cities by European standards— far larger and more impressive than anything yet established by English or French colonists. Universities were founded to train the priests and lawyers needed by the Spanish regime. The universities kept up close connections with the European world of learning and imported such novelties as the philosophical speculations of Descartes soon after they burst upon the European intellectual scene.

Not only were the Indians excluded from such activity, but their own cultural traditions were disrupted. To be sure, everyday routines in the fields and villages remained much as before. Even old religious rites and ideas persisted, usually in Christian dress. But the political and intellectual ideas and skills of Amerindian civilizations disappeared with the overthrow of the priests and rulers who had governed them. As a result, Spanish power and Spanish culture were secure and unchallenged in the New World, even

**European Expansion in the Americas, ca. 1700**

*Hudson Bay*

*Rupert L.*

NEWFOUNDLAND

Quebec

Port Royal

Boston
New York
Philadelphia
Jamestown
Charleston
Port Royal
St. Augustine

LOUISIANA

NEW SPAIN

El Paso

Pensacola

New Orleans

FLORIDA

Guadalajara
Mexico City

Belize

CUBA

PUERTO RICO

HISPANIOLA

Panama

Caracas

*Pacific Ocean*

NEW

GRANADA

Bogota

GUIANA

(Dutch) Fr.

Cayenne

*Atlantic Ocean*

Quito

Manaos

Belem

BRAZIL

Political Control

Lima

Cuzco

Bahia

NEW CASTLE
(PERU)

Sucre

Potosi

RIO

Sao Paulo
Asuncion

Rio de Janeiro

CHILE

DE LA

PLATA

La Serena

Santiago
Buenos Aires

Montevideo

*Treaty Line of Tordesillas 1494*

Valdivia

| | | |
|---|---|---|
| ■ | English | |
| ▨ | French | |
| ▤ | Dutch | |
| ▨ | Spanish | |
| ▨ | Portuguese | |

PATAGONIA

0    500    1000

Miles

MALVINAS IS.

Tierra del Fuego

though only a few persons of Spanish birth or descent shared in them fully.

## Portuguese Brazil

In Brazil, the Portuguese settlers created a much more variegated and disorderly society by importing large numbers of slaves from Africa to work the sugar plantations, upon which the prosperity of the colony soon came to depend. Since few Portuguese women left home, Portuguese men married African or Indian wives and recognized their children as legitimate. A gradation of racial mixtures therefore emerged in Brazil that was more complex than the Spanish-Indian-African social hierarchy. Moreover, since the African slaves brought their own cultural traditions with them to the New World, African elements blended with Indian and Portuguese cultures to make the Brazilian heritage unique.

Brazil's political history was also more complex than the bureaucratic system that prevailed in the Spanish Empire. First the French and then the Dutch tried to take over Brazil, but they were driven out by the colonists themselves. A bold buccaneering spirit led the Brazilians to penetrate deep into the Amazon forests looking for slaves for the sugar mills and, later, also for gold and diamonds, when they were discovered in the interior of the continent. Recurrent friction with Jesuit missionaries who controlled the Guaraní Indians of Paraguay and with Spaniards who settled along the Rio de la Plata gave local bands of Brazilians an excuse to raid and plunder far and wide. By doing so they extended the boundaries of their colony at a rapid rate.

## French and British Colonies in North America

By comparison with the Spanish Empire and even with Brazil, the British and French colonies in North America were still poor and undeveloped in 1700. Nowhere had settlement penetrated far from the coast. Colonial society was, for the most part, a crude, simplified version of the English and French model. Permanent settlement began at Jamestown in 1607 and at Quebec in the following year. But the infant colonies grew slowly at first. The easy wealth the first settlers expected was not to be found. Conditions were hard, food short, the climate unfamiliar. The arrival of religious dissenters (Puritans) in Massachusetts, beginning in 1620, added an unruly new strand to English settlements in the New World. The Puritans became a body of hardworking, disciplined people, ready to undertake the heavy labor of cultivating the stony soils of New England. But they preferred to govern themselves and were disinclined to obey a distant, and religiously suspect, English government.

Like the Spaniards, the French put great emphasis upon converting the Indians to Christianity and tried to protect them from unscrupulous traders. But European diseases proved fatal, even when communicated by well-meaning priests. As a result, only a few of the Indians of Canada and the northeastern United States survived contact with Europeans.

The French in Canada soon developed a profitable trade in furs. Explorers learned how to travel by canoe along the waterways of the continental interior. By going up the St. Lawrence River to the Great Lakes and then portaging from Lake Michigan to tributaries of the Mississippi River, the French outflanked the English colonists, who were blocked from the deeper interior by the Appalachian Mountains. The government of New France (the possessions of France in North America) was closely controlled from Paris. Governors, appointed by the king, managed all important affairs.

The English colonies were much more varied. Virginia and Massachusetts had both been founded by companies chartered by the king of England. New York was acquired from the Dutch in 1664 by conquest, having, however, already been granted to the king's brother, the duke of York. Pennsylvania was founded on the strength of a royal grant to William Penn, and many of the other colonies started through grants to other proprietors.

Between 1640 and 1660, England was troubled by civil wars. In 1688 the mother country suffered another revolution and then plunged into European wars that lasted until 1714. During most of this time the colonies were allowed to go their own way with only occasional efforts at supervision from England. Moreover, efforts to centralize control in London met with strong local resistance. When the royal charters for Virginia and Massachusetts were canceled, for example, and governors were sent out from England to conduct the public affairs of the colonies, they found themselves face to face with representative assemblies whose members were used to running their own affairs. Hence nothing like the orderly dignity and systematic thoroughness of Spanish or even of French administration ever prevailed in the English colonies. Instead, they became a refuge for religious dissenters (Catholic, Quaker, and Puritan) as well as for other misfits of English society.

Relations with the Indians were left largely to local decision. The settlers early found that they could not make the Indians work for them. They sometimes tried to treat the Indians fairly. William Penn was the chief exemplar of this policy. But in general, the settlers trampled on Indian rights and took what they wanted or could use without troubling themselves about what their actions might do to the Indians.

The fact was that the Indians could not defend themselves or make their wishes effective politically except by trying to play off the French against the English. Even with French guns and diplomatic encouragement, desperate acts of violence against the encroaching English could not restore Indian lands. Such attacks, however, convinced almost all the colonists that the Indians were cruel and dangerous enemies who could not be trusted.

Everywhere along the frontier where Indian communities confronted the newcomers, Indian populations withered and drew back, unable to offer much resistance. Disease deaths were always a factor. In addition, the Europeans had vastly superior knowledge and skills that put the Indians at a disadvantage they could never overcome.

# Africa and Oceania

The improvement of transportation, which resulted from the opening of the world's oceans by European explorers just before and immediately after 1500, meant that all the simpler societies of the earth that lay within easy reach of a coastline were in the same sort of danger as the Indians of North America. There were obstacles of distance which it took time to overcome, especially in the Pacific, where the smaller islands were, in general, not explored or disturbed by European sailors until after 1700. Australia, too, remained effectively isolated behind coastal mangrove swamps that obstructed approach from the north. Ice barriers meant that the coastlands of the Arctic were but slightly disturbed by the activities of English traders in Hudson Bay (from 1670) or in the White Sea

(from 1553). In these parts of the world, age-old hunting and gathering societies continued to live in their accustomed ways, without much disturbance from outside.

## Africa and the Slave Trade

The African continent was much more complicated. Ships could not penetrate far into Africa except along the Nile because rapids near the mouths of all the African rivers interrupted navigation. Even more important, tropical diseases like yellow fever, malaria, and sleeping sickness made it dangerous for outsiders to reside in sub-Saharan Africa. Local populations grew up exposed to these and other infections and developed resistances to them that newcomers lacked. Exactly the opposite condition prevailed in the Americas, where the native inhabitants lacked resistances to diseases Europeans and Africans brought into the New World and so suffered drastic die-offs in the first century and a half after transoceanic contacts started.

This disease difference was fundamental to the history of Africa from earliest times. It meant that strangers and intruders from north of the Sahara could not take over from disease-experienced local inhabitants, even when the local peoples, to begin with, were less well organized and less well equipped than the outsiders. As a result, Africa remained African, in full charge of its own fate and pattern of historical development in a way that the Amerindians did not.

To be sure, the heavy disease burden carried by African populations was a handicap as well as a protection. People carrying malarial parasites in their bodies could not work as hard as healthy persons, for example, and productivity inevitably suffered. Nevertheless, by the time the Portuguese began to sail along the West African coast, West and East African kingdoms had about a thousand years of history behind them, and of course North Africa was the site of one of the earliest of all human civilizations in Egypt. In the rest of the continent, trade was intensifying, kingdoms were arising, and contacts with the outside world were increasing in the decades when the Portuguese were exploring the entire length of the west coast, 1418–1486.

After the Portuguese rounded Africa in 1499, their main attention was fastened on the fabled wealth of the Indies because the African coast had less to attract them. Nevertheless, they set up a series of shore stations (some on off-shore islands) where they traded with local peoples and tried to convert them to Christianity. This established a new cultural frontier of African-European encounter. It ran all the way from the Straits of Gibraltar to about halfway up the east coast.

This new frontier supplemented a far older zone of encounter between Africans and Moslems. Even in Mohammed's lifetime (d. 632), converts to the new faith appeared in Africa as well as in Arabia proper. The whole of North Africa became an integral part of the realm of Islam by 700, and Moslem traders began to operate along the coast of East Africa at about the same time. In ensuing centuries, contacts between the Moslem world and the African interior gradually increased in importance. A major landmark was the conquest of Ghana in West Africa by Moslems from Morocco in 1076. Thereafter the rulers of most West African kingdoms were Moslems, and trans-Saharan caravans maintained close connections between West Africa and the heartlands of the Moslem world.

Another powerful current of migration and cultural influence came across the open savanna lands that lie south of the Sahara. After the collapse of the Christian kingdoms of Nubia (1504), nomadic tribesmen, moving from east to west, brought the grasslands firmly under Moslem control, all the way from the Horn of Africa to the Atlantic coast. By contrast, the savanna lands of East Africa remained beyond the reach of Moslem traders and conquerors, partly because the tsetse fly and the sleeping sickness it carried created very effective barriers to penetration from the coast. Nonetheless, at Zimbabwe in the interior of southern Africa, powerful kingdoms arose after about 1100. The rulers of Zimbabwe exported gold and ivory to Moslem cities on the east coast but, unlike the situation in West Africa, retained their own pagan religion.

Elsewhere in the interior of Africa far less is known about the rise of states and of the trade and warfare that supported royal courts and officials. Yet when the Portuguese showed up at the mouth of the Congo River in 1483, they discovered several powerful kingdoms in the region, some of which were probably of quite recent creation. Farther south, racially different peoples called San (Bushmen) and Khoikhoi (Hottentots) followed hunting and pastoral ways of life. They had been in retreat before the advance of Bantu-speaking black Africans for many centuries. The Bantus were farmers and herders and knew how to make iron tools. Some of them had become skilled miners as well and could build impressive stone fortifications, as they did at Zimbabwe.

During the early centuries of Africa's contacts with the outside world, the continent was famous for its exports of gold, ivory, salt, and slaves. But it was the slave trade that flourished most vigorously after 1500 and became indelibly associated with Africa in European (and American) consciousness. The trade was very old. Black Africans were valued as household servants in the Moslem world, sometimes holding key posts—for example, as guardians of the Ottoman sultan's harem. But African slavery took on new scale and significance in the course of the sixteenth century when European settlers in the New World discovered how to grow sugar in Brazil and later in the Caribbean Islands. Sugar required heavy labor for harvesting and processing the juice of the canes into crystalline form for transport to distant markets. The vulnerability of Amerindians to European diseases meant that efforts to compel them to work on sugar plantations failed utterly. But Africans were used to Old World diseases and proved to be far more resistant than Europeans, who could not easily endure the tropical infections that soon crossed the Atlantic from Africa. As a result, beginning in the 1520s, Europeans began to import African slaves to work on sugar plantations in the New World.

Numbers were small at first. Before 1700, the slave trade centered mainly in Angola, across the ocean from Brazil where the demand for slave labor was concentrated. But with each passing decade, the scale of sugar production and the numbers of Africans brought across the ocean to labor in the New World increased. In time, the majority of the inhabitants of the Caribbean Islands and of the sugar-growing regions of Brazil came to be descendants of black Africans who had come to the New World as slaves. Later, tobacco and cotton planters on the mainland of North America also started to rely on black slave labor, bringing a substantial black population into the southern British colonies. The transatlantic slave trade therefore carried African populations to vast new regions of the earth, in tandem with the expansion of European settlement across the ocean.

African slaves in the New World were always baptized to make them Christians, since saving souls was one justification Europeans used to defend the slave trade. But baptism could not erase the cultural traditions the slaves brought with them. Consequently, African as well as European and Amerindian heritages entered into the mix of cultures and peoples that arose in the Americas after 1492.

In sub-Saharan Africa itself, the effect of the slave trade was sometimes destructive. Raiders, often based in coastal cities, penetrated far inland seeking captives, and many of their victims died in chains while traveling to the coast or on shipboard afterward. Slave raiders ravaged innumerable villages and brought previously isolated communities into brutal contact with the outside world. But for the continent as a whole there is no reason to think that depopulation resulted, even though perhaps as many as 1.9 million Africans had been shipped away as slaves by 1700. (Incidentally, the export of slaves to the Moslem world also seems to have increased after 1500. In Moslem lands, however, male household slaves were not allowed to marry and have children. As a result, no separate and distinct black population, like that which arose in the New World, took form.)

One reason why the mounting intensity of the slave trade did not reduce African populations was that new crops from America allowed African farmers to raise more food than before. Maize was by far the most valuable of the new crops, and it eventually became a staple of African agriculture, although cassava, peanuts, and sweet potatoes were also important, especially in West Africa. No one knows for sure just when the new crops spread from the coastlands

to the interior, and it is quite impossible to balance the growth of population permitted by the increased food supply against the losses of the slave trade. All one can say is that the spread of the more productive American food crops tended to sustain African populations at the same time that slave raiders were destroying them. One therefore counteracted the other, allowing African peoples to survive and maintain their own ways of life in the general context of an increasingly militarized and commercialized society.

Since Europeans and Asians could not long survive in the African interior owing to their vulnerability to tropical diseases, slave raiding and transport to the coast remained always in African hands. Rulers and merchants imported cloth, iron, and guns from Europe in exchange for slaves. Access to guns transformed the prevailing techniques of African warfare and slave raiding, although old-fashioned armored cavalry long survived, partly for ceremonial reasons, at a court like that of Oyo in what is today western Nigeria.

The various states and peoples who thus entered more and more vigorously into the expanding trade nets that criss-crossed the continent maintained traditions and skills unique to Africa. Even those who became Moslem or Christian retained local customs that marked them off from the rest of the world. African art is the most obvious evidence of the continuity of local traditions and skills. Masks and sculpture, presenting haunting images of human and animal forms, had religious and ceremonial uses that cannot be shared by modern museum-goers; but this does not prevent such objects from arousing a powerful aesthetic response. Styles varied greatly in pagan Africa and merged into standard forms of Islamic art in those parts of Africa most firmly attached to the Moslem world. This reflects the fact that by 1500, North Africa, the savanna lands of West Africa, and the coasts of East Africa were well-established parts of the world of Islam. Moslem traders regularly doubled as missionaries of their faith; and as trade connections multiplied, conversions to Islam continued to occur over wide regions of the continent. By comparison, efforts of Christian missionaries met with rather modest success, although they, too, made some converts close to the western coasts where European influence concentrated.

Only in the extreme north and south of the continent, where cooler climates inhibited tropical diseases, did European settlement prove viable. As a result, when the Dutch established a shore station at Cape Town at the southernmost tip of Africa in 1652, it took root and eventually began to flourish. By 1700, Dutch farmers and herders had begun to move inland, displacing local Khoikhoi pastoralists by force. Elsewhere the population of Africa remained almost entirely African until French settlers started to establish themselves in Algeria after 1830.

Overall, between 1500 and 1700 Africa began both to enjoy and to suffer from its growingly intimate contact with the rest of the world. After the European voyages of discovery, Africans in effect found themselves caught between an expanding Moslem world to the north and east and an expanding European-managed world in the Americas and the Indian Ocean. Beginning about 1520 the transatlantic slave trade carried large black populations to the tropical and subtropical parts of the Americas. In Africa itself, during the next two centuries, long-distance contacts multiplied, social change accelerated, American food crops provided new sources of food, and the expansion of Islam continued. Africa, of course, had never been entirely isolated from the rest of the world, but after 1500 it was bound more and more closely into a worldwide economic system. Yet, protected by tropical diseases, African peoples remained in charge of their own affairs, building kingdoms, conducting trade, and dealing with outsiders pretty much on their own terms. Africa, in short, remained fully and uniquely itself, whereas the Americas, owing to their new transatlantic immigrant populations, experienced drastic demographic and cultural discontinuity.

## Conclusion

The appearance of European sailors, soldiers, and settlers in the Americas disrupted and, in time, destroyed almost all of the earlier Amerindian societies. Nowhere else, however, did the opening of the oceans to European ships have anything like such drastic consequences. In the civilized ports of Asia, mixing of peoples from different parts of the world was already quite familiar. European skills and knowledge did not persuade Moslems, Hindus, or Chinese to abandon familiar ways. There seemed to be no good reason why the Asians should not cling to what seemed good to them and let the Europeans do the same.

Yet the world did not stand still. The opening of the oceans led to the spread of American food crops, to population increase, and to a price revolution that affected all the civilized world, as we saw in Chapter 15. These changes had long-range consequences of the greatest importance. Within the 200 years from 1500 to 1700, another fundamental change took place within the Eurasian continent and in Africa, when the age-old superiority of cavalry to infantry came to an end. This was the result of the development of guns and muskets, which allowed foot soldiers to fire volleys that could break up a cavalry charge.

In Eurasia, consequently, the advantages that steppe nomads had enjoyed ever since about 700 B.C.E., when attacking farming peoples, ceased to exist. Rapid expansion of civilized control over the steppe regions resulted. Nevertheless, before that happened both India and China underwent one final conquest from the steppes. In India the conquest led to the establishment of the Mogul Empire, beginning in 1526, and in China to the establishment of the Manchu dynasty that ruled from 1644 to 1912.

The development of guns and muskets also meant, in all civilized countries, that central governments had growing advantages over more local authorities. Cannon could knock holes even in well-defended castles and city walls. But siege guns were expensive and conspicuous, which made it easy for a central authority to monopolize them. Local leaders, accordingly, had to submit to distant sovereigns far more completely than had been customary.

Everywhere in the civilized world, therefore, the size of political units and the effectiveness with which a single ruler could impose his will on distant regions increased sharply between 1500 and 1700. Almost all buffer zones between the separate civilized communities of Eurasia were rapidly gobbled up by one or another civilized goverment. Russia and China were the two powers that gained most from this situation; their territorial expansion in fact paralleled Spain's empire-building in the Americas both in time and geographical scale.

Improved communication among all the coastlines of the world increased the pace of social change everywhere. Many small and weak communities disappeared completely. In fact, only in Africa (and perhaps in New Zealand) were local peoples able to withstand and, in time, react successfully to the challenges that sudden exposure to alien styles of civilization presented to previously isolated peoples.

These changes in world relationships were fundamental and vastly important for human history. Yet it would be wrong to emphasize the novelties too much. Each of the major civilized traditions of the Old World continued along familiar and well-worn paths. Moslems continued to win converts along almost every frontier. Hindus underwent a religious revival that assured the continued vitality of that cultural tradition despite political subjection to Moslem rulers. The Chinese underwent the crisis of going from the rule of one dynasty to another in a completely traditional fashion. They did so rather more quickly than had often been the case in earlier centuries and emerged so strong and prosperous as to arouse the admiration of many Europeans when they learned how the Chinese governed their "Celestial Empire."

The western European world, to be sure, showed signs of its growing expansive power. European settlement of the Americas began to make inroads upon the continental vastnesses of North and South America. Until long after 1700, most of the New World was not occupied by settlers of European origin; but it was clear enough, all the same, that Amerindian populations could not stop westward expansion across North America, nor prevent occupation of the temperate parts of South America.

On Europe's eastern flank, Russia became more and more closely tied to the west. The relationship irritated the Russians, for they wished to keep their Orthodox faith and defend their cultural independence from western Europe. But they had to do so by borrowing western skills, importing western workers, and becoming more like the western nations of Europe. Russia's experience between 1500 and 1700 was thus a foretaste of the dilemmas other civilized peoples confronted later on when Europe's power finally compelled Moslems, Indians, Chinese, and Japanese to pay attention to what had happened in that remote peninsula of Asia called Europe.

# Bibliography

The most powerful description of early responses to the new European presence that I know of is in the form of a letter, written by Afonso I, king of the Congo, to Dom Manuel I, king of Portugal, dated October 15, 1514. It is available in English translation in W. H. McNeill and Mitsuoko Iriye, *Readings in World History: Vol. 9. Modern Asia and Africa* (1971). A similarly telling document expressing a similarly ambivalent response to western European pressure comes from a very different part of the world in the form of Jane Harrison and Hope Mirrlees, trans., *The Life of the Archpriest Avvakum by Himself* (1924). Avvakum became a leader of Russian Old Believers after 1653. Both of these texts illustrate the mixture of attraction and repulsion toward intrusive Europeans that was felt by other peoples of the earth. Similarly revelatory from the European side are the missionary reports sent back to Rome by St. Francis Xavier, available in H. J. Coleridge, ed., *The Life and Letters of St. Francis Xavier* (1890). But Europeans did not affect everyone, as is shown by the delightful account of his adventures written by the founder of the Mogul Empire and available in English as Baber, *Memoirs* (A. S. Beveridge, trans., 1922).

Four important recent works analyze the pattern of global relationship created by European discoveries and the new economic activities Europeans hastened to develop. Immanuel Wallerstein, *The Modern World System: Capitalist Agriculture and the Origin of the European World Economy in the Sixteenth Century* (1976), and Eric R. Wolf, *Europe and the Peoples without History* (1982), both approach the subject from a Marxist angle of vision; Philip D. Curtin, *Cross-Cultural Trade in World History* (1984), eschews that framework and draws mainly on anthropological concepts. W. H. McNeill, *The Age of Gunpowder Empires* (1989), offers a very brief introduction to the spread of gunpowder weaponry and the far-reaching impact of this change on non-Western peoples. On American silver and the onset of global exchange, see Dennis O. Flynn and Arturo Giráldez, "Born with a 'Silver Spoon': The Origin of World Trade in 1571," *Journal of World History,* 6 (1995):201–21.

For changes in the Americas, the following are of special interest: D. W. Meinig, *The Shaping of America, Vol. I Atlantic America 1492–1800* (1986); James Axtell, *The Invasion Within: The Contest of Cultures in Colonial North America* (1985); Gilberto Freyre, *Brazil: An Interpretation* (1941); Charles Gibson, *Spain in America* (1966); Lyle N. McAlister, *Spain and Portugal in the New World 1492–1700* (1984). On the slave trade, Edward Reynolds, *Stand the Storm: A History of the Atlantic Slave Trade* (1985), summarizes recent research on the subject, while David Brion Davis, *The Anatomy of Slavery* (1984), explores the role of slavery in the development of America. The peculiar importance that sugar came to play on both sides of the Atlantic is tellingly analyzed by Signey W. Mintz, *Sweetness and Power: The Place of Sugar in Modern History* (1985).

For the Far East, C. R. Boxer, *The Christian Century of Japan* (2nd ed., 1968); Jonathan D. Spence, *The Memory Palace of Matteo Ricci* (1984); Jacques Gernet, *China and the Christian Impact: A Conflict of Cultures* (1985); and Frederic Wakeman, Jr., *The Great Enterprise: The Manchu Reconstruction of the Imperial Order in Seventeenth-Century China* (1985), are books of unusual merit and readability.

For Russian entanglements and reactions to outside pressure, Raymond H. Fisher, *The Russian Fur Trade, 1550–1700* (1943); Donald W. Treadgold, *The West in Russia and China* (1974); Richard Hellie, *Slavery in Russia, 1450–1725* (1982); and Jerome Blum, *Lord and Peasant in Russia from the Ninth to the Nineteenth Century* (1961), are particularly interesting. For a general account, try George Vernadsky, *The Tsardom of Moscow* (1969).

For sidelights on the Ottoman-Christian encounter, see D. M. Vaughn, *Europe and the Turk: A Pattern of Alliances 1350–1700* (1954); S. A. Fischer-Galati, *Ottoman Imperialism and German Protestantism, 1521–1555* (1959); and Paul Coles, *The Ottoman Impact on Europe* (1968). For Islam as a whole, Marshall G. S. Hodgson, *The Venture of Islam, Vol. 3: The Gunpowder Empires and Modern Times* (1974), is the best guide.

For India, Ram P. Tripathi, *The Rise and Fall of the Mughal Empire* (1956), and Irfan Habib, *The Agrarian System of Mughal India 1556–1707* (1963), can balance against a more British point of view offered by T. G. P. Spear, ed., *The Oxford History of India* (3rd ed., 1958). For Southeast Asia, see Sanjay Subrahamanyam, *The Portuguese Empire in Asia, 1500–1700: A Political and Economic History* (1993), and C. R. Boxer, *The Dutch Sea-Borne Empire, 1600–1800* (1965).

This was the era of supreme artistic achievement in the world of Islam. Alexandre Papadopoulo, *Islam and Muslim Art* (1976); M. C. Beach, *The Imperial Image: Paintings from the Mughal Court* (1981); Ekrem Akurgal, ed., *The Art and Architecture of Turkey* (1980); and Arthur Upham Pope, *Persian Architecture* (1965), are among the books that can introduce you to its beauties.

# *Europe's Old Regime*
## 1650 to 1789

# 18

**How to Be Efficient** This etching was made to show Dutch soldiers how to fire a matchlock gun efficiently. The posture shown here (one of 42) is "Fire," and you can see how the trigger has just brought a smouldering cord into contact with gunpowder in the firing pan. Practice made perfect, and European armies used pictures like this to drill recruits until each move became almost automatic.

Between 1648, when the Peace of Westphalia ended the Thirty Years' War, and 1789, when the French Revolution began, Europe passed through a period of calm. But it was a calm and quiet time only by comparison with the storms that had gone before and those that came after. Wars did not cease, but they were conducted by professional armies with a decent respect for the fact that an enemy province might change hands at the peace table—and who wanted to acquire a smoking ruin? Challenging new ideas did not cease to arise in Europe; but they were advanced by professional writers and scientists who did not feel they had to go out and make their ideas come true, without delay, in the way the religious reformers of an earlier age and the political reformers of the age that was to come tried to do.

It was an age of moderation and compromise. People agreed to disagree on many matters and found, somewhat to their surprise, that they could do so and still get along with one another. An elaborate code of manners made this possible by cushioning collisions among individuals and between classes. Good manners often required men and women to disguise their feelings and betray their private characters by acting out a role. But individuals did in some degree become what they pretended to be—noble king or humble servant as the case might be; and the web of pretenses imposed by good manners did smooth over difficulties and helped to keep violence in check.

The restless energies that had helped to tear Europe apart in the age of religious wars was turned outward. The result was an enormous expansion of European empires in the Americas, in India, and throughout the forest and steppe zones of Eurasia. What had been a strictly West European civilization ceased to be so, when both Russian nobles and American pioneers began to share the culture and tradition that continued to have its center and main focus in northwestern Europe. European civilization, in short, became Western civilization, no longer tied to its original geographical cradleland.

Yet comparative calm did not involve inactivity or the end of rapid change. Kings and princes organized violence more effectively than ever before by maintaining professional standing armies. Most rulers claimed absolute power within their frontiers. But so-called absolute monarchs faced all sorts of practical limits to their power. Many local groups possessed traditional rights and privileges that had come down from medieval times. In addition, the soldiers and officials, who made royal absolutism effective, acquired a vested interest in maintaining their own special rights and roles. As such they resisted unwanted changes, even when those changes were decreed by a ruler who in theory held absolute power.

Absolutism was also counterbalanced by the development of communication networks that ran across political boundaries among people with similar interests or pursuits. Priests, bankers, and merchants had maintained such networks for centuries. What happened during the Old Regime was that scientists, writers, musicians, agriculturists, and others developed regular means of exchanging professional information about new discoveries and achievements. Thus, by one of the contradictory compromises characteristic of the Old Regime, Europe was divided into hundreds of separate states, each in theory completely independent of all the others. Yet it was also more united in matters of culture than before (when religious barriers had divided Europe into hostile parts) or after (when national differences did the same).

# Social and Economic Changes

Europe met with extraordinary success under the Old Regime. This showed up most dramatically in the way European settlers, merchants, and monarchs extended their reach into new regions of the earth. Expansion abroad was matched at home by stepping up the pace and intensity of economic activity so that larger populations lived better at the end of the Old

Regime than at its beginning and had some important new commodities at their disposal.

## Population Growth

Population growth was fundamental. In the eighteenth century every part of Europe began to undergo such growth. Epidemic diseases became less common and less severe. The last widespread outbreak of bubonic plague in Europe raged between 1663 and 1684. When plague broke out again in Marseilles in 1720–1721, effective quarantine limited its spread in a small area of southern France. Thereafter, one of the factors that in earlier times had kept down population ceased to affect western Europe, and the modern population explosion started, averaging a growth rate of about 1 percent per year.

Medical science had little to do with the first stages of this change, for doctors knew too little about the causes of disease to be very effective in stopping it. Quarantine of ships and of travelers from foreign parts may have been helpful sometimes (although often the fleas or rats or other carriers of disease were left alone because no one knew they were dangerous). Not until 1796 was the first successful inoculation against smallpox discovered by an English doctor, Edward Jenner (1749–1823). His idea of deliberately infecting people with a weak form of the disease met with some resistance, but soon became a standard practice (literally around the globe) when both the Spanish and the Russian imperial governments officially backed inoculation.

## The Agricultural Revolution

Improved agriculture was more important than medical science in forwarding population growth. Warmer climate, setting in after 1700, made crop failures in northern Europe less frequent, and increased the harvest in most years. On top of that, two valuable American food crops slowly but surely spread across Europe in the seventeenth and eighteenth centuries. Maize took hold in parts of Spain, Italy, and the Balkans, but its importance was eclipsed by the spread of potatoes in the north, where cooler climate and sandy soils were particularly favorable to them. In such regions, potatoes could produce nearly four times as many calories per acre as oats or rye, the only cereals that would ripen in Europe's less favored regions. Nearly four times as many people could therefore find nourishment by eating potatoes instead of oatmeal or rye bread. Only in Ireland did an almost total shift occur. Elsewhere, potatoes and maize supplemented bread but never entirely drove the older staples from the diet of even the poorest classes.

In addition to new crops for human nourishment, European farmers learned how to farm much more efficiently. By planting clover, alfalfa, or hay on grainfields, it became possible to do without fallowing. In medieval times, about a

---

**How to Get More to Eat by Working Harder**   In the Middle Ages, European farmers kept down weeds by fallowing one-third of their land and plowing the empty fields in summer before weed seeds had formed. A new and better way was found in the sixteenth century. Whenever enough labor was available, weeds could be killed by hoeing around fodder crops like turnips or potatoes, thus increasing overall productivity by at least a third.

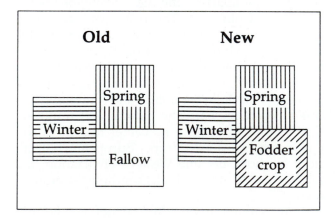

third of the arable land had to be left fallow each year to allow the extermination of weeds for two successive crops of grain. But by planting such fields with clover or alfalfa, the soil was improved, thanks to the activity of nitrogen-fixing bacteria that infest the roots of these plants; and at the same time, good winter fodder for horses and cows could be produced.

Better winter food meant larger and stronger animals. Improved plows, carefully designed to do the work with the least effort, could be pulled by a single team of horses, where four to six oxen had been needed in medieval times. Another crop, turnips, when planted in rows, allowed a careful farmer to cultivate his land repeatedly during the growing season and thus cut down on weeds while still getting a valuable fodder crop from the land. Drainage and flood control works, systematic experiment with a wide variety of fertilizers, and improved designs for such things as farm wagons, scythes, spades, and plows all increased yields or reduced the cost of production. In either case, the effect was to create a larger food supply with which the growing populations could be fed.

*Significance of Agricultural Advances*
Holland and England were in the forefront of agricultural improvement. Other parts of Europe lagged behind, and in some regions there was almost no change at all. Nevertheless, the agricultural improvers of the seventeenth and eighteenth centuries showed that great increases in yields and profits could be secured by using new methods, new crops, and new implements of cultivation. Improving farmers pioneered the idea of systematic experimentation. They tested results by keeping accurate records of how much seed, how much labor, and how much yield per acre were involved in using a new technique. And they communicated their results to other interested landowners through agricultural journals and newsletters, so that any really valuable discovery could spread rapidly and widely wherever soil and climate permitted.

Always before, agriculture had been in the hands of persons who assumed that what their predecessors had done was the only way things could be done. Disproving this notion was one of the most fundamental breakthroughs of modern times. Simple as it may seem today, the idea that farming methods could be improved shook age-old ways of life that tied the overwhelming majority of humankind to a fixed routine. And when a majority of the members of any society begin to alter their ways in important respects, then the scope and pace of historical change enormously increases. This, of course, is exactly what happened in modern times starting in northwestern Europe about 1650.

Looking backward, it is clear that an agricultural revolution had to come ahead of the better-known Industrial Revolution, which has been reshaping European and world society during the past 200 years. Without far-reaching changes on the land, Europe's industrial development could not have advanced as it did; for the Industrial Revolution required both food and labor to come from the countryside— and in ever-growing quantities. What permitted this to happen was the systematic application of the experimental method to techniques of farming, pioneered by a few hundred farmers, landlords, and scientists in England and Holland.

## Trade and Finance

Growing populations and improved agriculture sustained and were, in turn, sustained by a rising intensity of commerce. Important improvements in transportation made it easier to carry goods to market. Canals, for example, linked the major rivers of France. All-weather roads, smooth enough to allow wheeled vehicles to pass at any time of year, came slowly into existence as road builders learned how to drain the roadbed, cover the surface with gravel, and fill in holes before they got too big. Regular stagecoach connections between major cities were established so that anyone able to pay the price could travel scores or hundreds of miles at will and be more or less sure of arriving on schedule. The net importance of these improvements is difficult for us to imagine. But if you try to think of what life would be like without wintertime roads and without public transportation, the significance of these improvements for everyday life will begin to dawn on you.

Trade and commerce and all other economic enterprise were also stimulated by improvements in banking methods. Devices were found for assembling larger and larger quantities of capital. Such capital was then used to organize larger and more expensive undertakings. The effect was to allow Europeans to mobilize goods and labor for common enterprises on an ever-larger scale. War was always their biggest undertaking; and Europeans learned how to fight wars on credit, thereby mobilizing more and more of their resources in the pursuit of victory and empire.

*The Idea of a National Debt*     The decisive invention here was the concept of a national debt. Until about 1700, bankers and rulers tended to treat government borrowing as the personal debt of the reigning monarch. A new king or prince did not always feel obliged to pay off what his predecessor had borrowed. High interest rates were one consequence, and lending money to rulers remained a highly speculative business. In England, however, as we shall soon see, the king's powers over government were sharply reduced after 1689; and succession to the throne passed from one Stuart heir to another until it lodged in the House of Hanover in 1714. The result was that bankers began to make a clear distinction between the king's personal debts and the public debt.

The Bank of England was organized in 1694, in large part to manage the public debt. Its "bank notes," that is, promises to pay a given sum in metallic currency on demand, soon became a standard paper currency for large transactions. And, most important of all, anyone could buy a government bond and collect interest on it, secure in the knowledge that the Bank of England and the whole financial community of London would see to it that the promised interest would be paid on schedule. In this way, a large proportion of the English public (and foreigners too) became willing and eager to lend their spare cash to the government; and the government, in turn, could use borrowed money to pay the sudden extra costs of waging war or any other unusual expenditure. Taxes, of course, had to cover interest payments, but interest rates for government borrowing became much lower when the risk of repudiation no longer worried investors. As a result, financial and material resources could be mobilized more cheaply and on a larger scale than ever before.

Other governments lagged behind England in developing an efficient central bank and establishing public debts—but not by much, for the advantages of such a system for waging war were enormous.

## Techniques of Manufacture

Expenditures for war went, very largely, into the hands of merchants and manufacturers who supplied Europe's armed forces with the hundreds of items they required. New and expanded industries and transport systems resulted, some of which could be put to ordinary peacetime uses with little or no adjustment.

Yet all was not rosy. Between about 1650 and 1750, western Europeans faced a growing crisis as a result of the rapid disappearance of forests. Timber, fuel, and rough pasturage traditionally had come from Europe's forests. But as more and more people put greater demands upon the forests, big trees became scarce. The consequences of this scarcity for shipbuilding and metallurgy—both industries requiring large quantities of wood—were particularly important. The only solution for shipbuilding was to import timber, either from northern Europe—Sweden or Russia—or from the Americas. But English ironmasters discovered a far more effective way to solve their difficulty in getting enough fuel for their smelters by discovering how to make a new form of fuel—coke.

Ordinary coal, which existed abundantly in parts of western Europe, was useless for smelting iron ore. It had too many chemical impurities to produce usable iron or steel. Even a trace of phosphorous, for example, if allowed to penetrate the molten iron, would make a brittle and generally useless product. As a result, iron ore had always been smelted with charcoal; and to produce enough charcoal for Europe's iron smelters required enormous amounts of wood. For several decades in the early eighteenth century, therefore, Sweden and Russia had a special advantage in the iron and steel industries, since they still had sufficient forests to fuel the forges.

As early as 1709, an English ironmaster, Abraham Darby, discovered that he could purify coal of the objectional chemicals by burning it part way, just as wood had long been partly burnt to make charcoal. The coke that resulted from this process could then smelt iron ore just as charcoal did. For a long time, the Darby ironworks kept the method for making coke secret, and consequently the new technique did not come into general use until after 1750. When it did, coal, which was already an important fuel in western Europe for heating houses and for various industrial processes, acquired a much greater significance than before.

### New Sources of Power

Steam engines, which converted the energy of coal into mechanical motion, were invented as early as 1710 to drive pumps needed to lift water from coal mines. But the first such engines were extremely inefficient. Only when James Watt (1736–1819) invented an engine that did not have to be cooled to make the steam condense (1769) did steam power become really significant. Even then, the problem of making pistons and cylinders fit closely was very difficult to solve, so that the age of steam and power-driven machinery scarcely got started before 1789.

Watermills, windmills, and larger and better-designed ships were far more important sources of power than steam in the days of the Old Regime. Because horses provided the fundamental source of power for agriculture and land transportation, the most weighty improvement of all was the increased size and strength of systematically bred draught horses; and Europe's horse power multiplied as improved agricultural methods provided more and better fodder.

Overall, new techniques increased the amount of power—both muscular and mechanical—at the disposal of Europeans several times over between 1650 and 1789. This progress was fundamental. It opened all sorts of new possibilities for everyday activity.

### Precision Tools and Luxury Crafts

In other directions, too, European skills reached new levels during the Old Regime. Clockmakers, gunsmiths, lens grinders, glass blowers, jewel cutters, and diemakers learned how to shape metal and other hard materials very precisely. One of the great triumphs of Europe's technology was the invention of a clock so accurate and so insensitive to the pitching motion of a ship at sea that it could keep time within a few seconds for months on end. This invention, in turn, allowed ships' captains to calculate longitude. The first chronometer (as such clocks were called) accurate enough to measure longitude satisfactorily was invented in 1761 by an Englishman named John Harrison (1693–1776). He built upon a long tradition of mechanical ingenuity going back to the Middle Ages when the first mechanical clocks were constructed in church steeples to keep time for a whole town.

European artisans and inventors were also eager to borrow, and even improve upon, foreign skills when they found them useful. Two noteworthy examples were the discovery of how to make porcelain in imitation of the Chinese, who long kept the process secret, and the establishment of cotton manufacture in Europe in competition with Indian artisans. Since Indian weavers lived more cheaply than European workers could afford to live in the harsher climate of the north, it was only by inventing labor-saving devices that European manufacturers could come close to rivaling Indian production costs. They began to do so, with startling success, from about 1770; but, as in the case of the steam engine, the main impact of the new textile technology came later.

Luxury trades in the age of the Old Regime actually introduced much of the everyday equipment of an ordinary U.S. household of the twentieth century. Light, strong, and handsome furniture, "china" dishes, big windows filled with transparent glass, and printed wallpaper were among the new household items introduced between 1648 and 1789. Taken together, they made a more comfortable, cleaner, and attractive life possible—at first only for the upper classes and then, with mass production, for larger and larger numbers of people.

## Territorial Expansion

The advance of European settlement in North America is a familiar part of our national history. By the time the English colonies won their independence, they numbered about 4 million inhabitants—nearly half the population of England at the time. The frontier of settlement reached and, in places, had even crossed the Appalachian Mountain barrier. Far in advance of settlement, fur traders had explored the American west as far as the Rocky Mountains and the Mackenzie River, while Russian and Spanish activity expanded along the Pacific coast of North America. Claims overlapped, but in practice a gap remained between Russian and Spanish spheres of influence, for Russian fur traders seldom operated south of Vancouver Island, while San Francisco remained the northernmost regular Spanish outpost.

In Latin America, the decline of the Amerindian population reached its low point about 1650, after which a slow and then more and more rapid growth of population set in. Settlement in the Rio de la Plata region and in the interior of Brazil resembled what was happening at the same time in North America. In the La Plata region, ranching was more important than farming; in Brazil the discovery of gold and diamonds (ca. 1695) sparked the exploration and partial settlement of the interior. Meanwhile, the Brazilian coastlands and the islands of the Caribbean supported profitable sugar plantations, worked by slaves brought across the Atlantic Oceans from Africa. The importance of the sugar islands in international trade was extraordinary. Indeed, in 1763 the French preferred to give up all of Canada in order to

keep the island of Martinique; and as late as 1773, records show that Great Britain's trade with the Caribbean Islands was more valuable than trade with the mainland North American colonies.

Despite weakness at home, the Spanish and Portuguese empires survived all the wars of the seventeenth and eighteenth centuries, at least partly because yellow fever, to which local inhabitants of the Caribbean had become accustomed after 1648, when the disease arrived from Africa, had a way of destroying British and French forces sent to the region. A few weeks ashore within reach of the mosquitoes that carried the yellow fever virus was usually enough to defeat any expedition from Europe. This meant that even slender garrisons ashore could expect to defend fortified places long enough for the fever to paralyze vastly superior invading forces.

After 1750, Spanish power and wealth in the New World began to recover from the depression that had set in with the radical decay of Amerindian populations. Demographic turnaround about 1650 gave way to rapid population growth a century later. Mestizos, whose ancestors were partly white, partly Indian, outnumbered any other group in most parts of the Spanish Empire; but in Brazil and the Caribbean lowlands, a black element was also prominent in the emerging mixture of races. Increased population sustained a rising curve of trade and manufacture; this in turn supported urban populations that kept in touch with new currents of thought in Europe. In this way, ideas of the French Enlightenment took root in parts of the Spanish Empire; and when the English colonies of North America became independent in 1776, a few restless spirits in lands to the south began to think that they ought to follow the North American example by rebelling against Spain.

*The Eastward Movement in Eurasia* Overseas expansion in the Americas was matched by eastward expansion in Eurasia. The Hapsburgs, for example, conquered thinly settled lands along the Danube from the Turks

**From European to Western Civilization**   These two buildings symbolize the way the United States and Russia—one far to the west and the other far to the east of the main center of European civilization—both became part of what must henceforth be called Western rather than European civilization, since its seat was no longer limited to Europe. On the left is Independence Hall, Philadelphia, where the Declaration of Independence was proclaimed on July 4, 1776, and where the first seat of the new government was established. On the right is a view of the square in front of the Winter Palace in Leningrad, completed in 1784 during the reign of Catherine II. The buildings on this square housed some but not all of the officials who governed Russia in the eighteenth century. The difference in scale between what the Americans and Russians needed for housing their respective governments reflected the different structure of the two frontier societies that had arisen on the flanks of old Europe. In the one, freedom and equality were greater; subordination and control went much further than was customary in western Europe in the other. But the fundamental connection of America and of official Russia with Europe is clearly attested by the thoroughly European, so-called "classical," style of architecture evident in both photographs.

---

in 1699; and for seventy-five years thereafter, the Austrian government and Hungarian nobles shared the task of planting settlers on the grasslands of central Hungary. Farther east it was principally the Russians who took over the task of occupying the steppelands north of the Black Sea and bringing them into cultivation. Other settlers crossed the Ural Mountains into Siberia or traveled down the Volga River toward the Caspian Sea. It is impossible to know how many pioneers took part in this eastward movement, but the number was probably as great as, or greater than, the number of settlers and slaves who crossed the Atlantic.

*Characteristics of Frontier Society*    On the frontier, whether in the New World or in eastern Europe, society was simpler than near the centers of European civilization. Population was scant in proportion to land and other resources, and all the different levels and ranks, into which European nations divided, tended to break down. Two alternatives presented themselves. The first was for individuals and families to go off, more or less on their own, even though this meant giving up many of the advantages of civilized life—since schoolteachers, professionals, and other specialists could not support themselves in such a poor, crude, free-and-equal environment. The American frontier and parts of Siberia were, in fact, populated in this way. This produced a lawless, rough, half-barbarous frontier population, with a great ability to help itself and a fierce unwillingness to submit to anyone who was, or claimed to be, in any way superior.

The other alternative was to maintain some sort of social subordination by using force. In Europe, the poor had to work for the rich to be able to eat. On the frontier, the only way to make some people work for others was to enslave them. Slavery and other forms of forced labor, such as peonage and bonded servitude, played a big role in the New World. Such legal devices permitted a few plantation owners to remain far more cultured than was possible where rude equality prevailed. The same pattern dominated the eastward movement, where the legal powers of landowners over their serfs expanded throughout the period when settlement on new ground was most rapid and labor shortages were most critical. From the point of view of the Russian government, no other policy was possible. Landlords were needed to staff the government and to fill the officer ranks in the army. A strong and efficient army was needed to fend off attackers from the west and to overpower rivals in the south and east. The looser, freer, and more individualistic type of society that flourished in the northern English colonies

of North America could and did arise only because the colonists never had to support a trained and well-equipped army in order to defeat the Indians. Serious quarrels among the European states over possession of lands in the New World did of course arise; but they were fought out between England, France, and Spain mainly with soldiers trained, equipped, and paid for by the home governments. This was what tipped the balance in favor of freedom and equality on the North American frontier when freedom and equality were being systematically (but not completely) suppressed in the Russian lands.

# Politics and War

Intensification and expansion also dominated the politics of Europe. Until 1715 France held the center of the stage and led all other European states in developing an efficient army and bureaucracy. Between them, French soldiers and French officials were able to call on far greater resources than any other state of Europe could do—whether to fight a war or to build a palace at Versailles worthy of the self-styled "Sun King," Louis XIV, who reigned from 1643–1715.

## French Territorial Expansion

Early in Louis' long reign an armed uprising nicknamed the *Fronde* (French for "sling") broke out (1648–1653). Louis was thoroughly frightened when armed men struggled in his bedroom for control of the boy king, and when he grew up and took power into his own hands, he decided to permit absolutely no rivals within France. This required him to maintain an armed force, year in and year out, far superior to anything his own nobles or any foreign ruler could bring against him. Louis was able to keep such a standing army because France was a rich land, and ever since the Hundred Years' War the king

**The Sun King and His Palace at Versailles**   Louis XIV, who reigned in France from 1643 to 1715, took his duties as king very seriously. Convinced that God had personally and specifically chosen him to rule, Louis consciously worked at the task of behaving like a king. This meant playing a part from morning to night, imposing his will and presence upon everyone he met, not only by issuing orders and making decisions (which he did with great faithfulness), but also by looking and acting majestically. This portrait, painted in 1701 when the king was fifty-three years old and at the height of his powers, expresses the theatrical image Louis shaped for himself. To play the royal role effectively, Louis needed an audience. Accordingly, he attached hundreds of noblemen to his court, encountering them in stately levees each day, where his gracious word or carefully directed snub made everyone's standing rise and fall according to the king's good pleasure. To house the court, Louis built an enormous new palace at Versailles, shown on the right. Thousands of persons lived here, for each nobleman needed a train of servants to maintain him in the high style required for life at court, celebrating the greatness of the king.

---

had been legally entitled to collect taxes as he saw fit.

Louis XIV was a serious and hard-working monarch. He chose ministers who tried to develop French resources in every way possible. In particular, the controller general of finance, Jean Baptiste Colbert (in office 1662–1683), encouraged new industries, regulated old ones, adjusted taxes to make them more uniform and easier to collect, and always tried to make the king of France as rich and powerful as possible. The royal government and administration thus took over many functions that in earlier times had rested with guilds in separate towns or with other local authorities. The result, with Colbert's careful management of finances, was spectacular, for Louis XIV become able to maintain the greatest army and the most splendid court Europe had yet seen.

The king set himself the task of extending his kingdom to its natural frontiers, that is, to the Pyrenees, the Alps, and the Rhine. In 1659 he

## European States, 1789

signed a treaty with Spain that drew the frontier line along the watershed of the Pyrenees. During the rest of his reign Louis tried to reach the Rhine, but his efforts were checked by the Dutch and after 1689 by the English and Dutch together. In 1700 Louis undertook the last great venture of his reign, for in that year the king of Spain died without direct heirs and left a will assigning his kingdom to one of Louis XIV's grandsons, Philip of Anjou. When the French tried to make good Philip's claim to the Spanish throne, a general war broke out. England, Holland, the Austrian Hapsburgs, and several other rulers of Europe joined in a Grand Alliance to stop the French. The war was hard fought and strained French resources to the limit. In the end a compromise was agreed to by the Treaties of Utrecht and Rastatt (1713, 1714). Philip's claim to the Spanish throne was recognized by all con-

cerned, but Spanish possessions in Italy and the Low Countries (present-day Belgium) were transferred to Austria; while the British, as their part of the bargain, acquired Gibraltar from Spain, and Nova Scotia and Newfoundland from the French.

The result of the War of the Spanish Succession showed that the Austrian Hapsburgs and the British government had both caught up with the French when it came to waging war and managing the state. The power of the Dutch, by comparison, faded; so did the power of France's traditional allies—the Swedes, the Poles, and the Turks. From 1715 onward, the French advantage over neighboring states was gone. Instead, governments closer to the expanding edge of European civilization gained the advantage. By bringing new territory under their control, they could add to their resources,

**European Trade and Empire Overseas**

Pacific Ocean

Furs

ASIA

BENGAL

PHILIPPINE IS.

Silver

CEYLON

Tea

Silk

Indian Ocean

Silk

Spices

Coffee

Textiles

MOZAMBIQUE

AUSTRALIA

EUROPE

Furs

AFRICA

ANGOLA

PORT. GUINEA

Silver

CAPE COLONY

Manufactures

Atlantic Ocean

Manufactures

Timber

Fish

Furs

Tobacco

NORTH AMERICA

Silver

Pacific Ocean

Silver

Slaves

Sugar

SOUTH AMERICA

**Europe in 1492**

**European Empires in 1763**

→ European Trade Routes after 1500

British

Dutch

Russian

Spanish

Portuguese

457

while the French were stopped by one or another coalition of enemies from doing anything similar themselves.

# British Territorial Expansion

In the west, the country that benefited from these new possibilities was Great Britain thanks to its superior sea power. (Great Britain was itself a new creation resulting from the union of England, Scotland, and Ireland in 1707.) Each time the British fought the French in Europe, the struggle extended across the oceans of the earth and into the colonies. Sometimes fighting in the colonies began before war started in Europe. The most important instance of this came in 1754, when the French and Indian War began in North America two years before a full-scale war was joined in Europe between France and Great Britain. The upshot of this so-called Seven Years' War (1756–1763) was British victory in both America and India. By the Peace of Paris (1763), the French surrendered both Canada and India to the British.

To be sure, remnants of the French, together with the Spanish, Portuguese, and Dutch empires, still existed. But the British had secured a limited right to trade with the Spanish colonies as part of the Peace of Utrecht in 1713, and through smuggling they actually controlled much of the trade with South and Central America. Cooperation between the Dutch and British had become close and habitual. The same was true of British relations with Portugal. Hence British trade and British naval supremacy seemed all but unchallenged overseas after 1763.

Yet when quarrels between the government of George III (1760–1820) and thirteen of the British colonies of North America led to open warfare in 1776, not only the French but also the Spanish and even the Russian governments challenged Britain's predominance at sea, either by engaging in outright war or by an "armed neutrality" aimed against British naval power. Eventually the British had to yield. Through a second Peace of Paris in 1783, they agreed to the independence of their former American colonies and saw French power reestablished in North America in the Louisiana territory—a land that seemed much more promising than the snowy wastes of Canada to statesmen interested in sugar and other tropical products.

Despite this setback, British overseas trade and the empire built around that trade continued to be the largest in the world. British power and wealth increased with great rapidity. British business methods and parliamentary government, which took fresh hold on England when the "Glorious Revolution" of 1688 put the Dutchman, William III, on the throne, also began to arouse admiration among some Frenchmen who came to think that the successes of the British government—and the failures of their own after 1715—resulted from the superiority of the British constitution.

# Eastern European Expansion

In eastern Europe, expansion on land more or less matched expansion overseas. Not one but three new empires rose to greatness at the expense of older and less well-organized states. The rising powers were the Austrian Hapsburgs, based in the Danube Valley; the kingdom of Prussia, based in the eastern reaches of the north German plain; and the Russian Empire, based far to the north and east.

*Russian Agricultural Expansion*    Of the three, Russia had the most favorable position, being situated like Britain at the outermost edge of the European world where expansion into new and vast territories was comparatively easy. Yet Russia had special problems, too. Agriculture was inefficient. Peasants who worked as serfs for masters they disliked could not be made to work very hard. In addition, Russia had inherited a civilization and style of life from medieval times that derived in part from Byzantium and remained always a little different from the life of western Europe. After the Time of Troubles (1610–1613), when Polish armies occupied Moscow for a short time, the Russian gov-

## Partitions of Poland, 1772, 1793, 1795

SWEDEN

Baltic Sea

COURLAND

Riga

Libau

Memel

LITHUANIA

Vilna

WHITE RUSSIA

Danzig

Königsberg

EAST PRUSSIA

Neimen R.

Minsk

Dvina R.

Smolensk

Moscow

R U S S I A

Volga R.

PRUSSIA

Berlin

Posen

Vistula R.

Warsaw

Oder R.

Elbe R.

Bug R.

Pripet R.

Zhitomir

Kiev

Dnieper R.

A U S T R I A

Krakow

GALICIA

Lemberg

Vienna

Danube R.

HUNGARY

Buda

Pest

Pruth R.

Dniester R.

Odessa

OTTOMAN

EMPIRE

Black Sea

0      100      200

Miles

| | 1772 | 1793 | 1795 |
|---|---|---|---|
| To Prussia | | | |
| To Russia | | | |
| To Austria | | | |

ernment tried to safeguard the national tradition by holding Westerners at arm's length.

The policy worked pretty well. In particular, after a long competition with the Poles, the czars of Moscow took over the Ukraine (1667) and thereby added a broad and fertile agricultural land to their dominions. The problem, however, was to find settlers to cultivate its empty expanses, and then to find markets for the grain it could produce. Not until 1774 were these two problems really solved; for in that year, after a successful war against the Turks, the Russians made a treaty that gave them the right to send ships through the straits at the mouth of the Black Sea. Thereafter, a great boom came to the Ukraine, and the Russian government began to profit from its rich new agricultural base.

### The Western Ways of Peter the Great

Long before then, Russia's upper classes had accepted many West European ways. This was the result of deliberate policy on the part of Czar Peter I, the Great (reigned 1689–1725). Not until 1698, when he returned from a visit to western Europe, did Peter try to revolutionize his country. But once started he never rested. He forced every courtier to cut off his beard and put on Western clothes. He tried to teach the Russian court ladies to behave like French women. He also required every man of noble rank to serve the state in one capacity or another. Some acted as civil administrators, but most served in the army or navy. To equip his armed forces, Peter built factories to make all the things soldiers and sailors required, from cannon to uniform cloth and gaiter buttons.

The overriding goal Peter sought was military strength. He achieved it. After a long and difficult war, he compelled the Swedes to give up important territories along the Baltic Sea (1721). Without waiting for the peace, Peter built a new capital city on the newly acquired coast and named it St. Petersburg. Here he had a "window on the West" through which French governesses and German tutors soon swarmed to educate the children of the nobility in European manners and ideas.

One of the reasons that Peter could achieve such a sharp break from the Russian past was that many, perhaps most, peasants regarded him as Antichrist. In their eyes, therefore, it did not matter how wicked his actions might be. Each new shock simply seemed another sign that the end of the world was at hand, when God could be counted on to right all wrongs. The great conservative mass of the Russian people therefore remained remarkably passive while their ruler ordered them and their noble masters about. Even when Peter laid hands on the Holy Orthodox Church itself, deposed the patriarch of Moscow, and put the Church under the administration of ordinary state officials, there was no outcry. The Russian Church had already lost its hold on popular religious feelings due to Nikon's reforms of the preceding generation.

The other secret of Peter's success lay in the way he trained the nobles to serve him. He required noblemen's sons to serve as privates in special "Guards" regiments. There they learned all the newfangled ways of court. Those who caught the ruler's eye or had any unusual qualities were sent off to perform any of hundreds of special jobs for the impatient czar. Diplomats, factory managers, governors of a province, commanders of a fleet—any or every job might open; and for those who did well, wealth and power came with the job. Nor was noble birth the only path to advancement. Peter was always short of skilled subordinates. He welcomed foreigners, roughnecks, adventurers of any background, into his service. They could go as far as luck and their own abilities would carry them. This policy created a nobility almost completely alienated from the rest of Russian society and correspondingly dependent on the czar.

### The Greatness of Russia Under Catherine

Peter's successors, mostly women, had to rule over the Russian lands by keeping on good terms with the nobility. Catherine the Great (reigned 1762–1796) had the least claim to the throne yet was by far the most successful. A German princess by birth, Catherine came to power when a clique of courtiers murdered her husband, Czar

Peter III. She lived to see Russia become a European power of the first rank. By intervening in Swedish politics, she made Sweden a dependency and nearly conquered Turkey. She destroyed Poland by arranging three successive partitions of that country among its neighbors—Russia, Austria, and Prussia.

Nearly all of the nobles and officials, army officers and tax collectors, who served the Russian state in Catherine's time believed that what they did was worthwhile. They opened up new land to agriculture, built new towns, and in general made Russia more powerful, modern, up-to-date. As for the common folk, they had to work for their noble masters and for the benefit of the state—if need be, against their will. A widespread popular revolt (1773–1775), led by a Cossack named Emelian Pugachev, showed how great the gap had become between Catherine's government and the common people. But as long as most nobles served the state wholeheartedly and believed it was possible and right to westernize Russia by ordering the people to obey, the system worked pretty well. Russia's future greatness and superiority to the pygmy states of western Europe seemed assured.

## Austrian Expansion

The other growing states of eastern Europe were Austria and Prussia. Austria was ruled by the Hapsburg family, whose claim to the title of Holy Roman Emperor had become traditional. But the real strength of their state rested on the Hapsburg hereditary lands of Austria and Bohemia. From this core, Austrian power expanded eastward and southward by driving back the Turks, beginning with victory in a long war (1683–1699). After 1714, when the Hapsburg rulers added the former Spanish possessions in Italy and the Low Countries to their other territories, the great power status of the Hapsburg Empire was assured. But it never achieved administrative unification. Each separate duchy, principality, or kingdom kept its own forms of government and administration. To be sure, the empress Maria Theresa (ruled 1740–1780)

and her son Joseph II (ruled 1780–1790) tried hard to make the same laws and rules apply everywhere in their dominions. Yet they fell far short of success. The Austrian lands, like Germany and Italy generally, remained divided by all sorts of local differences. This weakened the empire and made it impossible to bring anything like the full resources of the various Hapsburg lands to bear on any common enterprise as the French, British, and Russians were increasingly able to do.

## Prussian Expansion

Prussia, on the other hand, was the most strictly centralized and carefully administered state in Europe. From the time of Frederick William, the Great Elector (ruled 1640–1688), everything was subordinated to making the army as strong as possible. The result was to make Prussia a far more powerful state than its sandy soil and scant population could otherwise have supported. A symbol of Prussia's rising importance came in 1701 when Frederick, whose highest title had been Elector of Brandenburg, became king in Prussia.

In the War of the Austrian Succession (1740–1748) and again during the Seven Years' War (1756–1763), Prussian soldiers proved their mettle to all Europe. In the first of these wars, Frederick II, the Great, king of Prussia (ruled 1740–1786), seized the province of Silesia from Austria and made his conquest stick. In the Seven Years' War he faced a far more dangerous coalition, for the French and Austrians, rivals for centuries, combined forces against the Prussians, and the Russians also joined them. Nevertheless, with help from Great Britain in the form of money and supplies, the Prussian army staved off defeat until Russia changed sides (1762), and the French and Austrians at length gave up the struggle and made peace. Prussia thus escaped from what had seemed overwhelming odds, and—as we have seen—Frederick II lived to divide Poland with his former enemies, Austria and Russia, making his state greater still.

## MARIA THERESA AND THE HUNGARIAN DIET

In 1740 a young queen, Maria Theresa, succeeded to the throne of the Hapsburgs. Her father had spent years trying to get his various subjects to
promise to obey his daughter, but the Hungarians were stubborn. According
to their ancient constitution, the Diet had to approve a new king; how could
they accept a woman as their ruler? A king was supposed to command in battle; no woman could do that. Nevertheless, in 1723, seventeen years before
she actually came to the throne, the Diet had reluctantly voted to accept
Maria Theresa as heir.

The question of what the Hungarians would do became acute soon after
Maria Theresa's reign began. Prussia attacked the Hapsburg lands, backed
by France and Bavaria. An army had to be raised and Hungarian help was required. Maria Theresa journeyed to Pressburg (called Bratislava today),
where the Hungarian Diet was meeting. She appeared before the assembled
nobles, carrying her infant son in her arms, and appealed for help.

In a sudden burst of enthusiasm, the Hungarians promised to fight for her
cause and did in fact take the field against the invaders with considerable
success. The Hapsburg power was saved, although Maria Theresa did lose
the valuable province of Silesia to the Prussians. For the rest of her long
reign, Maria Theresa remained grateful to the Hungarians for coming to her
rescue. She therefore did nothing to hurt the interests of the nobles or to alter the ancient Hungarian constitution that protected the nobles' privileges.

## New Challenges to Royal Absolutism

Prussia under Frederick the Great, Austria under Joseph II, and Russia under Catherine the
Great—all were ruled by monarchs who claimed
to be absolute and also "enlightened." This
meant, first of all, that they were not believers in
traditional Christianity. It also meant that they
tried, or talked about trying, to use the state to
promote wealth and well-being among the people as a whole. It meant, too, administrative cen-
tralization and concentration of authority in
the hands of officials who were themselves told
what to do by the ruler or by his or her ministers. These political principles worked wonders
in eastern Europe in the eighteenth century
where officials and noble landowners presided
over a growing population of enserfed peasants.

But in western Europe, royal absolutism failed
to cope successfully with the more complex urbanized societies that prevailed in France, England, and Holland.

## France

In France, which had once been the model of efficient government for the rest of Europe, all
sorts of vested interests prevented the king and
his ministers from changing established ways of
doing things. Many key government officials
bought their offices. As a result, they could not
be shifted around by the king. Under these
conditions the administration lost its flexibility.
French taxes ceased to produce enough money
to keep the French government in funds. The
army and navy suffered, and the French had to
endure humiliating defeats at the hands of the

British and Prussians. A growing number of writers were openly critical of the way things were run. In particular, professionals and business leaders were inclined to feel that they had too little voice in making governmental decisions. They began to look across the Channel toward Great Britain, where people like themselves played important roles in Parliament and helped run the government.

## England

Britain's internal political development was almost exactly opposite to the French experience. When the Stuart kings first came to the throne in 1603, they tried to build an efficient royal government like the French. This soon got them into trouble with Parliament, a medieval institution that got in the way of efficient administration by refusing to grant needed taxes and by defending unruly groups that refused to obey the king in matters of religion and taxation. Indeed, in 1642 relations between Charles I and Parliament got so bad that civil war broke out. Parliament won, and in 1649 a special commission decided that King Charles should be executed for failing to keep his promises to Parliament. But cutting off Charles' head solved nothing and, in fact, shocked many Englishmen.

Legal quarrels over the rights of the king as against those of Parliament were only part of the dispute. Many Englishmen believed that the church needed to be reformed and purified along Calvinist, biblical lines. Called Puritans by their opponents, they dominated both Parliament and the army that Parliament raised for the struggle against the king. But victory in the field presented Parliament with the difficult task of deciding how church and state should be reorganized. Members of Parliament could not agree. When the army made Oliver Cromwell—Parliament's greatest general—Lord Protector, a military dictatorship was fastened on England. But this soon became unpopular and indeed violated Cromwell's own convictions.

When Cromwell died (1658), the regime fell apart. Almost in desperation, a group of generals and other political figures called the Stuart heir to the throne. Charles II (reigned 1660–1685)

had grown up in France and had no wish to be exiled again. In general, he kept on reasonably good terms with Parliament. Nevertheless, King Charles tried to escape Parliament's financial control by making a secret arrangement with Louis XIV, whereby the French paid a considerable sum of money to Charles. In turn Charles agreed to keep England quiet while Louis attacked his neighbors in order to make the Rhine his frontier.

When James II came to the English throne in 1685, suspicion between king and Parliament came to a crisis once more. James was a Roman Catholic, and Parliament suspected that he wanted to make England Catholic again. They also suspected treasonable relations with France. In 1688, therefore, a coup d'état was organized. William of Orange came from Holland and claimed the throne jointly with his wife, Mary, who was the daughter of James II. The coup was successful, but Parliament made the new monarchs agree to a Declaration of Rights that defined the limits of royal power in a sense favorable to Parliament. Thereafter, the kings of England reigned but did not rule. Taxes had to be authorized by Parliament before they could be collected legally. No royal standing army could be maintained in England; the army's allegiance was to Parliament.

William was a vigorous king, but he was mainly interested in wars against Louis XIV on the continent. As long as his new kingdom supported such wars, he was well content to leave the government in the hands of ministers acceptable to Parliament. Queen Anne (reigned 1702–1714), George I of Hanover (reigned 1714–1727), and George II (reigned 1727–1760) followed the same policy. Neither George I or George II could speak English easily and stayed away from most of the meetings of the ministers at which government policy was discussed. They were satisfied to give the responsibility for choosing ministers to Robert Walpole, an ordinary member of Parliament who was able to win the confidence of both the monarch and of a majority in Parliament. In common speech he came to be called prime minister, and the group of ministers he selected was referred to as the cabinet.

Rules and traditions of parliamentary and cabinet government were not perfectly defined until after George III (reigned 1760–1820) tried to take a personal hand in governing his kingdom. For a while, he was able to get personal supporters elected to Parliament and to choose his own ministers. But the king roused opposition when his plan to bring the American colonies under tighter control led to rebellion and a disastrous war with France. The fact that George III soon afterward became intermittently insane hurt the king's cause even more and gave control of the British government back to Parliament and parliamentary leaders.

The advantages of the British system of government as it developed under the Old Regime were real. Members of Parliament represented the major propertied interests of the country. The election process allowed rising new interests to make themselves heard in Parliament at the expense of other groups whose importance was declining. In this way a rough match between political decision-making and the balance of British society as a whole could maintain itself, as it were, automatically. Moreover, closer partnership between government and the upper classes made support for government policies more reliable than was the case in a country like France.

The result was that an awkward representative assembly that in 1600 had looked like an outmoded survival from medieval times became, by 1700, the sovereign body controlling one of Europe's greatest and most rapidly growing states. The brilliant successes that came to the British government and nation in the decades that followed made parliamentary and cabinet government a model for reformers on the European continent who disliked their own royal, absolute governments.

Autocratic Russia, where society was divided between nobles and serfs and where the military model dominated all administration, stood on one flank of Europe and, with Prussia, represented one extreme of social and political organization. Great Britain, where the middle classes were more powerful than in any other great state and where religious and other kinds of pluralism were more widespread than in most other parts of Europe, stood at the other extreme. The rest of Europe fell somewhere between.

Thus Europe's enormous success under the Old Regime—and the territorial expansion that registered that success—meant the inclusion, within the circle of Western civilization, of a lot more variation, socially and economically as well as politically, than in earlier ages.

## European Culture

Pluralism and internal variety also characterized Europe's culture under the Old Regime. Different social classes and different nations, not to mention different professions and different cliques and parties, tended to develop their own distinct styles of thought and behavior. General patterns existed, but only vaguely and never in a way that prevented individuals and small groups from following their own particular bent.

French art and literature won a leading place in all Europe, particularly after the Polish and Russian upper classes in Catherine's time came under the influence of French culture. But there was also a Spanish-Italian-Austrian sphere of influence, built around the Hapsburg Dynasty and carrying the traditions of the Catholic Counter-Reformation into the eighteenth century. Finally, the English and Dutch made up a circle of their own; and by 1770 romantic poets had declared Germany's cultural independence of France as energetically as they knew how.

Science remained much more international, though French followers of Descartes clashed with English Newtonians; and the German Leibniz also quarreled with Newton on grounds that were at least partly nationalistic. However, in scientific matters, observation and measurement offered a means for settling most disputes quite quickly; whereas in fields where taste was the only thing to go by, preferences based on language, religion, personal whim, or local connections tended to create and support a number of separate cultural circles.

The leading characteristic of the culture of the Old Regime was growing professionalism. Writers became able to live from the sale of their work, creating a new, independent profes-

**How European Civilization Changed Between 1200 and 1800**   These four diagrams offer a schematic way of thinking about how the different elements of European civilization split apart and rearranged themselves between 1200 and 1800.

sion apart from both church and government. Painters and musicians still depended, usually, on noble patronage or on a church appointment. Scientists sometimes held university posts, and sometimes governments competed for their services. The Swiss mathematician Leonhard Euler (1707–1783), for example, took a job as professor at the University of St. Petersburg when only twenty-three years of age; then, at Frederick the Great's call, he moved to Berlin in 1741, but he returned to St. Petersburg in 1766. The prestige of scientists rose very high. Isaac Newton (1642–1727), the great English mathematician and physicist, was treated as a public monument during his own lifetime and, when he died, was buried in Westminister Abbey with England's kings and queens.

## Natural Science

Modern science got an enormous new energy after 1650. The task of observing, recording, and classifying all the plants and animals of the world was immense. In addition, with new instruments like the microscope and telescope, thermometer, barometer, sextant, and marine chronometer, Europeans had the tools to observe and record facts far more exactly than ever before. This great task of assembling information and arranging it in some sort of order was what kept most scientists busy and gave the whole enterprise of science such excitement. Everybody could understand what was being done, and no one could doubt any longer that Europe's knowledge far outstripped other peoples' knowledge, or even what the ancients had known. Making useful, workable classifications was, of course, the big problem. The two most successful classifiers were the Swede Linnaeus (1707–1778), who invented the system for classifying plants by genus and species that is still used today, and the French naturalist Georges Louis Leclerc de Buffon (1707–1788), who wrote a forty-four-volume *Natural History* in which he dealt with both animals and plants.

## The Newtonian Era

But the aspect of scientific discovery that mattered most for later ages was more mathematical and abstract. The key figure was Isaac Newton, born in the year that Galileo died and, in a real sense, Galileo's intellectual successor. Newton was a great mathematician who, among other things, developed calculus. A German, Gottfried Wilhelm Leibniz (1646–1716), also invented calculus and developed the kind of notation used today. Later, a nasty quarrel broke out between followers of the two great men over the question whether Leibniz had gotten his original idea from Newton or not.

Newton's greatest work was, however, in physics and astronomy. He experimented with sunlight and discovered that he could split it up into the colors of the rainbow and then recombine it into white light by use of glass prisms. He also invented a reflecting telescope that was superior in some ways to those using transparent lenses. But Newton's fame rests mainly on the theory of gravitation, as developed in his *Principia* (full title, *Philosophiae Naturalis Principia Mathematica*), first published in 1687. By assuming that all bodies attract one another with a force that varies inversely with the square of the distance between them, Newton was able to show that the motions of the moon and of the planets, as well as the motion of falling objects

**Reluctant Prophet of a New Age**     In 1687, when Sir Isaac Newton (1643–1727) published his famous book *Philosophiae Naturalis Principia Mathematica,* he showed that the same laws of motion applied to sun, moon, and planets in the skies and to moving objects on earth. By uniting heaven and earth in this way, he upset older ideas utterly. The world became a vast machine, moving predictably. What room was left for miracles? For God's intervention in human affairs? This greatly bothered Newton, and he spent his last years trying to show that biblical prophecies were, in fact, true.

near the surface of the earth, obeyed exactly the same laws. He put these laws in mathematical form, so that when appropriate data as to mass, distance, and velocity could be supplied, motions could be predictably calculated and could also be projected back into the past.

The marvelously simple world machine that Newton's theory revealed struck contemporaries with the force of a new revelation. The motions of the heavenly bodies suddenly fitted in with everyday things like the curving path of a thrown ball or of an apple falling in the wind. Everything could be explained with a few simple mathematical formulas. Some wondered about the mysterious nature of "gravitational force" that could work invisibly at a distance; others feared the mechanical, impersonal nature of Newton's vision of the universe. But when innumerable observations backed up his theories, and when planets and cannonballs kept on behaving as Newton's formulas predicted, who could doubt the essential accuracy of the new theory? Many felt, in the words of the poet Alexander Pope, "God said, 'Let Newton be,' and all was light!"

Scores of other ingenious experimenters and mathematical minds of the first rank surrounded Newton, in England and also on the continent. The scientific community founded special societies, the most famous of which was the Royal Society of London, where gentlemen interested in natural science could meet and exchange ideas. These societies corresponded with one another and published records of their meetings and of papers submitted to them from a distance. As a result, a lively network of communication among scientists and scholars came into existence, running from London to St. Petersburg, and from Florence and Madrid to Stockholm. A distant outsider like Benjamin Franklin (1706–1790) could communicate the results of his experiments with lightning and win recognition throughout the European world for proving lightning to be a form of electricity. The existence of such a network for communicating scientific results guaranteed the continued flow of data and ideas and made science a truly international enterprise.

No theoretical breakthroughs in astronomy and physics comparable to the importance of Newton's work came until long after 1789. Chemistry, however, achieved a new precision with the work of Antoine Lavoisier (1743–1794). He measured the weight of matter entering into and coming out of chemical reactions with greater accuracy than ever before. On the basis of such measurements, he was able to explain what happened in an ordinary fire, for he detected and measured the consumption of oxygen from the air and the discharge of carbon dioxide and other gases into the air. Lavoisier also cleared up the distinction between an element and a chemical compound and introduced many of the names used still by chemists (for example, *oxygen*). As a result of such work, chemistry was poised, by the close of the Old Regime, for all the technical and practical triumphs that came in the nineteenth century.

## Social Theory

Newtonianism changed Europeans' view of the world in fundamental ways. It was difficult to believe that God stood ready to intervene at a moment's notice in human affairs when the vast spaces of the universe all obeyed the same laws of motion. God seemed to be a master mathematician and craftsman who created the world in accordance with natural laws. He could not be expected to spoil His own handiwork or admit its imperfection by intervening to work a miracle. Thus, the whole world-view of the Reformation era was called into question.

As prevailing views of God and His way of controlling the universe changed, political theory had to be readjusted. The idea that God personally chose kings to rule and intervened in everyday affairs to reward and punish His people by sending them good and bad rulers seemed less and less convincing. But if God did not choose kings, what right had they to govern? The best answer theorists could find was to suppose that a contract, implied rather than real, between ruler and ruled gave kings their rightful powers. But the practical force of any such theory depended entirely on the terms of the contract. Thomas Hobbes (1588–1678), for example, argued that individuals, fearing one another, made a contract that transferred absolute power to their rulers. John Locke (1632–1704), on the contrary, asserted that subjects had the right to overthrow a ruler who broke the terms of the contract by endangering their lives, liberty, or property, since the only purpose for submitting to a ruler's authority in the first place was to assure the protection of these natural rights. Jean Jacques Rousseau (1712–1778) carried the argument to its democratic extreme by arguing that the social contract requires kings or other rulers to obey the "general will" of the people. If rulers failed to do so, it was a duty as well as a right to overthrow them.

Others concentrated their attention on economics and tried to find natural laws that governed human behavior in the marketplace. Two Scots, John Law (1671–1729) and Adam Smith (1723–1790), were particularly bold in their speculations. Law had a chance to put his theory of bank credit and currency management into practice in France, where his policies provoked a speculative boom and bust that discredited his ideas—perhaps unjustly—as well as his practice. Adam Smith was content to be a professor at Glasgow; but his treatise entitled *The Wealth of Nations*, published in 1776, became fundamental to all later economic theory. Smith's view was like Newton's in an important sense. He believed that if individuals were left alone to follow their private preferences in economic matters, enlightened self-interest would, in fact, create the best possible pattern of production and exchange. Just as gravitation kept the planets in their orbits, so Adam Smith believed private calculation of personal advantage was a universal force that made the economic machine work efficiently.

## Philosophy and Literature

Formal philosophy underwent a remarkable deflation during the Old Regime. At its beginning, René Descartes (1596–1650), Baruch Spinoza (1632–1677), and Gottfried Leibniz (1646–1716) still hoped to use mathematical rigor to reason out a complete system of truth that would explain everything in the whole world. Their disagreements focused attention on the question of how anyone can know anything at all. The more carefully critics considered this matter, the more uncertain knowledge of any kind seemed. John Locke (1632–1704), George Berkeley (1658–1753), and David Hume (1711–1776) made it increasingly difficult to believe that human minds could ever really know anything about the nature of things. Immanuel Kant (1724–1804) rescued philosophy from this dead end by pointing out that, even if the nature of things was forever unknowable, still the nature of the knowing mind could be explored. And since nothing that did not fit in with the capacities of the mind could

ever be known, to understand the qualities and capacities of the mind, in fact, allowed a philosopher to know the character and limits of all that could be known.

Such abstract ideas interested only a few; but there were others who called themselves "philosophers" and who wrote about social and political problems and often sought to reform the world around them. These philosophers were closely connected with the world of literature. They used novels, plays, or poems to convey their ideas more effectively to the audience they addressed. The main center for this kind of "philosopher" was in France where, especially after 1715, there seemed much to criticize in government and society.

Charles-Louis de Secondat, Baron de Montesquieu (1689–1755), was among the first to voice dissatisfaction with the French government. He wanted nobles like himself to play a larger part and argued that good government required the separation of legislative, executive, and judicial functions. His ideas, together with those of John Locke, were particularly influential among the men who wrote the Constitution of the United States.

The most famous of the French "philosophers," however, was Voltaire (real name, François-Marie Arouet, 1694–1778). Voltaire wrote plays, poems, histories, as well as pamphlets and books. His central idea was that reason and good sense would show people how to behave—if only priests and others who had a vested interest in appealing to human fears and superstitions would let the light of reason shine forth freely. He set himself, therefore, to attack religious superstition and to spread the light of reason. Everything he wrote contributed in one way or another to this general aim.

Voltaire and others like him believed they were helping humanity by spreading science and truth. The task of enlightening others, although immense, seemed very much worthwhile. Progress and social improvement could only come through the spread of reason and knowledge. One of the most powerful ways to spread knowledge was the preparation of a great encyclopedia. The articles, arranged alphabetically, dealt with almost everything under the sun. The main figure responsible for produc-

D. DIDEROT.

**The Third Estate**   From medieval times, European society had been divided into three legally different classes: nobles, who fought; clergy, who prayed; and the rest, who worked. But under the Old Regime this inherited structure twisted out of shape. Most nobles no longer fought; that was entrusted to professional soldiers. The high clergy were too busy with administration to have much time for prayer. But the biggest change came in the so-called Third Estate, where new ideas and new wealth changed older ways profoundly. Above, a painting of a French peasant family, made in the seventeenth century, celebrates the satisfactions of rest from work, food, and a sort of simple abundance, despite the bare feet and drab clothes appropriate to their humble status. Peasants were always the great majority in Old Regime Europe. Slow changes in their level of life sustained the more conspicuous changes in town life, one of which is illustrated below. The etching of Denis Diderot (1713–1784), pen in hand, registers the new role played by writers and intellectuals in eighteenth-century France. Diderot's most important achievement was editing the *Encyclopédie*, published between 1752 and 1772. This famous work publicized new ideas about science and society and the possibility of improvement by implementing deliberate, rational policies.

ing the French encyclopedia, published between 1751 and 1772, was Denis Diderot (1713–1784). Similar works were soon produced also in English and German. Like ordinary dictionaries, which also were first compiled in the Old Regime, this sort of reference work allowed anyone to look things up accurately and rapidly as never before.

This is not the place to try to describe the literary work of Europe's major writers in any detail. Poetry and drama—both tragedy and comedy—remained vigorous in France and in

England, too. The three great "classical" dramatists of France flourished under Louis XIV: Pierre Corneille (1606–1684); Molière, whose real name was Jean Baptiste Poquelin (1622–1673); and Jean Racine (1639–1699). John Milton (1608–1674) and Alexander Pope (1688–1744) were perhaps the two most important English poets of their age. England also saw the birth of the modern novel with the works of Samuel Richardson (1689–1761) and Henry Fielding (1707–1754). Other countries of Europe failed to produce writers of Europe-wide reputation, until a brilliant group of Germans emerged toward the end of this period. Chief among them were Gotthold Ephraim Lessing (1729–1781), Johann Christoph Friedrich von Schiller (1759–1805), and Johann Wolfgang von Goethe (1749–1832).

These German writers and important British literary figures like Robert Burns (1759–1796) and William Wordsworth (1770–1850) tended to seek inspiration from everyday language of the people. They declared that personal emotion and self-expression were the key to great art. Such "romantic" ideas stood in self-conscious opposition to the "classical" rules of correctness that had been fashionable in earlier times. Like the criticism of the "philosophers" and the smoke of the new steam factories, the "romantic" movement pointed ahead toward the age which was to follow the overthrow of the Old Regime.

## Art and Music

The Old Regime was not an age of major departures in the visual arts, but during that time European music evolved rapidly toward "classical" form.

Palaces, like that built for Louis XIV at Versailles, were designed for grandeur. Size and formal balance of doors, windows, and decorative elements were the ways in which architects chose to achieve these goals. Soon after 1700 a lighter, more graceful style called rococo came in, and exact balance of each part was deliberately abandoned. Then, toward the close of the eighteenth century, a reaction toward more "classical" simplicity and geometric regularity took place.

These shifts of style spread over most of Europe from France, where taste was, for the most part, defined. In painting there was some-what greater variety. Antoine Watteau (1684–1721) in France, Thomas Gainsborough (1727–1788) in England, Francisco Goya (1746–1828) in Spain, and Meindert Hobbema (1638–1709) in Holland—each embodied different national traditions. Yet differences, though real, were slight. The ideal of painting that had been defined so brilliantly in Italy, during the Renaissance, continued to be the norm for all of Europe.

What happened to European music between 1648 and 1789 was rather like what had happened to painting about two and a half centuries before. European musicians, first of all, had new or newly perfected instruments at their disposal. The violin and harpsichord were the most important. The scientific study of sound opened a better theoretical understanding of musical pitch, scales, and timbre. All this gave musicians the tools of their trade, just as Italian painters in Renaissance times had developed oil paints and canvas easels as the basic tools of theirs.

Using the new tools, a series of great composers created musical forms and works that still are performed regularly. Johann Sebastian Bach (1685–1750), George Frederick Handel (1685–1759), Wolfgang Amadeus Mozart (1756–1791), and Franz Joseph Haydn (1732–1809) are the most famous and familiar. Two general remarks about their achievement must suffice here. First, instrumental music became central and singing secondary, although, of course, all sorts of combinations of instruments and voices were experimented with. Few other musical traditions have given such prominence to instrumental music, but then few other musical styles have had instruments so flexible and various to put through their paces.

Second, secular music—opera, symphonies, and so forth—became as elaborate as, and perhaps even more important than, church music. This reflected musicians' roles as entertainers at royal courts and in great noble houses. The fact that they were classed just above the rank of servants explains the relatively low social status held by Mozart and Haydn. Fuller recognition of music among the arts had to wait for the development of concert halls open to the public and supported by the purchase of tickets. This did not become usual until after 1789. Until musi-

**Eighteenth-Century Aristocrats**  These two portraits, oddly, resemble one another, although one comes from France and portrays Madame de Pompadour, mistress to Louis XV (above), while the other comes from China and portrays an unnamed lady from another and quite different court (below). Both were painted in the mid-eighteenth century, at a time when admiration for chinoiserie had become something of a vogue in Europe. François Boucher, who painted Madame de Pompadour, was among those affected by chinoiserie; the resemblance perhaps arises from that fact. European admiration for aspects of Chinese civilization in the eighteenth century was a departure from the disdain for heathen ways that had dominated contacts between different civilizations up to that time. Incipient cosmopolitanism set in, reflecting a real resemblance that existed between the decorative courtly roles each of these ladies played at opposite ends of Eurasia.

cians had a way of making a living by public performance, they had to exist either on the patronage of the rich or by holding church positions (as, for example, Bach did).

## Religion and the Churches

Any brief survey of the cultural life of an age is likely to stress what was new and different and leave out the things that remained more or less the same. This is misleading, for most people are more influenced by the stable, old, and familiar ideas and styles of thought than they are by anything new, however attractive it may seem.

This is particularly true in the period we have been considering, when so many radical new ideas were put before the European public yet affected only small minorities in most cases.

We may be sure that nearly all Europeans remained Christian in some sense or other. The official churches, supported by the different governments of Europe, all continued to claim that their own version of Christian doctrine offered the one and only true path to salvation. Children were taught the catechism in school or at their mother's knee, and even those who in later life rejected some or all of what they had been taught in childhood remained deeply influenced by their religious training. Most people never really made up their minds between the traditional doctrines of Christianity and the impersonal "deist" view that portrayed God as the creator of the universe, who then abandoned his handiwork to let it run itself like a great machine. Many, particularly in the lower classes, never heard deist views expressed and thus remained loyal to traditional Christian ways of understanding the world. Still others reacted strongly against the new scientific vision of reality and consciously reaffirmed their faith in a personal and immediate relationship between God and individual human beings.

The powerful new religious movements of the age were all of this sort. In England, George Fox (1624–1691) founded the Society of Friends (or Quakers) on the strength of his own personal experience of God and of commanding visions that ordered him to preach to the public. The sect he founded had no clergy at all and put great emphasis upon following each person's own "inner light." Occasional persecution only hardened Quaker convictions. In the following century, John Wesley (1703–1791) took up a career as traveling evangelist after he, too, experienced a conversion and felt his "heart strangely warmed within him." His followers were known as Methodists. Both Quakers and Methodists became important in the English colonies of North America, where established churches were weaker than in England itself.

On the continent, Philipp Spener (1635–1705) founded Pietism. This was a religious movement that flourished within the Lutheran and Calvinist churches of Germany. Details of doctrine seemed unimportant to Spener and his followers. What mattered was direct personal experience of God, to be attained through meditation, prayer, and Bible study, conducted privately or within the family. Pietists felt that public worship in church was of little importance compared to the Christian duty of seeking direct, personal communion with God.

The Roman Catholic Church was disturbed by Quietism and Jansenism, both of which were eventually judged to be heretical and were therefore suppressed. Quietism was founded by a Spanish priest, Miguel de Molinos (1640–1697). He was a mystic and taught that the soul should wait quietly for God to come. Jansenism was named for a Dutch priest, Cornelis Jansen (1585–1638), but the main leader of the movement was a Frenchman, Antoine Arnauld (1612–1694). The Jansenists wanted to go back to St. Augustine's teachings, putting much stress on predestination and personal piety. They came into sharp controversy with the Jesuits, and for some years France was divided between those who sympathized with the Jansenists and others who went along with the Jesuits. The pope ruled against the Jansenists in 1713, and their center, Port Royal, just outside Paris, was closed down. But the Jesuit victory made many enemies in France. They also fell into disfavor with the rulers of Spain and Portugal for refusing to submit to royal decrees; and the combined pressure of the governments of Spain, Portugal, and France persuaded the pope to suppress the order in 1773. The Jesuits survived, however, by taking refuge in Orthodox Russia and Protestant Prussia, until in 1814 the papacy recognized their order once again.

Controversies like these, and the reaction all over Europe to Louis XIV's suppression of Huguenots in France (1685), showed the continuing hold Christianity had on the minds of men and women.

Europe's other religion, Judaism, suffered serious persecution and prolonged hardship in eastern Europe after 1648, when popular attacks on Jews in Poland and the Ukraine reflected rising peasant indignation against the commercialization of society in which Jews and their noble landlords were collaborating. The sufferings Jews experienced, in turn, prepared the way for a remarkable religious upheaval among them. It was triggered by the Messianic claim, made by a young Jew of Izmir in 1666 named Sabbatai Zevi. The self-proclaimed Messiah attracted numerous followers for a while, but the movement collapsed in disarray when Sabbati Zevi, having been arrested by the Turkish authorities, saved his life by converting to Islam. This fiasco troubled Jewish leaders profoundly. In Poland a new, popular form of Judaism emerged from the turmoil. Known as Hasidism, it valued mystical encounter with God, induced by song and dance. Such departures from older forms of worship gained a precarious respectability when a few learned rabbis fitted them into older mystical learning early in the eighteenth century.

A different response to the failure of the true Messiah to appear began to gain headway in Germany in the course of the eighteenth century when a few individual Jews began to explore the possibilities of making a career for themselves outside the segregated Jewish communities that existed in a number of German towns. Christians influenced by the Enlightenment were ready to respond. A God who created a Newtonian world machine and refrained from intervening in its operation thereafter was, after all, neither Christian nor Jewish but a sort of master intelligence, far surpassing all earlier human efforts to define his nature correctly. Moses Mendelssohn (1729–1786) was the main pioneer in opening intellectual communication between Jews and Germans along these lines.

## Conclusion

Even from this brief survey, it should be clear that Europe acquired knowledge and power at a faster rate than ever before during the Old Regime. Expansion on all fronts continued without halt; and with expansion went intensification, increasing variety, complexity, and an ever faster rate of change. The political and social balance that had been struck after the religious wars was never rigid and unchallenged. But by 1789 industrialism, arising primarily in England, and democratic political ideas, at home mainly in France and in America, had both begun to challenge the old order. Breakdown came with the French Revolution and the quarter century of war that the Revolution provoked.

Yet the eagerness with which later generations attacked the remnants of the Old Regime that survived the revolutionary struggles should not blind us—their descendants—to the positive achievements which that phase of Europe's long history had to its credit. No earlier age had been more brilliant or successful; the painful break with Europe's medieval frame, which had been the business of the Renaissance and Reformation, really paid off during the Old Regime when relative calm at home allowed Europe to take on the world—and to try to understand and appreciate, as well as trade and fight with, peoples of every kind. The impact of the European Old Regime on the rest of the world will be the theme of the next chapter.

## Bibliography

Several works of literature seem especially resonant as introduction to Europe's Old Regime: Henry Fielding, *Tom Jones*, a novel; Alexander Pope, "Essay on Man," a poem; Voltaire, *Candide*, a satire; and Jean Jacques Rousseau, *Confessions;* but there are many others almost as attractive and as readily available. This was a formative period for American ideals of government, and John Locke, *Two Treatises on Government* (1690), will acquaint you with ideas that colored much of the thought of the founding fathers of the United States.

For pan-European changes of intellectual outlook, an old standby, J. H. Randall, *The Making of the Mod-*

*ern Mind* (1926), remains interesting and lively. Norbert Elias, *The Court Society* (1983); A. N. Whitehead, *Science and the Modern World* (1948); Peter Gay, *The Enlightenment: An Interpretation* (2 vols., 1967–70); and Arthur O. Lovejoy, *The Great Chain of Being: A Study of the History of an Idea* (2nd ed., 1984), add nuances to Randall's overall portrait.

John Wolf, *Louis XIV* (1968), offers a biographical approach to the era of French dominance in Europe, and Franklin L. Ford, *Robe and Sword: The Regrouping of the French Aristocracy after Louis XIV* (1953), explains how the basis of royal absolutism, that had raised France so high, began to unravel. On the other side of the Channel, C. Wilson, *England's Apprenticeship, 1603–1763* (1965), and Christopher Hill, *The Century of Revolution, 1603–1714* (1961), analyze economic and political changes in England that propelled that country to the forefront in the next century.

For developments on the American flank of the expanding European world, in addition to books cited previously, Ralph Davis, *The Rise of the Atlantic Economies* (1973); Gary B. Nash, *Red, White and Black: The Peoples of Early America* (3rd ed., 1992); Jack P. Greene and J. R. Pole, eds., *Colonial British America* (1984); Mark A. Burkholder and Lyman L. Johnson, *Colonial Latin America* (1990); and James Lockhart and Stuart B. Schwartz, *Early Latin America: A History of Colonial Spanish America and Brazil* (1983), stand alongside innumerable others. For expansion eastward, W. H. McNeill, *Europe's Steppe Frontier, 1500–1800* (1964); W. E. D. Allen, *The Ukraine* (1940); and Donald W. Treadgold, *The Great Siberian Migration* (1957), show interesting likenesses and differences between the European expansion eastward and westward in the Americas.

On population growth, Michael W. Flinn, *The European Demographic System, 1500–1620* (1981), is a handy starting place. Thomas McKeown, *The Modern Rise in Population* (1976), and E. A. Wrigley and R. S. Schofield, *The Population History of England, 1541–1871* (1981), try to explain why population started sharply upward in the eighteenth century, without arriving at a definitive answer.

B. H. Slicher van Bath, *The Agrarian History of Western Europe, A.D. 500–1800* (1963), is the best book about agricultural improvements. On warfare and its consequences for Europe, G. N. Clark, *War and Society in the Seventeenth Century* (1958), and M. S. Anderson, *War and Society in Europe of the Old Regime, 1618–1789* (1988), may be balanced against the judgments of John U. Nef, *War and Human Progress* (1950).

On the changed world view that Newtonianism imposed on Europeans (and soon on the rest of the world as well), I. Bernard Cohen, *The Newtonian Revolution* (1980), and Albert van Helden, *Measuring the Universe: Cosmic Dimensions from Aristarchus to Halley* (1985), are particularly clear and informative.

# Development of Human Communication

Participation in communication networks turns helpless newborn babies into human beings, complete with all the knowledge, skills, habits, and abilities needed to survive in the particular human group into which each of them was born. The starting point for human communication is innate. A baby's smile (and answering smiles from those who come within a baby's range of vision) are instinctive, shared with chimpanzees and other primates. But most human communication has to be learned by consciously imitating what others do, and finding out by trial and error just what all the different gestures and symbols we use to communicate with one another actually mean.

Landmarks in the development of human communications networks include the following:

## DANCING AND SINGING

A first step, distinguishing us from apes, was learning to dance and sing together. Community-wide dancing that involves keeping together in time for hours on end is unique to humans and universal among human societies. It arouses a pleasant, shared excitement among all who take part. This had the effect of healing individual rivalries and frictions, making group cooperation stronger and survival a little surer.

Emotional response to keeping together in time remained a powerful way to consolidate groups even after other, more precise means of communication had been invented.

### Highlights

Community-wide dancing consolidated fellow felling on festival occasions. Such festivals are universal and age-old among hunters and gatherers and remained important in agricultural villages until very recently.

Religious gatherings made singing and dancing part of their worship from prehistoric times. All the world's religions resort to keeping together in time—varying all the way from slow, stately processionals to agitated singing, dancing, and trance.

Troops that drill for prolonged periods of time feel a warm esprit de corps that outweighs other emotional attachments. Modern governments, as well as the ancient Chinese, Greeks, and Romans, tapped this human trait, making their armies more flexible and formidable than would otherwise have been possible.

Since 1789 political parties and revolutionary leaders relied on salutes, marching, calisthenics, and other forms of coordinated muscular movement to express and intensify solidarity among their followers.

## THE INVENTION OF LANGUAGE

The invention of language inaugurated human society as we know it about 40,000 years ago. Like dancing, grammatical speech is both universal and unique to human beings, and it changed human behavior in far-reaching ways.

### Highlights

Language allowed people to develop far more precise rules for what to do in different circumstances. Simply by giving names to things—distinguishing, for example, between berries that were good to eat and others that were poisonous—everyday activities became more likely to get desired results, favoring survival.

Language sharpened memory of past situations so people could know what to do when a similar situation presented itself again. Hunters could agree in advance on how to encircle and capture their prey, for example; and elders could tell younger persons how to react successfully to once-in-a-lifetime emergencies and surprises.

Language permitted people to create a world of meanings that was largely independent of external things. In particular, dreams and trance opened up the spirit world for human exploration. Beginning in prehistoric times, experts developed special ways of communicating with the spirits. The world's religions all descend from their efforts to enter into the invisible world inhabited by powerful spirits.

Language also allowed people to create innumerable subgroups within larger societies. Shared special experiences, sometimes deliberately designed to mark an initiated group of insiders off from everyone else, could be passed on from generation to generation. This introduced a new complexity and variety to human life, for such subgroups had always to interact with others and with one another. Resulting frictions and borrowings enormously enlarged the possibility of elaborating human behavior, knowledge, and skill.

## INVENTION OF WRITING

A third landmark in the improvement of communications was the invention of writing. Ideographic scripts, as developed in Mesopotamia, Egypt, the Indus, and China between 3500 and 2500 B.C.E., used thousands of different symbols to record words and sentences unambiguously, so that learned experts could read what had been written years afterwards, or in a place far away from where the text had been written down. This allowed new skills to multiply.

### *Highlights*

Written records of tax receipts and expenditures allowed governments to mobilize resources drawn from ever-larger populations. Empires with millions of subjects became possible by 750 B.C.E.

Written laws made many human encounters more predictable so that even strangers could know what to expect. Social relations became correspondingly more efficient.

Writing down religious stories and recording how accurately priestly experts interpreted signs of what was going to happen started organized religion and science on their way.

Experts who mastered the art of reading and writing ideographic scripts became a small, privileged class, closely associated with the priests and rulers they served.

## ALPHABETS AND PRINTING

Two later inventions expanded the uses of writing.

1. Alphabets, invented about 1300 B.C.E., used fewer than thirty different signs so learning to read and write became comparatively easy.

### *Highlights*

Literacy therefore became far more common, and private persons began to take advantage of the precision with which writing could store and retrieve all sorts of information.

Alphabetic writing also made sacred scriptures accessible to private persons, thus allowing some faiths to leave the older priestly monopoly of religious truth behind. Based on sacred scripture, such religions could be practiced wherever fellow-believers gathered together. The so-called higher religions, shaped along these lines, spread throughout the Eurasian world, (beginning about 650 B.C.E.), and by offering authoritative guides for everyday conduct, made living in cities among strangers far easier than before.

2. Printing (and paper), invented in China about 600, allowed accurate reproduction of an indefinite number of copies of any text. As printing and paper spread across Eurasia (taking root in Europe only in the 1450s), far larger numbers of persons than before gained access to old texts, while new ideas and information could spread more rapidly and widely than before.

Yet the effect on different civilizations was not the same.

### *Highlights*

Printing in China allowed for larger numbers than before to study the Confucian classics and try to gain admittance to the official, ruling class by passing the imperial examinations.

Printing in Europe introduced pagan classics of Greece and Rome to a far larger public than before, presenting Christian writings with a rival body of learning. Simultaneously, printed reports of discoveries overseas added a third, discrepant element to European knowledge. And after 1517, religious reformers propagated their challenge to papal doctrines through the printing press as well.

Printing therefore split apart Europe's intellectual inheritance from the Middle Ages, while in China the same technique had the effect of consolidating and standardizing the Confucian heritage.

## MODERN FORMS OF COMMUNICATIONS

In the past 150 years, new mechanical, electrical, and electromagnetic forms of communication have accelerated the transmission of information beyond anything people of older times could imagine, with results for human society that are still unfolding.

### Highlights

High-speed rotary presses (1840s) allowed publication of popular newspapers on a daily basis.

Photography (1840s) allowed accurate reproduction of visual images as never before.

Electric telegraph (1837; trans-Atlantic cable, 1866) allowed instantaneous transmission of a limited flow of data wherever electric cables had been installed.

Telephone (1876; and long-distance amplifiers, 1899) allowed people to talk with others wherever the necessary network of wires, switching devices, and amplifiers connected them.

Phonograph (1889) allowed voices and music to be reproduced at will by using a simple machine to play easily portable records (then tapes).

Radio (1895; first broadcast station 1920) allowed listeners to hear words and sounds transmitted by electromagnetic waves propagated through the atmosphere.

Television (first broadcast, 1936) allowed moving images to supplement radio's words and sounds.

Computer link-ups (1946) allowed massive transmission of data with the speed of light wherever these machines are hitched to one another.

Communications satellites (1960s) allowed electromagnetic messages to travel around the globe in enormous volume and with minimal interference.

It is too soon to tell what the full consequences of these new forms of communication will turn out to be. Likely consequences include

the propagation of pop culture at odds with adult norms among young people in many, perhaps most, parts of the earth;

decay of local cultural autonomy as values and attitudes, spreading from a few urban centers, overwhelm local, provincial traditions;

increasing globalization of markets for commodities, manufactured goods, labor, and capital, with unforseeable consequences for both rich and poor countries caught up in this process.

Other consequences, some perhaps entirely unforeseen, may turn out to be far more important than anything mentioned here. As participants in an unprecedentedly capacious, speedy, and accessible communications network, we are launched on a global adventure whose upshot will define the human future in the same way that older systems of communication shaped the past.

# *World Reactions to Europe's Expansion*

## 1700 to 1850

# 19

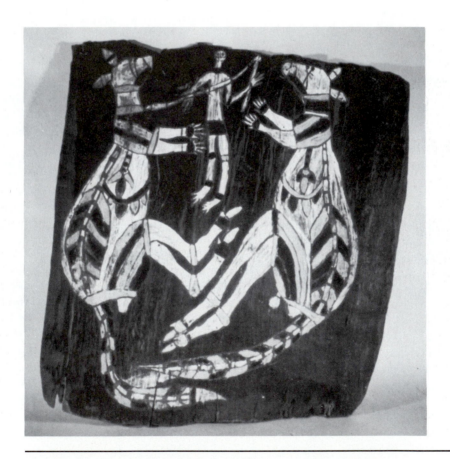

**Kangaroo Hunt in Australia** The human populations of the earth came increasingly into contact during the eighteenth and early nineteenth century. This meant that hunters and gatherers like the inhabitants of Australia, whose ways had not changed in any obvious way for millennia, suddenly had to adjust to intrusive strangers, while the intruders also had to alter their ways—far less drastically—when they started to share the Australian landscape with the aborigines.

Between 1500 and 1700, European merchants, explorers, soldiers, missionaries, and other adventurers had made their presence felt along almost every habitable coast. When first the newcomers appeared, local peoples often greeted them with curiosity and sometimes with hospitality, although both Moslems and Chinese were suspicious and aloof from the start. As soon as Europeans in any way threatened, or seemed to threaten, things that local peoples held dear, rulers reacted by trying to break off relations and withdraw from what had become a disturbing contact. The increasing power that Europeans acquired during the Old Regime meant that they threatened more and more to upset other people's ways. Almost everywhere, except in Russia, the response was to cut off or to cut down on contact with the source of the trouble. This was the policy of Asian and African peoples and states from 1700 to 1850.

## Withdrawal from Contact with Europeans

Stronger and more remote peoples could insulate themselves from Europe's influence successfully, but weaker or less favorably situated peoples could not. Thus, each of the great Asian civilized societies was able to cut off effective communication with Europeans, even when—as in the case of Moslems of India and of the Ottoman Empire—they had to endure the physical presence of foreigners in their midst. Their policy was to pay no attention to anything the Europeans had to say and to adhere to old tradition and patterns of behavior in the hope of seeing the intruders go away after a while. The Japanese and Siamese (modern Thailand) carried this policy to its logical extreme by completely prohibiting contacts with Europeans. The Chinese confined trade to a single port, Canton, and entrusted the task of dealing with foreigners to a special group of merchants, the Co-hong.

In other parts of the world, however, weaker and simpler societies were not always able to withdraw. This was the fate of the Amerindians,

for example, and of peoples of the Pacific Islands, of Australia, and of South Africa. In all of these regions, Europeans or people of European descent and culture kept pursuing the retreating natives, taking their land for farms or ranches, spreading diseases, and destroying traditional social discipline by defying it without punishment.

In the African interior, tropical diseases and comparatively well-organized kingdoms blocked European penetration. The simple geographical fact that sub-Saharan Africa's rivers have falls near their mouths created a barrier to inland travel. By requiring any traveler to come ashore and walk, the river falls exposed strangers to local human hostility and to insect-borne infections. As a result, the interior of Africa remained proof against European penetration until after 1850, although the slave trade left few parts of the continent unaffected.

Taking the world as a whole, the cost of withdrawal from disturbing contacts with Europeans was heavy. Closed minds, fearful of having to face awkward facts, could only repeat what had been thought and done in earlier ages. That was no way to cope with Europe's eager acquisition of new skills and knowledge. As a result, the gap between European accomplishments and the achievements of the rest of the world widened rapidly.

By the years 1850–1860, the great civilizations of Asia found themselves helpless in the face of Western superiority, which by then had become literally overwhelming. Hence, the effort to hold fast to old tradition and familiar ways of doing things backfired in the long run by requiring the non-Western peoples of the world to suffer an extremely painful and prolonged disruption of their various styles of life after 1850. But between 1700 and 1850, no one could foresee what was coming; and in the Far East particularly, the policy of withdrawal and insulation seemed to work fairly well.

## Population Growth

Another dimension of the worldwide scene between 1700 and 1850 made the "stand pat" policy easy in the short run and dangerous in the long run. This was the upsurge of population that set in among civilized peoples at a rate seldom equaled before. Japan was an exception, for late marriages and the custom of allowing unwanted newborn children to die from exposure—usually in some remote and unfrequented spot—kept Japan's population almost constant. But in China, in India, and in at least parts of the Moslem world, population spurted upward.

Four worldwide factors contributed to the remarkable growth of population. One factor was the fading away of epidemic diseases. A second factor was that American food crops enhanced the food-producing capacity of heavily populated parts of the world. Sweet potatoes in south China, cassava and maize in Africa, maize in southeastern Europe, and the potato in northern Europe and Russia came into their own between 1700 and 1850. Many millions of people came to depend on these crops.

A third factor was that the development of artillery allowed a few centers of political authority to control larger empires more effectively than in earlier ages. Thus, the Manchus in China established a higher level of peace and order over a larger territory and for a longer time than the world had ever seen before. In other parts of the world, kingdoms and empires were less majestic in scale. Nevertheless, rulers in Europe and Asia were in a better position than ever before to suppress banditry and small-scale raiding. In all probability, therefore, loss of life through local violence lessened at a time when deaths from disease were decreasing and food supplies were increasing.

In the fourth place, the big, new empires allowed merchants and local authorities to develop food storage and market systems that went a long way toward overcoming famines due to local crop failures. As long as fresh land lay uncultivated or more intensive tillage allowed food production to keep pace with growth of population, things went along smoothly and traditional ways of life were strengthened rather than weakened by growth in numbers. But when limits to traditional methods were reached, population did not stop growing. Mass desperation on the part of the peasantry, on a scale that traditional political methods could not cope with, was an inevitable result.

The world still finds itself affected by this crisis. It set in at different times in different parts of the earth, beginning, for example, about 1775 in China and about the same time in some of the European provinces of the Ottoman Empire. From the point of view of the great civilizations of Asia, therefore, this development meant that European pressures from outside became irresistible after 1850, at a time when fundamental internal problems were building up toward massive peasant revolt. Only Japan, where population was kept in check, escaped this difficulty.

With the benefit of hindsight we can see clearly how non-Western peoples eventually paid a heavy price for putting off fundamental transformation at home to take account of new things the restless Europeans kept on discovering. But at the time, when Europe was not yet equipped with the additional force that developed with the Industrial Revolution, the policy of withdrawal and conservative loyalty to traditional ways seemed adequate for coping with the situation that faced Moslem, Chinese, and Hindu peoples. A policy that was able to keep expectation and reality more or less in touch with each other during a century and a half should not be hastily condemned.

# The World of Islam

From the time of the prophet Mohammed until about 1700, the general course of history conformed to Moslem expectations. In spite of some serious defeats and disasters—such as the breakdown of political unity among Moslems, dating from 750, or the Mongol sack of Baghdad in 1258, Moslem missionaries and conquerors kept on adding new lands to the realm of Islam. No large or important territories had been lost by Mohammed's followers. Border wars with the Christians in Europe and against Hindus and other unbelievers in Asia and Africa tended for more than a thousand years to favor the Moslem cause. Who, then, could seriously doubt that Allah continued to favor His people as he had in the days of the Prophet and the first caliphs?

# Moslem Military Power Fades

It was, therefore, a tremendous blow to Moslems when the political and military balance rather suddenly reversed itself after 1700. In 1699 the Ottoman Empire was forced to make a humiliating peace with the Austrian Hapsburgs, surrendering most of Hungary. This was the first time the Ottoman Turks had been compelled to make a strategic retreat before superior Christian armies.

Immediately thereafter, the Mogul Empire in India began to founder. Aurangzeb died in 1707, leaving his empire distracted by revolt. Mogul power never recovered. Exactly half a century later, British traders emerged as the strongest military power in all of India. When the East India Company made the Mogul emperor its puppet, everyone knew that Moslems no longer really ruled India.

The third great Islamic empire was the Safavid, based in Iran and Azerbaijan. It, too, suffered a breakdown, beginning in 1709 with an Afghan revolt. Drastic political disorder invited the intervention of Russian, Chinese, and even British agents. Old-fashioned Moslem cavalry continued to charge across the landscape, brave and bold as ever; but their defeats and victories more and more depended on supplies of powder and shot that came from foreign, usually Christian, sources. The old independence and power were irremediably gone.

The overthrow of steppe warriors as a major force in the Eurasian balance of power lay behind these dramatic military-political setbacks. More than any other civilization, the Moslems had opened themselves up to the steppe. Their victories in India and in Europe had depended in large part on migration of steppe warriors from central Asia to the frontiers, where holy war against infidels promised booty. But when cavalry ceased to be decisive on the battlefield, the whole military-political tradition of the great Moslem empires became outmoded.

*The Janissary Corps*    Only the Ottoman Empire made a serious effort to develop an efficient infantry equipped with guns. But the Janissary corps, which won many famous victories by its discipline and firepower in the age of Suleiman the Lawgiver, fell behind European troops from the time when its members ceased to be recruited from the Christian villages of the Balkans. Village boys, pulled up by the roots from their places of origin, could be kept under a severe discipline and, as slaves of the sultan, were trained to serve him well. But after 1638, the corps came to be recruited instead from sons of Janissaries, and the character of the troops changed quickly. Because the sultan found it difficult to pay his soldiers a living wage, the Janissaries worked at various artisan trades during the winter when they were not in the field.

This soon resulted in merging the Janissaries with the Moslem artisans of the towns. By 1700 or 1750 most Moslem artisans in the European provinces of the empire held appointments in the corps. Positions were bought and sold freely, and little check was kept on whether or not the purchasers had military training or would submit to discipline. The efficiency of the corps could not survive such practices; the Janissaries nevertheless had the sultan and his ministers at their mercy. To protect their own privileges and traditions, they were ready to riot and revolt. They absolutely refused to allow any new body of troops to come into existence that might challenge their power at home.

*The Indian Armies*    Such experiences did not encourage other Moslem rulers to try to build up infantry forces that could make firepower really effective in battle. Neither the Mogul nor the Safavid rulers actually tried. The Mogul armies were poorly equipped, poorly trained, and poorly led by comparison with European armies of the Old Regime. But with European guns, uniforms, and drillmasters, Indian soldiers proved quite effective. Ironically, it was this that made it possible for the English East India Company to dominate India so easily. A mere handful of company employees from the British Isles were able to train *sepoy* (that is, native Indian) troops in the European manner—and thus by 1763 created what was by far the most efficient army in India.

**Retreat of Moslem Power, 1699–1856**

GREAT BRITAIN

NETHERLANDS
AUSTRIA-HUNGARY
Serbia
(Independent, 1804)
GREECE
(Independent, 1830)
ALGERIA
OTTOMAN EMPIRE

Black Sea
Caspian Sea
Mediterranean Sea

RUSSIA

SINKIANG

CHINA

MOGUL EMPIRE

Pacific Ocean

Indian Ocean

Atlantic Ocean

DUTCH EAST INDIES

British
Dutch

British
Dutch

Ottoman Empire, 1699
Mogul Empire, 1700
Boundary of realm of Islam, 1699

Territory lost to Russia
Territory lost to Austria-Hungary

Territory lost to Britain
Territory lost to Dutch
Territory lost to France

Hindu rebels in central India, called Marathas, also weakened the Mogul power. Sikhs, too, made good their independence in the northwest. Local governors, who in theory owed their position to the emperor's appointment, became independent in all but name. Invaders from the north, first Nadir Shah from Iran and then Afghan raiders, crossed the mountains and plundered northern India.

Many Moslem princes, faced with Hindu unrest at home and the danger of Afghan raids from the north, fell back on British protection. The East India Company adopted the policy of "indirect rule." Existing states and tax systems were allowed to stand as long as a British resident at court was kept informed and allowed to give advice, which, in most cases, had to be followed. This cost the Company less, opened the doors to trade, kept the peace, and aroused a minimum of local hostility.

However, the iron hand within the velvet glove appeared from time to time. In 1818, for example, British troops put down the last Maratha bid for genuine independence. And in the years 1839–1842, a British army invaded Afghanistan, across India's northwest frontier, to enforce the Company's will. By that time the mighty Mogul Empire had become a shadow and Moslem rule over India had become a hollow pretence. Moslem princes and their hangers-on had to submit. The Hindu majority was indifferent and politically inert, seeing little difference between one kind of foreign master and another. As long as the discipline of their Indian troops held, the British position in India was unshakable.

## The Growth of Russian Power

In central Asia and the former Safavid lands, Afghans, Uzbeks, Persians, Kazaks, Kalmucks, and Azerbaijani Turks engaged in a general melee. Successful captains like Nadir Shah (1736–1747) built vast empires that crumbled as fast as they had been constructed. Until after 1750, the power that made the greatest gains in this confused situation was China. A series of successful military campaigns extended China's northern and western borders to their present limits.

After that date the southward advance of Russian power became the most significant result of the continuing upheaval. Long leaps forward, such as that which brought Peter the Great's authority to the southern shore of the Caspian in 1723, were sometimes followed by withdrawal. But shifts back and forth usually tended to favor Russia because Russian armies and administration, tempered by participation in Europe's rivalries, were generally superior to anything the Moslems of central Asia could create.

Major landmarks of Russia's advance were the annexation of Georgia in 1800 and occupation of the Amu Darya Valley, south of the Aral Sea, in 1849. The net result, shortly after 1850, was to bring the Russians up against the Chinese frontiers in central Asia, while Afghanistan and Persia (Iran) constituted a buffer zone, separating the Russian frontiers from the outposts of British power in India's northwest provinces. These two countries suffered from continual intrigues and violence as local chieftains tried to play off Russian against British agents. The old tribal life survived, but what had once been the crossroads of the world had by 1850 become a backwater, bypassed by everything that really mattered.

*Ottoman Retreat*    The case of the Ottoman Empire was more complex. It, too, had to keep on retreating. The loss of Hungary in 1699 was followed by further losses to Austria in the Balkans in 1718, but the military tide was temporarily reversed in 1739–1740 when the Turks won several battles against Austrian commanders who had acted rashly. This victory came at an unfortunate time for the Turks because it convinced them that with only minor adjustments their old military establishment could cope with European armies. Hence, for the following quarter century, the Turks dropped efforts at military reform. Therefore, when the Russian armies, rested from their campaigns of the Seven Years' War, invaded the Ottoman Empire in 1768, the Turks found themselves woefully unprepared. Russian soldiers were completely successful and dictated a peace at

## Russian Territorial Expansion, 1699–1855

Alaska (Russian 1805–1867)

Kamchatka

Sea of Okhotsk

Okhotsk

Amur R.

Yakutsk

Lena R.

L. Baikal

CHINA

Arctic Ocean

Krasnoyatsk

Yenisei R.

Tomsk

Novaya Zemlya

Omsk

Ob R.

L. Balkhash

Archangel

Tashkent

Syr Darya

FINLAND

Samara

Aral Sea

Bukhara

Volga R.

Amu Darya

SWEDEN

St. Petersburg

Moscow

Baltic Sea

Astrakhan

Merv

Warsaw

Kiev

Georgia

Caspian Sea

POLAND

Odessa

PERSIA

Russia in 1689

Territory added by 1796

Territory added by 1855

0   400   800

Miles

484

Kuchuk Kainarji in 1774 that gave them control of the Black Sea and the right to send ships freely through the straits.

Turkish response to this blow was ineffective. Some thought the situation called for military reform along European lines, but preliminary efforts in that direction were stopped in their tracks by Janissary revolts. Local governors became independent in all but name. Serbs, Greeks, and Arabs rose in revolt. It looked as though the last days of the Ottoman Empire were at hand.

**How to Borrow from Europe, Ottoman Style**   On the left is Selim III (1789–1807), the Ottoman sultan who started to train a new infantry army in the European fashion. He paid for it with his life when the Janissaries of Istanbul revolted against the threat of their privileges. The fact that he allowed his portrait to be painted was itself an act of impiety; the further fact that the cloak he wears imitates the dress of European kings indicates departure from strict Islamic precedent. Yet his cross-legged posture is that of an Islamic ruler holding court. Selim, after all, was not prepared to borrow very much from Europeans. On the right the upstart ruler of Egypt, Mohammed Ali (ruled 1805–1849), is shown conferring with French engineers who were, presumably, in charge of the industrial plant partly visible through the window. Mohammed Ali not only succeeded in building an army along European lines but also tried to develop a tax base for his government by employing Napoleonic veterans to expand irrigation, improve transport, and establish factories. Yet Mohammed Ali remained traditional in dress and mentality and kept his distance from the French who served him, as we see here. He borrowed to become strong and rich so he could maintain the old ways. It paid off for a while. Mohammed Ali was on the verge of overthrowing his nominal overlord, the Ottoman sultan, in 1840 when a British fleet intervened and compelled him to withdraw to Egypt. He and his successors did not recover effective independence until the late twentieth century.

What saved Ottoman power until 1918 was the diplomatic intervention by the great powers of Europe. First the French and then the British came to Turkey's aid—sometimes with diplomatic notes, sometimes with a fleet, and sometimes with military instructors and advisers who tried to make the Turkish armies able once again to cope with the empire's foes. Success was only partial. Outlying parts of the empire became independent (Egypt from 1809, Greece in 1830) or autonomous (Serbia from 1815, Romania from 1828). Algeria, which had never been administered regularly from Istanbul, was annexed by the French in 1830. On the other hand, the sultan's administration became stronger in the parts of the empire left to him. The unruly Janissary corps was destroyed in 1826 and a new Turkish army took shape. But efforts to reform the law and administration in accordance with European ideas never achieved real success, although sweeping proclamations to that effect were issued in 1839.

# The Moslem Reform Movement

Most Moslems felt deep doubts about trying to imitate the West. To do so ran against their deepest convictions. It meant admitting, in effect, that Islam was not the true faith, for Islam was embodied in the Sacred Law, and the Sacred Law did not allow good Moslems to imitate European laws and customs. If Allah ruled the world and if He had revealed his will to Mohammed, as every Moslem believed, then it was folly to abandon the ancient ways. No doubt, shortcomings on the part of the faithful had angered Allah and persuaded him to withdraw his favor from the Moslem community. The answer, clearly, was to go back to the rigor of the Prophet's day, to follow every jot and tittle of the Sacred Law and wait patiently until Allah's favor was restored.

*Wahhabi Reform*     In different parts of the Islamic world many Moslems drew this conclusion. Efforts to get back to the purity of original Islam created disturbances in China, in Java,

and in parts of Africa; but the most successful and influential reform movement, appropriately enough, started in Arabia itself. Its spokesman was Mohammed ibn-Abdul-Wahhab (1703–1792), whose followers are often referred to as Wahhabis. A local chieftains of the Sa'ud family became the military leader of the movement and spread its power through most of Arabia. This brought on a collision with the Ottoman sultan, who claimed possession of the two sacred cities, Mecca and Medina. In 1818 Mohammed Ali, pasha of Egypt and only nominally subordinate to the sultan, sent troops, trained in European style, against the Wahhabis and defeated them with ease.

Yet this setback did not destroy the reform movement. On the contrary, Moslems in India and other parts of the Islamic world became interested in the Wahhabi reform only after it ceased to be identified with a strictly Arab military cause. The essence of Abdul-Wahhab's message was simple. He wanted exact and faithful obedience to the Koran and the Sacred Law—and the ruthless discard of all the Sufi encrustation that had grown up in Moslem practice since the prophet Mohammed's day. The movement had a strong puritanical element in it. In particular, the prohibition of wine was taken in the strictest sense, as were all the other injunctions of the Koran. The Wahhabi reform remains to the present day a great force within Islam and affects the conduct of millions of Moslems even beyond the borders of Saudi Arabia, where it is still the official form of religion.

Moslems unaffected by the Wahhabi movement remained passive for the most part. After all, other disasters had come and gone. This one, too, would finally pass. Allah would show his power only when it pleased him to do so. The wise do not demand reasons for God's acts. Such arguments pressed to their logical extreme could be used to prove that efforts at reform were futile and meaningless, since everything had to wait for Allah.

Only a tiny minority took seriously the idea of borrowing Western skills. Even when such individuals held high positions in government, they could not make their will effective. Until the twentieth century, no Moslem ruler was able to

# ALI PASHA OF JANINA

Ali Pasha of Janina (1740–1822) was thoroughly old-fashioned. Son of an Albanian chieftain, he had to flee for his life as a young boy from neighboring tribesmen who killed his father. Taking refuge in the barren mountains of southern Albania, Ali and his mother soon gathered a band of outlaws around them. His mother led the band until Ali was old enough to take command.

As soon as he could, Ali set out to revenge his father's death. But this was only a start. By hook and by crook he quickly extended his domain over most of what is today Albania and much of northern and western Greece. He became a complete despot. Riding through Janina, his capital, or in the country round about, he often ordered his bodyguard to behead someone accused of wrong-doing, immediately and on the spot. Ali never learned to read. He also never learned to trust anyone. He administered his government entirely on the basis of his memory for faces, names, and places.

All of this was quite traditional. But there was another side to Ali's career that made him different. His power peaked during the French revolutionary wars, when European secret agents were usually active in the Ottoman Empire. Consequently, Ali often played host to representatives of the European great powers, trying always to get promises of support and supplies of arms from them.

But Ali also cared about religious ideas. When he discovered that some of the French revolutionaries rejected Christianity, he was delighted. His own religious background was a heretical form of Islam which taught that official religions—both Moslem and Christian—were in error. Ali concluded that his views and those of the latest thinkers of Paris coincided. All he needed was to learn the rituals whereby the French got in touch with their God, and his armies might become as successful as Napoleon's.

Ali never abandoned this hope. It attracted him to negotiations with the secret revolutionary society that helped to start the Greek War of Independence in 1821. He sought their help against the Sultan in Istanbul who had resolved to destroy Ali's power. When fighting started, the Greeks' revolt did not save Ali because the Ottoman government decided to concentrate on overthrowing him first. But a long siege of Janina (1821–1822) gave the Greeks time to consolidate in the south, where they eventually succeeded.

Clearly, the effort to build a bridge between the world of an Albanian tribal chief and that of French revolutionary deists was not a success. Yet since Ali's time, many others have tried to bridge the gap between their own traditional ideas and those of the Western world. In this sense, the despotic, old-fashioned religious heretic of Janina was a forerunner of our own age.

create a clique of administrators whose careers depended on continuance of radical reform, as Peter the Great had done in Russia. Hence, efforts to borrow Western ways always flagged. Too few believed in such a program to make it work.

## Art and Literature

Under the circumstances, no one would expect to find important new art or literature arising within the Islamic world. Even the effort to stay safely within old forms fell short, for political upheaval meant that official patronage for artists, architects, and poets could not be depended on. Yet the breakdown of these traditional patterns had a negative virtue, since it opened the way for new beginnings. Ottoman Turkish, for example, was cast into new and simpler literary molds, far closer to everyday speech, by Akif Pasha (1787–1845). His literary efforts did not win much admiration, but his deliberate act of cutting Persian and Arabic words out of written Turkish inaugurated the creation of the literary language used in Turkey today.

## Moslem Missionary Work

The bad fortune that came to the Moslem heartlands between 1700 and 1850 was scarcely compensated for by the fact that in Africa and Southeast Asia, conversion to Islam continued to advance as it had for centuries. Individuals and small groups, especially those who began to take part in trade, found Islamic law useful. Acceptance of Islam offered a convenient way of entering into the great world at large. Arabs from Oman, in southern Arabia, became active in the slave trade of East Africa, operating mainly from the island base of Zanzibar, where European commercial activity remained unimportant until the 1890s. On the other side of the Indian Ocean, Malay pirates and traders sailed the South China Sea and traded with the islands nearby— Mindanao, Borneo, and points between. These traders acted as missionaries of Islam, as their predecessors had done for centuries. But conversions in these regions were a poor substitute

for the dominion over the entire Indian Ocean, which had once rested in Moslem hands. On the sea, as on the land, Moslem fortunes were at a low ebb indeed.

# Hindu and Buddhist Asia

Hindus and Buddhists of Southeast Asia found the presence of Europeans far less hard to take than the Moslems did. Both Hindus and Buddhists had already been forced to subordinate themselves to Moslem intruders, who expected to rule and to trade and who were ready to use force, when needed, to get their way. The European trading companies behaved in the same way.

From the Hindu point of view, habits that had been developed to deal with the Moslems worked perfectly well when applied to Europeans. They were simply treated as another caste, and appropriate rituals were at hand to remove any defilement that might come to a pious Hindu from having to deal with them. Hindu religion was strong and vibrant and therefore could easily resist Christian missionary efforts. Since religion and the entire way of life were intimately bound together, this meant, in effect, that Hindus were not inclined to inquire into European ideas or, indeed, into any other aspect of their civilization.

## Hindu-European Cultural Interaction

The British, however, were curious. Until 1837 the language of administration in India remained Urdu, the mixed Persian-Turkish speech used by the Moguls. This meant that British officials and the Hindu clerks who worked for them both had to learn Urdu. As a result, the British tended to view India through a more or less Moslem pair of spectacles. But a few individuals became interested in the other languages of India. The greatest pioneer was Sir William Jones (1746–1794), who translated works from Persian, Arabic, and Sanskrit and founded the Asi-

**The British in India**   A miniature painting by an Indian artist (above) shows an agent of the British East India Company taking his ease in private, attended by two Indian servants. The Englishman obviously lives between two different worlds. Dressed in European garb, he looks awkward on the settee, since sitting cross-legged did not come easily. Yet he is smoking a hookah (water pipe), and his servants and the furniture of the room are all thoroughly Indian. In the eighteenth century, when this miniature was painted, agents of the India Company often went over to elegant Indian styles of living, finding them better attuned to the climate. In the nineteenth century, however, when steamships shortened the trip to India and made it safer, strenuous efforts to impose European standards on India set in. The scene below shows a Christian missionary dying of fever in a village, far from the luxuries of upper class urban living. His dress and that of his two European assistants suggest that the missionary had made no concessions to Indian ways. Susceptibility to unfamiliar diseases remained a serious barrier to European penetration of tropical countries until after 1850.

atic Society of Bengal. He noticed the relationship between Sanskrit and European languages, a discovery that excited much attention in European learned circles and started quite a vogue for the study of Sanskrit. Enthusiastic scholars assumed that, as the oldest recorded form of Indo-European speech. Sanskrit must be closer to the original thought and language of their own ancestors than any other literary tradition.

European scholarly interest in Sanskrit studies was also fanned by the attraction many Europeans felt for Hindu philosophy and mystical doctrines. Filled with doubts about the truth of Christian dogma, yet repelled by the mechanical emptiness of a Newtonian universe, many sensitive Europeans became interested in Hindu doctrines that emphasized the illusory nature of the world of sense. Interest in India became, in fact, a trait of the romantic movement, especially in Germany.

*Christian Missions*     Christian missionaries provided a second and quite different channel for interaction between Hindu and European worlds. To be sure, until 1813 the East India Company carefully excluded Christian missionaries from its trading posts. The theory was that any attack upon local religious customs would damage trade and endanger the Company's position. In 1813, however, Parliament required the Company to admit missionaries freely. Once on the spot, the missionaries decided to put their message in the local vernacular language and, for the purpose, had to develop printing presses and standards of literary usage. The modern written Bengali language got its start in this fashion, though it was soon taken over by Hindu writers for their own purposes. Mission schools were also set up, in which secular subjects were taught as well as Christian doctrine, thus bringing Indian minds into contact with European ideas.

*Rammohun Roy*     Neither Hindus nor Moslems were much attracted to the doctrines of Christianity. Indeed, in one famous case, a Christian missionary lost his own faith after arguing with learned Hindus and emerged a Unitarian, convinced that all the great religions of the

world conveyed essentially the same message. This was also the conclusion arrived at by the first Indian who studied and tried to understand the cultural world of Europe. His name was Rammohun Roy. Born a Brahman, he first learned Urdu in order to qualify for a government job. He then learned English. This led to Greek and Latin, and soon his Bible studies required him to acquire a smattering of Hebrew also. As soon as he could afford to do so, Rammohun Roy resigned from his government job to devote himself more fully to religious studies. From Christianity he turned to the study of Islam, and the comparison of both with his inherited Hindu faith convinced him that all three religions needed to be revised in the light of modern knowledge. The truth conveyed by each of the world's great religions boiled down, he thought, to a simple belief in one God. Unitarians in England and America were much impressed by Rammohun Roy's message, which he brought to England just before his death in 1833. His efforts to reform Hinduism were not very successful. Yet he did persuade the British authorities to prohibit the custom of *suttee*, according to which a widow had been required to sacrifice herself on her husband's funeral pyre.

Rammohun Roy was the first of a long line of prominent Indians who learned English, and through English became acquainted with European civilization. In 1835 the East India Company set up schools to teach English and other European subjects. This opened the door wide for later generations of Indians to straddle two cultural worlds—one English and official, the other Hindu and private.

By and large, Indian Moslems stayed away from the new schools, leaving the pursuit of government clerkships to Hindus. Schooling in India was often defective, and graduates were usually more interested in getting a job in a government office than in interpreting Western civilization to their own people or in reforming Hindu customs in the light of European ideas or examples. Yet, for all its defects, the schools and administration of India began a process of interaction between Hindu and European civilizations on a scale and with an intimacy that was not achieved elsewhere until much later.

# Buddhist Retreat and Isolationism

Nothing of this sort bridged the gap between the Buddhist peoples of Southeast Asia and the outside world before 1850. These people lived in Sri Lanka, Burma, Thailand, Laos, Cambodia, and Vietnam. Most of these kingdoms found themselves squeezed between the vigorous and expanding land power of China on the north and an aggressive European, primarily British, sea power. The Chinese emperor claimed a vague traditional lordship over all of Southeast Asia, as well as over the British and other European traders who visited Chinese ports. In the years 1766–1769 the Chinese sent an army into Burma to try to enforce Peking's authority, but without lasting success.

British sea power was more difficult for these states to deal with. In 1802, for example, the kingdom of Kandy in Sri Lanka submitted to British guns. The Burmese had to give up part of their coastlands after a short war (1824–1826), and Thailand lost control of Malaya when local Moslem rulers shifted allegiance from the king of Siam to the East India Company's agents at various times between 1768 and 1824.

However disagreeable, neither Chinese nor British pressure persuaded the Buddhists of Southeast Asia to do anything drastic to change their traditional ways. Like the Moslems of Afghanistan and Iran, these peoples and kingdoms were far enough from the beaten track that they could afford to hold fast to old-fashioned ways, although their power of self-defense was clearly inadequate to keep European intruders away.

# China's Reversal of Roles

China prospered under two exceptionally long reigns. The K'ang-hsi emperor occupied the imperial throne from 1662 to 1722 and made the Manchu Dynasty secure for the first time. The Ch'ien Lung emperor ascended the throne in 1736 and abdicated in 1795 so as not to reign longer than his famous predecessor; yet in fact, he continued to fulfill the emperor's role from behind the scenes until his death in 1798. The Chinese ideal of stability and decorum was almost perfectly summed up in these two reigns. Virtue as defined by Confucius flourished. Scholarship was vigorous. Imperial patronage of pottery works produced the finest porcelains ever manufactured in China. Painting and poetry flowed from thousands upon thousands of brushes.

Peace prevailed at home; and along the distant frontiers of central Asia, Chinese armies overthrew the last nomad power that dared to defy the celestial emperor's will. Russia, by the Treaty of Kiakhta (1727), recognized the forward movement of Chinese frontiers to include Mongolia and Chinese Turkestan. Having made the northern border secure, the Chinese turned attention to the south and invaded, with varying success, Tibet (1751), Burma (1766), and Nepal (1792).

Population grew rapidly from about 150 million in 1700 to about 430 million in 1850. An increase in artisan manufactures and exports no doubt provided employment for a small part of the new population of China, but the great majority lived in the villages where rice lands were close at hand.

# China's Confucian Mold

Until about 1775 all seemed well. More people simply increased China's vast bulk. New land could be found for cultivation by moving higher up the hill slopes or deeper into swamps and other marginal lands. Everyone who worked hard enough could eat, and the peasants asked for nothing more than that. Their increasing numbers supported many landlords, whose sons studied the Confucian classics, sat for the imperial examinations, and, if they worked hard enough, could hope to pass the necessary tests and get jobs in the government. Since government jobs meant a chance to accumulate wealth, as well as the enjoyment of power and prestige, competition for appointments was intense.

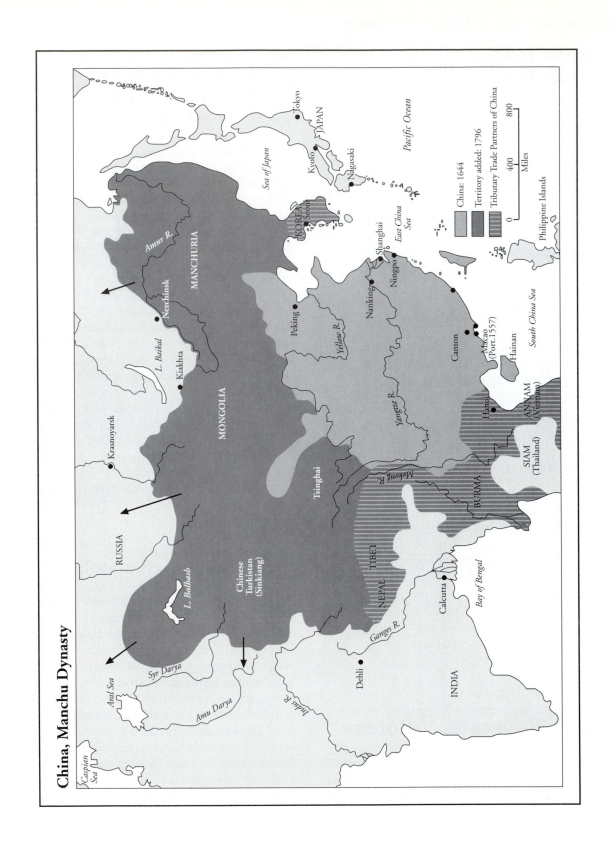

**China, Manchu Dynasty**

China: 1644
Territory added: 1796
Tributary Trade Partners of China

800
400
0
Miles

Pacific Ocean

Sea of Japan

Tokyo
Kyoto
JAPAN
Nagasaki

East China Sea

KOREA
Seoul

Shanghai
Ningpo
Nanking
Peking

South China Sea

Canton
Macao (Port. 1557)
Hainan

Philippine Islands

Yellow R.
Yangtze R.

MANCHURIA

Amur R.

Nerchinsk

L. Baikal
Kiakhta

MONGOLIA

Krasnoyarsk

Tsinghai

Chinese Turkistan (Sinkiang)

RUSSIA

L. Balkhash

Syr Darya

Aral Sea

Amu Darya

Caspian Sea

Mekong R.

ANNAM (Vietnam)
Hanoi

SIAM (Thailand)

BURMA

TIBET

NEPAL

Calcutta
Bay of Bengal

Ganges R.

Indus R.

Dehli

INDIA

The investment of time and energy in study was correspondingly immense. Study of the classics began in earliest youth and was often pursued day in and day out until middle age, since failure the first time did not mean that a student could not try the examinations again. The extraordinary effort required to pass the tests molded the rulers and leaders of Chinese society to the Confucian ideal and completely closed their minds to anything not tested in the examinations.

The government also patronized scholars directly. Men, famous for their learning, were assigned the task of editing ancient texts and compiling reference works of the most diverse sorts, such as bibliographies, familiar quotations, dictionaries, encyclopedias, lists of "best books," and the like. The grandiose scale of these labors is hard for us to believe. In 1726, for example, a famous encyclopedia of 5020 volumes was completed (although it should be pointed out that a Chinese volume was smaller than those European printers usually produced). By comparison with the bulk of such labors, however, really new work was hard to find. The attention of China's rulers was firmly fixed upon the past. It seemed self-evident that the more ancient a thing was, the more valuable it must be.

Of course, not everyone passed the examinations, and among those who did not make it a more self-indulgent cultural underworld came into existence. Novels or romances, the most famous of which is *The Dream of the Red Chamber* by Ts'ao Hsueh-Chan (d. 1764), reflected the life of such leisured but ineffective individuals. Since this sort of writing was regarded as unworthy of a scholar, the book was never published in the author's lifetime. It portrays the inner life of a large Chinese family with an intimacy modern readers find delightful but which seemed like undressing in public to Ts'ao Hsueh-Chan's contemporaries.

*Christianity Discredited*    As for European ideas and skills, Chinese scholars and officials had no time for such trifles. Until 1715, to be sure, the emperor often found it useful to employ Jesuit missionaries on various technical tasks at which they excelled, such as casting cannon and making a map of China with reference points established by astronomic observations. But in 1715, after years of bitter quarreling, the pope decided that the Jesuit view of Confucian rites was in error. This was a deep insult to the emperor, who only a few years before had come to the exactly opposite conclusion. Since a key point at issue was how the word "God" should be translated into Chinese, it seemed, to indignant Chinese, that the pope was trying to tell them how to use their own language. No greater insult could have been offered to an emperor who prided himself on his scholarship.

Thereafter, the Christian mission was completely discredited at court. The Jesuits were allowed to stay because they knew how to keep the calendar correctly, but they were forbidden to make converts. Christian missions, as far as they continued to operate at all, had to do so in defiance of the law. Limited underground preaching appealed mainly to poor and discontented groups in the cities. But in the eyes of the scholar class, this only discredited European ideas that much more.

## Peasant Revolt

In 1774 a peasant revolt disturbed the peace of China. It was put down, but secret societies, such as the White Lotus, which was associated with this revolt, kept on multiplying. The reason was that poor peasants no longer could live in traditional ways in those parts of the country where the growing population had begun to press on the supply of cultivable land. Impoverished peasants who went into debt risked losing their land to their creditors if repayment was not made. But foreclosure on loans soon created an angry, landless class ready for revolt. The result, therefore, was a series of disturbances—some small, others more serious—that kept the imperial authority on the defensive. The government's long success in maintaining peace and prosperity thus began to backfire after 1775 in a most distressing way.

**Old and New in Eighteenth-Century China**   Both these paintings are the work of Joseph Castiglione (1688–1766), a Jesuit missionary in China who brought the full array of European painting techniques to China for the first time. Painting was an important accomplishment for Chinese gentlemen. As a result, the novelty of Castiglione's use of bright color and mathematically accurate perspective attracted a good deal of attention at the court, where the Jesuit mission resided. How far toying with foreign novelties could go is illustrated on the left, where one of the emperor's concubines is pictured in European armor. Yet court routines remained thoroughly traditional, as we see on the right, where the emperor is shown observing archery, an exercise befitting gentlemen according to Confucius. Chinese painters soon decided that bright color was vulgar, while reliance on a single disappearing point in the European manner seemed unduly restrictive for scroll painting. European novelties were thus dismissed as unworthy of further consideration. Accordingly, Chinese court and society continued faithful to ancient models until the 1840s and beyond.

## Trade Problems Lead to War

At almost the same time, China's foreign trade began to present a serious problem too. In 1757 the emperor had decreed that Canton should be the only port at which foreign ships might put in. China's main European trading partner was the East India Company, which enjoyed a legal monopoly of Britain's trade with China. Dutch, French, and, after 1784, U.S. ships also put in at Canton occasionally; but the Chinese were able to keep them all under control by giving an association of merchants, the Co-hong, a monopoly of all dealings with strangers.

From the European point of view, the great problem was to find something the Chinese wanted to import. Chinese-made goods commanded a lively market in Europe and elsewhere, but about the only thing the Chinese wanted in exchange was silver. Europeans were reluctant to see their silver coins disappear into China, and it was not until a brisk market for opium developed that the Europeans discovered a commodity they could offer instead. Opium was produced cheaply in India, and it gave the English just what they needed to make their China trade really profitable for the first time.

In 1834 the British government canceled the legal monopoly the East India Company had long enjoyed and tried to put trade with China on the same basis as trade with any other part of the world. A swarm of private merchants therefore descended on Canton, eager to get in on the profits to be made from the opium trade.

The Chinese imperial authorities soon took alarm at the spread of the opium habit. They forbade the production or sale of the drug, but this simply drove the trade underground. European merchants began dealing with all sorts of shady characters, and smuggling became a large-scale, organized gangster affair. In 1839 the Chinese decided to crack down. A special commissioner came from Peking with instructions to break up the illegal trade. He seized 30,000 chests of opium within a few months and seemed on the point of cleaning up the whole mess when he collided with British authority.

*The Opium War*    The point at issue was trifling. Some English sailors had engaged in a brawl at Canton and killed a Chinese. The Chinese demanded that one of the sailors be handed over to them to be executed. From a Chinese point of view, this was only common justice and an ordinary assertion of sovereignty. From the British point of view, however, handling over a man to be executed without trial and without any proof of his guilt was an appalling miscarriage of justice. The British ship's captain therefore refused. He was backed up by a commissioner of trade, appointed by the British crown. When the Chinese then tried to use force, the British government decided to send a detachment of the Royal Navy to the scene.

British naval vessels and marine landing parties found the Chinese coast almost completely at their mercy. Chinese ports lacked effective harbor defenses, and Chinese troops could not move rapidly enough from one threatened place to another. When clashes did take place, the Chinese soldiers proved far inferior to the British detachments. In 1842 the bewildered and indignant Chinese had to make peace. By the Treaty of Nanking they opened four additional ports to British trade, agreed to levy a uniform 5 percent tariff on imports, ceded Hong Kong to the British, and officially recognized that Queen Victoria was not—as the Chinese had always before pretended—paying tribute to the emperor when British ships put in at Chinese ports.

*Unequal Treaties*    The French and American governments soon made similar and even more advantageous treaties with China. In 1844, the Americans secured the right of extraterritoriality. This meant that American citizens would be tried by American law, even on Chinese soil, and before American consuls. In the same year, the French secured official toleration of Christianity and of missionary activity in the port cities. By the principle of the "most favored nation clause," which was inserted into each of these treaties, any concession to one foreign power became a concession to all. Thus, a mere five years from the time when the clash had begun, China found itself the victim of unequal treaties and unable to stave off the intruding foreigners.

The shock to Chinese feelings was immense. The Celestial Kingdom, to which all barbarians ought to pay tribute, had suddenly ceased to occupy the center of the world. New and strange peoples, unknown to Confucius, had burst upon the scene. The ancients offered no rules for how to cope with such a situation. Stunned surprise and utter dismay were all that Chinese scholars and officials could feel at first; and in their state of shock they had no time to turn toward more constructive action before a new and violent civil war flamed up, the Taiping Rebellion, which for fifteen years (1850–1864) tore at the vitals of the empire.

The suddenness of China's fall needs to be emphasized. Until 1839 the internal troubles of the country remained marginal. Tried-and-true Confucian patterns of conduct seemed to be working well, and China's superiority over the barbarian world was completely taken for granted by every educated Chinese. The intellectual class, in other words, had been so homogenized that no one had any idea of how to deal with the crisis that burst so suddenly. The great bulk of China sprawled helpless, blind, angry—completely unprepared for the reversal of roles that events had thrust upon the nation.

# *The Land of the Rising Sun*

Japan's history from 1700 to 1850 was in almost every respect the exact opposite of China's. While China fought a series of victorious frontier wars, Japan remained at peace. While China's population nearly tripled, Japan's population remained almost constant. While Chinese scholars fixed their gaze upon their own past to the exclusion of everything else, Japanese intellectuals explored several different kinds of learning and paid considerable attention to what was going on in Europe, even though the official policy of isolation remained rigidly in force.

## Political Insecurity of the Shogun's Power

From the beginning, the Tokugawa shoguns had to face some awkward problems that refused to go away. Nothing like China's smug self-satisfaction could, therefore, arise in Japan, since both the ruling clique of the Tokugawa family and the "outside lords," who had been excluded from any part in the central government, realized that the whole system might fall apart again. Only the bitter memory of Japan's long civil wars and the political watchfulness of the shoguns kept the peace. But memories of a time when the Tokugawa family was just the equal, not the superior, of other noble families never died; nor could the Japanese forget that the emperor, kept in seclusion by the shoguns, was in theory supreme. No doctoring of the historical record could hide the fact that the shoguns' power was a usurpation.

## Economic Imbalance Between Warriors and Merchants

Another difficult problem arose from the success with which the shoguns kept the peace. The warrior class had no occupation when there was no war. It was a matter of policy (as established by Ieyasu Tokugawa in 1603) to require all important lords to spend part of the year in the capital, Tokyo, where they would be directly under the eye of the shogun; and when they were not in residence, they were required to leave sons and other close relatives behind as hostages. Hence, all of the fief holders had to keep houses in the capital, where they had nothing much to do.

Two consequences followed. First, fief holders had to convert at least a part of their income, which was in rice, into money that could be used in the capital to keep up the family establishment. This required merchants to buy surplus rice in the countryside and sell it in the cities, above all in Tokyo, the new magnet to which population and other resources flowed.

Second, the merchants who organized the distribution of rice and other necessary commodities grew rich; whereas the fief holders had to sell at the merchants' price and buy at the merchants' price and therefore grew poor. Or, at least they often found themselves too poor to live up to the standard of luxury that rapidly developed in Tokyo and other cities. Special amusement quarters catered to the taste of rich merchants for song and dance, good food and company. Warriors, whiling away their time idly in town, could not resist such attractions; and when they could not afford them, they ran recklessly into debt.

The result was a sharp discrepancy between what was and what most Japanese felt ought to be. The warriors and rulers were poorer than the merchants, who, according to Confucian ideas, were social parasites and pests, ranking, by rights, below hard-working peasants. The fief holders and the peasants agreed in deploring what had happened and tried all sorts of ways to remedy the injustice. Sometimes the government resorted to outright confiscation of merchant fortunes. More often a repudiation of debts was decreed, in whole or in part; or the currency was debased to make repayment of debts easier. All such measures failed. The merchants quickly made good their losses by charging more for services rendered. As long as the fief holders were not allowed to remain all year round on their lands, the merchants' services were literally indispensable, and they were, therefore, always able to regain the upper hand economically.

Toward the end of the period, some of the fief holders tried to solve their economic problem by developing mining and other enterprises on their holdings. New crops and skills spread—particularly the cultivation of silkworms. Japan, for the first time, became self-sufficient in silk. Another practice was to marry into a merchant family, thus refreshing the depleted fortunes of the noble warrior stock and endowing the merchant with a new respectability. Blurring of class lines in this fashion was forbidden by the warrior code of behavior, but the temptation was great on both sides and instances multiplied.

# Official Ideology

The shoguns' policy in face of these difficulties was to sit tight and hope for the best. Neo-Confucianism was official. Study of other schools of thought was formally prohibited. Great emphasis was put upon loyalty; and the code of approved conduct for the warrior class was spelled out exactly, both in formal decree and in literature and drama. Yet, the more the official line stressed loyalty to superiors, the more awkward it became to justify the shoguns' own disloyalty to the emperor. Indeed, public demonstrations of loyalty to the emperor became a way of expressing dissatisfaction with the shogun. But the government found it impossible to suppress sentiments that were outwardly so correct and proper.

*The Development of Shinto*    Accordingly, a school of thought arose that stressed the divine origin and descent of the imperial house. By degrees experts elaborated rites and ceremonies to celebrate the great events recounted in Japanese legend. These practices, referred to as *Shinto*, evolved rapidly to the level of an organized religion—complete with priests, different sects, and rituals for the everyday human emergencies of birth, marriage, and death. Borrowing from Christian and Buddhist rituals seems to have gone into the development of Shinto. An even stronger element was preference for an authentic Japanese, instead of a borrowed Chinese, doctrine.

The development of Shinto cults among the Japanese public at large was matched by the labors of a handful of scholars who set out to learn about Western thought. The medium was Dutch, for a single Dutch ship was permitted to put into Nagasaki harbor each year to carry on a carefully supervised trade. Foreign books were smuggled into Japan by this route, and a few persons learned how to read them and even made Japanese translations or adaptations of some medical and mathematical texts.

Admirers of Dutch learning and those who cultivated Japanese tradition got along with one another quite well. Both opposed the official

**Japan and the Europeans**   In 1638 the Japanese government limited foreign contact by allowing only a single Dutch ship to dock at an island in Nagasaki harbor each year. This law remained in force until 1854. On the left a Japanese artist recorded the outlandish appearance of a Dutch merchant of the early eighteenth century. The mingling of European and Asian cultures is clearly apparent, for the Dutchman carries a clay pipe from Holland and has a mongrel dog for company, while he wears a coat of Indonesian batik cloth, tailored in European style, and takes shelter from the sun beneath an enormous umbrella (of Indian provenance) held aloft by an Indonesian servant. Such isolated, rather comical visitors scarcely seemed threatening, which is why they were allowed to come ashore. Yet, in fact, European capabilities were building up throughout Japan's period of isolation to become as dangerous as the great wave, portrayed on the right by a famous Japanese woodcut artist, Katsushika Hokusai (1760–1849). As the wave inundates the fishing boats in the foreground and even overtops the snow-capped peak of Mt. Fuji that rises east of Tokyo, so European and American influence broke upon Japan immediately after Hokusai's death.

Neo-Confucian orthodoxy of the shogun's government; both were supported more or less secretly by the "outside lords," who never quite gave up their jealousy of the Tokugawa family; and both were looking for alternative lines of action for their country. Hence, when foreign pressures did persuade the shogun to open Japan again to foreign trade (1854), a few individuals in Japan were already familiar with some of the basic characteristics of Western civilization.

## The Life of the Arts

Japan's remarkable social structure was reflected in the arts. On the one hand, official culture conformed closely to Chinese models. Japanese painters, whose work can scarcely be distinguished from the work of Chinese masters, flourished at court. Literary scholarship along Chinese lines was brought to bear on the Japanese past. Chinese characters were used to write Japanese, and Chinese words were imported wholesale into the Japanese language to carry the proper Confucian distinctions. All this Chinese influence made Japan seem little more than a provincial variant of Chinese civilization.

On the other hand, there was a vigorously vulgar artistic life in the amusement sections of Tokyo and other cities, designed to appeal to the taste of merchants and other uneducated persons. Kabuki plays and the arts of geisha girls were examples of this sort of cultural tradition. In addition, artists produced cheap, multicolored prints that have since won the admiration of art critics and historians. They allow lively glimpses of the delights of city life as known in old Japan. In addition, novels and tales of adventure which were produced at this time gave literary expression to the same lifestyle.

Toward the end of the Tokugawa period, blurring of the distinctions between paintings done in the Chinese manner and the more popular styles faithfully mirrors the breaking down of the distinctions between merchant and warrior classes. Japan, therefore, saw the emergence of a more varied, complex, and pluralist society and culture—in a small way similar to the expanding pluralism of Western civilization—immediately before the nation plunged into new complexities by opening itself wide to imitation of and borrowings from the West in 1854.

# Less-Developed Regions of the World

The largest human population that remained on the fringes of civilized life lived in sub-Saharan Africa. Actually, the peoples of that continent were much involved overseas thanks to the slave trade, without, however, knowing much about the rest of the world, or themselves being known by it.

## Effects of the Trade in African Slaves

Black Africans experienced two powerful, contradictory changes between 1700 and 1850. Throughout the eighteenth century until the 1780s, the slave trade grew in scale and importance. Decade after decade, more captives were hunted down and shipped across the ocean. The demand for more and more slaves meant that slave hunting spread throughout almost all parts of the African continent. Slave raiders began to work inland from the east coast as well as from the west, where slaving had concentrated previously. But as the slave trade mounted in intensity, critical voices arose in England and France. After decades of agitation, in 1807 antislavery reformers prevailed upon the British Parliament to pass a law making the slave trade illegal. When the British ceased to be preoccupied by fighting Napoleon, the Royal Navy assigned some of its vessels to the task of preventing slave ships from carrying their human cargoes across the ocean. At first, they were too few to disrupt the trade very effectively, and trans-Atlantic slaving peaked a second time in the 1840s. Brazil and Cuba were the principal recipient countries. Thereafter the number of slaves leaving Africa began to shrink very fast, and by the 1860s only the sultan of Zanzibar in East Africa and a few Portuguese slavers moving between Angola and Brazil kept the trade alive.

The long intensification and sudden slackening of the slave trade had disruptive effects on African life. Weak and exposed village populations were ruthlessly assaulted by slave raiders, but local devastation seems not to have led to any general or widespread depopulation. Presumably, the productivity of crops derived from the New World improved African food supply so much that more children survived and thus counterbalanced the losses due to slave raiding.

But no one really knows because exact statistics cannot be discovered.

On the other hand, historians do now know a good deal about the number of slaves who crossed the Atlantic ocean because the trade was conducted by specialized ships, whose arrivals and departures were recorded at their ports of call, and whose carrying capacity can be figured out pretty accurately. On this basis, historians now believe that a total of about 11.3 million Africans were shipped across the ocean. Two thirds of them—7.5 million—crossed between 1700 and 1810; and despite British and French efforts to suppress the slave trade after that date, another 1.9 million left Africa before the trade finally came to a halt about 1880.

These are enormous numbers. Four to five times as many Africans as Europeans reached the New World by 1800; but as long as new slaves fresh from Africa were easy to get, not many of them were able to raise children. The establishment of a self-sustaining population of African descent in the New World came mostly after 1810, when the British navy began to intercept slave ships and compel them to return their captives to Africa. Many slave owners in the New World then found it cheaper to encourage their slaves to reproduce themselves instead of buying replacements as before. Not long thereafter, slavery was abolished throughout the French empire in 1815. (It was restored in 1815, however, and then permanently prohibited again in 1848.) The British abolished slavery throughout their possessions in 1832 and used the Royal Navy to intercept slave ships along the coasts of Africa as well. But slavery survived in the United States until 1863, in Cuba until 1886, and in Brazil until 1889. Emancipation made ex-slaves of African descent the largest element in the population wherever sugar plantations had prevailed. The burden of slavery thus resulted in the establishment of large black populations overseas, most notably in Brazil, the Caribbean Islands, and the United States of America.

Within Africa itself, the dwindling of the slave trade after 1850 had mixed consequences. Africa's political and economic system had been built around the trade to a very considerable degree, so when the export of slaves suddenly slacked off, the shock was correspondingly great. Slavery grew in importance within Africa itself

and was not finally abolished there until 1910. States that had drawn power and income from slaving raids had to find a new basis or crumble. Some survived and even flourished, like the Ashanti federation that had risen to power in the central part of Ghana in the eighteenth century. Other forms of economic production and trade had long existed in that part of Africa, and the Ashanti federation maintained its power because its people were able to shift from exporting slaves to exporting palm oil and other agricultural commodities.

In other parts of Africa the collapse of slave export had different and even destructive consequences. This was most apparent in southern Africa, where a series of wars between advancing whites and black farmers and herdsmen started in 1779 and achieved new intensity after 1836, when several thousand Boers, descendants of the original Dutch settlers at the Cape of Good Hope, migrated northward, across the Orange and Fish rivers. They did so to escape the British, who had replaced the Dutch at the Cape in 1815 as part of the peace settlement after the Napoleonic wars. In 1834, the British governors set out to abolish slavery in South Africa in accordance with Parliament's decree. A great many of the Boers objected; and in an effort to preserve their own way of life, which depended in considerable degree on using African labor for nasty jobs around the farm under conditions that amounted to slavery, they embarked on a Great Trek northward and eventually (1853–1854) set up two new republics of their own in the African interior.

The Boers had rifles and used them freely against Africans who tried to oppose them. Local tribesmen, armed only with spears, could not resist successfully. But in Natal, to the east of the Boer republics, an extraordinary military revolution was carried through by Shaka, who became chief of a small Zulu clan in 1816 and was assassinated by his half-brothers just twelve years later in 1828. In that short time, Shaka created a new and terrible form of warfare by training warriors to march in close order and fight hand to hand with short spears. Earlier, South African tribal warfare had been a matter of individual combat, featuring javelins thrown from a distance; and fighting was habitually broken off after a few champions had been killed or

# SHAKA, THE ZULU CHIEF

Shaka was the son of a Zulu chief, born about 1787 in Natal. His birth was scandalous because both his parents belonged to the same clan and marriage within the clan was prohibited by Zulu custom. As a result, when he was six years old his mother took him back to her homeland, where he grew up fatherless and despised as a bastard. When he was about fifteen, he and his mother fled from the persecution they suffered, taking refuge in land controlled by a rising new military empire, headed by the paramount chief of the Mtetwa people.

When Shaka finally came of age, he proved to be a man of fierce energy and found release for some of his pent-up anger by becoming a warrior in the Mtetwa army. For six years he served in the ranks, distinguishing himself for his bravery and skill. Then, in 1816, the paramount chief sent him to take over command of the Zulus, who were then a small tribe, part of the confederation of tribes headed by the Mtetwa.

Returning to his father's people in this way meant that Shaka had to overcome the disgrace of his illegitimate birth. He did so by dint of personality and ready resort to instant execution of anyone who opposed him. But what really confirmed Shaka's authority was a reform of military tactics and training that he inaugurated. Instead of relying on individual combat, as had been customary, he armed his warriors with short spears and formed them into units that maneuvered on the battlefield so as to take the enemy in flank and rear while simultaneously pinning the foe down by an intense frontal attack.

Close order drill had the same effect on Zulu warriors that it had once had on Spartan hoplites and Roman legionaries. Young men, trained to move together on the battlefield, achieved an intense esprit de corps that bound them together and separated them from the rest of society. As a result, Shaka created a professional army that easily defeated all rivals. He displaced the Mtetwa paramount chief in 1817 and rapidly extended his power in every direction. Conquered tribes were compelled to send their young men to join Shaka's regiments, where the psychological effect of close order drill made them over into proud Zulu warriors. In this way the Zulus rapidly became a numerous and powerful people, able to dominate a wide region of southern Africa.

Then in 1827 Shaka's mother died. His grief was bitter, and Shaka decreed that no crops should be planted and no children born for a year of mourning. He even ordered pregnant women and cows to be slaughtered so that everyone would know the greatness of his loss. He also ordered his army to keep fighting without the usual season's rest for the harvest season.

This was the last straw, and two of his half-brothers murdered him in 1828. But in twelve short years Shaka had built a Zulu nation. Even after British riflemen showed the limits of hand-to-hand combat by defeating Zulu regiments in battle in 1879, the Zulus continued to be a proud and powerful people and memories of Shaka's extraordinary career remain vigorously alive today.

wounded. Shaka, however, fought to win. His soldiers killed everyone who resisted them on the field of battle. Defeated tribes were compelled either to flee or to submit by sending their young men to serve in the Zulu units. Shaka's forces therefore grew very rapidly, and the range of their operations expanded every year.

The result was catastrophic. In the twelve years of Shaka's rule, his ever-victorious army devastated much of southern Africa and provoked flights and migrations that extended as far north as the Great Lakes and as far south as the borders of Cape colony. The political up-heaval Shaka's bloodthirsty victories created actually helped the Boers to advance because the Zulu army disrupted tribal societies that might otherwise have opposed the Boers more successfully than they did.

In other parts of Africa, the breakup of traditional political and economic patterns was not so sudden and violent as in the south. Yet there are signs that African states and peoples in all their variety were facing something of a general crisis about 1850. The rise of a number of Moslem reform movements, aimed at restoring true religion, was one sign of distress and dissatisfaction. As a result, efforts to achieve religious reform by military action kept much of West Africa in uproar, both before and after 1850.

In most of Africa, established ways of life were already under unusual strain at the time when the age-old disease barrier that had previously protected the continent from outsiders began to break down. The great breakthroughs of scientific medicine lay still in the future, but after about 1850 Europeans did become able to keep malaria at bay, and malaria had been the most common cause of the fevers that killed strangers in Africa. Europeans protected themselves from malaria by taking preventive doses of quinine, a drug derived from the bark of a tree native to Peru. Although they had known about quinine since the sixteenth century, Europeans secured a regular supply only after Dutch entrepreneurs took seeds from wild-growing (and relatively rare) trees in Peru and developed plantations of them in Indonesia. Regular and dependable supplies of quinine became available in Europe just about mid-century. As a result, exploration of Africa became far safer, even though other tropical diseases continued to endanger outsiders who lacked childhood exposure and inherited resistances to them.

Under these circumstances, European efforts to explore the interior of Africa became more and more systematic and successful. Geographical societies in London and elsewhere financed expeditions to find the source of the Nile, for example, or to explore the courses of the Niger and Congo rivers. Until the 1880s, important features of the African interior remained unknown to outsiders; but the main mysteries of what Europeans had dubbed the Dark Continent

**Shaka, Builder of the Zulu Nation** This portrait of the man who created the Zulu nation between 1817 and 1828 shows the shield and spear with which he equipped his soldiers, but it does not reveal the real secret of his success, which was to train his warriors to fight in close order and maneuver on the battlefield in disciplined units. Zulu armies, trained in this fashion, won a long series of victories against their neighbors and devastated much of southern Africa in the process.

were solved between the 1840s and the 1870s. Commercial, missionary, and military penetration of Africa swiftly followed, fueled by European rivalries and facilitated by the disorganization of African states and peoples that was reaching crisis proportions by about mid-century.

Thus, the special position of Africans in the world—exposed to contact with both the Moslem and European heartlands but safeguarded by the outsiders' vulnerability to tropical diseases—came to an end at a time when Europe's power and technical advantages over other peoples were reaching a climax. The suddenness with which almost all of the African continent came under European political and economic domination after 1850 was an inevitable, though still surprising, result.

## Explorations of the Pacific

The lands of the Pacific were thinly occupied by comparison with Africa. After the first few years of oceanic discovery, European ships stopped exploring for a long time. The reason was that nothing worthwhile attracted ships to the barren coasts of such lands as Australia, where the native inhabitants had nothing to offer Europeans in trade. In addition, there were serious problems for European vessels that wished to sail for long distances across an ocean so vast as the Pacific. Until an accurate marine chronometer had been invented (1761), the longitude of a small island could not be measured. Hence, the chance of returning to the same speck of land in the vastnesses of the open Pacific was slight. Moreover, on long voyages the crew suffered from scurvy—a serious disease brought on by lack of vitamins. No ship's captain could therefore afford to cruise around looking for an island that ought to be somewhere in the general area where the ship was, but whose exact location no one could tell for sure.

In the eighteenth century, organized European navies took over the work of exploration, and within a short time they had charted the coastlines of nearly the whole Pacific Ocean. The first official explorer was Captain Vitus Bering of the Russian navy. He made two voyages, in 1728 and 1741, and discovered the straits that bear his name, the Aleutians, and the Alaskan mainland. Russian fur traders soon followed in Bering's wake and set up trading posts on the American side of the straits. The French sent Captain Louis Antoine de Bougainville to cruise in the Pacific, 1767–1769; the British countered with Captain James Cook, who made three voyages to the same regions between 1768 and 1779. Captain Cook carried with him the first really successful marine chronometer and was able, therefore, to plot the longitude as well as the latitude of the coasts and islands he explored. The first usefully accurate maps of the Pacific region resulted from his careful labors. He also required his sailors to eat sauerkraut in order to protect them from scurvy by providing a supply of vitamin C in their diet. Later the British navy discovered that lime juice was even more effective as a protection against scurvy, whence the nickname "Limey" for British sailors.

*Settlement Patterns in the Pacific Area*
Whalers soon followed the explorers, with the result that Tahiti and Hawaii and other less-famous islands of the Pacific had to put up with boisterous whalers and other sailors who put ashore for a bit of relief from the cramped quarters of their ships and from the smell of whale oil. Diseases brought to the Polynesians by the mariners had the usual effect of spreading devastating epidemics, from which the old island life never recovered.

Around the shores of the Pacific, too, European settlers and traders began to leave their mark before 1850. Spanish missions moved north to Nootka to counter the Russian advance into Alaska. But the imposing Spanish Empire in the Americas began to break up after 1808 as local revolts gained headway. Not long after Mexico became independent of Spain (1821), the United States attacked (1846) and took over California. Almost immediately, the discovery of gold (1848) started a rush into that remote land.

Across the Pacific, in Australia, European settlement dated from 1788, when the British government sent the first shiploads of convicts there to make a new life for themselves on the other side of the world. Beginning in 1793, free settlers began to arrive. The effects of the arrival of the newcomers upon the Australian aborigines were drastic. They were driven toward the northern parts of the continent and into the interior, where deserts and heat made the land unattractive to the English. In addition, new plants and animals introduced by the Europeans upset the existing balance of nature in dramatic ways, so that, for instance, a plague of rabbits resulted from the absence of their natural predators.

The last important area of European settlement was New Zealand, where British colonists arrived for the first time in 1840. The Maori tribes, who lived in New Zealand, survived the shock of contact with Western civilization better than the native Australians. As a result, after the usual losses from disease and ensuing social disorganization, the Maoris, with the help of the new food resource supplied by the potato, made an astonishing recovery. In recent years they have begun to participate in the public life of New Zealand and now enjoy ordinary citizen rights.

## Amerindian Retreat

The fate of the Amerindians differed from that of the Maoris. Some tribes were utterly destroyed, but many survived, often only as a shattered remnant. As late as 1890, some of the Plains Indians in North America attempted armed resistance to the white settlers, but this was the last flicker of a century or more of hopelessly one-sided struggles. Repeatedly, Indians were assigned lands by treaty arrangements, only to see white settlers press into the areas supposedly reserved for the Indians. Only poor and unpromising land, which the white settlers did not want, was allowed to remain permanently in Indian possession. In South America, too, the last flicker of warlike resistance to advancing settlement came between 1841 and 1871, when the Araucanian Indians met defeat at the hands of Chileans who proceeded to extend their frontiers to the southernmost tip of South America.

By far the largest number of Amerindians lived in Peru, Mexico, and adjacent regions where village populations continued to work in the fields as their ancestors had done for centuries. Iron tools, domesticated animals and Spanish priests and rulers made life different; but within the village communities themselves, routines for raising maize and other traditional crops were little changed, and local Indian languages and other cultural heritages survived side by side with, and subordinated to, the Spanish life of landowners, towns, and officialdom.

When revolution broke out among the whites of Spanish America (after 1808), it did not make much difference for the Indians. In Mexico, some Indians took part in the revolt against Spain in 1810, but elsewhere the Indian element among the peoples in Spanish America remained passive politically.

Only in the remoter recesses of the Amazon jungles and in parts of the frozen Arctic did life continue almost unaffected by the presence in the New World of persons who shared the skills and ideas of Western civilization. Civilized ways had a remarkable reach. For example, metal hatchets, traded from hand to hand, often penetrated far beyond any face-to-face encounter between European traders and the people who ultimately put the hatchet to use. Moreover, even simple tools sometimes transformed life patterns in surprising ways. In this sense, we can be sure that by 1850 no part of the inhabited globe was immune to the impact of civilization; and the regions where isolated, simple societies still survived were shrinking faster than ever before.

## Conclusion

By comparison to the state of the world in our own time, the globe remained a relatively spacious place in 1850. It took months for persons, goods, or news to move from one side of the earth to the other. What occurred in China had no immediate impact upon what happened in Europe, Africa, or America. A lag in reaction time and defects in communication gave local peoples room to maneuver without immediately attracting the attention and intervention of world powers. But the Industrial Revolution, already well launched in Europe, soon made communication instantaneous through the installation of the telegraph, thus inaugurating a new age which we will consider in the last part of this book.

Before we do so, however, we must return to Europe and the West for a closer look at the two great movements that were to transform the world in the period after 1850: the Democratic and Industrial revolutions.

# Bibliography

Two diverse literary works allow special insight into unfamiliar words: on the one hand, Ts'ao Hsueh-Chan, *Dream of the Red Chamber* (Chi-Chen Wang, trans., 1958)—a lengthy tale written in eighteenth-century China, and portraying a well-to-do contemporary household; and, on the other, an autobiography written by a former slave, entitled *The Interesting Narrative of the Life of Olaudah Equiano, or Gustavus Vassa the African* (1789), available in an abridged form as Paul Edwards, ed., *Equiano's Travels* (1967). A powerful modern novel, James Clavell, *Shogun: A Novel of Japan* (1975), explores Japan's encounter with Westerners in this period also. Innumerable other texts exist, of course, some of which are accessible in collections of readings listed in previous chapter bibliographies.

Historians usually feel comfortable when dealing with only a single civilization or region of the world. A recent effort to look across such boundaries is David B. Ralston, *Importing the European Army: The Introduction of European Military Techniques into the Extra-European World, 1600–1914* (1990). Other books look at global economic links, most notably Immanuel Wallerstein, *The Modern World System, Vol. II, Mercantilism and the Consolidation of the European World Economy, 1600–1750* (1980) and *Vol. III: The Second Era of Great Expansion of the Capitalist World Economy, 1730–1840* (1989), and, a much briefer work, E. L. Jones, *Growth Recurring: Economic Change in World History* (1988).

For the Moslem world, in addition to books listed previously, H. A. R. Gibb and Harold Bowen, *Islamic Society in the Eighteenth Century* (2 vols., 1957); John O. Voll, *Islam: Continuity and Change in the Modern World* (1982); Albert Hourani, *A History of the Arab Peoples* (1991); and Bernard Lewis, *The Emergence of Modern Turkey* (2nd ed., 1968); are especially useful for this period.

For India, S. N. Mukherjee, *Sir William Jones: A Study in Eighteenth Century British Attitudes to India* (2nd ed., 1987); Eric Stokes, *The English Utilitarians and India* (1959); and Sophia D. Collet, *The Life and Letters of Raja Rammohun Roy* (3rd ed., 1962), deal with the emerging interaction of Hindu and English ideas; while Edward J. Thompson, *The Making of the Indian Princes* (1943), describes the growth of an alliance between the East India Company and Indian princes at the expense of the Mogul emperor's authority.

For China, John K. Fairbank, ed., *The Chinese World Order* (1968); Joseph Levenson, *Confucian China and Its Modern Fate* (3 vols., 1959–65); and Jonathan D. Spence, *The Search for Modern China* (1990), are particularly good general studies. For the fateful clash with British traders, see Peter Ward Fay, *The Opium War 1840–1842* (1975).

For Japan, George Sansom, *The Western World and Japan* (1950), and Donald Keene, *The Japanese Discovery of Europe* (1954), are elegant and instructive introductions to the encounter between Japan and the Western world. Charles D. Sheldon, *The Rise of the Merchant Class in Tokugawa Japan 1600–1865* (1973), and Thomas C. Smith, *The Agrarian Origins of Modern Japan* (1959), deal with the most important social transformations of the era; Irene Taeuber, *The Population of Modern Japan* (1959), and Susan B. Hanley and Kozo Yamamura, eds., *Economic and Demographic Change in Preindustrial Japan* (1977), explore the unique demographic pattern of modern Japan.

On African slavery, the following are of special importance. Patrick Manning, *Slavery and African Life: Occidental, Oriental and African Slave Trades* (1990); David Brion Davis, *The Problem of Slavery in Western Culture* (1966); together with two sequels by the same author, *The Problem of Slavery in the Age of Revolution, 1770–1823* (1975) and *Slavery and Human Progress* (1984). Paul E. Lovejoy, *Transformations in Slavery: A History of Slavery in Africa* (1983); Philip D. Curtin, *The Atlantic Slave Trade: A Census* (1969); Herbert S. Klein, *African Slavery in Latin America and the Caribbean* (1986); and, for the United States, John W. Blassingame, *The Slave Community: Plantation Life in the Antebellum South* (rev. ed., 1979). For South Africa, Monica Wilson and L. M. Thompson, eds., *The Oxford History of South Africa* (2 vols., 1969–71), is probably best.

On European discovery and settlement elsewhere in the world, J. C. Beaglehole, *The Exploration of the Pacific* (3rd ed., 1966), is standard. For Australian history, C. M. H. Clark, *A Short History of Australia* (1974), is a good place to start.

# The Democratic
# and Industrial Revolutions
## 1776 to 1850

# 20

**The Crystal Palace, London**   This etching records the opening ceremonies at the first modern World Exposition in 1851. The Exposition was intended to show off the new inventions that were beginning to change human life throughout the world. As you can see, the building in which it took place aptly symbolized the technical advances of the age by using iron and glass in entirely new ways.

In 1776 the states of western Europe were threatened by the giant power of Russia. Vast resources and an enormous population had been organized by the despotic government of Catherine the Great to support an immense army, which was about as well trained and equipped as any in Europe. Moreover, Russian power was on the move. Poland lost its eastern provinces to Russia in 1772; Turkey had been humbled in 1774; Catherine was laying plans to create a new, dependent Greek empire on the ruins of the Ottoman state; and only a royal coup d'état in Sweden in 1772 prevented that country from becoming a province or protectorate of the Russian Empire. Joseph II of Austria judged it better to cooperate with the Russians against the Turks than try to oppose them. The Prussians, unable to find allies to help them stop the Russian advance, came to the same conclusion and joined with Russia and Austria three separate times—in 1772, 1793, 1795—in successive partitions of Poland. When an independent Poland had thus been completely erased, the Russian frontier and the eastern boundaries of Prussia and Austria coincided, leaving no buffer zone between.

Three-quarters of a century had shown how rapidly the Russians could learn all they needed to know about Western military skills and organization. By 1775 they had come abreast of western European states in these respects, with the result that Russia's size was no longer a handicap but an immense advantage. The Germanies, divided among more than 300 sovereign states under the shadowy leadership of the Holy Roman Emperor, were clearly in no position to check Russian power. Even a one-time giant such as France seemed dwarfed by Russia's size and resources—quite apart from the fact that rivalry with England and frictions among the different classes at home made it impossible for the French government to devote more attention to what was happening in eastern Europe.

## Emergence of Europe's New Regime

Three-quarters of a century later, the aspect of Europe was strikingly different. By 1850, Russia was definitely old-fashioned. The czar's empire had fallen behind western Europe once again, in military matters as well as in industrial and political organization. The restless drive to expand Russian power in every direction, which had been so much in evidence in Catherine's reign, had given way to a conservative policy aimed at keeping things as they were. Internal difficulties were beginning to trouble the Russian state, which was still built upon serfdom for the majority and privilege for the few.

The fundamental difference between the situation in 1775 and the situation in 1850 was that the peoples of western Europe had been able to raise themselves again to a new and higher level of organization and in doing so outstripped Russia and the rest of the world. Thus, western Europeans postponed by a century having to face up to states as large as Russia and as well organized as they were themselves.

This remarkable reassertion of the primacy of western Europe was carried through on two fronts. No one planned it; no one foresaw the result. France took the lead in politics, Britain in economics. Between them, they transformed the life of Europe and moved that continent from the Old to the New Regime. The change in politics was simple in principle. Government and people came into closer partnership than before. As a result, the energies of a larger proportion of the total population could be brought to bear upon common, deliberately chosen goals. Routines of local life, particularly of village life, were broken in upon; service to the nation in war became the duty of every male citizen simply because the government was now "his" government and not the king's. Where the Old Regime had settled for political passivity on the part of the lower classes, the New Regime expected activity. As a result, the power, wealth, and energy at the disposal of governments that succeeded in taking their peoples into this kind of active partnership increased far beyond the limits imaginable to Louis XIV or Catherine the Great.

This "Democratic Revolution" gained much of its success from the fact that it got underway at the same time as the Industrial Revolution. The essence of the Industrial Revolution was the discovery of new ways to use mechanical power for producing useful goods. In particular, steam engines were used to drive textile and other kinds of machinery. Increased supply of power permitted the design of larger machines and new processes. As more and cheaper goods were produced, consumption increased. Then transportation and communication were revolutionized by the use of steam and electricity. As a result, industrialized nations became able to draw food and raw materials from all over the world to feed themselves and their factories. The pioneers of industrialization reaped enormous wealth. Some of the new wealth became available for state purposes, with the result that western Europeans could be both strong and rich at the same time. As wealth increased more rapidly than ever before, harsh and difficult choices between private and public, civilian and military, use of resources did not have to be made.

Europe's power and wealth under the Old Regime had also expanded rapidly. What happened from the 1770s on, therefore, was nothing new, although the pace of economic and technical change increased decade by decade. Internal balances between industry and agriculture and between the middle class and the aristocracy shifted sharply in favor of the former. This led to political transformations that gave the middle classes the leading role in public life because they, more than any other segment of society, were able to voice the public opinion to which the new governments of Europe paid attention.

Thus the New Regime that emerged by 1815 from the upheavals and wars of the French Revolution was, in a sense, a middle-class regime. Business people and professionals took over roles formerly reserved for nobles. High social status, wealth, and office were often earned by individual skill, luck, education, or personal characteristics. Such flexibility, in turn, allowed abrupt shifts of social energies into new activities—whenever they became profitable or seemed important for some other reason.

All the characteristics of the Old Regime that had distinguished Europe from other civilizations thus emerged from the crucible of the Democratic and Industrial revolutions in exaggerated form. In changing itself once again, western Europe remained true to its changeable past and became, more emphatically than before, the dominating center of the entire world.

# The American Revolution

As long as the English colonies in North America had to contend with unfriendly Indians and with French rivals in Canada and Louisiana, differences of opinion with the British government—intense enough at times—were always settled short of an open break. It was not safe to quarrel too much with the mother country because the British navy and, in time of war, British soldiers were necessary for the colonists' protection. After 1763, however, French power no longer existed in North America. This meant that the colonists no longer had anything to fear from their neighbors. The Spaniards were weak and distant; and without the French to arm them, the Indians could not hope to put up much resistance either.

The government of George III felt that the colonists had become too independent. In particular, British ministers in London thought the colonies should help to pay for the war that had just been won by submitting to taxes imposed by Parliament. The colonists objected. They had not been consulted and were not represented in the English Parliament. As the colonists saw matters, Englishmen had fought the Civil War of 1642–1649 to win the right of paying only those taxes agreed to by their elected representatives. They concluded that the sacred rights of Englishmen were endangered by the tyranny of King George, who was, in any case, trying to manipulate elections to Parliament in order to make it a rubber stamp for his own royal will.

Many people in England agreed with the colonists' arguments. Even when the dispute led to public violence and then to war, a party in Parliament criticized the king and sympathized openly with the rebellious colonists' cause. On the other hand, some people in the colonies believed that nothing justified open resistance to the king. Argument was fierce; and when fighting broke out, the patriot cause tended to become more radical. Not merely the "Rights of

Englishmen" but the "Rights of Man" were called upon to justify resistance to the British government. The theory that government derived its just powers only from the consent of the governed was formally proclaimed by the colonists in the Declaration of Independence (1776). Liberty and equality became the watchwords of the patriot group, although few of them took liberty and equality to mean the abolition of slavery or equalization of property. The words had, instead, a limited political meaning: the right of ordinary men of sound mind and modest wealth to take part in choosing representatives to shape government policy in elected legislative assemblies.

# France Supports the Revolution

The French were fascinated by the American uprising. The theoretical debate about political rights thrilled the ears of some, for their own position as subjects of an absolute monarch displeased many Frenchmen. In addition, by helping the colonists the French government could hope to undo the defeats of the Seven Years' War. Even if their own colonial possessions could not be recovered, at least the British position overseas would be weakened if the rebels won their independence.

After helping the Americans in unofficial ways, the French finally went to war in 1778. French soldiers joined the ragged forces under General George Washington's command with such effect that, when the British surrendered at Yorktown (1781), more French than Americans were on hand to witness the victory. Moreover, the French fleet made things extremely uncomfortable for the British at sea, and French diplomacy also brought the Spaniards and the Dutch into the war against King George. When the Russians, too, began to organize a diplomatic offensive against the British among all the Baltic powers, Great Britain was almost completely isolated. In 1783, therefore, King George made peace, recognizing the independence of the rebellious colonies and retroceding Florida to Spain.

# American Constitutional Government

Victory in war presented the colonists with the problem of governing themselves effectively. During the war, the Articles of Confederation (1777) had been agreed to by each of the colonies. This document committed them to a permanent union to be called the United States of America. But the separate colonies or states kept control of taxation with the result that the central authorities suffered from a crippling lack of income. The experience of the immediate postwar years did not solve the problem, although the decision made in 1785 to transfer control over the western lands to the federal government meant an important increase in its powers. In 1787, on the initiative of the state of Virginia and with the endorsement of the Congress of the United States, a new constitutional convention assembled. After four months of discussion, the delegates agreed upon a constitution that gave greater powers to the federal government. Having been ratified by two-thirds of the separate states, the new system of government began operation in May 1789.

Such a rational way of setting up a new government, after discussion and deliberation on the part of representatives of the people at large, seemed an extraordinary demonstration of political wisdom to many Europeans of the day. The rude and simple Americans had proved able to make a government according to reasonable principles and along lines to suit themselves. To be sure, there were skeptics who waited confidently for the arrangements embodied in the Constitution to fall apart. Aristocrats found it impossible to believe that the passions of common people would not upset orderly government. After all, the political experience of centuries seemed to show that republican government could only succeed in small city-states, and that monarchy was required to keep a large, sprawling country together.

*The Impact of the American Revolution*
But whether they looked hopefully and with sympathy upon the American experiment in rational self-government or waited, instead, for its

failure to prove the folly of trying to subordinate the operation of government to the will of the people, no European interested in political questions could remain indifferent. Theories of the rights of man and of the citizen had been talked about for decades in French drawing rooms and all over Europe. Now the Americans had been bold enough to act on them. The more successful the Americans seemed, the more restless Europeans felt in finding themselves subject to the authority of rulers they had no part in choosing, and over whose actions they had no legal control. The United States of America, in other words, became a shining beacon, proving to those who wished to believe it that reasonable citizens could govern themselves without needing kings, nobles, or priests to tell them what to do.

The idea that government is, in fact, a human creation and can be changed by human choice is accepted everywhere today. It is therefore difficult for us to realize how new and exciting such an idea seemed in 1789. Nearly all of Europe was then ruled by kings and emperors who claimed that God gave them the right to rule. They acted with the help of nobles and officials. These were privileged classes in the sense that different laws applied to them than to commoners. Differences of clothes and of manners also distinguished the privileged classes from the rest of society. They expected to be treated as superior beings by the common people.

The old idea that society was a great organism, requiring some at the head to do the thinking, while others were the hands and had to do the work, no longer convinced people of the middle class that they should remain in the station of life to which they had been born. Too many of their superiors were clearly incompetent. Too many individuals had, in fact, changed status. Legal theory and practical fact were too far apart. To such persons the simple truths, acted on by the Americans, alone seemed worthy of free and rational people. Government that failed to win the consent of the governed had no rightful claim to exist and should be changed. Or so it seemed to a vocal and energetic minority, especially in France, where the rigidities of the royal government were only partly redeemed by victory over Britain in 1783.

## The French Revolution

Widespread dissatisfaction with the way France was run became critical when Louis XVI (reigned 1774–1792) found himself in serious financial difficulties. The war with Britain (1778–1783) had cost a lot of money, and the French tax system could not produce the extra amounts needed to keep the government from bankruptcy. In theory, of course, Louis XVI was an absolute monarch and needed only to decree a new tax to make it legal. In practice, however, the bureaucracy that was supposed to serve the king had developed a will of its own. Many official posts were sold at auction. Those who purchased an office naturally felt that they owned what they had paid for and refused to change the way things were done unless the change was somehow clearly to their own advantage. In particular, high courts had the right to "register" the king's decrees. Originally, these courts were merely supposed to make sure that if any new decree contradicted some other law, the conflict would be drawn to the king's attention. Then, if the king wished, the new law was entered in the statute books or, on second thought, might be modified to avoid unnecessary confusion in the administration of justice. When, however, the high court of Paris refused to register new taxes decreed by the king, the judges became great popular heroes. The king's ministers decided that they could not afford to push through new taxes in the teeth of such opposition.

The royal government next tried calling together an assembly of notables (1787) in the hope that the great and powerful men of the realm would agreed to accept a new tax law. But the notables were unwilling to agree to anything that might require them to pay more taxes. The king next tried to revive the medieval institution of the Estates-General. This was a body rather like the English Parliament. Its members represented each of the three "estates" into which medieval political theory divided the country: clergy being the First Estate, nobility constituting the Second Estate, and commoners—everybody else—making up the Third Estate. The Estates-General had been called for the first time in 1302, when King Philip IV wanted to get support in his quarrel with Pope Boniface VIII, and had met for the last time in 1614, at the beginning of the reign of Louis XIII.

## The Meeting of the Estates-General

The Estates-General had been a gathering of representatives from the whole kingdom of France. But in 1789 great uncertainties existed as to how to choose representatives from each of the three estates. Even more critical was the question as to how the Estates-General would vote. If the representatives from each estate met separately and voted separately, conservatively minded clergy and nobles would control the Estates-General. If, however, all three estates met together, individual nobles and many of the clergy could be expected to sympathize with reform-minded representatives of the Third Estate who wanted to assure that in the future the king and his ministers would consult representatives of the nation regularly.

These uncertainties provoked a burst of political debate in France. The case was argued in numerous pamphlets. Each electoral district was invited to instruct its representatives in writing; consequently, all sorts of complaints and programs for reform were put on paper, with the result that even those who had not felt especially aggrieved before became aware of serious political injustices. A great many people, therefore, expected drastic reform when the Estate-General met in May 1789.

*Revolt of the Third Estate*    King Louis and his ministers agreed that, up to a point, reform was needed. New taxes certainly were necessary, but Louis XVI never decided what else ought to be done. The king was a well-meaning man but weak-willed. In the spring of 1789, he failed to decide how the Estates-General should sit and vote; and even after the first ceremonial meetings had taken place, he hesitated. Then, in June, he decided to order each estate to meet and vote separately. Before he got round to announcing his decision, however, someone locked the doors of the room where the Third Estate had been accustomed to assemble. The representatives reacted by jumping to the conclusion that a plot was afoot to dismiss them entirely. On June 20, 1789, they moved to a tennis court nearby and amid great excitement solemnly swore an oath that they would never disband until they had made a constitution for France.

Such an act was revolutionary. The representatives of the Third Estate, in effect, had announced their intention of curbing royal absolutism. Yet King Louis reacted mildly. He first went ahead and announced his decision that the representatives should sit and vote separately by estates. The Third Estate refused to accept his ruling. In the next few days, a growing number of clergy and nobles began to attend the meetings of the Third Estate. A week later the king yielded and ordered the representatives of all three estates to meet together and to vote individually. The Estates-General thus became the National Assembly, committed to making a written constitution for France just as the Americans had recently done for the United States.

## The National Assembly

Excitement ran high all over France. Louis XVI was by no means sure that the National Assembly could be trusted, and some of his advisers wanted him to call up soldiers and dismiss the troublesome representatives by a show of force. Troop movements stirred the people of Paris to action. They set up their own revolutionary authority, the Commune, to control the city; and on July 14, 1789, a great crowd attacked the Bastille—a royal fortress in the heart of Paris—and captured it. In later times this event was celebrated as the birthday of the French Revolution. It brought a new element into action—the people of Paris, who in the years that followed often demonstrated in fa-

# Declaration of the Rights of Man and of the Citizen

One of the first acts of the French National Assembly in 1789 was to approve the following declaration. Lafayette, hero of the American Revolution, proposed it, and members of the drafting committee conferred with Thomas Jefferson, then American ambassador in Paris, and also consulted the Bill of Rights for Virginia. This document therefore clearly reflects ideological connections between the American and French revolutions.

The National Assembly recognizes and declares, in the presence and under the auspices of the Supreme Being, the following rights of man and the citizen.

Art. 1. Men are born and remain free and equal in rights. Social distinction can be based only on public utility.

Art. 2. The aim of every political association is the preservation of the natural and imprescriptible rights of man. These rights are liberty, property, security and resistance to oppression.

Art. 3. The source of all sovereignty is essentially in the nation. No body, no individual can exercise authority that does not plainly proceed from it.

Art. 4. Liberty consists in the power to do anything that does not injure others. Accordingly, the exercise of the natural rights of each man is limited only by those that assure to the other members of society the enjoyment of the same rights. These limits can be determined only by law.

Art. 5. The law has the right to forbid only such actions as are injurious to society. Nothing can be forbidden that is not interdicted by law, and no one can be constrained to do what it does not order.

Art. 6. The law is the expression of the general will. All citizens have the right to participate personally or by their representatives in its formation. It must be the same for all, whether it protects or whether it punishes. All citizens, being equal in its eyes, are equally eligible to all public dignities, places and employments, according to their capacities, and without other distinction than that of their virtues and talents.

vor of radical measures and on several critical occasions were able to silence opposition.

The example of Paris proved infectious. Radical-minded reformers took control of other cities. Peasants, too, took the law into their own hands and began to attack their lords' houses. Often they set out to burn the charters that listed the obligations they owed their lords in the belief that if the documents were destroyed, the lords would never again be able to collect the rents and services listed in them.

The National Assembly responded by "abolishing feudalism" in the course of a hectic night, August 4–5, 1789, when, one after another, excited representatives renounced special rights and privileges. From that time onward, all Frenchmen were, at least in theory, equal before the law. All were citizens, owing the same duties and obligations to the state and enjoying the same rights and protection from it. Legally separate classes or estates and privileged corporations had been abolished. Liberty and equality had dawned. Before long, a third slogan was added to the revolutionary program: fraternity, meaning the brotherhood that ought to exist among free and equal citizens. These three ideals stirred

Art. 7. No man can be accused, arrested or detained except in cases determined by law and according to the forms it prescribes. . . .

Art. 8. The law ought to establish only penalties that are strictly and obviously necessary, and one ought to be punished only in conformity with a law established and promulgated prior to the offense and legally applied.

Art. 9. Every man is presumed innocent until he has been declared guilty. . . .

Art. 10. No one ought to be disturbed because of his opinions, even religious, provided their manifestation does not disturb the public order established by law.

Art. 11. The free communication of thought and opinions is one of the most precious rights of men; every citizen then can freely speak, write and print, subject to responsibility for the abuse of freedom in cases determined by law.

Art. 12. The guarantee of the rights of man and the citizen requires a public force; this force is then instituted for the benefit of all, and not for the personal benefit of those to whom it is entrusted.

Art. 13. For the maintenance of the public force and for the expenses of administration a general tax is indispensable. It ought to be distributed equally among all the citizens according to their means.

Art. 14. All citizens have the right to ascertain, by themselves or by their representatives, the necessity of the public tax, to consent to it freely, to follow the employment of it, and to determine the quota, the assessment, the collection, and the duration of it.

Art. 15. Society has the right to demand an accounting of his administration from every public agent.

Art. 16. Any society in which the guarantee of right is not secured, or the separation of powers is not determined, has no constitution at all.

Art. 17. Property being an inviolable and sacred right, no one can be deprived of it, unless legally established public necessity obviously demands it, and upon condition of a just and prior indemnity.

_____

Reproduced from William H. McNeill and Schuyler O. Houser, *Readings in World History*, Vol. 10, 1975, pp. 157–68, Margaret Maddox, trans.

enthusiasm not only in France but also in other parts of Europe. The English poet, William Wordsworth wrote:

"Bliss was it in that dawn to be alive"

—and many young men and women in Germany and Italy, as well as in England, felt the same.

*Financial Problems*    Events, however, refused to stand still in order to allow the National Assembly to draw up a constitution for France. In particular, the government's financial prob-

lem would not wait. As a stopgap, the Assembly decided to issue paper currency that would be redeemed by the sale of Church lands. But issuing paper currency proved such an attractive solution that more and more "assignats," as the bills were called, were printed to meet pressing government obligations. Even when in addition to the Church lands, the property of runaway nobles and the royal domains were put up for sale, the face value of assignats far exceeded the value of the lands that were sold. As a result, the paper currency could not be retired as intended. Inflation and a rapid rise in prices resulted;

wage earners suffered, but some businessmen and borrowers benefited.

The National Assembly's decision to sell Church lands and reorganize the Church as a branch of the state, by paying salaries to priests and bishops, was flatly condemned by the pope. This made the first great split in the revolutionary ranks. The many French men and women who remained good Catholics could not support the Assembly in opposition to the pope. Louis XVI was among those who refused to accept drastic reorganization of the Church. But for the time being, he was helpless. His secret appeals for assistance sent to the other monarchs of Europe produced no result, although when discovered later, they proved that the king had become a traitor to the Revolution.

## The Constitution of 1791

By the summer of 1791 the new constitution was finally ready. It made France a limited monarchy. Supreme authority was conferred upon an elected legislative assembly. It controlled taxation, exercised supreme judicial authority, and had the power to call royal ministers to account. Essential sovereign rights, in other words, were transferred from the king to the elected representatives of the French people. The king, nevertheless, kept important powers, such as the right to choose his ministers and to appoint army officers and diplomats, as well as a veto on legislation, which could, however, be overridden by the Legislative Assembly.

These provisions did not last, but the reorganization of local government written into the Constitution of 1791 proved durable. All France was divided into departments of about the same size. Church dioceses, judicial districts, and department boundaries were all made to coincide. All sorts of monopolies and special privileges were swept away. Simple, uniform administration, linking the individual private citizen with the government directly, was made to prevail all over France.

The effect of these changes was that in time of crisis the central government could demand more from each citizen than the government of the Old Regime had ever dreamed of doing. The thick tissue of privileged bodies that had grown up during the Old Regime meant that the king's ministers had seldom been able to get in touch with citizens individually, but had always to deal with guilds, town governments, high courts, provincial assemblies, and the like. Thus, the overthrow of privilege and the dawn of liberty, of which the revolutionaries were so proud, turned out to have a meaning they did not expect. Liberty, equality, and fraternity meant equal (and unlimited) service to the state—whether as a conscripted soldier or as a taxpayer.

The fatal flaw in the Constitution of 1791 was that Louis XVI, who no longer had the slightest sympathy for the Revolution, could not be trusted with the powers assigned to him. In June 1791, the king tried to flee abroad in disguise. But the royal party was recognized and compelled to return. The National Assembly could not do without a king. Outright republicanism was almost unthinkable still. All the same, when the new Legislative Assembly finally met in October 1791, suspicion of the king's good faith in accepting the Constitution ran deep.

Matters came to a crisis as a result of the outbreak of war against Prussia and Austria. King Louis and a circle of conservative "aristocrats" had tried to get these rulers to intervene against the Revolution for months and so welcomed war when it came in April 1792. Oddly enough, the most extreme radical faction represented in the Legislative Assembly also welcomed the war. An organized party of enthusiasts for the Revolution—called Girondins because some of their most conspicuous spokesmen came from one of the new departments in southern France, known as Gironde—were eager to bring liberty, equality, and fraternity to the other peoples of Europe. They also believed that foreign war would compel French citizens to rally to the cause of the Revolution and would help to silence internal frictions that were becoming acute.

The expectations of the Girondins turned out to be as false as those of the king. Revolutionary enthusiasm was not enough to win battles, and when the Austrians and Prussians began to advance into France, rumors that King Louis was in treasonable correspondence with the enemy roused the Paris crowds to fresh action. Under the leadership of Georges Jacques

Danton (1759–1794), they surrounded the legislators, demanding that they suspend the king. Reluctantly, the Legislative Assembly obeyed and organized new elections for a Convention to revise the Constitution once again.

## The Radical Phase: The Convention

Opinion shifted rapidly in the days of crisis that followed. To be sure, in September 1792 French armies turned the tide and a few weeks later started to march into the Austrian Netherlands (Belgium), where they were received as liberators. The Prussians also retreated, so that soon after the National Convention met in September 1792, French armies stood victoriously on the banks of the Rhine. But Louis' treasonable correspondence with the Austrians and the Prussians had been discovered. Accordingly, when the National Convention met, its first act was to abolish royalty and declare France a republic. In the following months, "Citizen Louis Capet" (Louis XVI) was brought to trial before the Convention, condemned for treason, and beheaded (January 1793).

This event shocked all of Europe. Kings and nobles everywhere felt threatened, and even those who had sympathized with the first stages of the French Revolution found it hard to justify the acts of the Convention. Britain, Holland, Sardinia, and Spain promptly joined Austria and Prussia in war against France. Discontent inside France became widespread, and the threat of revolt and civil war hung over the deliberations of the Convention.

The National Convention was also hampered by bitter factional fights within its own ranks. The Girondins, who had been the radicals of the year before, were challenged by a new faction, known as Jacobins, whose principal spokesman was Maximilien Robespierre (1758–1794). The Jacobins were or became leaders for the Paris crowds, and part of their power depended on being able to summon Parisians for mass demonstrations to back up their policies. The Girondins, in reaction, tended to become identified with the provinces, where, on the whole, less radical views prevailed. Danton tried to stand above party and, as a result, alienated both sides. Many delegates to the Convention belonged to neither faction but swung back and forth as the emergency of the moment seemed to require.

In the summer of 1793 it looked as though the Revolution would go down in defeat. The most successful French general, Charles François Dumouriez, with part of his army, went over to the enemy. In the south the British besieged Toulon, and the Prussians advanced across the Rhine toward French soil. A rash of revolts spread through France, particularly after the Girondins had been excluded from the Convention in June, leaving the Jacobin party in full control.

## The Reign of Terror

The crisis roused the Jacobins, supported by the people of Paris, to heroic effort. Executive power was concentrated in the hands of a Committee of Public Safety, of which Maximilien Robespierre became the leading spirit. A "Reign of Terror" began. Hasty trials of anyone suspected of disloyalty to the Revolution led to mass executions. Universal military service for all male citizens was decreed. Frantic efforts to assemble and equip vast new armies quickly bore fruit. By the fall of 1793 the revolutionary forces were once more on the offensive, and the most dangerous internal uprisings had been suppressed.

The effort to turn back the danger required strong, centralized control. Special "representatives on mission" carried the authority of the Convention to the provinces. Local dignitaries and officials were summarily executed if they seemed disloyal or merely inefficient. Jacobin societies sprang up in all important towns. These societies carried on a vigorous correspondence with the Jacobin club in Paris and, in effect, served as local propaganda agencies to spread enthusiasm for the latest policy decreed from Paris. The Jacobin societies also made it their business to oversee the activities of local officials. If they detected any lack of zeal, a letter to the Jacobin club in Paris would lead to prompt dismissal or even to the execution of the

**Two Faces of the French Revolution**
Both of these works of art were made by Jacques-Louis David (1749–1825). He became official artistic director of the French Revolution, entrusted with planning revolutionary celebrations like the "Festival of the Supreme Being" in Notre Dame cathedral (1794) and commemorating the great events of the revolution on canvas. Above is a painting of the Oath of the Tennis Court (1789), when representatives of the Third Estate swore not to disperse until they had made a constitution for France. Below, a sketch of Queen Marie Antoinette, arms tied behind her back, as she was carried through the streets of Paris to the public square where she was beheaded (1793). The Oath of the Tennis Court is not accurate to the event, for David was not present and the painting was made long afterward. But the heroic posturing of the deputies does capture the enthusiasm of the moment and the solidarity of all those who sought to reform France in 1789. Yet David's personal commitment to the revolution did not prevent him from capturing Marie Antoinette's disdainful defiance of her enemies, even in the face of death. Her humble dress, bringing her to the level of an ordinary Parisian housewife, does not disguise the fierceness with which she and other defenders of the Old Regime opposed the revolution.

accused. The same system worked inside the army to keep check on the officers.

In this fashion, something close to total mobilization of the French nation was achieved. Close mutual support between "the people," organized into the Jacobin societies, and their government achieved amazing results. The massed forces of the European Old Regime could not stand against the revolutionary armies. Everywhere the French took the offensive. The Revolution was once more secure.

Success in battle did not, however, solve the question of how France should be governed. Robespierre talked of a "Republic of Virtue." This frightened many delegates to the Convention, who were not sure they were virtuous

enough to satisfy Robespierre. The Paris populace, on the other hand, wanted to extend equality to economics. In particular, the Parisians were angry at the rise of food prices, believing that greedy bakers, or grain dealers perhaps, were responsible. Robespierre hesitated and eventually refused to go along with the Paris crowd. He tried to eliminate awkward criticism by executing the leaders of the Paris Commune in March 1794, and Danton in April 1794. His own turn was not long delayed. In July of the same year, some of his colleagues on the Committee of Public Safety arrested him. When news spread through Paris, a group of Robespierre's admirers tried to free him, but Paris, as a whole, did not rise. In the confusion that his supporters created, the man who had become identified with revolutionary extremism was shot, dying a few hours later (1794).

## Reaction and Consolidation

The politicians who conspired against Robespierre did not intend to end the Reign of Terror or to change policy in any important way. But Robespierre's overthrow sparked a sharp reaction all over France. Summary revolutionary justice was halted. Soon the Jacobin hold on the National Convention was broken; their meeting place was closed in November and the surviving Girondin deputies were recalled. When a new constitution was drafted and approved in October 1795, the Convention ended its sessions.

*Government by the Directory*    The new government was headed by five directors. Stability at home and victory abroad was the Directory's policy. With the help of brilliant young generals such as Napoleon Bonaparte (1769–1821), who led a ragged army into Italy and utterly defeated the Austrian forces there (1796–1797), the Directory at first met with general success. Prussia and then Austria made peace. According to the resulting treaties, revolutionary France, in a few short years, had achieved Louis XIV's ambition of extending French territory to the Rhine. Moreover, a client state in Holland, the Batavian Republic, and another in northern Italy, the Cisalpine Republic, extended French influence and revolutionary principles even farther into Europe. Plans for fundamental reorganization of the Germanies were left undefined; but France, Prussia, and Austria all were eager

**Two Faces of Napoleon**    On the left, another painting by David shows a young, heroic Napoleon crossing the Alps in 1796 to liberate Italy from the Austrians and, incidentally, make his reputation as a bold, successful general. On the right, a painting by Francisco Goya shows Napoleon's soldiers twelve years later executing citizens of Madrid who had tried to resist their seizure of that city. Both these images of Napoleon were real in the sense that millions of Europeans responded eagerly to the revolutionary invitation to share in the liberty, equality, and fraternity that Napoleon's armies spread in their wake, but millions also came to hate the French as foreign conquerors and oppressors.

to get rid of the hundreds of separate sovereign states into which Germany had been divided ever since 1648.

Great Britain remained a problem. The British navy guarded England's shores, and no French superiority on land could force the British government to make peace or recognize the territorial gains won by the revolutionary armies. In 1798 Napoleon proposed to invade Egypt, as a way of threatening India and bringing pressure on the English to make peace. The directors feared Napoleon's popularity and were glad to see him leave the country. They therefore promptly agreed with Napoleon's plan.

Soon afterward British diplomacy and subsidies raised a new coalition against the French. The Russians joined in, for the first time, with the Austrians and Prussians, and sent armies to fight in Italy and Holland. The French were driven out of Italy, and Russian armies even crossed the Alps but failed to invade France when supplies gave out. Napoleon's first victories in Egypt had been well publicized at home; later failures were overshadowed by the news of French defeats in Italy. Accordingly, when Napoleon suddenly appeared in France in November 1799, he seemed to be a savior and had little trouble arranging a coup d'état that made him First Consul and the effective ruler of France.

*Napoleonic Rule*    Napoleon soon restored French power in Italy. The Russians had already gone home, due to quarrels with the Austrians. After defeating the Austrians, consequently, Napoleon found himself in a position to make peace with all the enemies of France. He even negotiated an agreement with the papacy in 1801, by which the pope recognized the loss of the Church lands in France and made it possible for a Catholic once more to support the French government in good conscience. This was followed in 1802 by the Peace of Amiens, whereby the British government gave up the struggle to undo the achievements of the French Revolution in Europe. Napoleon was universally acclaimed at home, became consul for life in 1802, and two years later assumed the title "Emperor of the French."

Thus monarchy had been restored to France; but Napoleon was at pains to refer every change in his regime to the vote of the people and always claimed to rule only by virtue of the popular will. In large degree, the claim was justified. The French were proud of the greatness Napoleon thrust upon them and appreciated the peace and order he maintained at home.

The fundamental changes the Revolution had made were consolidated and written into law—the famous *Code Napoléon*—that gave exact definition to property and personal rights as they emerged from the revolutionary upheaval. Napoleon maintained a strictly centralized administration, appointing prefects over each department and mayors over all important towns. A special police kept track of suspects by means of a vast card file. Public opinion was managed by carefully controlled news releases. Discontent could not find open expression and, in fact, few French citizens felt anything but pride in what their nation, under Napoleon's leadership, had accomplished.

Abroad, matters were different. The Peace of Amiens soon broke down, and Napoleon started a new war against Great Britain in 1803. Austria, Russia, and Sweden joined Britain against Napoleon in 1805; but the Austrians met crushing defeat at the Battle of Austerlitz. The next year Napoleon defeated the Prussians and, in 1807, arranged a peace at Tilsit with the young czar of Russia, Alexander I. When Austria resorted to arms again in 1809, Napoleon was victorious once more. Then, by marrying the Austrian emperor's daughter, Marie Louise, in 1810, he entered the most select and exclusive ranks of European royalty.

Napoleon's power had reached its peak. He controlled Italy and Germany, having made both Austria and Prussia into subordinate allies. He had created the Grand Duchy of Warsaw on the ruins of the former Polish kingdom. His relatives were established on thrones in Spain, Italy, and Holland; and the Russian czar agreed to cut his country off from British trade as part of Napoleon's grand plan for bringing Great Britain, the "nation of shopkeepers," to its knees by economic boycott.

*Nationalist Resistance to French Rule*
Nevertheless, there were serious weaknesses in Napoleon's position. The British navy was undefeated, and British subsidies were always available to foment resistance against the French any-

# NAPOLEON'S CORONATION

Napoleon Bonaparte was born in Corsica. As a boy he was both very poor and very proud, for his family claimed noble rank but had little money. When he went to France he felt like an outsider, for the Corsicans spoke a language more like Italian than French. Napoleon never lost the feeling of being an outsider, even when he rose to undisputed power over all of France and a large part of Europe.

In 1804 Napoleon was approaching the peak of his career. Only Britain opposed him in war. At home, most Frenchmen admired his victories. Napoleon decided that he should make his power hereditary. But Napoleon was also a son of the French Revolution, and the French revolutionaries had set out to overthrow the hereditary privileges of kings and nobles. How could the Corsican upstart become a monarch without betraying his principles— and those of his most devoted followers?

Napoleon's answer was to put the question to a vote. If the people of France wanted him to hold hereditary power, then his rule would be based not on empty tradition or ancient privilege but on the will of the people. The vote was taken, and the people overwhelmingly approved the proposal that Napoleon should become emperor of the French.

From the time of Charlemagne, emperors had been crowned by the pope. Napoleon decided that his new title required a coronation, and he demanded that the pope come to Paris for the ceremony. After some hesitation, the pope agreed; and on December 2, 1804, the solemn ceremony took place in Notre Dame Cathedral at Paris.

But there was another difficulty for Napoleon. In the traditional ceremony, the pope put the imperial crown on the emperor's head. This seemed to say that the imperial crown was the pope's gift; and, again, Napoleon's revolutionary principles made any such idea unacceptable. For the French revolutionaries had also attacked the Church and denied that political rule came from the hand of God, or from any bishop, priest, or pope.

Napoleon solved this problem, too. As the ceremony of the coronation approached its climax, the imperial crown was carried forward. Just as the pope was about to pick it up and place it on Napoleon's head, the emperor himself leaned forward, seized the crown, and placed it on his own head. Thus he allowed no one but Napoleon himself to crown the new emperor of the French.

where on the continent. Overseas ambitions that Napoleon had briefly nourished after the Peace of Amiens had to be abandoned. Accordingly, he gladly sold Louisiana, recently acquired from Spain, to the United States in 1803. In Europe itself, the French provoked popular resistance in Spain. Soon a British expeditionary force added weight to the guerrilla warfare waged by the Spaniards. In Germany and Italy, many people asked themselves why France should be so powerful and their own nations so weak. National feeling, in other words, began to turn against the French and made the rising against Napoleon, when it came, strong and irreversible.

**Napoleonic Europe, 1810–1818**

KINGDOM OF SWEDEN

KINGDOM OF

DENMARK

AND NORWAY

*North Sea*

*Baltic Sea*

UNITED KINGDOM OF GREAT BRITAIN AND IRELAND

Edinburgh

IRELAND

Manchester

WALES

ENGLAND

London

Copenhagen

Hamburg

HANOVER

NETHERLANDS

K. of WESTPHALIA

CONFEDERATION

Leiden

Antwerp

BELGIUM

Waterloo

Amiens

Weimar

Halle

Leipzig

Auerstadt

Jena

Silesia

Prague

*Atlantic Ocean*

Paris

Versailles

Varennes

Valmy

LORRAINE

Luneville

Strasbourg

ALSACE

BADEN

Ulm

RHINE

OF THE

Weser R.

Oder R.

Elbe R.

Rhine R.

Meuse R.

Seine R.

Austerlitz

Wagram

Vienna

Nantes

VENDÉE

Orleans

Loire R.

Limoges

Bordeaux

FRANCE

Lyons

Geneva

SWITZER-

LAND

BAVARIA

TYROL

Gironde R.

Rhône R.

Avignon

PIEDMONT

SAVOY

Marengo

Milan

LOMBARDY

Po R.

VENETIA

Camporformio

Venice

ILLYRIA

*Adriatic Sea*

Marseilles

Nice

Genoa

PARMA

MODENA

KINGDOM OF ITALY

Florence

Pisa

TUSCANY

Elba

PAPAL STATES

Rome

KINGDOM OF NAPLES

PORTUGAL

SPAIN

Coimbra

Madrid

Lisbon

Tagus R.

Ebro R.

Guagalquiver R.

CORSICA (FRANCE)

BALEARIC IS.

MINORCA

SARDINIA

Naples

Cape Trafalgar

Gilbraltar (BRITAIN)

MALTA (Br.)

Palermo

SICILY

Empire of France

French satellites

Allied with France

⊗ Battle sites

0          5          10          15

FINLAND
L. Ladoga
Gulf of Finland
St. Petersburg
LIVONIA
Moscow
Borodino
COURLAND
W. Dvina R.
Vitebsk
Oka R.
Königsberg
Tilsit
Smolensk
Vilna
Friedland
Niemen R.
Napoleon's route, 1812
Warsaw
OF WARSAW
Kiev
GALICIA
R U S S I A
WHITE RUSSIA
EMPIRE OF
AUSTRIA
Dnieper R.
Dniester R. UKRAINE
Don R.
Azov
Pest
Buda
Prut R.
Caspian Sea
HUNGARY
Sevastopol
Belgrade
Morava R.
Danube R.
Black Sea
MONTE-
NEGRO
Kutchuk-Kainarji
O T T O M A N
PERSIA
Bosporus
Istanbul
Vardar R.
IONIAN Is.
(Br.)
Aegean Sea
E M P I R E
Dardanelles
Tigris R.
Euphrates R.
CRETE
CYPRUS
Mediterranean Sea
A R A B I A
Abukir Bay
Alexandria
Cairo
EGYPT

**Western Europe, 1798** PARTHENOPEAN
— Extent of French influence REPUBLIC

GREAT
BRITAIN
P R U S S I A
GERMANY
BATAVIAN
REPUBLIC
FRANCE
A U S T R I A
SWITZ.
CISALPINE REP.
LIGURIAN REP.
OTTOMAN
EMPIRE
SPAIN
CORSICA

The breaking point occurred in 1812 when Czar Alexander quarreled with Napoleon and went over to the British side. Napoleon organized a great army to invade Russia and marched to Moscow. But winter closed in and Russian resistance did not crumble. The proud French army had to withdraw, suffering enormous losses from cold and hunger en route. News of this defeat set all Germany ablaze. The Prussians entered the war against Napoleon; soon the Austrians did the same. A great battle at Leipzig, in 1813, ended in allied victory. Napoleon faced defeat.

The allies found it difficult to agree among themselves. Nevertheless, the alliance held until Napoleon surrendered in 1814. The victors exiled him to Elba, a small island off the coast of Italy. Then they set out to make peace, after the upheavals of twenty-three years of war. Scarcely had the peace conference met at Vienna when fierce quarrels broke out. Napoleon took advantage of the situation and secretly embarked for France. On his arrival, the French people and armies rallied once more to his banner, but the news of Napoleon's return brought the allies back together again. British and Prussian troops swiftly organized; and at Waterloo, in Belgium, not far from the French border, they met and defeated the French (1815). Napoleon surrendered once again, and this time he was shipped off to St. Helena, far away in the South Atlantic Ocean. He died there of cancer in 1821.

## The Congress of Vienna

The Congress of Vienna resumed its task of restoring the balance of power in Europe. The Bourbon monarchy was restored in France, in the person of Louis XVIII, brother to Louis XVI. (According to royalist principles, Louis XVI's son counted as Louis XVII, even though he never reigned.) The restored king issued a constitutional decree, giving legislative power to elected assemblies. In general, he made little attempt to turn back the clock. The basic revolutionary idea that people and government could and should cooperate remained in force. To be sure, not all the people were allowed to vote in elections; only the wealthy and better educated were invited to assume that responsibility. But despite this limitation upon the democratic

principle, the constitutional decree marked the restored Bourbon government of France as vaguely "liberal."

In Germany and Italy, where Napoleonic reforms had erased old boundaries, return to the Old Regime was equally impossible. Instead, Austria took over the task of guarding Italy against France and passed to Prussia the task of watching the Rhine frontier. The Prussians, therefore, annexed broad territories in the Rhineland in return for giving up Polish territories to Russia in the east.

By these and many other complicated deals a balance of power between the major states of Europe was carefully adjusted so that no one of them could dominate the rest. France, on the one side, and Russia, on the other, were the two chief threats—or so it seemed to Prince Metternich of Austria and to the British foreign minister, Lord Castlereagh, who, between them, arranged most of the important compromises. Czar Alexander was fond of thinking of himself as Europe's savior, and at different times he entertained various plans for establishing a new order. He toyed with the idea of uniting Germany and Italy in accordance with the will of their peoples. With himself as king, he restored Poland. A great crusade against the Turks attracted him, too. But most of all, he pinned his hopes on a Holy Alliance of Christian monarchs who would work in harmony and consult with each other regularly in order to end the warfare that for too long had brought such havoc to Europe.

## The French Revolution Overseas

The French Revolution provoked upheaval in the French and Spanish empires overseas. In 1791, for example, black slaves in Haiti, the largest of France's Caribbean colonies, responded to news of the revolution in France by proclaiming their own liberty and equality with whites and mulattoes. The National Convention eventually accepted the rebels' logic and prohibited slavery throughout the French Empire; but Napoleon tried to restore slavery, and it was permanently prohibited in France only in 1815.

When Napoleon sent an army to Haiti to reassert French authority in the island, he met with initial success. Toussaint L'Ouverture, who had led the slaves to freedom, surrendered; but soon yellow fever began to wreak havoc with the French soldiers, and in 1804 Napoleon had to withdraw the remnants of his army. Haiti became independent under black governance, for by then race war had almost eliminated the white population.

The Spanish Empire in Mexico and South America also responded to the revolutionary ideals of liberty and equality. Rebellions aiming at independence began when Napoleon overthrew the Spanish king in 1808 and put his brother Joseph on the Spanish throne. This allowed local rebels to claim that they were loyal to the legitimate king, Ferdinand VII. But when Ferdinand regained the Spanish throne in 1815, he proved himself very much opposed to liberal principles and set out to restore imperial administration. As a result, all the first efforts at independence collapsed, except in Argentina.

Nevertheless, Ferdinand's efforts soon backfired. The white population of the Spanish colonies had become used to taking part in public policy making; and when new officials sent from Spain disregarded them, revolts broke out afresh, and this time were successful. By 1825 all of Spanish South America had become independent, thanks to the leadership of Simon Bolívar, José de San Martin, and others.

In Mexico, independence came by a rather different route. In 1810 the early revolt against Spain attracted a substantial mestizo following. But when poor mestizos began to take the idea of liberty and equality seriously, white landlords and other members of the Mexican upper class took fright and were glad to see the movement collapse after 1815. But in 1820 Ferdinand's reactionary government provoked a new liberal revolution in Spain, whereupon the Mexican ruling elite decided to declare their country's independence (1821) in order to preserve their social position.

Self-government proved attractive to Brazilians also, and in 1822 that country followed the Spanish example by declaring its independence from Portugal. Brazil remained a monarchy, however, ruled by Pedro I, son of the Portuguese king. He soon proved himself a patriotic Brazilian, resisting his father's efforts to assert authority over his son and over Brazil.

Cuba and Puerto Rico remained Spanish colonies until 1898; and most of the other islands of the Caribbean stayed under European rule until the late twentieth century. One reason was economic hard times due to the fact that after 1815 European nations depended less on imported sugar, having discovered how to supply themselves from sugar beets grown at home.

On the mainland, in contrast, increasing populations meant economic growth as new land came under cultivation and urban life continued to expand. Development was slower than in the United States but still very rapid. Amerindians remained politically passive, many of them living in remote villages with few outside contacts of any kind. The new Latin American governments therefore presided over a split-level society. At the top were whites and some mestizos who took part in politics and commerce. Underneath was an Indian population of subsistence farmers who sometimes paid rent or performed services for white landlords but otherwise had little to do with outsiders.

## Revolution Versus Reaction in Europe

Meanwhile, in war-weary Europe, Czar Alexander's vision of a Holy Alliance of Christian monarchs boiled down to no more than an agreement among the powers to meet at intervals in order to agree upon joint action when any crisis required it. Congresses did meet until 1822, but after that date Great Britain withdrew and the system fell to the ground. In the meanwhile, Metternich had been able to persuade Alexander that Europe was threatened by a wicked conspiracy to spread "the revolution." Instead of toying with liberal ideas, therefore, the czar became wholeheartedly reactionary. As a result, the three eastern monarchies of Austria, Prussia, and Russia became stalwart defenders of the status quo. France and Britain, on the contrary, were more sympathetic with revolutionary aspirations and refused to agree to international intervention aimed at suppressing liberal movements. This lineup became clear when Britain

**European States after 1815**

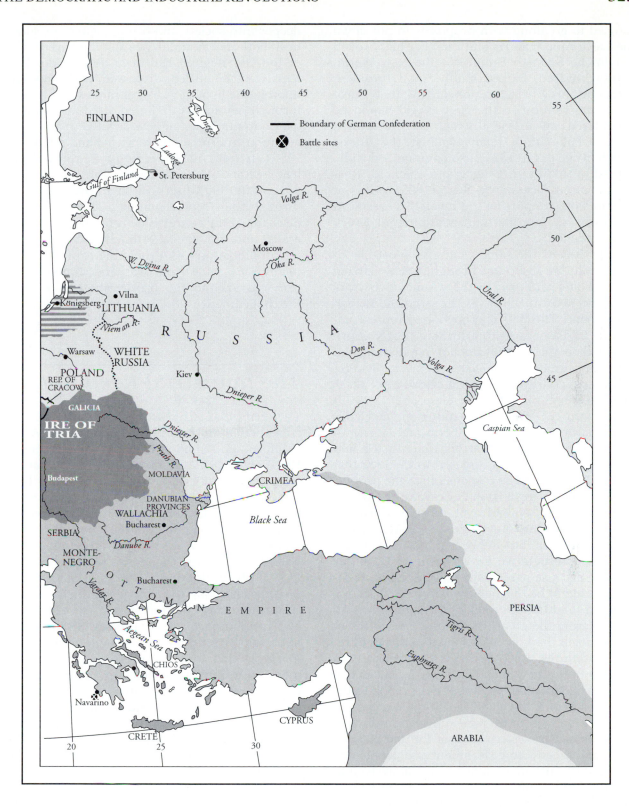

refused to go along with proposals to put down the Latin American revolutions that had broken out in the Spanish Empire of the New World. Britain, indeed, looked kindly upon President James Monroe's declaration (1823) that European intervention in the New World would be considered an unfriendly act by the United States. The Greek revolt against the Turks, which broke out in 1821, also commanded widespread sympathy in France and England. Russia, too, after Alexander's death (1825) could not refrain from supporting the rebels. The result in 1830 was an international guarantee of Greek independence.

In July of the same year, an almost bloodless revolution in France brought a new "citizen king," Louis Philippe, to the throne. Two years later, the Reform Bill of 1832 passed the British Parliament. This bill reapportioned representation in Parliament so that it more nearly corresponded to the distribution of population and gave the vote to middle-class taxpayers. The result was to confirm the liberal character of these two states and make middle-class political leadership secure. Germany and Italy remained a dubious battleground where liberal and conservative principles clashed. Farther east, Austria and Russia alone remained opposed to the idea that government should be responsible to the people.

In 1848, a fresh round of revolution, beginning in France, spread over most of Germany and Italy and into Austria as well. Metternich was overthrown, but the revolution failed to establish representative government in Germany or Italy because agreement on national unification could not be reached. By about 1850 among Germans and Italians most of the aspirations inherited from the great days of the French Revolution itself had been exhausted through repeated failures. Revolutionary enthusiasm was soon to find a new socialist form. As far as Europe was concerned, the era of the French Revolution had come to an end.

The change from 1789, however, was profound. In all the western parts of Europe, a closer partnership between government and people had brought the urban middle classes actively into politics. Public opinion mattered as never before. Governments rose and fell on the strength of it; and when supported by the enthusiasm of their people, governments had proved able to reach

deeper into society and bring greater energies to bear, both in war and in peace, than governments of the Old Regime had been able to do. Problems were identified, discussed, and then acted upon in the light of public opinion voiced mainly through newspapers. This allowed an extraordinary outpouring of activity devoted to all sorts of common enterprises both private and public.

City folk, instead of being merely subjects, had become citizens, responsible for the conduct of public affairs in their own right and through their representatives. The farmers and peasants of the countryside remained quiet, generally, and did not take much part in political and public affairs. But then, the acute problems of the day, aside from war and diplomacy, all centered around the transformation of urban life that came with the Industrial Revolution.

# The Industrial Revolution

The term "Industrial Revolution" was popularized about 1880 by an English historian, Arnold Toynbee, who applied it to the reign of George III (1760–1820). At the time, however, what contemporaries noticed were the wars and political upheavals of the age. The fact that cotton manufacturers in Manchester were making money by building new machines in dark and unpleasant factories hardly attracted the attention of anyone who was not in the cotton business.

Yet from the vantage point of our own age, it seems clear that the changes in the ways factories made things in Manchester and other cities had great importance for the world's history. By harnessing inanimate forms of energy, ingenious inventors and manufacturers added a new dimension to human power over nature. The use of coal and steam, and later of electricity, was comparable in importance to the discovery of agriculture in Neolithic times. A whole range of new possibilities opened up in both cases. Agriculture led to settled villages and then to cities and civilization. What power-driven machinery may lead to, we have still to find out. But it is already clear that where development of the new techniques has advanced most rapidly, human beings have been freed from the age-old round of the farmer's year. Instead of regulating our lives according to the seasonal necessities of planting and harvesting, industrialized societies have cut people loose from the soil and have enabled them to live under conditions very different from those their ancestors knew. The immensity of the change in the everyday experience of ordinary people has not been fully ex-plored even now, some 200 years after the critical breakthrough began.

## Invention of Steam Engines

Important improvements in spinning and weaving machinery had been made throughout the

**The Machine that Changed the World**   Here is a diagram of a 10-horsepower steam engine that James Watt patented. The machine looks flimsy today, and the gears and levers needed to convert vertical into rotary motion seem unnecessarily clumsy. But at the time, this engine constituted a new, flexible, and comparatively enormous source of power that could drive textile and other machinery tirelessly as long as coal was available to fire the boiler. Because production no longer depended on muscles or on variable wind and water, a vast expansion of output became possible, and the Industrial Revolution was underway.

M.ͬ WATT'S, PATENT ROTATIVE STEAM ENGINE
as constructed by Mess.ͬˢ Boulton & Watt, Soho, from 1787 to 1800.
10 Horse power.

Elevation

eighteenth century. But the fact that wool and linen production was firmly established as a cottage industry carried on in the homes of innumerable artisans—some of them part time—set limits upon the size such machines could attain. The first steam engine started operation in 1712. It was invented in England by Thomas Newcomen to pump water from a coal mine. Other engines were built for the same purpose in following years without making much difference to anyone.

But when James Watt (1736–1819) improved Newcomen's engine by making it unnecessary to cool the cylinder to make the steam condense, the consumption of coal became much less extravagant. When he further designed simple ways to convert the back-and-fourth motion of the piston in its cylinder into rotary motion that could be transmitted by gears or drive belts to other kinds of machines, the critical point in the Industrial Revolution had been achieved.

Watt took out his first patents in 1769, but his engines did not perform really well until decades of further work introduced further refinements to their design. In particular, when Watt tried to make large numbers of engines, he encountered new difficulties. The piston had to fit snugly into its cylinder or else too much steam escaped around the edges, wasting energy. Filing down a piston by hand to make it fit a cylinder exactly required skill and patience in extraordinary degree. No two cylinders were ever exactly alike; each fit had to be separately achieved. A few clumsy strokes of the file could spoil a piston entirely. This made large-scale production of steam engines impossible until 1797 when a skilled mechanic, Henry Maudslay, invented a lathe that could cut metal accurately within a thousandth of an inch.

The importance of this first "machine tool" can scarcely be exaggerated. It and others designed later for special purposes allowed skilled artisans to make parts for steam engines and other machines accurately. Eventually, instead of having to make each separate machine fit together by trial and error, standard parts could be assembled to make a standard machine that really worked. And even after temporary breakdown, standardized spare parts could be supplied, so that with relatively simple adjustments the whole machine would work again.

These things seem elementary to us, but it took time and skill to make such methods routine. For a long time, small adjustments with file and chisel had to be made by the skilled "engineer" who put the machine together or repaired it after breakdown. The first manufacturer who clearly worked out the theory of replaceable parts was Eli Whitney (1765–1825), an American; he was the inventor of the cotton gin and a manufacturer of muskets.

## Labor in the Machine Age

A second problem raised by the new machines was human rather than mechanical. When steam power was turned on in a new factory, all the machines started to move; but if their attendants were not on hand, something could go wrong and serious damage might occur. This called for mass punctuality. But weavers and spinners, accustomed to working in their own cottages on their own time and when they felt like it, could not easily get used to living by a clock. As a result, owners and managers used very high-handed methods to force their workers to submit to the routine requirements of the new machines. Women and children were easier to control and were often strong enough to tend the new machines; but the conditions under which they lived and worked, the brutality of the methods by which overseers forced them to be punctual and careful, and the long hours they were required to stay at their machines seem shocking today. Wages were low, barely above starvation levels. Workers' unions were illegal in Great Britain after 1799. In France the National Assembly had prohibited them, too, along with guilds and other combinations in restraint of trade.

The problems of factory life were multiplied by the rapid growth of industrial towns on or near coal fields. Housing was miserable and high-priced. Family life often broke up. Especially when the factory work force was wholly or mainly female, as was the case in many textile plants, men had no satisfying role to play in the family. They could not live on their wives' earnings and keep their self-respect. In addition, elementary city services—water supply, garbage removal, and schools—did not exist, and at first no one thought it necessary to provide them.

*Early Adjustments to Industrial Life*    But human inventiveness, so active in creating new machines, was not absent in the social field for long. Reformers began to demand legislation to protect the working people from oppressive hours and dangerous conditions in the new factories. In Great Britain the first such laws did not get through Parliament until 1833, and effective inspection and enforcement came even later. Organization of city services and local governments in the new industrial towns became systematic only after 1832. British workers could hardly afford to wait that long, since the great boom in textiles, coal, ironworks, and related industries started with the wars of the French Revolution (1792–1815). In Great Britain, therefore, two generations of industrialism passed before anything in the way of legislative regulation helped to improve human living conditions.

In the new factory and mining towns that began to deface the English countryside, the dreariness of working-class life was relieved in two meeting places: the church and the pub. In particular, thousands of Methodist chapels were built in raw industrial towns, where they offered evangelical religion and elementary experience in self-government to the new working class. A surprising number of later labor union leaders and labor politicians of Great Britain got their start as lay preachers in Methodist chapels, or were the sons of Methodist lay preachers. Pubs offered a different kind of assembly place, where alcohol helped to reconcile the laboring poor to their lot in life. In a later generation, labor unions and self-help societies such as the Rochdale Pioneers, from which the modern retail cooperative movement descends, also came into existence.

In Britain, therefore, the harshest impact of the new industrialism had become a thing of the past by 1850, through a combination of working-class self-help and regulation from Parliament. In other countries, adjustment was delayed. Without fail, the first stages of industrial development saw a widespread breakdown of older social networks, with correspondingly intense human distress. But as industrialism spread from Great Britain to the European continent, governmental and official regulation came faster and more sweepingly, leaving less to local makeshift and private initiative.

## The Napoleonic Wars and the British Economy

Britain prospered enormously during the French wars (1792–1815). Government need for uniforms put special demands upon the textile trades. As a result, mechanization spread from cotton mills, where it had started, to woolen mills. In the 1780s cotton mills—because they engaged in a new manufacture in England—did not displace artisans but opened new jobs for unskilled women and children. However, as soon as the extraordinary war demand ended, use of power machinery in woolen manufacture brought about the destruction of a great cottage industry in England. This involved much suffering on the part of poor weavers who could not compete with the price of mill-made cloth, but could not afford to pull up roots and leave their patch of land and little cottage either.

Military demand for guns and ships and all the equipment needed for land and naval forces had parallel consequences for the metal trades. New methods and larger-scale operations opened new uses for power-driven machinery. Mines went deeper, and more engines were needed for pumping. On every hand, fresh uses for steam power were found. The result was greater production and lower costs.

Sharp alternation between boom and bust hastened the transformation of the British economy. What made these alternations was the letting of massive government contracts for war supplies whenever the British government took on a new campaign or signed a treaty promising to supply the forces of one of their continental allies for war against the French. But whenever a campaign ended or an ally made peace with the ever-victorious French, such programs were canceled. Boom conditions then suddenly gave way to equally dramatic periods of depression. The effect of such conditions was to push and pull labor and resources into new industries and open the way for radically new techniques in periods of boom. Then in periods of depression, all the less efficient firms and old-fashioned methods had to be given up, since they could not compete with newer and more productive methods that had been pioneered in the boom times. The long-drawn-out Napoleonic wars therefore acted as both a whip and a carrot to reshape the British economy. It emerged in 1815 far more efficient than any other in the world.

*The Wars and the French Economy*    Until about 1780, France kept pace with Great Britain in the development of new industrial methods. War stimulated some branches of the French economy, too; but France lacked extensive coal fields and was therefore not in a good position to take advantage of steam power. Early steam engines were extremely wasteful of coal by comparison with those designed later. That made it much cheaper to bring labor and raw materials to the coal than to try to ship vast amounts of coal any distance from the place where it was mined. This handicapped the devel-

opment of French industry during and after the war years of 1792–1815.

In addition, the vast conscription of French manpower into the army and into government service drew human energy and inventiveness away from the grubby industrial process and into war and administration. Hundreds of thousands of Frenchmen spent the best years of their lives stationed in distant parts of Europe, either as garrison forces or simply marching to and fro. Many died, and those who lived did not learn the habits of the new industrialism or become interested in its skills and opportunities. In 1815, therefore, the demobilized French soldiers went back home to small farms, small towns, and an economy not nearly as much transformed by the war as Britain's.

*Other Parts of Europe*    Much the same was true of other parts of the European continent. The coal fields that run in a belt across Belgium, the Ruhr region of Germany, Saxony, and into Silesia, the Ukraine, and central Asia were a great treasure for the future; but until railroads

**Coal and Iron in the Industrial Revolution**    On the left, a painting of the pit-head of an English coal mine about 1820 shows the heavy and rather crude machinery for raising coal from below ground quite clearly; but the workings of the steam engine, fired by coal, that activated the ropes and pulleys remain unclear. The horses in the foreground show that animal power remained important long after steam engines began to change the industrial scene. On the right, the painting of a gun foundry illustrates one of the uses to which Europeans put their new technology. Iron had many uses, of course; but military requirements accelerated metallurgical development markedly in the early stages of the Industrial Revolution when the revolutionary wars (1792–1815) resulted in an urgent and enormously expanded demand for weapons.

opened up the continental interior, the cost of transporting bulky goods for more than a few miles overland made the industrial value of these coal fields almost nil. Coal fields and iron deposits, located on or near navigable water, were England's good fortune at a time when water transport was cheap and easy, and transport overland was still prohibitively expensive. In Belgium, however, where many of Napoleon's cannon had been forged, coal beds close to navigable rivers provided the basis for rapid development of industry on the British model after 1830.

## Postwar Industrial Progress

In the postwar period, to 1850, Britain kept the lead in industrial growth. The years 1815–1818 were difficult, for government spending decreased sharply and new markets were not immediately at hand to take up the slack. Overseas sales helped, for machine-made British goods were definitely less expensive and often of better quality than handmade products. As a result, the Indian cotton industry was almost wiped out by the competition of British-made cloth, carried halfway round the world. The trade of Latin America also fell largely into British hands. British arms and diplomacy sometimes helped trade, too, as we have seen in the case of China. And after prolonged diplomatic conversations, the Ottoman Empire, was opened freely to British goods in 1839, with the result that Ottoman artisans suddenly found themselves exposed to competition they could not meet.

The development of speedy, cheap mechanical transportation, in which the British pioneered, laid the groundwork for the later rise of Germany, the United States, and Russia to the first rank industrially. The key invention was the steam railroad. The first successful steam locomotive was built in 1804, but the first railroad was not built until 1825. Development was rapid

**The Impact of Railroads**   Beginning in the 1840s, railroads began to change the relation between town and country by cheapening transport and allowing peasants, like those shown in the painting on the left, to come to the city and return to their villages, all in a single day. The ancient gap between town and country, which had dominated all civilized history, began to narrow with this new mobility. Railroads also narrowed the gap between the European center of Western civilization and outlying lands like Russia and the United States. The construction of railroads cheapened and accelerated travel and transport across the vast continental interiors of Asia and North America and linked them with world markets as never before. The photograph on the right was taken in 1867 when the first transcontinental railroad in North America was still under construction. It shows passengers leaving the train and getting into stage coaches for the completion of their trip.

thereafter, and by the 1840s railroad building spread to the continent of Europe.

Railroads speeded overland transportation and lessened costs enormously. People and goods could move scores or hundreds of miles in a few hours. Iron ore and coal, even when separated by long distances, could be brought together to provide the basis for iron and steel production; and they, in turn, provided the fundamental material from which a larger and larger number of new machines were made. Railroads themselves became consumers of vast amounts of iron and steel. Bridges and steamships, storage tanks for the coal gas with which the cities were lighted, and literally thousands of other new uses for iron and steel developed, one after the other, between 1815 and 1850.

## Some Key Inventions and Breakthroughs

The extraordinary development of the iron industry that dominated the European industrial scene between the 1780s and 1850 required the use of the new fuel—coke—for smelting ore. Throughout the eighteenth century, Europe's iron and steel production had been limited by the scarcity of charcoal, which was the traditional fuel used for melting iron. How to make coke from coal became generally known in England after about 1750. The necessary fuel for the vast development of the iron industry thus became available.

As so often is the case with discoveries, the invention of coking involved useful by-products that changed European life in quite unforeseen ways. "Coal tars" left behind by the coking process provided important chemical raw materials for dyes, aspirin, and dozens of other products manufactured in the second half of the nineteenth century. Even before 1850, "coal gas"—produced by turning coal into coke—provided a cheap source of illumination for houses, streets, and public places of assembly. Inexpensive artificial light, in turn, opened all sorts of possibilities. Nineteenth-century theater and concert life, for example, would have been inconceivable without the utilization of artificial lighting for stage and concert hall.

Two other key inventions are worth mentioning here. In 1814 the first rotary press was installed in the printing office of the *London Times*. This made high-speed printing possible. Daily newspapers, reporting events within days or hours of their occurrence, linked government officials and other social leaders on the one hand and the reading public on the other. The flexibility and energy of nineteenth-century European society could not have been achieved without this sort of bond between the top and middle ranges of society.

A second key invention was the development in 1836 of a breech-loading handgun. The Prussian army was the first to adopt the new style of weapon. Superiority of the "needle gun," as it was called, was proven in 1866 when Prussian soldiers lay down on their bellies to fire at their Austrian foes, who had to stay on their feet to reload their muskets in the old fashion.

With this invention, therefore, the training of European armies had to be altered. Instead of standing close-massed in ranks, loading and firing on command, as had been necessary with muzzle-loading weapons, a far looser, open order became the key to success on the battlefield. New forms of discipline for the effective control of skirmish lines were called for, but it took European military experts a long time to adjust tactics to the requirements of breech-loading weapons.

Innumerable other inventions changed the character of human activity in less dramatic ways. The camera (1839), electric telegraph (1844), horse-drawn reaper (1834), screw propeller for ships (1836), revolver (1835–1836), bicycle (1839), and sewing machine (1846) are only a few of the new devices that were introduced or improved during these years. Invention became deliberate and expected. Ingenious inventors tinkered in their backyards or basements, hoping to make a fortune by some lucky patent. Few of them had much acquaintance with science or theory. Invention was still the province of the common-sense mechanic with a deft hand and three-dimensional imagination. Complicated mathematical calculations as well as academic physics and chemistry were largely irrelevant to the sorts of inventions that changed the texture of life in European cities between 1789 and 1850.

## Rural Conservatism

In the countryside the impact of the new inventions was delayed. Even after an American, Cyrus McCormick, invented the horse-drawn reaper in 1834, farming went on much as before. In Europe, particularly, farms were usually too small and peasants too poor and ignorant to take advantage of the reaper. Better transportation made it easier to get their produce to market, and growing city populations with ready money tended to push up farm prices in the more densely populated parts of Europe. More intensive cultivation, better seed, better tillage, and better rotations of crops all combined to increase Europe's food production sufficiently to keep pace with the rapid growth of its cities and population. Simplifying rights to particular parcels of land had been part of the legal reforms of the French Revolution, and this made agricultural progress much easier. Whenever the *Code Napoléon* applied, every particular piece of land was assigned to a single owner, and all overlapping and competing rights were abolished. In other words, the last remnant of manorial agriculture disappeared from western Europe; only in the Austrian and Russian empires did the older collective types of tillage survive until 1848 or even later.

Most Europeans remained on the land. Even in Britain, farming and occupations directly related to agriculture continued to engage a majority of the population until after 1850. This meant that European society as a whole could count on a generally stable and increasingly prosperous rural population. Farmers and peasants were, in general, willing to let city dwellers and their traditional superiors, the nobility or gentry, run political affairs, as long as the work on the land went on in familiar ways, and prices were not too bad.

Such basic stability, in turn, gave scope for city dwellers to push and pull against the conservative spirit of the landed element—lords and gentlemen, receivers of rents who were the tradi-

tional rulers of European society. In France, home of the Revolution, landed classes never recovered real political strength. Elsewhere in Europe, the balance varied with time and place; but in general it was the city people—rooted in industry, commerce, and the free professions—who advanced and the landed conservative classes who retreated.

## Cultural and Intellectual Developments

The upheavals of the Democratic and Industrial revolutions were mirrored by changes in prevailing intellectual and artistic tastes, often termed "romantic" as opposed to the ideals of the Enlightenment. But "romantic" has so many meanings that it does not do much to define innovations in European culture during the first part of the nineteenth century.

Romanticism in Germany, for example, was closely associated with the deliberate expression of intense, personal feelings together with a vigorous assertion of the value of the German language as against French, which had been fashionable in courtly circles before the French Revolution. Johann Gottfried Herder (1744–1803) argued that every language expressed a unique national spirit; and a cluster of writers, of whom Johann Wolfgang von Goethe (1749–1832) was the most famous, eagerly set out to explore the distinctive soul of their nation by using German for their poetry and prose. In Britain, too, romantic poets like William Wordsworth (1770–1850) and Robert Burns (1759–1796) deliberately used the simple language of the common people in order to express poignant personal emotions.

In music, the towering figure among romantic composers was Ludwig von Beethoven (1770–1827). Like the romantic poets, his music was deliberately more emotional than that of classical predecessors like Wolfgang Amadeus Mozart (1756–1791). On the other hand, the term "romantic" when applied to visual art seems mostly to mean an interest in portraying exotic places and circumstances. Architecturally, romanticism boiled down to the use of Gothic spires and arches for monumental purposes, as exemplified, for instance, in the Houses of Parliament in London (rebuilt 1840–1867).

Intellectually, two rather opposite innovations gathered headway in this period. On the one hand, a cluster of philosophers, of whom the German, Georg Wilhelm Friedrich Hegel (1770–1831), was the most influential, used reason to create a substitute for the Christian faith. Hegel argued that reality is in unending flux, moving in a "dialectical" pattern from thesis, to antithesis, and then to synthesis, which in turn becomes the thesis for the next stage in the unfolding of the Spirit that pervades the universe. Others preferred to reaffirm the truth of the Christian religion. Some, like the Frenchman, Réné du Chateaubriand (1768–1848), were inspired in large part by horror at the French Revolutionists' atheism. Others experienced personal conversions, which was the central aim and purpose of the Methodist churches and revival meetings that John Wesley (1703–1791) and his followers propagated very widely in Britain and the United States.

Hegelianism could appeal only to a small though influential number of intellectuals, whereas new ways of inviting personal, emotional encounters with God won far wider response and was undoubtedly more important. For example, the Russian Czar's sudden conversion to mystical Christian piety in 1815 realigned international politics in a conservative mould; but European society was stabilized far more powerfully as millions of common folk affirmed their Christian faith at a time when the Democratic and Industrial revolutions were putting unprecedented strain on their daily lives.

## Conclusion

Between 1775 and 1850, western Europe developed two new and strikingly successful sources of power. One was political: the closer alliance between government and people (at least, the upper and middle classes), pioneered in the United States (1776–1789) and carried triumphantly forward by the French (1789–1815). Even the defeat of Napoleon in 1815 did not reverse this Democratic Revolution—for Napoleon's enemies were able to defeat him only by taking their own public into partnership in some degree or other, and the restored French monarchy continued to try to find public support among the same groups that had been most important in supporting the revolutionary regime.

Western Europe's second major innovation was technical: the Industrial Revolution, pioneered mainly in Great Britain. Here the central fact was that inventors found ways to use inanimate sources of power—coal and steam primarily—to drive all sorts of new machines and perform other services for humankind's convenience. Cheaper, sometimes better, and far more abundant goods were the first result; radically changed living conditions for urban dwellers were a second, sometimes less pleasant, by-product of the new forms of industry.

Thus, the manufacture of more and cheaper goods plus a closer cooperation between political leaders and the public at large combined to produce far greater disposable power for those countries and peoples that were successful in making these twin transformations take root in their midst. Great Britain led the way, but Belgium, Germany, and the United States followed close behind. France lagged industrially, and so did all of Mediterranean and eastern Europe. Other parts of the world fell even further behind and, by 1850, found themselves entirely incapable of resisting the new kinds of power that western Europeans were able to bring to bear against them—commercially, diplomatically, and militarily.

Such an upsurge in Europe's power set the stage for the collapse of other civilizations' effective independence. Improved communication and transport laid the technical basis for closer and closer interaction of all parts of the world. After about 1850, the separateness that allowed Chinese, Japanese, Indian, and Moslem peoples—not to mention the inhabitants of Africa, Australia, and the Americas—to maintain their own distinct ways of life no longer existed. Such a change in human relationships marks the end of one historic era and the beginning of the global, cosmopolitan age, in which we ourselves are living. The inauguration of this new age was the most important historic achievement of Europe's Democratic and Industrial revolutions.

# Bibliography

So many important texts date back to this era that it is perhaps silly to try to pick any for mention here. All the same, carefully comparing the American *Declaration of Independence* (1776) with the French *Declaration of the Rights of Man and the Citizen* (1791) will be worth your while. Alexis de Tocqueville, *Democracy in America* (1835, and often reprinted), is also a thoughtful, familiar classic, worth looking at anew. For the Industrial Revolution in Britain, Robert Owen, *The Life of Robert Owen* (2 vols., 1857–1958, and often reprinted), provides a remarkably vivid insight, since Owen was in the forefront of what happened, first as a spectacularly successful factory manager and owner of cotton mills, and then as a socialist and reformer.

The classic work on the Democratic Revolution is Robert Palmer, *The Age of the Democratic Revolution: A Political History of Europe and America, 1760–1800* (2 vols., 1959–1964). For a survey of the subsequent political upheavals in Europe, Eric Hobsbawm, *The Age of Revolution, 1789–1848* (1962), provides a convenient overview.

For the American commencement of the Democratic Revolution, essays collected in Jack P. Greene, ed., *The American Revolution* (1987); Page Smith, *A New Age Now Begins: A People's History of the American Revolution (1976);* Bernard Bailyn, *The Ideological Origins of the American Revolution* (1967); and Don Higginbotham, *The War of American Independence* (1971); are good places to start.

For the French Revolution and its impact on Europe, Alexis de Tocqueville, *The Old Regime and the French Revolution* (trans. 1955), is a classic, first published in 1856, and still influential. For more recent scholarship, D. M. G. Sutherland, *France 1789–1815: Revolution and Counterrevolution* (1985), offers a general overview. Francois Furet and Nona Ozouf, eds., *A Critical Dictionary of the French Revolution* (1989), is a collection of essays, most of which are critical of older, especially Marxist, interpretations of the kind reflected in such works as Georges Lefebvre, *The French Revolution from 1793 to 1799* (1964); Albert Soboul, *The Parisian Sans-Culottes and the French*

*Revolution, 1793–94* (1964); and George Rudé, *The Crowd in the French Revolution* (1959). Louis Bergeron, *France under Napoleon* (1981); Peter Geyl, *Napoleon: For and Against* (1949); and David Chandler, *The Campaigns of Napoleon* (1966), deal with aspects of Napoleon's meteoric career. Gordon Wright, *France in Modern Times: From the Enlightenment to the Present* (4th ed., 1987), is a convenient guide to post-revolutionary France.

For Europe as a whole, Pricilla Robertson, *The Revolutions of 1848: A Social History* (1952), carries on with the history of liberal revolutionary movements; while Henry A. Kissinger, *A World Restored: Europe and Napoleon* (1964), is interesting both for what this book did for its author's career and for his sympathetic treatment of Metternich and other architects of the settlement of 1815.

Two standard authorities for the Industrial Revolution are David Landes, *The Unbound Prometheus: Technical Change and Industrial Development in Western Europe from 1750 to the Present* (1969), and Phyllis Dean, *The First Industrial Revolution* (1965). Two incisive, reflective, and readable discussions of what industrialism means for human affairs are E. L. Jones, *The European Miracle* (1981), and Ernest Gellner, *Plough, Sword and Book: The Structure of Human History* (1988). For a recent discussion of the Industrial Revolution in Britain, see Roderick Floud and Donald M. McCloskey, eds., *The Economic History of Britain Since 1700* (2nd ed., 2 vols., 1993); and for variety, a revisionist work that emphasizes the continuing primary of agriculture, see Patrick O'Brien and Caglar Keyder, *Economic Growth in Britain and France, 1780–1914: Two Paths to the Twentieth Century* (1978). Clive Trebilcock, *The Industrialization of the Continental Powers, 1780–1914* (1981), is a good place to start with the spread of industrialism to Europe.

For British political development, Eric J. Evan, *The Forging of the Modern State: Early Industrial Britain 1783–1870* (1983), and E. L. Woodward, *The Age of Reform, 1815–1870* (2nd ed., 1962), may be recommended. On social changes in Britain, E. P. Thompson, *The Making of the English Working Class* (new ed., 1968), is a classic. Ian R. Christie, *Stress and Stability in Late Eighteenth-Century Britain: Reflections on British Avoidance of Revolution* (1984), inquiries into the difference with the French experience, while C. A. Bayly, *Imperial Meridian: The British Empire and the World, 1780–1830* (1989), looks at the overseas dimension of British power in this era.

# Breakthroughs in the Use of Energy and Fuel

Muscles came first: arm, leg, and tongue. Then a few big animals were tamed, strong enough to carry heavy loads or pull great weights. The horse, ox, camel, and water buffalo were the most important of these power sources; and until 200 years ago they remained, with human muscles, the principal sources of power known to humans.

Yet from very early times people also tapped inanimate forms of power. Fire, for example, unlocked chemical energy—and from Paleolithic times, hunters used fire to warm themselves and to cook. Later civilized peoples made fire to bake pottery and smelt metals as well.

This was only the beginning. Wind, water, coal, electricity, and most recently nuclear energy have all been put to work for human purposes with consequences—good and bad, foreseen and unforeseen—that have entirely transformed our natural environment.

## NATURAL POWER OF WATER AND WIND

The Romans made the swift-flowing river Tiber grind grain into flour to feed the swollen populace of their city in the first century B.C.E. The principle was simple. A paddle wheel half in and half out of the river revolved as the flowing water pressed against each paddle.

Windmills worked on a similar principle but were invented later. The earliest known came from central Asia, where Buddhists used them to launch prayers to heaven. Later, windmills were put to more practical uses—for grinding grain, pumping water, and driving other machines.

### Highlights

Wind and watermills provided a new source of mechanical power that could be put to many uses.

Water Mill for Grinding Grain.

The great advantage was that, once a mill had been built, the power cost nothing and it could be put to work whenever the water flowed or the wind blew.

The main disadvantage was that, for many centuries, no one had a steady flow of grain to be ground or wood to sawed. The superior work capacity of water and wind was wasted.

Since it was expensive to build mills initially, they were not much used until the sixteenth and seventeenth centuries in Europe, when improvements in transportation did make it possible to keep water and windmills steadily at work.

## EXPLOSIVE POWER OF GUNPOWDER

Gunpowder is a chemical mixture that does not need to take oxygen from the air in order to "burn." When ignited, almost all of it turns into gas. The effect, in an enclosed chamber, is explosive.

The Chinese discovered how to make gunpowder about 1000. They used it first to blow up fortified gates by filling hollow chambers of bamboo with the explosive mixture and pushing them under the closed gates. Soon afterward the Chinese began experimenting with hollow metal pots, filled with gunpowder and open at one end, which they used as primitive guns.

Europeans started similar experiments in the fourteenth century, having learned about gunpowder from China via the Mongol Empire. By 1500, Europeans excelled in the manufacture of big guns, partly because they already had a highly developed metallurgy. Peaceful uses for explosives, as in mining, for instance, came later, mainly in the nineteenth and twentieth centuries.

### Highlights

Gunpowder altered warfare and government in far-reaching ways all over the world.

Big guns were expensive, and only a few rulers could pay for them. Those who did could knock down their rivals' castle walls. Large territorial states could be built with the help of big guns.

Handguns became important in warfare only in the seventeenth century. Infantry armed with guns overcame the age-old superiority of steppe cavalry. This allowed the Russian and Chinese empires, in the eighteenth century, to divide the steppelands of Eurasia between them.

## EXPANSIVE POWER OF STEAM

Modern steam engines let steam under pressure flow into a cylinder that is closed at one end by a close-fitting piston. Steam pressure then makes the piston move. There were different ways of bringing the piston back again. The earliest type of engine in common use allowed the steam to condense, so that atmospheric pressure pushed the piston back. James Watt in 1776 improved upon this method by using valves to let the steam both into and out of the cylinder. A heavy balance wheel carried the piston back, expelling the old steam and readying the cylinder for the next rush of high-pressure steam.

Such steam engines were soon put to work at many different tasks, like pumping, driving trains, and activating machinery in factories.

### Highlights

Steam engines could be set up where fuel was easily found.

Since coal fires were the easiest way to produce steam, available coal beds became the prime factor controlling the location of heavy industry after 1850, when the steam engine came into its own.

Because the steam engine was invented in Great Britain, the British achieved a head start over all other peoples in exploiting the potential of the new, cheap, and flexible source of power.

The many possibilities opened by the use of steam power between 1776 and 1850 made this the era of the Industrial Revolution in Britain and western Europe.

Steam Turbine.

## INSTANTANEOUS POWER OF ELECTRICITY

Lightning and static electricity awed and puzzled humankind from earliest times, but not until the nineteenth century did anyone begin to learn how to control the power of electrical currents. Electric motors on a toy scale were known as early as 1831, but it was the 1880s when engineers began to conceive of building large-scale dynamos to supply electric current to large numbers of customers.

Electric power was first used for interior lighting. But in the twentieth century innumerable uses for electricity in industry have been found, with the result that heavy cables have largely replaced steam engines as energy sources in modern factories.

### Highlights

Electricity as a source of power is clean, and it can be precisely controlled.

In time, electricity opened the possibility of modulating power at short intervals. This allowed refinements in manufacture otherwise unattainable.

In space, electrical power can reach down to the level of individual molecules and atoms by ionizing them. This opened the possibility for new kinds of processes, like silverplating.

Electrical power also allowed worldwide instantaneous communication, making precise information readily available to government, business, and other decision-makers.

## ENORMOUS POWER OF THE ATOM

All humanity's earlier adventures in harnessing diverse forms of energy have been dwarfed by the most recent breakthrough: the controlled release of nuclear energy. The first successful experiment took place in Chicago in 1942, and atomic energy was initially used for making the bombs dropped on Nagasaki and Hiroshima at the close of World War II. Peaceful uses of atomic energy include the

Water Power for Electricity.

Control Panel for a Nuclear Power Plant.

generation of electricity and underground blasting.

Atomic energy was developed by highly trained scientists acting on mathematical theory. Theory and practice had been closely linked in the development of electrical power too, but not as deliberately and consciously or on such a scale as in this case.

### Highlights

By converting matter itself into energy, atomic power offers an almost limitless supply of energy.

Yet drawbacks canceled gains, for safe disposal of radioactive wastes from atomic power plants is both difficult and expensive, and fear of accident soon aroused widespread distrust of the new energy source.

Moreover, military use of atomic energy has the potential for destroying all higher forms of life on earth.

## COSTS OF POWER OVER NATURE

Humanity's enormous triumphs in using power for its own purposes involve unexpected and unwished-for costs.

Rapid changes in machinery strained modern society by asking people to alter their habit too fast, and wholesale use of power for manufacturing products has upset the natural environment in ways we do not fully understand.

Still, some of the risks are clear. Carbon dioxide added to the atmosphere by burning coal and other fuels alters the way sunlight warms the earth. A "greenhouse effect" may melt glaciers, raise sea levels, and alter climates.

Toxic chemical wastes poison land, sea, and air, altering conditions of life for all kinds of organisms, from viruses and bacteria to large-bodied animals and humankind itself. No one knows what will happen to the earth's biosphere as a result of humanity's reckless exploitation of all the new forms of power.

# Epilogue: Part III
# The State of the World

## 1850

From the time when civilizations first began until 1850, the world had been big enough to find room for a dozen or more different civilizations, as well as for literally thousands of other societies. Patterns of communication and transportation set definite limits to the size of states. The Ottoman Empire, for example, could not grow beyond the radius of a three month's march from Istanbul for the simple reason that, if he had to march more than three months to reach the scene of combat, the sultan could not bring his armies into the field for long enough to win a decisive victory. Comparable limits existed for other empires in other parts of the world. The limits of political dominion were only outward signs of the limits to other forms of communication. Such limitations defined the circles within which people could interact continuously with one another and thus create and maintain a single civilization.

## Europe's Irresistible Inventions

By 1850, however, these old limits upon human interaction had been broken through. European inventions made worldwide interaction possible. After 1825, railroads opened up the possibility of penetrating continental interiors, making the most remote village no farther removed from the outside world than the nearest railroad station. The electric telegraph (invented 1835) opened still more amazing horizons, for all that was needed was to string wires across the lands and oceans of the world to create instantaneous communication around the entire globe. Steamships had a less revolutionary impact, for the oceans had already become highways for contact between the world's habitable coasts. Still, cheaper and faster ocean transport did make the worldwide net of communications and contacts so much the tighter.

In 1850 these new means of communication had been invented but had not yet been used outside of Europe and North America. Their global effect, therefore, lay still in the future. But Europeans clearly had both the will and the means to catch all the world in this new net of their devising. The Industrial Revolution had affected weapons, as well as transport and communications. The result was that European governments controlled ships, guns, and soldiers—all of which were far superior to the forces any other people in the world could put into the field.

As a result, armed resistance to Europeans had become all but impossible. The Chinese, to their surprise and dismay, discovered this fact in the Opium War of 1839–1842. The Turks learned that same lesson during the Napoleonic Wars, when French, British, and Russian forces took turns at being enemy or friend to the sultan but always enjoyed a clear upper hand when it came to military action. In India, British power was supreme by 1818. In central Asia, Russian advance was checked only by distances and the limited interest that the Russian czar felt in adding new deserts and barren steppelands to his domain. In the Americas European military superiority was apparent from the time that the conquistadors first set foot in the New World. And the same was true in Australia. Of the inhabited continents, sub-Saharan Africa alone remained safe from European penetration, but the disease barrier that had long protected Africa from outsiders was shattered in the 1850s when Europeans learned how to protect themselves from malaria and later from other mosquito-borne infections.

## Leading Role of Europe

Hence, after 1850 no part of the world could prevent Europeans from intruding if they wished to do so. Moreover, there was a second and no less powerful weapon in the European armory: cheap goods. With the help of machine production, it was possible for European factories to turn out a host of consumer goods—saws, hatchets, scythes, pocketknives, sewing machines, cooking pots, textiles, and hundreds of other items that were cheaper and better than anything which local artisans could produce by hand. European traders wished to sell such goods freely in order to get raw materials and other supplies they needed in return. Local peoples often welcomed the new goods. Local governments had little choice but to admit the Europeans. The futility of trying to prevent trade was sharply demonstrated by the Chinese defeat in the Opium War, and no other major civilized government ever again made the attempt.

But the availability of cheap machine-made goods, which could be supplied in almost any quantity if the demand were brisk enough, brought about a fundamental disruption of traditional society in all those parts of the world where artisan handicrafts had become important. Every civilized society, in other words, stood at Europe's mercy, for the disruption of handicrafts meant the breakdown of traditional city life, and cities were always and necessarily the centers of civilization.

The world had become one, in a way never known before. What happened in Peking, Delhi, Accra, or Istanbul depended on what was thought and done in London, Paris, New York, and Hamburg. The possibility of isolating one civilization from another had disappeared. All humankind had become part of a single, worldwide, interacting whole. Europeans played the lead role and, to begin with, enjoyed most of the advantages of this new world balance. The three major Asian civilizations suffered catastrophic breakdown, all at the same time and within a mere fifteen years, 1850–1865. During the same period, the less highly developed parts of the world felt the impact of European enterprise more forcibly than ever before; and disruption of tribal and other forms of local society became widespread, though not quite universal.

## World Cosmopolitanism

Europe and the Western world beyond Europe remained for a long time almost unaware of what was happening to the rest of humanity. From a Western point of view, it all looked like progress and the spread of Christian civilization, or the advance of science and technology. Inherited ways of thinking and doing, modified though they were by the Democratic and Industrial revolutions, provided a general framework for European life and thought that did not seem to need fundamental revision. How could it be otherwise when the world lay open to European curiosity and enterprise as never before, when everything seemed to work in Europe's favor, and when people of European culture could find nothing in the world that seemed equal, or nearly equal, to their own achievements?

Yet enough time has now passed since the end of the separateness of world civilization and cultures to make it plain that the worldwide interactions that started to take on such intimacy after 1850 were not entirely one-sided. World cosmopolitanism required Westerners to get used to living with people of backgrounds different from their own, just as much as it required the rest of humankind to get used to the Westerners.

After World War I ravaged Europe for four long years, 1914–1918, European civilization suffered a partial breakdown. Europeans, like Asians and Africans before them, began to feel that their traditional ways of life needed fundamental reorganization. But agreeing about what to do was impossible. The Communist Revolution in Russia offered one path; the United States of America affirmed another; and fascist revolutions in Italy and Germany proposed still

at third path toward the future. Fascism failed, but only after provoking World War II (1939–1945); communism collapsed in the former Soviet Union in 1991; but by that time the American combination of democratic government and a (more or less) free market faced a new challenge in the form of difficulty in keeping up with the economic performances of Japan and Germany, the latter situated in the center of an economically integrated western Europe. Mobilization of discontent among the poor of Latin America and Africa also presented a different sort of challenge to American world leadership. So did the problem of how the Russian lands would be reordered and how to deal with a still Communist China.

The last part of this book will explore the tumult of incipient world cosmopolitanism and the accelerating pace of interaction among all the peoples of the earth insofar as our present time and place allows. Getting things right becomes more and more difficult as we get nearer the present. Things that seem unimportant now may prove fundamental in time to come; and, conversely, matters that seem critical today may shrink to triviality after a few decades have passed. Human beings always face this sort of blindness, for we cannot know the future. All the same, trying to understand what is happening is the only guide we have to intelligent, effective action—public and private. Nothing is more important than doing it well, for our future success or failure hinges of what we know and believe and how wisely we act.

# *The Decisive Years*
## 1850 to 1865

# 21

**Ignorant Encounter**   Before the age of photography, artists portrayed newsworthy events by inventing appropriate scenes. This American example shows Commodore Perry coming ashore in Japan (1853) with gifts to sweeten his demand for treaty rights. Everything is wrong except the naval uniforms and American goods on display. The tent, telegraph wires, and wooden building are not Japanese, nor are the costumes correct. But of course Japanese ideas about Americans were just as inaccurate.

Interaction among the peoples of the world attained a new level of intensity between 1850 and 1865. During that short period of time, the impact of Europe's Industrial Revolution began to hit home in all parts of the globe. In particular, the great Asian civilizations found themselves unable to keep intrusive Europeans and/or Americans from doing more or less whatever they wanted to do, even on Chinese, Indian, Moslem, and (in much lesser degree) Japanese soil. This discredited old institutions, habits, and customs among more and more of the leaders of Asian opinion; but what to put in place of ancestral practices was difficult to agree upon. A time of troubles thus began, when almost everywhere outside the Western world people found themselves forced to experiment with new and unfamiliar ways of coping with daily emergencies. As a matter of fact, the world has not yet emerged from this time of troubles. We ought, therefore, to study the years 1850 to 1865 with particular attention if we want to understand how the world arrived at its present condition.

## The Breakdown of Traditional Social Order

The opening up of the world's oceans by European seafarers marked the start of modern times, not only for Europe but for all the world. The oceans ceased to be barriers to movement and became, instead, connecting links bringing individuals of diverse and different backgrounds into contact with one another on a scale and with a regularity that had never been possible before. Within thirty years after Columbus' first voyage in 1492, the main breakthroughs took place: Vasco da Gama's voyage around Africa in 1497 and Magellan's circumnavigation of the globe, 1519–1522.

Just as sharp a break came when new techniques of transportation and communication allowed Europeans to penetrate the continental interiors of the earth more or less at will, beginning about 1850. In the next fifteen years the traditional civilizations of Asia collapsed, in the

sense that their leaders no longer could follow customary ways, and were compelled more and more to react to European initiatives.

To be sure, western Europe was not particularly affected, at least to begin with. Europeans were merely pleased by the fact that their diplomats, armies, navies, missionaries, merchants, explorers, technicians, scientists, and settlers were able to break in upon almost every other human society on the face of the earth, without bothering about how their behavior might interfere with local customs or interests. This seemed to prove Europe's superiority beyond all doubt.

Indeed, by 1850 they were so sure of themselves that few Europeans really tried to understand the foreign peoples and different civilizations they met. In the 1700s, many Europeans were ready to admire the wisdom of Confucian sages, but the ways of the "heathen Chinese" struck their descendants of the 1800s as merely peculiar. Armed with such smugness, Europeans were not, therefore, particularly affected by the opening up of the continental interiors of the world, which took place during the fifteen years between 1850 and 1865.

In Great Britain, to be sure, the disruption of traditional rural life got seriously underway in the 1850s when cheap American grain started to arrive by railroad and steamer from across the Atlantic. But hard times in the countryside simply fed the booming cities with needed labor and sent a swarm of emigrants overseas to populate the colonies and dominions of the British Empire. Real disaster for villagers therefore looked like progress and expansion to the majority at home.

No such comforting thoughts cushioned the blows suffered by the rest of the world's peoples. Instead they found themselves plunged into a buzzing, blooming confusion when their forefathers' tried and true rules of conduct no longer produced expected and customary results. In the 1850s, therefore, traditional political, social, and economic patterns of life broke down in China, Japan, India, and the Ottoman Empire. These breakdowns were signaled and accelerated by the Opium War of 1839–1842 and two other wars: the Crimean War of 1853–1856 and the Indian Mutiny of 1857–1858.

In the next decade both Russia and the United States entered upon a particularly painful transformation. In Russia the abolition of serf-dom in 1861 gave legal expression to changes that ran from top to bottom of Russian society—changes that were triggered by the fact that Russia's Old Regime had failed in the Crimean War. In the United States the Civil War of 1861–1865 and the emancipation of the slaves in 1863 gave far more violent expression to the growing pains through which the American nation passed in these same years.

# Europe's Irresistible Impact

This widespread and sudden breakup of tradi-tional social orders had worldwide as well as lo-cal causes. For one thing, the impact of the In-dustrial Revolution (which had gotten underway one-half to three-quarters of a century earlier in Great Britain) began to be felt in the far parts of the world only after 1850. Being delayed, the impact, when it came, took a double form: one military, one economic. First of all, by 1850 Eu-ropean weapons and military organization had become overwhelmingly superior. Unprecedented mobility and firepower came easily to armies and navies equipped from Europe's new indus-trial workshops.

Secondly, after gunboats and marine landing parties had battered down political barriers, Eu-ropean merchants found themselves in a position to supply goods at lower prices, and often of bet-ter quality, than could be produced locally. A flow of such goods quickly changed consumers' tastes and ruined local artisans. With their ruin, the tra-ditional social structure of towns and cities was damaged beyond repair. This presented most of the world's peoples with a painful crisis. Societies and governments that lacked power machinery and factories had to find ways of creating them or else submit to foreign economic domination. The old routine of doing nothing in particular, and of paying no attention to what Europeans were up to, became quite impossible to follow when Eu-rope's guns, and the will to use them, opened the way for Europe's cheaply manufactured goods.

Industrialism was not the only factor caus-ing change, of course. Europeans were far better organized than were the other peoples of the world. Standing armies and navies, well-equipped and carefully trained, could operate thousands of miles from home and still get reinforcements, supplies, and strategic directives—if not always when most needed, at least eventually. As for trade, banks and other corporations coordinated the efforts of scores or of hundreds (and some-times of thousands) of individuals across as well as within national boundaries. As a result, com-mon purposes could be carried out anywhere in the world and across decades or even longer pe-riods of time. No other civilization could operate nearly so well at a distance.

In addition, Europeans were sure they were right: Adam Smith and others had proved that free trade was a good thing. If trade benefited Europeans more than others in the 1850s and 1860s, it merely proved how well thrift and a shrewd eye for business paid off. Moreover, the precious blessings of exposure to Christian civi-lization justified, in European eyes, the political subordination of peoples whose own past had kept them in heathen darkness.

A third aspect of Europe's moral armament for its great venture of smashing the idols long held dear by other peoples of the earth was the value Europeans placed upon heroic achieve-ment. Both as individuals and as representa-tives of the nation back home, Europeans valued deeds of daring and took risks most of us would shrink from. As in the days of the conquistadors, incredible expeditions carried tiny companies of adventurers into strange and hostile parts of the globe, blazing trails for the administrators who followed afterward. Nineteenth-century Euro-peans took their vision of heroism mainly from the Greek and Roman classics. Schoolboys read Plutarch, Livy, and Caesar and then tried to act on the model the ancient heroes offered them; and this was so whether the schoolboys pur-sued their activities in darkest Africa, in heathen Asia, or in desolate Australia—or whether, in-deed, they were merely chasing a fox across the hedgerows of England.

The combination of such traits made the mid-nineteenth-century Europeans literally irre-sistible. As Thucydides said of the ancient Athenians: "They were born into the world to take no rest themselves and to give none to others."

# Europe's Civilized Rivals

At the same time, we can point to special areas of weakness that afflicted China and Islam in particular. Both of these great civilizations had been psychologically on the defensive for centuries.

*China*     Ever since the Chinese had driven the Mongols out of their country (1368), the overriding aim of Chinese rulers and thinkers had been to keep themselves pure by preventing foreigners from again bringing in new and uncivilized habits. To be sure, the Manchu rulers were foreigners and the Chinese never quite forgave them for that. But at least the Manchus had the grace to accept Chinese civilization and tradition as fully and completely as any foreigners could. Foreigners who did not take the pains to meet the Chinese on their own terms by mastering the Confucian classics and the Chinese language were of no interest or concern to China's upper classes, except when they became unruly and had to be punished.

Such a policy worked very well indeed until about 1775, as we saw; it made China great and prosperous. But it had also allowed China to fall behind the European world in innumerable ways. Therefore, when military collision came, in the 1840s, Chinese minds and traditions were completely unprepared to face the crisis. Sticking to methods successful in the past seemed the only thing to do. It hurt dreadfully to acknowledge that foreigners had knowledge and skills that were actually superior to Chinese knowledge and skills. To admit such a thing was to admit that the whole policy of Confucian China had been a mistake. Indeed, the more obvious it became that something vital was lacking in traditional Chinese civilization, the more traitorous it became to say so in public—up to the time when it was too late to avoid being trodden upon by European intruders.

*Islam*     Islam had a similar though different history. The great divide, as far as Moslem skills and knowledge went, came about 1500. In 1499 the Safavid Shah Ismail challenged the prevailing compromises of Islamic society. But in the Ottoman Empire, where Islam's main contact points with Europe lay, this revolutionary religious movement was kept under control by administrative devices and military force. Debate was hushed up. Official Sunni Islam became dependent on the administrative structure of the Ottoman Empire. As a result, the official guardians of truth and knowledge could no longer afford to think freely and seriously for themselves. It seemed safer and better to memorize the Koran and ancient commentaries upon it.

But this intellectual attitude also required Moslems of the Ottoman Empire to turn their attention away from the new thoughts evident all over Christian Europe in the age of the Renaissance and the Reformation and to pay no attention to anything outside the official canon of Sunni Islam. Consequently, all the dazzling new ideas and techniques that grew up right next door were deliberately disregarded by Ottoman and the rest of Islamic society until, once again, it was too late to catch up and keep pace with the restless Europeans. Territorial retreat became necessary instead. Only complicated diplomacy prevented complete collapse. Time, the will, and the means to catch up with Europe were as utterly lacking in Islamic lands as in China.

*Japan and India*     Japan and the Hindu communities of India were in a less awkward position. The Hindus already had been overrun by Moslems. The religious ideas and caste organization of Hindu society made it easier for them to get used to having Europeans—in this case the British—ruling them and interfering in their economic and political affairs. One foreign master was much like another, after all; and if Europeans offered jobs in the government to clerks who could learn how to get along in an English-speaking world, there were plenty of bright and ambitious young men who were eager to qualify themselves as soon as suitable schools were set up after 1834.

Japan's case was almost the opposite. The Japanese had never been conquered. When Japan's rulers deliberately opened the country to contact with Europeans and Americans, they did so because they knew that their traditional military defenses against foreign attack could no longer keep the foreigners out. It seemed better, therefore, to learn the Westerners' secrets as quickly as possible. Only so could Japan be safe again from the danger of foreign conquest. After a shaky start, Japan's efforts along these lines proved remarkably successful. The nation was thus able to keep its traditional social structure and safeguard old values while working hard to modernize technology, the armed forces and government along Western lines.

Everywhere else in the non-Western world, among civilized and uncivilized peoples alike, the collision between Western ways and local traditions led to the disruption of old patterns of leadership. This was painful and confusing enough, but the difficulty grew greater as new ideas, new ideals, and new leaders struggled to cope with the ever-present white foreigners, who were always wanting something and would never take No for an answer. A century of paralysis, or near-paralysis, resulted. Moslems, Indians, and Chinese, not to mention the other less numerous and less mighty peoples of the earth, all found themselves helpless, unable to act together effectively toward clear and attainable goals. Anger and frustration were inevitable. Occasional outbreaks of violence gave vent to such feelings but led only to new defeats at European hands. Dismay, despair, and passive retreat while waiting out the storm were the inevitable results. No one, or almost no one, could act constructively amid the chaos created by the sudden collapse of traditional guidelines and landmarks in every walk of life.

Westerners, by contrast, had few or no hesitations before 1914. Some thinkers and artists did, indeed, foreshadow the collapse of Europe's New Regime—bourgeois, capitalist, parliamentary, reformist, progressive, and smug. But the great majority paid no attention. Westerners kept any doubts they may have had strictly to themselves when dealing with people who were less powerful than they were.

This extraordinary contrast dominated the history of the world from 1850 to about 1950. Then a new era set in. Western empires in Asia and Africa collapsed as local peoples reclaimed their independence, and Westerners' self-confidence suffered serious shock from the disasters of two world wars.

But for a century before 1950, our contemporary doubts about the uniqueness and superiority of Western civilization did not enter into the picture. Instead, triumphant Europeans asserted their power everywhere; and in a short fifteen years, between 1850 and 1865, old barriers to their supremacy everywhere crumbled.

## The Crimean War and Its Consequences

The Crimean War, 1853–1856, was one of the silliest wars ever fought; yet its consequences were extraordinarily important for Russia and for Europe as a whole, for the Ottoman Empire, and even for India. The struggle began with a quarrel between Roman Catholic and Orthodox Christian clergy over control of the holy places in Palestine. The Ottoman Turks were nominally in charge; but when the French backed the Roman Catholics and the Russians backed Orthodox claims, the sultan found himself in a delicate position. Turkish fear of the Russians was deep-seated. If the czar made good his claim to protect Orthodox interests in Palestine, the next step would be interference between the sultan and his Orthodox subjects in the Balkan Peninsula, where Serbs, Bulgars, and Greeks all belonged to the Orthodox Christian faith. English diplomats feared the same thing; and English journalists stirred up popular excitement in Great Britain by pointing with alarm to the consequences for the balance of power in Europe if the Russians should advance into the Balkans or, worse still, seize Istanbul and the Straits between the Black and the Aegean seas.

Hence, when Russian demands provoked the Turks to declare war on Russia, France and Britain came to the sultan's aid. Austria intervened by sending the Russians an ultimatum requiring them to withdraw from the provinces which later made up Romania or face the threat of Austrian attack. When the Russians did withdraw their troops from this territory, Austrian forces marched in. As a result, the Turks and Russians had no place to fight; and if British and French journalists had not been so blood-

# THE LADY WITH THE LAMP

When Florence Nightingale was seventeen years old, she heard a voice calling to her and believed that God had spoken. But for seven years she could not discover what she was called upon to do. Gradually, she decided that her mission in life was to nurse the sick; but her parents refused to permit her to do such a thing because at that time nursing was a very lowly occupation, and Florence Nightingale came from a wealthy English family.

But Miss Nightingale was nothing if not determined. She refused to marry and secretly read all she could about nursing and hospital administration. The more she read, the more she was sure that hospitals needed to be reformed, and that God had chosen her to accomplish the task. Eventually her parents gave way, and in 1851—when she was thirty-one years old—Florence Nightingale left home and went to Germany to get her first practical experience of nursing. The German hospital in which she worked was run by Protestant deaconesses, and it came nearer to her standards than any English hospital of the time.

On returning to England she began to set up a hospital, but she had scarcely started when the British government blundered into war against Russia, in the Crimea. Soon newspaper reports describing dreadful conditions in British military hospitals flooded into London. Officials of the government turned to Miss Nightingale and asked her to help. With thirty-eight nurses to assist her, in 1854 she sailed for the battle zone, and within a month had 5000 wounded and sick soldiers to look after.

To begin with, there were almost no medical supplies or facilities. But Florence Nightingale and her nurses set to work, cleaned things up, and did the best they could with what they had. They all put in long, hard hours; and Florence Nightingale worked harder than anyone else. Late at night, when her tasks for the day were done, she inspected each ward, carrying an oil lamp so as to be able to see. The sick and wounded soldiers soon nicknamed her "The Lady with the Lamp." She became a national heroine, universally admired and everywhere acclaimed.

Florence Nightingale used her position to demand, plead, and argue for a more adequate medical setup for the British army. Even after the close of the Crimean War, when she returned home and hid from her public admirers, Florence Nightingale continued to work from behind the scenes for much-needed reforms and improvements. Modern ideas about military hospitals and medical administration, as well as the modern profession of nursing, were created very largely through her work.

But after her hectic days in the Crimean War hospitals, she always remained out of the public eye—and most people assumed she had died. Actually, she worked at home with high officials of the British government until the 1870s. Thereafter she "retired" and spent much time in religious exercises. She lived until 1910, dying at the age of ninety. Having been idolized for two short years, during the Crimean War, Florence Nightingale remained mysterious, strong-willed, and independent all her life.

thirsty, the war might have ended before the French and British land forces even entered into action.

Instead, the French and British mounted an amphibious attack on the Crimea, hoping to eliminate the main Russian naval base at Sevastopol. A difficult campaign ensued, for both the Russian and the Allied forces had to operate at the end of very long supply lines. Supply and medical services were not set up to take full advantage of the new resources of science and industrial mass production; but the telegraph made it possible for journalists to send back daily new reports of everything that went wrong. Shortcomings revealed during the Crimean War made the British—and to a lesser degree the French also—realize the need for fundamental reorganization of their army supply systems and of their promotion policy for officers. Modern nursing started at this time, when Florence Nightingale organized emergency measures to help the British wounded. The French and British, who had been rivals ever since 1688, even became accustomed to cooperating with each other; they soon extended the practice to China, as we shall see. After a winter's siege, Sevastopol surrendered and peace followed. The Russians were humiliated but made peace anyway because, after Czar Nicholas died in 1855, his successor, Alexander II, felt that far-reaching internal reforms had to come first, before revenge would be practicable.

As far as Europe was concerned, the most important consequence of the Crimean War was the bitter feeling that arose between Austria and Russia. The conservative alliance that had keep Russia, Austria, and Prussia together since 1815 broke up completely. The Russians felt that their help in 1849, when a Russian army had invaded Hungary to put down rebels against the Hapsburg authority, had been repaid with the basest ingratitude. Instead of backing the status quo against any efforts toward change, as the Russians had done for forty years, the new czar was unwilling to raise a finger in their support when Prussia challenged the traditional Hapsburg leadership of central Europe. The result was the unification of Germany under Prussia between 1866 and 1871. Much of the world's history since then hinges upon Germans' efforts to make up for the lateness of their arrival upon the Euro-

pean scene as a united nation, but it seems best to postpone exploration of this by-product of the Crimean War until the next chapter.

Here we are concerned with the consequences of the Crimean War for Russia and the Ottoman Empire and with the echo that the Turks' victory over Russia had in India.

## Russian Reaction to Defeat

Russia's reaction to the defeats that the czar's armies suffered in the Crimea was confused and not very successful. The whole system of government had been built around the army, which had shown itself unable to defend Russian soil. Something was obviously wrong. Russia had again fallen behind the Western powers, and heroic efforts to catch up, as in the days of Peter the Great, seemed called for. But agreement on what had to be done and how to do it was never reached.

At first "liberals" had the upper hand in trying to meet the difficulty. The great problem, as they saw matters, was the absence of real freedom in Russia. What was needed was to unleash individual initiative by changing laws that made most Russians into serfs. Accordingly, in 1861 the government abolished serfdom and divided legal ownership of the land between landlords and their former serfs. Yet before the emancipation laws were put through, an opposite "Slavophile" point of view made itself heard at court. As a result, instead of assigning the land to individual ownership, as liberals would have done, the law assigned ownership of the serfs' fields to the village community as a whole. Provisions were made for periodic reassignment of fields among the villagers. This arrangement was customary in most of central Russia. The reform of 1861 gave it full legal force and thus set off Russian ways more sharply than ever from the patterns of land ownership current at that time in western Europe.

*Attempts at Social Reform*    This result was what Slavophiles wanted. Their idea was to preserve everything distinctively Russian. Some believed that in this way Russia could bypass the capitalist, individualist stage of society characteristic of nineteenth-century western Europe

**War in the Crimea and in India**   In the mid-nineteenth century, before photography had developed, artists recorded public events with drawings, which were then reproduced in books and magazines that reached the interested public soon after the events had occurred. Here are two such works of art. Above is an episode in the battle of Balaklava in 1854—a bungled maneuver made famous by Alfred Tennyson with his poem "The Charge of the Light Brigade." Below is a scene from India, showing the rebels scrambling for spoils while a battle against British is still in course. Neither of these representations is an accurate image of actual events. The artists were not eyewitnesses, and their purpose was to interpret what had happened for British readers safe at home. As a result, the image of war they conveyed was profoundly misleading. Old-fashioned cavalry dominate the pictures, but in fact it was rapid-firing handguns, heavy artillery, and trench warfare that controlled the battlefields of the Crimea during the war of 1854–1856. Sieges were also decisive in India, though the rebels' uncertain goals made their defeat comparatively easy once reinforcements from Great Britain arrived on the scene. Nevertheless, the survival of an outdated, heroic image of war among stay-at-homes was an important dimension of late nineteenth-century Europe. Images like these, showing victories over distant, alien foes, confirmed Europeans' sense of their superiority to everyone else and made it easy to mobilize support for continued imperial expansion in Asia, Africa, and Oceania.

and move directly into socialism—the social order of the future, according to their way of thinking. They argued that Russia might thus be able to leap ahead and, instead of being backward and despised, would find itself in the forefront of European social and historical development. Other Slavophiles feared and detested socialism and revolution; they believed in the past for its own sake and resisted every change, including the abolition of serfdom.

Both liberals and Slavophiles tended to extremes. They agreed that something fundamental was wrong with Russia but disagreed on practically everything else. In between was a body of officials and piecemeal reformers—practical administrators who worked within the limits of the possible. Their trouble was that the limits of the possible seemed uncomfortably narrow. Russia's poverty made any large-scale program for industrial development, or even for constructing an adequate railway network, prohibitively expensive. Tax income was not large enough to finance the necessary undertakings, and private enterprise and capital were not available. Moreover, fear that reform, if pressed too vigorously, might awaken the sleeping giant of the Russian peasantry and provoke some vast outburst of peasant discontent soon hampered reform, even when changes did not cost much money.

Half-measures and the endless delays of bureaucratic decision-making won no friends for the moderate middle road of gradual reform. Impatient young men began to gather in secret groups to talk of how Russia should be reborn. The spirit of revolution was fed by the fact that reform soon petered out. In 1864 the czar proclaimed a law setting up limited local self-government. Thereafter, the steam went out of the reform effort.

The basic fact was that the peasants were not satisfied with emancipation as handed down in 1861. They believed that the land was theirs by right. Some convinced themselves that wicked landlords had twisted the czar's intentions by keeping back part of the land. And while the peasant majority nursed its grievance, half in secret, the rest of the Russian society fell into hopeless disagreement. Fierce debate over whether Russia should imitate the Western nations or not, and how imitation

should be carried through if it should be tried at all, continued to distract Russian public policy until 1917.

In central Asia and the Far East, Russian armies were still able to advance and, in fact, annexed important new territories in the years 1850–1865. But at home everything was in confusion. Straightforward programs of economic development, aimed at catching up with the West, seemed impossible. Where would the money come from that was needed to build railroads, factories, mines, and steel mills on the scale that would be required to come abreast of Great Britain or France? But without such a program, really adequate defense against the Western powers was impossible, as had been shown in the Crimean War. On the other hand, the only justification for the czar's autocratic government was that compulsion and authority were needed to protect Russia from her enemies. If the czar's government could no longer perform that function, what claim had it to the obedience of the Russian people? After the scoffing irreligion of Peter the Great and Catherine II, it was hard to revive the theory of divine right; but the only alternative theory was popular sovereignty, which was too risky. The people, if consulted, would want to overthrow the landlords; but the czar's government was not ready, as it had been in the days of Ivan the Terrible and Peter the Great, to lead a revolution of that kind.

The effect of the Crimean War on Russia, therefore, was to open up a series of painful riddles. Cooperation between monarch and nobles, operating mainly by means of the military-civil bureaucracy, in which nobles occupied all important posts, had made Russia great in the eighteenth century. After the death of Catherine the Great (1796), however, this cooperation slowly wore itself out. For a while, the conservative policy of Alexander I (reigned 1801–1825) and Nicholas I (reigned 1825–1855) hid Russia's inner strains. But the failure of Russian arms in 1853–1856 discredited the czarist regime at home as well as abroad—without, however, provoking thoroughgoing breakdown, thoroughgoing reform, or thoroughgoing reaction. Instead a patchwork of half measures disfigured the Russian ship of state. Meanwhile, the western nations of Europe built up their power through the Industrial and Democratic revolutions, leaving

Russia to flounder, falling further and further behind.

# The Consequences of Ottoman Victory

The Ottoman sultan, though among the victors of the Crimean War, was no better off. The war left a Turkish debt, owed mostly to French and British bondholders. For a few years, the sultan's government met interest payments on the bonds by floating new loans; but when investors became more cautious, the cycle broke—and indignant creditors, with the help of their home governments, fastened a foreign-managed "Ottoman Public Debt Administration" upon the helpless Turks (1881). This administrative corporation had the right to collect specified taxes, mainly customs dues, to pay off the bondholders. It operated on Turkish soil without being subject to Turkish control. The victor of 1856, in other words, emerged from the war burdened with a foreign debt from which the Ottoman government was never afterward able to escape.

Special privileges for foreigners were nothing new in Turkey. Europeans resident in Turkey had enjoyed the right to be judged by their own law from 1569 when the Ottoman sultan first concluded treaties with Christian nations. The Turks took it for granted that foreigners, not being Moslems, could not be tried by Moslem courts. When the sultan was mighty and Christian traders existed on sufferance, the system worked well enough, from a Turkish point of view. When power relations were reversed, however, European consuls often gave protection to persons whose claim to be British or French subjects were very dubious. Shady characters sometimes escaped Turkish justice in this way. On the other hand, the unfairness of Turkish judges, especially when called upon to decide a quarrel between a Christian and a Moslem, gave European consuls grounds for extending their protection to persons who could not hope for a fair trial before a Turkish court.

*Moslem Reform*    The basic trouble with the Ottoman Empire was the lack of sympathy between Moslem rulers and Christian subjects. This, indeed, had been the real cause for the outbreak of the Crimean War. The Turks and their allies feared that if Russia were allowed to "protect" the interests of Orthodox Christians in the Ottoman Empire, before long the Russians would win over the loyalty of the Christians and be in a position to snuff out Turkish power in the Balkan peninsula.

The British ambassador to Turkey, Lord Stratford de Redcliffe, felt sure that energetic reform could cure this situation. If new laws were applied fairly to all the sultan's subjects—Moslem, Christian, or Jew—then the possibility of creating a stable, strong state would arise. Without reform, Lord Stratford felt, even the best efforts of the British government to prop up Turkish power would be in vain. The French and Austrian ambassadors agreed. Accordingly, just as the war was ending in 1856, the sultan proclaimed the equality of all his subjects before the law. Efforts to spell out this principle in detail continued for the next ten years. The European ambassadors and advisers wanted systematic codes of law. One by one, such codes were drawn up, usually modeled on the French *Code Napoléon*.

But the reform program did not work. The sultan's Christian subjects did not trust their Turkish masters. Secret revolutionary movements soon sprang up or took on new life. Prince Michael of Serbia (reigned 1860–1868), for example, plotted a general rising of all the Christian peoples against the Turks. The Turks for their part, felt that the only people who benefited from the reform were Christians and Jews. They found it difficult to give up the Sacred Law. After all, if Islam were the true religion—and who could doubt that and remain a Turk?—then the Sacred Law was in fact sacred, and no one had any right to annul its provisions. How, then, could the sultan take it upon himself to contradict the Koran and proclaim some newfangled nonsense about the equality of Jews and Christians? How indeed?

Nearly all Turks and other Moslems in the Ottoman Empire, therefore, tended to feel that the reform laws were mere window dressing. If the foreign ambassadors demanded such things, let them have them; but when it came to real,

**Ottoman Empire, 1865**

FRANCE · SWITZERLAND · AUSTRIA · HUNGARY · Vienna · Budapest · Danube R. · Dniester R. · Moldavia · RUSSIA · Caspian Sea · CORSICA · ITALIAN STATES · BOSNIA · SERBIA · ROMANIA · Walachia · BULGARIA · Dobrnia · CRIMEA · Sevastopol · Black Sea · ARMENIA · SARDINIA · MONTENEGRO · BALKAN PENINSULA · ALBANIA · Istanbul · BOSPORUS · Sea of Marara · PERSIA · SICILY · GREECE · Athens · ASIA MINOR · MESOPOTAMIA · Euphrates R. · Tigris R. · TUNISIA · CYPRUS · LEBANON · Mediterranean Sea · CRETE · PALESTINE · Jerusalem · SUEZ CANAL (Built 1859-1869) · ARABIA · LIBYA · EGYPT · Cairo · Nile R. · Red Sea

Semi-independent
Controlled from Istanbul

day-to-day personal relations, especially in the provinces, old habits persisted and the provisions of the new law codes were simply disregarded. This, of course, justified revolutionary conspiracy on the part of Christians; and the existence of such conspiracies, in turn, justified the Turks in disregarding the law.

*Ottoman Sovereignty*     Turkish efforts at reform were also damaged by the fact that the European powers continued to chip away at Ottoman frontiers. Romania became independent as a result of the diplomatic settlement of 1856. This was no great loss, since the provinces had been effectively freed from Turkish rule since 1828; but the Turks did not like giving up their claim to these rich territories. Turkish troops were pulled back from Serbia in 1867, after trou-

bles between the garrison of Belgrade and the Serbian populace provoked diplomatic intervention by the European powers. Turkish power over Lebanon was similarly hedged in with irritating restrictions after 1861.

On the other hand, the telegraph and, eventually, the railroad made it possible for the sultan to control what went on in remote provinces of his empire far more closely in the second half of the nineteenth century than had been possible before 1850. Hazy areas still existed in Albania, Armenia, Iraq, and Arabia, where tribal or other forms of traditional local government competed with the authority of the sultan's representatives. But even in the eastern portions of the empire—where tribalism was strongest—the authority of local chiefs tended to retreat into the desert regions, where nomadic life made any other kind of government impractical. This constituted a solid gain for the central government of the empire.

Some progress also was made toward modernization of the Ottoman army. Turkish troops, trained and equipped in the European fashion, had done well against the Russians in the Crimean War, and Turkish tradition made soldiering come easy. But the Ottoman government never even tried to build the industrial base needed to equip Turkish troops from home production. Instead, they relied on foreign-made equipment.

From 1839 on, the Ottoman government officially accepted the principles of free trade. This meant giving up any attempt to protect local artisans from the competition of European machine-made goods. As railroads were built inland, the disruption of artisan life, which resulted from this policy, moved inland, too. But no one in authority cared very much or even understood what was going on. Local resentments were fierce enough but usually found expression in rival nationalisms. Christian artisans, after all, suffered as well as Moslems. Each group blamed the other—and let it go at that.

In the aftermath of the Crimean War, therefore, the Ottoman Empire formally and publicly cut loose from the traditional Islamic ordering of society. Legal reform, along European lines, officially left the Sacred Law behind; but distrust among the different religious and national groups within the empire made the new laws unenforceable. The trouble was that laws imported wholesale from the West did not fit Ottoman society. Few Turks believed in the reform program, and Christians soon pinned their hopes on national independence.

The spread of nationalism was, of course, profoundly subversive of the Ottoman state, for the various nationalities that lived together under the sultan could not separate into independent nation-states without first destroying the empire. Yet this was what reform led to. How, then, would Turks and other Moslems support a program that asked them first to give up their religion and cultural identity, and then to watch their Christian subjects throw off Turkish control? But there seemed no alternative. The old traditions of Ottoman government

were dead and gone, and the heirs of that tradition could not come up with any practical line of action.

## Reforms in India

India, also, suffered drastic change between 1850 and 1865. The central event was what the British called the Sepoy Mutiny of 1857–1858. This was a rebellion of Indian soldiers, called sepoys, and it led to the destruction both of the Mogul Empire of Delhi and of the East India Company. The revolt, in turn, was touched off partly by news of Turkish (that is, Moslem) victories against Christians; but this was not the main cause.

The Indian soldiers, whom the East India Company hired to sustain its power in India, had many grievances. What started the mutiny was a rumor to the effect that a new drill routine would require the soldiers to violate religious taboos. To be exact, the British planned to pack powder charges for new muzzle-loading army muskets in little paper packets. In this way, an even amount of powder could be put in with each shot. To protect the powder from moisture, the paper was soaked with grease; and the Indian sepoys discovered—or assumed—that this was pig's fat, which was prohibited for Moslems, or else beef fat, which was prohibited for Hindus. The only way to open the packages was to bite off a corner, which, of course, meant ritual defilement.

This particular collision between new techniques and religious taboos was only one of many. British policy in India had changed. Before 1800 the East India Company went to great lengths to avoid offending local customs and respected all religious traditions. Christian missions, for example, had been forbidden, and the Mogul administrative language, Urdu, had been maintained even in provinces ruled directly by the Company. Once British military power in India became clearly superior to any rival (1818), the original grounds for this policy disappeared. Moreover, the Company came under attack at home for not admitting missionaries and for allowing various "wicked customs and heathen habits" to go on unchecked.

In 1837 it was decided to shift the language of administration from Urdu to English; but the change came slowly, since it required the establishment of schools to teach English to clerks and other subordinate officials of the government. However, by the late 1840s British power really began to bite into traditional Indian life. James Andrew Ramsay, Lord Dalhousie, governor general of India from 1848–1856, put the whole force of the East India Company's administration behind such improvements as building a rail and postal system, as well as the construction of telegraphic and road communications, irrigation projects, and similar public works. He also annexed important new territories, acting on the principle that when a ruling prince died without a direct heir, his territory ought to come under direct Company administration.

The Sepoy Mutiny of 1857 interrupted these enterprises, but only briefly. The soldiers acted in fear and anger. They knew vaguely what they were against: all the newfangled nonsense their British masters were bringing in so energetically. But they had no positive program, and the sharp differences between Moslems and Hindus failed to come into the open only because of their common enmity to the British.

For a few weeks the whole British position in India seemed threatened, for the Company had very few white troops under its command. Reinforcements soon arrived, however, and one by one the centers of resistance were reduced. Within two years, British power was fully restored. The British Parliament took the occasion to end the pretense of subordination to the Mogul emperor and abolished the East India Company as well. Instead, the government of India was entrusted to a viceroy appointed by, and responsible to, the British Cabinet in London.

The new regime plunged ahead with the task of remodeling Indian government and law. The overriding idea was to unite the country by a system of communications and administration and to station enough English troops in the land to make sure that any local disturbances—such as those that started the mutiny—could be snuffed out before the flame of rebellion spread. In addition, the British hoped and believed that

a just and fair administration, acting in accordance with published laws, would remove grievances and make the Indian people loyal and obedient subjects. In 1853, recruitment into the Indian Civil Service was put on the basis of competitive examination, with the result that graduates of Oxford and Cambridge, trained in the traditions of the English upper classes, began to staff the government of India. Legal reforms, separating administrative from judicial functions, followed. In 1861 legislative and executive councils were established in which British administrators and Indian subjects sat together to decide local problems of government.

In this way India came under the rule of a benevolent despotism, inspired by liberal principles. Those things that British custom assigned to the sphere of government were usually carried through with thoroughness, impartiality, and efficiency. Whatever belonged, by British practice, to the private sector was left strictly alone. The results were oddly lopsided. Efficient, limited government was superimposed upon age-old custom. Custom gave way where it had to, but elsewhere it remained little changed, since whatever was "private" in British eyes lay beyond the self-imposed limits of their jurisdiction. Private custom stood in the way of modern industrial development, for example. But because the government took British ideas of free trade and private business initiative for granted, public authorities did nothing to develop economic modernity.

Military security, however, was very much a part of the government's concern. In addition to making it routine to station significant numbers of British troops in the country, the government of India set out to erect a protective sphere of influence on every side of the subcontinent. The British occupied Aden, at the mouth of the Red Sea, in 1839; they intervened in Persia and Afghanistan to make sure that only rulers friendly to them should hold power there; they made similar arrangements in Zanzibar and Oman (1862). The situation in Egypt was more complicated, for there French influence competed, and sometimes cooperated, with the British. The great struggle was over whether or not to cut a canal through the Isthmus of Suez. In 1854 the ruler of Egypt agreed to let a French company build a canal, but the British opposed the scheme and managed to delay matters for several years. As a result, the Suez Canal was not opened for traffic until 1869. When the canal was completed, the British government bought the shares that had been assigned to the Egyptian government and thus secured an effective voice in the management of the canal company. With the opening of the Suez Canal the "life line of empire," connecting Great Britain with India, ran through the Mediterranean. In that sea, British naval power had to compete with French, Italian, and other navies; but farther south, beyond Suez, the shores of the Arabian Sea, the Persian Gulf, and the whole of the In-

dian Ocean were firmly under British-Indian management by 1865.

The new regime in India, together with British diplomatic activity in Arabia, Persia, and Afghanistan, reduced the eastern heartland of the Moslem world to nearly the same state of helpless dependency that afflicted the Ottoman Empire. By supplying a few guns, or refusing powder and shot to a stubborn sheik, the British could make and break dynasties and kingdoms along the shores of Arabia and the Persian Gulf. To the north lay Russia, whose appetite for Moslem territory was never in doubt. In 1849–1854, the czar's troops pushed back Persian frontiers, occupying the Syr Darya Valley. Then the outbreak of

**Opening of the Suez Canal, 1869**   The Suez Canal, built between 1859 and 1869, shortened the sea route from Europe to India by many thousands of miles and altered geopolitical relations by making the Middle East once again a crossroads for important traffic. This is an artist's drawing of the initial flotilla that started from the Mediterranean at Port Said in November 1869 and sailed southward to the Red Sea. The traditional clothing of the local inhabitants, who gathered on the bank to watch, contrasts with the new steam technology that propelled the larger ships shown here. To be sure, steamers were still in their infancy and needed sails as supplement since they could not carry enough coal for a long voyage. Hence tall masts still adorned these ships, though the plumes of smoke rising amidship attested the new power that had begun to transform sea transport, making it possible to carry larger cargoes more quickly, reliably, and cheaply than ever before. The Canal had a parallel impact, for it also made transport between Asia and Europe quicker, more reliable, and cheaper.

the Crimean War interrupted their advance. After the war, the Russians resumed expansion at the expense of the Kirghiz people, who lived as nomads on part of the central Asian steppe.

In such a situation, most Moslems despaired of public life and military-political action. Many concentrated instead on a more rigorous and exact performance of private religious observances. The central inspiration for this movement came from Arabia, where Abdul-Wahhab had founded a rigorist movement in the eighteenth century. At first, the Wahhabi reform was closely tied up with the military career of the Sa'ud family; but when Egyptian armies defeated the Sa'udis in 1818, Wahhabism began to spread more widely among Arabs and Indian Moslems.

Turks and Persians, on the other hand, were not much interested. The narrow emphasis upon Koranic lore could not appeal easily to these two peoples, whose native speech was not Arabic, and whose ancestors had brought the changes to Islam that the Wahhabi reformers set out to undo. Divided counsels therefore paralyzed action. For the world of Islam as a whole, the path toward a better future was not apparent.

# Collapse of the Far Eastern Citadels

Both the Manchu emperors of China and the Tokugawa shoguns of Japan found themselves in deep trouble in 1850. The key problems were internal. In China, the great mass of the peasantry had begun to stir. In Japan, it was the "outside lords" who were becoming restless. But in both cases, traditional methods of government seemed ineffective in meeting the new conditions. Dismay and uncertainty grew among the inner circle at court. No one knew what to do.

## China

China's case was by far the most critical. In 1842 the emperor had been forced to make terms with the British and to open key Chinese ports to European trade. Eight years later an obscure prophet, Hung Hsiu-ch'üan, announced the establishment of the "Heavenly Kingdom of Great Peace" in Taiping. Hung Hsiu-ch'üan had spent a short time in a Protestant missionary school; later he began to see visions, mixing old Chinese ideas with Christian teachings about the end of the world and the Second Coming of Christ.

In ordinary times the words of such a man as Hung Hsiu-ch'üan would not have attracted much attention, but in 1850 he was able to arouse smoldering discontents that had been accumulating for years. The Taiping movement was mainly a peasant revolt. Millions upon millions of poverty-stricken Chinese peasants responded to the promise of a heavenly kingdom, interpreting it to mean the end of rents and taxes. But, of course, it was impossible to create or maintain an army without some kind of tax income. Hence, when an army became necessary to hold off and then drive back Manchu forces, the Taiping movement came face to face with the crisis that always besets a successful peasant rebellion: how to organize a new government that can be strong enough to survive when the rebelling peasants want only to be left alone and not have to pay anything to anybody.

The Taiping leaders never solved this problem. Hung Hsiu-ch'ün himself was a seer of visions, not an administrator. Some of his followers proved to be good generals, but they never had a regularly organized administration to support them in the rear. Consequently, the Taiping armies had to live by plunder. This hurt their popularity with the peasants and eventually allowed the forces of the imperial court to win. For several years, however, when the vision of the Heavenly Kingdom of Great Peace was still fresh and bright, the weakness at the heart of the Taiping movement was not apparent. From their point of origin in the southern part of China, the Taiping forces moved northward, reached the Yangtze River, and in 1854 captured Shanghai. By then much of south China was in Taiping hands, and the peasants of the north were only waiting for their arrival to join in the revolt.

Moslems in the western provinces of China organized a revolt of their own; so did other minority groups. Banditry broke out in other provinces. Then, on top of these disasters, new

**European Trade in Canton, China**  This is a view of Canton harbor about the beginning of the nineteenth century, when it was the only Chinese port where European traders were allowed to come ashore. The artist was probably Chinese, but he suited his style to European taste, emphasizing the flags of six European nations and the separate shore establishments belonging to each, where exchanges actually occurred. The smaller boats in the harbor were designed for river and canal transport. The three bigger vessels in the foreground may be intended to portray European sea-going ships, but, if so, the artist did not know much about them, for European ships had multiple sails and yardarms on each mast. The double prows shown here also look completely unauthentic. Such discrepancies illustrate the gap that had opened between Chinese and European knowledge of one another in the decades before the Opium War (1830–1841) suddenly opened the country to European penetration.

quarrels with the British and the French led, in 1857, to hostilities and fresh humiliation for the Chinese armed forces. The Treaties of Tientsin (1858) restored peace briefly. But when the Chinese delayed making some of the concessions promised by those treaties, the French and British organized a military raid on Peking and in 1860 burned down the emperor's summer palace. Such an act confirmed Chinese detestation of the "south sea barbarians," but for the time being the imperial government had to give in on all points of dispute. New treaties admitted British, French, American, and Russian diplo-

mats, missionaries, traders, and adventurers to the capital and to any part of China they cared to visit.

During these same disastrous years, the Yellow River changed its course. Instead of flowing to the sea south of the Shantung Peninsula, as it had done for centuries, the river broke its banks and found a new course to the sea far to the north of its former channel. But before the river settled into its new banks, vast and destructive floods spread over the lower plain of the Yellow River. Millions of Chinese died as a result. Yet the floods helped to save the Manchu gov-

**China in the Era of the Taiping Rebellion, 1850–1864**

ernment. When the Taiping soldiers started north for Peking, still in the first flush of their early successes, and when the peasants everywhere were still ready to welcome them as liberators, the floods prevented their advance.

Thereafter, the Taiping cause began to suffer defeats. The framework of Manchu adminis-

tration had never broken down completely so the emperor was able to keep soldiers in the field, even if they were dispirited and inefficient fighters. Soon quarrels broke out in the ranks of the Taiping army. Hung-Hsiu-ch'üan expected miracles; none came. Instead, the imperial forces began to win victories until, by 1864, the Taiping

Rebellion was crushed. Hung Hsiu-ch'üan poisoned himself.

Millions upon millions of people died as a result of the disorders and natural disasters that descended upon China in these years. Yet, this calamity, by itself, made life a little easier for those who survived. There was more land to go around and innumerable old debts were washed away in the confusion. Thus the Chinese had a breathing space after 1865. Nevertheless, the government failed to use it effectively.

It is easy to understand why. The Taiping rebels had been put down by traditional measures. In the next few years, military operations against the Moslems and other unruly groups also proved successful. To be sure, the Westerners remained a thorn in China's side. Yet their impact was blunted by the poverty and disorder of the countryside, which interfered with trade and made missionaries' lives unsafe. Nearly all of China's rulers and learned men heartily disliked and despised the bad manners of the white barbarians from Europe and America. They hoped in time to be able to drive them away. In the meantime, the best thing to do was to neglect the intruders as much as possible.

This policy was foredoomed to failure, for China's weakness was too great. The traditional order that had achieved such brilliant heights a century before could not survive the combination of internal crisis and Western assault. The peasant problem had not been solved, only postponed; still less had the Western challenge been met. The old order, as in Moslem lands and in India, was in hopeless disrepair. Yet no one knew what to do; agreement on new courses of action could not be achieved; confusion and bafflement reigned, as in most of the other lands that were feeling the effect of Western superiority.

## Japan

Japan followed a very different course. A small, power-seeking clique of reformers set out to make Japan safe by making it strong. They soon realized that this required modern industry to supply an army and navy. But modern industry required new skills and knowledge, and these in turn required a new kind of school system and many other changes in traditional Japanese life. Yet, once launched on the path of radical change, the Japanese leaders never flinched from undertaking the next necessary step.

The first landmark of this extraordinary development came in 1854, when the shogun gave up the policy, in effect since 1638, of shutting Japan off from ordinary contact with the outside world. What triggered this decision was a U.S. naval mission sent to Japan under the command of Commodore Matthew C. Perry. When the American warships first appeared in 1853, they were rebuffed; but the next year, when Commodore Perry returned, the Japanese government meekly agreed to open two ports to foreign ships. In 1858 Japan agreed to a detailed commercial treaty with the United States, to which Holland, Russia, Britain, and France later adhered.

The shogun's weakness in knuckling under to the foreigners made a good rallying cry for patriotic warriors and clan leaders who were jealous of the position long held by the Tokugawa family. They focused their loyalty upon the person of the emperor. The ideas of Shinto, which had developed into an increasingly public religion, provided popular justification for the restoration of the emperor's powers. Behind the scenes, however, informal alliances and rivalries among the military clans stood at the center of politics.

The shogun's position was undermined by uncertainties about the right of succession, for direct heirs of the Tokugawa line had died out. The individuals who occupied the shogunate in its last years were weak and ineffective persons. In addition, they were by no means sure that the new policy of opening the country to foreign contacts was wise or safe. Consequently, they were divided and halfhearted while their rivals became more and more united around patriotic slogans—and the hidden figure of the emperor.

The upshot was a coup d'état in 1867. The shogun abdicated, and a new, young emperor officially took command of affairs. Members of the "outside clans" took over all the key positions around the emperor's person. Yet on their way to power, the new rulers of Japan had a sobering experience. In 1864 a combined British, French, Dutch, and American fleet bombarded

**The Wonders of the West as Seen from Japan**   Above a Japanese woodcut records the features of the paddle wheel steamer that carried Commodore Perry into Tokyo Bay in 1854, when he compelled the Shogun to sign a treaty opening Japan to foreign commerce. Inscriptions give further details: number of the crew, dimensions of the paddle wheel, information about the steam engine, and the like. Obviously the person who made this woodcut was fairly knowledgeable about the technology that supported American naval power and wished to communicate his information to others. A similar purpose pervades the woodcut to the left, which shows what the artist imagined things were like on the other side of the Pacific. He wanted his public to know that in America exotic architecture, exotic ladies, costumes, and a few other extraordinary things, like the American flag, provided a setting for such wonders as balloons that could carry people through the air and the great ships whose power had already impressed the Japanese so much.

and destroyed several Japanese coastal forts as a way of showing the displeasure of the Western powers at widespread antiforeign outbreaks in Japan. This demonstration of Western naval superiority convinced the men who took control in 1867 that anti-Western policies, without the power to defend the country, were not going to work. They therefore gave up their anti-Westernism, at least for the time being, in order to learn how to be strong.

Having once made this decision, there was no turning back and remarkably little hesitation. Whatever was needed for the creation of a strong, modern army and navy, they were determined to have. When it turned out that this meant an entirely new industrial technology with

drastic educational, social, and political reforms, the Japanese leaders never faltered. Peasants and commoners obeyed; the leaders commanded; and modern Japan began to emerge with amazing rapidity, within a single generation.

The Japanese were, of course, aware of China's difficulties when they made their fateful decision to open their country to Western contacts. The news also spread throughout Southeast Asia, where the British pushed into Burma and the French went into Annam, Laos, and Cambodia in the 1860s. When China trembled, these satellite states shook. Their rulers made little effort to resist the force of European arms. Siam remained independent, more as a buffer between French and British imperial spheres

**Siam's Tribute to the West**   Like Japan, the Kingdom of Siam was never conquered by Europeans, but in the 1860s, when Burma to the west had fallen to the British while on the east Cambodia and Laos were being subjugated by the French, the King of Siam appointed an Englishwoman as governess for his heir, who all too obviously needed to become familiar with the ways of the West. While still a minor, the young prince succeeded his father, becoming King Rama V (1868–1910) and eventually built himself the palace shown here. The King chose to erect an architectural hybrid that combined east and west by putting Buddhist spires on top of a wholly European facade. This matched his government, which erected a European facade featuring such novelties as a modern military establishment, telegraph, and railway, in order to defend his own sovereignty together with the other cultural traditions of the Thai people.

than because of any inherent strength that the ruling dynasty commanded. For another decade Korea, alone, remained an independent, hermit kingdom; but in 1876 that last, remote bastion of the Far Eastern circle of civilized communities also opened its ports to Western trade.

# Civil War in the United States

During the short period of time when these far-reaching changes were taking place in Asia, the United States of America came of age as a full-fledged participant in Western civilization. The national borders attained almost their present shape after a war with Mexico (1846) led to the annexation of California and Texas and territories in between. The Gadsden Purchase (1853–1854) added a strip of land in the extreme south of what is now New Mexico and Arizona, to facilitate construction of a transcontinental railroad. Then, in 1867 the federal government purchased Alaska from the Russians, thus attaining the country's present continental limits.

For a while it seemed uncertain whether a federal government would prove capable of holding such an enormous territory together. Loyalties to the separate states were strong; in the 1850s sectional loyalties began to create larger and scarcely less powerful political blocs. The issue that crystallized sectional feeling was slavery. In the Southern states, preservation of the "peculiar institution" of Negro slavery attracted fanatical support, partly, at least, because the Southerners were fearful of what would happen if the slaves were freed. Visions of economic disaster, if not of bloody revolution, haunted their dreams. In the Northern states, meanwhile, dislike of slavery increased. It seemed uncivilized, inhumane, and a disgrace to America. Fanatical abolitionists matched Southern fanaticism; compromise became more and more difficult.

In 1860 the Union fell apart. Abraham Lincoln was elected president but without an absolute majority. Moreover, his support was wholly in the North and West; the South feared and distrusted him as spokesman and leader of the new

**War in the United States** By the 1860s, photography became a practicable way to record events. As a result, a realistic image of the American Civil War entered the record in striking contrast to what patriotic artists had provided just a decade earlier. Here is a photograph of a wall and trench as it looked a few hours after Union forces had swarmed over it during the battle of Chancellorsville in 1863. Discarded weapons and Confederate dead dominate the scene, not men on horseback swinging sabres as before. Nonetheless, the long, drawn-out struggle of the Civil War did not convince military observers from Europe that the character of war had changed. They preferred to believe that Americans were merely amateur soldiers whose lack of professional skill prevented them from conducting quick, decisive campaigns like those that occurred in Europe during the wars of Italian and German unification between 1859 and 1871.

Republican Party. Southern states decided to withdraw and form their own confederacy, appealing to the same principles that had justified the American Revolution. But Lincoln and the North refused to admit that withdrawal was permissible. War ensued: long, bloody, and desperate. The war was popular in the sense that both governments commanded strong emotional support from the rear. In the end the North won because of superior numbers and superior industrial output; but until almost the very end, the Southern will to resist was never in doubt. Such tenacity raised difficult problems for a national government that professed to derive its just powers from consent of the governed.

At first, slavery was not officially the issue, but in 1863 Lincoln decided to publish an Emancipation Proclamation. Thereafter the advance of Union armies into Southern territory meant liberation of the slaves. Full citizen rights were conferred upon the liberated slaves by the Thirteenth, Fourteenth, and Fifteenth Amendments to the U.S. Constitution. These were adopted between 1865 and 1870; but in practice, systematic discrimination against the new black citizens continued to be a marked feature of American life.

The long years of civil war created a great demand for everything needed to equip huge armies. Rapid expansion of railroads also opened a vast new market for iron and steel. The result was a tremendous boom in the North that quickly made the United States an important industrial producer. American factory technology came abreast of the latest English and European practices, and in some fields, such as the mechanization of agriculture, the United States took the lead over the rest of the world. As a result, dramatic increases in the export of wheat became possible, even during the war years when large numbers of farm boys fought in the armies and had to be fed, without themselves helping to produce the crop.

Victory for the North, therefore, meant victory also for an expanding industry and for mechanized agriculture. Hoe cultivation and hand-picking lasted in the cotton fields of the defeated South for another eighty years or so, but it was precisely this sort of agriculture and the lifestyle built around it that had been defeated. The future of the United States would not rest with a sharply divided society, in which the forced labor of slaves maintained a few wealthy plantation owners. A much more varied and complex society prevailed, in which market prices and individual shrewdness—at least in theory—regulated personal status as well as the production and consumption of goods.

This new and growing American society differed in some respects from the pattern familiar across the Atlantic in England and western Europe. Aristocratic elements were almost absent from the American scene, and barriers to the rise of individuals from one social class to another were weaker than in Europe. Despite such differences, Americans shared the skills and ideas of western Europe, and the eastern seaboard of the northern United States had almost caught up with England and France by 1865. Moreover, the United States had begun to fill in its political frontiers by planting technically skilled communities all across the continent. The energies of the American people were engaged in this task throughout the next generation, when, except in the defeated South, both the work and the means to perform it stood ready at hand; and no really important doubts troubled the public mind.

America's success contrasted sharply with the doubts and difficulties that afflicted Russia, China, India, and the Moslem world. Yet it would be wrong to forget that the nation's success simply sidestepped the problems created by the South's defeat. That region of the United States took little part in the industrial upsurge. The South remained backward, poor, and ignorant—only a marginal sharer in the busy, greedy, restless, and increasingly urban world of the North, which had come into its own so suddenly during the Civil War years.

## The Rest of the World

Improved communication and transportation, which brought Western power to bear upon the Asian civilizations so dramatically between 1850 and 1865, also had important consequences elsewhere. For one thing, European governments organized expeditions to explore the parts of the earth still uncharted by European map makers; and many of the obstacles that had previously prevented Europeans from traveling in unknown lands were overcome by these new, systematic efforts.

Three regions of the earth remained to be explored by Europeans. Two of them, the Arctic and Antarctic, were frozen wastes; the other, tropical Africa, had always been protected by the prevalence of lethal diseases. In the 1840s two English expeditions penetrated Arctic and Antarctic waters. Between 1840 and 1843, Captain James Clark Ross got closer to the South

Pole than anyone before him. He skirted the shores of a considerable stretch of the Antarctic continent, discovering a mountainous coast, an enormous ice shelf, and the sea that bears his name. Then in 1845, Sir John Franklin set out to discover a "Northwest Passage" from the Atlantic to the Pacific across the seas and straits to the north of Canada, but his ship got caught in the ice and all the members of the expedition died. In the ensuing decade a series of relief expeditions were mounted to find out what had happened. Traces of Franklin's disaster were eventually found, and in course of the search most of the islands of the Canadian north were mapped for the first time. These efforts established both the reality and the impracticality of the Northwest Passage, which English explorers had dreamed of since the time of Columbus. The North and South poles remained out of reach until the twentieth century, when expeditions that traveled on foot reached first the North (1909) and then the South Pole (1911).

Learning how to travel safely in Africa was very different. In the 1840s, Europeans first began to secure a regular and dependable supply of quinine from Dutch plantations in Indonesia. This made it possible for them to travel in the interior of Africa with far greater chance of staying alive, since malaria ceased to be a serious threat. As a result, a series of explorers penetrated regions previously unknown to European map makers. The most famous was David Livingstone, a Scottish missionary who crossed Africa between 1853 and 1856, walking from the east coast to the west coast and back again and discovering Victoria Falls on the Zambesi River. He subsequently explored some of Africa's great lakes and died encamped on the shores of Lake Tanganyika in 1873. But the relation between the lakes and the sources of the Nile and Zaire (or Congo) rivers was not fully sorted out until an American, Henry Stanley, explored the upwaters of the Zaire between 1873 and 1877.

Exploration was, of course, only part of European expansion. In Australia and New Zealand, for example, British settlement advanced rapidly in the years 1850–1865, stimulated by gold rushes following the discovery of placer gold in Australia in 1851 and in New Zealand in 1861. In 1855, the British government abolished the last convict colony, setting up a series of self-governing colonies in Australia instead. (New Zealand became self-governing in 1846.) Sheep raising proved particularly successful in both lands; and even before gold was exhausted, commercial farming became the backbone of both the Australian and New Zealand economies.

British settlement provoked violent collisions with the native inhabitants, since the newcomers needed land for their sheep. The Maori inhabitants of New Zealand were sufficiently warlike to fight back. Although twice defeated (1843–1848 and 1860–1870), they won the respect of some British settlers, and in subsequent decades the Maoris secured full rights of citizenship and established a comparatively easy relationship with the whites. In Australia, on the contrary, the aborigines were unable to organize any effective resistance, and the gap between Stone Age hunters and gatherers, and the settlers proved to be quite unbridgeable. The fact that the Maoris were Polynesians, and impressed Europeans as being big handsome people, made the eventual reconciliation between the races easier, whereas the Australians were dark skinned, small of stature, and generally unattractive to Europeans. Race prejudice therefore sharpened the collision of interests and led the settlers to drive the aborigines away from all the best land in Australia, banishing survivors to the desert wastes in the center and north of the continent.

In Africa, race feeling also disfigured white–black encounters. Europeans had known and exploited black Africans as slaves for centuries, and the abolition of slavery in the nineteenth century did not change European attitudes toward blacks very noticeably. Within Africa itself, violent clashes concentrated in the south, where Boers, British, and black Africans fought one another in innumerable skirmishes and a few real battles. The upshot was the emergence of two Boer republics in the interior, and of two British self-governing colonies at the Cape of Good Hope and in Natal. The Boers made Africans work for them under conditions that approached old-fashioned slavery. In the English colonies a policy of protecting the blacks and (mostly mixed blood) descendants of the Khoikhoi (Hottentot) population prevailed, although full equality of legal rights was accorded only to a few of the mixed population known as "Cape Coloured."

Elsewhere in sub-Saharan Africa, local peoples and states continued much as before. The appearance of a handful of European explorers did not make any real difference at first, since it took a while before missionaries, traders, and soldiers followed in their tracks. European political and economic control of the continent may have been foreshadowed by the way explorers crisscrossed the interior, but the reality was delayed until the 1870s and 1880s.

## Latin America

In Latin America, the years 1850–1865 were not especially significant except in Mexico. In 1861 the Mexican government stopped payment of interest on government bonds. France, Spain, and Great Britain decided to intervene. The French sent enough troops to install a Hapsburg archduke, Maximilian, as emperor of Mexico in 1864. Mexican "liberals" resisted the French. Their main enemy had been the Church, whose lands they wished to confiscate. French intervention widened and deepened the conflict. For the first time, peasants of Indian descent began to take part in the resistance to Maximilian.

When the American Civil War ended in 1865, the United States government made clear that it regarded French interference in Mexico (or anywhere else in the New World) as an unfriendly act. As a result, the government in Paris decided to withdraw its troops from Mexico. Soon afterward, Maximilian was captured and killed (1867); and the liberals, led by Benito Juárez (d. 1872), himself a Zapotec Indian, came to power. The revolution did not go very far, although the Indian and mestizo majority asserted itself politically for the first time by challenging the dominance of a small upper class of purely Spanish descent.

## Conclusion

Although Latin America was not transformed between 1850 and 1865, and although these years were not particularly critical in western Europe, in most of the rest of the world the pe-

riod was crucial. The Moslem and Far Eastern worlds were shaken up badly. Russia and the United States reacted to Europe's Industrial and Democratic revolutions in sharply different fashions. Everywhere barriers to the advance of Westerners came tumbling down. As never before, world-girdling communications bound all people together into a single interacting whole. A new age of global cosmopolitanism, centered upon western Europe, leaped into being—full-grown and formidably armed. Humankind could never be the same, nor could Europe. We shall devote the next chapter to a closer look at what was going on in Europe, before turning back to study the world's reactions to European expansion in the period before World War I.

## Bibliography

Two brief books by Ivan Turgenev, *A Sportsman's Sketches* (1852) and *Fathers and Sons* (1862), are remarkably effective evocations of Russian life at the time of the Crimean War, when the Old Regime was about to collapse in that country. Alfred Lord Tennyson's well-known poem, "The Charge of the Light Brigade," can tell you something about the expansive, heroic style that was rife on the other side of that conflict. Stephen Crane, *The Red Badge of Courage* (1895), although written subsequently, is a powerful literary echo of the American Civil War. Mark Twain, *Life on the Mississippi* (1883), is comparable to Turgenev's portrait of the Russian countryside, harking back, as it does, to the decades before the Civil War. These all exist in many editions and are very much worth reading, for themselves and as historical documents.

On the Crimean War, Alan Palmer, *The Banner of Battle: The Story of the Crimean War* (1987), and John Shelton Curtiss, *Russia's Crimean War* (1979), tell what happened. For the war's consequences in Russia, W. Bruce Lincoln, *The Great Reforms: Autocracy, Bureaucracy and the Politics of Change in Imperial Russia* (1990) and Gerold T. Robinson, *Rural Russia under the Old Regime* (1932), are of special value. For the Ottoman upheaval that ensued, R. H. Davison, *Reform in the Ottoman Empire, 1856–1876* (1963), and Stanford J. Shaw and Ezel Kural Shaw, *History of the Ottoman Empire and Modern Turkey, Vol. II, Reform, Revolution and Republic: The Rise of Modern Turkey, 1808–1975* (1977), may be consulted. For echoes in India, see Thomas R. Metcalf, *The Aftermath of Revolt: India 1857–1870* (1964), and S. N. Sen, *Eighteen Fifty Seven* (1957), which is an account of what the British called the Sepoy Mutiny while Indians now regard it as a war for independence.

For changes in the Far East, in addition to books listed previously, the following are particularly useful: John K. Fairbank, *China: A New History* (1992); Immanuel C. Y. Hsu, *China's Entrance into the Family of Nations: The Diplomatic Phase, 1858–1880* (1960); Albert Feurwerker, *Rebellion in Nineteenth Century China* (1975); E. H. Norman, *Japan's Emergence as a Modern State* (1940); Thomas C. Smith, *Political Change and Industrial Development in Japan: Government Enterprise, 1868–1880* (1955); and Marius B. Jansen, ed., *Changing Japanese Attitudes towards Modernization* (1965).

For the American Civil War and its echoes in Canada and Mexico, see James M. McPherson, *Ordeal by Fire* (1982); James M. McPherson, *Battle Cry of Freedom* (1988); Kenneth M. Stampp, *The Peculiar Institution* (1956); Robin W. Winks, *Canada and the United States: The Civil War Years* (1960); Walker W. Scholes, *Mexican Politics during the Juarez Regime, 1855–1872* (1957).

# *Europe*
## 1850 to 1914

# 22

**Mastering Nature: The Eiffel Tower in Paris**   This soaring structure, almost a thousand feet tall, was erected in 1889 to commemorate the French Revolution. It remained the tallest man-made structure in the world until the 1930s, and it still expresses pride in the mastery of new engineering techniques that inspired the skillful bridge-builder, Gustav Eiffel (1832–1924), who designed it.

European political, economic, and cultural life in the second half of the nineteenth century and the first few years of the twentieth century was, for the most part, buoyantly self-confident. This was the great age of the European middle classes, who saw themselves and the rest of humankind becoming richer and wiser and, perhaps, even better as time went on. Not everyone believed in progress, but most Europeans who wrote and spoke about such matters took the idea pretty much for granted.

There were solid reasons for such confidence. New machines and new knowledge, especially in the physical sciences, came forward at an accelerating pace; and each new device or idea seemed clearly better than what it supplanted. Human life also became more comfortable, and health improved with the advance of medical skill. In politics, wider and wider circles of the population began to take part in elections and party organization. Education became more nearly universal. Riches increased, and even the poor and unskilled began to experience some benefits from Europe's advancing wealth.

To be sure, there was an underworld to all this progress. Women are legally subordinated to men in such matters as the right to hold property and to vote. Poor people were afraid of unemployment, and they suffered severely in time of illness. Labor in factories and mines was often dangerous and poorly paid. Strikes and the rise of socialist political parties expressed the discontent of industrial workers. Such problems were troublesome indeed for the European middle classes, but what toppled them from their privileged position as leaders of society was international instability. Each of the major European governments engaged in rivalries overseas, trying to build up its political and economic power in Asia, Africa, and other distant regions of the earth. Similar rivalries existed on European soil, too, dividing France from Germany, Russia from Austria, and lining up each Balkan nation against others in a tangle that puzzled and dismayed the diplomats of western Europe.

The upshot in 1914 was the sudden outbreak of World War I. The bloodshed lasted four long years, shattering Europe's smug sense of the superiority of its way of life.

## Political Changes

In the spring of 1848 a rash of liberal revolutions spread across Europe, starting from Paris and reaching all the way to Berlin and Vienna. Before the end of 1849 the hope of establishing constitutional governments in Europe had failed. In France, the Second Republic had come into existence when King Louis Philippe resigned; but in June 1848, bloody fighting broke out in the streets of Paris between the poor, who wanted improvements in their economic lot, and the regular army. After the "June Days" the French middle classes, as well as propertied peasants in the countryside, wanted a strong government. They therefore elected Louis Napoleon, the great Napoleon's nephew, first as president of the Republic (1848) and then in 1852 as emperor.

The failure of the 1848–1849 revolutions meant a split in the ranks of those who opposed the system of society and government that had emerged from the Congress of Vienna (1815). In continental Europe, middle-class liberals lost confidence. Kings, officials, and landlords continued to govern without paying much attention to middle-class demands for a voice in public affairs. Worse than that, in central Europe elected representatives had been unable to agree among themselves as to where national boundaries ought to run. Nasty quarrels between Germans and Czechs, Germans and Hungarians, Hungarians and Croats—to mention only the most bitter—made it clear that these nationalities would not willingly agree to work together peaceably. Who could really believe in the liberal ideal of popular self-government when representatives of the popular will had quarreled so bitterly?

A second fear eroded the liberal faith. Could the lower classes be trusted? Could workers, whose numbers grew rapidly with the onset of the Industrial Revolution, really have an

# Sentences Selected from the Communist Manifesto

In 1848, two young Germans, Karl Marx (1818–1883) and Friedrich Engels (1820–1895), published an eloquent summary of their ideas about how to transform existing society and inaugurate a just and equal Communist era. The text is far too long to reproduce here, and the argument is too tight to permit a single excerpt to represent the whole fairly. But by reproducing a series of sentences from the *Manifesto*, its scope, tone, and rhetorical force can be made apparent.

From Karl Marx and Friedrich Engels, *Manifesto of the Communist Party*

A spectre is haunting Europe—the spectre of communism.

It is high time, that Communists should openly, in the face of the whole world, publish their views, their aims, their tendencies and meet the nursery tale of the spectre of communism with a manifesto of the party itself.

The history of all hitherto existing society is the history of class struggles.

Our epoch, the epoch of the bourgeoisie, possesses however this distinctive feature: it has simplified the class antagonisms. Society as a whole is more and more splitting up into the great hostile camps, into two great classes directly facing each other—bourgeoisie and proletariat.

The proletarian is without property; his relation to his wife and children has no longer anything in common with the bourgeois family relations; modern industrial labor, modern subjection to capital, the same in England as in France, in America as in Germany, has stripped him of every trace of national character. Law, morality, religion, are to him so many bourgeois prejudices, behind which lurk in ambush just as many bourgeois interests.

The advance of industry, whose involuntary promoter is the bourgeoisie, replaces the isolation of laborers, due to competition, by their revolutionary combination, due to association. The development of modern industry, therefore, cuts from under its feet the very foundation on which the

---

equal share in self-government? Would they not try to seize the property of others and vote for socialist or communist agitators? Many business leaders and professionals concluded that revolution was dangerous and futile. Cooperation with nobles and monarchs and with the army and police seemed necessary to keep the lower classes quiet and in their place.

Some radicals stuck to the older faith in popular self-government and even welcomed the idea of expanding the ideal of equality to include economic equality. The most important spokesmen for this position were two young writers, Karl Marx (1818–1883) and Friedrich Engels

(1820–1895), who published a fiery little pamphlet in 1848—just before the revolutions began—entitled *Communist Manifesto*. It explained how all history had been a class struggle. First slaveholders, then feudal lords, and finally capitalists had dominated society by getting hold of the "means of production" (that is, first land and then, in more recent times, machinery and money). But, Marx declared, the capitalist system would bring about its own destruction by concentrating wealth in fewer and fewer hands, while making more and more workers propertyless.

Marx had in mind, in making this prediction, the fact that machine-made goods had bourgeoisie produces and appropriate products. What the bourgeoisie therefore produces, above all, are its own gravediggers. Its fall and the victory of the proletariat are equally inevitable.

The theory of the Communists may be summed up in a single sentence: Abolition of private property.

The working men have no country. . . . National differences and antagonism between peoples are daily more and more vanishing. . . . The supremacy of the proletariat will cause them to vanish still faster. . . . In proportion as the antagonism between classes within the nation vanishes, the hostility of one nation to another will come to an end.

The ruling ideas of each age have ever been the ideas of its ruling class.

We have seen above that the first step in the revolution by the working class is to raise the proletariat to the position of a ruling class to win the battle of democracy. The proletariat will use its political supremacy to wrest, by degrees, all capital from the bourgeoisie, to centralize all instruments of production in the hands of the state, i.e., of the proletariat organized as the ruling class; and to increase the total of productive forces as rapidly as possible.

When in the course of development, class distinctions have disappeared, and all production has been concentrated in the hands of a vast association of the whole nation, the public power will lose its political character. . . . In place of the old bourgeois society, with its classes and class antagonisms, we shall have an association in which the free development of each is the condition for the free development of all.

The Communists disdain to conceal their views and aims. They openly declare that their ends can be attained only by the forcible overthrow of all existing social conditions. Let the ruling classes tremble at a communist revolution. The proletarians have nothing to lose but their chains. They have a world to win. Working men of all countries, unite!

---

Reproduced from William H. McNeill and Schuyler O. Houser, *Readings in World History,* Vol. 10, pp. 191–215, in turn reproduced from *The Essential Left* (NY: Harper & Row/Barnes and Noble, 1961), pp. 14–36, 42–47.

been driving small artisans out of business all over Europe and in other parts of the world. Such people often did lose their property, tools, and shops and had to start working for wages. Many artisans resisted the process, hanging on grimly to the bitter end, in hopeless competition with machines. By assuming that the destruction of independent artisans would go on unchecked until a tiny number of great manufacturers controlled the whole industrial process, Marx envisioned a time when the propertyless proletariat, millions strong, would find it easy to seize the means of production from the capitalists. Such a revolutionary act, he

thought, would inaugurate the final communist stage of history, when the state would wither away and universal brotherhood, freedom, and equality would prevail.

Socialist ideals were not new in 1848. Radical advocates of equality had voiced their ideas in the days of the French Revolution, and social reformers had created a few experimental communities dedicated to sharing work and income equally among all members. But such efforts attracted little support, and Marx ridiculed them as utopian. He sought instead to organize followers into an international revolutionary association that would forward the day when property rights in the means of production would be overthrown, coercive government would wither away, and Communist ideals would prevail. As a result, from 1848 onwards the Democratic Revolution had a socialist as well as a liberal wing with sharply different ideas about how society should be reformed.

# Unification of Germany and Italy

Middle-class liberals who feared socialism found an alternative in nationalism. Marxists argued that workers had no real fatherland because they were without property. Patriotism was a trick property owners played on the poor, hiding their true interest: the international solidarity of the working class throughout the entire world. But in spite of Marxist arguments, most persons, including members of the industrial working class, proved more interested in identifying themselves with a great and powerful nation than with internationalism of any kind. The problem was especially acute in central Europe, where Germany and Italy remained divided into numerous separate states.

The diplomatic realignment of Europe brought about by the Crimean War (1853–1856) opened new possibilities. Moreover, leaders bold enough to take advantage of these possibilities arose in both Italy and Germany, so that by 1871 both these "geographical expressions" had become national states. Liberals supported the movement for the unification of Italy from the beginning. In Germany, they first opposed Otto von Bismarck's reliance upon "blood and iron" instead of elections as a way of settling matters. But when Bismarck turned out to be successful in defeating Austria (1866) and uniting north German states under Prussia, most of his liberal critics were silenced. He went on to pick a quarrel with France and after defeating Louis Napoleon (1870) persuaded the southern German states to join in a new German empire (1871), with Prussia's king as emperor. In the face of such a string of successes, liberal opposition to Bismarck's use of trickery and force evap-

orated. As "national liberals" they proved eager to cooperate with conservatives, such as Bismarck, to make a success of the new German empire.

Count Camillo Cavour (1810–1861) engineered the unification of Italy by using much the same methods that Bismarck used in Germany. The difference was that the kingdom of Sardinia, around which Italy united, was only a second-rate power and could not by itself hope to drive the Austrians out of Italy. Cavour, therefore, reached an agreement with Louis Napoleon of France, according to which the French agreed to help the Sardinians in war against Austria. Louis Napoleon wanted glory such as his uncle had won in Italy. He also wanted to upset the Vienna settlement—and believed that it was good politics to be on the side of the people, when possible. He furthermore made Cavour promise to give France two small bits of territory. Nice and Savoy, that would extend the French frontiers to the Alps.

Then Cavour picked a quarrel with Austria in 1859. The French came to his aid and defeated the Austrian armies in northern Italy but then tried to make peace before Italy's unification was complete. That did not satisfy Italian nationalists, who provoked popular uprisings all through central Italy. A dramatic expedition of volunteers known as the "Redshirts," led by Giuseppe Garibaldi against the kingdom of Naples, brought the south into the new kingdom of Italy.

In the northeast, Venetia remained under Austrian control until 1866, and the pope continued to rule Rome. But the pope's power depended on the fact that Napoleon III supported him against Italian nationalists by stationing French troops in Rome. These were hastily withdrawn when Napoleon blundered into war with Germany in 1870. The Italian government then marched in and made Rome the capital of united Italy. However, the pope refused to recognize its right to do so. Feuding between the papacy and the government of Italy continued until 1929, when a treaty gave full sovereign powers to the pope within the part of Rome where he lived (that is, the Vatican palace and some nearby areas). In return, the pope surren-

## Unification of Italy, 1859-1870

**Legend:**
- Kingdom of Sardinia before 1859
- To Kingdom of Sardinia
  - 1859
  - 1860
- To Kingdom of Italy
  - 1866
  - 1870
- "Claimed by Italy"
- ⊗ Battle sites

FRANCE — SWITZERLAND — AUSTRIA

SAVOY — LOMBARDY — Trent — VENETIA

Magenta — Milan — Custozza — Trieste
Novara ⊗ ⊗ Solferino — Verona
Turin — Po R. — Villafranca — Venice
To France 1860 — Genoa — PARMA — MODENA — Po R.
NICE — Bologna — ROMAGNA
Nice — Leghorn — Florence — "THE MARCHES"
TUSCANY

KINGDOM OF SARDINIA

CORSICA (French)

PAPAL — UMBRIA

Tiber R. — Rome — STATES

SARDINIA

DALMATIA

Adriatic Sea

Bari — APULIA
Naples — Taranto
KINGDOM

ALBANIA

OF THE

Tyrrhenian Sea

TWO

SICILIES — CALABRIA

Mediterranean Sea

Palermo — SICILY — Strait of Messina

Tunis

AFRICA

(Br.)
MALTA

0      100      200
Miles

Tripoli

## Unification of Germany, 1866–1871

**North Sea**

HELIGOLAND
(Br.)

Miles
0    50    100

**Baltic Sea**

SWEDEN

DENMARK

Königsberg

Danzig

Stettin

POMERANIA

BRANDENBURG

Berlin

P R U S S I A

Elbe R.

Vistula R.

RUSSIA

Posen

Oder R.

Oder R.

Breslau

SILESIA

Krakow

GALICIA

Lemberg

Sadowa

Elbe R.

Prague

AUSTRIA

Pilsen

SCHLESWIG

Kiel

HOLSTEIN

Lübeck

MECKLENBERG

Bremen

Weser R.

H A N O V E R

Hanover

OLDENBURG

NETHERLANDS

Münster

WESTPHALIA

Ruhr R.

Essen

Cologne

Rhine R.

WALDECK

Cassel

NASSAU

Ems

Coblenz

Moselle R.

Frankfurt

Darmstadt

HESSE

Leipzig

Dresden

SAXONY

THURINGIAN
STATES

Nuremburg

Main R.

B A V A R I A

Danube R.

Munich

Stuttgart

WÜRTTEMBURG

HOHENZOLLERN

B A D E N

SWITZERLAND

PALATINATE
(to Bavaria)

Metz

LORRAINE

Stras-
bourg

ALSACE

Sedan

LUXEM-
BOURG

BELGIUM

FRANCE

Prussia before 1866

Other states that joined Prussia to form North German Federation

States joining confederation to form German Empire

Territories annexed from France, 1871

Annexed by Prussia, 1866

Boundary of the German Empire, 1871

Boundary of North German Federation, 1866

⊗ Battle sites

dered the papacy's historic claim to sovereignty over the rest of Rome and the Papal States of central Italy.

# New International Alignments

Austria was the main loser in Italy and in Germany. And Austria lost largely because her old allies, Russia and Prussia, refused to continue to support the status quo in central Europe. Yet Bismarck was a thorough conservative in the sense that he believed in strong, authoritarian government, just as the Russian czar and the Hapsburg emperor did. As a result, when he had succeeded in creating the new German empire around the Prussian kingdom, Bismarck was eager to restore the conservative alliance with Austria and Russia that had kept Europe's boundaries stable between 1815 and 1859.

For a short period, the Hapsburg emperor, Franz Josef I (reigned 1848–1916), dreamed of revenge; but after the defeat of France in 1870–1871, he gave this up and, in 1879, agreed to an alliance with Germany. The major reason behind this move was that Austria suffered from internal frictions among the many different nationalities that made up the empire. In 1867 a constitutional settlement between the Hungarians and the rest of the empire sharpened the political appetites of Czechs and other Slavs who wanted similar privileges for themselves. But Austrian Germans and Hungarians were not willing to share their political privileges with Slavs. Resulting domestic confrontations meant that the Hapsburg monarch badly needed all the outside support he could get, and the German alliance of 1879 served this purpose admirably.

In 1882 Bismarck also brought Italy into the alliance, making it a Triple Alliance; and in 1887 he succeeded in making a secret treaty with Russia. Behind all of Bismarck's diplomatic activity after 1871 was his wish to keep France from being able to start a war of revenge with any prospect of success.

French pride had been deeply hurt by the German victory in 1870–1871. In addition, the Germans had taken the border provinces of Alsace and Lorraine from France and made them part of the new German empire; but despite the fact that many inhabitants of these provinces spoke German, the majority considered themselves to be French. French patriots, therefore, refused to forget the lost provinces. But as long as Bismarck was in charge of Germany's foreign policy, the French could find no allies and thus had to swallow their pride. Instead they concentrated on buildings an empire in Africa and Southeast Asia, an enterprise that kept them constantly at odds with British empire-builders, who were trying to do the same thing.

Bismarck left office in 1890 after a new emperor, Kaiser Wilhelm II (reigned 1888–1918), came to the German throne. Wilhelm had great ambitions for his country. By 1890 enormous economic success in building the world's most efficient industrial system had created a public that wanted to see Germany, too, start establishing an empire overseas. Naval officers argued that a powerful fleet was needed to defend German overseas commerce. Wilhelm agreed and thought that Germany should cut its ties with Russia and come to an understanding with the British instead. Accordingly, he dismissed Bismarck and set out to make Germany not just a European but a world power.

Wilhelm entirely failed to persuade the British to make a deal that would give Germany a share in world power. Instead, everything that Bismarck had most feared started to happen. First the French and Russians made an alliance (1893); then the French and British settled their colonial disputes (1904); and eventually the British and Russians did the same (1907). The result, therefore, was to align three great powers—France, Britain, and Russia—in a ring around the Triple Alliance of Germany, Austria, and Italy. Moreover, Italy gave clear signs, even before 1914, of not being reliable from a German point of view. The more Germany built up its navy and claimed the right to an equal voice in European councils about colonial matters, the firmer grew the hostile ring. The result was a series of diplomatic crises beginning in 1905 (first Moroccan crisis) and ending in 1914 with the crisis that triggered World War I. The alliance system worked in such a way that any quarrel anywhere in the world tended to line up the European great powers on opposite sides; and each time one or the other side backed down, it did so

**The Industrialization of War**  At the top, a scene
from the test firing ground that Alfred Krupp
established to demonstrate the capabilities of his guns.
Krupp was the first to discover how to cast steel so
perfectly that it became safe to use it for guns.

Krupp sold guns to armies, but for big guns his best
customers were navies, since armored ships could be
designed to carry very big guns indeed. The start of this
development is pictured in the center. There you see an
artist's rendition of the battle between the Merrimac
and the Monitor, which took place in 1862 off the
Virginia coast. This was the first time that ironclad
ships had fired in anger at each other, but the guns the
two vessels carried were too weak to do very serious
damage. What the ironclads did prove was that wooden
warships were helpless against them. Consequently, all
naval powers hastened to build warships—first of iron,
then of steel—and equipped them with bigger and
bigger guns to penetrate heavier and heavier armor.
The result by 1906 was *H. M. S. Dreadnought,* the
fastest, most heavily gunned warship of its time.

with the resolve not to do so next time. In 1914, therefore, the governments of Europe moved toward war as though hypnotized. Doing so, they plunged Europe and the world into a new and violent era, in which many of the familiar landmarks of Europe's past came tumbling down.

# Economy and Society

The central fact of Europe's history between 1850 and 1914 was the rise and progress of industry. Germany's great industrial boom left all other European nations behind. Russia, too, from about 1890 began to see the rise of large-scale modern industry, with consequences for the internal stability of the czar's government, which became critical in 1917. Everywhere cities grew in size, and rural life became less important; yet it is worth remembering that, in 1914, most Europeans still gained their living directly from farming. Among the great powers, only Great Britain had become a nation with more than half its population living in towns and cities away from the land.

## Conservative Social Forces

The agricultural elements of European society were basically conservative. Patterns of command and deference, as between upper and lower classes in European society, survived as strongly as they did because so many people either still lived in villages or had left them recently. The authority of landowner over farm workers, of the father over his children, and of men over women was an inheritance from rural custom and continued to define the daily conduct of most Europeans, even those who lived in great cities.

Religion was another important conservative force. Early in the nineteenth century, many persons reacted against the religious skepticism that had been so prominent among the leaders of the French Revolution. When liberal and nationalist movements came to the surface again, most churches opposed them. After some hesita-

tion, Pope Pius IX (1846–1878) repudiated all the new movements he saw rising around him in Europe. To get support for his views, he summoned the first Vatican Council (1869–1870). The Council obediently proclaimed the infallibility of the pope in matters of faith and morals at the very time that the papal government of Rome was being overthrown.

Papal policy presented the governments of western Europe with awkward problems. Bismarck tried to compel German Catholics to obey the laws of the new German empire instead of obeying the pope; this merely drove German Catholics into a single, opposition political party. Eventually Bismarck backed away from the fight because he felt that the socialist threat was even greater. In Britain, the Catholic issue took the form of the Irish question. Ireland was Catholic and oppressed, as well as poor; but Irish members of Parliament frequently held the balance of power between the Liberal and Conservative parties. In France the great issue was control of schools. This came to a crisis between 1901 and 1905 and ended in the legal separation of church and state and the suppression of most church-run schools.

Another problem that affected all European governments was created by the low cost of American grain. The price of grain became an acute issue about 1870 when railroad construction and the development of steamships made it possible for wheat from the American Middle West, or from the Argentine pampas, to be delivered to European ports at prices below European production costs. The British adhered to a free-trade policy and, as a result, nearly ruined British agriculture. Other European governments imposed special tariffs to protect peasants and landowners. This, of course, raised food prices for the cities and hurt the working class in the towns.

## New Problems of Industrialism

Problems of this kind were long familiar to European political leaders. Church and state, tariffs and taxes, had been at the heart of European politics for centuries. Problems raised by the galloping growth of industrialism, however, were far more difficult because they were so new. Everywhere, even in Russia, governments tried to win the support of the working class. By 1914 the idea that all adult males ought to have the right to vote in elections for some sort of representative assembly was accepted by all European governments, although in Germany and in Austria, as well as in Russia, such representative assemblies had only limited powers. In eastern Europe, emperors, their ministers, and other high officials kept ultimate decisions in their own hands, and neither trusted nor were trusted by ordinary workingmen. In western Europe, the gap between rulers and workers was almost as great, but political parties supported by working men's votes were powerful enough to influence official policies.

*Rise of Socialist Parties*      Karl Marx and other revolutionaries advocated one extreme solution to Europe's social problems. In 1864 they organized the International Workingmen's Association in order to spread the doctrines of the *Communist Manifesto* and prepare the way for socialist revolution. But before Marx attracted many followers, the revolutionaries quarreled bitterly among themselves.

Moreover, in 1871, the city of Paris went through another crisis. Many Parisians felt that the government, which had made peace with the Germans and given up Alsace and Lorraine, was full of traitors. The city had been besieged for several months and suffered accordingly. A coup d'état, followed by municipal elections, brought a revolutionary Paris Commune to power. Its leaders remembered the heroic days of 1793 when Paris had rallied all of France against foreign tyrants. They were eager to do the same again, but never had a chance. Instead, the French government sent in troops and suppressed the Commune, after bloody fighting. The end result was to discredit socialist plans for a popular rising to take power from the capitalists. The models offered by the French Revolution, when Paris crowds had been able to make and break governments, were becoming seriously out of date. As a result, the First International broke up in 1876.

Marx did not despair, however. Separate national parties, strongly under the influence of Marx's ideas, came into existence in most European countries during the 1860s and 1870s. The most important of these was the German Social Democratic party, organized in 1875. Bismarck responded by outlawing socialist agitation, and until 1890 the German party existed outside the law. In 1889 a Second International was founded to unite the socialists; but in spite of much talk about international solidarity, each national party went its own way in all essentials. By 1914, socialist parties had substantial representation in all of Europe's parliamentary assemblies. A French socialist had even cooperated with bourgeois politicians as a member of a short-lived government. A few socialists suggested that violent revolution might not be necessary. Reform might be able to win the rights workers were fighting for and introduce socialism gradually.

*Nonsocialist Initiatives*      From the other side of the political fence, conservatives, such as Bismarck, tried to blunt the effect of socialist propaganda by doing something about the grievances and hardships workers suffered. A series of social insurance laws resulted, whereby the state undertook to make payments to employees who fell ill or suffered disabling accidents. Such policies, combined with improvements in municipal services and the legalization of unions and of socialist parties, had the effect of reconciling many workers to their lot in life.

Great Britain followed a different path. Early experiments with socialist schemes for remaking the whole of society collapsed in the 1830s and left British workers deeply distrustful of what Karl Marx and his fellow revolutionaries were hoping to accomplish. Instead, beginning with the 1850s, labor unions arose, aimed only at improving working conditions through negotiation with employers or, if necessary, through strikes. The leaders of these unions, which to begin with were limited to skilled trades, avoided politics as a matter of principle. When the right to vote was extended to all adult males in 1884, miners and industrial workers supported Liberal party candidates for Parliament as a rule. Between 1900 and 1906, however, the unions changed policy and began to support a new Labour party; but unlike socialist parties on the continent, the Labour party paid little attention to Marxist ideas and always expected to carry out its program through parliamentary legislation, not through violent revolution.

Tensions between industrial workers and the rest of society were thus eased, though not erased, between the 1870s and 1914. Like the middle class before them, the working class had secured legal ways to make its interests heard, even in the highest quarters of government. During these years, socialism seemed well on its way to making the kind of elaborate compromises with older vested interests that revolutionary liberalism had made in the decades 1850–1870.

Where modern industry and the factory system had not taken root in Europe, other forms of violent revolution continued to find considerable support. Rapid population growth was making traditional rural life impossible for young people who could not inherit enough land to live even as poorly as their parents had done. In Italy, Spain, and Russia, anarchists captured most of the resulting anger and desperation.

**Bourgeois Europe at its High Noon**   This painting shows how prosperous Parisians took their ease on a Sunday afternoon in a park on an island in the Seine in the 1880s. It conveys the smug self-assurance of the age, when prosperous Europeans felt that all was well with a world in which such elegance, comfort, and leisure were attainable, if not by everyone, at least by a favored few who knew how to take advantage of business and professional opportunities.

The painting is interesting also for the way it exploited the latest scientific knowledge about light and visual perception for artistic purposes. The artist who made it, George Seurat, used tiny dots of contrasting colors throughout the painting, knowing that whoever looked at it would blend the separate dots into intelligible patterns, interpreting them as representations of human figures, trees, and all the rest. He believed that painting would become more entrancing just because observers had to take an active part in making sense of what they saw. Scientific discovery and technological improvements were very much part of the age. This painting therefore reflects that aspect of Europe's nineteenth-century achievement as well as portraying the serene self-confidence of the newly privileged bourgeoisie.

They advocated terrorist assassinations and carried through several successful attacks, beginning in the 1880s.

In the Balkans, however, rural frustration fueled rival nationalistic movements instead. After 1876, guerrilla bands began to roam the countryside, fighting one another, preying on the peasantry, and hoping to solve all problems by conquering new territory for their nation.

# New Forms of Industrial Organization

Adjustment to industrialism was not merely a matter of fitting the new working class into the preexisting structure of European society. New legal forms for business had to be invented. The limited liability company (or, as we call it in the United States, the corporation) met this need. Banking practices and the supply of capital were as critical as the supply of labor or of raw materials. Also, the boundaries separating private enterprise and profit from state operations and taxes had to be defined and constantly readjusted.

*British Laissez-Faire*    In general, British practice stood at one extreme. Until late in the nineteenth century the British government was reluctant to intervene in economic and social questions, and it lacked a large, well-trained bureaucracy like that which most continental European governments had inherited from the eighteenth century. Having allowed workers to develop unions, pubs, and chapels and having seen business leaders develop the corporation, free trade, and the gold standard for currency, British politicians felt, for the most part, that the economic machine should be left to run itself with minimal interference by government. This policy is called "laissez-faire"—a term borrowed from French economic theorists of the eighteenth century. The British economy did, indeed, run itself; but British manufacturers tended to fall behind what the Germans were able to do, partly, at least, because the Germans took it for granted that the forms of industrial organization that had worked so well between 1775 and 1850—and had given Britain the lead over all the world—could be improved upon.

*German Planning*    The Germans came late the industrial scene, for until railroads made low-cost overland haulage possible, German coal fields were of little value. But from about 1850, German industry grew rapidly, and by 1900 Germany had outstripped Great Britain in almost every branch of production. Three factors help to explain why Germany was so successful.

First, a few important German industrialists grasped the idea that theoretical science could help them in important ways. Beginning in the 1890s a few German corporations, mainly those working in chemicals and electricity, began to pay salaries to university-trained chemists and physicists whose only task was to discover new ways of doing things, or new products that could be manufactured and sold.

However familiar today, before 1914 this was a radical idea. Why pay good money to someone who, if successful, would outmode the machinery the company depended on for its profits? Why indeed? In earlier times, when an inventor hit upon some new method by tinkering in his attic or backyard, he secured a patent. This meant that no one else could use the invention without paying a fee. Then the inventor either sold the patent to someone else or went into business for himself, hoping to make as much money as possible from the invention. A successful effort to find a still better device would simply spoil the patent. From this point of view, it was absurd to hurry on the day when the company's patents might become valueless because of some new invention!

Yet the absurdity was amply justified by results. Just because they made old methods and machinery obsolete faster than anyone else, German electrical and chemical industries outstripped those of other countries before 1914. Their lead over other nations resulted directly from the use which German captains of industry made of the well-trained scientists and engineers produced by German schools and universities.

Secondly, German banks and businesses organized cartels on a scale unequaled elsewhere. A cartel is an agreement among producers of given commodities, coal for example, to divide the market among themselves and to sell at fixed prices. Such arrangements often led to increased profits; indeed, that was the aim. They also allowed managers to plan production schedules more exactly, and this sometimes evened out the "boom and bust" pattern that was so wasteful in British and American industry. Credit, also, was more highly centralized in Germany, so that financial as well as production planning operated with larger units and over longer time spans than was common in other countries. A firm could go deeper into debt and wait longer for returns on some new technique or product than was possible with the banking practices that prevailed in England. But, since some new technologies were very expensive and could not be tried except on a large scale, this meant that German financial arrangements and cartel organization could, if the managers so desired, take risks and introduce new things that small-scale businesses could not afford.

In the third place, the German government played a much more active role in economic policy than the British government did. Railroads were owned by the state, and freight rates could be adjusted to encourage or discourage any particular undertaking. The location of steel mills or of other important plants depended not only on geography but also on exactly how much it cost to haul a ton of ore or of coal from its place of origin to the place of manufacture. In setting up freight rates, military considerations were often taken into account. The German general staff cared where its ammunition came from and wanted to see a rail network that would permit troops to reach a threatened frontier faster than the enemy could bring up its forces. Thus the officials who managed the railroads and decided freight rates had a powerful tool at their command to affect the way German industry developed. They used this power to make Germany both prosperous and militarily strong.

*Industrialism Elsewhere*    Other European governments fell somewhere between the British and German extremes. No country relied as much on private initiative as did the British; none was nearly as successful as the Germans in manipulating and directing the growth of industry by governmental and quasi-governmental (bank and cartels) action. Southern Europe fell behind. Coal fields were lacking there, and until 1914 industry was based overwhelmingly on energy derived from coal. Water power and petroleum were only beginning to offer alternatives, and southern Europe was not particularly well endowed with either oil fields or waterfalls. Eastern Europe, being poorer agriculturally, had always lagged behind the western nations and continued to do so, despite the opening up of a few large mines and factories in Russia.

Underlying everything was a rapid expansion of population. During the nineteenth century, some 60 million people left Europe for America and elsewhere. In spite of this exodus, the population of the continent rose from about 187 million in 1800 to about 401 million in 1900. Factors that affect population are not fully understood, but it seems clear that one important cause for this extraordinary growth in numbers was the progress of medicine, which allowed doctors and public officials to take effective steps against diseases spread by contaminated drinking water. This check on the spread of disease allowed more babies to survive infancy; they grew up to have children of their own, thus setting off a population explosion of the sort that has become familiar, all around the globe, in our own time.

## Thought and Science

Europe's continued self-transformation under the twin impulses of the Industrial and Democratic revolutions in the years 1850–1914 must be counted as extraordinary. All the internal strains and struggles, one piled on top of the other, added up to progress in the eyes of nearly everyone who lived through them. A similar extraordinary achievement transformed science and the arts. There too, vigor and variety, in a reckless effort to expand the limits of the possible, were evident at every turn.

It seems useful to divide European thought and science in the period 1850–1914 into three schools: the "hard," the "soft," and the "crazy," or, in more formal language, the systematic, the evolutionary, and the irrational. The hard sciences were mathematics, physics, chemistry, astronomy and (more dubiously) economics. In each of these fields, the goal was to discover laws or patterns of behavior that were true everywhere and at all times. The fundamental point of view behind these efforts had been worked out in the 1600s by the great pioneers of modern science: Galileo, Descartes, Newton. Scientists in the later nineteenth century generalized the scientific laws they had inherited from their predecessors and found innumerable practical applications in industrial technology.

## The Systematic Sciences

On the theoretical side, mathematicians were able to do such surprising things as work out several non-Euclidean geometries and rules for converting one mathematical system into another. Chemists discovered how molecules and atoms could be combined and recombined according to more or less predictable patterns. Physicists were able to discern how mechanical motion, heat, light, and the entire spectrum of electromagnetic radiation were all forms of energy, and they worked out rules for converting one into the other. The key figure in this development was a Scotsman, James Clerk Maxwell (1831–1879), who first realized that light belonged in a much wider spectrum of electromagnetic radiation. No single chemist had quite the status of Maxwell among the physicists; but a Russian, Dmitri Mendeleev (1834–1907), first arranged the elements into a "periodic" table. This table showed gaps where hitherto unknown elements were needed to fill out Mendeleev's overall pattern. Later research discovered all of these missing elements. This confirmed in striking fashion the correctness of the pattern Mendeleev had first perceived.

Toward the end of the nineteenth century, both physicists and chemists had begun to zero in on the electron. At one and the same time, the electron was the smallest building block of matter (in which chemists were interested) and a particle that radiated energy (which physicists

found so fascinating). Puzzling problems multiplied. Electrons sometimes seemed to act like waves rather than like tiny billiard balls. Matter sometimes spontaneously emitted radiation. And radiation itself seemed sometimes to come in quanta, or bundles.

*The Theory of Relativity*   From a quite different angle of approach, astronomers also had turned up unexpected data. The planet Mercury seemed not to obey Newton's laws of motion perfectly. Most puzzling of all, light sent out from the moving platform of the earth seemed to travel at exactly the same speed, no matter what direction it followed. This contradicted common sense, as well as Newton's laws of motion, since in some directions the earth's motion should have added to the speed of light launched from its surface, and in other directions should have reduced the speed with which the same light traveled through space. Yet nothing of the sort could be detected, even with extremely sensitive instruments.

In 1905, a German Swiss, Albert Einstein, (1879–1955), proposed a special theory of relativity to explain some of these puzzles. Eleven years later he followed his first suggestion with a more general theory, and gave the fullest explanation of his ideas in a book published in 1929. Einstein took the four basic terms of Newtonian physics—space, time, matter, and energy—and suggested that they were not fixed, firm, and separate frames within which all natural objects existed, but, instead, interacted. It followed that measurements of space, time, and motion were relative to one another and that matter might be converted into energy, and vice versa, according to a simple mathematical formula, $E = mc^2$; that is, energy equals mass times the speed of light squared. Thus, at the very end of the period with which we are here concerned, Einstein arrived at the greatest generalization of all by giving a new definition to the basic terms of the physical sciences.

*Economic Theory*   Economics aspired to become a hard science, despite having to do with unpredictable human beings, because economists kept on trying to find universal laws that would explain, impersonally, how markets worked. They even hoped to learn how to predict what would happen, in the way that physicists, chemists, and astronomers were able to do. In this they were faithful to Adam Smith's habit of mind. In limited degree, they were successful in much the same way that the other hard sciences were successful. This is to say, succeeding theorists were able to bring more and more kinds of data into their system. A grand synthesis was achieved in the 1880s by an Englishman, Alfred Marshall (1842–1924), who introduced the concept of marginal utility as a master key to analyze fluctuations in prices, interest rates, wages, and rents. But Marshall's system, impressive and closely reasoned though it was, never explained adequately the boom and bust pattern of the business cycle.

The prestige of the hard sciences was reinforced by their practical applications. Chemistry, in particular, allowed the creation of new industries and new products, such as dyes, drugs, electroplated metal, and many more. Incandescent electric lights, invented in 1879 by the American Thomas A. Edison (1847–1931), began to replace gaslights in homes and offices; other electrical inventions, such as the phonograph and the telephone, followed one after the other. Yet, as we have already seen, it was not until the end of the period, and then only in a limited way—mainly in Germany—that scientific theory and technical processes of manufacturing were systematically brought together. The potentialities of this combination had only begun to dawn on the world by 1914.

## The Soft Sciences

By comparison, the soft sciences seemed impractical, since they had no distinct applications in industry, even though new ideas about the human past, present, and future certainly did change behavior and in this way altered the conditions of European life almost as much as the technical changes for which the hard sciences were responsible.

The basic philosophical approach common to the soft sciences was newer than the effort to discover mathematical, timeless, and universal laws that characterized the hard sciences. The soft sciences all emphasized change through time, but not until after 1800 did anyone try to work out the full implications of a world of ceaseless and universal change. More than any other single man, the German philosopher Georg Wilhelm Friedrich Hegel (1770–1831) was responsible for developing such a vision of reality. According to Hegel, everything changes always, doing so by a series of reversals or movements from one extreme to another. To use his own terms—a thesis confronts its antithesis and in time both are absorbed into a synthesis, which in turn becomes a thesis for the continuing unfolding of reality.

*The Theory of Evolution*    The concept of development through time particularly fitted biological and human affairs. Early in the nineteenth century, geologists discovered numerous fossils of plants and animals different from living forms. Studies of the distribution of different species of plants and animals also showed a pattern of resemblances and differences that made traditional ideas of the separate creation of each species difficult to believe. Charles Darwin (1809–1882) put these observations together to develop the idea of organic evolution. In his great book, *On the Origin of Species* (1859), he argued that since many more living creatures are launched upon life than ever survive to adulthood, there is a struggle for survival that goes on constantly. In such a struggle, some variations help the organism to survive. These survivors tend to spread because more such individuals grow up to reproduce their kind. In different environments different features help survival, so that in time such differences may become great enough to make what had been a single species separate into two or more different species.

Darwin's theory aroused angry debate because of its implications for religion. Some Protestants argued that belief in the literal truth of the account of creation in the Book of Genesis was fundamental to Christianity, since if the Bible could err in one passage, how could one believe it at all? The debate was complicated by the fact that scholars in Germany had already begun to subject the text of the Bible to critical methods that had been developed, ever since the

**Four Shapers of Modern Thought**   The men shown here changed prevailing ideas about the world and human life in different but complementary ways between 1859, when Charles Darwin (above left) revolutionized biology with his theory of evolution and 1916, and Albert Einstein (above right) revolutionized physics with his general theory of relativity. Between those two dates, Karl Marx (below left) published *Capital* in 1867, arguing the inevitability of proletarian revolution that would restore long-lost equality and freedom to human societies and, beginning in 1895, Sigmund Freud (below right) probed the subconscious levels of human minds and made older confidence in the power of reason seem naive. What emerged from the writings of these men (supplemented by the work of innumerable others) was an evolving universe in which physical and biological realities change with time and place.

Renaissance, for the study of ancient manuscripts. By treating the Bible as the work of human beings, such scholars had begun to unravel the various strands from which the biblical text had been put together long ago. But that sort of study, too, seemed to call the truth of Christian doctrine into question.

Some persons responded by arguing that religious truth, like everything else, develops and changes through time. Truths and insights valuable for one generation might cease to have the same meaning or importance for later generations. God's revelation, according to such ideas, could be a progressive and gradual process, even including the most recent and shocking discoveries of a scientist such as Darwin, or a philosopher such as Hegel. "Modernist" doctrines of this sort were emphatically repudiated by the Roman Catholic church at the first Vatican Council of 1870. Protestant churches divided, some pinning their faith on the literal truth of the Bible, others admitting, in varying measure, the idea that religious truth and knowledge changed and developed through time.

*The Study of Human Society*    The social sciences, with the exception of economics, also emphasized the idea of development. History achieved a new accuracy in detail as a result of seminar training in German universities, pioneered by Leopold von Ranke (1795–1886). The mass of facts that rapidly accumulated was kept in a sort of loose order by the idea of progress—in particular, the progress of limited constitutional government, of equality before the laws, and of personal, individual freedom. The historian who, more than any other, put this vision of the European past into focus was the Englishman Lord Acton (1834–1902). Sociology was inaugurated as a separate branch of learning by the Frenchman, Auguste Comte (1798–1857), who also believed in progress. Anthropology, likewise, when it emerged from the study of primitive customs and religions, was organized by such pioneers as the American Lewis Henry Morgan (1818–1881) in terms of a supposed development from savagery through barbarism to civilization. Behind and beneath these sciences lay the study of early civilizations, revealed with greater and greater detail by archaeologists. And

geologists probed still deeper into time through their study of sedimentary rock layers.

The results of the combined efforts of all these specialists was to create a panoramic vision of the nature of things in which change was universal. The whole human adventure on earth shrank to the proportions of a last-minute flourish, when measured by the geologic time scale or by the scale of organic evolution. But in a world in which everything changed—even the established truths of religion—what was there left to believe in, except the fact of change itself?

## Irrationalism

This chilling conclusion troubled many people even before 1914, when the violence and destruction wrought by World War I shocked millions more. There had been a small number of thinkers throughout the nineteenth century who emphasized the weakness of reason, the emptiness of progress, the folly of the age. Apostles of despair were listened to mainly by literary people and artists, who responded more to their feelings than to abstract debate. But the handful of philosophers who used their power of reasoning to argue how weak or useless reason really was, hardly mattered to scientists and professional specialists.

Yet, in Vienna, shortly before World War I the psychologist, Sigmund Freud (1856–1939), began to explore subconscious levels of the human mind. He found sexual drives and jealousies at the bottom of many kinds of behavior and concluded that human conduct was, for the most part, controlled by dark, elemental impulses over which we have only very limited conscious control. Freud's ideas won little attention before World War I, beyond the circle of a few personal followers. The widespread impact of his ideas came later. Other thinkers, the Italian Vilfredo Pareto (1848–1923), for example, emphasized the irrational aspects of social behavior and argued that myths and exaggerated slogans were the only means political leaders could use to mobilize their followers to action. Another school of thought tried to apply Darwinism to human affairs and interpreted history as a struggle in which only the fittest could expect to survive. Often this theory was thought of in racial terms, with the comforting (for Europeans) conclusion that the white race must be superior because it was then able to conquer everybody else. Others applied the idea of struggle for survival to conflicts between rich and poor; they concluded that any sort of political intervention to help the poor or weak members of society was dangerous in the long run because it would allow the unfit to survive.

Such ideas, together with those of Freud and others who emphasized the irrational side of human life, directly challenged the theory of democratic government. In the eighteenth century, when democratic political ideals were first clearly set forth, everyone assumed that all persons were fundamentally rational and could judge in a reasonable way the alternatives their political leaders set before them. If this was not, in fact, the case, then the original justification for democratic self-government would have to be abandoned.

Answers to this and other ultimate questions were not found; but European thinkers never drew back from any line of inquiry because it was too dangerous or too shocking to consider. A tremendous range of attitudes and ideas churned through questioning minds. New perspectives, new theories, new information competed for attention more and more urgently. In this, as in other respects, the years between 1850 and 1914 were something of a golden age for Europe's prosperous middle class.

# Art and Literature

Artists and writers valued originality above all else in the nineteenth century. Nearly all of them felt that superior craftsmanship within an established style was unworthy of true artistic genius. The result, of course, was that as time passed it became harder and harder to rebel because there was no established standard of taste against which to measure the personal originality of the artist.

From a historian's point of view, this characteristic of nineteenth-century artistic life makes it particularly difficult to say anything that is the least bit meaningful about countries, periods of time, or groups of artists. And outstanding individuals in the arts were so numerous it is hard to know whom to mention. There is some justification for making a distinction between the first half of the nineteenth century, when "romantic" art flourished, and the second half, when "realism" dominated the scene. But romantic attitudes lasted throughout the century, if by "romantic" we mean the effort to express inward personal feelings and an urge to explore remote times and places, fantasy, folklore, and things strange, new, and mysterious. Realists may have paid more attention to the lives of poor and humble people and dealt more frankly with ugly and brutal sides of human life than their predecessors usually cared to do. But this was a matter of degree. Moreover, realists who seized upon ugly and disgusting matter for their art were, in their own way, romantics. They, too, projected inward feelings upon the world. They, too, sought out strange and mysterious themes by exploring the slums of Europe's new industrial cities.

## Impact of New Techniques

One general factor that altered many forms of art during the century was the development of new techniques and materials. In architecture, for example, steel and concrete allowed buildings to rise much higher than before. The Eiffel Tower, 984 feet tall, erected in Paris for a world's fair in 1889, was a particularly dramatic example of what could be done with steel. Skyscrapers, first developed as office buildings in Chicago in the 1880s, gave practical use to the new techniques of construction. Musicians exploited a series of new instruments, and painters acquired innumerable new tints as a result of chemical discoveries. Some of them also tried to apply scientific theories of light and vision to their work by using tiny specks of different colors which, when seen from a distance, blended into a livelier, more interesting surface than could be attained by painting with solid colors. Literature, of course, was limited to words that could be understood, and language changed slowly even in the nineteenth century. In this sense it was the most conservative of the arts.

### Painting and Music

Painting, on the contrary, was the most radical. Until about 1875, the basic idea of how to paint a picture, which had been first defined in Italy in the 1440s, continued to be taken for granted. A picture, according to this tradition, ought to look like "real life," and rules for giving an illusion of three dimensions on a flat two-dimensional surface had been carefully worked out. In the latter part of the nineteenth century, however, a cluster of artists, who worked mostly in France, began to reject this idea. They wished to make their paintings not a "pretend window" to be looked through, but a thing to be looked at for its own sake. Violent colors, quite unlike those of nature, and distorted patterns vaguely resembling familiar objects were perfectly all right when the point of the picture was to be looked at for itself. Accordingly, such painters as Paul Cézanne (1839–1906), Vincent van Gogh (1853–1890), and Paul Gauguin (1848–1903) cut loose from older rules and restrictions and began to explore the possibilities of two-dimensional patternmaking by putting paint on canvas.

In the decade immediately before the outbreak of World War I, a new generation of artists began to abandon familiar shapes and to twist fragments of visual experience in playful and novel fashions. Henri Matisse (1869–1954) and Pablo Picasso (1881–1973) were among the most effective of these innovators. Strangely, the way they filled their paintings with twisted bits of familiar shapes and forms, seen from different angles or, as it were, at different times, seemed like a prophecy of the way in which traditional European culture was about to break up under the shock of World Wars I and II. Art often seems to hold a mirror to society. Europe's painters did so in the prewar years with unusual sensitivity and power. In this case, at least, the restless striving for new, original, and personal styles of expression seems to have had general significance for European society and civilization.

Musicians made attempts to experiment with such novelties as the twelve-tone scale, but with rather less success. The hold of the classics, from Johann Sebastian Bach (1685–1750) to Ludwig van Beethoven (1770–1827), was never shaken. Richard Wagner (1813–1883) tried to create a supreme art that would combine music, poetry, and dramatic spectacle. He found subject matter for his operas in Germanic folklore and pagan myth, believing that here could be glimpsed and expressed the innermost spirit of his own nation. Wagner gathered a circle of admirers around himself, but his notion of the priestlike role his art ought to play offended as many people as it attracted. Older, more classical ideas were upheld by Johannes Brahms (1833–1897) and, in some degree, also by Gustav Mahler (1860–1911).

### Literature and Journalism

European literature had divided itself up into separate language compartments beginning in the sixteenth century. Then, in the course of the nineteenth century, French began to lose the general currency its had enjoyed since the time of Louis XIV among the highly educated. This multiplied diversity, and authors' self-conscious efforts to be original worked in the same direction, making valid general statements about European literature as a whole all but impossible. One factor, however, affected writers everywhere, since in every nation of Europe, as public schooling became mandatory, a much wider reading public began to emerge. On top of that, public and lending libraries in the leading countries of the western world made books accessible to almost everyone who wanted to read them, beginning about 1850.

One consequence was a mounting flood of how-to-books, religious tracts, love stories, adventure novels, children's literature, and other sorts of popular writing. It became possible to make a good living by writing novels, plays, and even poems. Successful men of letters achieved public prominence, and a few of them, like the French poet and novelist, Victor Hugo (1802–1885), even played a (mildly) heroic role in national politics. Creativity was perhaps greatest among novelists who used what was then still a comparatively new literary form to explore the complexities of the human condition with enormous subtlety. Among the greatest of them were Charles Dickens (1812–1870) in England; Gustave Flaubert (1821–1880) and Victor Hugo in

France; and Ivan Turgenev (1818–1883), Feodor Dostoyevsky (1821–1881), and Count Leo Tolstoy (1828–1910) in Russia. These writers won wide readerships, using clear, simple, everyday language. But restless pursuit of originality pulled also in an opposite direction, so that, by the end of the century, a cluster of French poets— so-called symbolists—strained ordinary grammar and diction to their limits, thus replicating the way a few artists in Paris were simultaneously shattering established rules for painting.

Like the great novelists, journalists aimed at simplicity and clarity. They acquired greater public importance than ever before with the development of mass circulation newspapers, supplemented by weekly and quarterly journals, where all the political, intellectual, and literary issues of the day got a thorough airing. These publications shaped the public opinion that began to affect government policies and diplomacy from the time of the Crimean War (1854–1856). But before the end of the century, European governments learned how to affect journalists as much as they affected government by resorting to privileged leaks, secret subsidies, and occasional threats of legal action. In addition, a new style of "yellow journalism" won the race for enlarged newspaper circulation by taking special delight in exposing sex and money scandals among the famous, while interpreting public affairs as a matter of personal and national contests of will.

*Sports and Popular Amusement*    Sporting events started to attract journalistic attention after 1850, and published reports of the outcome of athletic competitions created public interest in several new sports. Football (soccer in the United States) acquired definite rules and nationwide organization in England in the 1870s, for example, and has since spread around the world, largely because the simple equipment, which recommended it to English workingmen in the first place, could be transplanted anywhere at almost no cost. Tennis, invented in England in the 1870s, like American college football (also invented in the 1870s), was limited at first to the middle and upper classes; but in France bicycle racing (started in the 1860s) soon

became as popular as baseball did in the United States after the Civil War. Journalism also allowed older sports—horse racing, boxing, bowling, cricket and the like—to enlarge their followings. And after 1896, when the Olympic Games were revived for the first time since antiquity, national rivalries in athletics started to compete with the ideal of amateur, individual sportsmanship that had inspired the first Olympic organizers.

Other sorts of popular amusements also proliferated in the cities of industrializing Europe. Vaudeville acts, featuring song and dance, toured the provinces, bringing a whiff of urban sophistication to otherwise dreary mill towns. On the other hand, priests and ministers, and a few traveling revivalists, vigorously tried to counteract what they felt to be modern corruptions of true religion. Between these opposite poles, innumerable choral societies, literary clubs, charitable organizations, and educational self-help associations sought to enrich or improve the lives of ordinary people.

In western Europe, traditional rural culture was in full retreat after 1850, since compulsory public schools began to introduce peasant children, along with everyone else, to national, urban standards of language and manners. In some instances, deliberate efforts to revive old rural customs met with some successes, as when a few Scotsmen began to wear kilts on ceremonial occasions. But this was artificial. Only in the poorer parts of eastern and southern Europe did village ways survive more or less intact into the twentieth century.

# Conclusion

The overwhelming impression that this hasty survey should leave is one of richness, variety, and confusion. European artists and thinkers reached for the sky. They did not quite make it; but, in failing, they expanded enormously the range of human achievement and knowledge. Their successes, however, created the problem with which we still struggle, for truth, beauty,

**Umberto Boccioni:** *Unique Forms of Continuity in Space* (1913) Bronze (cast 1931). $43\frac{7}{8} \times 34\frac{7}{8}$". *Collection, The Museum of Modern Art, N.Y. Acquired through the Lillie P. Bliss Bequest.*

**Where Are We Going and Why?**   Artists on the eve of World War I occasionally gave expression to urgent fears that lurked beneath the surface of everyday life even at the peak of Europe's dominion over the rest of the earth. On the left, *The Scream* by Edward Munch, a Norwegian, dates from 1895 on the right, *Unique Forms of Continuity in Space*, by Umberto Boccioni, an Italian, dates from 1913. The one conveys a sense of nightmare fear; the other a mechanized rush into an unknown, dehumanizing future. Such anxieties became more prominent among Europe's intellectual and cultural leaders in the decade before 1914 as faith in progress, which peaked sometime in the 1870s and 1880s, began to wane.

and goodness tend to get lost amid so many truths, so many beauties, and so many private, personal, or partial kinds of good and evil. The historian's problem of what to choose for attention becomes everyone's problem. Amid so many competing voices and ideals, where should one turn? How does it all fit together? Does anything make sense? Answers were not forthcoming before 1914—and what has happened since that

date has only added to the confusion in which Westerners, and humankind, find themselves.

Yet, for most of those who lived at the time and for us looking back, the gains in knowledge, power, and sensitivity were probably worthwhile. The nineteenth century, of all centuries, was an age of progress. Where it will lead remains to be seen; but, in and of itself, European civilization attained a final flowering between 1850 and

1914, before submerging itself, like the other civilizations of the world, into the still-emerging cosmopolitanism of the twentieth century.

Europe kept its traditions and its sublime self-confidence longer than other civilizations were able to do. In a paradoxical way, Europe was, therefore, both ahead of and behind the rest of the world. Ahead, because what the rest of the world had to adjust to was what the Europeans were doing and thinking. Behind, because until after 1914 Europeans remained smug and self-contained within the broad limits of their inherited civilization and had not yet come to realize, as other peoples had been compelled to do, that their way of doing things was only one of many ways and not always or necessarily the best.

# Bibliography

The novel was the leading form of literature in nineteenth-century Europe, and a fine sense of the texture of private life in this era may be gleaned from reading a book like Gustave Flaubert, *Madame Bovary* (1856), or Charles Dickens, *Great Expectations* (1961). Many other novels might serve the same purpose. A very different approach is offered by Mack Ridley, ed., *The Essential Darwin* (1987), a collection of excerpts from Darwin's writings. Since Darwin triggered a fundamental transformation of the European world view, it is worth reading what he actually said.

Good general accounts of European history in this period are C. J. H. Hayes, *A Generation of Materialism, 1871–1900* (1941), and A. J. P. Taylor, *The Struggle for Mastery in Europe, 1849–1914* (1954). For Britain, Asa Briggs, *The Age of Improvement* (1959), and G. M. Young, *Portrait of an Age: Victorian England* (rev. ed., 1977), are good reading. For France, D. W. Brogan, *France under the Republic, 1870–1939* (1940), and Eugen Weber, *Peasants into Frenchmen: The Modernization of Rural France* (1976), are the same. For Germany, Hans-Ulrich Wehler, *The German Empire, 1871–1918* (1985); James J. Sheehan, *German Liberalism in the Nineteenth Century* (1978); and Fritz Stern, *Gold and Iron: Bismarck, Bleichroder and the Building of the German Empire* (1977), are authoritative.

Saul Padover, *Karl Marx, an Intimate Biography* (1978), describes the career of the founder of "scientific socialism"; and David McLellan, *Marxism after Marx* (1979), describes how Marxism evolved into a powerful political movement.

For advances in science, Ernest Mayr and William B. Provine, eds., *The Evolutionary Synthesis: Perspectives on the Unification of Biology* (1980); Ronald W. Clark, *The Survival of Charles Darwin: A Biography of a Man and an Idea* (1984); and Albert Einstein and Leopold Infeld, *The Evolution of Physicis* (1938), are authoritative.

For the soft sciences, see Wolf Lepenies, *Between Literature and Science: The Rise of Sociology* (1992); William J. McGrath, *Freud's Discovery of Psychoanalysis: The Politics of Hysteria* (1986); Marvin Harris, *The Rise of Anthropological, Theory: A History of Theories of Culture* (1968); Dorothy Ross, *The Origins of American Social Science* (1991).

On sport and popular culture, Tony Mason, ed., *Sport in Britain, a Social History* (1989), and, Standish Meacham, *A Life Apart: English Working Class, 1890–1914* (1977), are particularly informative.

Widespread rejection of the ideal of creating illusory space by observing the rules of linear perspective in painting occurred in the decades immediately before 1914, and may be studied through a standard art history such as H. W. Janson, *History of Art* (4th ed., 1991). Francis D. Klingender, *Art and the Industrial Revolution* (1968), takes up a theme that is also worth exploring.

# *World Reactions to Europe's Achievements*

## 1850 to 1914

# 23

**A European Imperialist**   This carving shows
how intrusive Europeans looked to Africans in
the late nineteenth century. The superior status
Europeans claimed for themselves is registered by
the greater size of the seated figure, resting quite
literally on the backs of the Africans who are
carrying him.

Three developments changed the lives of nearly all humanity between 1850 and 1914. These were, first, the very much improved forms of transportation and communication; second, rapid population growth; and third, the imbalance arising from Europe's superiority to the rest of the world in a wide range of critical skills.

## Transportation and Communication

Before 1850, in nearly all the inland parts of the world, human beings lived in almost self-sufficient communities. News from outside a radius of twenty to fifty miles arrived only occasionally. Since it was difficult to carry goods for long distances, nearly all the basic requirements of life had to be found approximately within the same radius. Most people worked in the fields and raised most of what they consumed. Usually the surplus produce which they sold did not travel far, but was used in local towns. Because transportation was slow and expensive, people lived where there was food, rather than trying to bring food to where they lived.

Prevailing localism was modified by the fact that water transportation was comparatively cheap. This allowed the maintenance of large imperial states, such as China, Russia, and the Ottoman Empire. Canals, rivers, and seas made it possible to feed large populations in the Chinese capital at Peking, Russia's capital at Moscow (later at St. Petersburg), and the Ottoman capital at Constantinople by transporting food and other supplies by water across hundreds of miles. A state that depended largely on land transportation, such as the Mogul Empire of India, had to be weak, since wagons and animal packtrains simply could not bring enough supplies to a central point to make the emperor much more powerful than local governors.

When railroads began to spread from Britain (1840s) to the European and North American continents (1850–1870) and then to other continents (1870–1910), age-old limits upon the movement of goods and people disappeared. Cities,

hundreds of miles away, became easy to get to. And when the growing railroad systems were connected with oceangoing steamships, the lands and seas of all the world were caught up, by degrees, in a single mechanically-powered transportation network.

The effect upon human society was similar to the evolutionary emergence of animals with a central nervous system. Human communities had sprawled over the earth's surface throughout historic time, like a loosely coordinated assemblage of cells. Stimuli passed from one segment to another, but in a slow, haphazard fashion; and because conductivity was low, for long periods of time many stimuli failed to pass from one part of the world to another. The advent of railroads, steamships, and telegraph wires, and the appearance of newspapers with a mass circulation and of telephones meant that stimuli began to travel enormously faster and almost irresistibly.

Experts could communicate with experts all around the globe. The price of wheat in Chicago, of jute in Calcutta, of coffee in São Paulo, and of money in London governed decisions made halfway across the world. Technical skills, political ideas, and artistic styles moved as quickly as they attracted experts' attention. Sudden change could reach out to extremely remote regions of the earth. In the 1880s, for example, the Japanese deliberately went shopping for a constitution and, after careful study of European and American models, decided that the constitutional arrangements of Bismarck's Germany were best for them. Sometimes stimuli went the other way. Thus, Parisian artists in the 1890s borrowed motifs from African ceremonial masks, plundered from West Africa by French soldiers and sold in the Paris "flea market" at prices that even a poor artist could afford.

When it began, the new communications and transportation network was mostly controlled by Europeans. And as railroads were built inland, the effect was to extend the reach of European goods and of Europeans' political, military, and financial advantages. Nevertheless, the opening of the Suez Canal in 1869 and of the Panama Canal in 1914 changed the world's strategic patterns in a way that foreshadowed the weakening of Europe's dominance. The Suez Canal put the Middle East back into the center of Old World communications, where it had been before Europe's sailors had opened up the oceans; and the Panama Canal strengthened America's position in the world by improving the flexibility of the naval and military power of the United States. However, neither of these changes did much to undermine the reality of Europe's dominant political, military, and cultural position before 1914.

# Population Growth

Population growth acted in most parts of the world to check and limit the impact of the new communications and transportation. Poor peasants, on the edge of starvation, could take little advantage of new possibilities opened up by railroads and telegraphs. They continued to live much as their ancestors had done. This constituted a massive conservative force in world society. Yet the peasantries of the earth also nursed a potential for revolt. Inert and helpless they were, but hungry and resentful, too; and as their numbers increased, the old ways of life became more and more impossible to maintain, since tiny holdings had to be divided and divided again among the members of each new generation.

Why world population spurted upward so dramatically is not fully understood. Medical measures to check disease were important in some parts of the world, but they scarcely affected the immense numbers of rural Chinese and Indians before 1914. Increased food supplies due to better seeds, better methods of cultivation, or, in some parts, better fertilizers, irrigation, new crops, and pest control had some bearing on population growth. The pacification of great regions of the earth, brought about by improved communications, also allowed many persons to survive who in an earlier age would have perished through local violence. Famine relief was also important, especially in India where railroads made it possible to transport large amounts of food to regions where crops had failed. Lessening of epidemic diseases, through a more or less continual exposure to small doses of all sorts of infections, was another factor behind the world's population explosion. This re-

sulted from improved transport, which circulated disease germs as well as goods and ideas throughout the world.

Traditional authorities could not cope with rising population pressures in Asia, but neither could European administrators in India or missionaries in China. Only Japan was able to absorb its rapidly rising population by finding new industrial occupations for the rural surplus. But in the Americas, Africa, and parts of Southeast Asia, there was still room for expansion. Between 1850 and 1914, in all of these regions, uncultivated land could be brought under cultivation without much trouble and without any basic change in familiar farming methods.

For this reason, American societies did not undergo any very acute upheaval before World War I, and the establishment of European political administration in Africa made only minor differences to most Africans. Old ways went on much as before. The same was true in the New World, both for inhabitants of European and of African descent and for the Amerindian peasantry of central America and northern South America as well.

# The Impact of European Skills

The impact of improved communications and of population growth was largely unconscious, in the sense that no one decided in advance what to do about them. But the impact of superior European skills upon other peoples was very much a matter of conscious decision-making. People living outside of western Europe had to come to terms, in some fashion or other, with the facts of European superiority over local society and civilization. Although peasants could and did neglect the question, their cultural and political leaders could not afford to do so.

It is useful, perhaps, to distinguish between the attitudes of an "inner ring" of peoples who shared the European inheritance in greater or less degree and an "outer ring" of peoples who did not. Russians and Balkan Christians to the east were partially in and partially out of the circle of European civilization and felt both ashamed and proud of this fact. Overseas, the United States and the British Commonwealth countries, together with those parts of Latin America where Spanish and Portuguese settlers did not depend on Amerindians and Blacks to do the manual labor, also belonged to the "inner ring." Their problem was to catch up with Europe by settling the empty lands around them, after which the refinements of civilized life—which were still only poorly developed in these regions—could (they hoped) be expected to grow automatically.

The "outer ring" faced a much more difficult decision. Chinese, Hindus, and Moslems had to weigh the costs of giving up essential parts of their own treasured past in order to try to catch up with Europe. Japan chose to borrow wholesale from the West and soon forged ahead. No other proud and old civilized people was able or willing to make the hard decisions such a policy required. Instead, these communities hesitated, worried, floundered, and endured.

Africans south of the Sahara, and Amerindians in the middle regions of the New World, were subjected to European rule during the period with which we are now concerned. This was nothing new for the Amerindians. In their most developed centers, Amerindians had seen the Spaniards destroy their political leadership and higher culture before 1600. African kingdoms and tribes, however, were only brought under the control of European administrators during the later years of the nineteenth century. The degree to which African cultures and political organizations were altered by the arrival of Europeans differed a good deal from case to case. In general, the British tried to keep as much of the preexisting political and social system as possible; whereas the French, like the Spaniards in the days of the conquistadors, tried to impose their own patterns of government and education upon their African subjects.

Weaker peoples found the conditions created by improved world communications all but impossible to survive. In Australia, for example, the aborigines, who had inhabited the continent for many thousands of years, could not adjust their ways to those of the intrusive whites.

The same was true of Tasmanians and of some of the Pacific islanders; of Eskimos; and of the Amerindian tribes who inhabited most of North America and the more southerly parts of South America. In these regions, contact with the outside world resulted in destructive epidemics of disease and paralyzing breakdowns of custom. In most cases these populations did not die out utterly, but their customary framework of life fell apart drastically and dreadfully.

# How the "Inner Ring" Got Along

The United States of America was by far the most important overseas member of the "inner ring," corresponding, in many ways, with the vast overland semi-European power of Russia. Russia's relations with the Balkan Christians and with the western Slavs (Poles, Czechs, Slovaks) were similar to the relations of the United States with Canada and Latin America. In addition, interesting parallels as well as important differences may be detected in the internal development of Russia and the United States between 1850 and 1914.

## U.S. Domestic and Imperial Growth

Both the Democratic and Industrial revolutions had already gone a long way in the United States by 1850. Americans could proudly claim to be the earliest pioneers of democratic self-government, and "Yankee ingenuity" in matters industrial was as great as any in the world. What was lacking in the United States was capital, population, and cultural refinement. With the end of the Civil War (1865), Americans set out to remedy all three deficiencies as fast as they could.

Capital came from Europe, especially England, in the form of short-term and long-term credit. In addition, shrewd industrialists like Cornelius Vanderbilt (1794–1877), Andrew Carnegie (1835–1919), John D. Rockefeller (1839–

1937), and Henry Ford (1863–1947) quickly learned how to accumulate capital by plowing profits back into their businesses. They were free to set prices at what the market would bear. When very expensive plants became necessary to produce steel or oil or motor cars, competition (which in theory was supposed to keep prices close to the cost of production) worked imperfectly. Large profits reinvested in new enterprises thus created vast fortunes very rapidly. By 1914 the United States, although still a "debtor nation" in international money markets, had already begun to export large amounts of capital to the Caribbean, Mexico, Hawaii, and other foreign parts.

Population growth came from European immigration, as well as from the natural increase of people already living in the United States. As the decades passed, the flow of immigrants to North America from the British Isles and from Germany and Scandinavia slackened. Other nationalities from southern and eastern Europe became more numerous. Italians, Poles, Czechs, Croats, Jews, Greeks, Ukrainians, and many other ethnic groups swarmed across the ocean into the growing cities of the United States. There they provided labor for new factories, construction work, and the more menial services which city life required.

*Political Problems at Home*    Both the growth of capital and the flood of immigration created problems for a democratic political system. Farmers and small businesses often felt

**New York and Brooklyn in 1894**    New York became the principal commercial and financial center for the United States in the nineteenth century. Millions of immigrants from Europe, most of them fresh from peasant villages, arrived in New York between 1845 and 1914, and their labor helped to build the city seen here. The photograph features approaches to the Brooklyn Bridge, which connected Brooklyn with Manhattan. Started in 1869, it encountered a series of technical problems, so that fourteen years elapsed before it opened for traffic in 1883. At the time it was an engineering marvel, featuring the longest span (1595 feet) in the world. The use of steel wires to suspend the bridge from mighty pylons rising from the bottom of the East River was also a first. Such an achievement showed that Americans were not only catching up with European technological skills but actually surpassing them by increasing the scale with which new materials and methods were applied to engineering and industrial undertakings.

that the railroads and other big moneyed interests were squeezing them unfairly. Public regulation of railroad rates (1887) did something to remove the grievance, but a long agitation for cheaper money and credit failed to take the United States dollar off the gold standard. Similarly, popular movements aimed against immigrants succeeded only in closing the doors against Chinese and Japanese "cheap labor." Labor unions achieved a stable national existence after 1886, when the American Federation of Labor was founded. At first only a few skilled trades were organized. In these occupations cheap, unskilled immigrant labor was not much of a factor.

Political collisions between old and new immigrants and between workers and capitalists were cushioned by the fact that, until 1890 or so, the United States still had an agricultural frontier where public land could be acquired easily and quite cheaply by anyone willing to cultivate it. Hardships and grievances could never be very bitter when such a resource permitted the discontented to start afresh. Settlement of the western parts of the country tended to bypass the arid regions of the southwest at first. As a result, Arizona and New Mexico were not organized as states until 1912, at a time when American expansion had already been carried overseas to the Philippine Islands and Puerto Rico, which were acquired from Spain after a brief and victorious war (1898) against that decaying empire.

*U.S. Expansion Abroad*    With the Spanish-American war and with American diplomatic and military interventions in Panama, Nicaragua, Haiti, Mexico, and other Latin American states that swiftly followed, the United States joined the circle of imperialist powers. Germany, too, entered the field at about the same time, demanding its "place in the sun." Great Britain, in effect, made room for Americans and for the Japanese as well, who also built up a navy and began to create an empire for themselves in the Far East after a victorious war against China (1894–1895). The British simply gave up any pretense of controlling the seas in the Japanese and American parts of the globe. German rivalry close at home was too dangerous for any other policy to seem practical. The result was to keep

British and American policies harmonious, even in the absence of any formal treaty of alliance. This was a fact of the greatest importance for the lineup of powers in World War I.

*Culture and Society in the United States*
On all these fronts, the United States met with solid success. In the material sense, there was no doubt that the nation was catching up fast with the most advanced European countries. But cultural equality was harder to attain. Captains of industry, such as Vanderbilt, Carnegie, Rockefeller, and Ford, all arranged that a large part of their personal fortunes should be used to support institutions intended to improve the quality of American cultural life. As a result, universities, libraries, symphony orchestras, opera companies, and similar organizations sprang up like mushrooms in every large American city after about 1890. But real cultural creativity lagged behind the physical and financial support Americans provided so eagerly.

Before 1914, few artists or thinkers of the first rank lived in the United States. As a matter of fact, quite a few highly cultivated Americans, such as the novelist Henry James (1843–1916), preferred to live in Europe because they found their compatriots crude and unsympathetic. American culture had not really escaped from provincialism in 1914, in spite of all the money and conscious effort devoted to its cultivation.

Backward aspects of American life concentrated conspicuously in the Old South. After the Civil War, halfhearted efforts to allow blacks to participate in public life failed. By the late 1870s, relations between whites and blacks settled down to patterns not so very different from those that had prevailed in the days of slavery—patterns that enjoyed the legal sanction of so-called Jim Crow laws. Black sharecroppers, therefore, hoed cotton and tobacco in nearly the same way that slaves had done before 1863; and their education, skill, voting rights, and familiarity with newer aspects of modern life were not much greater than what had existed under slavery. In search of greater opportunities, some blacks did move into cities, mainly in the South. In fact, it was black musicians in New Orleans who invented jazz, the first truly original and compelling cultural innovation that bears the

## United States Expansion, 1783–1959

stamp *Made in America*. But in 1914 jazz remained hidden in the back streets of New Orleans, Memphis, and Kansas City; the majority of people in the United States, along with the rest of the world, discovered it only after World War I.

## Canada and Australia

In almost all respects, Canada lagged behind the United States by a generation or so but followed much the same curve of development. Australia and New Zealand differed in one important respect. From the 1880s both countries passed laws that made it difficult for anyone not of British origin to immigrate. This slowed population growth. In addition, elaborate laws for the protection of workers slowed down the development of industry in comparison to what was happening in the United States in the same period. When the separate Australian colonies united to form the Commonwealth of Australia (1901) and New Zealand also became a fully self-governing dominion (1907), both countries were almost entirely agricultural. They were divided between vast stretches of nearly empty sheep pasture and an extraordinary concentration of population at two or three port cities, where import-export businesses and the processing of raw materials for export were concentrated.

Clearly, such societies had a long way to go before they could hope to equal European complexity and sophistication. But, as in the case of the United States and Canada, the people from "down under" often asserted the superiority of their way of life to that of the Old World, where—they quite correctly pointed out—high civilization had been built partly upon the exploitation of the poor by the rich.

## South Africa

A different situation prevailed in South Africa. The Boer descendants of Dutch settlers kept their own language and, until 1901, defended their rural way of life, with guns in hand, against British intrusion. First the Boers withdrew inland; then when diamonds (1867) and gold (1886) were discovered on Boer soil, they tried to disfranchise the English-speaking miners who swarmed to the scene. Meanwhile, British empire-builders decided that all of eastern Africa, from Capetown to Cairo in Egypt, ought to come into British possession. The most active advocate of such an expansion was Cecil Rhodes (1853–1902). After making a fortune in gold mining, Rhodes turned to politics. His schemes led to a hard-fought war between the Boers and the British (1899–1902). In the end, the British won, but only after cutting off supplies for the Boer fighters by putting their women and children into specially guarded "concentration camps" and by burning their farmhouses and buildings.

Another feature of South African life was the presence of large numbers of Bantu-speaking Africans, as well as the "Cape coloureds" whose ancestry mingled European, Indonesian, and Khoikkoi strains. When the Union of South Africa was established (1910), Boers, British, and "Cape coloured" populations all secured voting rights; but the Bantus were excluded. Boers regarded the Bantus as servants and inferiors; the British, when they did not share Boer attitudes, thought that tribal government should be maintained to make the transition into modern life easier and smoother.

## South America

The situation of South America was again different. Argentina, southern Brazil, and Chile all remained hospitable to immigrants from Europe. But the distances involved made passage more expensive than to the United States, so fewer people made the ocean passage to those countries. Agricultural expansion inland, largely dependent on railroad construction, was rapid; and foreign capital, much of it British, was important. But the absence of coal fields severely handicapped the development of industry. On the other hand, agricultural exports from the "southern cone" of the continent made Brazilian coffee and Argentine beef and grain into major suppliers of world markets. Upper-class landowners who organized these export trades developed a style of life resembling that of pre–Civil War plantation owners of the southern United States,

## Latin America (After the Wars for Independence)

REPUBLIC OF MEXICO

CUBA (Sp.)

REPUBLIC OF HAITI

BELIZE (Br.)   JAMAICA (Br.)   PUERTO RICO (Sp.)

*Atlantic Ocean*

UNITED PROVINCES OF CENTRAL AMERICA

Caracas

VENEZUELA

Bogota

GREAT COLOMBIA

GUIANA

*Pacific Ocean*

ECUADOR   •Quito

*Amazon R.*

Lima•

PERU

EMPIRE OF BRAZIL

La Paz•

BOLIVIA

CHACO (Claimed by Bolivia and Paraguay)

PARAGUAY
Asuncion•

Rio de Janeiro•

PROVINCES OF LA PLATA (Argentina)
Santiago•

CHILE

Buenos Aires•

URUGUAY

Montevideo•

PATAGONIA

```
0      500     1000
|___|___|___|___|
      Miles
```

while a rough-and-tumble frontier style of life prevailed among those who actually did the work in the fields and pastures.

The miners, coffee growers, and entrepreneurs of the southernmost provinces of Brazil treated the rest of that enormous country, where black and Indian populations were numerous, as a sort of colonial domain. In addition, Brazilians, in alliance with Argentina, overthrew a remarkable regime in Paraguay, where, after the destruction of the Jesuit missions, three military dictators in succession organized the Guarani Indians into a tightly disciplined army. The war was bitterly fought (1865–1870), and it ended only when the Paraguayans had suffered enormous loss of life.

Somewhat later Chileans again proved that a population possessing European skills could exert superior military power, when they defeated Bolivia and Peru (where most of the population was Indian) in a war (1879–1884) aimed at seizing undisputed control of the valuable guano deposits of the coastal desert. These deposits, made from bird droppings, were rich in phosphates, and before 1914 constituted the world's cheapest and best source of commercial fertilizer.

# Russia

Overseas countries inhabited mainly by people of European descent enjoyed the advantage of having weak neighbors. In trying to catch up with Europe, they could, therefore, afford to pay little attention to building up military power. This was not true of Russia, whose landward frontier against western Europe had always been difficult to defend. Throughout the nineteenth century, Russia was a great power and wished to remain so. But this required heavy expenditure for the army and navy, and such expenditures left little to spare for building up industry. Yet modern industrial plants were vitally needed to equip the army and navy with efficient weapons. Financing railroad construction on the scale required by Russia's vastness also strained the resources of the country, though it was obvious that without railroads Russia could not remain a truly great power.

*Failure of Autocratic Government*  This difficulty was tied in with more strictly political problems. Ever since their defeat in the Crimean War (1856), many Russians had wanted to see changes in their government. But a Polish revolt (1863–1864) stopped the effort to set up some sort of representative system of government in Russia. Czar Alexander II (reigned 1855–1881)

had tried to win the Poles over by allowing partial self-government. Instead, the Poles revolted and fought a bitter guerilla war before being put down. The rulers of Russia drew the conclusion that it was dangerous to dabble with representative institutions. Absolute Russian dominance over all the subject nationalities of the empire seemed the only way of strengthening the state. Unbending autocracy, supported by the secret police and a strong army, looked like the only kind of government that could prevent open revolt.

Reaction fed revolution. Students plotted to overthrow the czar and his government, but efforts to rouse the peasants failed. As a result, in 1879 a small circle turned to terrorism and embarked on a plan to assassinate leading officials. In 1881 the czar himself was killed by one such terrorist.

This confirmed the worst fears of Russian reactionaries. In the next years, energetic police measures broke up most of the revolutionary circles. But the government could not rely only on repression. To keep strong, an active policy of building railroads and industry seemed absolutely vital. But Russia, like the United States, was short of capital. The people were already severely taxed to maintain the army and bureaucracy at existing levels.

A solution was found through a diplomatic alliance with France, concluded in 1891. The French government encouraged the Russians to float large loans in Paris. These loans enabled the Russian government to start a crash program of railroad building and industrial development. The Trans-Siberian Railroad, built between 1891 and 1903, was the greatest single achievement; in addition, many new armaments and textile plants came into existence in Moscow and St. Petersburg; and in the Ukraine, coal and iron mines provided the basis for a new and modern steel industry.

The difficulty with this policy was that it increased the danger of revolution. Factory workers, often miserably treated and badly housed, responded readily to preachers of revolution. A tiny Marxist party, the Social Democrats, founded in 1898, vigorously exploited this fact. Soon after, in 1901, a new terrorist group, the Socialist

Revolutionaries, organized themselves, intending to appeal primarily to the peasants by advocating abolition of landlord rights.

But as long as the Russian government remained successful abroad and the czarist police and army functioned with reasonable efficiency at home, the plans and hopes of Marxists and other revolutionaries attracted little support. And Russia was, on the whole, successful abroad. New stretches of central Asia were annexed to the czar's empire between 1865 and 1876. A victorious war against the Turks in 1876–1877 had a less satisfactory outcome because the European powers whittled away the "Big Bulgaria" the Russians had created in the Balkans. Even so, the czar annexed Bessarabia (1878). In the following years he added Merv (1884) in central Asia and acquired extensive rights in Manchuria and Outer Mongolia, in the Far East.

In 1903 the Marxists quarreled among themselves. A fiery and stubborn young leader, Vladimir Ilich Ulyanov (1870–1924), who went by the revolutionary alias Lenin, insisted that the party must become a secret group of professional revolutionaries who would obey without question whatever instructions the elected leaders of the party judged to be advantageous at the moment. Some of the delegates at the Party Congress refused to agree; but a majority, the Bolsheviks, accepted Lenin's doctrine and leadership. Most of the rank and file of the party, however, followed the anti-Leninist, or Menshevik, group.

Russia's internal situation changed suddenly in 1904–1905, when the czar's armies and navy met unexpected defeat at the hands of the Japanese in the Far East. Failure in war provoked revolution at home. The czar soon yielded, declaring that he would govern henceforth with the advice and consent of an elected duma (parliament). However, when the crisis had passed and the army came back to European Russia, reaction set in. The powers of the duma were reduced, and the government set out to improve the equipment of the Russian armies by buying armaments from France and retooling factories at home. The Russian rulers badly wanted a breathing space, such as that which had followed the Crimean War. Instead, a series

of crises in the Balkans (1908, 1912–1913) led the Russian and Austrian governments to such a pitch of rivalry that when still another crisis arose in the summer of 1914, neither would yield. The result was World War I and the downfall of both empires.

## The Asian "Outside Ring"

The gap between the Russian upper classes and the Russian peasantry was like the gap that opened between those Chinese, Japanese, Hindus, and Moslem individuals who mastered aspects of European civilization and the majority of their compatriots. In this, as in many other respects, Russia stood halfway between Europe and the societies of Asia.

### China

In China old ways of thought survived almost unshaken among the ruling class until 1895. After the severe crisis of the Taiping Rebellion (1850–1864), China enjoyed a kind of respite. But the respite was squandered; inactivity prevailed.

The trouble was that no educated Chinese who had spent his formative years studying the Confucian classics could really believe that fundamental changes should be made in the way China was governed. Nevertheless, some reforms were undertaken, often entrusted to foreigners. Thus, for example, a customs service was organized in 1863 by an Englishman, Robert Hart, who made it the most efficient branch of Chinese government. Other new enterprises, such as a nationwide postal system (introduced 1896), began as branches within the customs service, which, in fact, served as a training school in the methods of a modern bureaucracy.

Gestures were made toward creating a modern army and navy, but they remained half-hearted. Between 1875 and 1878, Chinese armies were able to reconquer Moslem and Turkish areas of central Asia, thus restoring China's bound-

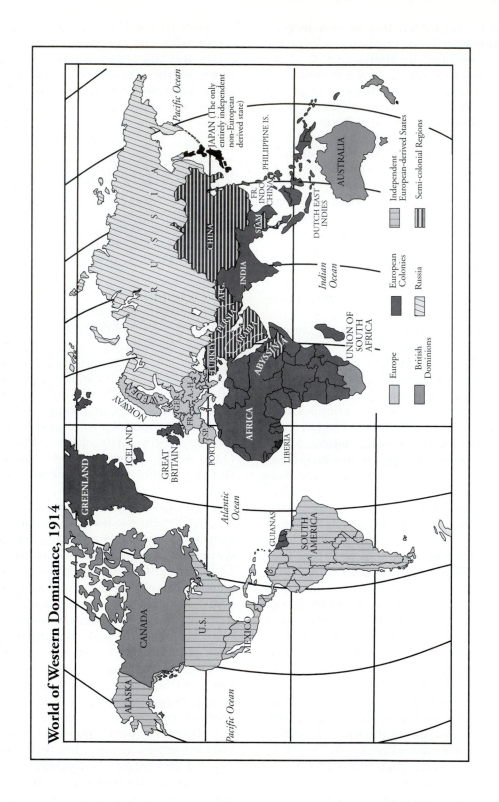

World of Western Dominance, 1914

aries to their former limits. Chinese control over Tibet and Mongolia was infirm but never formally surrendered. On the other hand, the Russians advanced into Manchuria, the French took over Annam (1883), and the British conquered Burma (1886), thus shearing off outlying territories that had previously recognized Chinese suzerainty.

Missionaries from Europe and the United States penetrated considerable distances into inland China, and in the 1880s railroads began to open up the Chinese interior to Western goods. In the north, some coal and iron mines, equipped along Western lines, also started operation. But none of these things altered the fundamental Chinese conviction that their old ways were the only right ways to live.

Then Japan and China quarreled over Korea. War broke out in 1894, and the Japanese won a series of rapid victories. This was a crushing blow to Chinese pride. For half a century, the Chinese had been forced to live with the fact that Western barbarians possessed the secret of winning wars. The Chinese had not really tried very hard to find out what that secret was. But now it was all too evident that the Japanese, who had started at no better a technological level than the Chinese, had somehow learned that secret. Inaction could no longer be justified; something drastic had to be done.

*Reaction to Foreign Powers*     The urgency of action was all the greater because Europeans began to make plans for dividing China into spheres of influence. Germany appeared on the scene and in 1897–1898 secured concessions from the Chinese government in the Shantung Peninsula. This set off a frantic scramble on the part of other imperial powers, each eager to pin down new rights. Control of railroad rights-of-way into the interior was the prize immediately at stake. Russia gained control of the railroads in Manchuria; Britain planned to open up the Yangtze with steamboats and railroads; the French concentrated in the south, driving a railroad northward from Hanoi to Yünnan. The Germans, as latecomers, concentrated in the region nearest Peking, where foreigners had hitherto been kept at arms' length. As for the United States, it advocated an "Open Door," meaning the right of every foreign power to enjoy equal access to all parts of China.

China's first reaction was a desperate effort to throw out the foreigners. A secret society, the so-called Boxers, preached hatred of all outsiders but made the mistake of relying on magical protection against European bullets. In 1900 when the Boxers attacked the European legations in Peking, tiny staffs fought them off until a relief expedition could be sent in from the coast. The Boxers were then shot down ruthlessly, and the Chinese government was required to pay an indemnity for losses suffered by the Westerners.

Failure of the Boxer Rebellion forced the reluctant Chinese to face the necessity of change. In 1905, accordingly, the imperial government abolished the ancient system of recruitment to the ranks of officialdom. Examinations testing mastery of the Confucian classics were abandoned. The effect upon Chinese life was profound. Young men who formerly had pored over the pages of the ancient sages now swarmed into missionary schools and colleges, hoping to prepare themselves for government jobs by finding the secret of Western greatness. Many young Chinese went to Japan, and the United States decided to use its share of the Boxer indemnity payments to bring Chinese students to study at American universities.

Obviously, it took time for Western-style education to take effect, since the language barriers to be crossed were unusually difficult. But the impatient Chinese could not wait for a new generation to arise, trained in Western-type schools. Revolutionary secret societies had long been a feature of Chinese life; and after the war with Japan (1894–1895), they took on new life. Sun Yat-sen (1866–1925) was the leader of one such group. He searched the political writings of Western and Japanese authors—hunting for ideas that might work in China—and came up with a hodgepodge of nationalist and socialist ideas.

In 1911 revolution broke out in China. The next year the emperor (a six-year-old boy) abdicated, and the Manchu Dynasty came to an end. Confusion only increased. Sun Yat-sen, now leader of the Kuomintang party, challenged more old-fashioned warlords who, for their part,

**How Westerners Penetrated China**   The drawing above portrays China's first railroad in action. It opened in 1876, but this drawing appeared about ten years later in a popular magazine published for Chinese readers in Shanghai. The dragon, breathing fire and smoke, had been the symbol of imperial power in China for centuries, but this mechanical dragon proved far more powerful than anything the emperor could summon to repel the foreigners, as the painting below illustrates. It was made by an American artist to record fighting in 1900 between a detachment of U.S. Marines, armed with rifles and bayonets, and the Boxers, whose weapons were swords and spears. Superior technology, both military and industrial, made the Westerners literally irresistible, even though millions of Chinese wished to have nothing to do with them.

probably dreamed of establishing a new imperial dynasty rather than carrying through a thoroughgoing revolution. Foreign diplomats and business interests added to China's troubles; and the Japanese, who had meanwhile annexed Korea (1910), showed signs of wishing to put a puppet of their choosing on the Chinese throne.

By 1914, China's political unity and independence seemed about to collapse. The cultural pride which had once made China utterly indifferent to the outside world was bearing bitter fruit indeed.

# Japan

Japan's history contrasted in every respect with China's unhappy experience. In 1867 the die had been cast for radical reform with the "restoration" of the emperor. By good luck, the young man who took the title *Meiji* for his reign (1867–1912) proved to be unusually wise, judicious, and strong-willed. Over and over again, in time of crisis, his decisions as to which advisers to appoint to office were of critical importance. Under the Meiji emperor, Japan was therefore able to pursue a consistent policy. It did so with a truly amazing success.

*Reforms in Government*    The first and central aim of the whole undertaking was to make Japan strong, so that the nation would no longer have to fear foreign gunboats. Very quickly the clique of warriors who engineered the overthrow of the shogun recognized that this required far-reaching changes in the Japanese social scene. Thus they "abolished feudalism" between 1869 and 1871. This meant destroying the rights of the warrior class to collect rice rents from the peasants. The dispossessed warriors received handsomely engraved government bonds instead.

A postal service, a daily newspaper, and a ministry of education, whose job it was to set up schools that could train the Japanese in what they needed to know about the West, quickly followed. In 1872, universal military service was decreed. It takes a moment to realize how radical this was for Japanese society, where the right to bear arms had always been a jealously guarded privilege of the warrior class. Now peasants and merchants, even the despised outcasts who had

traditionally been charged with menial tasks, were admitted to the ranks of the army. Appointment and promotion within the officer ranks were made to depend not on birth or traditional status but on competence and seniority. This established a career open to talent, appealing especially to poor peasant sons. It also provoked an armed rebellion on the part of disgruntled warriors of the old school (1877), but the new army stood the test by defeating the rebels. After the victory, the old order of things disappeared beyond all hope of recall.

The Japanese never looked back. In 1889, the emperor proclaimed a new constitution designed to resemble Bismarck's imperial system in Germany. Voting rights were limited to the richer classes. The elected Diet (parliament) had only modest powers. The Diet did, however, give the Japanese who mattered politically a way of making their will known to the highest circles of government. This was exactly what it was intended to do. Next came revision of the laws according to European ideas of property rights and judicial procedure. And in 1897, Japan attained economic respectability by putting its currency on the gold standard.

All the while, energetic efforts to introduce modern industry continued so as to be able to supply and maintain a modern army and navy. Usually the government tried new things first. Then, when a factory had begun to turn out the desired product, the government sold it, sometimes at very low prices, to private entrepreneurs. This meant, in effect, that the costs of starting up enterprises were carried by the government, which, with its tax income, was able to bear initial losses. But once private owners took over, more or less free market prices came into play. This required considerable efficiency on the part of the Japanese firms, for European and American factory-made goods were only lightly taxed on entry into the country. As a result, by 1914 some Japanese products, particularly textiles, were beginning to compete successfully with European and American products in the export markets of the Far East.

The Western powers recognized Japan's achievements by giving up extraterritorial rights (1899) which had been secured by the first treaties after the opening of Japan. Two years later, Great Britain concluded a military alliance

芝浦製作所
第二工場
發電機
製作場

**Modernizing Industry and Agriculture in Japan**    The Japanese worked hard to catch up with Western technology, not only in industry, as the woodcut indicates, but also in agriculture, as you can see in the photo. The woodcut was made about 1880, when electrical generators were still very new in the Western world, yet here we see how the Shibura Engineering Works put them into service in Japan. The man examining the generator coil in the foreground is wearing European clothes and may represent a foreign expert brought in to get the new machines started. What look like military costumes on the other workmen were equally exotic of course, but those wearing them were Japanese and may well have been soldiers in their new, Western-style uniforms who were assigned the task of serving the national interest by learning how to start up this new and important technology. For a long time, peasant life remained little changed, but eventually labor-saving machinery reached the paddy fields of Japan too, as can be seen in the photograph.

with Japan; and in 1904–1905, the Japanese amazed all Asia and most of Europe by defeating the Russians in Manchuria and driving them back across the Amur River. The Japanese also annexed Formosa (modern Taiwan) in 1895 after defeating the Chinese and took over control of Korea in 1910 by suppressing a Korean revolt aimed at driving them out of the country.

Throughout, the Japanese peasantry remained obedient, hard-working, poor to the edge of hunger, but energetic and ambitious all the same. At first, capital for industrial development came mainly from the peasants in the form of heavy taxes. Later, industry financed itself from profits, which came from Japanese consumers. Later still, when Japan was able to build up an East Asian colonial empire, the burden shifted in part to Koreans, Chinese, and others.

This success was made possible by the unwavering social discipline of the Japanese. The imperial authority, exercised by a changing circle of ministers and informal advisers, operated upon a society in which the habit of command and obedience had been cultivated for centuries. Military clan leaders had formerly been in control; now it was shifting cliques of advisers to the emperor, eventually diluted by a sprinkling of ordinary commoners, who gave commands. The aim was much the same, that is, military strength and greatness, not any longer for a single clan, but instead for Japan as a whole.

Universal elementary education opened Japanese minds to many aspects of Western civilization beyond the merely technical. But the idea of equality or of liberty, as developed in the West in the nineteenth century, made little impression. The Democratic Revolution, in other words, did not come to Japan with the Industrial Revolution. Instead, the speed and smoothness with which the Japanese adopted Western industrial and military technology depended on the survival of old-fashioned inequality.

## India

Hindu India was like Japan in one respect. A considerable number of Indians went to European-type schools and acquired some familiarity with European civilization. Yet the differences between Japan and Hindu India were far greater than the likenesses. The liberal principles of British administration in India required the government to keep its hands off most economic matters. These were thought to belong, as in England, to the sphere of private enterprise. But, except for a small number of Parsis (believers in Zoroastrianism) and other foreigners, no one in India was ready and eager to start up modern industry or bring in new techniques, as the Japanese government did so successfully.

Consequently, despite a fine railroad network, a remarkably honest government, and legal freedom to act, industrial development came very slowly to India. The government's policy of allowing free trade meant that Indian manufacturers were exposed to competition from British factories. The Japanese labored under the same handicap at the beginning, when their tariffs were fixed at a very low rate by treaty agreement with the Western powers. Free trade alone was not to blame, as Indian nationalists have often claimed. It was, basically, the lack of will on the part of any significant group of people to do anything about the business of factory production. To British-educated Indians, the prestige of work in a government office was so great that other careers seemed unattractive.

Population growth made famines frequent and serious. Systematic official countermeasures, begun in 1883, had the effect of keeping more people alive in time of crop failure. But this did not solve the problem and, indeed, only made it worse. Too many persons remained alive to be fed properly from the available land, given the existing level of agricultural practice.

In the sphere of politics, Hindu India was more active. In 1885, the Indian National Congress met for the first time. Delegates discussed political questions and petitioned for a larger share in government policy-making. The Congress leaders took the ideals of the British liberal parliamentary tradition seriously. And although they did not get all they asked for, little by little the British did bring Indian representatives into the higher councils of government.

In 1905, political agitation showed a different face. The viceroy decided to divide the large and wealthy province of Bengal in two. This roused suspicion that the British were really act-

## British Imperial Expansion in Asia and Africa, 1800–1914

**Asia**

British possessions in 1805
British possessions acquired 1805–1858
British possessions acquired 1858–1914
British protectorates

**Africa**

British possessions in 1805
British possessions in 1876
British possessions in 1876–1888
British possessions in 1888–1914

Campaigns by Indian Army

Shanghai

Yellow R.

CHINA

Hankow
Yangtse R.

Pearl R. Canton
Hong Kong (Br.)
1839–42

1860

Batavia

Hanoi

Mekong R.

SIAM

Saigon

Bangkok

Singapore (Br.)

Penang

1819

Indian Ocean

300    600
Miles
0

Brahmaputra R.

BHUTAN

NEPAL

Mandalay 1885
BURMA
1852–53
Prome
Rangoon
1825–28

Bay of Bengal

KASHMIR
Srinagar

Indus R.
Peshawar
Lahore
Dehli
Lucknow
Benares Ganges R.
Chandernagore (Fr.)
Calcutta

ORISSA

INDIA

AFGHANISTAN
Kabul
1878–79
Herat
1839–42

PUNJAB

RAJPUTANA

HYDERABAD
Ahmadabad
Diu (Port.)
BALUCHISTAN

Bombay

Madras
Pondicherry (Fr.)
Karikal (Fr.)

MYSORE
Hyderabad

CEYLON
Colombo

Goa (Port.)
Mahe (Fr.)

Karachi

Arabian Sea

PERSIA
Teheran

OMAN

Persian Gulf

OTTOMAN
EMPIRE

ARABIA

Mecca

ADEN

Red
Sea

BRITISH
SOMALILAND

ETHIOPIA

Ethiopia 1868

Ethiopia 1868

BRITISH
SOMALILAND

Mediterranean Sea

Suez Canal

AFRICA

EGYPT
Cairo

Port Sudan
Berbera
Khartoum
ANGLO
EGYPTIAN
SUDAN

ETHIOPIA

UGANDA
NAIROBI
L. Victoria
Mombasa
Zanzibar

L. Tanganyika

NORTHERN
RHODESIA

L. Nyasa

NYASALAND
Blantyre

RHODESIA

TRANSVAAL
ORANGE FREE STATE
NATAL
Pretoria
Durban

BECHUANALAND
Walvis Bay

UNION OF
SOUTH AFRICA
Cape Town

CABINDA

NIGERIA
Lagos

ASHANTI
GOLD Accra
COAST

GAMBIA

SIERRA LEONE
Freetown

500    1000
Miles
0    500

ing on the ancient precept of divide and rule, by creating a predominantly Moslem state in one half of Bengal (what is now Bangladesh) and a Hindu state in the other half. Protests were organized, not only among the educated upper class but also among the common people of Calcutta and other cities. A handful of terrorists also tried to use assassination to register their opposition to British policy. The British responded with repression but, in 1911, decided that the wiser course was to unite the two halves of Bengal once more.

Except for this flare-up of popular agitation in Bengal, most Indians remained politically inert. When the capital was moved to Delhi in 1911, the new king of England, George V, came to India to be crowned emperor of India. A splendid gathering of Indian princes was arranged to demonstrate the seeming loyalty and contentment of the Indian peoples under British rule.

# Islam

Indian Moslems seldom attended British schools, and few of them entered the Indian administration. They played larger roles in the army, but, by and large, the Moslems of India found it difficult to accustom themselves to Christian rule. This was also true of other Moslems, even though by 1914 a very large part of the Islamic world was under the political control of Europeans. The French began to move into North Africa in 1830, capturing Algiers in that year. In 1881 they took over Tunis to the east. In 1912 the French protectorate over Morocco, to the west, received international recognition, although only after German opposition had twice triggered international crises. French power also reached southward across the Sahara and overran most of the Moslem kingdoms of West Africa, and Moslem areas of Africa which escaped the French were conquered by the British.

Italy took Tripoli in 1911 after a war with the Turks, and Egypt fell under British control in 1882. When a sectarian leader proclaimed himself the Mahdi (that is, divinely appointed leader of all true Moslems) and drove Egyptian administrators out of the Sudan, British arms were summoned to impose Anglo-Egyptian control throughout the region. The Red Sea and Persian Gulf shorelines were also under British influence; so was the southern portion of Persia and Afghanistan. Most of these lands retained nominal independence, but by giving and withholding subsidies and supplies, the British were able to put their friends in power and keep their enemies on the run.

From the landward side, Moslem states fared no better. The Russians and Chinese, between them, squeezed out the last independent khanates of central Asia by 1884. Russia controlled the northern third of Persia as a result of a general agreement reached with Britain in 1907. In the Balkans, the Ottoman Turks lost ground to Bulgars and Albanians, as well as to the Serbs and Greeks who had won their independence in the first half of the century. No ray of hope relieved this dismal record of defeat and retreat. Everywhere Moslems continued to suffer defeat in war. Military failure was all the harder to endure because, from the days of the prophet Mohammed, success on the battlefield and the blessing of Allah had been closely linked in Moslem minds.

*Internal Problems*    Turks, Persians, and Afghans still ruled nominally independent states. Each had all the makings of a nation, with a history, language, and military tradition of its own. But the two strongest of these nations, the Turks and the Persians, faced a dilemma; for if they became out-and-out nationalists, they stood to lose an empire over other peoples.

In 1908, for example, a secret society of army officers and reformers, who went by the name "Young Turks," started a revolution in the Ottoman Empire. They wished to make the empire over into a secular state. In this fashion they hoped that the age-old conflict between Moslems and Christians would disappear. Everyone, it was hoped, could learn to be good "Ottomans," whatever his religion might be. The Young Turks took it for granted that Turks would continue to rule the state. When elections resulted in a parliament in which Bulgars, Greeks, Armenians, Albanians, and other nationalities all stubbornly defended their own self-interests, the Young Turks resorted in disgust to a coup d'état. They then established an authoritarian regime whose leading figures turned more and

more to Pan-Turkism as a substitute for Ottomanism. The idea was to arouse the Turkish-
speaking subjects of the Russian and Chinese
empires to a sense of their common destiny with
the Ottoman Turks. The leaders of the Young
Turks began to dream of a vast Asian empire, in
which Turks would be a majority of the population. This brought the Turkish government into
World War I on the German side, since Pan-
Turkism could only become a political fact after
the dismemberment of the Russian Empire.

As for the Persians, their subject nationalities were mostly of Turkish speech. What made
such Turks "Persian" was the Shi'a form of Islam they had inherited from the Safavid period.
Any shift from the traditional religious basis of
the Persian state therefore threatened an immediate breakup, which no Persian welcomed.

The Arabs and the Indian Moslems were,
of all Moslems, the most confused. Arabs found
it difficult to choose between the ideal of a local
nation-state—Egypt, Syria, and so forth—and
the ideal of a Pan-Arab empire. More important, they could not decide between trying to
build a strong secular state or remaining faithful to the Sacred Law of Islam. Yet the fact remained that one interfered with the other, and,
wanting both, the Arabs got neither. Up to 1914,
they remained puzzled, sullen and angry. As for
the Moslems of India, they had only a choice of
evils. Having no country of their own, they
feared the Hindu majority around them as
much as, or more than, they disliked being subjected to British rule.

To be sure, there were parts of the world
where Islam continued to prosper. In much of
Africa and in Southeast Asia, the faith of Mohammed continued to make converts, despite
the competition of Christian missionaries. Islam
offered peoples emerging from isolation all the
benefits of a civilized faith: literacy, a world view
that answered all fundamental questions, and a
code of conduct that could be used to guide
everyday behavior. It had the further advantages
of allowing a man to marry more than one wife
(an important consideration among polygamous
peoples) and of not being associated with the politically dominant whites from Europe. But continued Moslem missionary success in these regions of the world offered small comfort to the

Moslems of the heartlands. They scarcely knew
what was happening in such distant parts, and
even if they had known, it would not have helped
them to solve their own pressing problems.

## The Fate of Africans and Amerindians

The men who explored the interior of sub-
Saharan Africa between 1850 and 1880 were
only the advance guard for other Europeans
who followed hard on their heels, eager to bring
the blessings of Christian civilization to the
"Dark Continent." These blessings took different
forms, and the motives of the men who brought
them were no less varied. Some devoutly and
devotedly sought to save souls. Consequently,
Christian missionaries altered African life by
founding schools and hospitals as well as
churches. Others wished only to get rich, and
they tried to do so by making Africans work for
them, either on plantations or in mines. As a result, after the 1880s, gold and diamond mines in
South Africa and copper mines in the Congo
combined African labor with the most up-to-
date European technology.

Sometimes wages could not persuade
Africans, accustomed to subsistence farming, to
give up their traditional ways and work for the
European newcomers. In such cases, impatient
entrepreneurs resorted to forced labor, which
differed only in legal form from old-fashioned
slavery. Nevertheless, when news leaked out about
the way a company organized by King Leopold
of Belgium was using forced labor in the Congo,
widespread protests in Europe persuaded the
king to abandon the practice, and his company,
unable to make a profit, was taken over by the
Belgian government.

The decision by the Belgians to take formal
control over the Congo was an instance of another very powerful motive operating among
European imperialists in Africa. By annexing
new lands, European adventurers felt that the
greatness and prestige of their nation was enhanced. New colonies under the British, French,
Belgian, German, Italian, Portuguese or Spanish

flag—as the case might be—offered the colonizing power a chance at new wealth. Above all it meant that rival European powers were excluded from the area being taken over. Competition at first lay mainly between the French and the British. Not infrequently, ambitious officers, bored with garrison duty, set out to pacify some neighboring region, and having defeated local forces they took the initiative in annexing the new territory on behalf of their home governments. Newspapers made much of victorious colonial campaigns, and politicians at home went along when they did not actively encourage military adventures.

By the 1880s, Germany and Italy joined the scramble for colonies. This only made the French and British more anxious to get there first. When resulting competition in central Africa threatened to get out of hand, Bismarck called a conference that met in Berlin in 1884–1885. There the European powers drew more or less arbitrary boundaries on the map to delineate their respective colonial possessions. Frictions did not cease after the Berlin conference, however. France and Britain clashed again in 1898 over the upwaters of the Nile, for example. Troubles began in 1882 when the British occupied Egypt, excluding the French, who had previously been the most influential European power in that country. Beginning in the next year, fanatical Moslem dervishes, seeking to restore the purity of the faith, seized power in the regions of the upper Nile, throwing out Egyptians and their new British advisers. But the insurgent Moslem regime on the upper Nile soon got into difficulties, and the French saw a chance to gain control of the Nile's flow and embarrass the British in Egypt by sending an expedition into the region. They arrived at Fashoda on the banks of the Nile in 1898, a few weeks before a much larger British expedition, having defeated the dervishes, arrived to claim possession of the river banks. A brief and bitter diplomatic crisis ended only with French retreat. Yet five years later the two governments chose to bury their differences overseas by entering upon an informal alliance against the rising power of Germany.

Even so, Africa remained a bone of contention for the European powers. The main clash came in Morocco, where the Germans opposed French ambitions to control the sultan and his government. Two intense diplomatic storms resulted (1905, 1911). This time it was the Germans who backed down but not before hard feelings had been stirred on both sides of the European alliance system. In this way, colonial rivalries in Africa contributed a good deal to the psychological and diplomatic climate that triggered World War I.

Imperial rivalries and ambitions among the European powers met with only ineffective resistance. African states were in disarray; and the rapid development of new weapons—repeating rifles and machine guns became normal equipment for European armies between 1870 and 1890—meant that even small detachments of European-trained soldiers (many of them recruited in Africa itself) could defeat old-fashioned African forces with ease. European military and political organization also allowed their troops to move across previously insuperable obstacles. In 1868, for example, when the British invaded Ethiopia, they built a railroad to deliver supplies from the coast. Even after they withdrew, the railroad remained to connect that hitherto almost inaccessible kingdom with the outer world. Other railroads in other parts of Africa had similar effect, opening up the interior to European access as never before. River steamers and telegraph wires were also important in allowing Europeans to exercise political control over territory in a way that local kings and tribal chieftains could not match.

Yet even when facing enormous odds, African warriors and rulers often refused to submit. Thus, the Ashanti federation in West Africa clashed repeatedly with the British before 1900, when it was finally broken up. The French similarly destroyed the kingdom of Dahomey in 1892 after two wars. Other armed clashes occurred throughout East and Southern Africa, and sometimes desperate African resistance led to mass killings, or death through starvation and disease.

The imbalance of force was so great that by 1914 only two African states remained genuinely independent. One was Ethiopia, where King Menelik defeated an Italian effort to conquer his country in 1896. The other was Liberia in West

**Opening Africa: The European Viewpoint**   Above, an artist's imagined portrayal of how the American reporter Henry Stanley encountered the missionary-explorer David Livingstone on the shores of Lake Tanganyika in 1871. Livingstone had been reported dead, and Stanley set off to find him amidst a blaze of publicity. Subsequently, he informed an excited English-speaking world about the heroic explorer who had refused to leave Africa, even though he was ill. In fact, Livingstone died just two years later, still looking for the sources of the Nile and hoping by his example to inspire his fellow countrymen to promote Christianity, commerce, and civilization in Africa and suppress the slave trade. Below is a photograph that reveals a part of what European commerce meant for Africa. It shows the surface machinery needed by a mine at Bultfontein, South Africa, to wash diamonds out of the hard clay that enveloped them. By the 1880s, when this photograph was taken, Africans had been sent to work in the mines under conditions approaching slavery. They found themselves under the supervision of rough and ready white miners, some of whom are visible here in the foreground.

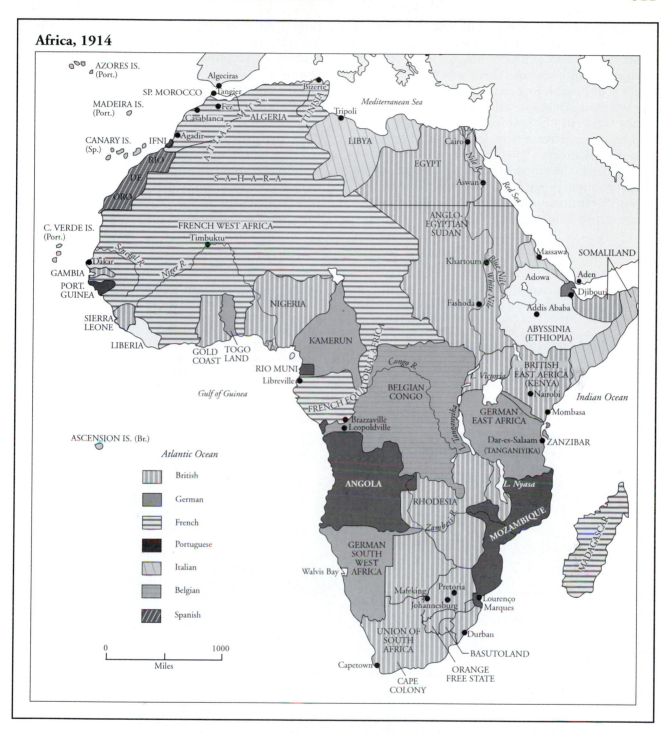

**Africa, 1914**

AZORES IS. (Port.)

SP. MOROCCO

MADEIRA IS. (Port.)

Algeciras
Tangier
Bizerte
Fez
Casablanca
ALGERIA
TUNISIA
Tripoli
*Mediterranean Sea*

CANARY IS. (Sp.)
IFNI
Agadir
RIO DE ORO
ATLAS MTS.
S A H A R A
LIBYA
EGYPT
Cairo
*Nile R.*
Aswan
*Red Sea*

C. VERDE IS. (Port.)
FRENCH WEST AFRICA
Timbuktu
ANGLO-EGYPTIAN SUDAN

GAMBIA
Dakar
*Senegal R.*
*Niger R.*
Khartoum
*Blue Nile*
*White Nile*
Massawa
SOMALILAND
Adowa
Aden
Djibouti

PORT. GUINEA
NIGERIA
Fashoda
Addis Ababa

SIERRA LEONE
ABYSSINIA (ETHIOPIA)

LIBERIA
GOLD COAST
TOGO LAND
KAMERUN
FRENCH EQUATORIAL AFRICA
*Congo R.*
BRITISH EAST AFRICA (KENYA)

RIO MUNI
Libreville
BELGIAN CONGO
*L. Victoria*
Nairobi
*Indian Ocean*

*Gulf of Guinea*
Brazzaville
Leopoldville
GERMAN EAST AFRICA
Mombasa

ASCENSION IS. (Br.)
*L. Tanganyika*
Dar-es-Salaam (TANGANIYIKA)
ZANZIBAR

*Atlantic Ocean*

ANGOLA
RHODESIA
*Zambesi*
*L. Nyasa*
MOZAMBIQUE
MADAGASCAR

British
German
French
Portuguese
Italian
Belgian
Spanish

GERMAN SOUTH WEST AFRICA
Walvis Bay

Mafeking
Pretoria
Johannesburg
Lourenço Marques
Durban
BASUTOLAND

0          1000
Miles

UNION OF SOUTH AFRICA
Capetown
CAPE COLONY
ORANGE FREE STATE

---

Africa, set up as a home for liberated American slaves in 1822. In many parts of Africa, to be sure, old kingdoms and tribal communities retained a shadowy sort of existence. The British liked to govern their colonies indirectly, depend-

ing on native leaders to collect taxes and carry out whatever new policies the British felt might be necessary. In other respects they deliberately left customs and traditional practices alone. In theory, the French aimed at making their African subjects into Frenchmen with black skins; in practice, they usually left the existing structures of African society and administration almost unchanged simply because there was nothing else a handful of French imperial administrators could do. German, Belgian, and Portuguese colonial rulers were in the same position, even when backed up by private businessmen and missionaries from Europe.

Indeed, the most marked feature of Africa in its colonial years was the discrepancy between the framework of European imperial administration and the human reality that con-

tinued to exist on the ground. The political boundaries drawn across the face of Africa seldom corresponded to geographical or social frontiers. Often very different peoples were grouped together in a single colony. Occasionally, kindred peoples found themselves split up between rival European administrations.

Africa as a whole remained extremely varied. The continent exhibited greater racial variety than existed elsewhere. Pygmies of the Congo rain forest and such extremely tall people as the Tutsi represent extremes of human stature, for example; and other differences divided the

---

**Two African Queens**   On the left, a bronze bust of a queen of Benin, cast by local craftsmen about 1600. On the right, a portrait of Queen Victoria carved by one of her African subjects about 1900. Insignia of rank differ, and probably Queen Victoria's thin lips and sharp nose were meant to emphasize how far her appearance departed from African norms, but the main purpose of both artists was to show how far above ordinary folk the two rulers were. Elaborate headdresses and haughty, half-threatening stares convey the power and dignity of royalty. It seems safe to say that the anonymous artist who carved this bust of Queen Victoria held fast to established African ideas of what royalty was and knew little or nothing of Queen Victoria's England.

inhabitants into numerous physically distinct groups. Hundreds of African languages also existed, some of them spoken only locally, while others, like Arabic and Swahili, served as languages of trade and culture among many different peoples. The Bantu family of languages can claim a certain preeminence in Africa, however, being spoken very widely in both western and southern Africa.

European administration constituted a thin veneer, half hiding the ancient human variety of Africa. New schools and laws and military service in European-style armed forces did make a difference, of course. So did the new modes of transport, new circulation of diseases, new taxes, and new economic activities. But most Africans remained in their villages and lived much as they had before Europeans appeared on the scene. Except in the extreme north (where French and Italian settlers became numerous in Algeria and Tunis) and in the south (where Boers and English occupied a good deal of the best farmland), Europeans always remained very few. Consequently, until after 1914, the European impact on Africa was drastic yet superficial. Old ways were in retreat, and old forms of political organization had been discredited or destroyed; but very few Africans had yet had time or opportunity to think of how to regain the initiative in their encounters with white men. Only after World War II did that possibility arise; and when it did, European empires crumbled even faster than they had arisen.

## Amerindian Peoples

The other large human population existing on the fringes of civilization between 1850 and 1914 lived in the central portion of the Americas, between Peru and Bolivia on the south and Mexico on the north. They were the descendants of Amerindians, who had inhabited these regions before the Spaniards came, with some admixture of Spanish and African blood.

In the parts of the Spanish Empire inhabited chiefly by people of European descent, the liberal ideals that had come to the forefront during the revolutionary years (1808–1824) fitted realities well enough. The Church was the main target of the liberals; after their victory, control over Church lands became the principal bone of contention among military and party leaders. In the regions where Amerindian populations were a majority, however, the liberals faced a special problem. Should the ideals of self-government extend also to the Amerindians? In South America, the white ruling classes answered this question in the negative. In Mexico, on the contrary, the answer was in the affirmative. Benito Juárez—the liberal champion against Emperor Maximilian and the French from 1860 to 1872—was of Indian parentage and got much of his support from the Indians and men of mixed blood. Later, to be sure, Mexico came under the control of Porfirio Diaz (1876–1911), who favored foreign investment and the white landowning class more than poor Indians. In 1911 he was overthrown by a revolutionary movement aimed both against rich landowners at home and U.S. businessmen who were operating mines and plantations in Mexico from abroad. Resulting diplomatic disputes between the United States and Mexico led in 1916 to minor military skirmishes along the border between the two countries.

Meanwhile, the ruling cliques of Peru, Ecuador, Bolivia, Colombia, and Venezuela quarreled vigorously among themselves for control of the government. But they always stopped short of appealing to the Amerindian villagers—partly, perhaps, because the peasants would not listen and partly because the whites feared for their position in society if ever the Amerindian majority should enter actively into politics. Therefore, being unable to mobilize wide support in their countries, all such regimes remained comparatively weak and were often unstable.

## Conclusion

In spite of the survival of remote Andean villages almost untouched by world events and the existence of similar village communities in some other parts of the globe, it still remained true that the world had become united as never before. Between 1850 and 1914, like a great spider, Europeans had spun a web of rails and telegraph lines around the globe. All humankind was caught in it. Struggles to escape, to withdraw, to get back to the good old times when strangers and outsiders didn't matter, where in vain. In the next chapters we will survey the whole globe, decade by decade, to see what people have, to date, done with the unparalleled opportunities and difficulties this new state of affairs created for humanity as a whole, and for each segment, class, group, and individual that, taken together, make up humankind.

---

## Bibliography

Two stories written at almost the same time, one by an Englishman, one by a Pole (who nevertheless chose to write in English), give human (and sometimes inhumane) reality to the European imperialism of this era. Rudyard Kipling, *Kim* (1901), is an upbeat portrait of British India; while Joseph Conrad's short story, "Heart of Darkness" (1902, and often reprinted), brings the costs of Europeans' penetration of Africa to life. Kipling's poem, "Recessional" (1897), revealing his sense of the fragility of Britain's hegemony, offers a surprising counterpart to the imperial assertiveness of *Kim*.

Two books by Daniel Headrick, *The Tools of Empire: Technology and European Imperialism in the Nineteenth Century* (1981) and *The Tentacles of Progress: Technology Transfer in the Age of Imperialism, 1860–1940* (1988), explain Europeans' technological advantages over other peoples. D. V. Glass and D. E. C. Eversley, *Population in History* (1965), give details of population growth in the era. For the financial dimension, Herbert Feis, *Europe: The World's Banker, 1870–1914* (1930), is a classic. W. L. Langer, *The Diplomacy of Imperialism 1890–1902* (2nd ed., 1950), and Wolfgang J. Mommsen, *Theories of Imperialism* (1980), treat the diplomatic and intellectual sides of the phenomenon masterfully.

For the experience of what I called the inner ring of European-style societies overseas, the following are of special interest: S. D. Cushman, *America in the Gilded Age: From the Death of Lincoln to the Rise of Theodore Roosevelt* (2nd ed., 1988); Walter P. Webb, *The Great Plains* (1931); C. Vann Woodward, *The Strange Career of Jim Crow* (3rd ed., 1974); Ernest R. May, *Imperial Democracy* (1968); Alfred Chandler, *The Visible Hand: The Managerial Revolution in America* (1977); J. M. S. Careless and R. C. Brown, eds., *The Canadians* (1967); Kenneth H. Norrie and Douglas Owrem, *A History of the Canadian Economy* (1991); F. K. Crowley, ed., *A New History of Australia* (1974); C. E. Carrington, *The British Overseas: Exploits of a Nation of Shopkeepers* (2nd ed., 1968); Theodore von Laue, *Sergei Witte and the Industrialization of Russia* (1963); Franco Venturi, *Roots of Revolution* (1960); Thomas E. Skidmore and Peter H. Smith, *Modern Latin America* (1984); Magnus Morner, *Race Mixture in the History of Latin America* (1967); and Philip D. Curtin, *The Rise and Fall of the Plantation Complex: Essays in Atlantic History* (1990).

For Asia and Africa, the following are also of unusual interest or importance: K. M. Panikkar, *Asia and Western Dominance: A Survey of the Vasco da Gama Epoch in Asian History, 1498–1945* (1953); Richard Koebner and Helmut D. Schmidt, *Imperialism: The Story and Significance of a Political World, 1840–1960* (1964); R. Suntharalingam, *Indian Nationalism: An Historical Analysis* (1983); Paul R. Bass and Francis Robinson, eds., *The Indian National Congress and Indian Society, 1885–1985* (1987); Benedict Anderson, *Imagined Communities: Reflections on the Origin and Spread of Nationalism* (1983); William K. Lockwood, *The Economic Development of Japan: Growth and Structural Change* (1968); John K. Fairbank, *The Great Chinese Revolution 1800–1985* (1986); Thomas Pakenham, *The Scramble for Africa, 1876–1912* (1991); Ralph Austen, *African Economic History* (1987); Michael Adas, *Prophets of Rebellion: Millenarian Protest Movements against the European Colonial Order* (1987); and for the fate of American Indians, James Axtell, *The European and the Indian* (1982).

# Transportation and Communication

To those who lack long-range means of travel and communication, walking is the only way to go and talking face to face the only way to communicate.

Through most of history this was the case, although from the beginning of civilization, ships and pack animals gave some people a longer reach. Using relays of horses or simple sailing vessels, a person could travel up to 100 miles a day, whether by land or by sea.

## BREAKING DESERT BARRIERS

Between 200 and 600 C.E. caravans acquired a new efficiency thanks to the domestication of camels. Thereafter, deserts became passable as never before. And since camels could live on wild herbage growing along the way, they cost very little. Cheap long-distance caravan transport gave Moslems an advantage over everyone else before about 1000, allowing Moslem traders to cross the Sahara to West Africa and penetrate all the deserts of Central Asia.

### Highlights

Overland transport by caravan could carry only small loads. Trade was therefore restricted mainly to luxuries.

Camels broke through desert barriers by 600 C.E., opening new frontiers to Islamic trade and civilization in Africa and Asia.

## BREAKING THE OCEAN BARRIERS

Between 1400 and 1500, Europeans learned how to make ships that could travel safely across stormy seas and in waters where tides ran swift and high. Strongly built hulls, a big rudder, and multiple masts with sails that could be put up or down, according to the strength of the wind, all played their part in making ships safer and more maneuverable.

With such vessels, long voyage across the oceans became easy. But how to get back? This required new methods of navigation, which would allow a ship to find its position by observing the sun or the stars. European sailors—especially the Portuguese—worked out this problem, too, by 1500.

Finally, how to protect oneself against strangers, whether on sea or land? The answer was to put cannon on board ship. Strong hulls, built to hold up against heavy waves, could also withstand the recoil of heavy guns.

### Highlights

Within less than thirty years (1492–1521), European seafarers broke through the vast ocean barriers that had previously divided humanity into separate continental blocks.

The opening of the oceans by European ships started new kinds of interaction among the peoples of the world. Trade, migration, and exchange both of diseases and of new food crops all took new paths.

## PRINTING

Printing from wooden blocks was invented by the Chinese before 800 C.E. Since Chinese writing uses thousands of different signs or characters, it was easier to carve a whole page at a time than to assemble separate bits of type made in advance.

In Korea and in Europe, however, alphabetic writing required only a small number of different signs. Therefore, it made sense to cast type for each letter in multiple copies ahead of time and then to assemble the movable type into words.

In Europe the first book printed in this manner was made in Germany by Johann Gutenberg in 1454.

### Highlights

Printing made it possible to produce large numbers of copies of a text cheaply and accurately. This had revolutionary effects in Europe but a conservative effect in China. In China, printing was used to reproduce the Confucian classics and commentaries upon them. Wider familiarity with these texts simply strengthened Confucian ideas and attitudes.

Among Europeans, an intensified interaction of old and new ideas and information shook established beliefs.

## INLAND TRANSPORT

Since the invention of ships, water transportation had always been much cheaper than land transport. Canals could extend the advantages of water transportation inland, even where natural riverways were absent. Locks allowed barges to travel up over a watershed, crossing from one river basin to another. The first country to take advantage of this possibility on a big scale was China, where the Grand Canal linked the Yangtze Valley with the Yel-

low River Valley after 605 C.E. By building feeder canals upstream (initially to irrigate rice paddies), a new, cheap transport system came into existence. Cheap transport, in turn, allowed trade to flourish, and China became the richest and most skilled country in the world for about five hundred years (1000–1500), thanks to its superior internal transport system.

In Europe, canal building became important for inland transportation between 1750 and 1850. Canals could carry heavy loads cheaply once they were built, but in many cases construction and maintenance were costly.

Roads used by wheeled vehicles must have some kind of drainage; otherwise, the rain softens the surface, mudholes develop, and the road soon turns into a quagmire. The Romans built narrow roads of paving stones. After 1700, Europeans discovered a much cheaper way of making durable roads by scat-

A 19th Century Printing Press.

tering gravel on the roadbed so that rain could drain away without leaving mudholes behind. Smooth roads allowed higher speed, so stagecoaches carried goods and passengers as much as 100 miles a day, reaching the old limit civilized peoples had known ever since they tamed the horse.

### Highlights

Cheaper movement of heavy goods by water and faster movement of goods and passengers by land intensified interaction across longer distances.

Rapid economic development resulted, with remarkable growth of both industry and agriculture.

## POPULAR PRESS

Early presses were worked by men using their own muscles to press a sheet of paper against a bed of ink-covered type. Even with the help of carefully designed levers this went rather slowly.

Faster printing came by making the type fit onto a curved, cylindrical surface. Such a cylinder could print by spinning around while a long sheet of paper rolled past. Cylinder presses made on this principle could print many thousands of sheets in an hour.

### Highlights

High-speed printing gave birth to mass-circulation newspapers and magazines.

Newspapers and magazines read by millions created a new kind of interaction between the government and the public.

Government action supported by the aroused will of a whole people attained much greater force than before, mobilizing greater resources, both human and material, to carry through common purposes.

## STEAM RAILROAD

Railroads reduce friction between wheels and the ground by concentrating comparatively

Passenger Train about 1950.

large weights on very narrow, hard rails. This principle was first used mainly in hauling coal, both inside the mines and on the surface.

The railroad came into its own when steam power was set to work moving whole trains of cars along metal rails. More powerful locomotives and carefully prepared roadbeds allowed the trains to reach speeds up to 100 miles per hour.

### Highlights

Railroads could carry people and goods overland faster than ever before and often more cheaply.

Railroads linked up with ocean-going steamships to deliver cheap grain to European ports from America, Argentina, and Australia. This damaged European agriculture and forced millions of European peasant farmers to emigrate to America.

The rise of Germany, Russia, and the United States as great powers depended on the development of the continental interiors of Europe, Asia, and North America. Railroads opened up these interiors between 1850 and 1914.

## GLOBAL COMMUNICATION

Smoke signals and fire beacons spread alarms in very ancient times. Semaphore flag stations carried more complicated messages during the Napoleonic wars. But from the 1830s the electric telegraph offered a far superior way of sending messages over long distances.

Waterproof cables, laid across the ocean beds, soon linked continent with continent. Key cities of the world came into instantaneous contact with one another.

After 1876, telephone communication speeded up the process, since words can be spoken faster than a telegraph operator can send letters by code. Over long distances, however, background noise often made spoken words unclear when telegraph signals could get through.

### Highlights

Telegraph and telephone extended the range of human communication enormously, by linking up the globe into a single communications network.

Orders for purchase and sales could reach around the world. This created a world market for standard bulk commodities like wheat.

Politics changed when central command and precise control, both in peacetime diplomacy and in war, became possible for the first time.

## MASS COMMUNICATION

Wireless communication uses electromagnetic waves to transmit messages at the speed of light. Complicated transmitters and simpler radio and television receivers allow massive communication at low cost. The only important limitation is that electromagnetic waves travel in straight lines and, unless bounced off reflecting layers of the atmosphere, soon leave the earth.

### Highlights

Radio and television stations create a new form of mass communication, since the same messages can be sent into millions of homes at small cost to the sender.

Mass marketing of standard consumer goods on radio and TV altered patterns of consumption all around the globe.

Political propaganda by radio and television exercise a strong influence, especially in countries where the government maintains control of sending stations.

Radio and television tend to reduce class and regional differences within the radius of the broadcast.

## AIR AND SPACE TRAVEL

Flying changed patterns of long-distance travel fundamentally. Old barriers fell. Mountains, deserts, and valleys ceased to matter much for overland travel; harbors, tides, and shoals ceased to affect travel across the seas. For long flights earth became a sphere, making the Arctic a particularly strategic region. This is because major population concentrations are in the Northern Hemisphere, and the shortest air routes between distant population centers always curve northward toward the Arctic. The earth became still smaller when rocket propulsion opened the possibility of escape from earth's gravity and exploration of the solar system.

### Highlights

Air travel changed transport routes and shortened time of travel between distant portions of the globe.

In case of a war, air and space travel mean that every state's territory is in danger.

Humanity's exploration of the earth and space beyond the earth continues with consequences—psychological, political, economic, and ecological—still unknown and unknowable.

## COMPUTERS, SATELLITE STATIONS AND THE INFORMATION HIGHWAY

Computers can store, sort, and retrieve enormous amounts of information almost instan-

An Illustration of the Westar IV Communication Satellite.

taneously. When connected together by wire or radio beams, they can send and receive data from anywhere on earth to anywhere else by bouncing radio waves off satellite relay stations hovering in space some 18,000 miles above the earth's surface.

These capabilities now link individuals and businesses with one another in entirely new ways by what is often called the "Information Highway." This is a picturesque way of describing the fact that personal computers in homes and offices can have ready access to a vast range of information stored in enormous data banks and can exchange messages with other individuals and organizations by e-mail and the Internet as well.

Pictures can also be transmitted by the same channels so that events in any part of the world can be viewed on home TV sets as they happen, if the news organizations think they are important or interesting enough to deserve such treatment. During the Gulf War (1992), CNN even broadcast live pictures from both sides of the battle and distributed these images throughout the world. To be sure, military censorship limited what was sent; but the visible results of modern air and missile warfare penetrated hotel rooms and private houses throughout most of the world.

### Highlights

No one knows what the consequences of these new forms of communication will be. Time will tell; but changes are sure to be far reaching. For example:

Office work can be done at home, making commuting into cities unnecessary. This may profoundly disrupt established urban patterns of life and work.

Private communication running across political boundaries might tend to reduce state sovereignty; yet governments may find ways to manage traffic in the Information Highway to suit their own purposes.

Overload may turn people off and make them indifferent to what comes incessantly into their homes and offices. Alternatively, easy private access to an enormous variety of information, ideas, and amusements may allow groups with common interests to link up with one another, creating quite new social and political associations with which old-fashioned territorial states and governments will have to come to terms.

# World Wars of the Twentieth Century

## 1914 to 1945

# 24

**Liberation (1945)**   Destruction and construction are inescapably intertwined in human affairs. Perhaps the fact that the wars of the twentieth century did little damage to the United States made it easy for an American artist, Ben Shahn (1898–1969), to greet the end of World War II with this celebration of human resilience amidst the ruins. Ben Shahn: *Collection, The Museum of Modern Art, New York. James Thrall Soby Bequest.*

The great wars of the twentieth century, World War I, 1914–1918, and World War II, 1939–1945, were similar in many ways and should be discussed together. Both began in Europe and pitted Germany against a coalition of allies, and in both wars Germany was eventually defeated. But Germany's defeat came only after American resources and manpower were brought into action on European soil; and by 1945 the national power of the United States had clearly outstripped all other nations, not just in Europe but all around the globe. American predominance was temporary, to be sure. But the rise of the United States, together with that of the Union of Soviet Socialist Republics (USSR) and of Japan, marked the end of the era of world leadership by nations of western Europe—an era that dated back to the sixteenth century.

The wars marked the end of an era in another sense as well. Before 1914, democratic and parliamentary government, together with the private pursuit of profit in the marketplace, seemed the wave of the future—the path of progress along which all peoples might be expected eventually to travel on the way to a peaceful and prosperous future. However, the wars showed that things were not that simple. The brutality and bloodshed of warfare itself—an experience more shocking in 1914 than in 1939—was obviously incompatible with former confidence in civilized progress. In addition, it became clear that politically organized effort, overriding the rules of private profit, could increase production and magnify national power far more efficiently than anyone had previously imagined. Managed economies worked wonders, more spectacularly in World War II than in World War I, making a return to unregulated private pursuit of profit impossible.

Democratic and parliamentary government also met with new challenges. The communist regime of Russia after 1917 and the fascist regime of Italy after 1922 both emphasized an ideal of *solidarity*—class solidarity for Lenin and his followers in Russia, and national solidarity for Mussolini and his followers in Italy. Communists and Fascists agreed that democratic parties and elections simply allowed selfish pursuit of private interests. This, they claimed, was both wicked and inefficient. Instead, some sort of so-cialist management or corporate organization of human effort would meet human needs far better and leave the old bourgeois selfishness of prewar society behind. Fascism was discredited by the defeat of Germany and Italy in World War II; and after World War II, Russian communism began to look more and more inefficient. But the pre-1914 confidence that the democratic, liberal, and parliamentary recipe for good government was universally applicable and adequate for all situations has not been fully restored.

Finally, the experience of World Wars I and II altered popular attitudes toward war. In 1914, the prospect of a short, victorious campaign was welcomed by millions of civilians who were called up to serve in European armies in accordance with mobilization plans laid down long in advance. War seemed a test of fitness, a way of asserting and preserving national greatness, and a useful instrument of statecraft. Years later, after two global wars, and after millions of people had been slaughtered, the glory and heroism of war diminished almost to the vanishing point. Yet fear of war did not prevent continued preparation for war. Instead, an ever more costly arms race broke out after 1945 even more vigorously than before 1914.

In all these respects, the two great wars of the twentieth century constitute a turning point in world affairs, whose full implications and long-range consequences we do not yet know. But it looks as though they will mark the end of what used to be called the modern era of world history—an era that began about 1450 and ended, perhaps, in 1945. We have no name for the new era, if indeed the course of future events will make it seem proper to call the period since 1945 a new era. We who live through it can only wonder and wait to see how things turn out.

## Outbreak of World War I

In Sarajevo, the capital of Bosnia, on June 28, 1914, an angry young man named Gavrilo Princip shot and killed Archduke Francis Ferdinand, heir to the throne of Austria-Hungary. Princip was a Serb, and the Austrians held the Serbian

**Triggering World War I**   This photograph shows the arrest
of Gavrilo Princip (right) moments after he had fired the shots
that killed the Archduke Franz Ferdinand, heir to the Hapsburg
throne, in Sarajevo on June 28, 1914. Princip swallowed a poison
capsule after firing his pistol but it only made him sick. He was
therefore brought to trial by the Austrian authorities and, being
a minor (he was eighteen years of age), received the maximum
penalty of twenty years' imprisonment. He died of tuberculosis
in April 1918, six months before the Hapsburg Empire collapsed
as a result of the war his act triggered. The diverse styles of dress
seen in the photograph reflect the clash of cultures that was then
taking place in Bosnia, where Western styles—both military and
civilian—mingled with traditional local costume. Moslems wore
the fez to permit them to put their foreheads to the ground when
praying (as their faith required), while Christians advertised
their different identity by wearing caps and hats with brims.

government responsible for the assassination.
Friction between Serbia and the Austro-Hungarian monarchy was already acute. Serbs lived on
both sides of the border between the two countries, and Serbian nationalists wanted to unite
their people into a single sovereign state. So
when Princip resorted to murder, the Austrian
government decided to teach the Serbs a lesson.
They believed, mistakenly, that other European
governments would not support assassins; and,
indeed, if Austrian demands on the Serbian government had been more moderate, or if the Serbian government had not gone very far toward
meeting Austrian demands, it is likely that the

crisis would have remained limited to the Balkan
cockpit where it started.

But the rival alliances into which the European great powers had divided since 1907 came
immediately into play, making a diplomatic crisis into a catastrophe. Russia backed the Serbs;
Germany backed the Austrians; France rallied to
the Russian side against Germany; and Great
Britain, after hesitating and trying to find a
peaceful solution, finally came in on the side of
France and Russia. Only Italy, which had been
formally allied with Germany and Austria, held
back. Thus the crisis escalated into full-scale
war, breaking out between July 28, when Austria

declared war on Serbia, and August 3, 1914, when Great Britain declared war against Germany and Austria.

One reason for the way things turned out was that the great powers of the European continent had worked out elaborate mobilization plans in advance. These could be put into effect by a simple order, but once started, could not be altered without paralyzing confusion. Each plan was designed to bring a maximal number of soldiers into action in the shortest possible time, using railroads to deliver troops and supplies to strategic locations in accordance with very precisely calculated timetables. Whichever army got going soonest with the largest forces would be able to impose its strategic plan on the enemy, and, according to plan, could then expect to win a decisive victory in a matter of a few weeks. Everything depended on speed, numbers, and the quality of troops and material brought to the field of battle. Delay or hesitation, once the first mobilization order had been given, was too risky to contemplate. As a result, the Austrian decision to attack the Serbs provoked Russian mobilization, quickly followed by German and French mobilization; and once rival mobilization plans went into action, there was no turning back.

As events showed, the German war plan was the most effective. A vast German army began to march across Belgium, intending to cross into northern France, surround Paris, and then take the French army, deployed along the German frontier, in the rear. The plan worked for the first few weeks, but as the Germans approached Paris, early in September, a gap opened between two of the advancing columns, and the French were able to attack through the hole that had opened up in the German front. Fearing that their vanguard might be cut off, the Germans decided to withdraw behind the Marne River on September 9, 1914.

## Stalemate and Intensified War Effort

This meant that the German plan had failed; but the French plan for attacking Germany directly across the frontier had also failed disastrously, and Russian armies, advancing into East Prussia, were turned back by September 15 as well. Even the Austrian forces assigned to conquer the little state of Serbia were unsuccessful. Machine guns and rifle fire proved far more lethal against attacking infantry than anyone had expected. The only thing to do was to dig in furiously, for even hastily built trenches could protect soldiers from rifle and machine gun bullets.

In France, accordingly, a system of trenches came into existence by the end of 1914 that ran unbrokenly from the Swiss frontier in the south to the shores of the English Channel in the north. Efforts to break through proved futile throughout the ensuing four years, though both sides tried, over and over again, to win decisive victory on this, the western, front. In the east, geographic distances were such that trench systems never ran continuously along the entire front. Armies were therefore able to take the offensive and move scores or even hundreds of miles at a time, forward and back. But until 1917 stalemate also prevailed on the eastern front. Even the most smashing victory soon petered out because an advancing army inevitably ran out of supplies, while the defeated forces recovered their fighting capacity by getting closer to their own sources of food and ammunition.

In this unexpected situation, European governments saw two ways of winning. One was to find new allies, thus extending the front, and strengthening one side at the expense of the other. By 1916, diplomatic pressure, promises of territorial gains, and a coup d'état in Greece divided most of Europe between the two sides. Italy, Romania, and Greece joined France, England and Russia (the Allies); Bulgaria and Ottoman Turkey joined Germany and Austria (the Central Powers). Even after Serbia was overrun by a combined German, Austrian, and Bulgarian offensive in 1915, the Serbian army fought on, based on Greek soil; and the Central Powers, despite their initial victories in Belgium and northern France, and subsequent advances into Polish territory in the east, remained almost completely surrounded by hostile forces. Until 1917, when the United States entered the war, the policy of finding new allies therefore proved

# World War I, 1914–1918

**Western Europe 1914–1918**

GERMANY
NETHERLANDS
LUXEM-BOURG
BELGIUM
Verdun
Argonne
Champagne
Chemin des Dames
FRANCE
Somme
Vimy
SWITZ.

Furthest German advance, Sept. 1914
Front at end of 1914
Battles
Armistice Line, 1918

IRELAND
GREAT BRITAIN
North Sea
Dogger Bank
Jutland
DENMARK
Amster-dam
NORWAY
SWEDEN
Baltic Sea
FINLAND
RUSSIA
Dnieper R.
UKRAINE
Caspian Sea
Black Sea
GEORGIA
AZERBAIJAN
ARMENIA
PERSIA
OTTOMAN
ARABIA
1918
Suez Canal
EGYPT
LIBYA
Mediterranean Sea
CRETE
GREECE
ALBANIA
MONTE-NEGRO
BULGARIA
ROMANIA
SERBIA
1915
Sarajevo
BOSNIA
AUSTRIA-HUNGARY
GALICIA
Danube R.
POLAND
E. PRUSSIA
Tannenburg
GERMANY
Rhine R.
BELGIUM
1914
SWITZ.
Seine
Loire R.
Rhône R.
FRANCE
SPAIN
Bay of Biscay
CORSICA
SARDINIA
SICILY
ITALY
Adriatic Sea

Allied Powers
Central Powers
Neutral States
Territory occupied by Central Powers
Allied Power advances
Limit of Central Powers advances

Battles
Central Power advances
Limit of Allied advances

ineffective in tipping the balance one way or the other in any decisive fashion. It simply engaged more countries and peoples in the struggle and made the eventual peace settlement more complicated.

The second way to win the war was to intensify mobilization, bringing more men into combat and equipping them with more and more artillery and other heavy weapons. Military experts agreed that a really massive preliminary bombardment by thousands of guns could smash the enemy's trenches and permit a decisive breakthrough. The flaw in this plan was that surprise became impossible as the open trenches of 1914 were turned into ever more elaborate underground fortifications and became able to withstand even a prolonged bombardment.

Consequently, an energetic British effort to win the war by building a new mass army equipped with hitherto unheard of quantities of artillery turned out to be in vain. A long and bloody Battle of the Somme in 1916 only sufficed to relieve pressure on the French, who were barely able to withstand an intense German assault aimed at the fortress of Verdun. But as before, the end result was stalemate.

Despite these failures, mobilization of the rear to provide more and more shells and other supplies for the front had important consequences for European countries. In effect, the principal combatant governments learned to make each belligerent nation over into a single war-making firm, maximizing output of goods and soldiers needed for the war effort by subordinating everything else to a national plan. Rationing of scarce goods, allocating critical materials, and keying industrial production to the needs of the armed forces all came on stream. The effect was to raise war-making capacity to unimagined heights, but all for naught, as one attack after another failed to achieve expected results.

## 1917–1918:
## The Years of Decision

Some governments were, nonetheless, better equipped than others to mobilize resources effi-

ciently. The Austro-Hungarian monarchy, for example, had to depend on help from Germany to make up for gaps in home production of artillery and other war goods. Internal frictions among the different nationalities of the empire became more intense as the war went on and paralyzed the state by 1918. Ottoman Turkey, too, depended on Germany for war supplies; and frictions between the Turkish government and some of its Arab subjects turned into a critical breakdown by the last months of the war.

But the most important country that got into serious trouble on the home front was Russia. The czarist government achieved remarkable results in increasing its armament production, but by 1917 food and other essential civilian commodities began to disappear from the cities where all the guns and ammunition were manufactured. Total food production declined because so many men were taken from their villages to serve in the army. In addition, those who remained on the land began to consume more of what they raised because there was nothing for them to buy in town.

Economic hardship fostered political discontent. Revolutionary parties had long existed in Russia, and the handful of Marxists who followed Lenin (original name, Vladimir Ilich Ulyanov, 1870–1924) soon began to win mass support in the hungry cities. Distrust and demoralization weakened the czar's government, and in March 1917 strikes by armament and other industrial workers in the capital, together with mounting criticism from the upper classes, persuaded the czar to abdicate. A provisional government then proposed to hold elections for a Constituent Assembly that would draft a new constitution for Russia; in the meanwhile the war had to go on.

Shortages simply got worse; and when Lenin proclaimed the slogan "Peace, Land, Bread," more and more Russians agreed. "Peace" was obviously needed to set things right. "Land" invited peasants on landlords' estates to seize control of the fields they cultivated. "Bread" meant life itself to hungry city dwellers, though how anyone would be able to deliver it to them was never made clear. Given the situation in Russia, Lenin's slogans were irresistible. In particular, peasants drafted into the army decided that they had to get back to their villages in a hurry so as to be

**World War I: The Glory and the Pain**   War became unpopular in Europe
and America during World War I in a new way because of the enormous
discrepancy between what everyone had expected and what actually happened
in the trenches of the Western Front. On the left is a photograph of parading
American soldiers, marching through London in 1917. Marching to music with
plaudits from the crowd was exhilarating in itself, and bringing victory to
the Allied side, as the Americans eventually were able to do, made war seem
glorious again. Such enthusiasm echoed the frantic enthusiasm that had
greeted the outbreak of fighting in 1914, when people in England, France,
and Germany welcomed release from the frictions and boredom of everyday,
confidently expecting glorious victory, according to plan, by or before
Christmas 1914. On the right, you may glimpse the painful reality of what the
war actually meant for those who got to the front. It shows a wounded soldier
about to be carried off to the rear on a stretcher. The narrow confines of the
hastily built trench are clear, but you have to imagine the mud, blood, rats, and
lice and the depressing daily routine of perpetual alert and ever-present danger
from machine gun bullets and shelling.

---

sure of getting their share of the land. Desertions
therefore multiplied, and the discipline of the
army wavered. Continuation of the war became
impossible.

On the night of November 6–7, 1917, Lenin
seized power in the capital city of Petrograd
(formerly St. Petersburg, later renamed Leningrad). Red Guards, organized by workers in the

# THE SEALED TRAIN

Vladimir Ilich Ulyanov (1870–1924) took the name "Lenin" when he became a revolutionary. The czarist government arrested him; later he fled from Russia and lived in Switzerland. He was there when World War I broke out. Switzerland remained neutral, completely surrounded by warring nations.

News of the March 1917 uprisings in Petrograd, the Russian capital, made Lenin desperate to get back. He wanted to take command of the Bolshevik party he had founded and carry the revolution onward to more and more radical stages. He wanted to end the war by overthrowing the landlords and capitalists, first in Russia and then in all the world. But how could he hope to escape from his Swiss refuge?

German agents in Switzerland knew a lot about Lenin and his plan for "turning imperialist war into class war." They thought, "Why not help Lenin to get back home and let him stir up the Russians to fight one another instead of fighting us?" The German Supreme Command had no objection. When the kaiser heard of the plan, he suggested that Lenin should be sent copies of all his latest speeches!

But Lenin was afraid. Perhaps the Germans only wanted to capture him by offering to let him ride a train through Germany to neutral Sweden. And his enemies might discredit him as a German agent if he took advantage of such an offer. All the same, he simply had to get back if all his dreams and life's work were not to fail.

On April 9, 1917, Lenin settled the issue. He would accept the German offer, provided the Germans would seal off the train so that no one could get on or off while passing through German territory. In this way, Lenin hoped that he could escape the charge of cooperating with the Germans. A train was made ready at once, and about twenty Russian revolutionaries, chosen by Lenin, got on board.

The trip lasted several days, with long delays in various switching yards. Each time the train stopped, the little group of Russians wondered whether they would all be arrested or perhaps killed. But the delays were caused by the fact that the German authorities had to clear the plan for sending Lenin and his friends to Russia through Sweden with officials of the Swedish government. By April 13, all was ready. Lenin crossed the Baltic to Sweden by ferryboat. The travelers continued by rail to Stockholm and then to Finland and so at last to Petrograd, Russia's capital. They arrived there on April 16, exactly a week after leaving Switzerland.

Both Lenin and the Germans got what they wanted from this deal. Lenin not only got back to Russia; within seven months he won supreme power and a chance to put his ideas into practice. From the start, his propaganda against the war proved very effective. Many Russian soldiers listened to Lenin and stopped fighting the Germans. As a result, the Russian army melted away and Germany was able to concentrate most of its remaining strength on the western front.

WORLD WARS OF THE TWENTIETH CENTURY

factories of the city, were the instrument he used; but the real basis of Lenin's power was the appeal of his propaganda and the frantic energy of the small corps of dedicated revolutionaries he had shaped into the Bolshevik faction of the Russian Social Democratic (that is, Marxist) party before the war. Marxist doctrine held that proletarian, socialist revolution was destined to occur first in the most industrialized countries, not in a predominantly peasant land like Russia. And so when Lenin took power, he confidently expected revolution to break out at any moment in Germany, France, and England. To hurry socialist revolution along, he declared peace unilaterally, denounced capitalist governments for continuing the war, and published secret treaties according to which the czar's government had agreed to share the spoils from the Austrian and Ottoman empires with France, Britain, and Italy.

Disintegration of the Russian army became almost complete after Lenin took power, and the Germans were therefore able to advance eastward more or less at will. But they did not want to go too far; instead, they wished to profit from Russia's collapse by concentrating their forces on the western front, where decisive victory remained to be won. Small bodies of German troops remained in the east, and in 1918 the Germans signed a peace treaty with the Bolsheviks at Brest Litovsk, making Poland, the Ukraine, Transcaucasia, and the Baltic provinces independent from Russia.

Success in the east was meaningless, however, unless the Germans could also defeat the French and British in the west. That became far more difficult after April 6, 1917, when the United States became a belligerent. Throughout the war, Americans had prospered by supplying food and munitions to the Allies. When the Germans responded by declaring unrestricted submarine warfare in the Atlantic and began to sink American ships, President Woodrow Wilson asked Congress to declare war. It took time to train American soldiers and send them to France; but as the Russian army disintegrated, a new American army was coming into being, thus counterbalancing Russia's collapse.

Moreover, American military power was matched by a powerful propaganda, designed in part to counteract Lenin's appeals for socialist revolution. In January 1918, President Wilson summed up American war aims in fourteen points, including the "right of national self-determination" and the establishment of a League of Nations that would settle future international quarrels peaceably. The United States, Wilson declared, was fighting a war to end war and make the world safe for democracy. Applied to central and eastern Europe, this was a program quite as revolutionary as Lenin's Marxism, and it appealed powerfully to war-weary people everywhere.

Early in 1918, German troops began their final offensive on the western front. For a while it looked as though a decisive breakthrough might be possible, but the weary French and British held, and fresh American units hurried into battle. Soon the balance tipped in the Allies' favor, and the Germans started retreating. Before the battle line reached the German border, however, revolution broke out in the rear of the German army, and a new, socialist German government signed an armistice on November 11, 1918. The war was over at last, for Turkey, Bulgaria, and Austria had also surrendered in the preceding weeks.

## The Peace Settlement: 1918–1923

The armistice ended the fighting but said nothing about the terms of peace. Peace-making was complicated by the fact that both Russia and the United States rejected treaties about postwar territorial arrangements that the Allies had made during the war. President Wilson advocated "open covenants, openly arrived at" and wanted to draw national boundaries anew on the basis of majority preferences among the local populations. Lenin continued to denounce the whole capitalist system and expected further revolutions to bring his fellow Marxists to power in other European countries. The communist government of Russia simply refused to have any dealings with the "Allied and Associated Powers," to give the victors the name they officially assumed at the peace conference. This meant that peace could not come to eastern Europe until 1921, when civil wars in the Ukraine and elsewhere had been fought to a finish. It took even longer for peace to come to the Near East, where a Greek-Turkish war lasted until 1923.

In the Far East, upheaval continued in China throughout the interwar period, though Japanese expansion was temporarily checked in 1922. During the war, Japan had overrun German colonial holdings in the Far East, then demanded special privileges in China; and when the Russian Empire seemed about to break up, the Japanese also sent an army into Russia's Far Eastern provinces.

The victorious allies entered the peace-making process with differing aims. The United States wished to check the Japanese in the Far East and to establish democratic governments in Europe so as to be able to get back to what soon came to be called "normalcy." The British government had similar goals and also wished to get control of Palestine and Iraq so as to safeguard the route to India. The French wanted the return of Alsace and Lorraine, provinces taken from them in 1871; but more important, they wished to make sure that Germany could never again become so powerful as to threaten French security. The Italians wanted territories along the Adriatic and in the eastern Mediterranean that they had been promised in 1916 in return for their entry into the war.

But the victors were only partly in control of the situation. Throughout eastern Europe, where the Austrian, Ottoman, and Russian governments had ruled before the war, confusion reigned. Socialists and nationalists collided, and rival nationalities disputed rights to nearly every territory and province. Germany, too, was in turmoil. Everywhere socialists split between those who supported Lenin's revolutionary recipe and others who preferred to cooperate with the Western powers. The choice for central and eastern Europe rested, in a sense, between Wilson's ideal of democratic, national self-determination and Lenin's ideal of proletarian revolution. But French and British wishes also

mattered; and they, burdened with war debts owed to the United States, hoped to punish the Germans and make them pay for the costs of the war by imposing heavy reparations payments.

When the Peace Conference met at Paris in 1919, therefore, the problem was how to combine Wilson's principles of democratic self-determination with punishment for Germany, while hoping that Lenin's challenge to the existing social order would soon disappear. It made for an unsatisfactory peace. The Treaty of Versailles, presented to the Germans for their signature in 1919, imposed unilateral disarmament and sliced off bits of German territory to allow Poland access to the sea, while prohibiting German Austria from ever uniting with Germany. Nearly all Germans felt that such provisions violated Wilson's promise of national self-determination. Even more deeply resented was the "war guilt clause," which declared that Germany had been responsible for starting the war and therefore had to pay reparations for all the war's costs. This provision was unenforceable in practice and threw a monkey wrench into the new League of Nations, upon which President Wilson pinned his hopes for future peace.

Farther east in Europe, events on the ground mattered more than decisions at Paris. The collapse of German power in 1918 provoked complicated civil wars in ex-czarist lands among Communists, "White" Russians, and various kinds of nationalists. France and Britain sent expeditionary forces to Russian ports and gave some help to the "Whites." The United States likewise sent a few soldiers to Russia's Far Eastern provinces, as much to watch the Japanese as to oppose the Communists. But war weariness was almost as intense in the West as in eastern Europe itself, and by 1920 the contestants were ready to make peace. Resulting treaties set up independent states throughout the western borderlands of the old Russian Empire. Russia's frontiers with the newly independent states of Finland, Estonia, Latvia, Lithuania, and Poland conformed pretty closely to the existing military lines of demarcation. But the Ukraine, Transcaucasia, and the Far Eastern

**Peacemaking in 1919: Warmaking in 1939**   On the left, the "Big Three" of the Paris Peace Conference, 1919–1920, are seen walking along a street between sessions. David Lloyd-George, prime minister of Great Britain, is on the left; George Clemenceau, premier of France, is in the middle; and President Woodrow Wilson of the United States is on the right. The three leaders differed about how to make a just and enduring peace, and their eventual compromises, embodied in the Treaty of Versailles, were imposed on Germany in 1920. Nearly all Germans felt that the treaty was unjust, and in the 1930s, after Adolf Hitler had come to power, Germany shattered the Treaty of Versailles bit by bit. Hitler first rearmed and reoccupied the Rhineland; then he demanded the right to bring Germans living in other lands into his Third Reich. He succeeded in extending German borders to embrace Austria and German-populated parts of Czechoslovakia, but when he also demanded parts of Poland, where Germans lived scattered among Polish populations, France and Britain reluctantly went to war. The photograph on the right shows the scene in the Reichstag on September 1, 1939, when Hitler announced that German soldiers had begun to march into Poland to liberate their fellow nationals, thus inaugurating World War II. Hitler stands in the exact center of this photograph, a small and almost inconspicuous figure, amidst a forest of arms raised in the Nazi salute.

provinces all returned to Russia within a very few years.

Hunger and disease were rampant, and in 1921 Lenin announced a "New Economic Policy" whereby private trading was allowed. It looked as though the communist principle of public ownership of the means of production had proved unworkable, just as critics in the West had always said. Lenin's ideals, as much as Wilson's, had indeed been compromised, but

**States of Europe, 1923–1939**
**Interwar Boundaries and Alliance Structure**

Boundaries in 1914
Post war in boundaries
**F** Allied with France
Shaded areas reflect territorial changes and formation of new nations

SOVIET UNION

*Volga R.*

Moscow

TURKEY

CYPRUS

*Don R.*

*Black Sea*

FINLAND

Petrograd
(Leningrad, 1924)

*Dnieper R.*

Kiev

ESTONIA

LATVIA

LITHUANIA

Vilna

*Baltic Sea*

EAST
PRUSSIA

POLAND

Warsaw

**F**

*Vistula R.*

RUMANIA

**F**

Bucharest

*Danube R.*

BULGARIA

Sofia

To
Greece

Constantinople

SWEDEN

Danzig

CZECHOSLOVAKIA

**F**

Budapest

HUNGARY

Belgrade

YUGOSLAVIA

**F**

ALBANIA

GREECE

Athens

CRETE

NORWAY

Copenhagen

Prague

Berlin

Vienna

AUSTRIA

to
Italy

*Adriatic
Sea*

Rome

ITALY

*Elbe R.*

GERMANY

Munich

SWITZ.

*Po R.*

*North Sea*

*Rhine R.*

SAAR

Strasbourg
to
France

*Rhône R.*

CORSICA

SARDINIA

*Mediterranean Sea*

NETHER-
LANDS

BELG.

Paris

Versailles

*Seine R.*

FRANCE

NORTHERN
IRELAND

GREAT
BRITAIN

London

*Loire R.*

*Bay of Biscay*

IRISH FREE
STATE

Madrid

SPAIN

PORTUGAL

500

250

Miles

0

Lenin's new economic policy helped the heartlands of the old Russian Empire (renamed Union of Soviet Socialist Republics in 1923) to regain a modicum of internal stability in the following years. Europe seemed about to settle into a new mold, giving France primacy on the continent, thanks to German disarmament and to alliances the French concluded with most of the new states of eastern Europe.

To the south, the treaty prepared at Paris for the Ottoman Empire proved unenforceable. Turkish national feeling rebelled against the provisions of the treaty that assigned territory on the eastern shore of the Aegean to Greece; and when the Greeks tried to enforce the treaty, Mustafa Kemal organized a makeshift Turkish army, which defeated them and proceeded to drive all Christians from the Asian side of the Aegean. A million and a half refugees fled to Greece. In return, Turks and Bulgarians were expelled from Greek soil to make room for the newcomers. The Treaty of Lausanne ratified and regulated this mass exchange of populations in 1923.

The Arab lands of the Ottoman Empire were assigned as "mandates" to France (Syria and Lebanon) and Britain (Palestine and Iraq). A mandate was a new legal invention, requiring the administering power to treat the territory in question as a temporary trust under the supervision of the League of Nations. Eventually, it was assumed, mandated lands would become capable of democratic self-government. Former German colonies in Africa and the Pacific were also made into mandates and assigned to one or another of the victors, including Japan. Local populations sometimes resisted, as happened in Syria, but not for long.

Palestine presented a more complicated problem. During the war, the British government had endorsed the idea of establishing a national home for Jews in Palestine. This Zionist ideal had begun to gain momentum among European Jews from the 1890s, but Arabs in Palestine opposed the idea vigorously. The new British administrators antagonized both parties by trying to find a compromise.

In the Far East, Japan's wartime activities in China and the Russian Far Eastern provinces had aroused intense American suspicion. Britain, allied with Japan since 1903, felt compelled to cooperate with the United States. When the Japanese realized this fact, they decided to draw back. The decisive negotiations took place in 1922 in Washington, where a naval limitations treaty defined the number of warships the principal naval powers of the world could have. Britain, the United States, and Japan agreed upon a 5:5:3 ratio for capital ships. Japan's overall inferiority nevertheless assured the Japanese navy of the preponderance in Far Eastern waters it already enjoyed, since neither the British nor the Americans could ever expect to concentrate their whole fleet so far away from home bases. But the Washington treaties of 1922 did nothing to stabilize conditions in China, where local disorders dating back to the overthrow of the Manchu Dynasty in 1911 tore the country apart.

The peace settlements, 1918–1923, were therefore imperfect and partial. Seeds of future troubles were all too apparent, especially in Europe, where a disappointed Italy became the seat of an ambitious fascist government in 1922, and where German resentment against the Treaty of Versailles was deep and abiding.

# Stabilization and Renewed Crisis: 1923–1933

Soviet economic recovery came slowly under the New Economic Policy. The communist regime was weakened first by Lenin's incapacity (an assassin's bullet followed by a stroke) and then by his death in 1924. The United States, too, withdrew from European affairs in 1920 when the Senate refused to ratify the Versailles treaty. Relations between the two remaining victors, France and Britain, also unraveled when the French attempted to enforce their rights under the Versailles treaty by occupying part of Germany in 1923 in order to compel the delivery of reparations. Economic collapse then threatened to provoke either a communist or a fascist revolution

# THE LONE EAGLE

Charles Augustus Lindberg (1902–1974) was too young to take part in World War I, but he learned to admire the aviators who dueled in flimsy airplanes high above the trenches in France. As soon as he could, he enlisted as a flying cadet in the United States Army Air Corps. When he graduated, the Air Corps put him on reserve status, and he got a job flying the mail between St. Louis and Chicago.

After doing this for two years, learning a lot about wind and weather and the ways of airplanes, he decided to compete for a prize offered for the first non-stop flight between New York and Paris. Backers in St. Louis paid for a plane built to his specifications. They named it *Spirit of St. Louis*.

On May 20, 1927, all was ready. A few minutes before 8:00 A.M., Lindbergh lifted the overloaded plane off the grass of Roosevelt Airfield at Garden City, Long Island, New York, and headed for Paris. Flying in those days was rather hit-or-miss. For long hours Lindbergh could not be sure where he was, for everywhere the ocean looked the same and he had to guess how much the winds were blowing his plane from its compass course.

A second problem was sleepiness. He took off early in the morning and landed in Paris late in the evening of the following day, after more than thirty-three hours in the air. The noise of the engine and the whistle of the wind sounded monotonously; yet Lindbergh had to stay awake and keep the plane headed on a steady course. Otherwise he might waste precious gas by swerving to and fro across the ocean, or he might even plummet into the sea and drown. The struggle to stay awake was his most difficult task, for the plane functioned perfectly and his guesswork about the winds turned out to be very nearly right. He sighted Ireland on the second day and could then fly on to Paris by following the map from point to point across southern England and northern France.

As he approached Paris a new problem arose. A vast crowed streamed out to greet him as news of his approach spread through the city. (His plane had been recognized over Ireland, and newspapers had followed its progress hour to hour thereafter.) And it was getting dark. How could the weary aviator see the landing place? Cars with their headlights gleaming were hastily arranged to show Lindbergh where to land, and the police kept the runway clear until the plane touched down safely.

Then the crowd broke through police lines. Excited people even started to tear the canvas skin off the *Spirit of St. Louis* for souvenirs. Lindbergh was completely taken aback. He struggled to get his plane safely locked in a hangar. Then he collapsed from fatigue. He awoke to worldwide renown.

Lindbergh's later life was anticlimatic. He soon came to hate the publicity and hero worship that surrounded him. In 1932 his eldest son was kidnapped and killed. Lindbergh was later accused of being too much impressed by Hitler's achievements, and President Roosevelt refused to allow him to fight in World War II. Thus politics clipped the "Long Eagle's" wings; Lindbergh became an inconspicuous civilian consultant to airplane manufacturers.

in Germany, and this prospect brought the United States back into action. An economic settlement of sorts was agreed upon (the Dawes Plan), whereby American bankers lent money to Germany, thus allowing the Germans to pay reparations to France and Britain, who, in turn, paid installments on their war debts to the United States. This arrangement worked for a while and even provoked a burst of industrial prosperity in Germany. The United States, too, enjoyed a postwar boom as new mass-produced consumer goods—automobiles, radios, washing machines, and so forth—came into more and more American homes and profoundly changed old patterns of living.

In 1929 boom turned into bust, following a rhythm that had existed for centuries but which no one really understood. Bank failures in Austria triggered panic in the United States. Suddenly the loans that had sustained the German recovery were no longer available. The same financial panic closed off credit for factories in the United States, so manufacturers had to shut down or cut back production drastically. In earlier times, crises of this kind had been endurable because most economic activity was agricultural and many of the people thrown out of work when factories shut down could take refuge with relatives on the farm and wait until new jobs opened up again. In the 1930s this was no longer possible in countries like Germany and the United States. Too many people lived in cities, without relatives in the country whom they could turn to.

Private charity and public relief were the alternatives if unemployed workers were not to starve. But why were idle factories unable to produce goods, and why were idle workers unable to buy what they needed to live? No one had a good explanation at the time. Marxist prophecies about the crisis of capitalism seemed to be coming true. The situation was made more acute by the fact that beginning in 1928 the Soviet government, now controlled by Josef Stalin (1879–1953), had launched a vast Five Year Plan of industrial development and continued to announce new victories in the struggle to build modern power plants and factories at a time when economic depression made life miserable for millions in the West. Soviet peasants paid the cost

of Stalin's forced pace of industrialization by providing both labor and food for the industrial effort without getting anything back in return; but this was not clear at the time.

## The Drift Toward War: 1933–1939

Economic suffering and discontent in Germany and the United States triggered drastic political departures. In Germany, Adolf Hitler (1889–1945) and the National Socialist German Workers' Party (Nazis, for short) came to power in January 1933. In March of the same year, Franklin D. Roosevelt (1882–1945) became president and launched what he called the New Deal to cope with the Great Depression. Hitler and Roosevelt, despite many contradictory currents that flowed among their supporters, had this in common: They both fell back on World War I methods of national mobilization to meet the crisis of the Depression and were fairly successful in doing so. On other matters, the two regimes differed profoundly for Hitler was a fanatic nationalist, intent on undoing the Versailles settlement, while Roosevelt was a Democrat and an optimist, with no very deep convictions about international affairs.

Hitler set out to establish a fascist dictatorship, far more efficient and powerful than the original fascist regime in Italy. Between 1922 and 1927, Benito Mussolini (1883–1945) had fastened the dictatorship of his Fascist party on Italy; but Mussolini's praise of national solidarity at home and imperial expansion abroad met with a mixed reception among Italians. Old patterns of peasant life still prevailed in the south, and the Roman Catholic Church together with other conservatives acted as a second restraining force. Mussolini's initial efforts to build a Mediterranean empire at the expense of Yugoslavia and Greece were successfully checked by France and Britain, acting through the League of Nations. But in 1933, when Mussolini attacked Ethiopia to revenge the defeat Italian soldiers had suffered in 1896, the League huffed and puffed but failed to prevent the Italians from conquering the whole of Ethiopia by 1936.

Before coming to power, Hitler partly modeled his Nazi party on Mussolini's Fascists; but national socialism, as defined by Hitler, differed from Italian fascism in being racist. Hitler proclaimed the superiority of the so-called Aryan race and asserted that German Aryans had been corrupted by Jews and other inferior races. One of his goals on coming to power in 1933 was to drive Jews from all walks of German life. He also wanted to restore German military power and hoped to cope with all the millions of unemployed whose votes had helped him come to power. Vast public works, especially road building, reduced unemployment; and after 1935, when Hitler felt it safe to denounce the Versailles treaty and begin rearmament openly, the unemployment problem disappeared.

By 1936, French and British opposition to Italy's invasion of Ethiopia made Mussolini into Hitler's ally; and between 1936 and 1939 Italy and Germany helped a fascist government, headed by Francisco Franco (1892–1975), come to power in Spain after a bitter civil war. The demoralization of the French, torn by domestic strife and unwilling to accept a wartime style of national mobilization, had become plain. Hitler therefore turned attention to building up the German armed forces so as to be able to undo the territorial settlement of 1919 on Germany's eastern border. Appealing to the right of national self-determination, Hitler annexed Austria and then dismembered Czechoslovakia in 1938; in 1939, he turned on Poland. This time resistance was better organized, and when Hitler persisted, World War II broke out.

In the United States recovery from the depression remained precarious until late in the 1930s, when armament programs designed to face up to German and Japanese threats had the effect of mopping up most of the country's unemployment. Americans began rearmament reluctantly, but events in Europe together with a resumption of Japanese expansion on the mainland of Asia tipped the balance of opinion within the United States.

Japan's aggression against China began in 1931. It was triggered, at least in part, by the fact that after years of disorder and sharp division among local warlords, China seemed about to unite under the leadership of Chiang Kai-shek (1887–1975). Chiang became leader of the Kuomintang Party with Communist support. But in 1927 he quarreled with them, expelling all of the Communist faction from the Kuomintang Party and killing all he could lay hands on. Survivors fled to the countryside. Under the leadership of Mao Tse-tung (1893–1976), the Chinese Communists eventually made their way to the province of Yenan, on the Mongolian border, where a trickle of supplies from the Soviet Union helped them keep going. In the rest of China, however, old warlords were compelled, one by one, to come to terms with Chiang's forces or meet destruction.

Before China's unification could be completed, however, the Japanese intervened in Manchuria. Swiftly they occupied the entire province and proclaimed the heir of the Manchu dynasty as emperor of Manchukuo. The League of Nations denounced but failed to check Japan's aggression, and neither the Chinese nor the Americans were willing to recognize the new state of affairs in the Far East. Instead, animosity increased and in 1936 the Japanese invaded north China, pushing southward along the coast and trying vainly to subdue the vast bulk of China completely. Rapid build-up of heavy industry in Manchuria helped to support the Japanese armed forces, which began to play a more and more independent role, not only on the mainland of Asia but within Japan itself. The so-called "China incident," committing the Japanese army to operations on the mainland, merged into World War II after 1941. Indeed, the conventional date for the beginning of the war, September 1, 1939, is arbitrary. Active operations in Asia dated back to 1932, when, from a Far Eastern point of view, the war really started.

Before describing World War II, a few words should be said about other parts of the world and how they fared during the interwar years. The Depression of the 1930s hit especially hard at countries that depended on the export of raw materials. As prices fell and demand slackened, farms and mines piled up unsaleable surpluses. Local governments were completely unable to solve the problem. On the other hand, where subsistence agriculture prevailed, the Depression made little difference, and urban unemployed could find refuge with relatives in the countryside when jobs disappeared.

As a result, Africa remained politically quiet under colonial rulers. Even Italy's conquest of Ethiopia had little obvious effect on the rest of the continent. India, on the other hand, became the scene of a struggle between the British rulers and the Congress party, whose leader, Mohandas Gandhi (1869–1948), demanded independence and national self-determination. He preached passive resistance, relying on "soul force" to overcome opposition. The British found Gandhi's campaigns very embarrassing, for how could they support democracy and self-determination in Europe and deny it in India? Several times Gandhi went to jail after defying British regula-

**Two Men Who Shook the British Empire**   This photograph shows Mohandas Gandhi and Jawaharlal Nehru conferring in 1942.
At that time, the Congress Party they headed was debating what to do about Britain's war with Japan that had just begun. The two leaders decided to demand that the British grant India independence at once and proposed to resist all efforts at mobilizing their country against the Japanese. The British promptly jailed them for the duration of the war, but mass protests that had stirred all India in the 1920s and 1930s, when Gandhi first organized civil disobedience against British rule, were muted by the fact that most Indians did not want to be overrun by the Japanese. That risk seemed very real when a Japanese army occupied India's neighbor, Burma, in 1942, and in fact the British were able to use Indian manpower and resources in their struggle against the Japanese quite effectively. When the war ended, India's independence followed swiftly in 1947, accompanied by bloody riots between Moslems and Hindus. Gandhi's efforts to halt the violence led to his assassination in 1948. Nehru, on the other hand, became the first prime minister of India and retained that office until his death in 1964.

tions; but this only increased his following in India. On the other hand, Indian Moslems were uncomfortable with Gandhi's movement, fearing that an independent India would become a Hindu India in which their religious identity and social status might be undermined. By the late 1930s some Indian Moslems had begun to demand an independent state of their own, separate from India. This may have strengthened the British position in India in the short run, but in another sense it simply consolidated opposition among another segment of the Indian population against continuation of British imperial rule.

In Latin America, the interwar years brought no very conspicuous changes. A bitter war between Paraguay and Bolivia ended in 1935 when mediators arranged a new boundary between the two nations. Further north, relations between Mexico and the United States entered upon a comparatively friendly era after 1933, when President Roosevelt proclaimed a Good Neighbor policy, which meant, in effect, that old U.S. claims to compensation for properties confiscated by the Mexican government during and after the revolution of 1911 would not be pursued any further.

Elsewhere, in the islands of the Pacific and in the British Dominions of Canada, Australia, and New Zealand, for example, politics revolved around the Depression and what to do about it; but no solutions were found.

World affairs were dominated by the drama of European politics where Hitler's challenge to existing international relationships had become obvious and urgent by the mid-1930s. When war began in Europe in September 1939, the struggle soon spread round the globe, making it a world war, more truly than in 1914–1918.

## World War II: Initial Axis Victories, 1939–1941

France and Britain reluctantly came to Poland's aid in September 1939 when the German army launched its attack. Memories of World War I weighed on everyone's mind, in Germany as well as elsewhere. Rejoicings like those of 1914 were conspicuously absent everywhere. But Hitler had prepared the ground for victory this time rather more skillfully than the German government of 1914 had done. First of all, he signed a non-aggression treaty with Stalin on August 23, 1939, just a week before the war began. Secret clauses partitioned Poland between the two powers and provided that the U.S.S.R. would supply Germany with food and other raw materials needed for the war effort. Stalin, who had previously been among the most vehement of Hitler's enemies, had changed sides and by doing so prevented a repetition of the World War I blockade, which had done a good deal to weaken the German war economy.

## Blitzkrieg

Hitler had also prepared his armies for what the Germans called "Blitzkrieg"—lightning war. This referred to the use of tanks, trucks, and airplanes to speed up the pace of military action. Columns of tanks, supported by motorized infantry and low-flying airplanes, could break through on a narrow front, penetrate many miles into the rear, and, by attacking headquarters, disrupt the enemy command and control system. In such a situation, it was always unclear just who had surrounded whom, for tanks needed fuel and ammunition in enormous quantity and without it were helpless. But troops cut off from headquarters, with an enemy in the rear, and with hostile airplanes overhead, were likely to panic; and an armored column, probing the enemy rear, could often capture the gasoline it needed to keep advancing.

Hitler hoped and believed that blitzkrieg would bring quick victory and make war profitable once again. His long-range goal was to seize territory in eastern Europe to assure the German "race" of a sufficiently large geographic space to become a world power. This meant displacing Slavs, of course; but in 1939 he also had to cope with the French and British, who, to his surprise, had not backed away from war

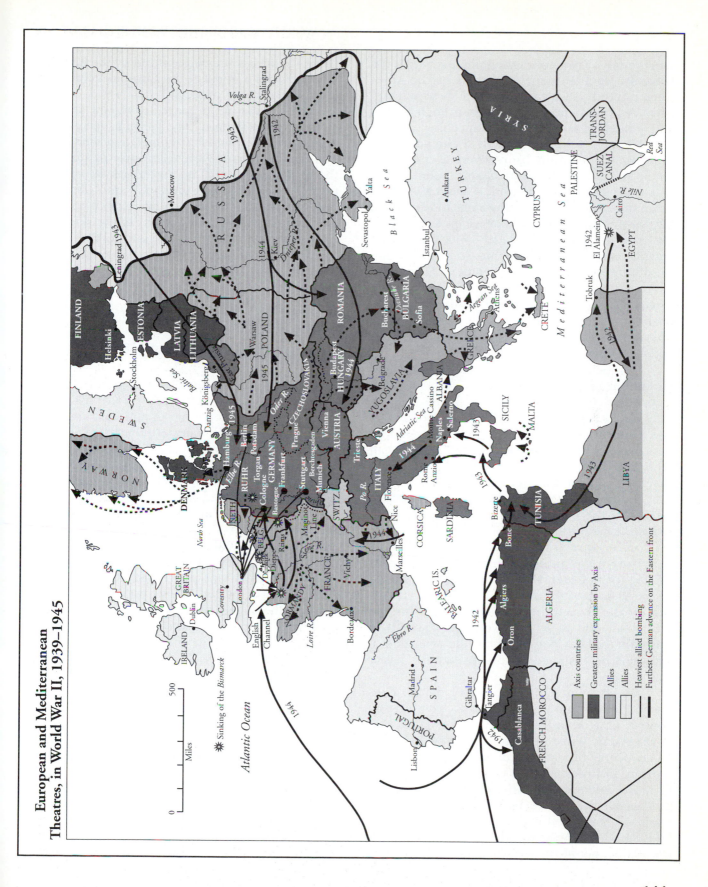

**European and Mediterranean Theatres, in World War II, 1939–1945**

FINLAND

Helsinki

SWEDEN

Stockholm

Leningrad 1943

Moscow

Volga R.

Stalingrad

1943

1942

R U S S I A

1944

Kiev

Dnieper R.

ESTONIA

LATVIA

LITHUANIA

Königsberg

Danzig

Vistula R.

Warsaw

POLAND

1945

Hamburg

Berlin

Potsdam

Torgau

Oder R.

Prague

CZECHOSLOVAKIA

Vienna

AUSTRIA

Budapest 1944

HUNGARY

ROMANIA

Bucharest

Danube R.

BULGARIA

Sofia

Belgrade

YUGOSLAVIA

Trieste

Black Sea

Sevastopol

Yalta

Istanbul

Ankara

TURKEY

SYRIA

TRANS-JORDAN

Red Sea

PALESTINE

SUEZ CANAL

Nile R.

Cairo

EGYPT

1942

El Alamein

1942

Tobruk

LIBYA

Mediterranean Sea

CYPRUS

CRETE

Aegean Sea

Athens

GREECE

ALBANIA

Adriatic Sea

Monte Cassino

Naples

Salerno

Anzio

Rome

1944

Florence

Po R.

ITALY

Nice

1943

1943

SICILY

MALTA

CORSICA

SARDINIA

Bizerte

Bône

TUNISIA

1943

Algiers

Oran

ALGERIA

Tangier

Casablanca

FRENCH MOROCCO

1942

Gibraltar

SPAIN

Madrid

PORTUGAL

Lisbon

BALEARIC IS.

Ebro R.

Marseilles

Vichy

1944

FRANCE

Loire R.

Bordeaux

Seine R.

Reims

NORMANDY

Dieppe

Dunkirk

BELG.

NETH.

Maginot Line

Siegfried Line

SWITZ.

Munich

Berchtesgaden

Stuttgart

Frankfurt

GERMANY

Cologne

Bastogne

RUHR

Elbe R.

DENMARK

North Sea

Baltic Sea

Sinking of the Bismarck

NORWAY

Coventry

London

Dublin

IRELAND

GREAT BRITAIN

English Channel

1944

Atlantic Ocean

500

Miles

0

**Legend:**
Axis countries
Greatest military expansion by Axis
Allies
Allies
Heaviest allied bombing
Furthest German advance on the Eastern front

when news of the non-aggression pact with the U.S.S.R. reached them. Nevertheless, the Allies were unready to attack; instead they manned prepared fortifications along the French border and waited for something to happen.

Happen it did. First of all, Stalin set out to improve his position by recovering control of lands lost to the Russian Empire after World War I. He sent soldiers into Estonia, Latvia, and Lithuania and tried to do the same to the Finns, but they resisted and even drove back an invading army in the winter of 1939–1940. The French and British saw an opportunity in this situation to end the cooperation between the U.S.S.R. and Germany by sending an expeditionary force across Norway into Finland while simultaneously attacking oil fields in the Transcaucasus, thus cutting off oil supplies for both the U.S.S.R. and Germany.

But before the Allies were ready to act, Hitler seized the initiative by first sending troops into Norway and Denmark and then, in May, attacking France, Belgium, and Holland. It was 1914 all over again with the difference that tanks and airplanes moved much faster than men and horses, and this time there was no eastern front for the Germans to worry about. French morale soon cracked, and in a mere six weeks the campaign was over. Most of the British expeditionary force escaped from the beaches of Dunkirk in small boats, leaving all their heavy equipment behind. After this surprising turn of events, the British public reacted to the disaster as though it had been a victory. But for the French there was no escape. Instead they concluded an armistice on June 22, 1940, in the same railway car in which the armistice of 1918 had been signed. To all appearance, Hitler had won.

But Britain refused to admit defeat. British failures to stop the Germans from seizing control of Norway had provoked a change of government. Winston Churchill (1874–1965) became prime minister and brought a new resolution and recklessness to the British war effort. He embarked on all-out mobilization and mortgaged the future by buying what Britain could not produce for itself in the United States and elsewhere. Most of all, his speeches rallied the British people against the Nazis, even when

German success seemed assured by the fact that the resources of most of the European continent lay at Hitler's beck and call.

Hitler was not prepared to mount an invasion of Great Britain. The German navy could not control the English Channel, and that meant that landing barges were vulnerable to attack by the British navy. Hitler, nevertheless, ordered preparations for an invasion and launched heavy air attacks on British airfields. When that failed to drive British planes from the skies, the Germans attacked London and other cities, without changing the strategic situation. In September 1940, Hitler's invasion plan had to be postponed—as it proved, forever.

# Invasion of the U.S.S.R.

Prolonging the struggle with Great Britain threatened to distract Hitler from his main goal—seizure of territory in the east in order to build a great Germany. He therefore decided in November 1940 to attack the U.S.S.R., thinking that when the Communist power had been destroyed, Britain would have to make peace. This decision proved fatal to the Nazis, and in retrospect it seems amazingly reckless. Why invite a war on two fronts when Stalin was doing everything he could to cooperate? But at the time, almost every military expert believed that the Soviet army was poorly led and lacked the will to fight. The Red Army's poor performance against the Finns seemed to prove what prewar treason trials, followed by massive purges of disloyal officers in the late 1930s, had led outsiders to suspect. Hitler therefore counted on a swift and easy victory against the U.S.S.R., like the easy victories he had already won against Poland and France. And by attacking communist Russia, he could again live up to his principles, for one of the main themes of Nazi propaganda had been denunciation of communism.

Before his planned invasion, however, Hitler was distracted by a brief Balkan campaign. This was because shortly before the end of the campaign in France, Mussolini declared war against France and Britain. Fighting in North Africa between British forces stationed in Egypt and Italian troops in adjacent Cyrenaica (Libya) followed, and the Italians suffered some embarrassing defeats. Then in October 1940 Mussolini attacked Greece, hoping to restore his damaged prestige. Once more the Italians were defeated, and in the spring of 1941 British troops arrived from Egypt to help the Greeks. This threatened the German flank, so Hitler ordered an attack on Yugoslavia and Greece in April 1941. As before, victory came quickly and the British were driven back to Egypt.

On June 22, 1941, a few weeks later than first planned, the German war machine was finally ready for the assault on the Soviet Union. As before, blitzkrieg tactics worked wonders at first. Vast Soviet armies surrendered without much of a fight. But the Russian spaces were immense, and German columns could not advance more than about 100 miles at a time without pausing to bring up supplies. Roads were miserable, and the deeper the Germans got into Russia, the more difficult it became to deliver everything needed to renew the offensive. Soviet morale wavered but did not crack, and eventually the onset of cold weather began to hamper German mobility, for the Nazi army was not equipped for winter operations, lacking even the proper clothing for subzero temperatures. By December 6, 1941, although the Nazis were within a few miles of Moscow and had almost surrounded Leningrad, Hitler had to call off the offensive, ordering the German armies to hold fast to everything they had conquered.

Easy victories had stopped. Instead, the Germans faced a two-front war once again, and their situation was worsened by the actions of the United States, where sympathy for Britain and dislike of the Nazis led President Roosevelt to offer Hitler's enemies all help short of war. Americans started by selling armaments and other strategic goods to France and Britain. Then, when the British began to run out of funds, Congress passed the Lend Lease Act (March 1941), whereby the United States offered to supply what Britain and Hitler's other enemies needed without charge, on the theory that they were contributing to the security of the United States by opposing Hitler and

should not be required to pay back the costs of things actually used up in the course of the struggle. Then, when the war ended, whatever was left over could be returned or paid for at some agreed price. In this way, war debts, like those that had plagued international relations between the wars, would not accumulate, and by becoming "the arsenal of democracy" the United States might escape having to send its own soldiers into battle.

## Pearl Harbor and Initial Japanese Victories, 1941–1942

Affairs took a new turn on December 7, 1941, only a day after the German offensive in Russia halted, when the Japanese attacked the American naval base at Pearl Harbor. Anchored U.S. battleships were sunk, but U.S. aircraft carriers were at sea and remained unscathed.

Japanese strategists thought that if they could paralyze the U.S. Pacific fleet, then it would become possible for them to capture oil fields in the Dutch East Indies (Indonesia) and thus assure themselves of sufficient oil to maintain the army and navy indefinitely. By creating a vast "Co-Prosperity Sphere" throughout Southeast Asia, China, and islands of the Pacific, the Japanese hoped that they would be able to hold off counterattack indefinitely. Given existing methods of warfare, and the difficulties of landing on a defended beach, this hope was not unreasonable.

For six months after Pearl Harbor, everything the Japanese military had counted on seemed to be coming true. A series of brilliantly successful campaigns brought the Philippines, Malaya, Burma, and the Dutch East Indies under Japanese control, and the Japanese also garrisoned a number of smaller islands of the Southwest Pacific. "Asia for the Asians" was a slogan that appealed to many inhabitants of former British, French, and Dutch colonies; but the Japanese had difficulty in converting hostility to European colonialism into active support for what amounted to an empire of their own. Moreover, Chinese resistance continued, and the pop-

World War II
Asian and Pacific Theatres, 1941–1945

ulation of India, after hesitating, settled down under British management to create a vast new army to protect its exposed frontier in Burma from further Japanese advance.

## Turning the Tide: American Mobilization and Allied Offensives, 1942–1945

Despite these initial successes, the Japanese were no match for American power, once the resources of the United States were fully geared for war. And the American response to Pearl Harbor was all-out mobilization, harnessing all available manpower and know-how to the task of creating a truly formidable army and navy as quickly as possible. How to manage an all-out war effort had already been worked out by the British, building on World War I precedents. The American government, helped by British advice and example, was therefore able to achieve a remarkably efficient system for channeling resources into the war effort, all in conformity with strategic plans devised by the Joint Chiefs of Staff. Production goals, once seemingly impossible, were soon achieved and surpassed. American industrial and agricultural productivity was so great that the flow of Lend Lease goods to Britain, Russia, and other Allied powers actually increased while the American armed forces were being built up and then sent into action overseas.

Hitler declared war on the United States just after the Pearl Harbor attack, even though the Japanese had not informed him of their plans and refused to attack the Soviet Union in the Far East, despite German requests that they do so. Hitler's declaration of war made it easy for the United States to confirm and strengthen cooperation with Britain and with the Soviet Union by deciding, in spite of the Japanese attack at Pearl Harbor, to concentrate first against Germany, on the ground that if Hitler were left alone to defeat Russia in a second campaign, he would become difficult or impossible to overthrow. As a result, Allied military campaigns were far better coordinated than anything the Germans, Italians, and Japanese were able to achieve.

Results of American mobilization and Allied planning began to show toward the end of 1942. By far the biggest military action was on Germany's eastern front, where a second German advance was turned back at Stalingrad on the Volga, beginning in late August. The Soviets had to rely almost entirely on their own resources, for Lend Lease shipments were still small owing to shortages of shipping. But factories in the Urals and still farther east were able to produce large numbers of tanks and guns; and once the harshness of Nazi rule became clear, the Soviet peoples rallied behind the Communist regime.

On the other fronts, too, the balance began to favor the Allies in the second half of 1942. Japan's victories ended in June, when the Americans won a sea battle off Midway Island; and later in the year, hard fighting on Guadalcanal, in the Southwest Pacific, led to a second American victory, this time on land. Against Germany, the first important Anglo-American success came in the Atlantic, where German submarines threatened for a while to sink so many ships as to prevent the successful deployment of American forces overseas. By midsummer 1942, that danger had been largely overcome; and in November the Americans and British were able to combine forces for a large-scale landing in North Africa. A few weeks earlier, British troops had won a decisive victory in Egypt over a combined German and Italian army; and by May 1943 the whole southern shore of the Mediterranean was in Allied hands. From there, the Anglo-American forces invaded first Sicily (August) and then the Italian mainland (September). By this time, most Italians were anxious to make peace, and a coup d'état in Rome overthrew Mussolini. Prompt German reaction, however, meant that northern Italy remained under their control. A German task force even freed Mussolini from prison, but he was no more than a useless puppet from then on.

On the Russian front, a third German offensive, launched in July 1943, was quickly

# THE SECOND BEST IS NOT THE PACIFIC

In July 1942, the war was going badly for the Allies. Japan controlled a vast region of the Pacific. The Germans' second summer offensive in Russia was thrusting toward the Volga. In the North African desert, other German soldiers were at Egypt's doorstop.

Earlier in the year, the United States, Britain, and Russia had agreed upon their strategy for 1942. Anglo-American forces were to land in northern France and open a second front to relieve the Russians. Everything else was to be subordinated to that effort. But by July, the British decided that the plan would not work. Landing craft and other supplies were lacking. Reinforcing the defenses of Egypt and of India seemed even more important than landing in France, for it took only a little imagination to believe that the Axis' next move would be for Japanese forces to move into India while the Germans drove past Egypt to meet them somewhere in the Indian Ocean.

The Americans were very reluctant to change the agreed-on plan. What if Russia should collapse or make a separate peace? But without the British, a landing in France was clearly impossible. What to do? On July 10, the Joint Chiefs of Staff recommended that in such a case major effort should be shifted to the Pacific against the Japanese.

This brought President Franklin D. Roosevelt up against the most important strategic decision of the war. If he accepted the advice of his chiefs of staff, each of the great Allied nations would in effect be conducting its own war, with little real cooperation. This seemed unwise. It seemed even more unwise to concentrate on Japan when everyone agreed that the Germans were a more serious threat to the long-range security of the United States.

On July 15, 1942, President Roosevelt talked the problem over with his friend, Harry Hopkins. The two men sat in the White House on a summer's evening, wondering what to do. In the end, Roosevelt decided to try once again to work out a plan for joint action with the British. He sent Harry Hopkins and General George C. Marshall to London to make the attempt. Ten days later, they agreed on a landing in North Africa. In greatest haste, a vast expedition was made ready under the supreme command of a young American general, Dwight D. Eisenhower. As a result, on November 8, 1942, less than four months after the decision had been made, American and British troops went ashore in French North Africa.

The Russians were not fully satisfied with this second front. But British and American cooperation became closer and more intimate than ever before. Soon afterward, the turning point of the war came: at Stalingrad in Russia, at Guadalcanal in the Pacific, and in North Africa. And as the Allies took the strategic initiative, they made it a genuinely cooperative effort—all because President Roosevelt had decided on July 15, 1942, that even if a landing in France was not possible in 1942, "the second best is not the Pacific."

turned back; and from that time onward, it was the Red Army that advanced, while the Germans fought desperately to hold them back. Lend Lease deliveries began to supplement Russian home production significantly by 1943; in particular, American trucks, shoes, and food kept the Red Army mobile.

## Problems of the Peace

The Soviet Union's growing military success meant that concerting plans with American and British leaders became necessary. A conference at Tehran (November 1943) brought Stalin, Roosevelt, and Churchill together for the first time, and they were able to agree on future strategy. In particular, the United States and Britain promised to attack across the Channel in 1944, in spite of the very great technical difficulties of landing on the French coast. Everyone expected that a successful landing would lead to Germany's defeat, since the Soviets promised a massive offensive in the east to coincide with the landings in France.

On June 6, 1944, Allied landings on the Normandy beaches proved successful, and within a few weeks German armies were driven from France. But the Allies barely got across the German border before bad weather set in, and in December Hitler was even able to launch a counteroffensive. Soviet armies in the east got into Poland but had to stop short of Berlin. Victory in Europe was thus delayed until May 1945, when Russian and American forces finally met at the Elbe River. Hitler had killed himself a few days previously. With his death, the Nazi movement collapsed utterly, though only after murdering millions of Jews and others in special extermination camps and bringing massive destruction to most of Europe.

How to arrange the postwar map of Europe was more than the Allies could agree on. Until Hitler had been destroyed, differences could always be prepared over, as happened at Yalta in February 1945, when Roosevelt, Churchill, and Stalin met for a second time. But when German resistance finally collapsed, hard decisions had to be made, and it soon became obvious that the sort of "friendly" governments the Russians wanted in eastern Europe were undemocratic

**The Big Three of World War II**   This photograph, taken during the Yalta Conference in February 1945, shows Winston Churchill, prime minister of Great Britain, Franklin D. Roosevelt, president of the United States, and Josef Stalin, generalissimo of the Soviet Union, seated with senior staff advisors standing in the rear. This was the second time the three heads of government came together to draw up plans and policies. At Tehran in 1943 strategic decisions about a second front in France were agreed upon; at Yalta political questions about the future of Europe were more urgent than military planning. Even in the Far East, where Stalin did commit himself at Yalta to enter the war against Japan within three months of the end of the hostilities in Europe, military cooperation soon seemed less important than political agreement about what sort of postwar governments were to exist in liberated and conquered lands. On this issue, real cooperation proved impossible, and polite fictions accepted at Yalta soon proved unworkable in practice. The Great Alliance of World War II was already wearing thin when this photograph was taken. It evaporated entirely two years later.

and unacceptable by British and American standards. For a while, the United States continued to hope that such differences could be amicably settled, especially since they wanted Soviet help against Japan.

Toward the end of 1944, however, the limitations of Japanese war-making ability became

**Horrors of World War II**    Between 1914 and 1918, the long stalemate in the trenches took the romance out of war. The revival of mobile warfare in 1939, thanks to the tactics of *blitzkrieg*, might have restored the glamour of successful combat if World War II had not also turned into a prolonged and bloody struggle that was eventually decided by the Allies' superior industrial production and strategic cooperation. As victory drew near, two new horrors of war struck home. Above is a photograph taken in May 1945 of the Nazi concentration camp at Buchenwald. It shows Jews and other enemies of the Nazi regime on the verge of starvation by the time the American army reached them. Many others had already died, and their bodies lay exposed in open mass graves. Photographs like these shocked American public opinion profoundly. Earlier reports of Nazi death camps had often been discounted as mere war propaganda. But here were certain proofs of unprecedented brutality and bureaucratic mass murder—a new horror indeed. On the bottom is a photograph of the mushroom cloud that rose above Nagasaki, Japan, on August 9, 1945. It signaled a new kind of horror—the mass destruction wrought by nuclear weapons.

clearer and the American wish for help in the Far East diminished accordingly. United States submarines succeeded in sinking so many ships that the Japanese became unable to tap the resources of their "Co-Prosperity Sphere." Moreover, beginning in November 1943, the Americans learned how to send task forces thousands of miles from base with everything needed for a successful assault on a defended beach. This meant that the Japanese defense perimeter in the Pacific became vulnerable, since even the bravest garrisons, cut off from home, could not survive very long without food and ammunition. With giant steps the Americans were therefore able to advance first toward the Philippines, then toward the Japanese home islands.

The final blows came swiftly. On August 6 and 9, 1945, American airplanes dropped newly invented nuclear bombs on Hiroshima and Nagasaki. Then, on August 9, the Russians began marching into Manchuria. These disasters persuaded the Japanese government to sue for peace on August 15. Formal surrender was arranged on September 2, 1945, just six years and a day after the war in Europe had begun.

# Conclusion

World War II was over, at least officially. Urgent unsolved questions remained; and in the hurly-burly of everyday decision-making, no one really took time to wonder whether the two world wars of the twentieth century, and the changes they had brought about, marked the end of an era. But with more than half a century's perspective, it now seems probable that historians will need a new label for the period since World War II.

The modern era that began with the great European voyages of discovery in the latter part of the fifteenth century was marked by the rise of western Europe to world predominance. But European world power came to an end with the breakup of colonial empires after 1945, and with the rise of new superpowers, east and west of the old center of world leadership. To be sure, both the U.S.S.R. and the U.S.A. inherited or borrowed a great deal from western Europe; but

neither Americans nor Russians were quite the same as the peoples of the west European nations who had lorded it over the rest of the earth before the wars.

The era of the two world wars also marked an end to the delicate balance between public and private enterprise that had characterized bourgeois Europe. That balance had initially been struck in a few city-states of Italy and the Rhinelands in the fourteenth century; it had spread to the Netherlands, England, and France during the sixteenth and seventeenth centuries, and had then been imperfectly imitated in central and eastern Europe in the eighteenth and nineteenth centuries. It gave wide scope to private accumulation of capital and pursuit of gain by buying and selling at prices negotiated anew for each deal in accordance with the best estimate of personal advantage each party could make at the time. Intervention in the market by political and military authorities was always important. Taxes and tariffs affected market prices, often in very important respects; and fixed "fair" prices for food and other necessities were often enforced as well, especially in times of crisis. But as compared to other times and places, bourgeois Europe gave the market far freer scope than was usual elsewhere.

The two world wars reversed this trend. Rationing, price control, direction of labor, compulsory military service, planned industrial production—all took over. In each of the principal belligerent countries, military and civilian planners set out to make economic production fit strategic war plans. Careful calculation and management proved able to achieve wonders. Goals that seemed impossible were in fact achieved, over and over. As long as everyone agreed that the effort was worthwhile, and millions of common folk willingly put up with all the discomfort and deprivation that wartime conditions involved, the efficiency of what we may call "command" economy as against the traditional "market" economy was undeniable.

Bourgeois society could never be the same after such a demonstration of what state intervention in the market was able to achieve, even though the problem of maintaining general agreement on the goals to be pursued in peacetime turned out to be far more difficult than it was to agree that wartime enemies must be defeated. After 1917, the Soviet Union defiantly rejected bourgeois free-market rules and set out to build a new socialist society. The nations that remained "capitalist" and democratic compromised between free-market and command principles for the management of their economies. But everywhere the role of the state and of deliberate public planning was much increased as compared to conditions before 1914, while the scope for strictly private pursuit of profit was correspondingly reduced by all sorts of new regulations and taxes aimed at narrowing gaps between rich and poor, or in other ways advancing political goals. In this respect, as much as in the displacement of world leadership from western Europe to the United States and the Union of Soviet Socialist Republics, the world wars of the twentieth century seem likely to mark a new era in world history.

We will discuss some characteristics of that era in the remaining chapters of this book.

---

## Bibliography

Two front line soldiers left especially poignant literary monuments of how shocking World War I was: Erich Maria Remarque, *All Quiet on the Western Front* (1929); and the war poems of Wilfred Owens, reproduced in many anthologies. For the interwar years, Hitler's *Mein Kampf* (1925) and John Steinbeck, *Grapes of Wrath* (1939), illustrate contrasts of the time; and for World War II, Anne Frank, *Diary of a Young Girl* (rev. ed., 1967), and Ernie Pyle, *Brave Men* (1983), both give vivid day-by-day accounts of what it was like for an extraordinary German Jewish girl to face death in a concentration camp, and for very ordinary American soldiers to face death in combat.

We are still too close to events to have a reliable sense of how to grasp the history of the twentieth century as a whole, or even of its first half. Historians do far better with smaller segments. For World War I, Marc Ferro, *The Great War, 1914–1918* (1973), and Gerd Hardach, *The First World War, 1914–1918* (1977), offer interesting interpretations of the social and economic aspects of the conflict. John Keegan, *The Face of Battle* (1977), contains an excellent chapter on why stalemate set in in the trenches. For a general military narrative, Cyril B. Falls, *The Great War* (1959), is conveniently short.

John Reed, *Ten Days That Shook the World* (1919, and often reprinted), gives a vivid eyewitness account of how the Bolsheviks took power in Russia. George F. Kennan, *Russia and the West under Lenin and Stalin* (1961), explains the subsequent development of the communist movement inside and outside of Russia. For the rise of the United States as rival and counterpart to the Russians, N. Gordon Levin, Jr., *Woodrow Wilson and World Politics: America's Response to War and Revolution* (1968), and Arno J. Mayer, *Politics and Diplomacy of Peacemaking: Containment and Counterrevolution at Versailles, 1918–1919* (1967), are available.

For the interwar years in Europe, Raymond J. Sontag, *A Broken World, 1919–1939* (1971), and Charles S. Maier *Recasting Bourgeois Europe: Stabilization in France, Germany and Italy in the Decade after World War I* (1975), are excellent; and so is Akire Iriye, *After Imperialism: The Search for a New Order in the Far East, 1921–1931* (1965), for Asia. For the colonial world, Raymond F. Betts, *Uncertain Dimension: Western Overseas Empires in the Twentieth Century* (1985), offers an introduction.

The following cast light on various aspects of the drift toward war in the 1930s: Anthony P. Adamthwaite, *The Making of the Second World War* (2nd ed., 1979); Alan Bullock, *Hitler: A Study in Tyranny* (rev. ed., 1962); Mack Smith, *Mussolini's Roman Empire* (1976); Martin Gilbert, *The Roots of Appeasement* (1966); Donald C. Watt, *Too Serious a Business: European Armed Forces and the Approach to the Second World War* (1975); Francis C. Jones, *Japan's New Order in East Asia, 1921–1931* (1954); Robert J. C. Butow, *Tojo and the Coming of the War* (1961); and Herbert Feis, *The Road to Pearl Harbor* (1950).

On the Depression, John A. Garraty, *The Great Depression* (1987), and Charles P. Kindelberger, *The World in Depression, 1929–1939* (rev. ed., 1986), are authoritative. On American domestic affairs, two books by William E. Leuchtenburg, *The Perils of Prosperity, 1914–32* and *Franklin D. Roosevelt and the New Deal, 1932–40*, are delightfully crisp and comfortably brief. For the Soviet Union, Donald W. Treadgold, *Twentieth Century Russia* (5th ed., 1981), is a good place to start.

For World War II, Gordon Wright, *The Ordeal of Total War, 1939–1945* (1968), is admirable for the European theaters; Akire Iriye, *Power and Culture: The Japanese American War, 1941–1945*, is the same for the war in the Pacific. Gerhard L. Weinberg, *A World at Arms: A Global History of World War II* (1994), is both massive and comprehensive.

On Allied politics during the war, Robert E. Sherwood, *Roosevelt and Hopkins: An Intimate History* (1945), was revelatory when it first appeared and remains a vivid and compelling account. Herbert Feis, *Churchill, Roosevelt and Stalin: The War They Waged and the Peace They Sought* (2nd ed., 1967), and John Lewis Gaddis, *The United States and the Origins of the Cold War, 1941–1947* (1972), are clear, readable, and more formal histories.

On economic mobilization, Albert Speer, *Inside the Third Reich* (1970), records his memoirs of how he presided over Hitler's war economy. John Barber and Mark Harrison, *The Soviet Home Front, 1941–1945: A Social and Economic History of the USSR in World War II* (1991), Alan S. Milward, *War, Economy and Society, 1939–1945* (1977), and Jerome B. Cohen, *Japan's Economy in War and Reconstruction* (1949), are formal histories.

For the two greatest catastrophes of the war, Martin J. Sherwin. *A World Destroyed: The Atomic Bomb and Grand Alliance* (1975), and Paul Hilberg, *The Destruction of the European Jews* (3 vols., 2nd ed., 1985), may be consulted. On demographic aspects, Eugene M. Kulischer, *Europe on the Move: War and Population Changes, 1917–1947* (1948), is authoritative, and if you want a little relief from disasters and wholesale destruction, try books by Ronald Lewin, *Ultra Goes to War* (1981) and *The American Magic: Codes, Ciphers and the Defeat of Japan* (1982), which deal with Allied cryptographers' remarkable successes in breaking German and Japanese codes.

# World Views

People need to make sense of the world around them. Across the ages they have done so by accepting different world views. Details varied from person to person and from place to place, but despite all their diversity, the world views that gave meaning to human lives and guided actual behavior are elaborations and mixtures of only four core ideas: animism, theism, natural law, and evolution. The first three believe the universe remains fundamentally the same; the fourth believes that change is universal and unending.

## ANIMISM

**Animism** is the oldest of these organizing ideas. It arose in prehistoric times, before human beings dispersed across the face of the earth from their African cradle. According to this view, everything (or perhaps only everything that moves) has a soul or spirit that acts and feels like a human being. Resembling breath, spirits are invisible and can leave the body they usually inhabit in order to travel about in the spirit world, encounter other spirits, and even enter into a new body. Interaction among the spirits is like the interactions of human society, or, more accurately, human conduct is an example of how spirits interact, since what we do is governed by the spirits inhabiting our bodies.

Some spirits are thought to be powerful, some protective, some malicious, some merely whimsical. It follows that everyone needs to know how to keep evil spirits away and maintain good relations with spiritual protectors. Song and dance, working up to trace states, allowed experts to enter the spirit world and act as mediators between the spirits and ordinary people. Shamans, living among Siberian hunters today, are modern examples of this sort of religious specialist.

Animism explained human dreams, trance, and, above all, death as what happened when the spirit left the body it usually inhabited, traveled off into the spirit world, and then either returned (dreams and trance) or stayed away permanently (death).

Physical and mental illness was explained as the result of a bad spirit taking up residence in someone's body. Rituals to drive evil spirits away were therefore needed to cure the sick, and they often met with success.

The failure of human plans to work out as expected was explained as the work of unfriendly spirits; conversely, when things went well, protective spirits deserved at least part of the credit. Thus, everything that happened, good or bad, was understood to be the result of how spirits perpetually activated every visible thing.

No other world view ever spread so widely or explained so much in such an easily understood way. Millions still believe in spirits and try to appease them and win their protection. Civilized learning sometimes elaborated on animism. Examples are the Hindu doctrine of the transmigration of souls, and Chinese family rituals for communicating with ancestors. The world's oldest world view is therefore very much alive and continues to meet the needs of large numbers of persons.

## THEISM

**Theism** differs from animism by affirming that one or more spirits are so much more powerful than all the rest that they require special attention and must be worshiped as god(s). Three variations of this world view, each arising initially in the ancient Middle East, are known as polytheism, henotheism, and monotheism.

The most influential form of **polytheism** (many gods) emerged in ancient Sumer between 4000 and 3000 B.C.E. Experts in the supernatural among the Sumerians brought a new orderliness to the spirit world by discerning seven great gods, each of whom controlled an aspect of the natural environment that affected human life in important ways. These were sun, moon, sky, earth, fresh water, salt water, and storm, the leader of them all. To bring these gods closer, the Sumerians built magnificent temple-homes for them, complete with cult statues where, it was hoped, one of the great gods would take up residence—at least from time to time—and thus receive the prayers, praise, and offerings of food, clothes, and other amenities that their household servants, the priests, brought to them every day.

When new, the idea that the world was controlled by seven great gods, who could be persuaded to take up residence in special temples, seemed like a very effective way to get access to the top of the spirit world and thus gain really effective protection. The idea spread widely among surrounding peoples and (with local modifications) lay behind the polytheism of ancient Greece, Rome, Aryan India, and other pagan peoples of Europe and western Asia.

### Highlights

Sumerian polytheists believed that the Great Gods met each New Year's Day to decide what they would do to and for humans during the following twelve months. The gods did not always agree; but the superior strength of Storm ordinarily prevailed. Thus the governance of the universe was conceived as a political process whereby clashes of will among the great gods were resolved by face-to-face consultation. Unpredictable disasters from war, flood, epidemic disease, and crop failure, which often affected Sumerian cities, were explained in this way.

Polytheism in the Sumerian and subsequent forms left plenty of room for animism. The high gods were deemed to control public events—especially war and natural disasters—but personal concerns of ordinary people were beneath their attention. For these, old animist rituals were needed to establish connection with local, ordinary, everyday spirits. In other words, the public religion of the state became separate and distinct from the private religion of common people.

**Henotheism** arose after about 2000 B.C.E. when increasing communication across cultural and political boundaries compelled more and more people to admit that the gods of their own state and region were different from those worshiped elsewhere. The view that different gods had jurisdiction over different peoples and places is known as "henotheism."

### Highlights

Henotheism explained success and failure in the military and political struggles of the ancient Middle East as due to one people's gods being stronger and so able to defeat their rivals.

Defeated peoples were tempted to transfer their worship to victorious, stronger gods. But shopping around for the most effective divine protection eroded firm and enduring faith in old and new gods alike. As a result, human commitment to official forms of polytheism weakened as the incessant turmoil of war raised and then discredited a particular set of gods protecting each successive conqueror.

**Monotheism** came to the fore as the credibility of polytheism diminished in the ancient Near East. It started to emerge at the same time as henotheism, but did not achieve firm and lasting definition until the first millennium B.C.E. when prophets of Israel and Judah proclaimed the universal jurisdiction of Yahweh, the Hebrew God of Battles, and declared that all other gods were false and powerless idols. At almost the same time, Zoroaster in Persia said the same about Ahura Mazda and denounced earlier faiths as a lie.

In the following fifteen hundred years, first Christianity and then Islam reaffirmed the monotheistic idea, as proclaimed initially by Jewish prophets. In subsequent centuries missionaries spread these two faiths very widely through the world. As a result, more than half the world's inhabitants now inherit one or another form of monotheism.

### Highlights

Monotheism has several strengths. In the first place, it closes the gap that polytheism had created between public, official religion and private, personal search for spiritual help. The one and only supreme God, all-powerful and all-knowing, hears everyone's prayers. Humble persons have the same access to God as kings and emperors; and, conversely, rulers are subject to God's law and God's will just as much as ordinary persons are.

In the second place, God revealed himself to humankind by inspiring prophets to proclaim his will and purposes. Their message, recorded in sacred scripture, became the basis of true religion. Each of the major monotheistic faiths—Judaism, Christianity and Islam—can therefore spread anywhere and still remain true to itself, thanks to sacred texts, accurately reproduced.

In the third place, when human hopes and plans failed, God cannot be blamed. His purposes are beyond human comprehension. Dutiful obedience to the precepts of sacred scripture is the only appropriate human response to any and every circumstance of life.

Finally, monotheism did not entirely banish ancient animistic practices. Many persons felt they needed intercessors with God and therefore invoked the aid of one or another of the saints in Heaven.

## NATURAL LAW

**Natural law** constitutes a third world view. It arose initially among a handful of Greek thinkers after 600 B.C.E. They were aware of the multiplicity of gods worshiped by different peoples around them and decided to disregard the resulting confusion. Instead they set out to explain the natural world by seeking for laws that governed things in the same way that written laws governed the behavior of citizens of the polis. Modern science descends from this stab in the dark.

### Highlights

Ancient Greek philosophers proposed natural laws about how the world came into existence by using ordinary words—condensation, rarefaction, atoms, and the like. Different schools advocated different natural laws, and agreement was impossible, except in astronomy, where by Ptolemy's time (ca. 140 C.E.) exact measurement, careful observation, and geometrical modeling proved capable of predicting eclipses and the movements of the sun, moon, and planets quite accurately.

In the seventeeth century, Europeans, building on ancient astronomy, formulated laws of motion mathematically. To general amazement, Isaac Newton's formulas (1687) applied to movements on earth and in the heavens alike, turning terrestrial physics into a predictive science. Other natural laws were soon discovered for chemistry, geology, and other sciences as well.

In the nineteenth century, newly formulated natural laws found practical application in the design of steam engines, the manufacture of artificial chemical compounds, and much else. Practical devices generated from this world view proved capable of increasing human wealth and power enormously.

Natural laws, everywhere the same, conflicted with older ideas about Divine miracles. But most people did not bother very much about such logical discrepancies, believing in God and the new science simultaneously.

## EVOLUTION

The **evolutionary view** of reality that emerged in the nineteenth century and expanded to embrace astronomy, physics, and other natural sciences in the twentieth century offered a different challenge to monotheism by asserting that the entire universe changes across time, beginning with the Big Bang, when laws of physics were different from those prevailing afterwards; and proceeding through successive generations of stars toward an unknown and unpredictable future. An eternal, omniscient, and unchanging God is hard to fit into such a view, and when Charles Darwin first advanced the idea of organic evolution (1859) the collision between traditional Christianity and new-fangled evolutionary biology became acute. Controversy continues, for the discrepancy between modern science and inherited religion persists.

But in the twentieth century the surprising way in which an evolutionary world view supplanted older notions of unchanging natural laws in physics and astronomy perhaps softened the clash. At any rate, the Big Bang resembles Creation as described in sacred scripture, and evolutionary science and traditional religion agree in discerning a beginning and anticipating an end to the world as it now exists.

### Highlights

Evolutionary science undermined the view that the world was ruled by unchanging natural laws, claiming that such laws were merely local and temporary. Simultaneously, the way observers affect what they observe compelled physicists to accept the mathematics of relativity and quanta.

More recently, mathematical chaos theory set out to analyze the evolutionary process, whether exhibited in the birth and death of stars, the surprises of human history, or the genesis and decay of weather systems in the earth's atmosphere. Success in finding uniformities among such different evolutionary processes remains problematic.

## IN CONCLUSION

The more we know, the more new questions arise. Certainty and predictability, once the goal of natural science, seem less and less attainable for the universe as a whole. Yet, in detail and within the limited time and space of planet earth and the adjacent solar system, engineers and inventors have multiplied human capability of controlling natural processes enormously, with no end in sight.

All the major historic world views remain vigorously alive in this strange new world of ours. Most persons subscribe to them all in appropriate circumstances, regardless of logical discrepancies. In effect, we make sense of our world by drawing on the whole human heritage, consciously and unconsciously. That, undoubtedly, is the human way, using whatever works best for us in ever-changing circumstances without worrying much about consistency.

# Science, Thought and Culture

RENAISSANCE  AND  REFORMATION

**Humanism**     **Jesuit Order**     **Council of Trent**
**1500**     **1534**     **1545–1563**     **1600**

Shah Ismail (d. 1524) Shi'a vs Sunni

Luther (d. 1546) Protestant vs. Catholic

Erasmus (d. 1536)

**1550**   Michelangelo (d. 1564)

Ricci (d. 1610) to China

Copernicus (d. 1543)

Chaitanya (d. 1527) Hindu revival

Calvin (d. 1546)

Machiavelli (d. 1527)

OLD REGIME

**Royal Society**     **Scientific Revolution**
**1600**     **1650**     **1700**

Shakespeare (d. 1616)

Bacon (d. 1626)

Galileo (d. 1642)   Descartes (d. 1650)   Molière (d. 1673)

Nikon (d. 1681)

Newton *Principia* (pub. 1687)

Locke (d. 1704)

Jansen (d. 1638)

ENLIGHTENMENT        ROMANTIC MOVEMENT

**1700**     **1750**     **1800**

Leibniz (d. 1716)

Montesquieu (d. 1755)

Voltaire (d. 1778)

Herder d. 1803   Goethe (d. 1832)

Spener (d. 1705)

Bach (d. 1750)   Linnaeus (d. 1778)

Mozart (d. 1791)

Rousseau (d. 1778)   Lavoisier (d. 1794)

Kant (d. 1804)

Adam Smith (d. 1790)

Wesley (d. 1791)

Adb-al-Wahhab (d. 1791)

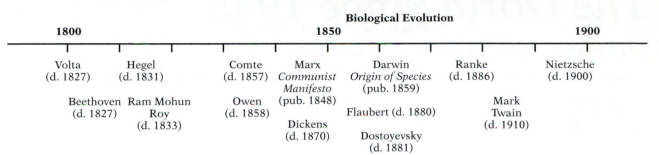

ROMANTIC MOVEMENT        REALISM        MODERNISM

**Biological Evolution**

1800        1850        1900

Volta
(d. 1827)

Hegel
(d. 1831)

Comte
(d. 1857)

Marx
*Communist
Manifesto*
(pub. 1848)

Darwin
*Origin of Species*
(pub. 1859)

Ranke
(d. 1886)

Nietzsche
(d. 1900)

Beethoven
(d. 1827)

Ram Mohun
Roy
(d. 1833)

Owen
(d. 1858)

Dickens
(d. 1870)

Flaubert (d. 1880)

Dostoyevsky
(d. 1881)

Mark
Twain
(d. 1910)

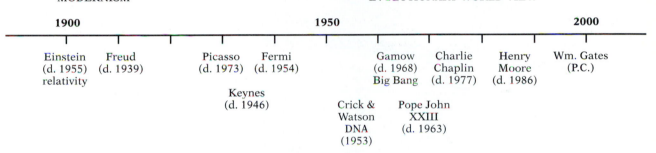

MODERNISM        EVOLUTIONARY WORLD VIEW

1900        1950        2000

Einstein
(d. 1955)
relativity

Freud
(d. 1939)

Picasso
(d. 1973)

Fermi
(d. 1954)

Gamow
(d. 1968)
Big Bang

Charlie
Chaplin
(d. 1977)

Henry
Moore
(d. 1986)

Wm. Gates
(P.C.)

Keynes
(d. 1946)

Crick &
Watson
DNA
(1953)

Pope John
XXIII
(d. 1963)

# *The World Since 1945*
## Public Affairs

# 25

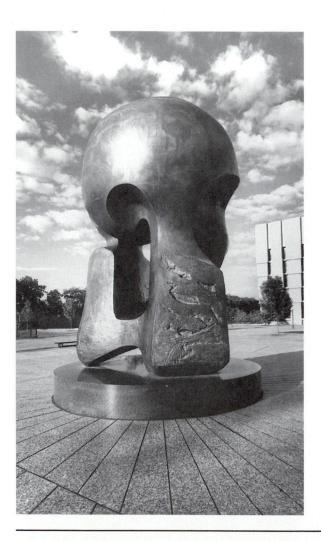

**Henry Moore, Nuclear Energy**   This statue stands on the spot where Enrico Fermi and a team of other physicists achieved the first controlled release of nuclear energy in December, 1942 on the campus of the University of Chicago. The statue aptly expresses the threat and promise inherent in the event it commemorates. Its rounded top is reminiscent of the mushroom cloud created by the atomic explosions to which Fermi's experiment led. Yet the statue's crouched form and bulging head also suggests the shape of a human embryo, with all the unrealized potentialities of that first stage of life.

Deciding what matters most in public affairs becomes harder and harder as we come closer to the present simply because we do not know what is coming. Little-noticed innovations of today may turn out to have enormous consequences, while noisy disagreements may blow over, leaving little trace behind. The course of history has always been surprising and will continue to be so. All this chapter can do is to sift out what, from today's point of view, seems fundamental in the record of the past half-century, knowing full well that perspectives will change as time goes by.

## Two Leading Phenomena

As of 1996, two themes seem predominant in the public affairs of humankind since 1945. One was the political and economic rivalries among the world's rich and powerful peoples. Politically, the aptly named Cold War pitted the United States and its allies against the Soviet Union and its allies between 1945 and 1991, when the U.S.S.R. broke up into its constituent republics and officially abandoned the Communist faith that had ruled in Russia since 1917. Economically, an expensive arms race stabilized the internal economies of the two superpowers while also handicapping them in global market competition with Japan and Germany. Ironically, the two defeated powers of World War II, initially prohibited by the peace treaties from armament production, became the most successful producers of civilian goods in the postwar era, though they have recently seen smaller "Asian tigers" along the Pacific rim outstrip them in some lines of production.

**Occupation Zones of Germany and Austria, 1945**

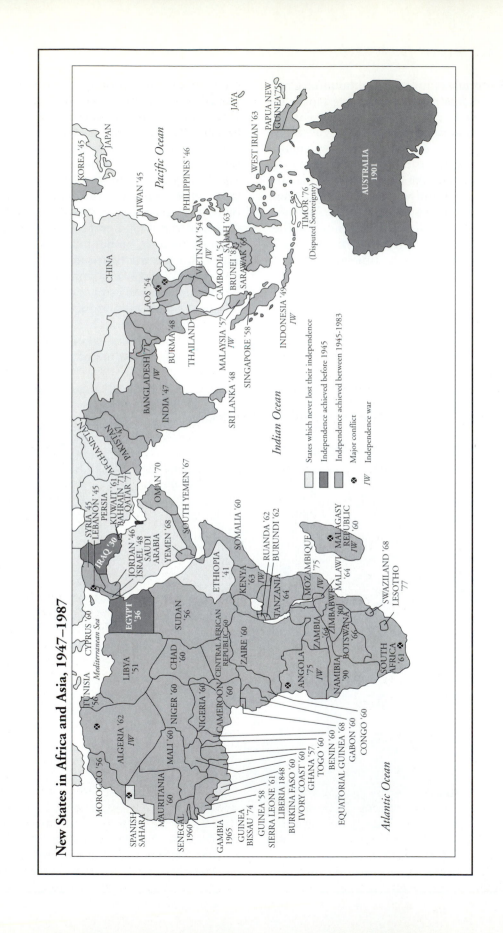

## New States in Africa and Asia, 1947–1987

KOREA '45
JAPAN
TAIWAN '45

*Pacific Ocean*

JAVA
WEST IRIAN '63
PAPUA NEW
GUINEA '75
TIMOR '76
(Disputed Sovereignty)

AUSTRALIA
1901

PHILIPPINES '46

CHINA

LAOS '54

VIETNAM '54
*IW*
CAMBODIA '54
BRUNEI '83
SABAH '63
SARAWAK '63

THAILAND
BURMA '48
MALAYSIA '57
*IW*
SINGAPORE '58

INDONESIA '49
*IW*

BANGLADESH '71
*IW*
INDIA '47

SRI LANKA '48

*Indian Ocean*

States which never lost their independence
Independence achieved before 1945
Independence achieved between 1945–1983
Major conflict
*IW*  Independence war

AFGHANISTAN
PAKISTAN
PERSIA

OMAN '70

SOUTH YEMEN '68

SYRIA '45
LEBANON '45
KUWAIT '61
BAHRAIN '71
QATAR '77
JORDAN '46
ISRAEL '48
SAUDI
ARABIA
YEMEN '68

IRAQ '30

CYPRUS '60
*Mediterranean Sea*

EGYPT
'36

TUNISIA
'56

LIBYA
'51

SUDAN
'56

ETHIOPIA
'41

SOMALIA '60

RUANDA '62
BURUNDI '62

MALAGASY
REPUBLIC
*IW* '60

SWAZILAND '68
LESOTHO
'77

CHAD
'60

CENTRAL AFRICAN
REPUBLIC
'60

ZAIRE '60

KENYA
'63
*IW*
TANZANIA
'64

MOZAMBIQUE
'75
*IW*

MALAWI
'64

ZIMBABWE
'80

ZAMBIA
'64

BOTSWANA
'66

SOUTH
AFRICA
'61

MOROCCO '56

ALGERIA '62
*IW*

MAURITANIA
'60

NIGER '60

MALI '60

NIGERIA '60

CAMEROON
'60

ANGOLA
'75
*IW*

NAMIBIA
'90

SPANISH
SAHARA

SENEGAL
1960

GAMBIA
1965

GUINEA
BISSAU '74

GUINEA '58

SIERRA LEONE '61

LIBERIA 1848

BURKINA FASO '68

IVORY COAST '60

GHANA '57

TOGO '60

BENIN '60

EQUATORIAL GUINEA '68

GABON '60

CONGO '60

*Atlantic Ocean*

The second leading transformation of public affairs in the post–World War II world centered among the poorer, mainly agricultural, peoples of Asia, Africa, and Latin America. They experienced massive population growth and wrenching social change that was triggered in large part by rapidly increasing numbers. Migration from rural communities into cities became massive. Simultaneously, subsistence agriculture decayed among those who stayed behind in the villages.

A side effect of population growth among the poorer peoples of the earth is that increasing numbers of them migrated across political and cultural borders to seek jobs in richer, more developed countries. The fact that birth rates in rich, urbanized countries fell very fast when a postwar "baby boom" subsided after 1960 meant that reproduction rates fell below what was needed for maintaining existing numbers among some of the world's richest, most urbanized, and most industrialized peoples. If this continues—and population trends sometimes shift with surprising rapidity—mingling of peoples of different cultural traditions, different physical appearance, and different expectations will become far more widespread, and the political ideal inherited from the American and French revolutions of separate nations, each with definite borders and a sovereign, democratic government, will become less and less easy to apply to mixed populations in the world's richer countries.

# Political and Economic Rivalries, 1945–1991

## Onset of the Cold War, 1945–1953

Even before hostilities ceased in World War II, quarrels had broken out among the victors. A conference at Yalta (February 1945), where Roosevelt, Stalin, and Churchill met for a second time, produced promises on paper without solving the differences between Russia and the Anglo-American powers over the postwar settlement of Europe. By July 1945, when the Allied heads of government met at Potsdam, just outside Berlin, frictions were sharper, but the need to end the war with Japan, arrange for peace treaties, and agree on how to administer defeated Germany kept the alliance from breaking apart. Earlier in that year the victors had assembled representatives from fifty nations for a conference in San Francisco where they agreed to replace the discredited League of Nations with a redesigned international authority, the United Nations. Long-term peace-keeping and other international problems were entrusted to this new body; but it got off to a rocky start because the victors could no longer even pretend to cooperate on most issues.

Instead, open quarrels, openly arrived at, prevailed. Stalin carved out a sphere of influence in eastern Europe, where Soviet troops were able to enforce his will. A matching Anglo-American sphere of influence formed in western Europe, though by the end of 1946 it was clear that Great Britain could no longer afford to play the role of a great power. By 1947, therefore, the Americans confronted the Soviets across what Churchill had dubbed an "iron curtain," splitting Europe into Communist and non-Communist parts. Defeated Germany was divided between the two blocs.

In Asia a similar division took place. Japan fell within the American sphere of influence, but China became Communist in 1949, thanks to the victory of Mao Tse-tung's Red Army over Chiang Kai-shek's forces. Korea and Vietnam, like Germany, were divided between a Communist north and non-Communist south, depending on where rival occupying forces were located at war's end.

As the line of demarcation between the Soviet and American spheres of influence hardened, rivalry focused on restoring war-damaged economies in the lands each controlled. The Americans had an enormous advantage, for the United States had prospered during the war whereas the Soviet Union had suffered extensive destruction. Americans could therefore afford to extend large credits to their friends through the so-called Marshall Plan (1948–1952), and encouraged the governments of western Europe to cooperate in the tasks of economic reconstruction. Administrative and industrial skills,

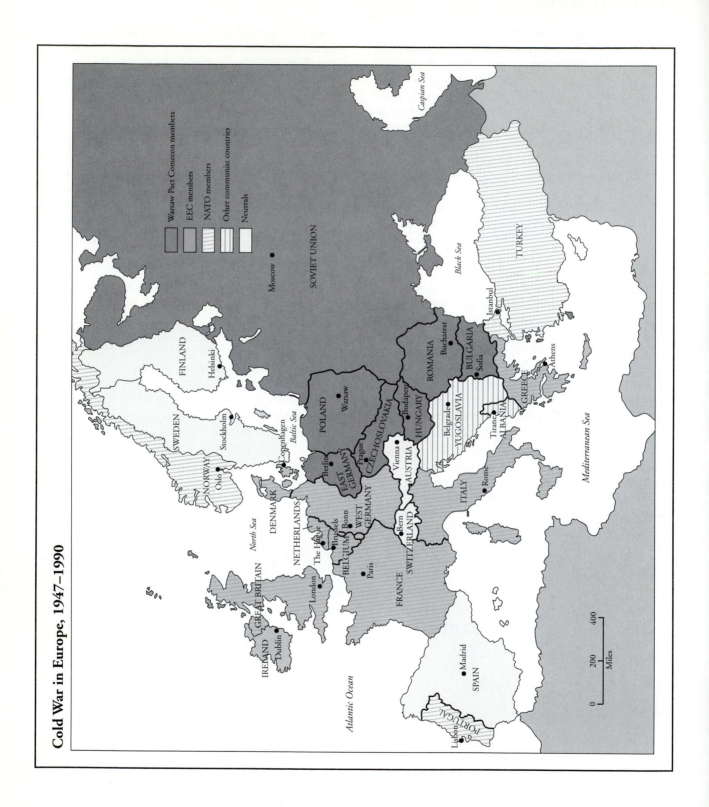

**Cold War in Europe, 1947–1990**

Warsaw Pact Comecon members
EEC members
NATO members
Other communist countries
Neutrals

SOVIET UNION

Moscow

FINLAND

Helsinki

SWEDEN

Stockholm

NORWAY

Oslo

Baltic Sea

Copenhagen

DENMARK

North Sea

NETHERLANDS

The Hague

Brussels

BELGIUM

Bonn

WEST GERMANY

Paris

FRANCE

Bern

SWITZERLAND

Vienna

AUSTRIA

POLAND

Warsaw

Berlin

EAST GERMANY

Prague

CZECHOSLOVAKIA

Budapest

HUNGARY

Belgrade

YUGOSLAVIA

ROMANIA

Bucharest

BULGARIA

Sofia

Tirane

ALBANIA

GREECE

Athens

Istanbul

TURKEY

Black Sea

Caspian Sea

ITALY

Rome

Mediterranean Sea

GREAT BRITAIN

London

IRELAND

Dublin

Atlantic Ocean

Madrid

SPAIN

PORTUGAL

Lisbon

0    200    400

Miles

which had been applied to war-making with remarkable results, were suddenly applied to economic reconstruction and soon met with equally remarkable success. In particular, the western part of Germany achieved an "economic miracle," outstripping the pace of recovery in Britain, France, and other west European countries.

Recovery in eastern Europe was also rapid, though the Soviets could not afford to extend credits to other governments, and in fact plundered east Germany and other occupied lands in the first postwar months to help with their own reconstruction. But after severe initial difficulties, Communist command planning worked surprisingly well in eastern Europe, where large numbers of underemployed peasants could and did leave their native villages for work on industrial construction projects. The Communists had done exactly the same in Russia before the war. Hardships were greater and living standards never caught up with those of western Europe; but the planned economies of the Soviet Union and of its satellites—Poland, Romania, Hungary, Bulgaria, Albania, Czechoslovakia, and East Germany—recovered from wartime damages about as rapidly as the rest of Europe was doing. As a result, Communists could plausibly claim to offer a way to the future that was capable of competing with the modified capitalism of the West.

Japan's economic revival began as a byproduct of a war in Korea, 1950–1953. Communist rulers of the north invaded South Korea in 1950, expecting a walk-over. But Americans were still unreconciled to the Communist victory in China, and President Harry Truman decided to use the United Nations to organize resistance against this clear case of Communist aggression. As it happened, the Soviets had walked out of the U.N. Security Council to protest another issue and so were unable to veto the American initiative. A U.N. force, in which American troops played the largest part, therefore came to the aid of South Korea and drove the invading northerners back. When complete victory seemed at hand, however, the Chinese Red Army intervened and drove the U.N. forces back to almost the same demarcation line from which the struggle had started. Then, after lengthy negotiations, a truce was agreed upon in 1953. It still prevails.

During this war, the U.N. forces found it convenient to order all sorts of supplies from Japan. This demand kindled Japan's industrial recovery and started a boom that eventually left all other countries behind. Japan's economic success depended on producing better goods at lower prices than anyone else. That in turn reflected the skill and discipline of the Japanese people, who accepted a work ethic derived from their rural past and combined that tradition with a rigorous educational system and effective governmental management of key aspects of the national economy.

Rivalry between the United States and the Soviet Union did not completely dominate public affairs in the first postwar years. A second key political process was the dismantlement of European overseas empires, starting, most notably, with the decision of the British government to withdraw from India in 1947. In fact, the British had no choice, for a large Indian army, recruited during the war to fight against the Japanese, obeyed officers who were resolved to win India's independence, if necessary by fighting against their British comrades-in-arms. But among the Indians, a large Moslem population demanded separation from the Hindu majority, so after hurried consultation the British divided their Indian empire between a new Moslem state of Pakistan (organized into separate eastern and western parts) and a larger Hindu-dominated state of India. Angry riots between Hindus and Moslems ensued in many parts of the former empire. Order was restored only after Mohandas Gandhi, the principal architect of Indian independence and world-famous advocate of non-violence, was assassinated by a Hindu extremist (1948) while trying to stop crowd violence.

The establishment of the sovereign state of Israel in 1948 was a different sort of landmark in the process of decolonization. Substantial numbers of Jewish Zionists lived on land purchased from Arabs in Palestine between the wars; and after 1945 a flood of Jews who had somehow survived the Nazi holocaust in Europe emigrated to Palestine, where they were determined to set up a state of their own. The

# *Charter of the United Nations*

President Franklin Roosevelt, Winston Churchill, and Josef Stalin endorsed the idea of setting up a new international authority during their meeting at Yalta in February 1945. Accordingly, delegates from fifty-one countries gathered at San Francisco, California, in April and spent two months drafting a charter for the new United Nations. They tried to make rules more realistic by giving four Great Powers (United States, U.S.S.R., Great Britain, and China) a veto on critical questions; but the aim of making peace permanent reaffirmed the central ideal of the League of Nations.

The charter is a lengthy document, comprising nineteen chapters. But excerpts from the Preamble and first three chapters, reproduced below, define the purposes, hopes, and instruments for their accomplishment approved by the delegates on June 25, 1945. The charter duly came into force four months later after most of the signatory governments had ratified it. It remains operational to the present.

Charter of the United Nations

Preamble

We the peoples of the United Nations, determined to save succeeding generations from the scourge of war which twice in our lifetime has brought untold sorrow to mankind, and to reaffirm faith in fundamental human rights, in the dignity and worth of the human person, in equal rights of men and women and of nations large and small, and

to establish conditions under which justice and respect for the obligations arising from treaties and other international law can be maintained, and

to promote social progress and better standards of life in larger freedom

and for these ends

to practice tolerance and live together in peace with one another as good neighbors, and

to unite our strength to maintain international peace and security, and

to ensure acceptance of principles and the institution of methods, that armed force shall not be used, save in the common interest, and

to employ international machinery for the promotion of the economic and social advancement of peoples,

have resolved to combine our efforts to accomplish these aims.

Accordingly, our respective Governments, through representatives assembled in the city of San Francisco . . . have agreed to the present Charter of the United Nations and do hereby establish an international organization to be known as the United Nations.

Chapter I. Purposes and Principles

Article 1. The Purposes of the United Nations are:

1.  To maintain international peace and security. . . .

2.  To develop friendly relations among nations. . . .

3.  To achieve international cooperation in solving international problems of an economic, social, cultural and humanitarian character. . . .

4.  To be a center for harmonizing the actions of nations in the attainment of these common ends.

Article 2. The Organization and its Members . . . shall act in accordance with the following Principles:

1.  The Organization is based on the principle of the sovereign equality of all its Members. . . .

3.  All Members shall settle their international disputes by peaceful means. . . .

5.  All Members shall give the United Nations every assistance in any action it takes in accordance with the present Charter. . . .

6.  The Organization shall ensure that states which are not Members of the United Nations act in accordance with these Principles so far as may be necessary for the maintenance of international peace and security.

7.  Nothing contained in the present Charter shall authorize the United Nations to intervene in matters which are essentially within the domestic jurisdiction of any state. . . .

Chapter II. Membership

Article 4.

1.  Membership in the United Nations is open to all other peace-loving states which accept the obligations contained in the present Charter. . . .

Article 6.

A Member of the United Nations which has persistently violated the Principles contained in the present Charter may be expelled from the Organization by the General Assembly upon the recommendation of the Security Council.

Chapter III. Organs

Article 7.

1.  There are established as the principal organs of the United Nations: a General Assembly, a Security Council, an Economic and Social Council, a Trusteeship Council, an International Court of Justice, and a Secretariat.

The charter then goes on to specify the composition and duties of each of these organs in detail.

**Super-modern Japan**    Japan's economic success since World War II arose in large part from the readiness of government and industry to introduce the newest technology with the least delay. When transport between Tokyo and Kyoto began to clog seriously, the Japanese government decided to build a completely new high speed railway running for over 300 miles between the two cities. Heavy, wide-gauge tracks that avoided sharp curves and steep grades were designed to allow the trains to travel at speeds above 120 miles an hour; double tracks permitted trains to shuttle back and forth along this heavily travelled route at frequent intervals. From its opening in 1961, Japan thus achieved the swiftest and most efficient train service in the world. Below is a scene from a Japanese automobile factory, where robots are seen welding a car body automatically and without human intervention. Labor-saving machinery like this helped to make Japanese cars cheaper and more reliable than cars built elsewhere.

# THE CONQUEST OF MOUNT EVEREST

Mount Everest rises 29,028 feet above sea level, higher than any other mountain on earth. Icy winds blow fiercely around the high slopes of the mountain; temperatures of 30 or 40 degrees below zero are common near the top. Not only that, the air gets thinner with every increase in altitude. Men whose bodies are built to breathe at or near sea level cannot get enough oxygen into their bloodstream to keep their muscles strong at altitudes as high as Everest's peak. For many years, this seemed to make it impossible to climb to the earth's highest point.

But the word "impossible" was a challenge. Improved equipment for dealing with rock, ice, and snow at high altitudes allowed skilled mountain climbers to get higher and higher. In 1921 the first effort was made to use these skills on Everest. The expedition did not get anywhere near the top, but it proved one very important thing: tanks of oxygen, strapped to a climber's back, allowed oxygen-starved muscles to revive their strength in spite of the thin air. So the extra weight was worthwhile; and with this discovery, the conquest of Mount Everest became a real possibility.

But difficulties were immense. Between World Wars I and II, five Everest expeditions set out, each better equipped than the previous one had been; and five times they failed. Then World War II interrupted mountaineering in the Himalayas until the 1950s. All the early expeditions had approached Mount Everest from the north, only to reach an impassable face near the very top. In 1951 a new route, approaching from the south, was reconnoitered. A Swiss expedition tried this approach in 1952 and almost reached the top before bad weather interfered. The next spring a British party, helped by Sherpa tribesmen who were accustomed to living at very high altitudes, renewed the assault.

Day after day the climbers leapfrogged higher. Toward the top, the party divided up into smaller groups of two or three men. One such group went on ahead to explore the best line of ascent and set up a camp, from which the next group could take off and do the same thing over again. On May 28, a camp only 1,100 feet below Mount Everest's crest was set up. The honor of making the final climb fell upon two men: Edmund Hillary, a New Zealander, and Tenzing Norgay, a Sherpa. Starting from the advance camp in the early morning, the two men reached the highest point on the surface of the earth before noon, May 29, 1953. Unlike many of those who had tried before, they got back down safely.

Thus another landmark in the restless effort to test strength and skill by doing what has never been done before entered the record of human achievement.

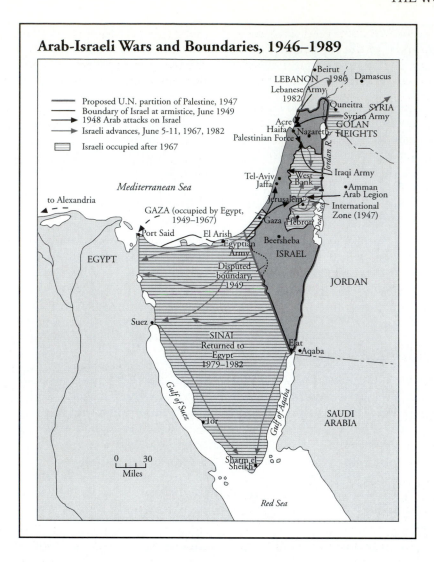

British, who administered Palestine as a mandate from the League of Nations, could neither stop them nor persuade the Palestinian Arabs to accept a Jewish state and so referred the issue to the United Nations. That body speedily ratified what had already been decided on the ground when Jewish fighters defeated the Palestinian Arabs, driving many thousands off land they had occupied for centuries. Bitter hostility divided the new Jewish state from the displaced Palestinians, who found sympathy and rather ineffectual support from neighboring Arab governments.

Both in India and in Palestine, therefore, hostility rooted in religious heritages came to the fore in the first postwar years, introducing an issue into international politics that had previously been carefully swept under the rug. Two other hopes for the future competed with religion for popular support in the so-called "Third World"—that is, all the peoples and governments that were not closely tied into the American and Soviet spheres of influence. One such hope was national independence, the other was socialism—usually in Marxist dress. Marxists often sought help from the Soviets; nationalists tended to look toward the Americans; and religiously inspired movements ordinarily opposed and distrusted both superpowers. But political leaders often combined nationalism with socialism and mingled traditional religious identities with both of these newer faiths. Political alignments among the peoples of Africa, Asia, and Latin America with one or other of the superpowers therefore remained tentative and unstable.

## Precarious Stabilization: The Cold War, 1953–1973

For twenty years between 1953 and 1973, world affairs settled down to an awkward balance between the United States and the Soviet Union. Neither superpower dared to interfere very much with the other's sphere of influence; but the Third World was up for grabs, and the rival governments competed for prestige and influence in the Middle East, Africa, Latin America, and southeast Asia by granting aid, supplying arms, and engaging in covert actions intended to help their friends and overthrow their enemies. Their rivalry stopped well short of open warfare. The main reason for holding back was that each side came to fear horrendous destruction from rapidly proliferating atomic warheads.

The United States had pioneered the development of atomic weapons during World War II, but the Russians exploded their first atomic warhead in 1949, and immediately after that, when first the Americans and then the Russians discovered how to build unimaginably powerful H-bombs, both sides became desperately afraid of all-out conflict. The balance of terror was reinforced after 1957 when the two powers started to build rockets capable of carrying city-destroying warheads across the oceans of the Northern

Hemisphere. No way of intercepting such missiles existed. Hence the outbreak of war between the two great powers seemed likely to bring sudden destruction to most of the home population of the two combatants—and, by damaging global ecosystems, might even end human life entirely. No one wanted that sort of disaster, so Americans and Russians both began to back away from situations in which resort to full-scale war seemed possible.

An unexpected side effect of this deadlock was that other states had more room to maneuver between the two superpowers. Yugoslavia had already quarreled with the Soviets in 1948, and Stalin was unable to overthrow his fellow Communist, Tito, who headed the Yugoslav government. The United States soon extended some modest aid to Yugoslavia, to keep the country independent; but by the time Hungarians revolted against their Communist rulers in 1956, the balance of terror was in place, so the United States and the NATO alliance it had created in 1948 to safeguard western Europe did not intervene and instead allowed Moscow to restore a Communist regime by force. Similarly, when the East German government erected a wall to prevent its subjects from fleeing to the west in 1961, the Americans and NATO remained inactive as before.

All the same, these events reflected increasing difficulties within the Communist bloc. A far more important setback for the Soviet Union came to a head in 1960 when Communist China accused the Russians of having abandoned true Marxism. Russian advisors and technical helpers were withdrawn, while the Chinese plunged ahead with what Mao Tse-tung called "The Great Leap Forward," aiming at achieving socialism in a hurry. Mismanagement soon provoked a famine from which as many as thirty million people died; and most of the hastily constructed industrial plants proved sadly inefficient. But despite the withdrawal of Soviet technical help, China exploded its first atomic warhead in 1964, and Mao's advocacy of heroic action created a following in other lands that seriously embarrassed Soviet claims to revolutionary world leadership.

The United States, too, found it hard to keep its sphere of influence in order. In 1959 Fidel Castro seized power in Cuba after a brief

**Recent Revolutionaries**   These photographs record two successful revolutions of the post-World War II era. Above, Mao Tse-tung, chairman of the Chinese Communist Party, makes a public appearance in 1959 at a time when the Great Leap Forward was in midcourse. In 1959 Mao was near the peak of his influence and prestige as a revolutionary leader. He had brought the Chinese Communists to power in 1949 and then defeated United Nations troops in Korea in 1952–1953. In 1958 he undertook the Great Leap Forward to show Marxists everywhere (and especially the Russians) how to achieve the goals of real communism without suffering from the bureaucratic socialism that, Mao claimed, had diverted the Soviet Union from the true path of revolutionary Marxism. Subsequently, the failure of the Great Leap Forward dimmed Mao's reputation at home and abroad, and the increasingly obvious failures of Marxist regimes made religiously inspired revolution of the sort that came to Iran in 1979 far more attractive. Below is a photograph of an Iranian crowd demonstrating in front of the American Embassy in Tehran in 1979. Placards of Ayatollah Khomeini and a crude caricature of U.S. President Jimmy Carter show the two poles of the movement: revulsion against the influence of the United States, on the one hand, and an effort to return to old-fashioned Moslem righteousness, as defined by the Ayatollah, on the other. Yet for all their desire to get back to a religiously defined way of life, the revolutionaries in Iran consciously used television to influence opinion in the United States, as the symbols and writing on the Carter caricature plainly show.

guerrilla campaign and established a Communist regime just ninety miles off the Florida coast. His efforts to forward revolutions in other Latin American countries annoyed the Americans but met with little success. On the other hand, Castro's decision to threaten the United States directly by allowing the Soviet Union to install rockets on Cuban soil in 1962 provoked a first-class diplomatic crisis. After very tense negotiations between Moscow and Washington, the Soviets backed away and offended Castro by withdrawing their missiles. This was the nearest the Cold War ever came to igniting World War III.

The United States also saw France withdraw from NATO in 1966; and as Japan's economy and the European Economic Community (founded in 1957) started to prosper mightily, American industry (automobile and electronic manufacturers, in particular) began to face damaging competition from both Japan and Germany.

Even more troubling was the way American efforts, beginning in 1955, to back up the anti-Communist government of South Vietnam gradually sucked American armed forces into a war that proved unwinnable. China and the Soviet Union kept the Communist forces in the field by providing weapons and other war supplies. But the Communists relied mainly on the widespread sympathy they aroused among civilians in the south. That was because, in the minds of most Vietnamese—North and South—the Communist cause and national independence converged, since, in their eyes, American soldiers looked just like the French imperialists whom the Communists had already defeated.

The precarious balance of the Cold War did not interfere with the breakup of European colonial empires that had started in the immediate postwar years. French efforts to restore their power in Vietnam were abandoned after 1954, and, as we just saw, Americans then tried vainly to prop up the unpopular government of South Vietnam that the French left behind. In Algeria, where more than a million French settlers lived, France fought a far more bitter war between 1956 and 1962 but reluctantly agreed to Algerian independence when the costs of the struggle became too heavy to bear. Great Britain offered less resistance to colonial independence movements, though in Kenya, where white settlers owned a good deal of the best land, and in Malaya, British forces conducted nasty anti-guerrilla wars before conceding independence. Elsewhere in the British Empire, transfer of government to local political leaders went far more smoothly, beginning with Sudan in 1956 and Ghana in 1957. After their failure in Algeria, the French followed suit. Other European governments soon did the same, until only a few scattered remnants of European overseas empire remained in places like Hong Kong (until 1997) and a few other islands.

Independence of former colonies gave Third World countries a numerical superiority of votes in the United Nations General Assembly. But this did not do much to increase their power or prosperity. Instead, the new governments depended heavily on grants of aid (often in the form of military equipment) from the rich countries of the world. Efforts to improve local living standards met with very limited success, largely because both population growth and global prices for their exports and imports were entirely beyond their control.

Often, too, boundaries inherited from colonial days did not match local realities. Tribal, ethnic, and religious groups remained important, and some bitter civil wars broke out among them, especially in Africa. In many new countries the army constituted the most cohesive and readily mobilized element in society, with the result that military dictatorships became widespread. Yet such regimes remained weak, since other segments of society were either indifferent to, or actively alienated from, upstart soldiers.

The Middle East remained bitterly divided between Moslem countries and the new state of Israel. Three wars in 1956, 1967, and 1973 led to quick Israeli victories over their Arab neighbors—Egypt, Syria, and Jordan. As a result, the Israelis took possession of all of Jerusalem (initially partitioned into Israeli and Palestinian sectors) and extended their control to the Jordan River. Other governments, even those most sympathetic to Israel, did not recognize the legitimacy of these conquests; and a Palestine Liberation Organization, operating in exile, did all it could to keep Palestinian grievances before the United Nations, while organizing resistance among Palestinian refugees and those subjected to Israeli occupation.

Religiously rooted antagonisms also distracted south Asia, where India and Pakistan fought an inconclusive war over Kashmir in 1965. Subsequently, in 1971–1972, the Indian army helped the Bengali Moslems of East Pakistan to win independence by founding a new state of Bangladesh.

Race was comparably divisive in some parts of the world. For example, white South Africans tried to separate themselves from the black majority by confining blacks to special reserves, but the policy of apartheid (separation) was widely condemned by others from the time it was introduced in 1948.

Race relations in the United States moved in an opposite direction. President Truman ended racial segregation in the American armed forces in 1948, and in 1954 the Supreme Court declared segregated public schools unconstitutional. The next year, Martin Luther King (1929–1968) borrowed Gandhi's non-violent methods to protest against other segregation laws, dating back to post–Civil War decades. King's campaigns won wide support and helped to persuade Congress to pass a Civil Rights law in 1964 prohibiting practices that had previously legalized inequality between blacks and whites in American society. But civil rights laws and changes they made in actual behavior did not erase racial frictions in the United States. Efforts to redress old injustices sometimes discriminated against whites, who often resented it; while a few black leaders contributed to keeping race relations uneasy by advocating black cultural and even economic separatism.

By comparison, in Brazil and other Latin American countries, race relations remained far more comfortable. Inequalities existed, but the poor and disadvantaged did not organize along racial lines, largely because most of the population was of mixed ancestry. Elsewhere, for example, in Malaysia, where Malays and Chinese collided, or in the Fiji Islands, where Indians were opposed by native Fijians, race sometimes be-

**Civil Rights in the United States**  Segregation of blacks on buses and in other public places became law in most southern cities in the 1870s, and private agreements prohibiting blacks from owning or renting houses in a white neighborhood were common in the north. Pictured here is the man who first challenged these and similar forms of discrimination effectively. Martin Luther King, Jr., was a Baptist minister who borrowed Mohandas Gandhi's idea of attacking unjust laws by organizing nonviolent disobedience on a mass scale. He began in 1955 with a boycott of the bus system in Montgomery, Alabama, and after about a year succeeded in abolishing segregated seating there. Soon he was leading a nationwide movement for civil rights. This photograph was taken in 1963 at the height of King's career as a political activist, as he addressed a vast crowd of sympathizers from the steps of the Lincoln Memorial in Washington, proclaiming his dream of achieving racial equality and brotherhood. As a result of his agitation, in 1964 Congress passed a Civil Rights Act prohibiting racial segregation, and King won the Nobel Peace Prize. Four years later, aged 39, he died of an assassin's bullet, after having compared himself with Moses in his last public speech, saying: "I may not get to the promised land with you, but I want you to know tonight that we as a people will."

came a political issue. But in most of the world the ideal of common citizenship prevailed, overriding or disregarding religious, racial, and other differences.

This ideal was sustained by the extraordinary economic expansion that took place between 1953 and 1973. Increasing productivity among the rich industrial nations brought substantial improvements in living standards. In the United States, for example, the GNP (Gross National Product) doubled between 1960 and 1970. Even in Communist lands, where increases in productivity began to lag after about 1960, millions of newly urbanized workers escaped most of the hardships of peasant life from which they had come.

# New Dilemmas and End of the Cold War, 1973–1996

In the first twenty-five years after World War II it looked as though Communist management by command in the Soviet sphere and fiscal management of the market by fine-tuning interest rates, taxes, and government expenditures in the American sphere had left the old boom-and-bust economy behind. But in 1973 world markets were jolted, when, in response to Israel's victories against its Arab neighbors, an association of oil-producing countries in the Middle East (OPEC) quadrupled the price of oil by agreeing to ration oil production and sell only at the new rates. This move had a drastic impact on oil-importing countries and provoked a worldwide depression. It also helped the Soviet Union to stave off its internal economic problems by exporting increasing quantities of oil to pay for food and other necessary imports.

Fiscal management of separate national economies, which had worked so well for western Europe and the United States ever since 1945, began to sputter. Instead of maintaining full employment and steady prosperity, political tinkering with tax and interest rates provoked rapid inflation without restoring prosperity. No one knew what to do. The rich industrial nations of the world suddenly confronted a situa-tion like that which poor, raw-material producers had confronted before. International trade in oil and other commodities had grown so great during the postwar boom that the domestic economies of the major industrialized nations were at the mercy of world markets. Poor and weak peoples had long been in that situation. Now it appeared that even the biggest and most powerful industrial nations were caught in the same dilemma. Techniques of nationwide economic management, pioneered and perfected during World War II for war mobilization, could not cope with an increasingly global economy. As a result, rich and poor peoples alike faced economic perils that their governments could not control.

Transnational economic management was a partial but inadequate step up from the national scale of trying to regulate economic processes. To be sure, the European Economic Community survived and indeed expanded its membership to include Great Britain among others, but this merely made the EEC into a big, imperfectly consolidated, economic unit that remained at the mercy of world markets. Even the OPEC cartel, after enriching its members enormously, soon broke down when individual countries started to pump more than their agreed-upon quotas. Oil prices therefore sank considerably after 1970–1980 because OPEC could not enforce its rules.

Oil importers benefited, but competition from low-wage countries located along the Pacific rim of Asia soon began to trouble industrialists in Europe and the United States and drove even the formidable Japanese out of some lines of production. As a result, in 1980s and 1990s, the international division of labor started to shift painfully fast. Individual firms could profit either by setting up manufacturing branches overseas or by buying parts abroad. But abandoned factories meant loss of jobs in old industrial centers, and no merely national government could do much to stop the process. Cutting off connections with the rest of the world was too costly to contemplate. Where would the oil come from, and all the other essential imports? As long as that remained true, participation in an increasingly global economy was inescapable as well as painful.

The response of the United States was complicated by the fact that the oil shock coincided with an ignominious withdrawal from Vietnam. American opposition to the war had become intense after 1968; but other Americans felt just as strongly that national prestige and the cause of freedom required nothing less than total victory. When costs began to outweigh any conceivable gains, the American government reluctantly decided to withdraw its soldiers in 1973, whereupon the puppet government of South Vietnam soon collapsed. This was profoundly troubling to Americans of all political persuasions, and for a long time the extra costs of the war obscured the more general breakdown of the postwar style of economic management.

Then, when economic prosperity continued to sputter even after the war ended, the United States went recklessly into debt. President Ronald Reagan (1981–1989) prescribed self-confidence, tax reduction, and an expanded arms program ("Star Wars") aimed at intercepting hostile rockets before they could reach their target. He hoped to end the balance of terror that had prevailed between the two superpowers since the 1950s, but success eluded the effort. Instead, the United States doubled its national debt in a decade, creating a problem that still distresses the nation's public life.

But strains and stresses within the Soviet Union turned out to be far greater than anything Americans experienced. After the Cuban crisis of 1962, the Soviet government decided to build a big navy to prevent recurrence of the humiliation they had suffered when the U.S. Navy intercepted ships bound for Cuba. This added to the costs of an already overstrained military budget; and further efforts to compete with Reagan's high-tech arms program only intensified the problem.

Soviet difficulty, however, rested fundamentally on the fact that the recipe for economic management that the Communists had used successfully ever since the first Five Year Plan of 1928 wore out soon after they completed reconstruction of war damages in the 1960s. Communist planning had always been wasteful of manpower and materials; but as long as undeveloped resources and underemployed labor abounded, even wasteful production increased national wealth and allowed the government to devote an extraordinary proportion of the country's resources to the manufacture of arms and high-tech prestige undertakings like the exploration of space.

But after 1940 birth rates dropped precipitously in the U.S.S.R. so that collective farms no longer had surplus labor that could be transferred to more productive kinds of urban employment. Equally, after the best natural resources—coal fields, oil reserves, dam sites, and the like—had been developed, material windfalls disappeared. Instead, economic expansion came to depend on efficiency; but Communist managers could not afford to be efficient. Instead they had to hoard materials and labor in order to be able to fulfill the plan and overcome all the temporary interruptions of supply that frequently created crises in their factories. Moreover, prices were arbitrary, and quantitative measures of output were what the planners paid attention to. As a result, quality, especially of consumer goods, often suffered.

Instead of continued expansion of wealth and productivity, therefore, the Soviet Union began to experience economic slowdown. This was most evident in agriculture, where bad harvests required large-scale import of grain, beginning in 1963. Living standards remained far behind those of western countries, and almost everyone lost faith in Communist promises of future betterment. Marx's prediction that after socialist revolution the state would wither away was contradicted by everything the Soviet regime did; and the privileges Soviet officials reserved for themselves began to resemble the privileges Russia's landowning nobles had once enjoyed. As a result, cynical disillusionment spread, slowly but irresistibly, even among the most privileged classes of society.

Demoralization came into the open between 1979 and 1989 when the Soviets suffered an embarrassing and unexpected military setback in Afghanistan. Intervention by the Red Army failed to prop up a Communist government in that country against Moslem guerrillas, who were supplied in large part from the United

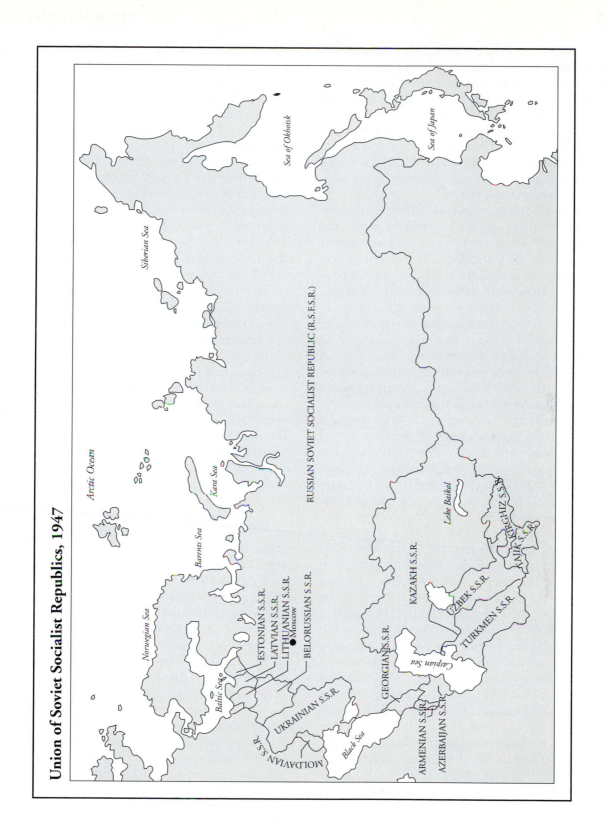

**Union of Soviet Socialist Republics, 1947**

Arctic Ocean

Siberian Sea

Sea of Okhotsk

Sea of Japan

Kara Sea

Barents Sea

Norwegian Sea

RUSSIAN SOVIET SOCIALIST REPUBLIC (R.S.F.S.R.)

Lake Baikal

KIRGHIZ S.S.R.

TAJIK S.S.R.

KAZAKH S.S.R.

UZBEK S.S.R.

TURKMEN S.S.R.

ESTONIAN S.S.R.

LATVIAN S.S.R.

LITHUANIAN S.S.R.

Moscow

BELORUSSIAN S.S.R.

Baltic Sea

GEORGIAN S.S.R.

Caspian Sea

UKRAINIAN S.S.R.

MOLDAVIAN S.S.R.

Black Sea

ARMENIAN S.S.R.

AZERBAIJAN S.S.R.

States. As a result, the Afghan war was as demoralizing for Russians as the war in Vietnam had been for Americans, and, in 1985, when Mikhail Gorbachev became General Secretary of the Communist Party, he decided to change things by "openness" (glasnost) and "restructuring" (perestroika). This meant public admission of past failures, withdrawal from Afghanistan, and installing younger and perhaps more efficient economic managers.

But Gorbachev soon found that limited reform from the top could not solve the problems he faced. As a result, first in eastern Europe and then in the U.S.S.R. itself, he had to embark on more radical reforms than he had first imagined; and, when he hesitated, other leaders, most prominent of whom was Boris Yeltsin, came to the fore by appealing to increasingly vigorous popular discontent.

The first effect was that within a year of the start of Gorbachev's reforms, the countries of eastern Europe, one after another, broke away from Russian domination by overthrowing their Communist governments. After the failure in Afghanistan, Gorbachev decided not to suppress these upheavals with military force and agreed instead to bring Soviet garrisons home. This was swiftly followed by the breakup of the Soviet Union into its constituent republics, each of which claimed sovereign independence.

The sudden demise of the U.S.S.R. in 1991 deprived Gorbachev of his job, and Yeltsin, as president of the Russian Republic, became the most powerful figure among the leaders of the successor states. He persuaded most but not all of them to join with Russia in a loose federation, but a number of local ethnic groups were not satisfied and demanded full independence. Some violent collisions ensued, the most conspicuous of which was in Chechnya, where Russian efforts to repress armed resistance met with only limited success.

These truly surprising political upheavals did nothing to resolve the issues of economic management that had provoked the crisis in the first place. Yeltsin started to privatize industrial enterprises and introduce market prices, but this aroused new discontent because a handful of successful wheelers and dealers began to enrich themselves without doing much to repair the inefficiencies of the Russian farms and factories. It therefore remains unclear whether Yeltsin's reforms will improve the Russian economy quickly enough to win popular support. As long as economic inefficiency prevails, discontent will remain lively, making fresh upheavals likely. No one can foretell what will happen, least of all those in charge of the new governments of Russia and eastern Europe.

Soviet collapse, and the Russian government's repudiation of Communist recipes for social and economic management, were both sudden and amazingly peaceful. Return to a command economy, with or without Marxist window-dressing, remains possible. The apparent change in world relations that took place so suddenly in 1991 may therefore turn out to be less drastic than first appeared.

Yet, up to now, at least, the Cold War seems over. World politics is taking a new shape, but what that shape may be remains unclear. Conflicts aplenty continue throughout the world. Contradictory claims on human loyalties and faiths struggle against one another everywhere. Only in retrospect will historians know which really matter. For now, confusion reigns.

All the same, other notable changes seem worth mentioning here. The Chinese government reacted to the collapse of Soviet Communism by reaffirming its own version of the Marxist faith. But Deng Xiaoping, who dominated the Party and government after 1980 from behind the scenes, decided to allow free market prices to spread through a large part of the Chinese economy while retaining strict political control in the hands of the Chinese Communist party. Very rapid increases first in agricultural, and then in industrial, output resulted, and China began to export some industrial goods on an unprecedented scale.

Political discontent, manifested mainly among students, was forcibly repressed in 1989. Whether widespread disillusionment with Communist ideas and ideals festers beneath the surface, as it did in Russia, is unsure. And whether the Communists can maintain their political monopoly and satisfy popular hopes by relying on free markets to raise living standards remains altogether uncertain. China's future and the future of the world will depend in considerable degree on how that question is resolved.

The Middle East also experienced dramatic political upheavals in the years since 1973. The region's ethnic and religious rivalries are also sure to affect the world's future in unpredictable ways, if only because so much of the world's oil reserves are located around the shores of the Persian Gulf.

The most important single event in the Middle East came in 1979, when religiously inspired opponents overthrew the Shah's ruthless, modernizing regime. By smuggling his tape-recorded sermons into the country; the exiled Ayatollah Khomeni—Iran's leading expert in the Shi'a version of the Sacred Law of Islam—had inspired this successful campaign; and on his return he continued to advise and direct the new government's effort to regulate society in accord with the Sacred Law.

The Iranian revolution sent a quiver of excitement through the Moslem world when excited crowds in Tehran took American diplomats hostage and vilified the United States as "The Great Satan." After suffering centuries of defeat by westerners, Moslems could dare to hope that political success did not require abandonment of the faith and customs of their forefathers. But Moslems were irreconcilably divided among rival sects and peoples. Hence, when the revolutionary Iranian government thought of rescuing fellow Shi'a believers from the secularizing government of neighboring Iraq, the Iraqi government (with some American encouragement) took the initiative by declaring war in 1980. After a long and bloody struggle, mutual exhaustion set in by 1988, when the United Nations negotiated an armistice.

Then suddenly in 1990, the ruler of Iraq, Saddam Hussein, raised the stakes in the Middle East by ordering his army to occupy oil-rich Kuwait. This put him in a position to intimidate (or conquer) Kuwait's neighbor, Saudi Arabia, where the world's richest oil deposits were located. Oil-importing countries, chief among them the United States, were unwilling to allow Iraq to control all the oil of the Persian Gulf area. The Americans therefore abruptly turned against Saddam Hussein and took the lead in getting the United Nations to authorize a campaign to drive the Iraqis back. The resulting Gulf War was an easy victory for the heavily armed Americans, helped by token detachments from many other countries, including Saudi Arabia and several other Arab countries. The armistice that ended the war in 1991 required Iraq to disarm; and U.N. efforts to enforce the armistice provisions continue to the present.

Moslem disunity could not have been more dramatically demonstrated; yet religiously inspired revolutionary movements, sometimes relying on terrorism, continued to thrive among Moslems despite all disappointments. In this inflamed atmosphere, the United States tried to persuade Israel and its Arab neighbors to make peace. Successes were real but limited. Israel made peace with Egypt and withdraw from the Sinai Peninsula in 1982; and after making peace with Jordan and secret negotiations with the PLO, Israeli troops also withdrew from Gaza and from part of occupied Palestine in 1995. But whether real pacification will ever be achieved between Israel and its neighbors remains problematic.

In South Africa, the white government abandoned racial apartheid, and Nelson Mandela, leader of the African National Congress, came to power in 1994 after winning an election in which black voters participated equally with whites for the first time. The new government proved able to keep race relations surprisingly peaceable, owing largely to Mandela's personal influence and readiness to forgive past injustices. At the same time, an opposite spectacle unfolded in Rwanda, where Hutu and Tutsi peoples, long intermingled on the ground, began to slaughter one another wholesale.

In the world as a whole, quite contradictory political trends seem to prevail. A great many subordinated ethnic groups demand self-government and sometimes are able to organize local violence against constituted political authorities. As a result, countries as diverse as Sri Lanka (Tamils versus Sinhalese), Turkey (Kurds versus Turks), Spain (Basques versus Castilians), and Russia (Chechens and several other local peoples versus Russians), to mention only a few, have endured long-drawn-out secessionist violence. Canada is also convulsed by controversy between French- and English-speakers; Czechoslovakia split up between Czechs and Slovaks, while in Bosnia three years of fighting came to a halt in 1995 when a precarious agreement split the country up between Serbs, Croats, and Moslems.

Yet in important parts of the world, national sovereignty has been willingly subordinated to new trans-national organizations. NATO was the main military example of national subordination to a transnational administration. The European Economic Community (renamed European Union (EU) in anticipation of still closer linkages agreed to in 1991) offers by far the most conspicuous example of a significant surrender of national sovereignty in the economic sphere. But the North American Free Trade treaty of 1993, projecting a common market for Mexico, Canada and the United States (NAFTA), moved in the same direction, and other regional free trade areas in South America, in some of the former Soviet lands, and perhaps in south East Asia as well may be poised to take off if NAFTA and the EU continue to flourish.

Transnational organizations, if large enough and well-managed, may do something to relieve the frustration created when merely national governments cannot correct economic injustices. But agreeing on common policies on a transnational scale is difficult, and any and all policies are bound to reward some more than others. Disputes over appropriate ways to manage our increasingly global economy are therefore bound to continue; and it is not clear that even the largest of existing transnational organizations can control global economic processes in ways acceptable to their peoples.

Other grounds for quarrel abound as well: religious, ethnic, ideological. Accordingly, public affairs are sure to remain turbulent in time to come, as they have been throughout the recorded past. What is new is the extent of human power, both for construction and destruction. This raises the stakes enormously, making the future both more threatening and more promising than ever before. Only time will tell which way things will go.

# Population and Society
## Growth of Human Numbers

The human population of the earth grew by about 100 million in 1995 according to demographers' estimates. This was the largest increase ever recorded; and short of some enormous catastrophe, future years will see additional millions. The pace of recent growth is altogether extraordinary. Sometime about 1800, world population crossed the one billion mark for the first time, and it took until 1930 for human population to reach two billion. But the pace picked up enormously thereafter, as the following table shows:

**Estimated World Population Totals**

| 1930 | passed 2 billion |
|------|------------------|
| 1960 | passed 3 billion |
| 1974 | passed 4 billion |
| 1990 | passed 5 billion |

Source: *Encyclopedia Britannica*, s.v. "Population," Vol. 25, p. 1041.

It is almost certain that before 2000 more than 6 billion people will share the face of the earth, more than tripling human numbers in less than three generations. Nothing remotely like this explosion of human numbers ever took place before. It makes the second half of the twentieth century unique in human history.

Improvements in public health explain most of what happened. One-third to one-half of the world's children had regularly died from infections before the World Health Organization launched a global effort in the 1950s to reduce or eliminate most of the diseases that killed them. Local governments cooperated everywhere; and thanks to vaccinations, some simple sanitation and an array of new antibiotics, the effort was spectacularly successful. Smallpox, one of the principal killers, was entirely eliminated by 1977. Other infections were drastically reduced. Human lives were suddenly relieved from a dreadful burden.

Children no longer died as before. Nearly all of them grew up and had children of their own, just as their parents had done before them. High birth rates, once needed to compensate for high rates of child mortality, meant very rapid population growth when, all of a sudden, most infants survived to adulthood. Human society is still adjusting to this extraordinary change.

Population growth rates peaked in the 1960s, reaching about 2 percent per annum. Since then birth rates have begun to diminish, but since absolute numbers are growing so fast, the total number of births and the annual increment to human population continue to rise. Changes are sure to curb the growth of human numbers eventually, and some are already apparent. As they come into force, the demographic history of our times will begin to look more and more extraordinary.

## The Green Revolution

Tripling human numbers of course required a corresponding increase in the production of food. At first, most of the villages where population growth concentrated could find enough uncultivated land nearby to feed themselves by extending accustomed methods of farming to new land. Extra work was needed and yields from new lands were usually lower, but extra hands were on the spot and knew what had to be done. This was how villagers had always reacted to growing numbers, ever since farming started in the Neolithic era.

But empty land started to run short in more and more localities after 1950 when child mortality sank so suddenly in Asia, Africa, and Latin America. What might have been a brutal collision between growing population and available food was cushioned in the world's most densely occupied regions by what came to be called the "Green Revolution." This refers to the introduction of new breeds of rice, corn, and other cereals that yielded up to as much as three times more calories per acre, if properly cultivated and provided with enough fertilizer, pesticides, and (especially for rice) irrigation water. Hard-pressed village farmers did not take much persuasion to adopt the new methods; and total food production in such countries as India and China grew even more rapidly than total population—at least for a while.

But paying for fertilizer, pesticides, tools, and other necessary inputs required food producers to sell at least part of their harvest. Hence local self-sufficiency characteristic of subsistence agriculture disappeared as the Green Revolution spread. In other ways, the rural majority of humankind also entered into far closer contact than ever before with the urban world around them. In particular, first radio, and then television brought villagers into daily contact with urban ideas and outlooks. Innumerable young people, dazzled by what they heard and saw, decided that life in town was what they wanted for themselves. Cities therefore grew enormously. Swarms of newcomers moved into shanty towns that grew up around old city centers everywhere in the Third World.

## Urbanization and the End of Village Autonomy

Indeed, it is probably true today that more than half the world's population now lives in towns and cities, eating food they have not raised themselves. This is an enormous change. Ever since the invention of agriculture, most people produced their own food by cultivating land around the villages where they lived. City folk were a minority—until two hundred years ago, a small minority—whose food came from the countryside in the form of rents and taxes as well as from exchange of goods and services

**Poverty, Rural and Urban**   Rapidly growing populations put an enormous strain on Asian, African, and Latin American societies. When young people come of age in the villages, new land to cultivate as their ancestors have done before them is often hard to find. But migration into town does not solve the problem if urban employment is not available in sufficient amount. These two photographs suggest the rural and urban sides of this dilemma. Above, Indonesian peasants are busily transplanting rice plants; below, a street scene from Calcutta in India shows people sitting idly on the sidewalk. The backbreaking work of the paddy fields is age old, but in Indonesia, as population has grown, there is less and less rice land to go round. In India, massive emigration from an overcrowded countryside into Calcutta has helped to create a concentrated mass of poor and discontented people. The Communist party of India tries to win their support, as the slogans and symbols painted on the walls in this photograph show. Nevertheless, religious and other conservative influences have preserved both India and Indonesia from large-scale civil violence and revolution since their liberation from European imperial control in the aftermath of World War II.

with the rural population around them. Now, for the first time, most of the world's inhabitants depend on buying and selling to sustain daily life. Innumerable poor peasants have begun to buy fertilizer to attain the high crop yields they must have to survive at all. They also long to share more fully in the comforts and conveniences of urban life as portrayed by radio voices and on television. Harder work, more efficient farming, and selling more of the harvest is the only way for them to keep food on the table and begin to realize at least part of their dream of a better life.

As a result, the enormous gap that used to divide town from countryside has begun to narrow. But cities are still privileged, most frequently by government policies that keep food prices low. And poor, hard-working farmers commonly feel that city folk are dishonest, buying cheap and selling dear, without earning an honest living by doing real, muscular work. This sort of rural discontent lay behind Communist victories in Russia in 1917, in China in 1949; and in Vietnam in 1954–1975. Village resentment is not exhausted. Uprisings and guerrilla wars in Africa, Latin America, and parts of Asia continue to reflect rural discontent and personal frustration due, largely, to local overpopulation and unequal landholdings. Acute discontent is sure to continue as long as rapid population growth requires rural folk to work harder and harder merely to stay alive. This weakens Third World governments because so many villagers feel estranged from public officials who, as a matter of course, tend to favor the interests of city folk like themselves.

The millions of villagers who migrated to cities—nearby or across cultural and political boundaries—also have a hard time. Competition for jobs is intense, and living conditions in city slums are often deplorable. Moreover, the tight-knit village communities that guided individual behavior in traditional rural society dissolve in urban settings where everyone must deal with strangers every day. Under these circumstances, moral dilemmas and personal distress multiply, magnifying merely economic hardships. But village communities, too, are un-

der pressure. Old ways and customs do not fit well with the growing importance of buying and selling. In particular, sharing of surpluses on festival occasions, that once knitted whole communities together, turns into a reckless waste of private resources when a family can use such surpluses to buy things in town for its own use. Moral dilemmas thus penetrate the countryside as well, making the human majority on earth into an unusually dissatisfied, politically and religiously volatile mass, capable of sudden and surprising twists and turns in the search for a better life.

This is probably the most fundamental feature of contemporary society. Among the majority of human beings, old village ways of life, little changed for centuries, have begun to break down. The ancient autonomy of village communities has been shattered. New, urban practices and expectations have infiltrated the countryside almost everywhere. How private guidelines for living a good life can be defined afresh, how vivacious communities can form anew amidst the hurly-burly of an ever-changing global economy, and how the skills and attitudes of adult life can be transmitted across the generations under these radically new circumstances seem likely to become key questions for human societies everywhere in the next century.

The transition underway among us appears to be as drastic as what happened when hunters and gatherers had to learn how to live as food producers. Village communities, shaped in that far-off time, have ceased to be viable as autonomous, almost self-contained units. But the overwhelming majority of our ancestors lived in such communities, and it was emigrants from them that kept cities going. No substitute for village life and nurture seems immediately available. But humans are social creatures and we need to live in a community that guides our private behavior and gives meaning to our lives. How such communities can form in an increasingly urban, cosmopolitan world remains to be seen.

Yet the dilemma is clear enough. The second half of the twentieth century destroyed the ancient compromise between city dwellers and semi-autonomous village communities upon which all historical civilizations depended. City-based exchanges have swiftly engulfed the world's villages. Yet all the new, intensified connections between food producers and food consumers arising from market exchanges need to be reinforced by shared moral expectations. Otherwise, relations among participants in the global flow-through economy of our time will remain precarious and liable to angry interruption.

## Population Decay in Urbanized Societies

Although growing numbers imposed wrenching changes on something like three-quarters of earth's human inhabitants after 1950, a contrary trend simultaneously set in among the world's rich, urbanized minority. It has equally complex and awkward consequences.

Demographers were surprised by a post–World War II "baby boom" in the United States and a few other countries as veterans demobilized. But after 1960 prewar trends toward lower birth rates resumed among all the rich industrial nations in Europe, in lands of European settlement overseas, and in Japan. Eventually, birth rates sank below the point at which these nations could reproduce themselves without an influx of newcomers.

For a while migration disguised what was happening. Immigrants were predominantly young adults who brought comparatively high birth rates with them from their rural background. Accordingly, when census returns made no distinction between newcomers and native-born citizens, national population figures continued to rise, though far more slowly than in Africa, Latin America, and Asia. But if newcomers were counted separately, as happened in Germany after 1961, when immigrants from southern Europe and Turkey were assigned a special status as "guest workers," an absolute decline in the number of Germans soon showed up, beginning in 1973. Increasing numbers of guest workers more than made up for fewer Germans, so

total population grew slowly. But the ethnic composition of the total began to change rather rapidly.

Similar developments took place in other European countries—including the Soviet Union—and the United States. As a result, growing immigrant populations, often distinguished from the host population by racial and cultural differences, now fill many of the least attractive jobs in most rich countries. Assimilation of these newcomers into the host population may occur eventually, as prevailing law usually assumes. Alternatively, urban, industrial countries, where the host population's birth rates have fallen below replacement levels, may allow a sort of caste hierarchy to develop, whereby different ethnic and cultural groups occupy distinct niches in society, each performing different kinds of work, with matching social statuses.

Japan took a different path from the countries of the western world. Among industrial nations, it faces the sharpest demographic shock. Relatively high birth rates prevailed there until World War II; but defeat was accompanied by a drastic drop in births. Rural migrants from the countryside staffed the factories that made Japan so successful in the postwar decades; but, crowded into cities where housing was persistently short, they had fewer children than Europeans or Americans. Nonetheless, when labor shortages showed up, the Japanese refused to admit immigrants. Instead they built factories overseas, bringing industrial production to alien workers instead of allowing alien workers to staff home factories, as Europeans and Americans were doing.

Japan thereby avoided the frictions between newcomers and native-born citizens that showed up in the 1980s and 1990s in Europe and (rather less acutely) in the United States, where hospitility to immigrants was of long standing. But even in the United States, Canada, and other countries accustomed to immigration, the tensions arising from the juxtaposition of declining numbers of the host population and an increasing number of newcomers strain established social and political behavior. Whether legal equality can be translated into common citizenship and a shared national life, as democratic theory assumes, is uncertain.

Three factors make assimilation of newcomers more difficult than it was in the nineteenth century. First and foremost, in the European lands, outward differences of appearance are now reinforced by the religious gap between Moslem and Christian heritages, since most newcomers come from Turkey, North Africa, and in the Russian case, from Central Asia, bringing their Islamic religion with them.

Second, modern transport and communication allow immigrants to keep in touch with their homeland—wherever it may be. Instead of cutting ties with the old country, as trans-Atlantic emigrants had to do in the nineteenth century, newcomers can easily telephone their relatives or return for a visit. In effect, it becomes possible to live in two quite different worlds simultaneously, instead of having to cut old ties off completely and adjust as quickly as possible to the new environment.

Last but not least, the Jewish experience of the Holocaust and the difficulty Blacks continued to have in the United States called into question the ideal of assimilation to a common national culture and standard of behavior. How multiplicity of cultures and ways of life can exist side by side without dividing society into separate, unequal parts is hard to see. But the fact that the ideal of assimilation has been vigorously challenged means that newcomers find it easier to retain their distinctiveness, whatever the long-term social consequences may be.

Thus, the combination of population decay among urbanized nations and rapid population growth in rural communities puts both rich and poor under serious strain. So far, poor villagers have faced by far the hardest challenges. Traditional, self-sustaining village communities simply cannot accommodate their growing numbers. Drastic, often painful, efforts barely kept up with the need to feed more and more people. But rich, urban populations also find it hard to accept newcomers among them while maintaining the flow-through economy that allows them to enjoy a high standard of living when the rest of the world is so poor.

**Schooling in Nigeria**   The poor countries of the world are poor because their people lack skills and habits of cooperation that are necessary for efficient use of modern machinery and for the effective coordination of human effort. The most obvious way to escape the trap of poverty is to set up schools in which the young may learn needed new skills, beginning with the simple ability to read and write and do arithmetic. Accordingly, since World War II much effort has gone into schooling in the newly independent countries of Africa and Asia. Here we see a school in Nigeria, housed in a rather makeshift fashion and with minimal furniture. But the presence of the two TV screens attests to the impact of new technology, and the way the children are dressed shows the influence of Western and specifically American styles on the young.

## Cultural and Biological Continuity Under Urban Conditions

The massive growth of cities since 1945 created yet another dilemma of far-reaching importance. In villages, children learn everything they need to know as adults simply by growing up with their parents and watching them as they work in the home and in fields nearby. From

### Old and New in the Third World

Extraordinary discrepancies result from the importation of high technology into countries where older ways of living continue unchanged, at least for a while. Above, women and children in India gather on a river bank to wash clothes and fill their water jugs, while across the river a new electric generating station, built with World Bank funds, stands stark and square. But since ordinary households still lack electricity and running water, age-old household routines persist indefinitely into the future, creating scenes like this. Below is a similar juxtaposition of old and new from Kuwait, where oil wealth allowed a good many residents to acquire such new gadgets as TV sets and automobiles. Even the porter, carrying his exotic load in a thoroughly traditional fashion, is wearing tennis shoes!

very early ages children shared in household tasks; and since everyone in the community did the same, everyone expected the young to do what needed to be done. Open rebellion against such universal expectation was rare and exceptional. Hence the young acquired the habits and outlook of their elders by the mere fact of growing up. Everyday routines therefore assured massive cultural continuity.

Urban living has become very different. Work and home are now usually separated so children cannot readily accompany their parents to work. Moreover, employers seldom allow it. Transmission of skills and attitudes of the workplace from generation to generation thus ceases to be automatic. Schools take up some of the slack, but formal schooling segregates the young from other age groups for most of the waking day, allowing age-specific attitudes and outlooks to take root and spread in spite of, and often in conscious opposition to, teachers and other adult authorities. Under such circumstances, youthful rebelliousness finds much enlarged scope. Cultural continuity across the generations becomes correspondingly fragile.

Cities, in short, appear to be inhospitable to human reproduction, both biological and cultural. In former times, intensified infections prevented cities from reproducing themselves biologically, and newcomers from the countryside were constantly needed to fill nasty jobs. In the twentieth century, when infections ceased to matter very much, plummeting urban birth rates required cities to import workers from rural backgrounds as before.

In contrast to the fundamental continuities of village life, cities were always where cultural change concentrated. But when power machinery and high-tech communications substituted factory and office work for home-based artisan shops, and when married women followed men into the workplace (mainly during and after World War II), an unprecedented gap opened between parents and children. This intensifies the pace of cultural change in urban settings throughout the world, sometimes calling adult rules of conduct and all the achievements of the past into question. Emphatic,

sometimes angry conservatism also feeds on the disarray of the older, unthinking transmission of traditional attitudes and values. No one can tell what the upshot will be, but it seems obvious that basic continuities of human life and society are far less assured than was usual in times past.

## Conclusion

Adjustment to all these novelties proceeds, partly by deliberate actions but largely by other means. We can be sure that the recent surge of population will not last indefinitely, and when it subsides, the chief phenomenon disrupting rural life in our time will peter out. Thus, declining birth rates already have started to slow the rate of population growth, even though absolute numbers continue to grow.

In addition, biological evolution among bacteria and viruses shows signs of catching up with human ability to discover new antibiotics. Resistant strains of several infections have appeared, and cures have not yet been found.

It therefore begins to look as though the medical victory over infectious disease, which seemed so certain in the 1950s and 1960s, may have been only a passing phase in humanity's long coexistence with disease organisms. If so, the principal cause of the recent population explosion will disappear. Alternatively, doctors may discover new ways to destroy disease-causing viruses and bacteria by attacking them at the genetic and molecular levels.

Ecological considerations suggest that absolute limits to the growth of human numbers exist and may be close at hand since we have been exploiting natural resources at a rate that cannot be long sustained. Fish populations of the North Atlantic, for example, have been depleted so much that a formerly important source of human food has dwindled drastically. Fields, newly cleared for agriculture, accelerate erosion everywhere; and in parts of Africa, overgrazing has allowed the Sahara Desert to engulf grasslands where rainfall was already marginal. Serious famines resulted in parts of Africa, beginning in the 1970s.

Industrial processes also put chemicals into air and water, altering the atmosphere globally and affecting fresh water (eventually also the oceans) in ways only imperfectly understood. Climate is changing as a result of the way human activities (primarily the emission of carbon dioxide into the atmosphere) intersect with natural variations in the sun's activity and other global (and even cosmic) changes. Impacts on human and other forms of life are likely to hurt more often than not by upsetting long-standing, complex relationships among the earth's innumerable organisms.

In effect, human beings are tinkering with a system no one fully understands, and we are doing so on a rapidly increasing scale. More powerful technology magnifies the impact of our increasing numbers. Nasty, disruptive surprises that endanger human survival locally or even globally may be within the bounds of possibility. Yet human ingenuity is enormous, and in time past people have learned to alter their ways after meeting local ecological disasters. The same may be so in future as well, though recent changes in oceans and atmosphere raise the specter of genuinely global catastrophe, unparalleled in previous human experience on earth.

Given what we know and can surmise about the impact of human activity on the world around us, trends of the past fifty years cannot be expected to continue far into the future. Perhaps we are riding the crest of a breaking wave. As always, opportunity and danger both confront us. Human beings, like everything around us, are part of a vast evolutionary process whose past is only dimly apparent and whose future remains obscure. In this great adventure humanity has done very well for itself so far by using intelligence and imagination to find new ways of getting what people wanted. These capacities are undiminished among us, however complex the problems we face as the twentieth century approaches its close. Who knows what human inventiveness will achieve in time to come? Despair is foolish. So is blind confidence. Mud-

dling through is the way human societies do things. Perhaps the next century will be no different.

# Bibliography

As we approach the present, the quantity of available information about the state of the world multiplies about as rapidly as human population is doing; and both sorts of growth create confusion. Fitting details into the larger picture is further hampered by rapid changes in perspective as new, surprising events take place. Nearly all recent books will therefore soon be superceded.

In the meanwhile, here are some titles that try to interpret the course of public affairs since 1945: Peter Calvocoressi, *World Politics since 1945* (6th ed., 1991); Raymond F. Betts, *Uncertain Dimensions: Western Overseas Empires in the Twentieth Century* (1985); R. F. Holland, *European Decolonization, 1918–1981: An Introductory Survey* (1985); Lawrence Freedman, *The Evolution of Nuclear Strategy* (2nd ed., 1989); Walter A. McDougall, *The Heavens and the Earth: A Political History of the Space Age* (1985); Joan E. Spero, *The Politics of International Economic Relations* (4th ed., 1990); Peter R. Odell, *Oil and World Power* (8th ed., 1986).

On the Cold War, John L. Gaddis, *The Long Peace: Inquiries into the History of the Cold War* (1987), is a lot cooler and probably wiser than the more critical tone of Walter LaFeber, *America, Russia and the Cold War, 1945–1992* (6th ed., 1992). For the rival alliance systems in Europe, Lawrence S. Kaplan, *NATO and the United States: The Enduring Alliance* (1988), may be compared with Charles Gati, *The Bloc That Failed: Soviet-East European Relations in Transition* (1990). For recent summaries of domestic developments of the two superpowers, see William H. Chafe, *The Unfinished Journey: America since World War II* (2nd ed., 1991), and John B. Dunlop, *The Rise of Russia and the Fall of the Soviet Empire* (1993). For the economic and social dilemmas each faced, see E. A. Hewitt, *Reforming the Soviet Economy: Equality vs. Efficiency* (1988), and William L. O'Neill, *Coming Apart: An Informal History of America in the 1960s* (1971).

For other parts of the world, the following are useful introductions: Stephen Wright and Janice N. Brownfoot, eds., *Africa in World Politics: Changing Perspectives* (1987); Cole Blasier, *The Hovering Giant: U.S. Responses to Revolutionary Changes in Latin America, 1910–1985* (1985); Mohammed E. Ahari, *OPEC: The Falling Giant* (1986); James A. Bill, *The Eagle and the Lion: The Tragedy of American-Iranian Relations* (1988); Richard Ovendale, *The Origin of the*

*Arab-Israeli Wars* (2nd ed., 1992); Mark Urban, *War in Afghanistan* (2nd ed., 1990); S. B. Linder, *The Pacific Century: Economic and Political Consequences of Asian-Pacific Dynamism* (1986); Wang Gungwu, *China and the World since 1949: The Impact of Independence, Modernity and Revolution* (1977); George C. Herring, Jr., *America's Longest War: The United States and Vietnam, 1950–1975* (2nd ed., 1986).

On population growth and social consequences, see George Tepinos and Phyllis T. Piotrow, *Six Billion People: Demographic Dilemmas and World Politics* (1978); G. Robina Quale, *Families in Context: A World History of Population* (1992); David Grigg, *Population Growth and Agrarian Change* (1980); Richard Critchfield, *The Villagers: Changed Values, Altered Lives, the Closing of the Urban-Rural Gap* (1994); William H. McNeill, *Population and Politics since 1750* (1990); Ansley J. Coale and Susan Cotts Watkins, eds., *The Decline of Fertility in Europe* (1986); Daniel Patrick Moynihan, *Pandaemonium: Ethnicity in International Politics* (1993); Andrew Hurrell and Benedict Kingsbury, eds., *The International Politics of the Environment: Actors, Interests and Institutions* (1992); John L. Seitz, *The Politics of Development: An Introduction to Global Issues* (1988); and Michael P. Todaro, *Internal Migration in Developing Countries* (1976).

# *Thought and Culture*
## 1914 to the Present

# 26

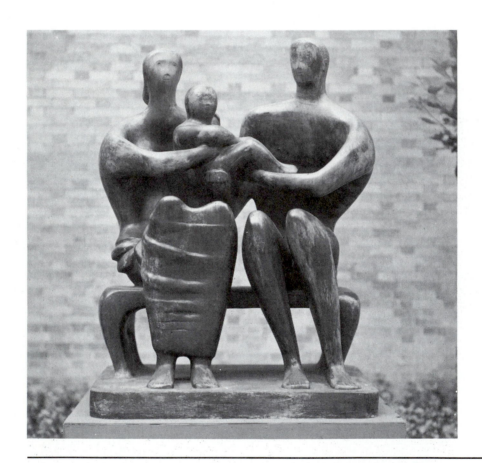

**Human Nature and Nurture**  This statue by the Englishman Henry Moore (1898–1986) shows how we differ from the rest of creation, being born helpless and having to learn everything from our parents, teachers, and peers. Because we learn, we change what we do, generation after generation, and keep on upsetting the world around us with new thoughts, new skills, new deeds.

Since 1914 deep and far-reaching changes have come very quickly in the way people think and act. From country to country, great differences appear; and even within a single country, different age groups and different economic classes, different races and different religious bodies, sometimes disagree with one another about nearly everything. Or so it seems to anyone who reads the newspaper headlines and listens to all the quarreling voices that compete for public attention all round the world.

General trends are difficult to detect. Certainly, communication has increased. We know far more about events in distant parts of the earth than our grandparents or great-grandparents did, and far more people travel than ever before. This may tend to even out differences—but only in the long run. In the short run, as people become more aware of their many differences, more frequent contacts may merely underline the disagreements that split humankind into quarrelsome parts.

Since World War I, scientists have mastered new secrets at a great rate; atomic physics, genetic codes, Big Bang cosmology, continental drift, humanity's evolutionary past—these and many other fields have opened important new vistas. Yet we have also learned how much human action depends on unconscious impulses. Artists have tried to express and explore the subconscious levels of life, both in words and through the visual arts.

Some people feel that the result of so much change amounts to a breakdown of all civilized traditions. Others argue that the Western world is undergoing one more internal transformation, like the shift from medieval to early modern or from the Old Regime to nineteenth-century industrial and liberal society. At the moment, no one knows which of these judgments will stand up in time to come. Caught as we are in the midst of it all, no one is wise enough to foresee the outcome or understand everything that is happening. In this chapter, therefore, we can only make an attempt to point out some things that seem important, and may turn out to be lastingly so—or may not.

# Rise of Popular Culture

From close up, at any rate, it looks as though specialization and professionalization of art and thought had run riot since 1914. Artists who are so original that no one understands them are easy to discover in any art colony. Scholars whose interests are so specialized that only a few others in the entire world know what the argument is about also exist on many university campuses. On the other hand, the gap that used to exist between local folk cultures and the concerns of the upper classes was probably no greater than the gap between experts and the rest of us. But popular culture has achieved new visibility through mass communications, whereas before it survived inconspicuously from generation to generation, passed on by word of mouth and by example.

Taking the world as a whole, the dominating fact about popular culture is the break it represents with folk traditions of every kind. Wherever economic conditions allowed, peasants and ex-peasants left traditional local styles of living behind them as fast as they could. People emerging from traditional peasant ways of life find their most fascinating introduction to urban civilization in studying an illustrated mail-order catalog or the advertisements in a glossy magazine. This allows them to learn about what can be wished for. The next thing is actually to possess a bicycle, then household appliances; and the climax is a car. But to have a car in such societies is still reserved for a tiny few who have made it all the way to the top.

## The Impact of Mass Media

Somewhere about midway in this curve of rising expectations, people start to pay serious attention to the mass media. To begin with, it was nearly always government initiative that brought the radio and roads to the countryside and to urban slums. During World War II, for example, the United States Information Service distributed thousands upon thousands of cheap radio speakers to villages in many different parts of the world. These radios were tuned to a central radio station and were usually planted in a public place near the center of the community. In many regions of the world where official propaganda and news had never penetrated on a regular basis, it now became possible to speak daily to the villagers. An entirely new kind of political life thus became possible.

Even the busiest politicians have to stop talking sometimes. This means that national radio and television hookups filled the time with other sorts of material, exposing hundreds of millions of human beings to new forms of cultural expression. Popular music, and popular TV programs, differing from country to country, did something to close the gap between city and village populations. Performers attracted a following among the vast numbers of persons who became able to listen to them or see them on the screen. And new art forms arose as well: westerns, crime shows, soap operas, quiz shows, jazz, rock music, and the like.

The effect on human lives of these new forms of mass communications is only beginning to be felt. Yet it is sure to be profound. After all, contentment and distress arise from what people expect for themselves and others; and that, in turn, depends on communications. In villages where traditional subsistence agriculture prevailed, food might become scarce each year in the weeks before the harvest, while in bad years everyone starved. But as long as economic differences between families remained slight and reflected how hard each family worked, no one felt poor. Hardships were part of life: normal, natural, and shared by all alike. Custom and habit sustained individual lives and defined what to expect, individually and collectively.

Buying and selling introduced new complications and new possibilities of economic differentiation. Contact with townspeople who never worked in the fields and lived far more comfortably than villagers often made rural life seem harsh and unattractive. Landlords and moneylenders, where they existed, could sometimes lead an even easier life without working at all. Civilized societies endured these contrasts for many centuries, and village custom somehow accommodated the inequity, usually by treating urban folk and landlords as alien beings. By refusing to compare themselves with such outsiders, villagers could retain their own community values and way of life, regardless, or almost regardless, of what happened outside the village itself.

This sort of psychological insulation of rural from urban standards of expectation arose and flourished when communications were slender, so that the great majority of individuals lived out their lives in a village context and encountered outsiders only a few times a year. As long as villagers' communication with outsiders continued to be mainly oral and face to face, this ancient accommodation between the rural majority of humankind and the urban minority survived. Printing, although extremely important for urban specialists, was slow to affect rural communities. In European lands, rural schooling was seldom available before 1850, while in other parts of the world, school systems that reached villages came a good deal later, and are not universal today. In the twentieth century, however, movies, radio, and television created a powerful shortcut for spreading urban attitudes and ideas among rural dwellers.

Movies existed before World War I but came into their own during the 1920s as a new form of popular entertainment. Radio networks began to attract large audiences during the 1930s in Europe and the United States and became important in poor countries after World War II. TV broadcasting started in the 1940s but soon caught up with radio in the sense that broadcast stations became nearly universal, even though receiving sets, since they cost more, remained far fewer. But display in public places made TV broadcasts available to hundreds of millions. The same was also true of movies and radio broadcasts, although cheap receiving sets made it far easier to own a radio privately and use it in the home. From the 1970s, recorded tapes added still another dimension to the new forms of communication and made smuggling prohibited messages across political frontiers comparatively easy.

An important feature of all these means of communication was that they did not depend on literacy and schooling. As long as the movie sound track or broadcaster used a language familiar to listeners, messages came across very much in the way face-to-face encounters had always brought messages to the attention of ordinary people in everyday life. TV's visual images reinforced spoken words with a different sort of communication, comparable to the effect that travel to new lands and experience of strange societies would have on those watching the screen.

The political impact of these communications was sufficiently obvious that nearly all governments monopolized the control of broadcasting at home and sometimes tried to jam messages coming from abroad.

In West European and some other democratic lands, laws prescribed more or less equal access to radio and TV for political parties during election campaigns. But daily decisions about how to present the news went a long way towards shaping public opinion, giving those in control of the media enormous political power.

In Communist countries (before 1989) and in lands where a single party or military faction ran the government, access to radio and TV was tightly controlled to prevent dissenters from broadcasting criticism of official policies and points of view. In such circumstances, tapes sometimes played an important role in spreading a rival version of the truth.

The United States was unusual in consigning control of radio and TV to private companies whose main concern was making money from paid advertising. The political or social impact of their programming took second place to the aim of appealing to the largest possible audience, so as to increase advertising income. Even political campaigns began to be conducted with the powerful aid of paid advertisements. Equal access rules for formal political speechmaking by the major candidates and parties modified without canceling the resulting commercialization of American elections.

Sports, criminal violence, and sex proved powerfully attractive in the competition for mass attention that American broadcasting companies engaged in. Programs often set out to shock viewers by pressing against conventional and legal limits. Movies went even further, and a new market for pornographic films arose when laws against them were voided by American courts.

What the effect of such programming may be on actual conduct and attitudes is a matter of considerable debate in the United States and elsewhere. No one knows for sure, but it is hard to doubt that family relations as well as political and religious attitudes have been changed by movies, radio, and TV, working alongside other aspects of contemporary life.

In the world's rich countries, modern communications fostered the emergence of a distinct youth culture, expressed and propagated primarily by musical recordings and performances celebrating sexual and other forms of sensory excitement. In poor countries family ties were stronger, and the young for the most part could not afford the material instruments—guitars, blue jeans, and the rest—through which youthful rebelliousness found expression. Yet the attraction was strong; and in Communist lands, where official efforts to insulate the public from capitalist corruption went very far, it still happened that the outward marks of American and European youth culture took root—at first in secret and after 1985 more and more publicly.

This was a striking instance of another important feature of modern communications: their ability to cross political boundaries, whether or not governments approved. Agitation via the media which led to the Iranian revolution of 1979 offered a spectacular example of successful defiance of an established government. The sudden collapse of Communist regimes in eastern Europe was another.

## Effects of American Media

News and information services aimed at foreign listeners are broadcast daily by the world's leading governments in hope of affecting public

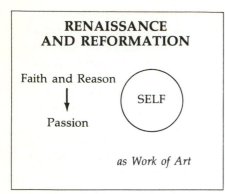

**RENAISSANCE AND REFORMATION**

Faith and Reason

↓

Passion

SELF

*as Work of Art*

**FRENCH REVOLUTION**

Reason

↓

Passion

SELF AND STATE

*as Works of Art*

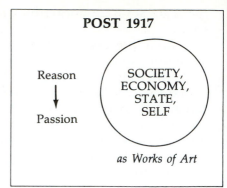

**POST 1917**

Reason

↓

Passion

SOCIETY, ECONOMY, STATE, SELF

*as Works of Art*

**LIBERAL COMPROMISE, 1850–1914**

Conscious Control

POLITY

ECONOMY   SOCIETY

Natural Relationships

**WORLD WAR I, 1914–1917**

POLITY

ECONOMY

SOCIETY

War Effort

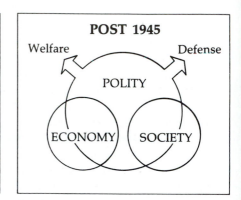

**POST 1945**

Welfare          Defense

POLITY

ECONOMY   SOCIETY

**Two Ways to Think About Modern Times**   These diagrams summarize long-term changes in the way peoples of the western world think and act. In the first three diagrams, the expanding scope of conscious, deliberate management—from self, to state, economy, and society—is represented along with schematic suggestion of changing relationships among the guides to human action as they were understood at the time. The diagrams below describe the same historic process over a shorter period of time, emphasizing the growth of governmental activity since the French Revolution. Such diagrams simplify historic processes, leaving out local differences and much else. But simplification may also make the main lines clearer, as long as you remember to take account of specific differences when thinking of any particular event, time, or place.

opinion beyond their borders in ways favorable to the senders. A more subtle yet perhaps more powerful effect on human consciousness arises unintentionally from entertainment programs whose messages, political or otherwise, are only implied. This side effect makes the widespread showing of American movies and TV programs in foreign lands one of the most significant cultural phenomena of our time.

Mass media exports are not an American monopoly. Other countries have some success in exporting entertainment as well. Great Britain produces several programs shown in the United States, for example; Egyptian films circulate widely to other Moslem lands, and there is a market for Indian films in southeast Asia and parts of Africa as well. But these are all dwarfed by the sale of suitably dubbed American films and tapes to the TV stations and movie houses of other countries. American films and tapes command popular attention by appealing to elemental human emotions, by having no overt political message, and, above all, by being available in abundance, whereas in smaller countries locally produced programs simply cannot fill all the broadcast time.

The effect of such broadcasting in poor and backward countries is even more uncertain than the effects within the United States itself. Many foreign viewers perhaps react to screen portraits of the streets of Los Angeles and other American cities as a sort of never-never-land and treat the whole thing as a fairy story. But patterns of personal behavior, exemplified in westerns, soap operas, and other staples of the American entertainment business, are likely to suggest new possibilities to viewers in distant lands where family traditions and expectations are profoundly different from those prevailing in the United States. How the old and new will combine remains to be seen. Change in patterns of personal behavior seems sure to follow from the mingling of such discrepant elements. It is too soon to tell.

Countercurrents to the mass culture of the broadcast media as commercialized in the United States are powerful and obvious. Most of the world's governments produce at least a few radio and TV programs of their own, intended to assert and maintain local traditions and values. Some countries prohibit some or all forms of American entertainment, so its circulation becomes clandestine. This was true of the Soviet Union and of most other Communist countries before 1989. Many Moslem lands also prohibit or censor American programs.

Even within American society itself, and in other countries where the mass media are not strictly controlled by official authority, private persons and organizations deliberately reject some or all of the values implied by commercialized mass entertainment. Religious groups, seeking to uphold old certainties, are by far the most important of these counterweights in American society. Some of them use radio and TV to propagate their teachings in direct competition with secular entertainment. Ethnic groups also sometimes seek to maintain their unique heritage despite the attractions of the American melting pot and rely on radio as well as ethnic newspapers to do so.

All this is a counterpart, within American society, of similar movements in the world at large among peoples who wish to be modern, rich, and powerful, but who also wish to maintain their customs, their language, their religion, and their uniqueness against all the temptations and corruptions of the outside world. Since nearly everyone feels pulled in both directions—toward the new and toward the old—how any particular group or country will choose between alternatives remains very uncertain.

Even more uncertain is the way individual access to information and entertainment through personal computers will affect broadcasting. Individualized dissemination of ideas and tastes may result; and the power of newscasters to shape public opinion may decay. But the growth of the Internet and other such linkages is so recent that their importance cannot even be guessed at.

*Standardization of Language*    An important by-product of the mass media is standardization of language. A few "world languages" attained greater importance. English has profited most, as U.S. and British radio programs, movies, cassettes, CDs, and phonograph records spread literally around the world. The Russian language also met with great success inside the borders of the Russian Republic, where all the other nationalities used Russian increasingly in daily encounters. In other parts of the world, the pattern is unclear. In India, for example, government effort to make Hindi a national language met with organized local resistance, and English still retains some importance for the well-educated. The future of European languages in Africa remains completely uncertain; but in Latin America, Spanish and Portuguese seem to be encroaching on the Indian languages that still survive. In China and Moslem lands, however, the old classical languages, enriched by new coinages to fit new conditions, have had their power reinforced by the advent of mass media. The end result, in all probability, will be to reduce quite sharply the number of living languages. Speech patterns familiar to only a few people will have trouble resisting the new means of communication.

# The Sciences

Although enormous amounts of new data have been gathered since 1914, the hard sciences that allow prediction have not achieved any radically new breakthrough since Albert Einstein proposed his theories of relativity between 1905 and 1915. All the same, it took physicists some time to get used to the sort of universe that Einstein's formulas implied; and ordinary people found it still more puzzling to be told that space and time were not clearly separate, and that waves and particles, as well as matter and energy, were somehow different forms of the same thing.

## Advances in Physics

In the 1930s, new machines were invented for accelerating electrons and other charged particles to great speeds. With these instruments, exploration of atomic nuclei became possible. High-speed particles could be made to hit an atom nucleus, and special instruments could then record information about the fragments that resulted from the collision. By measuring sizes and speeds, scientists could figure out what had been in the nucleus before the collision took place. As time went on, more and more powerful accelerators were constructed, and the number of particles that could be detected and measured increased.

For a while, it seemed possible to explain all observations by making a geometrical model of atomic structure. A Danish physicist, Niels Bohr (1885–1962), developed the idea that the nucleus was surrounded by revolving electrons, moving in more or less fixed orbits at different distances from the nucleus. Bohr's atom was a little like a miniature solar system, with the nucleus as sun and the electrons as planets. But during the 1930s, various new observations could not be fitted into this geometrical model. Physicists gave up the whole effort, preferring mathematical and statistical expressions to describe subatomic relationships. To ordinary people who habitually think of physical matter in spatial, geometrical terms, this breakdown of visual models was very puzzling. Fanciful names for subatomic particles made advanced physics into a sort of Alice-in-Wonderland world, where quarks come in flavors and leptons spin and collide with dozens of other odd entities.

Even though the language of physics, as it became more mathematical, became more unintelligible to everyone but experts, new practical applications continued to appear. During World War II, for example, Einstein's formula for the equivalence of matter and energy was translated into the controlled release of nuclear energy. The atom bombs dropped on Japan in 1945 were the first and most dramatic result of this application of theory. Atomic reactors that energize electrical generators and drive submarines are among the more important later applications of the nuclear techniques that physicists and engineers began to explore after World War II.

The potential importance of these inventions staggers the imagination. Total destruction of human life is one possibility. An almost unlimited supply of energy, if difficulties in disposing of atomic wastes can be met, might be another. In either case, old limits on human powers have been broken through; whether for good or ill remains to be seen.

## Computers and Their Applications

The development of capacious and dependable electronic computers during World War II promises to have even greater influence among us. In the more advanced countries, computers have already changed everyday life in countless ways. Grocery check-out counters have been computerized, for example, and so have ticket sales and flight information on airlines. Personal computers, linked up with one another and with various data banks, bring an enormous store of information and entertainment into home or office at the will of the user. Business corporations keep account of material and cash flows on computers. Governments collect taxes and disburse payments by computer. As storage capacity and speed of retrieval improve, new uses like these multiply every year.

Computers are equally important for engineering and industrial production. They allow engineers to test the design of new products and eliminate potential glitches before building test models out of real materials. Computers can also be programmed to control automated machinery used in assembly lines. Thanks to other computer programs, so-called "smart weapons" can home in on their targets far more accurately than before. In addition, mapping, printing—and the task of writing itself—all became faster, more accurate, and more easily revised or kept up-to-date by exploiting the capacity of computers for storing, sorting, and deleting information. Moreover, teaching and learning can be tailored to individual interests and ability by appropriately programmed computers.

Finally, computers open new possibilities for the theoretical sciences by making calculations and picking out answers to fit given conditions far faster than unaided human beings can ever do. This makes it possible to solve mathematical problems that were insoluble before. Another frontier of inquiry opened by computers was investigation of how the brain handles data. As computers became more flexible, they began to resemble human brains more closely, so that theoretical insight into the one seemed likely to rub off onto the other.

New understanding of language and of logic may also arise from the way computers mimic, surpass, and fall short of human intellectual capacities. Sociology and history might be transformed if sufficiently massive data describing individual human lives become available for analysis by computers since, at least in principle, such data ought to make generalizations about society far more precise than at present. But these dimensions of the computer revolution have yet to pan out and may prove illusory. The emotional dimension of human behavior and thought escapes computerization and may turn out to be so pervasive as to thwart the quantitative, mechanical accumulation of bits of data upon which computers depend.

But computers have not even begun to approach their limits in storing, processing, and retrieving information, or in affecting technology, industrial production, weaponry, and social management. As a result, far-reaching changes in everyday life and work are sure to continue as computer programs and networks expand around the globe, transforming patterns of human interaction far more thoroughly than has yet become apparent.

## Earth Sciences

Another area in which scientists have been unusually active since 1914 is exploration of the earth and of space. Rockets introduced new ways to explore the atmosphere and the regions of space close to the earth after World War II. As a result, new data have come in much faster than anyone has been able to put them together into a tidy theory.

The first rocket to put an artificial earth satellite into space went up from Kazakstan in 1957. Since then, hundreds of rockets have thrust their payloads into orbit around the earth where they perform many new tasks: photographing the surface of the earth; relaying radio and TV signals around the earth; measuring gravity, magnetic fields, and other variables with a new precision; and observing the heavens without the fuzziness created by the atmosphere. Other rockets escaped earth's gravity entirely, extending probes toward Venus, Mars, and Jupiter. These probes sent back limited information about the earth's fellow planets. Far more spectacular, however, was the assault upon the earth's nearest neighbor in space, when the United States sent a man to the moon for the first time in 1969. American moon flights not only put in position various "sensors" (devices that respond to physical stimuli) to detect moonquakes and other changes on the moon but also were able to bring back rock samples from different regions of the moon's surface.

Spectacular photographs and a lot of detailed information about the moon resulted from these efforts. In addition, space explorers wrote a new chapter in the record of human venturesomeness and technical achievement. But so far, theoretical understanding of earth and sky has not been much affected by these first efforts to extend humanity's domination into the fringes of earth-space.

**Exploration of Space**   Powerful rockets, designed to deliver atomic warheads to any part of the earth's surface, could also be used to explore space.
Artificial satellites, like the one pictured on the left, could circle the earth, or
alternatively, could rotate with the earth and thus always appear in the same
location. This opened enormous new possibilities for collecting information
about the earth below and the skies above. Reflectors collected energy from the
sun and converted it into radio and other electromagnetic waves. Connected
with cameras and scanners sensitive to different wave lengths and pointed
in different directions, these waves could then carry detailed information to
receivers on the earth. Both weather patterns and military movements became
visible as never before with such devices hovering overhead. When pointed
toward the depths of space, artificial satellites also discovered new objects in
the heavens. The most spectacular feat of space exploration, however, was
sending men to the moon and bringing them back again safely. On the right is
a photograph of an American astronaut walking on the surface of the moon
in 1969, just twelve years after the Russians had launched the first artificial
satellite into orbit.

Exploration of the world's oceans also
achieved a new thoroughness and scope after
World War II. Accurate plotting of ocean bot-
toms revealed a complicated pattern of ridges
and deeps, together with differences in the underlying rocks. These new observations prove
that North and South America are slowly drift-
ing away from Europe and Africa, making the
Atlantic wider and the Pacific narrower, inch by
inch. Earthquakes and mountain-building are
related to this newly discovered pattern of conti-

nental drift, and the possibility of understanding
and perhaps someday predicting movements
deep within the bowels of the earth now seems
open.

But this is still in the future. So far, the
principal practical application of new data is
better weather prediction. Satellites are capable
of photographing wide areas of the earth continuously and can transmit the picture to the
ground. This technique allows the paths of
storms to be plotted and their course predicted

with much greater precision than before. In addition, the military significance of photographic reconnaissance from space is obvious. Orbiting cameras make military secrets much harder to keep than they used to be.

## Molecular Biology

In biology, a dramatic new idea was broached in 1953 when Francis H. C. Crick and James D. Watson deciphered the spiral structure of DNA—the giant molecule that carries biological inheritance from generation to generation for every form of life. Even though DNA spiral chains could be very long, they had a relatively simple repetitive structure. Small changes in the exact order in which sets of atoms appeared in such a molecule made all the difference between the genetic inheritance of human beings and even the simplest of living forms, such as bacteria and algae.

Many other, less spectacular discoveries extended detailed understanding of biological processes. More and more of what happened in living tissues could be explained in chemical terms. Numerous applications of this knowledge came in medicine, as doctors invented chemical treatments for conditions that previously had been incurable. Some breakthroughs came by accident. In 1928, for example, Alexander Fleming noticed in some "spoiled" experiments that the growth of certain kinds of mold destroyed germs. This led to the discovery of penicillin (1929), the first of numerous antibiotic drugs that have since saved innumerable lives.

## Advances in the Social Sciences

In the hard sciences, little difference existed between the Communist and non-Communist worlds. Stalin did, for a while, try to impose Marxian linguistics and Marxian biology upon Russian scientists; but the effort was given up after Stalin's death. Physicists, chemists, mathematicians, and earth scientists have little trouble understanding one another or agreeing upon new discoveries as they are made, no matter where they live.

The soft sciences were different, for until 1989 Marxist doctrine crippled Communist research in social science. The fact was that many of the predictions Marx and Lenin made did not come true. Yet Communists treated the writings of Marx and Lenin as though they were sacred scripture. Basic truths, Communists claimed, had been laid down forever and ever, and if the facts failed to conform to the doctrine, it was too bad for the facts.

*New Perspectives in Social Science and History*     This attitude made honest thought about society impossible, and the collapse of dogma after 1989 left Russians and other ex-Communists desperately confused. In the Western world, however, the half-century following World War I gave birth to three far-reaching new ideas. The first was the "new economics," developed after 1936 by John Maynard Keynes (1883–1946), together with his critics and followers. Keynes set out to explain what went wrong during the Great Depression of the 1930s when unemployed workers and unemployed machinery in his native Britain and elsewhere existed side by side with unsatisfied human wants. He argued that countercyclical government expenditure and taxation could and should flatten out the harmful rhythm of business boom and bust. During World War II such ideas gained greater scope and precision when the British and American governments began to collect national statistics, allowing them to direct economic activity into new paths with striking practical success.

After the war, a somewhat relaxed style of nationwide political management of the economy became normal in the leading non-Communist countries and, as we saw, the new techniques worked well until 1973. Thereafter governments of even the largest nations ran into difficulties in getting the results they wanted. As a result, Keynes' ideas and reputation began to fade and economists disagreed about what wise public policy should be. Nonetheless, after Keynes (and Lenin) no one could doubt that political management could in fact redirect economic activity in far-reaching ways. Yet it now appears that macroeconomics on the national scale was

# THE DOUBLE HELIX

As a senior in college, James Dewey Watson decided he would try to discover the chemistry of genes. Genes were what carried biological inheritance from one generation to the next; but though biologists had been talking about them for a long time, no one knew exactly what genes were. From the University of Chicago, Watson went to Indiana for a Ph.D. in genetics; then he was awarded a postdoctoral fellowship for study in Europe. He resolved to use it to get started on his dream project: unraveling the chemical structure of genes.

At Cambridge, England, he found a colleague in Francis H. C. Crick. Crick was thirty-five years old, brilliant, and brash. Watson was also brilliant and brash—and eleven years younger. The two men hit it off from the start; and they agreed that to get at the secret chemistry of heredity, the thing to do was to construct a model of a molecule known as DNA. DNA is short for deoxyribonucleic acid—a material found in the nucleus of all living cells.

But DNA molecules are among the biggest known to exist. These enormous molecules were made up of hundreds of thousands of atoms, grouped in thousands upon thousands of subassembly blocks. How could anyone hope to discover how such a thing was put together? It was like trying to assemble the millions of parts of a big computer while blindfolded, for even the giant DNA molecules were far too small to be seen. Other research biologists thought that the staggering complexity of DNA would have to wait until the structure of smaller molecules—like the proteins that also exist in all living cells—had been worked out.

But Watson wanted to find out about genes, and he believed that DNA, not proteins, held the secret. So he plunged stubbornly ahead. When Crick and Watson started on the project, they had the advantage of others' work. The separate building blocks out of which DNA was made were already known. The proportions of each kind of material in DNA had been measured quite ac-

not an enduring answer to the problem of boom and bust since economic and political boundaries and diverged too widely for national controls to work.

Freudianism was a second powerful intellectual current that came into fashion in parts of the Western world during the 1920s only to fade from the forefront of serious thought about forty years later. Sigmund Freud (1856–1939) was a Viennese doctor who began by studying hysteria. He soon broadened his psychological investigations and convinced himself that unconscious drives dominated much of human behavior. A long series of books, many of them published before 1914, developed a schema for classifying subconscious human motivation. The terms he used—ego, superego, id, and the like—had no relation to the structures of the human brain and are largely discredited today. But Freud did show in thoroughly convincing ways that people often act in response to subconscious impulses; and that some of our deepest urges are sexual. His ideas were shocking to many people in the 1920s; but for that very reason, Freudian psychology appealed to a post–World War I rebellious generation, eager to shed traditional inhibitions.

Just as Keynes and other economists showed that under some conditions politics can control economics, so Freud and his followers showed curately. Most important of all, a way to fix DNA molecules into crystal form had been invented. This allowed x-ray photographs to be taken of the molecules. The difficulty was that what showed on such photographs was not a shape or even a shadow of the molecule itself, but patterns of x-ray reflections as they bounced off the various atoms that made up a DNA molecule.

Such bits of information added up to a vast puzzle. What could be done with it? What Watson and Crick did was to make guesses, and then try to build a model—out of wire and bits of metal—that would have a place for everything that had to fit into the giant DNA molecule. They made several false starts: leaving not enough space for all the necessary building blocks, or attempting a chemical bond between next-door neighbors that would not work. But in less than two years, they hit upon what turned out to be the right form—a double helix—after seeing some new x-ray photographs of DNA that had been made in London.

By the beginning of April 1953, the model had withstood all tests. The two young men were ready to announce their discovery. They did so by publishing a short article—only slightly over 900 words long. It began thus:

> We wish to suggest a structure for the salt of deoxyribose nucleic acid (DNA). This structure has novel features which are of considerable biological interest.*

This was grandiose understatement. Biologists everywhere soon realized that the double helix form allowed reproduction of similar molecules. By splitting the two strands of the double helix apart, a new strand could form to fit the old half. Thus the structure of the DNA unraveled part of the mystery James Dewey Watson had set out to solve. He had in truth learned something about the chemistry of genes—the innermost machinery of life itself.

---

* J. D. Watson and F. H. C. Crick, "Molecular Structure of Nucleic Acids," *Nature* 171 (1953): 737.

that human beings are not entirely, or perhaps not even usually, rational. Though details of both arguments have since collapsed, these residues of their thought changed the way almost all experts in the Western world approach the study of human society, although the repercussions of these simple notions have not yet been fully absorbed. That is not surprising, for they are, or appear to be, contradictory. Keynesianism sought to expand rational management to new domains of human behavior, whereas Freudianism argued that irrational drives dominated our conduct and that words commonly disguised real motives. Deliberate, conscious manipulation of other people's subconscious drives may perhaps

reconcile the contradiction. Advertising and political campaigns have moved a long way in that direction. But what about the subconscious drives of the manipulators? And, more generally, how does human reason mesh with emotion in actual practice for individuals, for societies, and for human groups? The problem has not been solved.

A third, and very surprising, scientific transformation was the broadening of the developmental view of reality to embrace astronomy, physics, earth sciences, biological evolution, and human history in a single, all-embracing stream of change through time. Seeds of this view had been laid in the nineteenth century with geological investigations and Darwin's *Origin of Species*. But the prestige of Newtonian physics and astronomy remained unshaken until the twentieth century, and sciences like biology, geology, and history seemed inferior because they lacked the mathematical form and predictive capability of astronomy and physics.

Physics began to lose some of its predictive power when the indeterminacy of subatomic particles emerged from experiments in the 1920s. Far more radical reshaping took place after World War II when physicists and astronomers began to accept the idea that the physical universe had begun with a Big Bang about ten billion years ago. Moreover, they concluded that stars were not eternal, but had passed through at least three generations before arriving at their current state of complexity. Existing stars, galaxies, and laws of physics suddenly appeared to be only a passing phase of physical reality. According to some, the universe was destined to collapse anew into a cosmic egg after which another Big Bang might, or might not, ensue. Others foresaw a state of complete entropy, in which matter would gradually melt away as energy dissipated itself thinly and evenly throughout space. But whichever vision of the long-term future experts chose, all agreed that Newton's stable, predictable astronomical universe was local and temporary. Instead their observations and calculations compelled them to accept a tumultuous, chaotic, ever-changing and, in the long term, entirely unpredictable universe.

While this astounding expansion of a historical, developmental vision of reality was taking place among astronomers and physicists, archaeologists and historians expanded their domains as well. To be sure, the time and space they explored remained trivial by astronomical standards. Yet the cumulative expansion of their subject was substantial. As a result, understanding of the human career on earth reaching back a million years or more took on fresh precision and attained an ever-widening scope.

In 1914 most Westerners still knew little and cared less about other civilizations. Indeed, many Europeans and Americans believed that Asian peoples had no history. Progress, they believed, was limited to the West. But as changes came to all the world, this naive misunderstanding of the facts lost any shred of plausibility.

Many careful scholars, both Westerners and Asians, set out to discover and write histories of all parts of the non-Western world.

At the same time, archaeologists discovered evidences of the beginnings of civilization in Sumer (1920s), China (1930s), and India (1920s). In 1914 Egypt was believed to be the oldest civilization. By the 1940s it was known that this was not true, because the ancient Egyptians had borrowed some important items from the Sumerians. Then, in the 1950s archaeological discoveries in Africa began to reveal new details of prehuman and human evolution.

The result of these lines of inquiry was to make it possible to see all the separate histories of nations, civilizations, barbarian peoples, and simple hunting and gathering societies as part of the larger adventure of humanity. Much disagreement over details and even over the pattern as a whole remained. Oswald Spengler (1880–1936) and Arnold J. Toynbee (1889–1975) suggested that civilizations rose and fell according to a uniform pattern, and remained distinct from one another. This book, on the contrary, has tried to portray different civilizations and other less complex societies all at once, in the belief that they acted and reacted upon each other from the beginning. Still other patterns have their supporters; for instance, the Marxian view that all societies pass through slave, serf, and wage labor stages of development. Whatever room for argument remains—and it is very wide—it still holds true that a far more spacious and inclusive vision of the human past has become available as a result of progress in historical study in the past half-century. History, once the stepchild of the sciences, has in fact begun to pervade all branches of knowledge. The evolutionary approach to truth, pioneered in the nineteenth century, seems everywhere triumphant as the twentieth century comes to its close. This probably constitutes the most fundamental intellectual change of our time.

# Music, Art, and Literature

In the 1920s musicians, artists, and writers experimented with new forms. Jazz was perhaps the most original musical innovation. It emerged from the Black ghettoes of New Orleans and Memphis and spread around the world in the 1920s and after. On a more highbrow level, a few composers experimented with twelve-tone scales and electronic sound without, however, displacing classical music from pride of place in the world's concert halls.

Painters had only to carry on with the effort begun before World War I. Bits and pieces of ordinary visual experience were jerked out of context or distorted to the point where recognition by the viewer became hit-or-miss. Symbols aimed at affecting the subconscious mind were deliberately sought after. The greatest names had already emerged to fame before World War I: Pablo Picasso (1881–1973), Georges Braque (1882–1963), and Henri Matisse (1869–1954) among them.

Nonobjective paintings that made no effort whatever to look like anything else carried the breakaway from the Renaissance ideal to its logical conclusion. Piet Mondrian (1872–1944) and Vasili Kandinski (1866–1944) were among the pioneers of this kind of painting. The ideal of nonobjective painting was "pure design," mathematical, geometrical, like music in its underlying principles.

**Modern Sculpture: Brand New and Age Old**  *Bird in Space* by the Rumanian sculptor Constantin Brancusi (left) and *King and Queen* by the English sculptor Henry Moore (right) both depart from older notions of artistic excellence by not trying exactly to resemble anything seen in nature. This makes them modern. But these two works are opposites too. Despite its title, Brancusi's slender, geometric shape soars from its base more like a rocket than like a bird, aptly expressing the extraordinary mastery over nature that science and technology have achieved in the twentieth century. The haunting, only half-human faces of Moore's gaunt figures, on the contrary, hark back to myth and subconscious memory, expressing a different side of twentieth-century scientific accomplishment.

In Germany an influential group of architects and industrial designers, inspired by the same ideas, created the so-called international style of architecture in the 1920s. It was characterized by the free use of new materials such as concrete, steel, and glass for walls, and by spare, rectangular shapes. One great advantage of the new style was lower costs of construction. Walls of glass were lighter, less expensive, and resulted in bright, open interiors. This style spread round the world within a couple of decades.

Writers such as the novelist James Joyce (1882–1941) or the poet Thomas Stearns Eliot (1888–1965) experimented with words. By in-venting new expressions, using fragmentary sentences, and stretching grammar, they and other writers tried to affect subconscious levels of their readers' minds in much the same way that artists were trying to do. But even in the hands of a master, tinkering with language quickly degenerated into total unintelligibility; so this was not a very promising field to explore—nothing to compare with what painters were able to do. Accordingly, in the period after World War II, this line of literary development almost stopped. Writers, instead, concentrated on other ways of breaking with the past. One technique was the shock value of exploring previously forbidden

**How to Be Architecturally Different**
The international style of architecture soon generated an opposite tendency, emphasizing what made each particular place different from everywhere else. Here are two spectacularly successful examples of how to be different. Above is the opera house in Sydney, Australia, with the bridge connecting the two sides of Sydney Harbor in the background. The concrete arches of the opera house roof mimic the sails of ships that brought the first English settlers to Australia. Perched on the water's edge with the bridge behind it, this spectacular building erected in the 1960s, aptly symbolizes the way European settlers and civilization were suddenly implanted in a strange new environment. The spare rectilinearity of the Central Library of the University of Mexico, seen on the bottom, is countered by the brilliant mosaic decoration of its surface. Juan O'Gorman, who designed this mosaic in 1950, set out to portray the history of Mexico all the way back to Aztec times to celebrate the uniqueness of his country and its blending of Indian and European heritages.

themes, such as sex. Another was to celebrate the antihero, that is, to create a fictional character who did not impose his will on people and things around him in the way heroes had done since the time of Homer but became instead the helpless victim of circumstances.

Amidst all this striving for novelty, it is impossible to foresee what will endure and what will simply wither away. All we can be sure of is that the high culture of the future is being shaped by the music, art, and writing of our age, since that is what future generations will have to react against and elaborate upon.

## New Genres of Old Forms

If popularity is any standard to depend upon, the really outstanding authors of the post–World War I period were the writers of murder mysteries. This branch of literature became popular before World War I with the tales by Arthur Conan Doyle (1859–1930), about a private detective, Sherlock Holmes. Hundreds of authors followed in Sherlock Holmes' footsteps, and millions of people read their works.

Still another new form of writing that came to the fore after 1914 was children's literature. Better understanding of how children grow from year to year made it possible to write more effectively for different age levels. Some stories became so well known as to populate the English-speaking world with a host of new characters: Pooh, Dr. Doolittle, Charlie Brown, and many more. Talking animals and clever children, generally speaking, took the place of the witches and fairies of older nursery tales.

Comic books, too, first gathered together from already published newspaper strips and then printed as an independent form of literature, also became very popular, appealing mainly to young and not fully literate readers.

Perhaps the most influential form of writing in the last fifty years has been manuals on how to raise infants and small children. Once upon a time, skills for the care and feeding of infants was handed down from generation to generation without being written down. In the 1920s, however, the movement of people from country to city meant that millions of young women married later in life and had no close relative nearby to pass on traditional lore. In addition, new information about vitamins and infant development gave doctors something new to say to mothers. The result was a rash of "How to" books. Millions of middle-class Americans raised their babies according to instructions laid down in such books. Since then, "How to" books have covered a vast range of other subjects, replacing or supplementing older "hands-on" ways of transmitting practical skills from one generation to the next. The impact upon the national life was tremendous. In other countries, such manuals had less importance, perhaps; but everywhere the breakdown of oral tradition, linking the generations, required writings of this kind.

## Religion and Philosophy

Most of the recent developments in science and thought have paid little attention to traditional religion. Yet Christianity, Judaism, Islam, Hinduism, and Buddhism remain. Their power over human minds is probably as great as ever. After all, religious groups also can use the mass media to spread their doctrines.

Among Christians, one striking development of the years since World War I was a growing willingness to seek common ground. For a long time, this ecumenical movement was the work of Protestant churches, especially in the English-speaking world. Pope John XXIII (1958–1963) brought the Roman Catholic Church into a much more sympathetic relationship with this movement. He summoned the Second Vatican Council (1962, 1963), which defined Roman Catholic relationships with Jews and with other Christian sects in a conciliatory way.

A contrary trend was equally strong, for new sects—with uncompromising views—continued to arise and flourish, especially among poor and disadvantaged people. Jehovah's Witnesses, for example, founded in 1872, spread from the United States to Africa and Latin America among peoples emerging from traditional peasant life. Pentacostalists, founded in 1901, spread even faster and further among the same populations and are by far the fastest growing Christian sect in the Third World today.

## Church and Society

A second important, new emphasis within Christianity was the result of efforts to apply Christian principles to changing social, political, and economic conditions. Missionaries in Asia and Africa tended to shift away from emphasis on religious salvation and instead put medical and educational service in the forefront. In the English-speaking world, members of the clergy took leading parts in movements for social reform. The Labour party in England, for instance, was deeply colored by Methodism; and the civil rights movement in the United States, whose most famous leader, Martin Luther King, Jr. (1929–1968), was himself a Baptist minister, attracted much Church support.

All around the world, Marxism rivaled Christianity (and other religions) by preaching atheism. Nevertheless, when communism collapsed in eastern Europe (1989–1991), traditional forms of Catholic and Orthodox Christianity reemerged and attracted young and old.

The Nazi movement in Germany also challenged Christianity by glorifying teutonic paganism and rejecting Christian morality. A few Germans, inspired by Christian ideals, plotted actively against Hitler; indeed, Christian faith proved the most effective rallying ground for the German opposition to Nazism. In other European countries, too, Christian belief played an important role in inspiring resistance movements against the Nazis during World War II. As a result, after the war, powerful new Christian-Democratic parties emerged in France, Italy, and Germany and continued to dominate the post–World War II governments of Italy and West Germany until the 1990s.

On the other hand, in Spain and some of the Spanish-speaking countries of South America, the Roman Catholic Church pursued a conservative if not downright reactionary policy. In these lands the Church remained a target for liberal and anticlerical reformers.

A third issue for Christians was how to react to secular thought and science. Many Protestants rejected Darwinian evolution and put their faith in the literal accuracy of the Bible. This was challenged by "Modernists" who believed that religious truth (like other kinds of truth) evolved over time, so that Bible writers were mistaken on some points and headed in the right direction on others.

Among Roman Catholics, modernism had been prohibited by the Vatican Council of 1869–1870. Yet a Jesuit philosopher and archaeologist, Teilhard de Chardin (1881–1955), developed an evolutionary philosophy which included religion. In this, as in other ways, the gap between Protestant and Roman Catholic thought seemed to be narrowing, as both found it possible to adjust to the progress of science without giving up older tradition and doctrine.

## Judaism

Among Jews, the Nazi persecution in Germany, climaxing in the death camps of World War II, had tremendous impact. Nearly all European Jews were uprooted. Of those who survived, many went to Israel after the war or followed earlier emigrants to the United States, South Africa, Argentina, and elsewhere. The Israeli War of Independence in 1948–1949 provoked another wave of persecution that ran through the entire Moslem world. As a result, nearly all "oriental" Jews were forced to flee to Israel.

Within Israel, opinions differed widely as to how a Jewish state ought to handle religion. At first, secular-minded Jews predominated; but there were also Orthodox Jews who regarded any departure from rabbinical rules as heresy. In recent years, religious parties have held the balance of power in Israeli politics, giving them greater power than their numbers would otherwise permit.

The outbreak of vicious anti-Semitism in Nazi Germany and the rise of Israel as a Jewish state persuaded many Jews in other lands that it was neither possible nor desirable to try to merge into the general population by giving up all ties with traditional Judaism. This "assimilationist" idea had flourished in Germany ever since the later 1700s, when special laws against Jews began to be repealed. Intermarriages between Christians and Jews had become quite common, and differences between Jews and other Germans were less than in almost any other land. If Hitlerism could break out in Germany, therefore, the whole ideal of assimilation into secular society and of ceasing to be a separate social group seemed to be proved dangerous and false.

At the same time, in the United States and England, widespread reaction against Nazi barbarism discouraged open expression of anti-Semitic feelings; and various social barriers against Jews tended to fall, one by one, without the public outcry and legislation that was needed to batter down discrimination against American Blacks. In Russia, however, traces of old anti-Semitic feelings, which had been strong before World War I, survived in spite of official Communist disapproval and came to the surface again in the confusion of communism's collapse.

## Islam

The ecumenical movement among Christians tried also to reach out toward Jews in order to soften the historic clash between the two faiths. This was not true of Islam. Few Christians knew much about the faith of Mohammed, and the Moslems had no interest whatever in associating with Christian clerics, whom they regarded, as they did the Jews, as hereditary enemies and preachers of false doctrine.

Yet Islam found itself in an embarrassing position. The Moslem Sacred Law, like the Jewish law, was at the heart of traditional religion. Its rules were plainly incompatible with Western thought and made it next to impossible to build up a strong and modern Moslem state. Still, to reject the Sacred Law meant losing the past. The Turks tried to do so in the 1920s. But in the 1950s Islam began to come back and even won official recognition in Turkey because voters remained Moslem despite efforts by the revolutionary government to discredit the faith. On the other hand, in Arabia, where red-hot Wahhabi

reformers had come to power in the 1920s, the discovery of vast oil reserves brought huge sums of money into the country. With this new wealth some of the warmth of the Wahhabi faith vanished, at least in court circles. Pakistan was a religious state, carved out of British India in 1947, because its citizens were Moslems. But when it came to deciding what a Moslem state ought to be like, the old dilemma of how to treat the Sacred Law proved insoluble. A military coup d'état brought Westernized army officers to power who systematically sidestepped the issue by concentrating on inherited quarrels with Hindu India.

Throughout the Moslem world, Communist doctrine collided with traditional religion. Marxist atheism and materialism contradicted Mohammed's revelation, and neither side tried to disguise the fact. As a result, there were few Communists in Moslem lands. Only people who were willing to throw away their cultural heritage could become Communists, and this was always a small minority. The mass slaughter of the Indonesian Communist party in 1965–1966 was a bloodthirsty demonstration of how Moslems felt about Marxists.

The collision between Islam and the modern secular outlook achieved new intensity in Iran in 1979 with the victory of Shi'a fundamentalists over the shah's government. But how to apply the Sacred Law under contemporary conditions remains problematic, and how to combine the pursuit of holiness with other goals has not been resolved. For the Iranian revolutionaries, like other people, want wealth and power as well as wishing to obey Allah; and the two are difficult to combine.

This is the crucial dilemma of the world of Islam. No resolution of the problem seems in sight.

## Hinduism, Buddhism, Confucianism, and Shinto

Hindus and Buddhists, on the contrary, saw no vital contradiction between Western secular ideas and their traditional religions. Long ago, both these faiths made room for an infinite variety of doctrines. Atheism was nothing new or shocking to Hindus and Buddhists. Buddha was an atheist, and many Hindu philosophers were, too. Marxism thus was able to fit in as another partial truth—mistaken, of course, inasmuch as Marxism taught that the material world was real—yet, perhaps, useful in its own limited way if it helped social reform or forwarded national independence.

As a result, Indians living in the southern part of India, where various local languages survived, often became Marxists as a way of protesting against domination from the north, where Hindi was the common speech. Similarly, in Vietnam and other parts of southeast Asia, all kinds of halfway-houses between Buddhism and communism existed, without provoking any sense of strain on either side.

Confucianism in China and Shinto in Japan, however, appear to be dying faiths. The schools that once trained generations of Chinese in the Confucian classics were abandoned after 1905,

and a new generation grew up with little acquaintance with that past. Since 1949 the Communists have done all they could to discredit old ways of thought. Maoism was deliberately invented to replace Confucianism, but in many ways it resembled what it displaced. Anything else would be strange, for Mao was educated in a traditional way until his twenties, when as a young college student he first met Lenin's ideas and began his career as a Marxist. Other Chinese Communist leaders, as well as many in the rank and file, have similar personal histories. Massive carryover from the Confucian past is, therefore, inescapable, even if the old doctrines have been officially repudiated.

As for the worship of the sun goddess and of her divine descendant, the emperor of Japan, the events of World War II thoroughly discredited that form of Shinto. After the war, the emperor publicly denied his divinity, and the crown prince of Japan married a commoner before succeeding to the throne in 1989. Nothing much remained of the old Shinto beliefs, though

**Our Changing World**   The flux of energy and flow of air and water vapor in the earth's atmosphere is made plain in this photo taken from outer space. We live amidst these flows and also the flows of matter and energy within the seas and the core of solid earth. This is our world, perpetually in flux like human society itself.

temples and rituals from the Shinto past remained attractive to many Japanese. Traditional religion was represented in Japan mainly by remodeled forms of Buddhism, some forms of which entered politics by sponsoring political parties.

# Conclusion

Human societies, thought, and culture have changed fast and fundamentally since 1945. No end is in sight, although past ages of really rapid and far-reaching change have all been relatively brief—a matter of two or three generations, usually. But this time, older limits have been left behind. The majority of human beings no longer must work in the fields to feed a privileged few who are doing other things. For the first time in history, modern machines and methods allow a few to feed the majority. Cultural consequences of this shift remain unclear. All we think and do reflects and contributes to this basic departure from life patterns that prevailed throughout previous civilized history. It makes our age a time of adventure into the unknown.

How future generations will evaluate the time in which we live is impossible to know but interesting to wonder about. If the pace of change levels off eventually, as seems inevitable in the long run, it is possible that our remote descendants will regard this as a great, heroic time in which the ground rules of their own societies were laid down by us—stumbling, uncertain, and anxious though we be. Confusion, which seems to dominate every aspect of our age, even its science, can be immensely fertile. It offers future generations a multitude of models from which to pick and choose. This, perhaps, may be the long-range historical importance of the twentieth century.

# Bibliography

The rise of audio and visual modes of recording made written literature a less current register of the climate of the age than were performers like the Beatles, Pete Seeger, and innumerable others, whose works are available in the form of records or audio cassettes. Here, and in old movies, the new youth culture that has spread almost around the earth is best sampled. A literary counterpart is J. D. Salinger, *Catcher in the Rye* (1951).

For books about audio-visual communication, try John Wyver, *The Moving Image: An International History of Film, Television and Video* (1989); David W. E. Rees, *Satellite Communication: The First Quarter Century of Service* (1990); A. G. Smith, ed., *Communication and Culture* (1966); and Edwin Emery, P. H. Ault, and W. K. Agee, *Introduction to Mass Communications* (3rd ed., 1970).

On the transformation of science and world views connected with science, see George O. Abell, *Exploration of the Universe* (4th ed., 1982); Donald Goldsmith, *The Evolving Universe* (2nd ed., 1985); Joseph Silk, *The Big Bang: The Creation and Evolution of the Universe* (1980); Stephen Toulmin and Jane Goodfield, *The Discovery of Time* (1982); Emilio Segre, *From X-Rays to Quarks: Modern Physicists and Their Discoveries* (1980); Lily E. Kay, *The Molecular Vision of Life: Caltech, the Rockefeller Foundation and the Rise of the New Biology* (1992); Robert C. Olby, *The Path to the Double Helix* (1974); Ursula B. Marvin, *Continental Drift: The Evolution of a Concept* (1973); George J. Stigler, *Essays in the History of Economics* (1965); Alwyn McKay, *The Making of the Atomic Age* (1984); and the quasi-autobiographical account of the discovery of DNA by James Watson, *The Double Helix* (1968).

On computers and their implications, try Tom Forester, ed., *The Information Technology Revolution* (1984); Walter M. Mathews, ed., *Monster or Messiah? The Computer's Impact on Society* (1980); Herman H. Goldstine, *The Computer from Pascal to Von Neumann* (1972); and Pamela McCorduck, *Machines Who Think: A Personal Inquiry into the History and Prospects of Artificial Intelligence* (1979).

For art, a pair of books by Herbert Read, *A Concise History of Modern Painting* (1959) and *A Concise History of Modern Sculpture* (1969), offer an overview and sampling of the break away from old forms and conventions that took place before and after World War I, but I do not know of any comparable survey of more recent changes, nor can I recommend any general survey of recent world literature.

On religion and society, try James Hastings Nichols, *History of Christianity, 1650–1950: Secularization of the West* (1956); Jerald C. Brauer, *Protestantism in America: A Narrative History* (rev. ed., 1965); Howard M. Sachar, *The Course of Modern Jewish History* (1977); Joseph Blau, *Modern Varieties of Judaism* (1966); John O. Voll, *Islam: Continuity and Change in the Modern World* (1982); Heinrich Dumoulin and John C. Maraldo, eds., *Buddhism in the Modern World* (1976); and D. S. Sarma, *Studies in the Renaissance of Hinduism in the Nineteenth and Twentieth Centuries* (1944).

# Epilogue: Part IV
# The Study of History and its Meaning

At the close of a book like this, that attempts to portray the human adventure on earth in its entirety, it is well to remind readers of how tentative and uncertain its assertions and judgments remain. Historians have expanded their knowledge of the human past very rapidly in recent decades; but what historians see and think important is influenced as much by the concerns and sensitivities of their time as by anything in the sources they use for constructing their accounts of what happened. An enormous and ever growing amount of information about the past is beyond dispute. But the meaning and significance of all those facts, and how to weave them together into an intelligible pattern provokes persistent disagreement.

Surprises abounded in times past; and the recent collapse of Communism in the Soviet Union is an example of how surprising current events can be in our time as well. We are always blind to some of the signs of what is to come and exaggerate the importance of circumstances and problems that actually weaken or even disappear. Indeed, it is worth reminding ourselves that perhaps an obscure group of outsiders holds the future in its hands today, as followers of Buddha, Christ and Mohammed once did. Or again, biochemists may discover entirely new ways to affect the way people behave; and by using that power could transform themselves and the rest of humankind in ways we can barely imagine.

No one knows what the future will bring; and until it comes the meaning and shape of past and present remain subject to revision. Each generation therefore has to reshape its understanding of the recent past to fit its present and assist the inevitable transition to a still different future. The more distant past also changes shape more slowly, but just as surely, because

708

historians acquire new information and ask new questions in the light of events and experiences of their time.

But if the meaning of history is so changeable, so uncertain, and so much a product of a particular time and place, you may well ask whether it is worth bothering with at all. So many names, outmoded ideas, and vanished institutions to keep in mind! Such brutal violence, so many mistakes! What is worth learning from such a past? Why not leave it all behind and make the world better instead?

As a matter of fact, secular revolutionaries and religious reformers have often set out to discard the past by starting anew. Trying to do so, they changed society around them, sometimes quite radically. But no matter how much they wished to make a clean break, they were never able to escape the past or erase continuities between old and new. That was because grown ups inevitably incorporate a personal past into their innermost selves since, as infants, they had to learn how to behave and what to think from those around them. Indeed, the myriad of individual pasts, distilled into rules of thumb about what to do in different circumstances, is what makes us human.

History extends individual experience deeper into time and further in space than any single person's private encounters can ever hope to do. Its principal function is to define the various groups to which individuals belong, and thereby tell them who they are and how they ought to conduct themselves in public affairs. Families and other small groups—by far the most important ones for ordinary life—transmit their history orally in the course of everyday activities. Stories about who did what, and how a particular problem was met provide guidance needed to allow such groups to function in customary fashion. To be sure, moral rules and religious injunctions also provide general instruction for human behavior, but only when embodied in historical examples does their actual, practical meaning become clear.

Written history comes into play among larger groups when customary rules for behavior wear thin. Laws, general principles and religious revelation were also put into writing to guide for the public management of large groups

of people from soon after the time that writing was invented. But, as with small, face-to-face groups, stories about what whole peoples had done before—especially in crisis situations—brought general rules to life, and explained more exactly what ought to be done by providing examples that could be imitated in comparable circumstances.

As we all know, during the past two centiries the most important sort of historical writing was national political history. This was not accidental. The democratic revolutions of the late eighteenth century in America and Europe expanded the power of national states enormously, and citizens needed instruction about their rights and duties. Laws and abstract principles were not enough. Accordingly, from about the middle of the nineteenth century, patriotic national histories were taught in state-supported schools to turn children into good citizens. The aim was to create a citizen body prepared to combine with their fellows to carry out agreed-upon public purposes more effectively than ever before. That was what the abstract ideal of freedom meant, and insofar as it was realized, the practical power of national states increased very rapidly indeed.

Accordingly, separate national histories were constructed to teach children what it meant to be French, British or German. In the same decades, New Englanders constructed a national past for the United States by making the Pilgrims central and leaving the founders of the other colonies on the margins. As nationalism spread, other peoples constructed their own national histories, and the process is still in train among the "new nations" of the earth. Patriotic feelings and participatory citizenship—the special hallmarks of European states in the nineteenth century—flourished on the strength of a shared national past. Nation-wide cooperation in peace and more especially in war became possible on an unprecedented scale when citizens felt a sense of common identity as a result of their schooling in national history.

Creating and sustaining coherent citizen bodies by teaching national history remains the principal role for the study of the past in nearly all existing societies, including the United States of America. But the United States was unusual because many American schools supplemented national history by teaching English and European history, then by introducing courses in Western Civilization, (beginning soon after World War I), and more recently, by offering world history (a subject explored and elaborated only after World War I).

The reason Americans felt a need for supplementing national history in this unusual fashion was that so much of our national culture and tradition had come from across the ocean. And the recent shift of attention from a merely European past to the history of the whole wide world reflects the global involvement of the United States since 1941, as well as the increasing number of recent immigrants from Latin America, Asia, and Africa. Other countries lag behind in supplementing national history by globalizing their sense of the past. So far, at least, the United States is the undisputed pioneer of the study of world history in schools and, less prominently, in universities as well.

Reconciling national history with world history is not automatic or altogether easy. Readers of this book probably noticed how little attention it pays to the separate history of the United States. That is partly because the author assumes that readers already know a great deal about the nation's past. But most national history treats the United States as unique, different and specially blessed by circumstance and by the virtues of its citizens. Other national histories also go to great lengths to emphasize the separate distinctiveness of the people concerned. But a world history, like this one, challenges national particularity by emphasizing what happened across national and civilizational boundaries. Anything else would not be a world history but a history of separate regions and peoples.

To be sure, before 1500, separate parts of the earth did have separate histories, and any sensible historian recognizes that fact by treating the early history of the Americas, the interior of Africa and Australia separately from the history of Eurasia. But since Eurasian skills far outstripped those of the rest of the world, and since European bearers of those skills began to intrude upon and transform the lives of other peoples once they had learned to navigate the oceans of the world, what happened in Eurasia before 1500 played a dominating part in defining what occurred throughout the world subsequently. That, indeed, is why Americans felt the need to supplement national history with world history. Only so can we know who we are in the larger sense, heirs (like everyone else) to the human past in its entirety. What marks Americans off from other, older nations, is that our merely local past is clearly inadequate for the centuries before 1500, and is becoming increasingly so for the events of our own age as we become more and more entangled with world-wide trends and influences.

By contrast, national histories of the leading European peoples and of such an imposing civilization as that of China can, and often do, pretend to be self-contained and self-sufficient. But as they, too, become enmeshed more and more intimately in global networks of informational and economic exchange, the need to supplement national and civilizational history with some sort of world history seems likely to assert itself for them as well as for Americans.

Two considerations push in that direction. One is the increasingly obvious fact that local national states no longer can exert full control over economic affairs within their boundaries. Too many goods and services have to come from abroad if existing levels of wealth are to be sustained, much less improved. Trying to live on what can be made locally has become too costly to contemplate, even if dependence on imports and exports puts all concerned at the mercy of world-wide flows of goods and services whose interruption by war or natural disaster would be catastrophic. Imagine, or instance, what a year's interruption of deliveries of foreign oil to the United States (or to any other modern industrial country) would be like! Within a few months, tractors would not be able to plow the fields. Crops could not be planted, food supplies would dwindle, and a crisis of monumental proportions would swiftly ensue.

In such an interdependent world, knowing something about the other peoples who share the earth with us is obviously desirable; and acquaintance with their history—and with the history of all humanity—looks like a prudent way to decrease the likelihood of unpleasant surprises.

The second consideration that makes world history an attractive supplement to national histories is also connected with the decay of national sovereignty in economic matters. Among other things, national histories prepared citizens for waging war with greater energy than ever before; but the outbreak of war between states armed with nuclear weapons now constitutes the most obvious threat to the existing web of economic exchanges upon which everyday life depends.

How the peoples and governments of the world will deal with this issue remains to be seen. Formal commitment to peaceful ways of resolving quarrels through the United Nations may or may not suffice to stave off nuclear war indefinitely. No one can tell ahead of time. Hatreds and fears abound; and some reckless leader of a desperate people may someday decide to risk everything on surprise attack.

On the other hand, anyone who thinks about the risks of all-out nuclear war recognizes the disproportion between costs and any conceivable gain; and it is not hard to see that the whole of humankind has a very lively interest in avoiding such a disaster. In other words, national and other local interests and identities compete with a wider human identity, shared by all the peoples of the earth. And just as study of national history is one of the most effective ways to create and sustain national consciousness, so study of world history is an obvious way to create and sustain a global consciousness that might help to restrain even the most powerful national governments from recklessly engaging in nuclear war.

All too obviously, economics and politics have become more and more global. World history, and only world history, shows how contemporary global entanglements evolved from the initial exchange patterns that sustained the earliest civilizations, gradually becoming further ranging and more complex as modes of transport and communication improved. That is the story this book sets forth, together with an account of key inventions and innovations that changed human life along the way until we arrived at the skill, knowledge and power over nature and over one another that prevails among us today. This makes world history an essential introduction to the world we inhabit. As such, it is worth your attention, however imperfect and partial our understanding of it may be.

## The Meaning of History

If we try to contemplate human history from the earliest times to the present and ask what does it all add up to, an obvious answer obtrudes itself. So far, at least, the human adventure on earth is a success story, in spite of all the hurts and damages people have wreaked on one another, and on the natural world around them. It is a success story because no one can doubt that little by little our predecessors learned how to satisfy their material wants more and more effectively, learning how to manipulate more and more of the energy flows on the surface of planet Earth in order to use them for human purposes.

To be sure, power of destruction always kept pace with the power of construction. Both risks and gains multiplied as humans altered the ecological balances of nature more and more radically. Moreover, enhanced power and wealth did not assure greater happiness. Quite the contrary. Our personal wishes and hopes commonly outrun what is available to us, and envy of those more fortunate than ourselves finds more scope as material possessions multiply. Nearly everyone wants respect, deference and even love from daily encounters with others; but one person's success may merely frustrate rivals. As a result, satisfying material wants, however essential that may be for human happiness, by no means guarantees it.

It follows that there are real psychological and social limits to the human success story. Physical limits to the multiplication of human power and wealth must also exist since the earth is finite and the prospect of human colonization of other planets or outer space looks very bleak. But physical limits—whatever they are—have not yet been reached. What look like insoluble problems for one generation may fade away, as happened repeatedly in the past when human ingenuity found a way of doing something that had previously been impossible. Computers, nanotechnology, biotechnology and who knows what still stranger possibilities loom on the horizon of today's accomplishments. They may suffice to cope with the forseeable increase in human numbers—or, again, may not. Conceivably the traditional inequalities between village and city folk can be erased by new technologies and improvements in transport and communication. Other injustices may be relieved as well.

On the other hand, human affairs might move in an opposite direction. Perhaps new quarrels and grievances will multiply, and the recent increase in wealth and comfort that many millions of human beings have experienced will be reversed. Assuredly, catastrophe to our global economy would provoke massive starvation. Or the appearance of a new and highly infectious lethal disease might kill off hundreds of millions of persons. Humanity encountered comparable disasters in the past and may again in future. No one can be sure in advance.

Yet the general pattern of the human career on earth as outlined in this book is at least mildly reassuring. Our predecessors survived in-numerable local disasters, and over the millennia succeeded in enlarging their share of earth's resources enormously. Human intelligence and adaptability allowed them to muddle through—somehow. Future generations will probably do the same. That, assuredly, is the human way. And since there is no obvious limit to the process of invention and discovery that has made humankind so amazingly successful among earth's creatures, perhaps human successes will continue indefinitely into the future.

Yet the enduring ambiguity of human power can never be escaped. Our capacity to destroy ourselves and others is greater than ever before. Whether our heirs and successors will learn to share the earth with one another and with all the other forms of life in some mutually acceptable fashion remains unclear. From today's perspective that looks like the most critical question humanity faces. How things will turn out remains unknown and unknowable. Hence the ultimate meaning of history will continue to elude exact definition just as long as human beings inhabit and keep on transforming the face of the earth.

# Photo Credits

**Chapter 15:** **361** National Maritime Museum, London. **367** Art Resource, New York. **371** Zdenek J. Pivecka. **373** (*top*) Rare Book Division, The New York Public Library, Astor, Lenox, and Tilden Foundations; (*bottom*) University of Chicago, Department of Art. **379** McGraw/Three Lions. **381** Bettmann Archive.

**Chapter 16:** **388** Alinari/Art Resource, New York, **391** (*top*) Alinari/Art Resource, New York; (*bottom*) Public domain. **393** (*left*) © National Museum, Stockholm; (*right*) Art Resource, New York. **399** Alinari/Art Resource, New York. **406** Art Resource, New York. **409** (*top*) Public domain; (*bottom*) Courtesy of United Artists Corporation. **411** The Metropolitan Museum of Art, New York, gift of Henry G. Marquand, 1889.

**Chapter 17:** **415** Courtesy of the Trustees, British Museum, London. **420** (*right*) The Metropolitan Museum of Art, New York, bequest of Benjamin Altman, 1913; (*above*) Art Resource, New York. **423** (*left and right*) William H. McNeill slide collection. **426** Werner Forman. **428** (*left*) Marion H. Levy; (*right*) Sekai Bunka Photo. **432** The Granger Collection. **435** New York Public Library Picture Collection.

**Chapter 18:** **446** Library of Congress. **453** (*left*) The Convention and Visitors Bureau of the Chamber of Commerce of Greater Philadelphia; (*right*) Leslie Deeb. **455** (*left*) The New York Public Library, Prints Division, Astor, Lenox, and Tilden Foundations; (*right*) Giraudon/Art Resource, New York. **466** © 1934 by Regents of the University of California, courtesy of Niels Bohr Library. **469** (*top*) Cliché des Musées Nationaux; Giraudon/Art Resource, New York. **471** (*top*) Public domain; (*bottom*) Museum of Fine Arts, Boston.

**Chapter 19:** **478** Art Gallery of New South Wales. **485** (*left and right*) William H. McNeill slide collection. **489** (*top*) William H. McNeill slide collection; (*bottom*) New York Public Library Picture Collection. **494** (*left and right*) William H. McNeill slide collection. **498** (*left*) William H. McNeill slide collection; (*right*) Courtesy of the Museum of Fine Arts, Boston, the Spaulding Collection. **502** The Granger Collection.

**Chapter 20:** **506** Bettmann Archive. **516** (*top*) Fogg Museum, Harvard University, Grenville L. Winthrop bequest; (*bottom*) Giraudon/Art Resource, New York. **517** (*left*) Giraudon/Art Resource, New York; (*right*) Museo del Prado, Madrid. **527** Library of Congress. **530** (*left*) Bettmann Archive; (*right*) Buckingham/Putnam County Historical Society. **531** (*left*) The Metropolitan Museum of Art, New York, bequest of Mrs. H. O. Havemeyer, 1929, the Havemeyer Collection; (*right*) Southern Pacific Photo.

**Illustrated Essay 3:** **536** Bruce Roberts/Photo Researchers. **537** News Bureau/General Electric Company. **538** New York Power Authority. **539** Wide World Photos.

**Chapter 21:** **543** Public domain. **550** (*top*) Bettmann Archive; (*bottom*) The New York Public Library Picture Collection. **556** Bettmann Archive. **558** Courtesy of the Peabody Museum of Salem/photo by Mark W. Sexton. **561** (*top*) Courtesy of the Museum of Fine Arts, Boston, Bigelow Collection; (*bottom*) Library of Congress. **562** Harrison Forman. **563** National Archives.

**Chapter 22:** **568** French Government Tourist Office. **576** (*top*) Bettmann Archive/BBC Hulton; (*middle*) The Granger Collection; (*bottom*) Bettmann

Archive/BBC Hulton.   **579** Courtesy of the Art Institute of Chicago.   **584** (*top left*) New York Public Library; (*top right*) Neils Bohr Library; (*bottom left*) Library of Congress; (*bottom right*) UPI Bettmann Newsphotos.   **589** (*left*) National Gallery of Art, Washington, D.C., Rosenwald Collection; (*right*) Collection, The Museum of Modern Art, New York, acquired through the Lillie P. Bliss bequest.

**Chapter 23:** **591** Field Museum of Natural History, Chicago.   **595** Museum of the City of New York. **604** (*top*) William H. McNeill slide collection; (*bottom*) Painting by John Clymer, Defense Department Photo (Marine Corps).   **606** (*top*) Courtesy of the Toshiba Corporation, Tokyo, Japan; (*bottom*) William H. McNeill slide collection.   **612** (*top*) New York Public Library Picture Collection; (*bottom*) Bettmann Archive/BBC Hulton.   **614** (*left*) Museum fün Volkerkunde, Berlin; (*right*) William H. McNeill slide collection.

**Illustrated Essay 4:** **618** Library of Congress.   **619** Santa Fe Railway.   **621** Western Union Corporation.

**Chapter 24:** **623** Collection, The Museum of Modern Art, New York, James Thrall Soby bequest.

**625** UPI/Bettmann Newsphotos.   **629** (*left and right*) National Archives.   **633** (*left*) Bettmann Archive; (*right*) UPI/Bettmann Newsphotos.   **639** UPI/Bettmann Newsphotos.   **647** Library of Congress.   **648** (*top*) U.S. Department of Defense Photo; (*bottom*) UPI/ Bettmann Newsphotos.

**Chapter 25:** **658** The University of Chicago, University News Office.   **666** (*top*) Japanese Airlines; (*bottom*) Michael Heron.   **670** (*top*) Bettmann Archive; (*bottom*) UPI/Bettmann Newsphotos.   **672** AP/Wide World Photos.   **680** (*top*) United Nations; (*bottom*) Paolo Koch/Photo Researchers.   **683** Marc Riboud/ Magnum.   **684** (*top*) Magnum for World Bank; (*bottom*) Bruno Barbey/Magnum.

**Chapter 26:** **688** Collection, The Museum of Modern Art, New York, A. Conger Goodyear Fund. **696** (*left and right*) NASA.   **701** (*left*) Philadelphia Museum of Art, Louise and Walter Ginsberg Collection; (*right*) Hirshhorn Museum and Sculpture Garden, Smithsonian Institution, Washington, D.C. **702** (*top*) Courtesy of the Australian Overseas International Service; (*bottom*) Mexican National Tourist Council.   **706** NASA.

# Index

Abbas I the Great, Shah, 422
Abdul-Wahhab, Mohammed ibn, 486
Aborigines, 565, 594
Absolute monarchs, 404
Absolutism, 447
  challenges to, 462–64
Acton, Lord, 585
Afghanistan, 483
Africa, 386, 440–43, 639
  interior of, 479
  Islam in, 416
  North, 609
  South, 479
  sub-Saharan, 499–503
  tropical, 564
Africans, 594
  fate of, 610–15
Agricultural exports, 598
Agriculture
  in European society, 577
  revolution in, 448–49
  Russian expansion of, 458–60
  U.S., 596
Air travel, 620
Akbar, Emperor, 422, 425
Akif Pasha, 488
Alfonso, King, 382
Alaska, U.S. purchase of, 563
Albert of Wallenstein, 402
Alexander, Czar, 522, 523
Alexander I, 551
Alexander II, 549, 600
Algeria, 486, 671
Ali Pasha, 487
Allies, 626
Alphabets, 476
American Federation of Labor, 596
American Revolution, 508–10
Americas, 363, 416, 437–40
  Catholic Church in, 379–82
Amerindians, 386, 437, 479, 594
  and disease, 384
  fate of, 610–15
  population decline of, 452
  retreat before Europeans, 504
Anabaptists, 394
Anarchists, 579
Angola, 441
Animism, 652
Antarctic, 564

Anthropology, 585
Apartheid, 679
Archaeologists, 585
Architects, 470
Architecture, 586, 702
Arctic, 564
Argentina, 598
Aristotle, 407
Armies, 412, 454
  equipping, 404
  Indian, 481–83
  modernization of Ottoman, 554
  in Prussia, 461
  standing, 454
Arnauld, Antoine, 472
Art, 410, 470, 586–88, 700–703
  African, 442
  in China, 491
  French, 464
  Islamic, 488
  in Japan, 499
  Moslem, 422
Articles of Confederation, 509
Artificial light, 532
Artillery, development of, 480
Artisans, 571
  local, 545
Asia
  Europeans in, 488–91
  as outside ring, 601–10
Assembly of notables, 510
Assimilation, ideal of, 683
Astronomers, 582
Astronomy, 429, 466
Atheism, 704
Atomic power, 538–39, 669
Aurangzeb, Emperor, 422
Australia, 479, 503–04, 565, 594, 598
Austria, 507, 638. *See also* Hapsburgs.
  bitter feelings against Russia, 549
  expansion of, 461
  outbreak of war against, 514
  pre-World War I, 575
Austro-Hungary, 625
Ayatollahs, 421

Babur, 422
Bach, Johann Sebastian, 470

Bacon, Francis, 408
Balboa, Vasco Nuñez de, 375
Banking, improvements in, 450
Bank of England, 450
Bantu, 441
Barometer, 406
Baroque, 410
Baseball, 588
Battle of the Somme, 628
Beauty, pursuit of, 410–12
Beethoven, Ludwig von, 533
Belgium, 531
Belief, system of, 407
Bering, Captain Vitus, 503
Berkeley, George, 468
Berlin conference, 611
Bible, 394, 410
Bicycle racing, 588
Big Bang, 700
Biology, Molecular, 697
Bismarck, Otto von, 572, 575, 577
Blacks, 596
Blitzkrieg, 640–42
Boers, 500, 565, 598
Bohr, Niels, 694
Bolivar, Simon, 523
Bolivia, war with Paraguay, 640
Bolsheviks, 601
Books, sale of printed, 412
Borrowing, for exploration, 369
Bosnia, 678
Botticelli, Sandro, 388
Bougainville, Captain Louis Antoine de, 503
Boundaries, European national, 569
Boxer Rebellion, 603
Brahmans, 425
Brahms, Johannes, 587
Braque, Georges, 701
Brazil, 382, 598
    independence from Portugal, 523
    Portuguese, 438–39
Britain, 507, 603, 625. *See also* England.
    colonies of in North America, 439–40
    and France, 518
    and Hitler, 642
    in India, 483, 489
    labor in, 578–79
    Napoleonic Wars and, 529–31
    new French war against, 518
    in North Africa, 609
    pre-World War I, 575
    territorial expansion of, 458
British traders, in India, 481
Brooklyn Bridge, 595
Brueghel, Pieter, 410
Bubonic plague, 448
Buddhism, 705–07
Buddhists, isolation of, 491
Burns, Robert, 470, 533
Bushmen, 441

Cabot, John, 374
Calendar making, 429
Calvin, John, 396–98, 406, 410
Calvinism, 401, 407
Camels, 617
Canada, 439, 598, 678
    surrendered to British, 458
Canals, 618
Cannons, on ships, 366
Canton, 495
    European trade in, 558 *fig.*

Cão, Diogo, 369
Cape coloureds, 598
Capitalism, crisis of, 637
Caravans, 617
Caravels, 366
Caribbean colonies, and French Revolution, 522–23
Carnegie, Andrew, 594, 596
Cartels, Germany, 580–81
Cassava, 384
Caste, elimination of, 425
Castiglione, Joseph, 494
Castlereagh, Lord, 522
Castro, Fidel, 669
Catechisms, 400
Cathedral, oldest American, 379 *fig.*
Cathedral of St. Basil, 435 *fig.*
Cathedral of St. Peters, 391 *fig.*
Cathedral of Santo Domingo, 379 *fig.*
Catherine the Great, 460–61, 507
Catholic Church, 378, 407, 585
    in the Americas, 379–82
    quarrel with Orthodox church, 547
    reform of, 399–401, 436
Catholics, 577
Cavour, Count Camillo, 572
Cervantes, Miguel de, 410
Cézanne, Paul, 587
Chaitanya, 425
Charles I, 463
Charles II, 463
Charles V, 389–92, 395, 396
Chateaubriand, Réné du, 534
Chemists, 582
Chiang Kai-shek, 638
Ch'ien emperor, 491
Children's literature, 703
Chile, 598
    conquest of, 375–78
China, 427–30, 546, 601–05, 632, 635,
        661, 676
    Christian missions to, 429–30
    communist, 669
    geography of, 362
    internal problems of, 557–60
    military campaigns of, 483
    plans for dividing, 603
    rising unrest in, 491–96
    western penetration of, 604
China incident, 638
Chinese, 479, 594, 609
Christianity, 583, 653, 704
    Chinese discrediting of, 493
    stamping out of in Japan, 433
Christians, 703
    Japanese, 382
    as subjects of Moslems, 552
Chronometer, 451, 503
Churches, reformed, 396–98
Churchill, Winston, 642, 647, 664
Church lands, selling of, 514
Church of England, 398
Civil rights law, 672
Civil war, in United States, 563–64
Class lines, blurring of in Japan, 497
Clemenceau, George, 633
Clock, accurate, 367, 406, 451
Coal, as fuel, 450
Coal fields, 530–31, 581
Coal gas, 532
Coal tars, 532
Code Napoléon, 518
Code of manners, 447
Co-hong, 479
Coke, as new form of fuel, 450–51

Coking, 532
Colbert, Jean Baptiste, 455
Cold War, 659, 669–73
  end of, 673–78
  onset of, 661–69
Colonies
  fighting in, 458
  scramble for, 611
Columbus, Christopher, 368, 372–74
Communication, 592, 617–22
  development of, 475–77
Communications satellites, 477
Communism, 624
Communist Manifesto, 570–71
Communist Revolution, 542
Computer, 477, 620–22, 694–95
Comte, Auguste, 585
Concentration camps, 648
Concept of marginal utility, 583
Confession, 394
Confucianism, 705–07
  in China, 491–93
Congregational singing, 411
Congress of Vienna, 522
Constitutional government, American, 509–10
Constitution of 1791, 514
Conversion, 380
Cook, Captain James, 503
Copernicus, Nicolaus, 407
Co-Prosperity Sphere, 643
Coracles, 364
Corneille, Pierre, 470
Coronado, Francisco Vásquez de, 378
Cosmopolitanism, world, 541–42
Cotton, 451
Council of Trent, 399–400
Coup d'état, in Japan, 560
Credit, 581
Crick, Francis H.C., 697, 698, 699
Crimean War, 544, 547–54
Cromwell, Oliver, 463
Crops, spread of new, 384–85
Crystal Palace, 506
Cuba, 669
Cultivable land, shortage of in China, 493
Cultural conservatism, China's, 430
Cultural developments, 533–34
Culture
  European, 464–73
  Japanese, 433–34
  rise of popular, 689–93
  in United States, 596
Customs service, 601
Czechoslovakia, 638

da Gama, Vasco, 369, 370
Dancing, 475
Danton, Georges Jacques, 514
Darby, Abraham, 451
Darwin, Charles, 583, 584, 654
David, Jacques-Louis, 516 fig.
Dawes Plan, 637
Debt
  Turkish, 552
  United States, 674
Declaration of Independence, 509
Declaration of Rights, 463
Declaration of the Rights of Man, 512
Democratic Revolution, 507
Deng Xiaoping, 676
Dervishes, 421

Descartes, René, 407, 408, 468
de Secondat, Charles-Louis, 468
de Soto, Hernando, 378
Diamond mines, 612
Dias, Bartholomeu, 369
Diaz, Porfirio, 615
Dickens, Charles, 587
Dictatorships, military, 671
Diderot, Denis, 469
Diet, 605
Diet of Worms, 394, 395
Directory, government by, 517–18
Disease
  fading of epidemic, 480
  resurgence of, 685
  spread of, 383–84
DNA, 697, 698
Don Quixote, 410
Dostoyevsky, Feodor, 588
Doyle, Arthur Conan, 703
Drake, Francis, 402
Dreadnought, H.M.S., 576
Drilling, close order, 501
Dürer, Albrecht, 410
Dutch
  in Africa, 443
  scholastic influence on Japan, 497
Dutch East India Company, 424
Dutch Republic, 405
Dynastic wars, 401–06

Earth sciences, 695–97
Eastern Europe, expansion in, 458–61
East India Company, 481, 483, 490, 554
  in China, 495
Ecological considerations, 685
Economic change, in Europe, 447–54
Economic decay, 424
Economics, 468
  new, 697
  transnational, 673
Economic theory, 582–83
Economy, pre-World War I European, 577–81
Edict of Nantes, 401
Edison, Thomas A., 583
Education, universal in Japan, 607
Egypt, 440, 486, 555, 611
Eiffel Tower, 568, 586
Einstein, Albert, 582, 584, 694
Eisenhower, General Dwight D., 646
Electricity, 538
Electric light, 583
El Greco, 410
Eliot, Thomas Stearns, 702
Elizabeth I, 398
Emancipation, 500
Emancipation Proclamation, 564
Empires
  breakup of colonial, 671
  dismantlement of, 663
  expansion of European, 447
  more effective control of large, 480
  Spain's overseas, 372–83
Encyclopedia, 469
  Chinese, 493
Energy
  breakthroughs in use of, 536–39
  harnessing, 526
England
  challenges to absolutism in, 463–64
  parliamentary government in, 405

English, 410
    as official language of administration in India, 555
    as world language, 693
English East India Company, 424
Epidemic diseases, lessening of, 593
Erasmus, Desiderius, 410
Esprit de corps, 501
Estates, 404, 405
Estates-General, 510, 511
Ethiopia, 611
Ethnic composition, changing, 682
Euler, Leonard, 465
Eurasia, eastward expansion in, 452
Europe
    culture in, 464–73
    economic change in, 447–54
    leading role of, 541
    new regime in, 507–08
    reaction of to French Revolution, 523–26
    recovery in Eastern post World War II, 663
    under Old Regime, 447
    Western, 363
    worldwide impact of, 545–47
European Economic Community, 673
Europeans, withdrawal of local peoples from
            contact with, 479–80
European Union, 678
Evolution, theory of, 583–85
Evolutionary view, 654–55
Exile, of Napoleon, 522
Expansion, United States, 596
Exploration, 362
    of African interior, 502–03
    consequences of European, 383–85
    Portuguese, 369–72
    problems of organizing, 368–69
Extraterritoriality, American right of in China, 495


Factory life, 528
Faith, act of, 406
Fallowing, farming without, 448
Famine relief, 593
Fascism, 542, 624
Ferdinand, Archduke Francis, 390, 401, 624, 625 fig.
Ferdinand II, 402
Ferdinand III, 404
Ferdinand VII, 523
Ferdinand and Isabella, 372
Feudalism, abolishing, 512, 605
Fief holders, 497
Fielding, Henry, 470
Finance, under Old Regime, 449–50
Financial problems, in France, 513–14
First Estate, 511
Flaubert, Gustave, 587
Fleming, Alexander, 697
Food
    increased supplies of, 593
    production of, 679
    storage and marketing of, 480
Food crops, American, 480
Forbidden City, 428 fig.
Forced labor, 454, 610
Ford, Henry, 595, 596
Foreign trade, opening of Japan to, 560
Forests, disappearance of, 450
Formosa, 607
Fox, George, 472
France, 401, 507, 603, 625
    alliance with Russia, 600
    armistice with Hitler, 642
    challenges to absolutism in, 462–63

colonies of in North America, 439–40
economy of, 530
missionary work in China, 495
    in North Africa, 609
    pre-World War I, 575
    Second Republic of, 569
    and Spain, 402
    support of American Revolution, 509
    territorial expansion of, 454–57
    World War II landing in, 646
Franco, Francisco, 638
Franklin, Benjamin, 467
Franklin, Sir John, 565
Franz Josef I, 575
Frederick II, 461
Frederick William, 461
Frederick the Wise, 395
Free trade
    in India, 607
    in Ottoman Empire, 554
French and Indian War, 458
French Revolution, 510–26
Freud, Sigmund, 584, 585, 698
Fronde, 454
Frontier society, 454
Fur trade, 439


Gadsden Purchase, 563
Gainsborough, Thomas, 470
Galen, 408
Galileo, 408, 409 fig.
Gandhi, Mohandes, 639 fig., 663
Garibaldi, Giuseppe, 572
Gauguin, Paul, 587
Geisha girls, 499
Geography, knowledge of based on books, 362
George I, 463
George II, 463
George III, 458, 464, 508
German Social Democratic party, 578
Germany, 389, 507, 625
    defeated, 661
    industrial planning in, 580–81
    revolution in, 526
    unification of, 549, 572–75
Girondins, 514
Glasnost, 675
Global economy, dawn of modern, 427
God, world-view of, 467
Goethe, Johann Wolfgang von, 470, 533
Gold, 375, 378
Golden Bull, 389
Golden Horde, 434
Good Neighbor policy, 640
Gorbachev, Mikhail, 674
Government, remodeling Indian, 555
Governors, 372
Goya, Francisco, 470
Grain, low cost of American, 577
Gravitation, theory of, 466
Great Depression, 637, 638
Great Leap Forward, 669, 670
Great Trek, 500
Greece, 486
    independence of, 526
Greek-Turkish war, 632
Green Revolution, 679
Grotius, Hugo, 405
Grunewald, Mathias, 406 fig.
Gulf War, 677
Gunpowder, 366, 536–37
    in Russia, 437

Guns
  breech-loading, 532
  in Japan, 430
  matchlock, 446
  suppression of, 432
Gustavus Adolphus, 404

Haiti, 523
Handel, George Frederick, 470
Hapsburgs, 452, 458, 461. *See also* Austria.
  limits of power of, 402–04
  Moslem peace with, 481
Hapsburg Empire, 389–92
Harrison, John, 367, 451
Hart, Robert, 601
Harvey, William, 408
Hasidism, 473
Hawkins, John, 402
Haydn, Franz Joseph, 470
Hegel, Georg Wilhelm Friedrich, 534, 583
Hegelianism, 534
Henotheism, 652, 653
Henry IV, 401
Henry VII, 374
Henry VIII, 398, 399
Herder, Johann Gottfried, 533
Heresy, 392
  struggle against, 401
Heroic achievement, 545
Hideyoshi, Toyotomi, 427, 431, 432, 433
Hillary, Edmund, 667
Hinduism, 373 *fig.*, 705–07
  and geography, 362
  revival of, 425–27
Hindus, 546, 594, 607, 663
  interaction with Europeans, 488–90
Hitler, Adolf, 633, 637, 640
Hobbema, Meindert, 470
Hobbes, Thomas, 467
Hong Kong, 671
Hopkins, Henry, 646
Horse
  in Americas, 384
  draught, 451
  winter fodder for, 449
Hottentots, 441
How to books, 703
Hugo, Victor, 587
Huguenots, 401, 473
Humayun, 422
Hume, David, 468
Hungarian Diet, 462
Hung Hsiu-ch'üan, 557, 559–60
Hus, John, 392
Hussein, Saddam, 679

Ideology, official Japanese, 497–98
Ieyasu, 433
Ignatius of Loyola, 400
Immigrants, growing population of, 682
Immigration, 598
  to U.S. from Europe, 595
Imperial examinations, 491–93
Independence, national in Third World, 668
Index of prohibited books, 400
India, 546–47, 607–09, 672
  armies in, 481–83
  British in, 481, 489
  British withdrawal from, 663
  English schools in, 490

  independence for, 639 *fig.*
  Moslem rulers of, 422
  reforms in, 554–57
  surrendered to British, 458
Indian Civil Service examinations, 555
Indian Mutiny, 544
Indian National Congress, 607
Indian Ocean, 363
Indians, American, 440
Indirect rule, 483
Indulgences, 392
Industrialism
  adjustments to, 580–81
  problems of, 577–80
Industrial processes, 686
Industrial Revolution, 507–08, 526–34
  impact of, 545
Industry
  modern in Japan, 605, 606
  progress of, 577
Inflation, 513
Inner ring of peoples, 593–94
Inoculation, first successful, 448
Inquisition, 400
Instability, international, 569
*Institutes of the Christian Religion*, 396, 410
Intellectual developments, 533–34
Intellectual history, of Europe, 406–10
International Workingmen's Association, 578
Inventions, 406, 532, 540–41
Iran, 677–78
Iraq, 677
Irish question, 577
Iron curtain, 661
Irrationalism, 585–86
Islam, 386, 416–25, 481–88, 546, 609–10,
    653, 705
  weaknesses of societies, 422–25
Ismail Safavi, 418–21
Isolation, Japan's policy of, 433
Israel, 671
  establishment of, 663
Israeli War of Independence, 704
Italy, 390, 625
  fascist regime of, 624
  in North Africa, 609
  revolution in, 526
  unification of, 572–75
Ivan the Terrible, 417–18, 434, 435 *fig.*
Ivan III, 434

Jacobins, 515
Jahan, Shah, 422
James, Henry, 596
James II, 463
Jamestown, 439
Janissaries, 485 *fig.*
Janissary Corps, 481
Jansen, Cornelius, 472
Jansenism, 472
Japan, 370, 382, 416, 496–99, 546–47, 605–07,
    632, 635, 661
  closing of, 432–33
  culture in, 433–34
  defeat of Russia by, 601
  economic revival post World War II, 663
  expansion by, 638
  initial victories in World War II, 643
  internal problems of, 560–63
  modern, 666
  nuclear bombing of, 649
  Portuguese ship in, 371 *fig.*

refusal to allow immigrants into, 682
shifts of policy in, 430–34
unification of, 431–32
Japanese, 479
Java, Islam in, 417
Jazz, 596, 700
Jefferson, Thomas, 512
Jehovah's Witnesses, 703
Jenner, Edward, 448
Jesuit mission, 430, 436
Jesuits, 400–401, 472
Jim Crow laws, 596
Joint stock company, 412
Jones, Sir William, 488
Joseph II, 461
Journalism, 587–88
Joyce, James, 702
Juarez, Benito, 615
Judaism, 473, 653, 704–05
June Days, 569

Kabuki plays, 499
Kalmucks, 418
Kandinsky, Vasili, 701
K'ang-hsi emperor, 491
Kant, Immanuel, 468
Kemal, Mustafa, 635
Kenya, 671
Keynes, John Maynard, 697
Kepler, Johannes, 408
Khomeini, Ayatollah, 670, 677
King, Martin Luther, 672
King, right of to govern, 467
Korea, 661
Japanese control of, 607
quarrels over, 603
Korean War, 663
Krishna, 425
Krupp, Alfred, 576
Kuwait, 677

Labor
international division of, 673
in machine age, 528–29
in pre-World War I Europe, 569
Labor unions, 578, 596
Labour party, in Britain, 578–79
Lafayette, 512
Laissez-faire, British, 580
Land grants, 374
Languages
African, 615
invention of, 475–76
standardization of, 693
Las Casas, Bartolemé de, 380
Latin, 410
Latin America, 566
Latitude, determining, 366
Lavoisier, Antoine, 467
Law, John, 468
Law, remodeling Indian, 555
League of Nations, 632
Leclerk, Georges Louis de Buffon, 466
Legal reform, in Ottoman Empire, 554
Leibniz, Gottfried Wilhelm, 466, 468
Lend Lease Act, 643
Lenin (Vladimir Ilich Ulyanov), 601, 628–31
Lessing, Gotthold Ephraim, 470
Liberia, 611
Liberty, equality, fraternity, 512

Libraries, 587
Limited monarchy, in France, 514
Lincoln, Abraham, 563–64
Lindberg, Charles, 636
Linnaeus, 466
Literature, 410, 468–70, 586–88, 700–703
French, 464
Islamic, 488
Moslem, 422
Livestock, spread of new, 384–85
Livingstone, David, 565, 612
Lloyd-George, David, 633
Localism, 592
Local peoples, withdrawal from contact with Europeans, 479–80
Locke, John, 467, 468
Longitude, measuring, 367
Louis Napoleon, 569
Louis Philippe, 526
Louis XIV, 454, 455
Louis XVI, 510, 511, 514, 515
L'Ouverture, Toussaint, 523
Luther, Martin, 392–96
Lutheranism, 390
Luxury crafts, 451–52

Macao, 370, 371, 427
McCormick, Cyrus, 533
Machine-made goods, 570
Magellan, Ferdinand, 375
Mahler, Gustav, 587
Maize, 384–85, 448, 480
in Africa, 442
Malaria, 502
Malaya, 671
Manchu conquest, 428–29
Manchu dynasty, end of, 603
Manchukuo, 638
Mandate, 635
Mandela, Nelson, 677
Manufacturing, new techniques of, 450–52
Maoism, 706
Maori, 565
Mao Tse-tung, 638, 669, 670
Marco Polo, 362
Maria Theresa, 461, 462
Marie Antoinette, Queen, 516 fig.
Marshall, Alfred, 583
Marshall, General George C., 646
Marshall Plan, 661
Marx, Karl, 578, 584
Mary, Queen, 398
Massachusetts, 439
Mass media, impact of, 689–91
Mathematics, theoretical, 582
Matisse, Henri, 587, 701
Maudslay, Henry, 528
Maximilian, Emperor, 389, 566
Maxwell, James Clerk, 582
Media, American, 689–93
Medicine, checking of disease by, 593
Mediterranean Sea, 363
Mehmed II, 366
Meiji emperor, 605
Mendeleev, Dmitri, 582
Mendelssohn, Moses, 473
Menshevik group, 601
Merchant class, 433
Merchants, 362
Moslem, 370
warriors and in Japan, 496–97
Merrimac, 576
Mestizos, 452

Metal lathe, 528
Metal trades, 529
Methodist chapels, 529
Methodists, 472
Metternich, Prince, 522
Mexico, 437, 523, 566
    conquest of, 375–78
    and United States, 640
Michael, Prince of Serbia, 552
Microscope, 406
Middle-class regime, 508
Middle East, 677
Military drill, 475
Military power, fading of Moslem, 481–83
Military security, in India, 555
Military service, universal, 605
Milton, John, 470
Mines, 437
Ming dynasty, 427
Mining, organization of, 378
Ministry of education, 605
Missionaries, 603
    Christian, 610
Missionary thrust, in Americas, 378–82
Missionary work, Moslem, 488
Missions
    in Americas, 380
    Christian, 490
    Christian to China, 429–30
    Portuguese, 382–83
Mobilization
    of French, 516
    U.S., 645
Mobilization plans, 626, 628
Modern army and navy, 601
Modernist doctrines, 585
Mohammed Ali, 485 fig., 486
Molière, 470
Molinos, Miguel de, 472
Monarch, cooperation of Russian with nobles, 551
Mondrian, Piet, 701
Monitor, 576
Monotheism, 652, 653–54
Monroe, President James, 526
Monsoons, 363
Montezuma, 375, 376
Moore, Henry, 658
More, Thomas, 410
Morgan, Lewis Henry, 585
Morocco, 611
Moscow, Polish invasion of, 434
Moslems, 368, 382, 594, 609, 663
    art of, 422
    fading military power of, 481–83
    missionary success of, 610
    reform movement of, 486–88
    reform of, 552–53
    territorial advances of, 416–17
    wars against, 372
Mosques, 423 fig.
Most favored nation clause, 495
Mount Everest, conquest of, 667
Movies, 690
Mozart, Wolfgang Amadeus, 470, 533
Murder mysteries, 703
Music, 411, 470, 587, 700–703
Mussolini, Benito, 637, 642, 643
    overthrow of, 645

NAFTA, 678
Napoleon, 517–22
Napoleonic Wars, and British Empire, 529–31

National assembly, French, 511–14
National Convention, French, 515
National debt, idea of, 450
Nationalism, 572
    spread of, 554
NATO, 678
Natural law, 654
Natural sciences, 654
Naval tactics, revolution in, 370
Navigation, 364–68, 617
Nehru, Jawaharlal, 639 fig.
Neo-Confucianism, 433, 497
Newcomen, Thomas, 528
New Deal, 637
New Economic Policy, Soviet, 635
New Regime, 507
Newspapers, 588, 592, 605
Newton, Isaac, 465, 466–67
Newton's laws of motion, 582
New World, 437–40
New York, 439
New Zealand, 504, 565, 598
Nicholas I, 551
Nightingale, Florence, 548, 549
Nikon, 436
Nomads
    eclipse of, 416
    religious community of, 418
Non-aggression treaty, 640
Norgay, Tenzing, 667
North America
    colonies in, 439–40
    European settlement in, 452
North Atlantic, 363
Northwest Passage, 565
Nuclear power, 658
Nuclear weapons, 648, 649
Nursing, modern, 549

Oath of the Tennis Court, 516 fig.
Obo of Benin, 416
Ocean currents, detection of, 367–68
Oceania, 440–43
Oceans, exploration of, 696
Oil, price of, 673
Old Believers, 436
Old Regime, Europe under, 447
Olympic Games, 588
OPEC, 673
Open Door policy, 603
Opera, 411
Opium trade, 495
Opium War, 544
Orthodox church, 436, 460
    quarrel with Roman Catholics, 547
Ottoman Empire, 390, 546, 635
    retreat of, 483–86
Ottomanism, 610
Ottoman Public Debt Administration, 552
Ottoman Turks, 547
    consequences of victory of, 552–54
    sovereignty of, 553–54
Outer ring of peoples, 593–94
Outside ring, 601–10

Pacific, exploration of, 503–04
Pacification, 593
Paddle wheel, 536
Painters, 586, 701
Painting, 470, 494, 587

Pakistan, 663, 672
Palace of Chambord, 391 *fig.*
Palestine, 635, 668
Palestrina, Giovanni, 411
Panama Canal, 592
Pan-Arab empire, 610
Pan-Turkism, 610
Papacy
    feuding with Italian government, 572
    Napoleon and, 518
    power of, 389
Paper currency, 513
Paracelsus, 408
Paraguay, 599
    war with Bolivia, 640
Pareto, Vilfredo, 585
Paris Commune, 578
Paris Peace Conference, 632
Parliamentary government, 464
Parsis, 607
Patriotism, 572
Peace of Amiens, 518
Peace of Augsburg, 396
Peace of Paris, 458
Peace settlement, post World War I, 631–35
Pearl Harbor, 643
Peasant revolt, 394–96, 436
    in China, 493, 557
Peasants, 362
    Japanese, 607
    Russian, 551
Pedro I, 523
Penicillin, 697
Pennsylvania, 439
Pentacostalists, 703
Peonage, 381
Perestroika, 675
Perry, Commodore Matthew, 560
Persia, 483
Persian miniature painting, 422
Peru, 437
    conquest of, 375–78
Peter the Great, 436, 460
Philip of Anjou, 456
Philip II, 401, 402
Philosophy, 468–70, 703–07
Phonograph, 477
Photography, 477
Physicists, 582
Physics, 466, 694, 700
Picasso, Pablo, 587, 701
Pietism, 472
Pirates, Japanese, 427
Pius IX, Pope, 577
Pizarro, Francisco, 375
Plato, 407
Plows, improved, 449
Plundering, 402
Po, Fernando, 369
Poland, 638
    invasion of Moscow by, 434
    Russia and, 461
Police measures, in Russia, 600
Polish revolt, 600
Political development, internal, 404–06
Political dominion, limits of, 540
Politics
    changes in late nineteenth century, 569–77
    and religion, 389–401
    and war in Old Regime, 454–62
Polytheism, 652–53
Pope, 435
Pope, Alexander, 470
Pope Leo X, 393 *fig.*
Pope Paul III, 399–400

Population, 678–85
    decay of in urbanized societies, 682–83
    destruction of by disease, 437
    growth of in China, 491, 493
    increase in, 384, 448, 579, 581, 593
    Indian, 607
    massive growth of, 661
    self-sustaining African in the New World, 500
    worldwide growth in, 479–80
Porcelain, 451
Portugal, 368
    and claims with Spain, 374
Portuguese
    missions of, 382–83
    in shipbuilding, 366
    trade with China, 427
    trade and exploration by, 369–72
Postal system, 601, 605
Postwar Europe, arranging map of, 647
Potatoes, 384, 448, 480
Power, new sources of, 451
Precision tools, 451–52
Predestination, 396
Prester John, 369
Prince Henry the Navigator, 366, 368
Princip, Gavrilo, 624, 625 *fig.*
Printing, 476–77, 617, 619
Printing press, 412
Professionalism, 464
Protestant Reformation, 392–96
Prussia, 458, 507
    expansion of, 461
    outbreak of war against, 514
Ptolemy, 362
Public debt, 450
Public health, improvements in, 678–79
Public schooling, 587
Public works, 555
Pubs, 529
Puritans, 439, 463

Quakers, 472
Quebec, 439
Queen Anne, 463
Queen Victoria, 614
Quetzalcoatl, 376
Quietism, 472
Quinine, 502, 565

Race, 672–73
Race feelings, in Africa, 565
Racial mixtures, in Brazil, 438
Racine, Jean, 470
Radio, 477, 620, 690
Railroads, 531–32, 540, 553, 592, 603, 611, 619
    German, 581
    public regulation of rates of, 596
Rama, 425, 562 *fig.*
Rammohun Roy, 490
Ramsay, James Andrew, 555
Ranchers, in Americas, 437
Ranke, Leopold von, 585
Reagan, Ronald, 674
Reaper, horse-drawn, 533
Rearmament, U.S., 638
Redshirts, 572
Reformation, in England, 398–99
Reform Bill of 1832, 526
Reformed churches, 396–98
Reign of Terror, 515–17
Relativity, theory of, 582

Religion, 472–73, 703–07
  in European society, 577
  politics and, 389–401
  and theory of evolution, 583
Religious dissenters, 439
Religious taboos, clash with new technology, 554
Religious wars, 401–06
Rembrandt van Rijn, 410
Replaceable parts, 528
Republic, France as, 515
Revolutionary movements, Christian, 552
Revolutions, liberal in Europe, 569
Rhodes, Cecil, 598
Ricci, Matteo, 429
Richardson, Samuel, 470
River steamers, 611
Roads, 618
Robespierre, Maximilien, 515, 516
Rockefeller, John D., 594, 596
Romania, 486, 553
Romanov, Michael, 436
Romanticism, 533
Roosevelt, Franklin D., 637, 646, 647, 664
Ross, Captain James Clark, 564–65
Rotary press, 477, 532
Rousseau, Jean Jacques, 467
Royal rule, establishment of direct, 374
Royal Society of London, 467
Rudders, 365
Rudolph of Hapsburg, 389
Rural conservatism, 533
Rural life, disruption of in Britain, 544
Russia, 416, 600–601, 603, 609, 625
  abolition of serfdom in, 545
  bitter feelings against Austria, 549
  communist regime of, 624
  growth of power of, 483–86
  and Moslems, 418
  poverty of, 551
  pre-World War I, 575
  reaction of to defeat, 549–52
  secret treaty with, 575
  as threat to Europe, 507
  troubles in, 628
  war on Turks, 547
Russian army, disintegration of, 631
Russian autocracy, rise of, 434–37
Russian language, 693
Russians, in steppelands, 453
Rwanda, 677

Sacred Law, 486, 552, 705
Safavid state, rise of, 418–22, 481
St. Francis Xavier, 382, 430, 431
St. Thomas Acquinas, 407
Samurai class, 433
San Francisco conference, 661
San Martin, José de, 523
Sanskrit, 490
Schiller, Johann Christoph Freidrich von, 470
Scholars
  Chinese, 493
  study of Western thought by Japanese, 497–98
School
  control of in France, 577
  English in India, 490
Science, 464, 465–66, 581–86, 694–700
  development of, 407–10
  soft, 583–85
Scurvy, 503
Seafarers, exploration of European, 362
Seafaring, 385, 544
  problems of, 363–69

Second Estate, 511
Second Republic, French, 569
Secret societies, 493, 603
Selim the Grim, 420, 485 fig.
Sepoy, 481, 554, 555
Serbia, 486, 553, 625
Serfdom, 434
  abolishment of, 545, 549
Seurat, George, 579 fig.
Seven Years' War, 458, 461
Shah, Nadir, 483
Shaka, 500–502
Shakespeare, William, 410
Shi'a Muslim, 418, 421–22, 610
Shinto, 705–07
  development of, 497
Shipbuilding, 364–68
  timber for, 450
Ships, 617
Shiva, 425
Shogun, 432
  political insecurity of, 496
Siam, and the West, 562 fig.
Siamese, 479
Silk, 497
Silver, 375, 378
  price of, 383
Silver mines, 380
Singing, 475
Skills, impact of superior European, 593–94
Skyscrapers, 586
Slavery, 563
Slaves, liberation of, 564
Slave trade, 440–43, 499–503
Slavophiles, 549
Smith, Adam, 468, 545
Soccer, 588
Social change, in Europe, 447–54
Social Democrats, 600
Social insurance laws, 578
Socialism, 551
  response to, 578–80
  in Third World, 668
Socialist parties, rise of, 578
Social order, breakdown of traditional, 544–45
Social sciences, 697–700
Social theory, 467–68
Society, pre-World War I European, 577–81
Society of Friends, 472
Society of Jesus. See Jesuits.
Sociology, 585
Solidarity, 624
South Africa, 598, 523, 672, 679
South America, 598–600
Southeast Asia, Islam in, 416
Soviet Union, cold war with United States, 659
Space, exploration of, 620, 695–97
Spain, 368, 638
  and claims with Portugal, 374
  France and, 402
  overseas empire of, 372–83
  persecution of non-Catholics by, 404–05
Spanish Armada, 402
Spanish empire, in Americas, 437–38
Spanish Inquisition, 379
Speed, measuring ship's, 367
Spener, Philipp, 472
Spengler, Oswald, 700
Sphere of influence, around India, 555
Spice Islands, 371
Spice trade, 369–70
Spinoza, Baruch, 468

*Spirit of St. Louis*, 636
Spiritual Exercises, 400
Sports, 588
Stalemate, pre-World War I, 626
Stalin, Josef, 637, 640, 647, 664
Stanley, Henry, 565, 612
Steam engines, 451, 527–28
Steam power, 537
Steamships, 540, 592
Steppe warriors, overthrow of, 481
Stratford, Lord de Redcliffe, 553
Suez Canal, 556, 592
Sufi Islam, 382
Sugar islands, 452
Sugar plantations, 382, 438
    slaves to work, 441
Suleiman the Lawgiver, 390, 421
Sun, in navigation, 366, 367 *fig.*
Sunni Islam, 421–22, 546
Sun Yat-sen, 603
Supply lines, 626
Sur Das, 425
Suttee, 490
Sweden, 404
    Russia and, 461
Swedes, 434
Sweet potatoes, 384–85, 480
Switzerland, 396, 405
Symbolists, 588

Taiping movement, 557, 559
Taiping Rebellion, 496
Taj mahal, 422
Tantrism, 425
Taxes, 455
Tax-farming, 424
Tax system, French, 510
Tehran peace conference, 647
Tekkes, 421
Telegraph, 477, 540, 553, 592, 611, 620
Telephone, 477, 620
Telescope, 406
Television, 477, 620
Tennis, 588
Territorial expansion, 452–54
Terrorism, in Russia, 600
Textile trades, 529
Theater, 412
Theism, 652–54
Theoretical science, and industry, 580
Thermometer, 406
Third Estate, 469 *fig.*, 516 *fig.*
    revolt of, 511
Third World, hopes of, 668
Thirty Years' War, 402–04
Time of Troubles, 435–36
Tintoretto, 410
Titian, 410
Tobacco, 385
Tokugawa, Ieyasu, 432
Tokugawa shoguns, 427, 432–33, 496
Tokyo, 496
Tolstoy, Count Leo, 588
Toynbee, Arnold, 526, 700
Trade
    with Japan, 430
    Portuguese, 369–72
    problems in China, 495–96
    under Old Regime, 449–50
Trade routes, 363
Trans-national organizations, 678

Transportation, 592, 617–22
    improvements to, 449
Trans-Siberian Railroad, 600
Treaties of Tientsin, 558
Treaty, with China, 495–96
Treaty of Karlowitz, 417
Treaty of Kiakhta, 491
Treaty of Lausanne, 635
Treaty of Nanking, 495
Treaty of Nerchinsk, 437
Treaty of Rastatt, 456
Treaty of Utrecht, 456
Treaty of Versailles, 632
Treaty of Westphalia, 404
Trenches, in France, 626
Triple Alliance, 575
Tropic zone, 365
Truman, Harry, 672
Ts'ao Haueh-Chan, 493
Tulsi Das, 425
Turgenev, Ivan, 588
Turks, 401, 483
    defense against, 390
    Russian war against, 601
Turnips, 449
TV, 690
Twelver sect, 421

Ukraine, civil wars in, 632
Uniates, 435
Unification, of Germany and Italy, 572–75
Unitarians, 490
United Nations, 661
    charter of, 664–65
United States, 594–98
    civil war in, 563–64
    cold war with Soviet Union, 659
    culture in, 596
    debt of, 674
    entry into World War I, 631
    and Mexico, 640
    in World War II, 645–49
Urbanization, 679–82
Urban living, 685
Urdu, 488
    changing language of administration from, 555
U.S.S.R.
    demise of, 676
    invasion of, 642–43
    problems in, 674–76
*Utopia*, 410
Uzbeks, 418

Vanderbilt, Cornelius, 594, 596
van Gogh, Vincent, 587
Vatican Council, first, 577
Vaudeville, 588
Vedas, 425
Velásquez, Diego, 410
Vermeer, Jan, 411 *fig.*
Veronese, Paolo, 410
Vesalius, Andreas, 408
Vespucci, Amerigo, 375
Viceroy, 378
Vietnam, 661, 674
Vietnam War, 671
Vikings, 364, 368
Village, end of autonomy of, 679–82
Virginia, 439

Vishnu, 425
Voltaire, 468


Wagner, Richard, 587
Wahhab, Abdul, 557
Wahhabi reform, 486–88, 557
Waldseemüller, Martin, 375
Walpole, Robert, 463
War
   politics and in Old Regime, 454–62
   popular attitudes toward, 624
   religious and dynastic, 401–06
   trade problems leading to in China, 495–96
Warfare, new form of by Zulus, 500
War guilt clause, 632
War of the Austrian Succession, 461
War of the Spanish Succession, 456
Warriors, and merchants in Japan, 496–97
Watson, James D., 697, 698, 699
Watt, James, 451, 527 *fig.*, 528, 537
Watteau, Antoine, 470
Weapons, development of new, 611
Wesley, John, 472, 534
Whalers, 503
White Heron Castle, 428 *fig.*
White Lotus, 493
Whitney, Eli, 528
Wilhelm II, Kaiser, 575
William of Orange, 463
Wilson, President Woodrow, 631, 633

Windmills, 536
Winter fodder, 449
Women, in pre-World War I Europe, 569
Wordsworth, William, 470, 513, 533
Workers, voice in government of, 569
Working class, 578, 579
World Exposition, 506
World leadership, end of European, 624
World War I, 624
   outbreak of, 624–31
World War II, 624
   initial Axis victories, 640–49
   prelude to, 637–40
Writing
   invention of, 476
   popular, 587


Yalta conference, 661
Yankee ingenuity, 594
Yellow journalism, 588
Yellow River, 558
Yeltsin, Boris, 676
Young Turks, 609
Yugoslavia, 669


Zevi, Sabbati, 473
Zulus, 500–502
Zwingli, Huldreich, 396